NEW DEVELOPMENTS IN INTERNATIONAL COMMERCIAL AND CONSUMER LAW

New Developments in International Commercial and Consumer Law

Proceedings of the 8th Biennial Conference of the International Academy of Commercial and Consumer Law

Edited by
JACOB S. ZIEGEL
Professor of Law Emeritus, University of Toronto

Consulting Editor
SHALOM LERNER
Professor of Law, Bar Ilan University

·HART·
PUBLISHING
OXFORD
1998

Hart Publishing
Oxford
UK

Distributed in the United States by
Northwestern University Press
625 Colfax
Evanston
Illinois
60208–4210 USA

Distributed in Australia and New Zealand by
Federation Press Pty Ltd
PO Box 45
Annandale, NSW 2038
Australia

Distributed in Netherlands, Belgium and Luxembourg by
Intersentia, Churchillaan 108
B2900 Schoten
Antwerpen
Belgium

Hart Publishing is a specialist legal publisher based in Oxford, England.
To order further copies of this book or to request a list of other
publications please write to:

Hart Publishing, 19 Whitehouse Road, Oxford, OX1 4PA
Telephone: +44 (0)1865 434459 or Fax: (0)1865 794882
e-mail: hartpub@janep.demon.co.uk

British Library Cataloguing in Publication Data
Data Available
ISBN 1–901362–07–8 (cloth)

Typeset in 10pt M. Sabon
by Hope Services, (Abingdon) Ltd.
Printed in Great Britain on Acid-free paper
by Bookcraft Ltd, Midsomer Norton, Avon.

Contents

Detailed Contents

PART V THE CHALLENGES OF ADAPTING TO MARKET ECONOMIES

Editor's Preface

The International Academy of Commercial and Consumer Law is pleased through this volume to be able offer the international legal community access to a revised and edited version of the papers that were presented at the Academy's eighth biennial conference held at the Bar Ilan University in Israel from August 18-22, 1996.

The Academy is an eighteen year old institution whose members, prominent legal scholars located on an all five continents, meet every two years in a different country to present and discuss papers across a broad spectrum of commercial and consumer law topics of current relevance. Biennial meetings of the Academy have been held in Mexico City, Austria, Melbourne, Boston, Oxford, Stockholm and St. Louis as well as in Israel. The 1998 conference will be held from August 8 to 11 at Bond University in Queensland.

"Collegial", "stimulating" and "wonderfully hospitable" are certainly apt words to describe the outstandingly successful conference held at Bar Ilan. The credit for this accomplishment belongs to Prof. Shalom Lerner, a former dean in the Faculty of Law, and his most supportive colleagues in the University's administration. We were also fortunate enough to be able to spend a memorable day in Jerusalem as the guests of the Supreme Court of Israel and its president Prof. Aharon Barak (also a member of the Academy) and, later that day, as the guests of Tana Spanic, Deputy Attorney General (Private Law) and Allen Zysblatt, Senior Director of Legislation and Legal Counsel (Commercial and Consumer Law), at the Israel Ministry of Justice.

As can be gleaned from the contents of this volume, the Bar Ilan conference generated a large number of papers during the four days of active sessions. We have subsumed them in this volume under the same seven major headings in which they were summarized and discussed at the conference: I Basic International Commercial and Contract Law Developments, II Banking Law, Payment Systems and International Finance, III Secured Transactions in Movable Property, IV Conflict of Laws, V International Trade Law, VI The Challenge of Adapting to Market Economies, and VII Consumer Law Developments. The papers cover such a broad spectrum of topics of current relevance that I am confident they will provide intellectual nourishment to an equally broad range of readers.

Publishing an array of papers by scholars with such diverse linguistic, stylistic and geographical backgrounds presented a special editorial challenge. I am most grateful to all the authors for helping me to meet the challenges. The Academy is equally indebted to the Bar Ilan University for financial assistance in the preparation of this volume and to Richard Hart, director of Hart

Publishing in Oxford, for agreeing so readily to publish the papers and for producing what is by any visual measure a most attractive volume. Martha Hundert, a second year law student at the University of Toronto, performed admirably as a proof reader. Gabriel Cavazos Villanuerva, then a graduate Mexican law student at the University of Toronto, was of great assistance in editing the papers by the Spanish speaking authors as was Edward Wu Xiaohui, a doctoral student, in preparing the subject matter index at very short notice. My secretary, Dace Veinberga, responded with her usual cheerfulness and resourcefulness to the demands of communicating effectively with the community of scholars who comprise the authors of this volume.

March 1998

Jacob S. Ziegel, President,
International Academy of
Commercial and Consumer
Law, 1994–96.

PART I

Basic International Commercial and Contract Law Developments

1

Usage and its Reception in Transnational Commercial Law

ROY GOODE*

I. INTRODUCTION

The study of what has become known as transnational commercial law[1] is fraught with hazards. What do we mean by transnational commercial law? Is it the same as the *lex mercatoria* or something broader? What are its sources? Can we identify general principles of commercial law and, separately, uncodified international trade usage? If so, what happens to these principles when they become embodied in convention or contractually incorporated uniform rules? Do they disappear, maintain a parallel existence in their original form, or change their shape to match the convention or rules? And how far do conventions and rules either evidence pre-existing principles and usages or influence the creation of new ones?

If one examines the literature on public international law, one finds an astonishing correlation between the kinds of issue discussed by the international lawyers and those that have perplexed the scholars of transnational commercial law. Indeed, international law provides a rich harvest for the commercial lawyer, not least because the International Court of Justice has on numerous occasions given rulings directly bearing on the relationships between the different sources of international law, and in particular between treaties and customary international law. Yet the two streams of literature, on international law and transnational commercial law, appear so far to have developed in almost total isolation from each other.

This paper focuses on international trade usage: its nature, its normative force, the means by which its existence is established and its relationship to other elements of transnational commercial law. In so doing it seeks to

* Norton Rose Professor of English Law in the University of Oxford and Fellow of St. John's College, Oxford. I am indebted to Lady Fox and Professor Christine Chinkin for their very helpful comments and suggestions on the public international law aspects of this paper. I hope that I have accurately reflected these in the final text.

[1] The concept of transnational commercial law was pioneered by Professors Berthold Goldman, Clive Schmitthoff and Aleksander Goldstajn in the early 1960s. There is now an enormous literature on the subject.

ascertain how far parallels may be drawn with principles of public international law. The paper concludes with a discussion of the relationship between the *lex mercatoria* and the conflict of laws and the implications of the diversity of approaches adopted in international commercial arbitration.

(a) Terminology: Transnational Commercial Law and *Lex Mercatoria*

The phrase "transnational law" seems first to have been given prominence by Philip C. Jessup, whose work *Transnational Law* was published in 1956. Yet his conception of it seems markedly different from what we understand, in the field of commercial law, by the phrase "transnational commercial law". He considered the terms "international" and "international law" misleading since they suggested a concern only with relations between States. He therefore used transnational law, instead of international law, to embrace "all law which regulates actions or events that transcend national frontiers", including public and private international law and other rules not fitting wholly into such standard categories. But in relation to commercial law, at any rate, this description is too broad, for it includes the *national* law of international trade and *national* conflict of laws rules. By contrast, "transnational commercial law" is conceived as law which is not particular to or the product of any one legal system but represents a convergence of rules drawn from several legal systems or even, in the view of its more expansive exponents, a collection of rules which are entirely anational and have their force by virtue of international usage and its observance by the merchant community. In other words, it is the *rules*, not merely the actions or events, that cross national boundaries.

But there is no agreement as to the meaning or content of transnational commercial law. Some equate it with the new *lex mercatoria*,[2] though this too is given different meanings by different writers. If transnational commercial law is taken to mean the product of the convergence of rules of commercial law through all means, including conventions and other international instruments, then its ambit is plainly far wider than law fashioned by merchants. Yet that, surely, is the essence of the *lex mercatoria*. It is by nature uncodified, non-statutory and non-conventional. Rules embodied in an international convention can legitimately be described as part of transnational commercial law but *qua* conventional law they are not part of the *lex mercatoria*, for the convention in which they are incorporated operates only by the will of States who become parties to it or otherwise adhere to it.

Similarly, the codification of unwritten usages in a standard set of rules adopted by contract, subjects them to national law, namely the law governing the contract. Accordingly an international convention or a contractually

[2] See Ole Lando, "The *Lex Mercatoria* in International Commercial Arbitration" (1983) 34 *ICLQ* 747 at 748 ff.

adopted codification is at most evidence of the uncodified rules previously existing; and by itself it is not very reliable evidence, because the purpose of most conventions or contractual codifications is not to reproduce an existing set of universally adopted usages—for in truth no such universality exists—but rather to build on existing usage and to provide best solutions to current problems. It is in the nature of conventions and codifications that they do not simply reproduce the *status quo*, they change it, and sometimes quite radically. The extent to which they are evidence of pre-existing customary rules cannot be determined solely, or even primarily, from the instrument itself except where it expressly states that it is declaring existing custom (a declaration which is not always reliable) or where it replaces earlier codified rules; what is required is an examination of the *travaux préparatoires* and, if this is not sufficient, an analysis of other materials or the reception of oral or documentary evidence of practice to determine the content of the pre-existing rules.

So for the purpose of this paper the phrase "transnational commercial law" is used to describe the totality of principles and rules, whether customary, conventional, contractual or derived from any other source, which are common to a number of legal systems, while the phrase "*lex mercatoria*" is used to indicate that part of transnational commercial law which is unwritten and consists of customary commercial law, customary rules of evidence and procedure and general principles of commercial law, including international public policy.[3]

(b) The Elements of Transnational Commercial Law

It has been said of the *lex mercatoria*, as of public international law, that it is not possible to provide an exhaustive list of elements. In a widely cited article[4] Professor Ole Lando identified eight elements of the *lex mercatoria*, namely public international law, uniform laws, the general principles of law, the rules of international organisations,[5] uncodified customs and usages,[6] codifications of customs and usages by international organisations, standard form contracts and reported arbitral awards. In the terminology adopted in this paper only general principles and uncodified usages constitute the *lex mercatoria*; collectively the various elements make up transnational commercial law. Curiously, no reference is made to the decisions of the Court of Justice of the

[3] See *infra* n. 19 and *post*, 18. For a masterly comparative survey of the whole field of transnational commercial see Filip De Ly, *International Business Law and Lex Mercatoria*.

[4] *Supra* n. 2.

[5] In which are included formulations of general principles prepared by scholars and issued by an international organisation, such as the *Principles of International Commercial Contracts* published by Unidroit and the *Principles of European Contract Law* prepared by the Commission on European Contract Law.

[6] The two terms are nowadays used interchangeably, and for brevity are hereafter referred to as "usages". But see *infra* n. 20.

European Communities, which has itself developed general principles, or of national courts when interpreting or applying international instruments or usage, though these obviously carry a much more general authority than arbitral awards and should be regarded as constituent elements of transnational commercial law.

It is not without significance that Professor Lando uses the term "elements" rather than the more usual "sources". "Elements" is more exact, since it is evident that the items in the shopping list are of very different kinds. Some create law, some declare law,[7] some are not themselves law but are sources of rights and some are evidence of law. Instruments that create law may also serve evidential purposes.[8] Transnational commercial law shares with public international law the characteristic that it raises fundamental jurisprudential questions such as "what is law?" and "what are the sources of law?". It is outside the scope of this paper to examine issues of this kind. My concern is to examine briefly the nature of uncodified international trade usage, its role in transnational commercial law, the methods by which courts and arbitrators satisfy themselves of the existence of a usage and the effect on uncodified usages of their reduction to a convention or to a set of uniform rules promulgated by international organisations and effectuated by incorporation into contracts.

(c) Hierarchy of Norms

As a matter of impression, if a commercial lawyer were asked to rank norms of transnational commerce in descending order of importance he or she would probably rank international trade conventions at the top and compilations of scholars at the bottom, with international trade usages somewhere in between. But things are not always what they seem, and a good case can be made for standing this ranking completely on its head. At the time of its making a convention is not law at all; at most its existence signifies that States are contemplating its adoption. By contrast an international trade usage has normative force through the conjunction of *usus* and *opinio juris*.[9] Again, since conventions are effectuated only by ratification or some other adoptive act, the agreement of States to the text of a convention indicates a provisional view only of the acceptability of the text, whereas a compilation of scholars, such as the Unidroit Principles of International Commercial Contracts or the Principles of European Contract Law published by the Commission on European Contract Law, represents a commitment to the text by the scholars concerned and carries the weight appropriate to their international standing.

[7] This is the theory of the common law, but it is recognised that in reality the existing law represents a framework within which the judge has a limited power to create law.

[8] See *post* 20.

[9] See *post*, 10 ff.

Moreover, even in countries where a convention has become operative its dispositive provisions will be, and will very often be expressed to be, subordinate to the contrary agreement of the parties, which would include any contractually incorporated codifications of usages. So the UNCITRAL Convention on Independent Guarantees and Standby Letters of Credit, most of the provisions of which are purely dispositive,[10] will usually be displaced by the non-binding UCP or URDG issued by the International Chamber of Commerce, one or other of which is likely to be incorporated into the relevant contract. Nor can we necessarily conclude that an apparently normative international usage takes precedence over, say, the Unidroit Principles or the Principles of European Contract Law, for it would be open to courts and arbitrators to say that this product of the collaboration of a group of internationally known scholars points the way to what should now be seen as the best rule of contract law on the relevant point and should be adopted in preference to existing rules or usages.

(d) The Impetus for the Concept of Transnational Commercial Law

The development in the past few decades of a theory of transnational commercial law represents in some degree a desire, part pragmatic, part intellectual, part emotional, to recreate the internationalism of the mediaeval law merchant. No doubt the usages of merchants, accepted by the mercantile community as binding and applied by the merchant courts, were a significant unifying factor in the regulation of international trade and transport. There is, however, a tendency to romanticise the law merchant and to treat it as an integrated corpus of universally applied law akin to the canon law, when in truth it was never an organised body of legal rules at all, rather a diverse and constantly changing aggregation of mercantile customs which might from time to time be brought together in a more or less authoritative compilation. Most of these focused heavily on maritime customs rather than on general commercial usage, and they consisted of a collection of detailed rules which addressed very specific, albeit common, problems.[11] Nevertheless, a number of these rules can be regarded as indicative of broader principles of more general application. They thus represent an important source of general principles of law applicable to international trade.[12]

[10] See art. 1(1) and the various arts. (arts. 13, 14, 16) referring to generally accepted rules, usages and accepted standards of international practices; and, for a general discussion, Rafael Illescas-Ortiz, "International Demand Guarantees: The Interaction of UNCITRAL Convention and the UROG Rules of the ICC", below p. 161.

[11] Sec *post* 18.

[12] See *post*, 19.

Though national courts and arbitral tribunals continue to make extensive use of conflict of laws rules to determine the law applicable to a transaction with a foreign element, arbitrators in international commercial arbitrations have shown a growing desire to throw off the shackles of private international law and to avoid dependence, or exclusive dependence, on any particular national law, however selected, and instead to resort to a modern *lex mercatoria*. The reasons for this are discussed later in this paper.[13]

(e) The Influence of the Dispute Resolution Method on Substantive Rights

It is clear that while litigation and arbitration are alternative methods of dispute resolution, the difference between them is not purely procedural but has a significant effect on substantive rights. There is nothing new in this. Even in the Middle Ages the law merchant as administered by the merchant courts was significantly different from that administered by the courts of common law, and, indeed, was given pre-eminence over the common law within its legitimate sphere of application.[14] Necessarily, therefore, the principles of law to be applied varied with the tribunal. This is even more true today. Arbitrators undoubtedly have a greater freedom than national judges. While the requirements of the *lex loci arbitri* have to be observed in relation to matters such as capacity to act, jurisdiction and the conduct of the arbitration if the award is to be enforceable under the New York Convention, it is primarily for the arbitrators, within the limits agreed by the parties, to determine their own procedure and the admissibility of evidence; and it is widely (though far from universally) held that even in the absence of express authority from the arbitration agreement or any rules it incorporates[15] arbitrators may apply their own conflict of laws rules to determine the applicable law, in the absence of a choice of law by the parties,[16] or even choose directly the law or rules of law they consider appropriate,[17] and can more freely invoke general principles of law or international trade usage to define the rights and duties of the parties. Again, it is the view of some scholars that an arbitrator, unlike a national judge, is free to recognise the contractual adoption of an otherwise inapplicable convention as a valid choice of law, not merely a contractual incorporation of terms.[18]

[13] See *post* 31 ff.

[14] Statute of the Staple, 27 Edw. III, stat. 2 (1353) cc. 5, 6, 8 and 21.

[15] E.g. the ICC Rules of Conciliation and Arbitration (1998 revision), art. 17(1).

[16] Since while a national judge is obliged to apply the conflict rules of his own jurisdiction as the *lex fori*, there is no particular *nexus* between an arbitrator and the place or seat of the arbitration and thus, on one view, no arbitral *lex fori*. However, views remain divided on this question. See further *post* 28, as to international trade usage and the conflict of laws.

[17] See *post* 29.

[18] See *post* 25.

Moreover, since finality is one of the key attractions of arbitration it is an almost universally accepted principle of national laws, as reflected in the UNCITRAL Model Law on Arbitration, that courts should be slow to interfere with arbitral awards, even if they appear to be erroneous in fact or law, with the result that it is inherently harder to upset an award than it is to reverse a judge on appeal. To the extent that national laws limit the ability of national courts to interfere with arbitral awards the arbitrators are in practice able to disregard any theoretical limitations on the way they reach their decisions and the law they apply. Even so, arbitral tribunals have a moral, as well as legal, obligation to act in a disciplined fashion and according to settled principles unless they are dispensed from such obligation by the agreement of the parties. So the fact that the control exercised over their functions is relatively light is not a ground for treating the legal basis for their decisions as unimportant.

II. THE NATURE, ELEMENTS AND SCOPE OF INTERNATIONAL TRADE USAGE

(a) The Nature of Unwritten International Trade Usage

Unwritten[19] trade usage is a practice or pattern of behaviour among merchants established by repetition which has in some degree acquired normative force. There are two theories as to the nature of unwritten trade usage. One is that it is a particular form of international customary law.[20] The other, adopted by (*inter alia*) English law and by Article 9(2) of the Vienna Sales Convention, is that it takes effect as an implied term of a contract. Though the contract theory has been criticised as artificial, in that it ascribes to the parties a knowledge of the usage which they may not possess, this is entirely consistent with the objective theory of contract by which terms are interpreted not according to the subjective intention of the parties but as a reasonable

[19] The term "unwritten" is here used to denote a principle or rule that has not been reduced to writing, whether in binding form (such as a judicial decision, statute or convention) or in non-binding form (such as a private codification or scholarly or mercantile publication).

[20] The subject of trade usage and custom is bedevilled with problems of linguistic ambiguity. Usage is sometimes used to denote practice or behaviour, sometimes to indicate a pattern of behaviour which has risen to the level of a norm. It has been traditional to distinguish custom from usage, but the distinctions have been drawn in widely differing ways. For example, according to some authorities custom is the practice of a particular locality, usage the practice of a trade, profession or vocation. Others consider that usage is merely a pattern of behaviour and that custom is the application of the usage from a sense of binding obligation. Others again divide custom into different categories, according to the degree of their antiquity or universality. The modern approach is to treat the two terms as interchangeable. In transnational commercial law the term "usage" or "usages" is that generally adopted; in international law the reference is usually to custom. For convenience, "usage" is the term adopted in this paper to denote a settled practice which has acquired normative force and is thus equated with custom. But since "usage" does not have an adjectival form, reference will also be made to customary law or customary rules of law. Mere repetitive behaviour will be referred to as such or as practice.

person would interpret them. Usages depend for their efficacy on the settled practices of parties to contracts; they are essentially contractual in nature. Proponents of the *lex mercatoria* tend to be hostile to the contract theory, seeing it as inconsistent with the status of international trade usage as "law". But the practical effect of the distinction between the two theories appears to be slight.

(b) The Normative Force of Unwritten International Trade Usage

Until relatively recently it has been widely accepted that in order for an international trade usage to have normative force it is not sufficient to establish a pattern of repetitive behaviour among merchants; it must also be shown that this pattern of behaviour is observed from a sense of legally binding obligation, not from mere courtesy, convenience or expediency.

> "There is, however, the world of difference between a course of conduct that is frequently, or even habitually, followed in a particular commercial community as a matter of grace and a course which is habitually followed because it is considered that the parties concerned have a legally binding right to demand it."[21]

The point was strikingly illustrated by the decision of Staughton J in *Libyan Arab Foreign Bank* v. *Bankers Trust Co*,[22] in which the above passage was cited.

The plaintiffs maintained a Eurodollar deposit account with the defendants in London. The United States government imposed a freeze on transfers by American banks from and to accounts of Libyan nationals. The plaintiffs contended that the freeze had no effect outside the United States and demanded repayment in cash in London or by any other means not involving activity in the United States. The defendants did not argue that the freeze order had extra-territorial effect but contended that it was a usage of the Eurodollar deposit market that transfers from an account outside the United States denominated in US dollars could be made only through a United States clearing system i.e. through CHIPS or Fedwire, and that this necessarily involved acts in New York on which the order would bite.

It was held by Staughton J. that while there might be a habitual practice of transferring Eurodollars through CHIPS or Fedwire, the evidence did not establish that this was because such methods of transfer were considered the only ones a depositor was legally entitled to demand. Accordingly the plaintiffs were entitled to payment in cash[23] or by some other means which did not involve going through CHIPS or Fedwire.

[21] *General Reinsurance Corp.* v. *Forsakringsaktiebolaget Fennia Patria* [1983] QB 856, *per* Slade LJ at 874.

[22] [1989] QB 728.

[23] A fairly dramatic finding, given that the amount of the demand was US $292 million! In the end, the US regulatory authorities agreed to authorise the transfer, thus obviating the need for an appeal against the decision.

This principle finds an exact parallel in international customary law, which requires a conjunction of *usus* and *opinio juris sive necessitatis* to establish a principle or rule of customary law.[24] Thus Article 38(1) of the Statute of the International Court of Justice identifies as one of the sources of international law the Court is required to apply: "b. international custom, as evidence of a general practice accepted as law". To much the same effect is the elegantly worded rule in the *American Restatement (Revised), Foreign Relations Law of the United States,* § 102:

> "(1) A rule of international law is one that has been accepted as such by the international community of states
> (a) in the form of customary law;
> . . .
> (2) Customary international law results from a general and consistent practice of states followed by them from a sense of legal obligation."

The problem with the requirement of observance of custom from a sense of *legally* binding obligation is that it is based either on circularity or on paradox, for it presupposes a belief in an existing legal duty which, if correct, would make the belief itself superfluous and if erroneous would convert non-law into law through error. It is interesting to note that § 1–205 of the American Uniform Commercial Code and Article 9(2) of the 1980 UN Convention on Contracts for the International Sale of Goods have jettisoned the *opinio juris* element. Under § 1–205(2):

> "A usage of trade is any practice or method of dealing having such regularity of observance in a place, vocation or trade as to justify an expectation that it will be observed with respect to the transaction in question."

Article 9(2) of the Sales Convention (which as previously mentioned attributes the binding force of usage to implied agreement[25]) takes the same position, though in rather more prolix terms:

> "The parties are considered, unless otherwise agreed, to have impliedly made applicable to their contract or its formation a usage of which the parties knew or ought to have known and which in international trade is widely known to, and regularly observed by, parties to contracts of the type involved in the particular trade concerned."

Yet these two formulations are not without their problems either, for they fail to distinguish usage observed as binding from usage followed purely as a matter of habit, courtesy or convenience or simply a desire to accommodate one's business counterparty voluntarily where this is not detrimental to one's own

[24] See generally Michael Akehurst, "Custom as a Source of International Law" (1974–75) XLVII *B.Y.I.L.* 1; G. M. Danilenko, *Law-Making in the International Community*, chaps. IV and V; G. J. H. van Hoof, *Rethinking the Sources of International Law*, chap. VI; Karol Wolfke, *Custom in Present International Law* (2nd revised edition).

[25] See *ante* 9.

interests. Clearly there must be some perception of obligation, even if it is not obligation in the full legal sense of that which has been ordained by law. Perhaps the most satisfactory way of capturing the element of obligation without reference to law is to say that the usage relied on must be one which is considered by the relevant mercantile community to bear on the making, proof, interpretation, performance or enforcement of the parties' commercial engagements towards each other.[26]

A vexed question, which has long been debated in discussions on the nature of customary law and, indeed, of the common law itself,[27] is whether the combination of *usus* and *opinio juris* suffices or whether it is also necessary that the customary rule contended for has received judicial, arbitral or legislative recognition. What exactly is the status of an uncodified usage before it has been the subject of an adjudication in a dispute? There are at least two divergent views on this question. The first is that before the usage has been formally recognised it does not exist, for its normative force is dependent on satisfying certain criteria—consistency of practice, reasonableness, notoriety and conformity with international public policy and any applicable national mandatory law—which are imposed externally by the law and which can only be shown to be satisfied by a decision of a court. This Austinian view of custom fails to address the paradox that if the function of the court or the arbitrator is to *declare* the law, including any rule of customary law, then the rule contended for must exist already. The decision is the authority for the existence of the rule but is not the rule itself. Moreover, if the custom has no normative force until declared, how can it affect the rights of the parties under a contract necessarily made before the decision? The alternative position, advocated by Hart, Salmond and others,[28] is that a ruling by the court in favour of a custom as meeting certain legally defined criteria is purely declaratory and is not the source of the custom's legal force any more than it is the source of, say, subordinate legislation that is challenged but upheld by the court as *intra vires*. This position, which is paralleled in the field of transnational commercial law by advocates of the new *lex mercatoria*, seems

[26] A alternative approach is to think in terms of the sanctions that the relevant sector mercantile community would consider an aggrieved party entitled to exact if the usage were not observed. But this would be appropriate only for usages governing performance, not those relevant to the interpretation of contract terms.

[27] Jeremy Bentham considered the common law to be "a fiction from beginning to end" (*Collected Works*, vol. IV, 483). Ewart (he of estoppel fame) took the same view of the law merchant, conceived as a body of law, in his splendidly iconoclastic article, "What is the Law Merchant?" 3 *Columbia L. Rev.* 135 (1903). See also A. W. B. Simpson, "The Common Law and Legal Theory", in *Oxford Essays in Jurisprudence* (2nd series, ed. A. W. B. Simpson, Oxford, Oxford University Press), who favours the approach taken by Blackstone that the common law is a system of customary law. The question is less meaningful in public international law, where there is neither compulsory recourse to adjudication nor the expectation of adjudication.

[28] For a sophisticated theory, based on a distinction between a practical judgement as to what would be a desirable pattern of conduct to be adopted as an authoritative rule and a practical judgement that such a pattern has been adopted warranting treatment as an authoritative rule, see John Finnis, *Natural Law and Natural Rights*, (Oxford, Clarendon Press) 238 ff.

the preferable solution. It also surmounts another problem, namely that a finding of usage in an arbitration binds only the parties to it and cannot be constitutive of the usage as regards third parties. Only a consistent upholding of the usage in a series of awards could have this effect. To a lesser degree this is true of decisions of national judges at first instance, for these too are not binding on anyone except the parties. And if this is the case as regards local usage, how much more so of international usage, which cannot be ruled on authoritatively by any national court so as to bind the courts of other jurisdictions. The problem, then, is to determine by whom or by what standards the external criteria against which the validity of an international trade usage must be tested are to be set.[29]

(c) Scope

Trade usage, like custom in public international law, may vary widely both in its sphere of influence and in its degree of specificity. Its sphere of influence may be delineated in a number of different ways, for example:

(1) *geographically*, by reference to a particular town, port or region;
(2) *politically*, by reference to a particular political grouping or affinity;
(3) *economically*, by reference to a particular economic grouping or affinity;
(4) *legally*, by reference to a particular legal tradition;
(5) *commercially*, by reference to a particular trade or market.[30]

Each of these groupings is to some extent independent of the others, so that, for example, an international trade usage may be confined to a particular type of business activity (e.g. bank documentary payment undertakings) but may be near-universal in geographical scope, whilst on the other hand there may be usages which apply to business activities generally but only within a defined geographical area or a particular legal family.

In content the usage may express a very broad principle of required behaviour or a very specific one. Usages that express very broad norms of behaviour may, if extended beyond a given type of international contractual activity, become elevated into general principles of law or become embodied in international conventions and lose their distinctive status as usages of trade. An example is the principle *pacta sunt servanda*, a principle common to domestic and international trade law and public international law, which can be said to have developed from customary law to become a general principle of law[31] or, in the case of international law, a rule codified in Article 26 of the Vienna Convention on the Law of Treaties.

[29] See *post*, 17 ff.
[30] Either geographical (as in the case of a commodities market) or organisational (as in the case of the financial markets).
[31] See further *post* 18.

Just as the sphere of application of each trade usage grouping has no necessary relationship with that of the others, so also the level of generality or specificity of a usage is not necessarily related to the generality of specificity of its sphere of application. For example, the principle that a party cannot take advantage of his own fault to escape from a contract on the ground of his own or the other party's inability to perform is a very broad principle which is not specific to a particular trade, location or legal system. It is interesting to find that virtually every rule identified from arbitral awards as a rule of the *lex mercatoria* in the brilliant essay by Mustill LJ (now Lord Mustill) on the new *lex mercatoria*[32] is of this broad character. Yet there are many widely adopted trade usages that are highly specific: for example, in the sphere of international banking, that a reasonable time for examination of documents presented under a letter of credit is no more than a few days,[33] or that banks are concerned only with the apparent good order of documents, not with their genuineness or authenticity.[34] The degree of specificity of an unwritten international trade usage may be relevant to the ease or difficulty with which its recognition before an arbitral tribunal can be secured, for the more general the asserted usage the greater its affinity with a general principle of law and the lower the burden of showing that it is generally known.

III. HOW UNCODIFIED USAGE IS ESTABLISHED

(a) The Nature of the Problem

The difficulty with uncodified usage, as with any other customary law, is to establish its existence. Individual members of the commercial community may have, or believe that they have, a broad perception of what a given usage is or means, but typically the postulated usage will lack definition, its boundaries and qualifications will be hazy and even its central core may prove to be a matter of debate.

That this is so can readily be demonstrated by everyday experience and by the process of litigation, and it applies with equal force to asserted but previously unexplored rules of the common law. A young lawyer practising in England and not familiar with the workings of English bank settlement systems attends a gathering of experienced bankers who are discussing problems of daylight exposure arising from a multilateral settlement system which nets out obligations only at the end of the day. The young lawyer is curious to know whether a payment order given by a customer to his bank can be coun-

[32] "The New *Lex Mercatoria*: The First Twenty-five Years" in *Liber Amicorum for Lord Wilberforce* (ed. Martin Bos and Ian Brownlie), (Oxford, Clarendon Press) chap. 11, at 174–7.

[33] *Bankers Trust Co* v. *State Bank of India* [1991] 2 Lloyd's Rep. 443. See now UCP arts. 13(b), 14(d)(i), allowing a maximum of seven days.

[34] UCP art. 15.

termanded after it has gone into the bank clearing but before the conclusion of the daily settlement. He would like to ask about this but is reluctant to expose his ignorance on what must obviously be such an elementary matter. Eventually he plucks up courage and poses the question. He may then quite possibly find to his surprise that half the assembly replies yes and the other half no. He would almost certainly have had a similar experience if, before the decision in the *Banque de l'Indochine* case,[35] he had enquired as to the meaning and effect of a payment "under reserve" to the beneficiary of a documentary credit. One group of bankers would have said that the paying bank could recover the payment from the beneficiary if the account party could demonstrate that the documents were not in conformity with the credit, whilst the other half would have answered (correctly, as it would turn out) that the bank could recover if the account party declined to take the documents, even if the reason for his refusal to take them was not legitimate.

In fact, every case in which there is a dispute between expert witnesses as to the fact and content of an unwritten trade usage makes the point that, not being reduced to writing, the usage is exposed to challenge as to its meaning or even its very existence. Precisely the same situation obtains where there is a dispute as to whether a right or remedy is given by the common law on a point not previously the subject of a judicial decision or scholarly writing. It is worth emphasising this point because there are arbitrators who seem willing to infer international trade usage on the flimsiest of evidence or even on no evidence at all beyond their own personal experience.

(b) Usage as It Exists and Usage as the Merchants Would Like It to Be

Before considering the various conditions in which an international trade usage may be received by a court or arbitral tribunal I should like to focus on a point which hitherto appears to have escaped attention, namely whether so much emphasis should be placed on usage as it stands, and whether there is not a case for admitting evidence that the usage is no longer acceptable to the mercantile community and is observed solely because it has been given contractual force. In international law it is recognised that there may be a fine line between *lex lata* and *lex ferenda*.[36] Indeed, *lex ferenda* may quickly become *lex lata*, as in the case of scholarly compilations such as the Unidroit Principles of International Commercial Contracts, where what are offered are in effect best solutions adapted from existing principles, solutions which within a year or two of publication of the Principles have already been applied in a number of arbitrations and at least one court decision.[37]

[35] *Banque de l'Indochine et de Suez SA* v. *J.H. Rayner (Mincing Lane) Ltd* [1983] QB 711.

[36] See G. M. Danilenko, *op. cit.*, 16–22.

[37] M. J. Bonell, "The UNIDROIT Principles of International Commercial Contracts and the Principles of European Contract Law: Similar Rules for the Same Purposes?", *Uniform Law Review* 1996–II, 229.

What should a tribunal do when a rule of codified usage becomes seen as obstructive or unhelpful and in need of replacement and is observed solely because it is seen as having contractual force? The problem is less acute in the case of uncodified usage, for all the business community has to do is to abandon the usage and replace it with a new one.[38] But where a usage becomes embodied in a codification incorporated into contracts it acquires contractual force and, unless negated or modified by express contractual provision, can only be changed by altering the code. It might be said that the duty of the tribunal is to ignore dissatisfaction with the existing rule and to apply it. But in the typical case where a tribunal applies a codified rule as evidence of existing usage it is usually prompted to do so because the rule is seen to reflect what is desirable, not simply what is done.

By way of illustration, when the Uniform Customs and Practice for Documentary Credits was first published by the International Chamber of Commerce in 1933 it contained a rule that credits were to be deemed revocable unless otherwise indicated. Given the fact that a beneficiary under a revocable credit was almost wholly unprotected, it was not surprising that the vast majority of credits were issued as irrevocable credits. In other words, the rule, if it had ever reflected the needs and practices of the merchant community, had long ago ceased to do so. Nevertheless the rule remained in force for sixty years; not until the 1993 revision was it changed to make credits irrevocable unless otherwise indicated.[39] Now suppose that in 1990 a documentary credit had been issued which was in traditional form and appearance in all respects except that it did not state whether it was revocable or irrevocable and omitted any reference to the UCP, and that an arbitral tribunal was called upon to decide whether, in mercantile usage, the credit was to be considered revocable or irrevocable. What position should it take? On the one hand, there was a clear rule of the UCP that a credit was to be presumed revocable unless otherwise indicated; on the other, a long-settled practice of calling for irrevocable, rather than revocable, credits. Should not the tribunal rely on the practice (if duly proved or capable of judicial notice) rather than treating the rule as evidence of usage or of a general principle of documentary credits law? To generalise the question, if parties to a set of contractually incorporated rules consistently exclude one of them, should that rule continue to be presumptive of the intention of business generally so as to bind parties who have not adopted the rules and thus have no contractual commitment to apply the presumptive rule if they have not excluded it?

Unfortunately a negative answer to this question confronts an immediate difficulty, namely, that most parties do in fact adopt the UCP and therefore the presumptive rule. There is no argument about what the former rule was, merely about what it ought to be. It is not, therefore, a case where the par-

[38] The transition may, of course, raise intricate questions as to whether at a certain point there are two competing usages in operation or alternatively none at all.

[39] UCP art. 6(c).

ties decided to create a new usage by acting outside the former UCP; on the contrary, what they did was to apply the freedom given by the UCP itself to displace the presumptive rule by declaring the credit irrevocable. Thus, however much the commercial world might have thought the rule out of touch with commercial needs, there can be no doubt that they accepted its binding force. So while the *usus* of issuing irrevocable credits could readily have been established, there would have been no basis for inferring an *opinio juris* that the issue of a credit imposed an irrevocable commitment on the part of the issuer.

(c) The Reception of Usage by a Court or Tribunal

There are three principal conditions in which a court or an arbitral tribunal can be led to accept the existence of a trade usage. The first is where the usage is so well known that the tribunal can take judicial notice of it; the second, where written or oral testimony is given by expert witnesses; and the third, where the usage can be inferred from international conventions, uniform rules prepared by international organisations, standard contracts, scholarly writings, and the like. The first two of these require no particular comment here, except to note that international arbitrators appear much readier than courts to make confident statements about international trade usage and to take judicial notice of them. But the inference of usage from conventions and other international instruments and writings raises questions of acute difficulty both as to what can legitimately be inferred and as to the impact of such an instrument or writing on existing usage. Indeed, in many respects the role of international trade usage *vis-à-vis* other elements of transnational commercial law remains obscure, despite the considerable volume of literature devoted to the subject.

(d) Determining the Relevant Sphere of Influence

A usage may be international without being universal; indeed, there can be very few usages that are universal, and finding them poses almost insurmountable difficulties. However, the application of an international usage presupposes that both parties are operating within its sphere of influence. This is relatively easy for transactions conducted on an organised market or exchange with an identified seat or location, for usually both parties will be bound. But in other cases the problem is more difficult. Trade usages are most highly developed in those parts of the world that have well developed legal systems which attach importance to party autonomy. Suppose that one party to an international supply contract has its place of business in one such part of the world while the other party is based in a country in which law is relatively undeveloped or is subordinate to political and economic goals, so that the role of contract is diminished. An attempt by the former party (who will typically be the supplier) to invoke international usage is likely to be met by the other party's challenge: why should we be bound by a usage which our countries and others of like philosophy or stage of development had no part in shaping and which runs quite counter to that philosophy? If there is nothing else to indicate into which of the two possible spheres of influence the transaction falls, that of the supplier or that of the customer, there seems no alternative but to resort to the applicable law as determined by the conflict of laws rules of the forum.

IV. THE INTERRELATION OF INTERNATIONAL TRADE USAGE AND OTHER ELEMENTS OF TRANSNATIONAL COMMERCIAL LAW

(a) International Trade Usage and General Principles of Law

In my view it is an inherent feature of an international trade usage, and that which distinguishes it from a general principle of law, that it is particular to a given form of international trade, or to finance or other contractual activity linked to international trade. It may be a usage related, for example, to the international sale or carriage of goods, international construction contracts, or the provision of security for payment or performance through letters of credit and demand guarantees. But once a usage has acquired such general acceptance as to become independent of any particular form of international trading activity, it ceases to be a usage and becomes elevated into a general principle of law. Examples are the principles *pacta sunt servanda* and *rebus sic stantibus*. It is not a great over-simplification to say that general principles of law, to the extent that they are not overriding rules of public policy, are generalised (though not necessarily universal) expressions of former international trade usages or conventions. General principles of law recognised by civilised nations are also identified as a source of public international law in Article 38(1)(c) of the Statute of the International Court of Justice (and some writers contend that they can also be derived from international law itself), but in practice they are invoked relatively infrequently.

The various maritime codifications of the Middle Ages show, as one might expect, that merchants and mariners were not concerned with broad principles or sweeps of policy; what they wanted was a more or less consistent application of current usage by tribunals of their peers. A good example is provided by the fifteenth-century Catalonian compilation known as *The Consulate of the Sea*,[40] one of the most detailed and influential compilations of its time. This consists of no fewer than 334 Articles covering almost every known eventuality, from the responsibility of a patron of a vessel to his partners and his merchants to the punishment of a sailor improperly undressing

[40] Translation by Stanley S. Jados (University of Alabama Press, 1975).

for the night,[41] and from waterlogged cargo carried in an open boat to the liability of shareholders in a boat construction venture.

Yet it is also true that the detailed rules contained in *The Consulate of the Sea* have certain recurrent themes from which one may legitimately extract a surprising number of underlying principles. These include the duty of disclosure,[42] the binding force of agreements,[43] including informal and unwitnessed agreements concluded by a handshake,[44] the immunity from liability to pay for unrequested benefits,[45] the duty of care owed by the patron to merchants and passengers,[46] *force majeure* as an excuse for non-performance,[47] but no excuse where the inability to perform is self-induced,[48] immunity of bailee of goods lost without fault,[49] the duty to account for profits or proceeds made from the joint-venture vessel,[50] and the buyer's right to damages for breach of warranty by the seller, measured by the difference between the value of the goods as warranted and their value as delivered.[51] The common thread that links all these rules is the duty to act reasonably and in good faith; and where life or limb is at stake, a high degree of importance is attached to the exercise of proper care and skill.[52]

General principles of law, other than rules of international public policy, are so broad as to be of little practical utility except to give comfort to an arbitrator or respectability to his award. The principle *pacta sunt servanda* is everywhere accepted. What we need to know is the circumstances in which performance is excused. *Rebus sic stantibus* is all very well as a general principle but is too vague to be of great practical assistance and in the field of public international law appears never to have been successfully invoked, despite its embodiment in Article 62 of the Vienna Convention on the Law of Treaties. Increasingly, issues of this kind are dealt with expressly in international conventions[53] and international restatements of contract.[54] General

[41] Which was, for each transgression, to be tied and dunked in the ocean three times while held by a rope (art. 170).

[42] Art. 47, dealing with the duty of a patron to give certain information publicly to prospective investors.

[43] Arts. 48, 89, 90, 102, 194.

[44] Arts. 48, 89.

[45] Arts. 50, 51 (no liability of shareholders to pay additional sums to the patron for constructing a vessel larger than agreed).

[46] Arts. 61, 69.

[47] Arts. 66, 262, 282.

[48] Art. 85 (inability of merchant to ship cargo by reason of sale to a third party).

[49] Arts. 206, 255.

[50] Arts. 241, 256, 287.

[51] Art. 293.

[52] Some of the rules of the sea were of long standing. The 12th century Sea-Laws of Oléron, for example, decreed that if a pilot failed to exercise due skill in bringing a vessel to port and was not able to make satisfaction he should lose his head. 300 years later the option of giving satisfaction had apparently disappeared; instant decapitation was the price of failure.

[53] E.g. the Vienna Sales Convention, art. 79.

[54] E.g. the Unidroit *Principles of International Commercial Contracts* and the Commission on European Contract Law *Principles of European Contract Law*.

principles of law are still capable of being derived from conventions as well as from usage, but the scope for this source is shrinking with the increasing adoption of the rule of interpretation laid down in the Vienna Sales Convention requiring resort to general principles of the convention itself and, where there are none, reference to the applicable law under conflict of laws rules. By contrast there are principles of international public policy or morality of such overriding importance that they will displace any contrary usage. For example, it is almost universally held that a contract procured by bribery is void or unenforceable, and it is not to the point that in the locality with which the transaction is connected bribery is an everyday occurrence of which all parties were likely to be aware.

(b) Trade Usage and International Conventions

The relationship of conventions to usages is as complex in transnational commercial law as it is in international law.[55] A convention may be evidence of a usage, so as to allow its admission where the convention would not as such be applicable; it may operate concurrently with the usage; it may displace the usage; and it may create or evidence new usage through consistent adoption in cross-border commercial transactions or by non-contracting States. Further, if a convention is evidence of usage it may equally be the case that its non-adoption negates its significance as evidence of usage.

(i) International Trade Conventions as Evidence of Existing Trade Usage

An international trade convention may legitimately be relied on in given conditions as evidence of pre-existing usage, in the same way as an international treaty may be relied on as evidence of international customary law.[56] It is a characteristic of conventions that they can never exhaustively determine the scope of their own application, which may be extended by contract, usage or acquiescence.

The crucial question is whether the convention does in fact reflect pre-existing usage or whether on the contrary it changes the usage. It has been pointed out by a number of writers that it is impossible for *ius scriptum* accurately to capture any unwritten law, if only because the scope of the latter is inherently uncertain and changeable and may also, when reduced to writing, be found in some respects to be incomplete or unsatisfactory. The notion that "codifiers" sit down faithfully to reproduce rules of customary law is pure mythology, particularly at the international level, where there are likely to be significant differences between the rules of one legal system and those of

[55] As to which see the citations in n. 24, *supra*, and the *North Sea Continental Shelf Cases* [1969] ICJ Rep. 3.

[56] See the citations in n. 24, *supra*.

another. When legal experts gather together to frame a convention or a set of uniform rules they will normally have the advantage of a report by the secretariat of the sponsoring international organisation setting out in broad terms the existing law and practice in selected jurisdictions. Each of the participating experts will bring to bear a knowledge of his or her own legal system and, understandably enough, can be expected to test each proposed rule against the rules of that system to see whether it overlooks a problem or on the contrary represents an improvement. But the drafters of the convention or uniform rules would make no progress at all if they conceived their task as being to assemble before them all the known rules and practices and strive to create an amalgam of them all. Even if such a task were feasible its product would negate any notion of mere reproduction of existing law, for necessarily the amalgam could only be created by changing in some degree the existing rules of its various constituents. In any event, that is simply not how the process of harmonisation works. What those involved in the project seek to achieve is best solutions to typical problems, being solutions which are not so far removed from existing practice as to make them unacceptable. Accordingly, change is inherent in any redaction of rules, whether written or unwritten. The resulting text will thus be a combination of rules that existed before, modifications of existing rules and entirely new rules.

How, then, is a court or arbitral tribunal to determine whether a convention or codification reproduces existing usage or changes it? If the usage has already been embodied in an earlier convention or codification the task is relatively easy, for all the tribunal has to do is to compare the two texts. But where the convention or codification is relied on as evidence of existing unwritten usage this resource is not available. If the alleged usage is disputed then unless it is of the near-universal kind of which judicial notice can be taken a national court is likely to require it to be established by evidence. Such evidence could take a variety of forms, of which the most compelling would be the *travaux préparatoires* and the rapporteur's report.[57] What is interesting is the readiness of some arbitral tribunals to assume, without any evidence whatsoever, that the best reflection of existing usage is the provisions of an international convention or codification.

A striking example of this is the award in an ICC arbitration, case no. 5713 of 1989.[58]

The seller of goods under a contract of sale made in 1979 brought arbitration proceedings to recover the balance of the price. The buyer claimed the right to set off loss suffered from the fact that the goods did not conform to

[57] It should be borne in mind that we are not here talking of *interpretation* of a convention or codification, for which reference to *travaux préparatoires* would normally be inadmissible unless the text to be interpreted was ambiguous or would lead to a manifestly absurd or unreasonable result (see, for example, the Vienna Convention on Treaties, art. 32), but its relationship to pre-existing usage, which cannot be determined solely from the text of the convention or codification itself except in those cases where it is expressed to be declaratory of existing usage.

[58] 1990 *XX ICCA Yearbook* 70; Jarvin *et al.*, *Collection of ICC Arbitral Awards*, vol. II, 223.

the contract of sale. An issue arose as to whether the buyer had given notice of the lack of conformity in due time. The tribunal applied generally accepted conflict of laws rules to decide that the law governing the contract was that of the seller's country. However, the applicable law as thus determined was considered by the tribunal to impose time requirements for the giving of notice of defects that were so short and specific as to run counter to generally accepted trade usages. The tribunal therefore declined to apply the law applicable under conflicts of laws rules, and instead applied Articles 38 and 39 of the Vienna Sales Convention.

> "The Tribunal finds that there is no better source to determine the prevailing trade usages than the terms of the United Nations Convention on the International Sale of Goods of 11 April 1980, usually called 'the Vienna Convention.' This is so even though neither [the country of the Buyer] nor [the country of the Seller] are parties to that Convention. If they were, the Convention might be applicable to this case as a matter of law and not only as reflecting the trade usages.
>
> The Vienna Convention, which has been given effect to in 17 countries, may be fairly taken to reflect the generally recognized usages regarding the matter of the non-conformity of goods in international sales."

The Tribunal went on to hold that the buyer had given notice of non-conformity within the time laid down by Articles 38 and 39, that in any event the Seller was debarred by Article 40 from invoking the time limits laid down in those Articles because he had known of the non-conformity and did not disclose it, and that accordingly the Buyer was entitled to compensation which could be set off against the seller's claim. It can reasonably be inferred from the rather truncated report of the award that under the applicable law the buyer would have been held to have given notice of non-conformity out of time.

What is surprising about the award is not that it extended the scope of the convention beyond its own stated boundaries—for this can happen in a variety of ways, including treatment of the convention as the embodiment of existing usage—but that it completely disregarded the applicable law[59] and, in doing so, assumed without discussion that the Vienna Sales Convention did in fact embody relevant trade usage. On the latter point there are least four matters which should have given the tribunal pause for thought.

(1) When the contract was concluded (which is accepted as the point where rights and duties are established) the Vienna Convention not merely lacked the necessary number of ratifications to bring it into force, it had not even been made! All the more curious, then, that the tribunal indicated that the convention could have applied directly if both parties had carried on business in contracting states.

(2) There *was* a convention in force at the time of the contract, namely Vienna's predecessor, the 1964 Uniform Law on International Sales. Why,

[59] A point developed *post* 29.

then, did the Tribunal not apply (or even refer to) ULIS? One can only speculate. Perhaps the Tribunal considered that the ULIS rules on the time for examination were too rigid[60] and would have left the buyer remediless. Another answer might be that by 1979, fifteen years after it was made, ULIS had attracted only eight ratifications and one accession, compared with the seventeen ratifications, etc., referred to in the award, and that a total of nine adopting States was not considered strong enough evidence of prevailing international trade usage. But if this is true of ULIS, then how much more so of a convention that was still only in draft at the time of the contract and might conceivably have proved as unsuccessful as ULIS.

(3) At the 1980 Diplomatic Conference there was protracted debate on what became Article 39 and was then Article 37, and two delegates on separate occasions made the point that the article in question was one of the most controversial in the entire Convention[61]—hardly the strongest basis for treating the article as evidence of an internationally established usage! It is true that the UNCITRAL Commission text which came forward for consideration by the Diplomatic Conference and embodied what is now Article 39 could be given some weight as representing the views of the Working Group and the full UNCITRAL Commission, but why should it be accorded greater weight than the stricter provisions of a convention which had then already been in force for fourteen years?

(4) International trade conventions are made by States, not by businessmen, and accordingly are not formulated by the members of the community whose usages they are supposed to embody. Not uncommonly conventions fail to gain acceptance precisely because they do not reflect the practices or perceptions of the dominant commercial community. A good example is provided by the Hamburg Rules, which though technically operative have proved very much of a damp squib. Nowadays more determined efforts are made to consult business interests on a proposed international trade convention—indeed, their representative organisations may be involved in the preparatory work as observers—but the policy decisions and the drafting are undertaken almost entirely by lawyers, and it is primarily lawyers who will lead the representation of their governments at a Diplomatic Conference to conclude a convention.

Unfortunately there is no indication from the report of the award (which, as is customary, has been filleted to preserve the anonymity of the parties) as to whether any of the above arguments were placed before the tribunal or, indeed, whether there was any opportunity given, or any attempt made, to

[60] See John Honnold, *Uniform Law for International Sales* (2nd edn.), paras. 250–252. Professor Honnold comments (in para. 250) that "[i]n the UNCITRAL proceedings it was possible to make the rules on examination of goods more flexible and consistent with current commercial practice".

[61] Mr Khoo (Singapore) at the 16th meeting; Mr Inaamullah (Pakistan) at the 21st meeting. See John Honnold, *Documentary History for the Uniform Law on International Sales*, 542, para. 51, 566, para. 6.

challenge the assumption that Article 39 of the Vienna Sales Convention reflected current usage at the time of the contract or, indeed, at the time of the making of the Convention.

There is a further problem to be considered. A purely dispositive provision of an international trade convention, even if accurately reflecting existing usage, may be displaced by subsequent usage.[62] How can a tribunal be sure that the convention still reflects trade usage? No doubt there is a presumption in favour of continuing validity of a convention as evidence of usage but it should certainly be capable of being rebutted by evidence.

The drawing of inferences of uncodified usage from an international trade convention raises a number of other conundrums. How far is the tribunal entitled to rely on hindsight? In the arbitral award referred to above the tribunal, deciding a case ten years after the contract, relied on the fact that the Vienna Sales Convention had been carried into effect in seventeen countries. Suppose that the hearing had taken place not in 1989 but in 1981, when there had been no ratifications at all. Would that have made a difference? Certainly there would be no clear indication at that stage of the level of support the convention would command. The absence of ratifications would have had no significance either, because it would have been too soon to draw any inferences. Suppose that, at the time when the case was in fact heard, there had still been no ratifications. That would be a clear indication that the convention had attracted no support from governments and was unlikely to do so. Should the tribunal take this fact into account in giving an award in 1989, when if it had made the adjudication in 1981 no real significance could have been attached to the lack of ratifications?

If the adoption of a convention is to be relied on as evidence of usage, or its non-adoption as evidence to negate usage, do we not need to know why it gained acceptance or, on the contrary, did not. It is conceivable that the particular provision invoked in the dispute was highly controversial and considered out of touch with commercial reality[63] but that the benefits of the convention as a whole were considered to outweigh the drawbacks of this one provision. Conversely, States may have been unanimously in favour of the provision as reflecting current usage but opposed to the convention on other grounds.[64] Further, the fact that a convention may not have come into force does not necessarily deprive it of significance, for it may be sufficiently persuasive within the commercial community to generate new usages. Similarly, in the field of international law the ability of treaties to generate customary law prior to their coming ito force is widely recognised, as in the case of recognition of the 200-mile exclusive economic zones in the course of negoti-

[62] Whether in public international law a treaty may be displaced by subsequent state practice is highly controversial. See the citations in n. 24, *supra*.

[63] As was the case on the provisions of ULIS for automatic termination of the contract on a fundamental breach.

[64] See Mark E. Villiger, *Customary International Law and Treaties*, at 164.

ation and after adoption of the final text of the 1982 UN Convention on the Law of the Sea.

Reliance on conventions as evidence of international trade usage is at once a virtue and a danger. As previously indicated, the effect may be to extend the scope of the convention well beyond its stated sphere of application. Reference has already been made to an arbitral award which applied Article 39 of the Vienna Convention to a case where the convention was not in existence at the time of the contract, and even at the time of the award many years later the convention would not have been applicable on its own terms, since neither of the parties carried on business in a country that had become party to the convention. Extensions of this kind may not trouble arbitrators; they are of much graver concern to national judges, for their effect may be to impose on a national court the duty to apply the provisions of a convention which its own state has declined to ratify. The same objection applies to the theory advanced by some scholars that parties may subject their contract to the terms of a convention not as a method of incorporation of contractual terms but as the choice of an applicable law under conflict of laws rules. There is no objection to the former, for the incorporated terms of the convention become subject to the mandatory rules of the applicable law in just the same way as any other contract terms, but strong objection to the latter, which if valid would give private parties the right to invoke the convention against the wishes of a non-ratifying state in which the dispute was tried. Again, however, it has been argued that while this is a valid argument as regards national judges it should have no application to arbitrators, who typically will not occupy any position of authority in, or indeed have any connection with, the state where they sit.[65]

Of course, it has to be recognised that courts and arbitral tribunals and the parties appearing before them are unlikely to have detailed knowledge of more than a very small number of legal systems and that they cannot be expected either to engage in a major comparative study or to expend huge effort in tracking the antecedents of conventions presented to them. In meeting the exigencies of dispute resolution they cannot be said to be acting unreasonably in assuming, in the absence of evidence or argument to the contrary, that a particular convention reflects pre-existing usage. But that is a matter of evidence and of onus of proof. The difficulty in using prior arbitral awards as precedents is that we know so little about the facts and arguments. Often the reports do not show even the date of the contract in dispute, though that may be highly relevant. The countries involved and the commercial background to the dispute will usually be omitted for reasons of confidentiality, and it can be difficult even to deduce the arguments advanced or to know to what extent the arbitral tribunal was relying on its own knowledge rather than on evidence.

[65] See the note by Yves Derains [1995] *Clunet* 1020, criticising the award in ICC case no. 6754 of 1993.

(*ii*) *Effect of International Trade Convention on Existing Usage*

It may be equally difficult to determine the effect of an international trade convention on existing usage. To the extent that the convention indicates a change of direction it may establish a new usage, or induce courts and arbitrators to adopt a new rule, in place of the existing usage. It is also possible, however, for the existing usage to continue in force and to run in parallel with the convention as regards transactions to which the convention does not apply, or even to supplement the convention on matters on which the latter is silent.

(*iii*) *The Expansion of the Scope of International Trade Conventions through International Trade Usage*

Just as a convention may change unwritten international trade usage, so also usage may qualify or override the dispositive provisions of a convention. Moreover, insofar as the convention is evidence of usage its provisions may become applicable *qua* usage even where the connection to a contracting State prescribed by the convention is missing, e.g. where, in an international sale of goods, one of the parties does not have its place of business in a contracting State. Again, this finds a counterpart in international law, where a State may be taken to have adhered by practice to a convention to which it is not a party.[66]

(c) **Trade Usage and Formulations by International Organisations**

Similar considerations apply where reliance is placed on a codification promulgated by an international organisation. Such codifications take a variety of forms: uniform rules or trade terms incorporated by contract, legal guides, formulations of legal principles by scholars, and the like.

Prominent among organisations publishing uniform rules and trade terms is the International Chamber of Commerce, which over the years has prepared and published numerous sets of uniform rules and trade terms which are carried into effect by incorporation into contracts. Examples are the Uniform Customs and Practice for Documentary Credits, the Uniform Rules for Demand Guarantees, the Uniform Rules for Contract Bonds—all of which lay down rules to be observed by participating banks and other parties to transactions of the types in question—and Incoterms, standard price and delivery terms for contracts of sale, each term carrying with it a defined set of duties for seller and buyer respectively. Such rules do not in themselves have nor-

[66] See Christine Chinkin, *Third Parties in International Law*, (Oxford, Clarendon Press), Chapter 3.

mative force; indeed, even the contracts which incorporate them cannot be regarded in themselves as part of transnational commercial law, for though they are the source of entitlements they operate only as between the parties and do not constitute law in themselves but are dependent on law for their effect. It follows that if these contractually incorporated rules are to play any part in the scheme of transnational commercial law they do so as evidence of existing usage or as fashioners of new usage.

Of a different kind altogether are the Unidroit *Principles of International Commercial Contracts* and the *Principles of European Contract Law* prepared by the Commission on European Contract Law. These are formulations of general principles and rules of contract law prepared by two different (though overlapping) groups of scholars. They have no binding force as such, though it would be open to contracting parties to incorporate them by reference into their contracts. More significant is their availability as a tool for courts and arbitrators seeking to identify current norms of contract established by mercantile usage or general principles of law, to ascertain what in modern legal thinking are conceived as best solutions to typical contract problems and to fill gaps in existing conventions. Such formulations are likely to be particularly persuasive in relation to cross-border transactions where the tribunal, recognising that at least one of the parties is from another jurisdiction, may be more receptive to the application of principles or rules deviating in some degree from those of its own national law. Publications by outstanding scholars have long been influential in shaping legal principles, particularly (though not exclusively) in the field of public international law. In this field their status is now enshrined in Article 38(1)(d) of the Statute of the International Court of Justice, which includes among the materials the ICJ is to apply "the teachings of the most highly qualified publicists of the various nations". The enormous interest attracted by the Unidroit Principles shows the impact of the fruits of top-level intellectual collaboration from distinguished scholars drawn from a number of different legal families and systems. More generally, the growing influence of non-formal "soft" law sources is to be seen in transnational commercial law as it is in public international law.

Both sets of principles defer to mandatory rules of the applicable law under conflict of laws rules, a realistic recognition of the fact that general principles of law and usages cannot wholly displace national law since they do not constitute complete systems of law. What is interesting is that both sets of principles also incorporate a few mandatory rules of their own, such as the requirement of good faith and the rules on unilateral price determination. It may be asked how principles which are themselves non-binding in character can sensibly include mandatory provisions. There are at least two reasons why this is not as strange as it may seem. First, the parties may choose to incorporate the principles into their contract, in which event they will be bound by the provisions declaring certain principles mandatory or non-excludable.

Secondly, the stated mandatory principles provide strong evidence of a general acceptation of types of rule that are to be considered to have such a strong policy content that they should not be capable of exclusion by the parties, whatever the applicable law—i.e. they should be given the character of *ius cogens*.

V. INTERNATIONAL TRADE USAGE AND THE CONFLICT OF LAWS

(a) The Antipathy Between the Lex Mercatoria and the Conflict of Laws

National conflict of laws rules developed as part and parcel of the overall process of nationalising law. To the extent that law was unified by the canon law, the *ius civile* and the mediaeval *lex mercatoria*, it was unnecessary to devise rules to determine which State's law applied. But with the gradual replacement of the merchant courts by the central courts and of international rules with national laws it became necessary for each legal system to develop its own rules for determining (among other things) what law was to govern disputes involving a foreign element.

In his essay on the *lex mercatoria*[67] Mustill LJ pointed out that the purpose of the conflict of laws is antithetical to the premise of the *lex mercatoria*, in that the former seeks to identify the applicable national law whereas the latter is conceived as anational in character.

(b) The Application of Conflict of Laws Rules

National judges for the most part continue to regard themselves as bound to determine a dispute by reference to a national law determined by the conflict of laws rules of the forum. Arbitrators in international commercial arbitration also regularly resort to conflicts rules to determine the applicable law.[68] Nevertheless the difference in approach between courts and arbitrator has perceptibly widened over the past two decades. There is a strong body of opinion which denies the existence of any arbitral *lex fori*, on the ground that the arbitrator is appointed by the parties, not by the State, and that the connection of an arbitrator with the seat of the arbitration is usually temporary

[67] *Supra*, n. 32.

[68] An approach supported by the Resolution on Arbitration in Private International Law prepared by the XIV Commission of the International Law Association and approved at its meeting in Amsterdam in 1957. However, a resolution adopted at the 1992 meeting of the Association in Cairo declared that the fact that an award was founded on transnational rules (general principles of law, principles common to several laws, international law, trade usage, etc.) should not by itself affect its validity if the parties (1) had agreed that the arbitrators might apply transnational rules or (2) or had remained silent concerning the applicable law.

and tenuous, so that there is no reason why the arbitrator should necessarily feel obliged to apply the conflict rules of the State in which the arbitration has its seat. So a number of arbitrators would feel free to decide which legal system's conflict of laws rules should be applied. Others go further still; they would not regard themselves as bound to apply the conflict rules of any *system* of law but (in the absence of an express choice of law by the parties) simply apply general principles of the conflict of laws or alternatively the conflict *rule* (i.e. the connecting factor) that seems to them appropriate, e.g. that in a contract of sale the rights of the parties are governed by the law of the seller's place of business. Such a power is enshrined in the 1998 ICC Rules on Conciliation and Arbitration,[69] though it would seem not to be exercisable where the Rome Convention applies.[70]

(c) The Supplementation or Disregard of the Applicable Law

These diverse routes to the selection of the applicable law can, of course, lead to strikingly different results. But we have not exhausted the possibilities. If not otherwise constrained by the *lex loci arbitri* or contractually adopted arbitrtion rules, the arbitrator may bypass conflict of laws rules altogether and go directly to the law, or rules of law, which he considers appropriate.[71] There have also been a number of arbitrations in which the arbitral tribunal has applied international trade usage or the *lex mercatoria* either to supplement or to displace the applicable law as determined by the arbitral tribunal. It is generally accepted that the tribunal cannot override the parties' own choice of law. More delicate is the question whether, in the absence of party choice, the arbitrator can invoke the *lex mercatoria* either in addition to or in substitution for what he has found to be the applicable law.[72] As regards supplementation of the applicable law, Article 10 of the Organisation of American

[69] Art. 17(1) of which provides that in the absence of any agreement by the parties as to the applicable law, "the Arbitral Tribunal shall apply the rules of law which it determines to be appropriate". Even in English law, which has tended to take a restrictive view of the powers of arbitrators, the courts have accepted that the references to "law" and "proper law" in Art. 13(3) embrace rules of law or general principles of law and do not require the application of a particular national law. See n. 74 *infra*.

[70] Since this is generally taken to require reference to a legal system. However, if it be the case that arbitrators are not bound to apply the conflicts rules of the seat of the arbitration or, indeed, the conflicts rules of any particular national legal system (which is the position taken here), then it would seem to follow that they are not obliged to apply the Rome Convention, even if sitting in a Convention State. They are, however, obliged to respect rules of international public policy. For a masterly analysis of this complex topic see Pierre Lalive, "Transnational (or Truly International) Public Policy and International Arbitration" in *Comparative Arbitration Practice and Public Policy in Arbitration* (ICCA Congress series no. 3), 256 ff.

[71] The legislation of several jurisdictions now expressly confers the power to do this. See below.

[72] Whether the arbitrator can choose the *lex mercatoria* as being itself the applicable law is a separate question, discussed *infra*.

States Inter-American Convention on the Law Applicable to International Contracts (1994) is of particular interest.

> "In addition to the provisions in the foregoing articles, the guidelines, customs and principles of international commercial law as well as commercial usage and practices generally accepted shall apply in order to discharge the requirements of justice and equity in the particular case."

The application of the *lex mercatoria* in disregard of the applicable law is the threshold objection to the approach taken by the arbitrators in the ICC award to which reference was made earlier. It is not clear why the tribunal found it necessary to disregard the applicable law in arriving at the result they wanted to teach. In general, legislative provisions regulating non-consumer sales are dispositive only; they can be displaced by contrary agreement and they can also be displaced by relevant trade usage, whether that usage be local or international. So in most cases it is unnecessary to reject the dispositive application of the law applicable under conflict of laws rules, for that law will also provide for its dispositive provisions to yield to contract and usage. It is only where the law in question is mandatory that there need be an urge to bypass it at all.

(d) The *Lex Mercatoria* as the Applicable Law

Assuming that for some reason the applicable law under traditional conflict of laws rules does not allow its provisions to be displaced by contrary international usage, the question is whether, instead of expressing itself as disregarding that law, the tribunal could not reach the same result more subtly by applying what they consider to be an appropriate rule of conflict to treat the *lex mercatoria* itself as the applicable law. To the extent that the *lex mercatoria* represents general principles of law common to relevant States[73] there seems no reason why it cannot be applied as the proper law governing the substantive rights of the parties. This approach has been adopted in case law.[74] Whether that part of the *lex mercatoria* represented by international trade usage that has not been expressly or impliedly incorporated into the parties' contract can be invoked in this way is a separate question. Before addressing it we need to see why a number of arbitral tribunals might wish to avoid reference to a national law to determine the dispute.

[73] The question which States are relevant is not discussed here.

[74] See, for example, the landmark decision of the English Court of Appeal in *Deutsche Schachtbau- und Tiefbohrgesellschaft mbH* v. *R'As al-Khaimah National Oil Co* [1987] 3 WLR 1023, upholding an award in which the arbitrators, under an agreement to arbitrate held to be governed by and valid under Swiss law, applied "internationally accepted principles of law governing contractual relations" to determine a dispute arising under an oil exploration agreement.

(e) The Reasons for Applying Anational Law

As the essay by Lord Mustill has shown, most of the reported cases in which the arbitrators chose to apply the *lex mercatoria* could just as well have been decided under the applicable law as determined by a conflict of laws rule. Why, then, should the parties or the arbitral tribunal strive to avoid applying the relevant national law?

At the contract stage this may be done because the parties are unable to agree on a national law to govern their contract. Where the concern is to avoid choosing the law of one or other of them this is sometimes dealt with by subjecting the contract to general principles common to the two legal systems. This was the approach adopted in the Channel Tunnel agreements and is a recipe for uncertainty, since there is a high risk that common principles either cannot be identified at all or are applied in very different ways or are too general to be of help in resolving the particular issue. A better solution is to choose the law of a neutral State. But parties do sometimes elect to avoid any reference to national law, perhaps with a view to giving the arbitral tribunal greater flexibility and responsiveness to international trade usage.

At the arbitration stage there are at least seven possible reasons why the tribunal might wish to avoid determining the applicable law or relying on the law which would ordinarily be applicable. First, there may be cases where the putative applicable law is so undeveloped that it is incapable of furnishing a solution to the issue under consideration. No developed secular legal system would admit to such a possibility[75] but the problem has been experienced in Islamic countries where the law is primarily religious in character, and with this in mind parties to contracts have sometimes made express provision for recourse to general principles of law or international trade usages in cases where the applicable law does not furnish an answer. In such a case, disregard of the applicable law is seen as the only practical solution. Secondly, the laws of the two parties are in conflict and the use of conflict rules would lead to the selection of the law of the winner; recourse to the *lex mercatoria* is thus seen as a neutral method of resolving the dispute without offending the sensitivities of the loser. Thirdly, the laws of the two parties or of the different States with which the contract is closely connected are the same as to the issue in contention, in which case the arbitral tribunal may understandably feel that no useful purpose is served by undergoing an exercise to determine which law should be treated as the applicable law. The identity of rule in the two systems provides the tribunal with a justification for declaring it to be a rule of the *lex mercatoria*. Fourthly, the rules of the competing systems are different

[75] It is thus surprising that in *SPP* v. *Arab Republic of Egypt*, ICC case no. 233 of 1992, the arbitral tribunal found that Egyptian law did not furnish an answer to the question from what date interest should run, so that this had to be resolved by reference to international law, a ruling described by Professor Gaillard as "*si caricatural qu'il suffit à discréditer la méthode*" (Emmanuel Gaillard, "Trente ans de Lex Mercatoria" [1995] *Clunet* 5 at 13.

and the choice between one national law and another under conflict rules is so finely balanced that the tribunal finds it difficult to prefer one to the other,[76] in which case reference to the *lex mercatoria* provides a way out of the problem. Fifthly, choice of a national legal system, whether by recourse to the conflict of laws or otherwise, is seen by the tribunal as inherently unsatisfactory because it involves the application to an international transaction of a national law fashioned primarily for domestic transactions. Sixthly, the tribunal simply does not like the rule of the applicable national law, or the result it would produce, and is determined to find a method of avoiding it. This was the case in the above-mentioned ICC award. Finally, the tribunal is wedded to the concept of the *lex mercatoria* and wishes to avail itself of every opportunity to apply it and to expand its influence.

(f) **Applying the** Lex Mercatoria **as "Rules of Law"**

Most of the reasons given above for seeking to bypass the conflict of laws have at least some merit,[77] and they suggest that it is fruitless to insist that arbitrators are obliged to apply conflicts of laws rules[78] or a particular national legal system, or that an international usage must be shown to have received recognition in any particular national law before it can be accorded normative force. This conclusion is reinforced by the widespread recognition that arbitral awards should be set aside only in exceptional circumstances. The parties have made their bed; they must lie on it. To the extent that the arbitral award falls beyond the purview of judicial review under the *lex loci arbitri* or on grounds for refusal of enforcement under the New York Convention it will be enforceable, and any objections to its application of the *lex mercatoria* as the applicable law are largely of theoretical interest. In such cases the arbitral tribunal is effectively free to draw on whatever materials it chooses in order to reach the result it wants to reach. This is not because the failure of the parties to designate an applicable law constitutes an implied choice of the *lex mercatoria*[79] but because, having omitted to choose the applicable law, the parties cannot complain if the arbitral tribunal looks to what it regards as

[76] Consider, for example, a dispute between multinationals over a pipeline running through six different countries.

[77] Only the last two are in my view illegitimate, the one because having found the applicable law the arbitrators have no right to disregard it merely because they think another rule is better, the other because the parties should not serve as cannon fodder for an arbitrator's personal crusade.

[78] For a powerful attack on conflicts scholarship and its dedication to the concept of an applicable national law in every case see Frederick K. Juenger, "American Conflicts Scholarship and the Law Merchant", 28 *Vanderbilt Journal of Transnational Law* 487 (1995).

[79] See K. P. Berger, *International Commercial Arbitration*, who argues persuasively (at 561) that there is usually no way of knowing the exact reason for the omission of a choice of law clause, so that it is dangerous to deduce from this an intention to be governed by the *lex mercatoria*.

the best solution to the problem. So far, national courts have shown themselves reluctant to refuse enforcement of an award solely on the ground that the tribunal applied the *lex mercatoria*.[80] If this is so where the *lex loci arbitri* is silent on the matter, *a fortiori* it will be the case where the *lex loci arbitri* authorises selection of the *lex mercatoria* as the applicable law. It is considered to do this where, though not referring *eo nomine* to the *lex mercatoria*, it authorises the arbitrator to apply *rules of law* and does not constrain him to select a "law" in the sense of a legal *system*. Article 1496 of the French Code of Civil Procedure gives statutory blessing to such an approach:

> "*L'arbitre tranche le litige conformément aux règles de droit que les parties ont choisies; à défault d'un tel choix, conformément à celles qu'il estime appropriées.*"

Provisions to similar effect are to be found in Article 1054(2) of the Netherlands Arbitration Act 1986 and in Article 42 of the 1965 Washington Convention governing investment disputes involving a state. But it appears that this option is not open in arbitral proceedings governed by the UNCITRAL Model Law, article 28 of which requires the application of "the law determined by conflict of laws rules".

(g) Is the Lex Mercatoria **Anational?**

Does this mean, then, that the *lex mercatoria* is truly anational and autonomous? Put in this way the question is ambiguous, as becomes apparent when one considers the diversity of ways in which objections to the whole concept of *lex mercatoria* have been expressed.[81] The first objection is that the *lex mercatoria*, consisting of general principles of law and international trade usage, is not a complete legal system, so that it is futile for the parties to seek to designate it as the law applicable to their contract. It is certainly the case that the *lex mercatoria* is not a complete legal system. But that does not mean that to choose it as the applicable law is wholly ineffective; merely that so far as its principles do not cover the question in dispute it will be necessary to refer to some applicable national law. Whether they do cover the question is for the tribunal to decide, drawing on whatever materials are at hand. Secondly, it is objected that the *lex mercatoria* is not an autonomous body of principles, for it is controlled by rules of public policy and mandatory rules of national law. This also is true, but it does not follow that the *lex mercatoria* lacks normative force, merely that it is subordinate to higher norms, in much the same way as principles laid down by the courts may be affected by

[80] See, for example, the protracted and ultimately unsuccessful attempts in Austria and France to upset the award in the celebrated *Norsilor* case (*Pabalk Ticaret Sirketi* v. *Ugilor/Norsilor SA* (ICC case no. 3131 of 1979)); and, for a general discussion, David W. Rivkin, "Enforceability of Arbitral Awards Based on *Lex Mercatoria*" [1993] *Arbitration International* 67.

[81] See the discussion in Craig, Park and Paulsson, *International Chamber of Commerce Arbitration* (2nd edn.), 603–9.

legislation. Thirdly, it is contended that every international usage depends for its normative force on recognition by national law. To the extent that it consists of general principles of law common to States (or to relevant States, however these might be defined) this condition is met. More debatable is whether the usage has to be shown to have been received into national law. If by this is meant a particular national law then it necessarily predicates selection of a given legal system as the applicable law, for that is the national law that is relevant to the question. Since arbitrators do from time to time decide cases according to international trade usage without reference to a national law and have their awards upheld by courts it would be rather futile to deny the efficacy of awards made on this basis. Nor can we even say, conformably with arbitration practice, that international usage is necessarily to be found in a convergence of rules in different legal systems, for such usage can also be inferred from conventions which have not yet come into force or, if in force, have not yet been ratified by the relevant States.

It is everywhere admitted that the normative force of usage, whether domestic or international, depends on its satisfying certain essential criteria.[82] But where do we look to find what these are? The usage itself cannot speak as to its own validity. There are no doubt some usages that are so broad in character and so universal of application that they would be recognised in any developed legal system, and would, indeed, be likely to have lost their distinctive status as trade usages and to have acquired the status of a general principle of law.[83] But broad principles of this kind, such as *pacta sunt servanda*, are so hedged about with qualifications which vary from one legal system to another that they serve little purpose except as a device by which an arbitral tribunal can claim support for its conclusions without having to determine an applicable law.[84] Outside these broad principles we cannot point to some universal law against which to measure the validity of a usage, for such a law does not exist; both the character of a trade usage and the conditions of its validity vary from jurisdiction to jurisdiction.[85] How, then, can arbitral tribunals satisfy themselves that an international usage is valid without resorting to national law?

A short answer to this is that if the usage is truly international then it cannot depend for its existence on any particular national law or decisions of any particular national court. That would localise and domesticate what is *ex hypothesi* international.[86] But the admission of international usage as a determinant of rights *is* dependent on national law in a different sense in that (quite

[82] See *ante* 10.

[83] See *ante* 18.

[84] Why arbitrators should want to do this is discussed *ante* 31.

[85] See Clive M. Schmitthoff, *Interpretation and Application of International Trade Usages*, a study prepared for the International Chamber of Commerce.

[86] That is not to say that national law has nothing to say about it. See, for example, s. 62(2) of the UK Sale of Goods Act 1979, which expressly preserves in relation to contracts of sale of goods "the rules of the common law, including the law merchant".

apart from mandatory rules and rules of public policy) the existence of international usage can only be ruled upon by a tribunal of competent jurisdiction,—and in the case of an arbitral tribunal, jurisdiction is determined by the *lex loci arbitri*. It is everywhere the case that an award may be set aside where the arbitrators have exceeded their jurisdiction, and that is also a ground for refusing enforcement under the New York Convention.[87] It is primarily the *lex loci arbitri* which controls the conditions in which arbitrators can make valid awards. Within the limits set by those conditions, and in the absence of a choice of law by the parties, arbitrators can draw on whatever sources seem to them proper in order to determine the rights of the parties. Accordingly the normative force of international trade usage depends not on what national law says about the usage but upon whether the power to decide on the existence and content of such usage has been exercised by a tribunal having competence under the *lex loci arbitri* and conforming with its procedural requirements.[88] National laws, through their conferment of decision-making powers on arbitral tribunals, have delegated to them the power to decide whether the requisite criteria for recognising an international usage have been satisfied and for that purpose to draw on such materials as seem to them proper.[89] As Professor Clive Schmitthoff so perceptively observed many years ago:

> ". . . the new law merchant, as an autonomous legal regulation, is founded on the complementary interaction of party autonomy and arbitration".[90]

VI. INTERNATIONAL TRADE USAGE AND THE SEARCH FOR UNIFORMITY

The underlying motive power for the new *lex mercatoria* is the desire to return to a perceived golden age when commercial law was relatively universal and the outcome of a dispute was likely to be the same in whichever country it was decided by the merchants according to international trade usage.

The first point to make is that such a golden age never truly existed. International usage was interwoven with local usage, each codification in a particular locale differed from its contemporaries and its predecessors, the rules were fragmented and in many cases uncertain in their content an ambit, and many of them were only transient.

[87] New York Convention on the Recognition and Enforcement of Foreign Arbitral Awards, art. V(1)(c).

[88] It is the need for controls of this kind which makes the concept of a *lex loci arbitri* indispensable and is the most powerful argument against the notion of delocalised arbitration. Accordingly the provisions of art. 177 of the Belgian *Code Judiciaire* depriving Belgian courts of the power of judicial review where neither party is a Belgian national are particularly unfortunate.

[89] See, for example, art. 1496 of the French Code of Civil Procedure.

[90] "International Business Law: A New Law Merchant", in Clive M. Schmitthoff's *Select Essays on International Trade Law* (ed. Chia-Jui Cheng), 20 at 33.

But even if we allow (as we must) that some unifying effects are created by an international law merchant the diversity of approaches now adopted tends to undermine it. First, we have noted the marked differences between the approaches and powers of courts and those of arbitrators, leading to the increased likelihood that the outcome of the dispute on contested issues of law will depend on the procedure adopted. Secondly, the widely diverse approaches to the inference of international trade usage from conventions that are not applicable according to their own terms mean that in one group of cases the applicable law is applied and in another group its dispositive rules are treated as displaced by international trade usage applicable to the contract. Thirdly, the difference in view as to whether there is an arbitral *lex fori* means that, unless otherwise agreed by the parties or provided by the arbitration rules to which they have subjected themselves, one arbitral tribunal will apply the conflict rules of the jurisdiction where the arbitration has its seat while another will resort to the conflict of laws rules of a different State and a third will determine the *rule* it considers appropriate without reference to the conflict rules of any particular legal *system*. Fourthly, one arbitral tribunal will seek to find an applicable law under a conflicts rule or system while another will choose a national law directly, without reference to any conflict rule, and a third will disregard all national laws and simply apply what it perceives to be the *lex mercatoria*. Finally, while arbitral tribunals are trying to escape from the application of national conflict of laws rules, modern international trade conventions almost invariably include at least some provisions laying down a uniform conflicts rule on a particular point or referring particular issues to the applicable law under rules of private international law.

Yet what some will see as anarchy will be stoutly defended by others on the ground that it is in the nature of arbitration that it is flexible and admits of a variety of approaches, and that whereas decisions of courts build up a pattern of principle and rule which contributes to the common law and to which resort may be had to predict or determine the outcome of future disputes, it is not the function of arbitral awards to develop international jurisprudence. All that matters at the end of the day is that the arbitral tribunal reaches a result that commends itself to the reasonable man as just *in the particular case*. That this is so is shown by the private nature of arbitration (which is inconsistent with its function as a law-making institution) and by the reluctance of parties to arbitration proceedings to allow the full text of awards to be published. So perhaps the growing recourse to international trade usage, to the exclusion of national law, is not such a bad thing after all.

2

Internationalization of Sales Law—Practice under the Convention on International Sale of Goods—A Primer for Attorneys and International Traders*

LOUIS F. DEL DUCA AND PATRICK DEL DUCA**

I. MORE COURTS CONFRONT THE CISG

Since the 1995 installment of our review[1] of "Practice Under the Convention On International Sale of Goods",[2] the number of reported cases involving the CISG has increased from forty-four to one hundred and forty-two and the number of States which have ratified the CISG has grown from thirty-eight to forty-seven.[3] In this installment we address developments pertaining to

* The United Nations Convention on Contracts for the International Sale of Goods, Official Records of the United Nations Conference on Contracts for the International Sale of Goods, UN Doc. A/Conf. 97/19 (1981); (1980) 19 ILM 668. The UN English-language text is reproduced in 52 (1987) *Federal Register* 6264.

** Louis Del Duca, Associate Dean and Professor of Law at Dickinson School of Law, Carlisle, PA; BA Temple; JD Harvard Law School and Dott. di Giur., University of Rome School of Law. Patrick Del Duca, Partner, Kelley Drye & Warren, Los Angeles; BA Harvard; JD Harvard Law School; Dott. di Giur., University of Bologna; Ph.D European University Institute in Florence, Italy; DEA University of Lyon (France).

The authors gratefully acknowledge the research assistance of Laura J. N. Failing, 3rd year law student and Julia M. Glencer, 2nd year law student, at The Dickinson School of Law, in the preparation of Part Two of this article.

[1] L. F. Del Duca and P. Del Duca, "Practice Under the Convention on International Sale of Goods (CISG): A Primer for Attorneys and International Traders (Part I)" (1995) 27 UCC 331.

[2] The UN Convention on Contracts for the International Sale of Goods, Official Records of the UN Conference on Contracts for the International Sale of Goods, UN Doc. A/Conf. 97/19 (1981); (1980) 19 ILM 668. The UN English-language text is reproduced in (1987) 52 *Federal Register* 6264.

[3] Systematic reporting of CISG cases has been undertaken by the UNILEX and CLOUT systems. UNILEX is a CD-ROM system that provides the case name, the case number, the date of the decision, the country, and the court for each reported case. CLOUT is a hard-copy reporting system that provides the same type of identification and also assigns a sequential number to each

contract formation, performance and remedies in connection with contracts for international sales of goods.

We also amplify in light of recent cases our earlier discussion of the "applicability" provisions of the CISG to suggest the desirability of including a

case as it is reported. The nn. in this article use this identification for each of the cases reported by tribunals outside the USA.

The "UNILEX" database was originally conceived as a research project of the Centre for Comparative and Foreign Studies (a joint venture of the Italian National Research Council, the University of Rome and the International Institute for the Unification of Private Law—UNIDROIT). The database was created and is updated by a team of experts under the supervision of Prof. M. J. Bonell, Director of the Centre. It is published by Transnational Juris Publications, Inc., One Bridge Street, Irvington, NY 10533, telephone: (914) 591–4288. Order Line: (800) 914–8186. Fax: (914) 591–2688. A hard-copy looseleaf edition of the UNILEX database has also recently become available.

UNILEX is a comprehensive database that contains, *inter alia*, the text of the Convention. It also includes summaries in English of all the cases so far reported in the different countries and is scheduled to be updated every 6 months to provide a complete collection of the existing international case law. The cases are reported both in the form of an abstract in English summarizing the essential elements of the decision along with the complete decision of the tribunal in the language in which it was originally rendered.

CLOUT ("Case Law on UNCITRAL Texts") is a system for collecting and disseminating information on court decisions and arbitral awards relating to conventions and model laws that have emanated from the work of the UN Commission on International Trade Law. The purpose of the system is to promote international awareness of such legal texts elaborated or adopted by the Commission, to enable judges, arbitrators, lawyers, parties to commercial transactions and other interested persons to take decisions and awards relating to those texts.

The national correspondents collect court decisions and arbitral awards and prepare abstracts of them in one of the official languages of the UN (i.e. Arabic, Chinese, English, French, Russian or Spanish). The Secretariat stores the decisions and awards. The abstracts are then translated by the Secretariat into the other 5 UN languages and published in all 6 languages as part of the regular documentation of UNCITRAL (under the identifying symbol: A/CN.9/SER.C/ABSTRACTS/). Documents containing abstracts are published whenever a sufficient number of abstracts has been received to justify the cost of publication. Thus, the abstracts are published at irregular intervals.

Each abstract bears a case number based on the order in which the abstracts are published, irrespective of the legal text to which the decision or award relates or of the country of its origin.

The CLOUT system was established by the Secretariat of the UN Commission on International Trade Law (UNCITRAL) pursuant to a decision by UNCITRAL at its 21st session in 1993 (A/43/17, paras. 98–109). Copies of decisions and arbitral awards available to the public will be sent to interested persons upon request addressed to UNCITRAL Secretariat, Vienna International Centre, PO Box 500, A–1400 Vienna, Austria, for a fee covering copying and mailing. Additional charges will be made for any requested fax transmission or use of courier service. The UNCITRAL Secretariat prefers not to levy such fees or charges for each individual request. Therefore, it suggests that users of the system, when making their first request for copies, make a down payment of $30.00, and once that amount is exhausted, an additional down payment, and so forth. All requests by others for permission to reproduce or translate copyrighted publications or parts thereof should be referred to the Secretary of the UN Publications Board, United Nations Headquarters, New York, NY 10017.

As at 8 May 1996, the following States have ratified the CISG: Argentina, Australia, Austria, Belarus, Bosnia and Herzgovina, Bulgaria, Canada, Chile, China, Cuba, Czech Republic, Denmark, Ecuador, Egypt, Estonia, Finland, France, Georgia, Germany, Ghana, Guinea, Hungary, Iraq, Italy, Lesotho, Lithuania, Mexico, Moldova, The Netherlands, New Zealand, Norway, Poland, Romania, the Russian Federation, Singapore, the Slovak Republic, Slovenia, Spain, Sweden, Switzerland, the Syrian Arab Republic, Uganda, Ukraine, the United States of America, Venezuela, Yugoslavia, Zambia.

supplementary choice of law clause in the sales contract to cover issues which the CISG does not address. Our goal is to address issues raised by practice under the CISG, with particular emphasis on issues raised by reported cases. As at 1 January 1996, one hundred and forty-two CISG cases (mostly from courts of first instance) have been reported as noted in Table 1.

Table 1. Reported CISG decisions

Country	*Number of Cases*
Argentina	3
Australia	1
Austria	4
France	9
Germany	62
Hungary	3
Italy	4
Mexico	1
Netherlands	22
Switzerland	9
USA	9
Arbitral Tribunals	
International Chamber of Commerce	11
Iran–United States Claims Tribunal	1
Hungarian Chamber of Commerce Court of Arbitration	1
Italian arbitration panel, Florence	1
Internationales Schiedsgericht der Bundeskammer der gewerblichen Wirtschaft (International Arbitration of the Federal Chambers of Business in Germany)	2
Total Number of Reported Cases	142

There is an especially high number of cases from the Netherlands and Germany. In the case of the Netherlands the high number can be attributed to the general openness of the Dutch legal system to international law rules and to the use of CISG as a model for many of the provisions governing domestic commercial law under the new 1992 Dutch Civil Code. In the case of Germany, it can be attributed at least in part to the early preparation of a translation of the CISG from its five official languages into German, and the significant role of German-speaking jurists in the drafting of the CISG.

II. WHAT TO DO ABOUT SIGNIFICANT ISSUES WHICH THE CISG DOES NOT ADDRESS

Fifty-two of the one hundred and forty-two cases of disputes thus far reported arising from contracts to which the CISG applies in fact involve disputed issues of law which the CISG does not address. In some instances, the parties wisely specified in a contractual choice of law clause that the law of a given nation should govern the issues to which the CISG does not speak. In the case of the United States, the preferred way to do this would be to choose the law of a specific state with particular reference to the UCC. In some instances, the parties included specific contractual provisions to cover the disputed issues to which the CISG does not speak. The risk, of course, with reliance on specific contractual provisions to address issues to which the CISG does not speak, as an alternative to a general choice of law clause, is that the parties may not be able to anticipate all of the issues that they may eventually dispute with each other. The reported cases discussed in this article in which the parties failed to agree to a contractual choice of law clause or to a contract clause pertaining specifically to the disputed issues illustrate the uncertainties which the parties face when the judge of their dispute must apply conflict of laws (i.e. private international law) rules of the forum State to determine what provisions of positive law govern the disputed point.[4]

The CISG specifically provides that it does not cover "validity" and "passage of title" issues.[5] The cases discussed in the balance of this heading illustrate other legal issues which have substantial practical significance and to which the CISG does not speak. Of the issues in this category, it is not surprising that issues related to the payment of money have to date been the most frequently litigated.

(a) What Interest Rate on Late Payments?

Forty-two of the one hundred and forty-two CISG cases reported thus far deal with the determination of the rate of interest applicable to late payment by the buyer or to refund of a purchase price payment due to the seller.[6] This

[4] CISG, *supra* n. 2, art. 7(2).

[5] CISG, *supra* n. 2, art. 4 provides:

"[t]his Convention governs only the formation of the contract of sale and the rights and obligations of the seller and the buyer arising from such a contract. In particular, except as otherwise expressly provided in this Convention, it is not concerned with:

(a) the validity of the contract or of any of its provisions or of any usage;
(b) the effect which the contract may have on the property in the goods sold."

See also Del Duca and Del Duca, *supra* n. 1 at nn. 63–71 and accompanying text.

[6] (Parties not reported), 3 KfH 0 97/89, 31 Aug. 1989 (Germany, Landgericht Stuttgart) UNILEX, CLOUT (Case 4); (Parties not reported), 410 O 198/89, 3 Apr. 1990 (Germany, Landgericht Aachen) UNILEX; (Parties not reported), 5C 73/89, 24 Apr. 1990 (Germany,

group of cases illustrates the importance of using a choice of law clause which specifies what law will govern questions to which the CISG does not speak or, in the absence of the ability to agree to such a clause, at least including a provision which specifies the rate of interest to be applied to late payments and refunds. Although the CISG contains specific provisions awarding

Amtsgericht Oldenburg in Holstein) UNILEX, CLOUT (Case 7); (Parties not reported), 5 O 543/88, 26 Sept. 1990 (Germany, Landgericht Hamburg) UNILEX, CLOUT (Case 5); (Parties not reported), 5 U 261/90, 13 June 1991 (Germany, Oberlandesgericht Frankfurt am Main) UNILEX, CLOUT (Case 1); (Parties not reported), 3/11 O 3/91, 16 Sept. 1991 (Germany, Landgericht Frankfurt am Main) UNILEX; CLOUT (Case 6); (Parties not reported), 15/91, 16 Dec. 1991 (Switzerland, Pretura della giurisdizione di Locarno-Campagna) UNILEX, CLOUT (Case 55); (Parties not reported), 7153/1992 1992 (ICC, Court of Arbitration of the International Chamber of Commerce) UNILEX, CLOUT (Case 26); (Parties not reported), 7197/1992 1992 (ICC, Court of Arbitration of the International Chamber of Commerce (Paris)) UNILEX, CLOUT (Case 104); (Parties not reported), AZ 12.G.41.471/1991, 24 Mar. 1992 (Hungary, Court of the Capital City of Budapest) UNILEX; (Parties not reported), O 42/92, 3 July 1992 (Germany, Landgericht Heidelberg) UNILEX; (Parties not reported), 19 U 97/91, 22 Sept. 1992 (Germany, Oberlandesgericht Hamm) UNILEX; (Parties not reported), 1 C 216/92, 14 Oct. 1992 (Germany, Amtsgericht Zweibrücken) UNILEX; *H* v. *K*, 12 O 153/92, 24 Nov. 1992 (Germany, Landgericht Krefeld) UNILEX; (Parties not reported) (no number assigned), 21 Dec. 1992 (Switzerland, Zivilgericht, Kanton Basel-Stadt) UNILEX, CLOUT (Case 95); (Parties not reported), 6653/1993 1993 (ICC, International Chamber of Commerce (Paris)) UNILEX, CLOUT Case (103); (Parties not reported), 9 O 85/92, 8 Feb. 1993 (Germany, Landgericht Verden) UNILEX; *Gruppo IMAR SpA* v. *Protech Horst*, 920159, 6 May 1993 (Netherlands, Arrondissementsrechtbank Roermond) UNILEX; (Parties not reported), 2 U 1230/91, 17 Sept. 1993 (Germany, Oberlandesgericht Koblenz) UNILEX; *Nieuwenhoven Vichandel GmbH* v. *Diepeveen-Dirkson BV*, 1992/1251, 30 Dec. 1993 (Netherlands, Arrondissementsrechtbank Arnhem) UNILEX, CLOUT (Case 100); (Paries Unknown), 17 U 146/93, 14 Jan. 1994 (Germany, Oberlandesgericht Düsseldorf) UNILEX; (Parties not reported), 5 U 15/93, 18 Jan. 1994 (Germany, Oberlandesgericht Frankfurt am Main) UNILEX, CLOUT (Case 79); (Parties not reported), 2 U 7418/92, 24 Jan. 1994 (Germany, Kammergericht Berlin) UNILEX, CLOUT (Case 80); (Parties not reported), 7 U 4419/93, 2 Mar. 1994 (Germany, Oberlandesgericht München) UNILEX, CLOUT (Case 83); (Parties not reported), 6 U 119/93, 10 Feb. 1994 (Germany, Oberlandesgericht Düsseldorf) UNILEX, CLOUT (Case 82); (Parties not reported), SCH–4318, 15 June 1994 (Arbitral Award, Internationales Schiedsgericht der Bundeskammer der gewerbli) UNILEX; (Parties not reported), SCH–4366, 15 June 1994 (Arbitral Award, Internationales Schiedsgericht der Bundeskammer der gewerbli) UNILEX; (Parties not reported), 6 O 85/93, 5 July 1994 (Germany, Landgericht Gieaen) UNILEX; (Parties not reported), 7660/JK, 23 Aug. 1994 (ICC, Court of Arbitration of the International Chamber of Commerce) UNILEX; (Parties not reported), G O 85/93, 26 Aug. 1994 (Germany, Landgericht Gieaen) UNILEX; *Delchi Carrier SpA* v. *Rotorex Corp.*, 88–CV–1078, 9 Sept. 1994 (USA, US Dist. Ct., ND, New York) UNILEX; CLOUT (case 85); (Parties not reported), 2 C 395/93, 21 Oct. 1994 (Germany, Amtsgericht Riedlingen) UNILEX; (Parties not reported), 12 O 674/93, 9 Nov. 1994 (Germany, Landgericht Oldenburg) UNILEX; *R. Motor snc* v. *M. Auto Vertriebs GmbH*, 7 U 1720/94, 8 Feb. 1995 (Germany, Oberlandesgericht München) UNILEX; (Parties not reported), 11 U 206/93, 8 Feb. 1995 (Germany, Oberlandesgericht Hamm) UNILEX; (Parties not reported), 12 O 2028/93, 15 Feb. 1995 (Germany, Landgericht Oldenburg) UNILEX; (Parties not reported), 2 C 600/94, 8 Mar. 1995 (Germany, Amtsgericht Wangen) UNILEX; *Société Camara Agraria Provincial de Guipuzcoa* v. *Andre Margaron*, 156, 29 Mar. 1995 (France, Cour d'Appel de Grenoble, Chambre Commerciale) UNILEX; (Parties not reported), 54 O 644/94, 5 Apr. 1995 (Germany, Landgericht Landshut) UNILEX; *Marques Roque Joachim* v. *Sàrl La Holding Manin Rivière*, RG 93/4879, 26 Apr. 1995 (France, Cour d'Appel de Grenoble, Chambre Commerciale) UNILEX, CLOUT (Case 85); (Parties not reported), 20 U 76/94, 24 May 1995 (Germany, Oberlandesgericht Celle) UNILEX; (Parties not reported), 41 O 111/95, 20 July 1995 (Germany, Landgericht Aachen) UNILEX. *See also* Franco Ferrari, "Uniform Application and Interest Rates Under the 1980 Vienna Sales Convention" (1995) 24 *Ga.J Int'l & Comp.L* 467.

interest for late payment to buyers[7] and reimbursement of the purchase price by sellers required to refund the price,[8] it does not specify which country's law should be applied in determining the applicable rate of interest.

Thus far the reported cases have generally ruled that the law of the country of the creditor's place of business applies, an unsurprising result given that creditors are likely to bring their actions in their home country. The implicit reasoning behind this kind of holding appears to be based on the hypothesis that in the absence of timely payment, the creditor will cover its need for funds by borrowing in the credit markets of the country in which it has its place of business. In simple cases this reasoning appears plausible. However, it does not address the realities of currency exchange risks, differing national inflation rates, multinational corporate creditors and debtors, the availability of hedging instruments and the international character of financial markets. Because of these realities, both parties to a contract are well advised to address the issue at the time of contracting rather than rely upon a judge or arbitrator attempting to identify a private international law criterion to determine what interest rate should apply.

If the parties fail to address the issue at the time of contracting, the judge of their dispute may be forced to select an interest rate which will hopefully approximate the creditor's loss.[9] The general principles of the CISG are that damages for breach of contract are to consist of a sum equal to the loss suffered by the aggrieved party as a consequence of the breach.[10] The common sense approach of the reported cases in selecting the interest rate indicated by the law of the creditor's country is generally consistent with this notion; however, as the CISG comes to be used for larger and more complex contracts, the parties to such contracts may wish to avoid arguments about what kind of risk as to the cost of money a debtor contracting party assumed by simply

[7] CISG, *supra* n. 2, art. 78 provides:

"[i]f a party fails to pay the price or any other sum that is in arrears, the other party is entitled to interest on it, without prejudice to any claim for damages recoverable under article 74."

[8] CISG, *supra* n. 2, art. 84(1) provides:

"[i]f the seller is bound to refund the price, he must also pay interest on it, from the date on which the price was paid. *See also* (Parties not reported), 7660/JK Aug. 23, 1994 (Arbitral Award, ICC Court of Arbitration (Paris)) UNILEX."

[9] (Parties not reported), 3KfH 0 97/89, 31 Aug. 1989 (Germany, Landgericht Stuttgart) UNILEX, CLOUT (Case 4); (Parties not reported), SCH–4366, 15 June 1994 (Arbitral Award, Internationales Schiedsgericht der Bundeskammer der gewerblichen Wirtschaft) UNILEX.

[10] CISG, *supra* n. 2, art. 61 (1)(b) provides:

"[i]f the buyer fails to perform any of his obligations under the contract of this Convention, the seller may . . . (b) claim damages as provided by in articles 74–77."

CISG, *supra* n. 2, art. 74 provides:

"[d]amages for breach of contract by one party consist of a sum equal to the loss, including loss of profit, suffered by the other party as a consequence of the breach. Such damages may not exceed the loss which the party in breach foresaw or ought to have foreseen at the time of the conclusion of the contract, in light of the facts and matters of which he then knew or ought to have known, as a possible consequence of the breach of contract."

specifying the applicable interest rate, and of course currency in which overdue funds are to be paid.

At least one reported case makes the further point that, in addition to specifying the country whose law should be applied to govern issues to which the CISG does not speak, it is also desirable to pinpoint a specific interest rate because national law as to the applicable interest rate may itself be unclear. In that case the German court, after deciding that Swedish law governed the question, wrestled with whether Swedish law made applicable a Swedish statutory or a Swedish discount banking rate, which at the time differed by 8 per cent.[11] Thus, the well drafted contract will specify a governing law to address questions to which the CISG does not speak, and it will also specify the parties' contractual agreement on the specific interest rate payable by either party in the event of a late payment or a refund.

(b) Other Issues which the CISG does not Address

Other recent CISG cases which have required courts to use private international law (i.e. conflicts of law rules of the forum State) to determine which State's law should apply in resolving non-CISG issues pertain to:

(a) burden of proof of non-conformity of goods;[12]
(b) validity of penalty clauses;[13]
(c) prescription (i.e. statute of limitations);[14]

[11] (Parties not reported), 7 U 4419/93, 2 Mar. 1994 (Germany, Oberlandesgericht Munchen) UNILEX, CLOUT (Case 83).

[12] (Parties not reported), 6653/1993 1993 (ICC, Court of Arbitration of the International Chamber of Commerce (Paris)) UNILEX, CLOUT (Case 103).

[13] A Bulgarian buyer and an Austrian seller who had contracted for the sale of goods submitted this case for arbitration before the Court of Arbitration of the International Chamber of Commerce. The seller: (1) alleged that the buyer had not performed its obligations under the contract; and (2) challenged the validity of the contract's penalty clause limiting the amount of damages. Noting the absence in the CISG of any provision governing penalty clauses, the court applied Austrian law in holding that the seller was entitled to full damages despite the limitations of the penalty clause in the contract: (Parties not reported), 7197/1992 1992 (ICC, Court of Arbitration of the International Chamber of Commerce (Paris)) UNILEX, CLOUT (Case 104).

[14] An Italian seller and a Czech buyer agreed that their contract would be governed by Austrian law and that any disputes would be submitted to the ICC Court of Arbitration. The buyer submitted the case for arbitration when a piece of assembly line machinery (which the seller had guaranteed for up to 18 months) was found to be defective. The buyer claimed partial avoidance of the contract, reimbursement of the purchase price for the equipment which had not yet been delivered and damages for breach of contract by the seller. The seller in turn alleged that the buyer had commenced the arbitral proceedings after the expiration of a contractually fixed period of 18 months within which the buyer was to exercise its right to give notice of non-conformity. The court concluded that by inserting this 18-month clause in their contract the parties had used CISG Art. 6 to derogate from Art. 39(2) which *inter alia* sets forth a 2-year maximum time limit for the buyer to give notice of non-conformity. It ruled that the buyer's claim was time-barred by this contractual 18-month warranty period. It also noted that since the CISG does not mention the prescription period within which a buyer who has given timely notice of non-conformity has to commence legal action, the prescription period is a question outside the CISG

(d) selection of forum for dispute resolution;[15]
(e) the existence of a "company";[16]
(f) existence of an agency relationship;[17]
(g) the right of a party to off-set claims;[18] and,
(h) the currency in which price should be made.[19]

If international traders become more sophisticated in explicitly resolving in their contracts the issues not covered by the CISG, or at least sophisticated enough to realize that the choice of the CISG to govern their contracts does not obviate the need to select a national law to govern issues to which the CISG does not speak, they will achieve greater predictability in their contractual relations.

and is therefore governed by applicable domestic law. Since the parties had chosen Austrian law, the contract was governed by the CISG under the conflicts of law basis for its application: (Parties not reported), 7660/JK, 23 Aug. 1994 (ICC, Court of Arbitration of the International Chamber of Commerce (Paris)) UNILEX, *see also* (Parties not reported), 11 U 191/94, 9 June 1995 (Germany, Oberlandesgericht Hamm) UNILEX.

[15] An Argentine court held that the issue of the validity of the forum selection clause did not fall within the scope of the CISG and was to be decided according to the applicable domestic law. Applying Argentine law, the court found that the Argentine buyer had implicitly accepted the forum selection clause in favor of an Italian forum by failing to object to it when signing an invoice containing the clause in question. *Inta SA* v. *MCS Officina Meccanica SpA*, 45626, 14 Oct. 1993 (Argentina, Camara Nacional en lo Comercial, sala E) UNILEX.

[16] (Parties not reported), 5 0 543/88, 26 Sept. 1990 (Germany, Landgericht Hamburg) UNILEX, CLOUT (Case 5).

[17] Two German courts have held that the issue of agency is excluded from the scope of the CISG. In one case, an Italian seller and a German buyer contracted for the sale of wine. The seller assigned his right to payment arising from the contracts to an Italian company. The assignee brought an action to recover the price when the buyer did not pay. The court held that since the CISG does not contain any rule on agency, Italian law was applicable to agency issues relating to the assignment of the contract price: (Parties not reported), 2 U 7418/92, 24 Jan. 1994 (Germany, Kammergericht Berlin) UNILEX, CLOUT (Case 80).

The second case also involved an Italian seller and a German buyer. However, upon holding that the CISG did not apply, the court in this case applied German rather than Italian law to determine the question whether the buyer was acting as an agent: (Parties not reported), 5 0 543/88, 26 Sept. 1990 (Germany, Landgericht Hamburg) UNILEX, CLOUT (Case 5).

[18] One court in Germany and two in The Netherlands have held that the question of a party's right to off-set another party's claim for damages falls outside the scope of the CISG and must be determined by domestic law: (Parties not reported), 1992/182, 25 Feb. 1993 (Netherlands, Arrondissementsrechtbank Arnhem) UNILEX, CLOUT (Case 99); *Gruppo IMAR SpA* v. *Protech Horst*, 920159, 6 May 1993 (Netherlands, Arrondissementsrechtbank Roermond) UNILEX; (Parties not reported), 2 U 1230/91, 17 Sept. 1993 (Germany, Oberlandesgericht Koblenz) UNILEX.

[19] (Parties not reported), 13 U 51/93, 20 Apr. 1994 (Germany, Oberlandesgericht Frankfurt am Main) UNILEX; CLOUT (Case 84).

III. UPDATE ON RECENT APPLICABILITY AND SCOPE CASES

(a) More on the "Four Bases for Applying the CISG"

Part One[20] of this article notes that the CISG is applicable if:

(1) The parties to the contract have their places of business in different States and such States are Contracting States (hereafter referred to as the "place of business" basis for applying the CISG);
(2) The rules of private international law lead to the application of the law of a State that has ratified the CISG (hereafter referred to as the "private international law-conflict of laws" basis for applying the CISG);
(3) The parties to the contract include a choice of law clause making the CISG applicable (hereafter referred to as the "opt-in" basis for applying the CISG); or
(4) The CISG can be applied because it is part of the *lex mercatoria*.

A recent International Chamber of Commerce arbitration award involves an interesting interplay between the "opt-in" and Article 1 "Conflicts of Law" basis for applying the CISG. In that case an Italian seller and Czech buyer agreed to a contract which provided that Austrian law governed without, however, specifying "including" or "excluding" the CISG.[21] The arbitral court reached that right result by holding that Austria's ratification of the CISG made the CISG part of Austrian law, and that therefore Austrian law "including" the CISG should be applied. Although the logic of the arbitral court's ruling is so clear that it is hard to understand how the parties could litigate the point in good faith, drafting a choice of law clause to specify a governing national law "including" the CISG would seem to obviate any basis for such a claim.

A recent German case reached the same result.[22] In response to a party's claim that contractual reference to German law as the law governing the contract impliedly excluded application of the CISG, the German court concluded that, in the absence of explicit exclusion, a clause choosing the law of a contracting State as applicable law will not constitute an "opt-out" under Article 6 of the CISG.[23] Similar reasoning was applied by another German court in a case between a Swiss buyer and a German seller in which the CISG was applicable under the Article 1(1)(a) "places of business" rule. The court there

[20] *See* Del Duca and Del Duca, *supra* n. 1, at 339 ff.

[21] (Parties not reported), 7660/JK, 23 Aug. 1994 (International Chamber of Commerce Court of Arbitration (Paris)) UNILEX.

[22] (Parties not reported), 7 U 3758/94, 8 Feb. 1995 (Germany, Oberlandesgericht München) UNILEX.

[23] CISG, *supra* n. 2, art. 6 provides:

> "[t]he parties may exclude the application of this Convention or, subject to Article 12, derogate from or vary the effect of any of its provisions."

ruled that reference by the parties in their pleadings to provisions of the German Civil Code was not sufficient to exclude application of the CISG even though the reference to the German law was a valid choice of law under German conflicts of law.[24]

In all three of these cases, the court reached the right result by holding that a reference to the law of a contracting State, i.e. a State which has ratified the CISG, included application of the CISG as well as the other law of the contracting State. Other courts in the absence of compelling circumstances requiring a contrary ruling should reach the same result because the CISG becomes part of the laws of a contracting State, and also because CISG Article 7(1) calls upon all courts to attempt to interpret the CISG in a uniform manner. However, there is no "supreme" court to provide authoritative rulings on CISG issues. Parties to contracts would therefore be well advised more firmly to close the door to unfounded litigation claims by clearly "including" or "excluding" the CISG as the law to be applied in such situations.

(b) What is a "Contract for Sale of Goods"?—Transactions Included or Excluded by CISG

Article 1 of the CISG states that the CISG applies "to contracts of sales of goods between parties whose places of business are in different contracting states".[25] The CISG does not contain any definition of "contract of sale of goods".[26] However, Article 2 *inter alia* excludes from CISG coverage sales of goods for "personal, family or household" use and other sales such as sales by auction, execution or otherwise by authority of law, etc.[27]

Questions regarding what types of transactions qualify as a "sale of goods" subject to the CISG will have to be resolved without the availability of a UCC Section 2–106 definition of "contract of sale"[28] or a Section 2–105 definition of "goods".[29]

In a recent case, a German company ordered market research from a Swiss company.[30] The German court held that the CISG was not applicable because

[24] (Parties not reported), 54 O 644/94, 5 Apr. 1995 (Germany, Landgericht Landshut) UNILEX.

[25] CISG, *supra* n. 2, art. 1.

[26] Del Duca and Del Duca, *supra* n. 1, at 347 ff.

[27] Del Duca and Del Duca, *supra* n. 1, at 351 ff.

[28] UCC § 2–106 provides:

" '[c]ontract of sale' includes both a present sale of goods and a contract to sell goods at a future time."

[29] UCC §2–105 provides:

" '[g]oods' means all things (including specially manufactured goods) which are movable at the time of identification to the contract for sale other than the money in which the price is to be paid, investment securities (Article 8) and things in action. 'Goods' also includes the unborn young of animals and growing crops and other identifiable things attached to realty as described in the section on goods to be severed from realty" (Article 2–107).

[30] (Parties not reported), 19 U 282/93, 26 Aug. 1994 (Germany, Oberlandesgericht Köln) UNILEX.

the contract was neither a contract for the sale of "goods" as required by CISG Article 1(1) nor a contract for the "supply of goods to be manufactured or produced", governed by CISG Article 3(1). Instead, the court found the contract to be one for performance of work rather than for sale of goods.[31]

On the matter of sale of "made-to-order" goods, the CISG specifies that it is applicable to contracts for the sale of goods to be manufactured unless the party who orders the goods "undertakes to supply a substantial part of the materials necessary for such manufacturing production".[32]

Exclusion of contracts in which the party who orders the goods undertakes to supply a "substantial part of the materials necessary for such manufacture or production" under CISG Article 3(1) has been litigated in several cases. For example, where a German buyer and a French seller entered into a contract ordering textiles to be produced by seller, the German court found the contract to be one for "supply of goods to be manufactured or produced", since the buyer had not undertaken to supply a substantial part of the materials necessary to manufacture or produce the textiles.[33] However, in a 1994 Austrian case[34] the court ruled the CISG inapplicable where an Austrian company had entered into an agreement with a Yugoslav company to deliver to the Yugoslav company the necessary raw materials for processing finished goods thereafter to be delivered back to the Austrian company.

With reference to mixed transactions involving labor or services, the CISG also does not apply to contracts in which "*the preponderant part* of the obligation of a party who furnishes the goods consists in the supply of labor or services"[35] (emphasis added).

Where the charge for the services of dismantling a second-hand airplane hangar that a French seller sold to a Portuguese buyer was approximately only 25 per cent of the total purchase price, a French court applied the "preponderant part" provision of Article 3(2) to the hybrid "sale-service" transaction and held the contract subject to the CISG.[36]

[31] *Ibid.* The German court, referencing the French and English versions of the CISG, defined "goods" as "tangible, corporeal things which are typically sold in a commercial setting": *ibid.*

[32] CISG, *supra* n. 2, art. 3(1). *See also* Del Duca and Del Duca, *supra* n. 1, at 352 ff.

[33] (Parties not reported), 12 O 2028/93, 15 Feb. 1995 (Germany, Landgericht Oldenburg) UNILEX. *See also Marques Roque Joachim* v. *Sàrl La Holding Manin Rivière*, RG 93/4879, 26 Apr. 1995(France, Cour d'Appel de Grenoble, Chambre Commerciale) UNILEX; *Fa. N. GmbH* v. *Fa. N. GmbH & Co KG*, 8 Ob 509/93, 27 Oct. 1994 (Austria, Oberster Gerichtshof) UNILEX.

[34] (Parties not reported), 8 Ob 509/93, 27 Oct. 1994 (Austria, Oberster Gerichtshof) UNILEX.

[35] CISG, *supra* n. 2, art. 3(2). *See also* Del Duca and Del Duca, *supra* n. 1, at 353 ff.

[36] *Marques Roque Joachim* v. *Sàrl La Holding Manin Rivière*, RG 93/4879, 26 Apr. 1995 (France, Cour d'Appel de Grenoble, Chambre Commerciale) UNILEX.

IV. WHEN THE CISG CREATES A CONTRACT

(a) Oral Contracts are Binding: No Statute of Frauds

Article 11 of the CISG[37] abolishes the Statute of Frauds for contracts to which it applies. Unlike the Statute of Frauds requirement of the Uniform Commercial Code[38] section 2–201,[39] a contract for the sale of goods can be concluded under the CISG without any written agreement.

However, the CISG provides a compromise between nations which utilize a Statute of Frauds requirement as a prerequisite for enforcing an oral contract for the sale of goods and those which permit enforcement of oral con-

[37] CISG, *supra* n. 2, art. 11 provides:

"[a] contract of sale need not be concluded in or evidenced by writing and is not subject to any other requirements as to form. It may be proved by any means, including witnesses."

[38] Uniform Commercial Code (hereinafter UCC).

[39] UCC §2–201 provides:

"(1) Except as otherwise provided in this section a contract for the sale of goods for the price of $500 or more is not enforceable by way of action or defense unless there is some writing sufficient to indicate that a contract for sale has been made between the parties and signed by the party against who enforcement is sought or by his authorized agent or broker. A writing is not insufficient because it omits or incorrectly states a term agreed upon but the contract is not enforceable under this paragraph beyond the quantity of goods shown in each writing.

(2) Between merchants if within a reasonable time a writing in confirmation of the contract and sufficient against the sender is received and the party receiving it has reason to know its contents, it satisfies the requirement of subsection (1) against such party unless written notice of objection to its contents is given within 10 days after it is received.

(3) A contract which does not specify the requirements of subsection (1) but which is valid in other respects is enforceable

(a) if the goods are to be specially manufactured by the buyer and are not suitable for sale to others in the ordinary course of the seller's business and the seller, before notice of repudiation is received and under circumstances which reasonably indicate that the goods are for the buyer, has made either a substantial beginning of their manufacture or commitments to their procurement; or

(b) if the party against who enforcement is sought admits in his pleading, testimony or otherwise in court that a contract for sale was made, but the contract is not enforceable under this provision beyond the quantity of goods admitted; or

(c) with respect to goods for which payment has been made and accepted or which have been received and accepted" (Sec. 2–206).

But see UCC Revised Art. 2. Sales §2–201 (The American Law Institute Proposed Council Draft No. 1, 1995) which would revise §2–201 to provide:

"[a] contract or modification thereof is enforceable, whether or not there is a record signed by a party against whom enforcement is sought, even if the contract or modification is not capable of performance within one year after its making": *ibid.* at 15.

Comment 3 to this proposed revision of Art. 2 suggests:

"[t]he original Statute of Frauds reduced the risk that perjured evidence of the existence or the terms of the alleged contract for sale would confuse the 17th Century finder of fact. The Drafting Committee concluded that this risk is neutralized by the modern fact finding process and that current §2–201 was frequently used to avoid liability in cases where there was credible evidence of an agreement and no evidence of perjury. Moreover, there is no persuasive evidence that the valuable habit of reducing agreements to a signed record will be adversely affected by the repeal": *ibid.*, at 15–16.

Those for retention of the provision cite evidentiary functions of the Statute of Frauds deemed desirable, particularly in a litigation system as in the US where the right to a jury trial is broadly guaranteed.

tracts for sale of goods. CISG Article 96 permits a ratifying country to make a reservation[40] which has the effect of nullifying the CISG Article 11 abolition of the Statute of Frauds requirement.

The United States has not filed an Article 96 reservation to the abolition of the writing requirement (see Appendix A, *infra*). Accordingly, while US domestic contracts for the sale of goods are subject to the UCC Section 2–201[41] Statute of Frauds, US international sale of goods contracts to which the CISG applies are not normally subject to the Statute of Frauds writing requirements.

A recent Mexican case[42] illustrates this difference in handling Statute of Frauds issues in transactions subject to the UCC as distinguished from transactions subject to the CISG. In that case, the Mexican Commission for the Protection of Foreign Trade (COMPROMEX) held enforceable an oral contract for the sale of twenty-four tons of garlic between a Mexican seller and a Californian buyer. The seller delivered the goods and an invoice with the purchase price to the buyer, who then refused to pay the balance due. In the arbitration proceeding, COMPROMEX found that because of the CISG's applicability the contract need not be in writing. In addition, the invoice and documents of carriage were deemed sufficient proof of the contract's existence. It also found that the buyer had breached its obligations under the contract and ruled that the purchase price be paid.[43]

In another interesting case,[44] a German court applying the CISG held enforceable an oral contract between a German buyer and a French seller, noting that "a contract of sale . . . may be proved by any means, including witnesses".[45] The court utilized order forms which contained the signatures of the parties and the testimony of two witnesses to conclude that a valid

[40] CISG, *supra* N. 2, art. 96 provides:

"[a] Contracting State whose legislation requires contracts of sale to be concluded in or evidenced by writing may at any time make a declaration in accordance with article 12 that any provision of article 11, article 29, or Part II of this Convention, that allows a contract of sale or its modification or termination by agreement or any offer, acceptance, or other indication of intention to be made in any form other than in writing, does not apply where any party has his place of business in that state."

CISG, *supra* n. 2, art. 12 provides:

"[a]ny provision of article 11, article 29, or Part II of this Convention that allows a contract of sale or its modification or termination by agreement, or any offer, acceptance, or other indication of intention to be made in any form other than in writing does not apply where any party has his place of business in a contracting State which has made a declaration under article 96 of this Convention. The parties may not derogate from or vary the effect of this article."

[41] *See supra* n. 130.

[42] *Jos Lois Morales y/o Son Export, SA de CV, de Hermosillo Sonora, Mexico* v. *Nez Marketing de Los Angeles California, EUA*, M/66/92, 4 May 1993 (Mexico COMPROMEX, Comision para la Proteccion del Commercio Exterior de Mexico) UNILEX.

[43] *Ibid.*

[44] (Parties not reported), 2HO 1434/92, 1 Dec. 1993 (Germany, Landgericht Memmingen) UNILEX.

[45] *Ibid. See also supra* n. 116; *V. Russian German joint venture* v. *Fa. Va. Gesellschaft für Wirtschaftskooperation mbH*, 7 U 5460/94, 8 Mar. 1995 (Germany, Oberlandesgericht München) UNILEX.

contract had been entered into.[46] Although different legal routes would have to be followed, the result in this case probably would be the same under the UCC or the CISG. Under the UCC Section 2–201 Statute of Frauds,[47] the order forms would probably qualify as writing sufficient to indicate that a contract of sale was made and therefore enable the plaintiff then to attempt actually to prove the existence of the oral contract.

One US case suggests that many international traders, and perhaps some judges, are as yet unaware of the CISG, and in particular of how it changes the substantive law otherwise applicable to Statute of Frauds issues. In *GPL Treatment, Ltd.* v. *Louisiana-Pacific Corporation*,[48] the Oregon state court appellate judges adhering to the majority opinion appear to have overlooked the applicability of the CISG. As a result of not focusing on the applicability of the CISG, they undertook a complicated application of the UCC Statute of Frauds requirement. The decision that they reached, as the dissenting opinion makes clear, is consistent with the result provided by the CISG; however, had they relied on the CISG, as the dissenting opinion states was required, their reasoning would have been better founded. The responsibility for overlooking the applicability of the CISG cannot, however, be squarely assigned to the appellate judges authoring the majority opinion; the reported opinions of the appellate court suggest that the plaintiff *failed timely to raise* the applicability of the CISG in the trial court.

In *GPL Treatment, Ltd.*, a Canadian seller of wood products sued a US buyer for breach of an oral contact in the Oregon trial courts. The majority opinion of the Oregon state appellate court ruled that the buyer's silence in response to confirming communications sent by seller to buyer constituted confirmation of the oral agreement. In the absence of a response by buyer objecting to its contents, the seller's confirming communication was deemed to satisfy the UCC Section 2–201 Statute of Frauds writing requirement against the non-objecting buyer and therefore could be used as a basis for enforcing the oral agreement against the buyer.[49]

[46] (Parties not reported), 2HO 1434/92, 1 Dec. 1993 (Germany Landgericht Memmingen) UNILEX.

[47] UCC §2–201(1) provides:

> "(1) Except as otherwise provided in this section a contract for the sale of goods for the price of $500 or more is not enforceable by way of action or defense unless there is some writing sufficient to indicate that a contract for sale has been made between the parties and signed by the party against who enforcement is sought or by his authorized agent or broker. A writing is not insufficient because it omits or incorrectly states a term agreed upon but the contract is not enforceable under this paragraph beyond the quantity of goods shown in each writing."

[48] 894 P.2d 470 (Ore. App. 1995); *GPL Treatment, Ltd* v. *Louisiana-Pacific Corp.*, 9209–06143 CA A81171, 4 Apr. 1995 (USA, Ct. of Appeals of Oregon) UNILEX.

[49] UCC §2–201(2) provides:

> "(2) Between merchants if within a reasonable time a writing in confirmation of the contract and sufficient against the sender is received and the party receiving it has reason to know its contents, it satisfies the requirements of subsection (1) against such party unless written notice of objection to its contents is given within 10 days after it is received."

The dissenting appellate opinion in *GPL Treatment, Ltd.* concluded that the communication sent by seller to buyer after the alleged oral contract was entered into did not qualify as confirmation of an oral contract. Accordingly, the seller would be barred by the UCC Statute of Frauds from enforcing the oral agreement. However, the dissent noted that application of the CISG would enable the seller to enforce the oral agreement. The CISG's treatment in the court's opinions is limited to a footnote in the dissenting opinion which states:

> "I would, however, address plaintiffs' cross-assignment that the trial court erred in refusing to apply the United Nations Convention on Contracts for the International Sale of Goods (CISG) . . . instead of the UCC Article 11 of the CISG does not require a contract to be 'evidenced by writing' and, thus, would defeat [appellee's] statute of fraud defense if the trial court abused its discretion . . . in ruling that plaintiffs' attempt to raise the CISG was untimely and that they had waived reliance on that theory."[50]

This footnote reference recalls the kind of "surprise" reflected in Part I's discussion of the Southern District of New York's *Filanto* decision. That is, at the time of contracting, just as the Italian and the US parties to the contract for the sale of shoes at issue in the *Filanto* case had no clue what law really governed their contractual relationship, so the Canadian and US parties to this contract had no clue at the time of their dialog about what law governed when that dialog gave rise to the formation of a contract. And, just as the plaintiff's failure in the *Filanto* case at the time of trial court proceedings to understand the applicability of the CISG and the implications of the applicability led the trial court to reject its effort to bring suit in the USA, so the Canadian plaintiff's apparent failure in the instant case to raise in timely fashion the CISG's applicability led to the case's resolution on principles of law other than the CISG.

The *Filanto* and *GPL Treatment, Ltd.* cases just discussed suggest several lessons for US international traders in respect of the Statute of Frauds. First, the CISG elimination of the Statute of Frauds provision requires additional caution on the part of sales and procurement personnel in the negotiation of contracts for the international sale of goods in order to avoid unintentionally becoming contractually bound. At the very beginning of the negotiation process, the US participants would be well advised to state in writing that no agreement will be concluded until formal writing is executed, and that all negotiations are simply to be considered negotiations on which the other party has no right whatsoever to rely until the formal writing is executed. Once a contract is made, it is generally advisable also to provide that contractual modifications are to be in writing because the CISG provides that a contract

[50] *Ibid.*, at 477. In both the *Filanto* and *GPL Treatment Ltd* cases the parties to the contract had their places of business in different contracting States, thereby making the CISG applicable under Art. 1(1)(a). The countries involved in the cases (i.e. Canada, Italy and the USA) have all ratified the CISG.

in writing which contains a provision requiring any modification or termination by agreement to be in writing may not be otherwise modified or terminated by agreement.[51] The UCC contains a comparable provision.[52]

It is prudent to include as part of any written offer a requirement that any acceptance must be in writing. In addition, the offeree may wish to include in a written acceptance the terms of the original offer and further specify that the acceptance contains all the terms and conditions of the parties' agreement, which are not subject to variation except in writing.

(b) Offer and Acceptance Rules

Articles 14 to 24 of the CISG contain special rules pertaining to offer and acceptance. Comparison of these rules with the UCC "mail box", "firm offer", and "battle of the forms" rules illustrates some of these provisions.

(i) Status of the "Mail Box" Acceptance Rule

Under the CISG, acceptances are effective when received.[53] Under the US common law "mail box" rule acceptances are effective on dispatch. On its face, this is an important difference between the UCC and the CISG. Although no cases directly on point on this issue have yet been reported, it should however be noted that the impact of the CISG "receipt rule" may be softened by Article 16(1),[54] which on the important issue of timeliness of revocation of offers provides: "(1) Until a contract is concluded, an offer may be revoked if revocation reaches the offeree before it has dispatched an acceptance." For the limited purpose of determining the timeliness of a revocation of an offer, this

[51] CISG, *supra* n. 93, art. 29(2) provides:

"[a] contract in writing which contains a provision requiring any modification or termination by agreement to be in writing may not be otherwise modified or terminated by agreement. However, a party may be precluded by his conduct from asserting such a provision to the extent that the other party has relied on that contract."

[52] UCC §2–209 provides:

"[a] signed agreement which excludes modification or recision except by a signed writing cannot be otherwise modified or rescinded, but except as between merchant such a requirement on a form supplied by the merchant must be separately signed by the other party."

[53] CISG, *supra* n. 93, art. 18(2) provides:

"[a]n acceptance of an offer becomes effective at the moment the indication of assent reaches the offeror. An acceptance is not effective if the indication of assent does not reach the offeror within the time he has fixed or, if no time is fixed, within a reasonable time, due account being taken of the circumstances of the transaction, including the rapidity of the means of communication employed by the offeror. An oral offer may be accepted immediately unless the circumstances indicate otherwise."

[54] CISG, *supra* n. 2, art. 16(1). The United States "mailbox" rule, which generally makes an acceptance effective on dispatch, is incorporated into the UCC under § 1–103, which provides that "[u]nless displaced by the particular provisions [of the UCC], the principles of law and equity . . . shall supplement its provisions". There is no provision in the UCC on whether the acceptance is effective on dispatch or on receipt.

CISG provision in substance arguably makes the acceptance effective on dispatch rather than on receipt.

(ii) Unintentionally Irrevocable Offers

Both the UCC and the CISG permit irrevocable offers to be made without consideration. However, the CISG broadens enforceability of such offers beyond the scope of the UCC rule.

The UCC provides that "an offer by a merchant to buy or sell goods in a signed writing which by its terms gives assurance that it will be held open is not revocable for lack of consideration".[55] The CISG instead provides that an offer is irrevocable if:

> "it indicates, whether by stating a fixed time for acceptance or otherwise, that it is irrevocable, or if it was reasonable for the offeree to rely on the offer as being irrevocable and the offeree has acted in reliance on the offer."[56]

Unlike the UCC, the CISG does not require "signed writing which by its terms gives assurance that it will be held open" as a condition for making the offer irrevocable. In addition, under the CISG, an offer is irrevocable merely because it was reasonable for the offeree to rely on the offer as being irrevocable and its offeree acts in reliance on the offer. To avoid accidentally making an irrevocable offer under the CISG as a result of stating a fixed time for acceptance, such offers should state something like "[t]his offer expires after thirty days, but can be revoked at any time".

(iii) Battle of the Forms Lives On

The CISG initially makes most "acceptances" with different or additional terms a counter-offer rather than an acceptance.[57] It does not explicitly contain the UCC concept of an "expression of acceptance" which has the same effect as an acceptance.[58] However, the CISG compromises between the old common law "mirror image" approach and the UCC approach to contract formation which merely looks to agreement on essential terms.

Under the CISG[59] a reply to an offer which purports to be an acceptance but which contains additions, limitations or other modifications is initially classified as a rejection of the offer and constitutes a counter-offer. However,

[55] UCC § 2–205.
[56] CISG, *supra* n. 2, art. 16(2).
[57] CISG, *supra* n. 2, art. 19(1).
[58] UCC § 2–207(1) provides:

> "[a] definite and seasonable expression of acceptance or a written confirmation which is sent within a reasonable time operates as an acceptance even though it states terms additional to or different from those offered or agreed upon, unless acceptance is expressly made conditional on assent to the additional or different terms."

[59] CISG, *supra* n. 2, art. 19(1).

the rigidity of this counter-offer approach is softened by the language immediately following it, which by implication adopts an "expression of acceptance" type approach. This language states that a reply to an offer which purports to be an acceptance but contains additional or different terms which do not "materially" alter the terms of the offer constitutes an acceptance, unless the offeror, without undue delay, objects orally to the discrepancy or dispatches a notice to that effect.[60] If the offeror does not so object, the terms of the contract are the terms of the offer with the modifications contained in the acceptance.[61] This movement in the direction of permitting a contract to be created on the basis of agreement on essential terms is in turn altered by the immediately following provision which states:

> "[a]dditional or different terms relating among other things to the price, payment, quality and quantity of the goods, place and time of delivery, extent of one party's liability to the other or the settlement of disputes are considered to alter the terms of the offer materially."[62]

Despite this broad coverage of what constitutes a "material term" making the response to an offer a counter-offer under the CISG, some cases involving "non-material" additional or different terms have already been reported. An example of a non-material modification is found in a recent German case in which a German buyer had ordered goods from an Italian seller.[63] The seller replied in writing which included a provision calling for all claims of defect to be made within thirty days. When the buyer alleged that the goods were non-conforming and refused to pay the entire purchase price, the court held that the additional term in the seller's acceptance requiring notification of the defect within thirty days had become a part of the contract since the offer had not been materially altered.[64]

Even the addition or alteration of those terms which, under CISG Article 19(3), are stated materially to alter the terms of an offer and therefore create a counter-offer may not necessarily be held to do so. Recall that CISG Article 19(3) *inter alia* provides that "the settlement of disputes are considered to alter the terms of the offer materially".[65] In *Filanto* v. *Chilewich*,[66] the seller (offeree) claimed that its response to the buyer's offer which contained an objection to the incorporation of an arbitration clause in the buyer's offer constituted a counter-offer. The Southern District of New York Court held

[60] CISG, *supra* n. 2, art. 19(2).

[61] *Ibid.*

[62] CISG, *supra* n. 2, art. 19(3).

[63] (Parties not reported), 4 O 113/90, 14 Aug. 1991 (Germany, Landericht Baden-Baden) UNILEX, CLOUT (Case 50).

[64] *Ibid.*

[65] *See* discussion *supra* page 000.

[66] *Filanto* v. *Chilewich*, 789 F. Supp. 1229 (SD NY 1992), 91 Civ. 3253 (CLB), 14 Apr. 1992 (USA, US Dist. Court, SD, New York) UNILEX, CLOUT (Case 23).

otherwise. Citing CISG Articles 18(1) and 18(3),[67] it found that the seller's conduct and delay of five months in replying to the buyer's offer indicated its intention to accept it. The court held that the seller was under a duty to notify the buyer in a timely fashion of its objections to the arbitration terms due to the parties' extensive prior dealings. The court also noted that the seller had begun its performance under the contract by shipping part of the goods, and the buyer had issued a letter of credit naming the seller as beneficiary to cover part payment of the goods during the five-month delay period.

Unlike the UCC, the CISG does not address the question of what happens when conflicting offers and acceptances are exchanged, performance nonetheless begins and problems then arise.[68] Because the CISG does not provide an answer in such cases, recourse will have to be to general principles of the CISG and private international law to resolve such questions.[69]

V. SELECTED PERFORMANCE ISSUES

(a) Open Price Term

The CISG permits a contract to be formed even if the parties have not specified the price by providing that a proposal is sufficiently definite if it indicates the goods and expressly or implicitly fixes or makes provision for determining the quantity and the price.[70] In addition, where a contract has been validly concluded but does not expressly or implicitly fix or make provision for determining the price, in the absence of any indication to the contrary, the market price charged at the time of the conclusion of the contract for such goods sold under comparable circumstances in the trade is applicable.[71] The open price

[67] CISG, *supra* n. 2, art. 18(1) provides:

"(1) A statement made by or other conduct of the offeree indicating assent to an offer is an acceptance. Silence or inactivity does not in itself amount to acceptance."

CISG, *supra* n. 2, art. 18(3) provides:

"(3) However, if by virtue of the offer or as a result of practices which the parties have established between themselves or of usage, the offeree may indicate assent by performing an act, such as one relating to the dispatch of the goods or payment of the price, without notice to the offeror, the acceptance is effective at the moment the act is performed, provided that the act is performed within the period of time laid down in the preceding paragraph."

[68] UCC § 2–207(3).

[69] CISG, *supra* n. 2, art. 7(2).

[70] CISG, *supra* n. 2, art. 14(1) provides:

"[a] proposal for concluding a contract addressed to one or more specific persons constitutes an offer if it is sufficiently definite and indicates the intention of the offeror to be bound in case of acceptance. A proposal is sufficiently definite if it indicates the goods and expressly or impliedly fixes or makes provision for determining the quantity and the price."

[71] CISG, *supra* n. 93, art. 55 provides:

"[w]here a contract has been validly concluded but does not expressly or implicitly fix or make provision for determining the price, the parties are considered, in the absence of any indication to the contrary, to have impliedly made reference to the price generally charged at the time of the conclusion of the contract for such goods sold under comparable circumstances in the trade concerned."

term provision of the UCC[72] produces essentially comparable results. However, the UCC provision states that in such a case the price is a reasonable price at the time for delivery rather than the market price at the time of the conclusion of the contract. Because of the currency exchange risks associated with international contracting, the establishment of the CISG rule as the market price at the time of contracting was an essentially foregone conclusion.

(b) Warranties

The CISG warranty provisions[73] produce seller warranty accountability substantially similar to the express and implied merchantability and fitness

[72] UCC §2–305(1) provides:

"(1) The parties if they so intend can conclude a contract for sale even though the price is not settled. In such a case the price is a reasonable price at the time for delivery if:
(a) nothing is said as to price; or
(b) the price is left to be agreed by the parties and they fail to agree; or
(c) The price is to be fixed in terms of some agreed market price or other standard as set or recorded by a third person or agency and it is not so set or recorded."

[73] CISG, *supra* n. 2, art. 35 provides:

"(1) The seller must deliver goods which are of the quantity, quality and description required by the contract and which are contained or packaged in the manner required by the contract.
(2) Except where the parties have agreed otherwise, the goods do not conform with the contract unless they:
(a) are fit for the purposes for which goods of the same description would ordinarily be used;
(b) are fit for any particular purpose expressly or impliedly made known to the seller at the time of the conclusion of the contract, except where the circumstances show that the buyer did not rely, or that it was unreasonable for him to rely, on the seller's skill and judgment;
(c) possess the qualities of goods which the seller has held out to the buyer as a sample or model.
(d) are contained in the manner usual for such goods or, where there is no such manner, in a manner adequate to preserve and protect the goods.
(3) The seller is not liable under subparagraphs (a) to (d) of the preceding paragraph for any lack of conformity of the goods if at the time of the conclusion of the contract the buyer knew or could not have been unaware of such lack of conformity."

Compare CISG art. 35 with the analogous UCC provisions §§2–313, 2–314, and §2–315 reproduced below. UCC §2–313 provides:

"(1) Express warranties by the seller are created as follows:
(a) Any affirmation of fact or promise made by the seller to the buyer which relates to the goods and becomes part of the basis of the bargain creates an express warranty that the goods shall conform to the affirmation or promise.
(b) Any description of the goods which is made part of the basis of the bargain creates an express warranty that the goods shall conform to the description.
(c) Any sample or model which is made part of the basis of the bargain creates an express warranty that the whole of the goods shall conform to the sample or model.
(2) It is not necessary to the creation of an express warranty that the seller use formal words such as 'warrant' or 'guarantee' or that he have a specific intention to make a warranty, but an affirmation merely of the value of the goods or a statement purporting to be merely the seller's opinion or commendation of the goods does not create a warranty."

UCC §2–314 provides:

"(1) Unless excluded or modified (Section 2–316), a warranty that the goods shall be merchantable is implied in a contract for their sale if the seller is a merchant with respect to goods of that kind. Under this section the serving for value of food or drink to be consumed either on the premises or elsewhere is a sale.
(2) Goods to be merchantable must be at least such as

quality warranties of the UCC. However, the CISG does not contain any provisions comparable to the disclaimer procedures sellers are authorized to use under the UCC.[74] This omission may result from the fact that such disclaimer provisions may be considered to address issues pertaining to the validity of the contract and therefore would be excluded from CISG coverage under Article 4[75] of the Convention.

The CISG also contains provisions which are substantially in accord with the implied warranty of title provided for by the UCC.[76] These provisions

(a) pass without objection in the trade under the contract description; and
(b) in the case of fungible goods, are of fair average quality within the description; and
(c) are fit for the ordinary purpose for which such goods are used; and
(d) run, within the variations permitted by the agreement, of even kind, quality and quantity within each unit and among all units involved; and
(e) are adequately contained, packaged, and labeled as the agreement may require; and
(f) conform to the promise or affirmation of fact made on the container or label if any.

(3) Unless excluded or modified (Section 2–316) other implied warranties may arise from the course of dealing or usage of trade."

UCC §2–315 provides:

"[w]here the seller at the time of contracting has reason to know any particular purpose for which the goods are required and that the buyer is relying on the seller's skill or judgment to select or furnish suitable goods, there is unless excluded an implied warranty that the goods shall be fit for such purpose."

74 UCC § 2–316 provides:

"(1) Words or conduct relevant to the creation of an express warranty and words or conduct tending to negate or limit warranty shall be construed whenever reasonable as consistent with each other; but subject to the provisions of this Article on parole or extrinsic evidence (Section 2–202) negation or limitation is inoperative to the extent that such construction is unreasonable.

(2) Subject to subsection (3), to exclude or modify the implied warranty of merchantability or any part of it the language must mention merchantability and in case of a writing must be conspicuous, and to exclude or modify any implied warranty of fitness the exclusion must be in writing and conspicuous. Language to exclude all implied warranties of fitness is sufficient if it states, for example, that 'There are no warranties which extend beyond the description on the face hereof.'

(3) Notwithstanding subsection (2)

(a) Unless the circumstances indicate otherwise, all implied warranties are excluded by expressions like 'as is,' 'with all faults' or other language which in common understanding calls the buyer's attention to the exclusion of warranties and makes plain that there is no implied warranty; and
(b) when the buyer before entering the contract has examined the goods or the sample or model as fully as he desired or has refused to examine the goods there is no implied warranty with regard to defects which an examination ought in the circumstances to have revealed to him; and
(c) an implied warranty can also be excluded or modified by course of dealing or course of performance or usage of trade.

(4) Remedies for breach of warranty can be limited in accordance with the provisions of the Article on liquidation or limitation of damages and contractual modifications of remedy" (Sections 2–718 and 2–719).

75 CISG, *supra* n. 2, art. 4 provides:

"[t]his Convention governs only the formation of the contract of the contract of sale and the rights and obligations of the seller and the buyer arising from such a contract. In particular, except as otherwise expressly provided in this Convention, it is not concerned with:

(a) the validity of the contract or any of its provisions or of any usage;
(b the effect which the contract may have on the property in the goods sold."

76 UCC § 2–312 provides:

"(1) Subject to subsection (2) there is in a contract for sale a warranty by the seller that

(a) the title conveyed shall be good, and its transfer rightful; and
(b) the goods shall be delivered free from any security interest or other lien or encumbrance of which the buyer at the time of contracting has no knowledge.

(2) A warranty under subsection (1) will be excluded or modified only by specific language or by circumstances which give the buyer reason to know that the person selling does not claim title in himself or that he is purporting to sell only such right or title as he or a third party may have.

cont./

require the seller to deliver goods which are free from any right or claim of a third party, including claims based on industrial property or other intellectual property, unless the buyer agreed to take the goods subject to such rights or claims.[77] In the case of claims based on industrial property or other intellectual property, the CISG explicitly specifies that the obligation of the seller does not extend to cases where, at the time of the conclusion of the contract, the buyer knew or could not have been unaware of the right of claim, or the right or claim results from the seller's compliance with technical drawings, designs, formulae or other such specifications furnished by the buyer.[78]

(c) Risk of Loss

Risk of loss rules are based on the premise that a buyer's obligation to pay arises when the seller has performed its obligations. Once the seller has performed, because the risk of loss has passed to the buyer, the buyer is required to pay even if the goods are subsequently destroyed or damaged.

The CISG provides that once the risk has passed to the buyer, the buyer must pay the full price, even if the goods have been accidentally damaged or destroyed. However the buyer is not required to pay the price if the loss or damage was "due to an act or omission of the seller".[79] In this latter situation, the loss or damage is not an accidental loss, but rather a loss for which the seller is responsible. The seller's action releases the buyer from its obligation to pay and also gives the buyer a claim for damages for breach of contract.

The CISG sets forth three sets of risk of loss rules for:

(1) contracts for sale of goods involving carriage of the goods;[80]
(2) contracts for sale of goods sold in transit;[81] and
(3) contracts for sale of goods which are neither "carriage" of goods contracts nor "in transit" contracts.[82]

(3) Unless otherwise agreed a seller who is a merchant regularly dealing in goods of the kind warrants that the goods shall be delivered free of the rightful claim of any third person by way of infringement or the like but a buyer who furnishes specifications to the seller must hold the seller harmless against any such claims which arise out of compliance with the specifications."

77 CISG, *supra* n. 2, art. 41 provides:

"[t]he seller must deliver goods which are free from any right or claim of a third party, unless the buyer agreed to take the goods subject to that right or claim. However, if such right or claim is based on industrial property or other intellectual property, the seller's obligation is governed by article 42."

78 *Ibid.*

79 CISG, *supra* n. 2, art. 66 provides:

"[l]oss of or damage to the goods after the risk has passed to the buyer does not discharge him from his obligation to pay the price, unless loss or damage is due to an act or omission of the seller."

80 CISG, *supra* n. 2, art. 67.

81 CISG, *supra* n. 2, art. 68.

82 CISG, *supra* n. 2, art. 69.

The third category involves pick-up of the goods by the buyer at the seller's place of business or at some third location, as for example when the goods are in the hands of a third party bailee.

(i) Sales of Goods Involving Carriage

If the contract of sale involves carriage of the goods and the seller is not bound to hand them over at a particular place, the risk passes to the buyer when the goods are handed over to the first carrier for transmission to the buyer in accordance with the contract of sale.[83] If the seller is bound to hand the goods over to a carrier at a particular place (i.e. a destination contract), the risk does not pass to the buyer until the goods are handed over to the carrier at that place.[84] These provisions do not split the risk in cases of multi-modal transportation involving a combination of road, sea or air transportation unless special provisions of the contract specify otherwise.

While the language of the CISG differs from the analogous UCC provisions, these risk of loss rules applicable to sales of goods involving carriage appear to be essentially similar to the rules applicable to shipment and destination contracts under the UCC.[85]

(ii) Sales of Goods in Transit

Under the CISG, the risk of loss of goods sold in transit passes from the seller to the buyer at the time of the making of the contract.[86] Professor John Honnold, who was intimately involved in the drafting of the CISG, has advised:

> "If you are drafting a contract for the purchase of goods that are already afloat at the time of the contract, one would want a clear provision on whether the buyer bears the risk for damage (such as seeping sea-water) that occurs throughout the voyage. The Convention's rules on this awkward problem are probably no better than you find in domestic law."[87]

[83] CISG, *supra* n. 2, art. 67.

[84] *Ibid.*

[85] UCC §2–509(1) provides:

> "[w]here the contract requires or authorizes the seller to ship the goods by carrier
> (a) if it does not require him to deliver them at a particular destination, the risk of loss passes to the buyer when the goods are duly delivered to the carrier even though the shipment is under reservation (Section 2–505); but
> (b) if it does require him to deliver them at a particular destination and the goods are there duly tendered while in the possession of the carrier, the risk of loss passes to the buyer when the goods are there duly so tendered as to enable the buyer to take delivery."

[86] CISG, *supra* n. 2, art. 68.

[87] John Honnold, "The New Uniform Law for International Sales and the Uniform Commercial Code: A Comparison" (1984) 18 *Int. Law* 21, 27.

(iii) Sales of Goods not Requiring Carriage and not in Transit

Where the sales contract does not require carriage of the goods and the buyer is to pick up the goods at the seller's place of business, the CISG provides that the risk passes to the buyer when it takes over the goods. If the buyer does not do so at the time specified by the contract, risk of loss then passes at the time when the goods are placed at the buyer's disposal, and the buyer commits a breach of contract by failing to take delivery.[88] If the goods are in the hands of a third-party bailee and the buyer is bound to take over the goods at a designated place, the risk passes when delivery is due and the buyer is aware that the goods are at his disposal at that place. This latter situation requires that the buyer have a receipt or notice that the goods are ready for delivery.[89] If the contract relates to goods not then identified, the goods are considered not to be placed at the disposal of the buyer until they are clearly identified to the contract.[90]

The UCC risk of loss rules where the goods are held by a bailee to be delivered without being moved, or where delivery is to be at the seller's place of business, are set forth in Section 2–509(2) and (3).[91] They are substantially similar to the CISG rules.

(iv) Effect of Seller's Breach on Risk of Loss

Both the CISG and the UCC have provisions pertaining to the effect of a seller's breach on the risk of loss. The CISG provides that the normally applicable risk of loss rules discussed above do not impair the buyer's remedies if the seller has committed a fundamental breach.[92] The UCC provides that

[88] CISG, *supra* n. 2, art. 69(1) provides:

"[i]n cases not within articles 67 and 68, the risk passes to the buyer when he takes over the goods or, if he does not do so in due time, from the time when the goods are placed at his disposal and he commits a breach of contract by failing to take delivery."

[89] CISG, *supra* n. 2, art. 69(2) provides:

"[h]owever, if the buyer is bound to take over the goods at a place other than a place of business of the seller, the risk passes when delivery is due and the buyer is aware of the fact that the goods are placed at his disposal at that place."

[90] CISG, *supra* n. 2, art. 69(3) provides: "[i]f the contract relates to goods not then identified, the goods are considered not to be placed at the disposal of the buyer until they are clearly identified to the contract."

[91] UCC §2–509 (2) and (3) provide:

"(2) Where the goods are held by a bailee to be delivered without being moved, the risk of loss passes to the buyer

(a) on his receipt of a negotiable document of title covering the goods; or
(b) on acknowledgment by the bailee of the buyer's right to possession of the goods; or
(c) after his receipt of a non-negotiable.

document of title or other written direction to deliver, as provided in subsection (4)(b) of Section 2–503.

(3) In any case not within subsection (1) or (2), the risk of loss passes to the buyer on his receipt of the goods if the seller is a merchant; otherwise the risk passes to the buyer on tender of delivery."

[92] CISG, *supra* n. 2, art. 70.

where a tender of delivery of goods so fails to conform to the contract as to give a right of rejection, the risk of their loss remains on the seller until cure or acceptance.[93]

(v) Overview

Like the UCC, the CISG's rules on risk of loss have abandoned the approach of making risk of loss turn on the question whether "property" (i.e. title) has passed from the seller to the buyer. Both the CISG and UCC risk of loss rules are applicable on the basis of concrete commercial events such as handing over the goods to the carrier or the buyer taking over physical possession from the seller. To the extent that these physical events rather than metaphysical concepts of passage of title determine the substantive rights of the parties, a great improvement in achieving predictability and certainty of results has been made. However, the CISG risk of loss rules are stated in language yet to be interpreted by courts. In addition, no definitions of transportation terms is contained in the CISG. Accordingly, where negotiation postures permit, the parties may wish to insert their own specific risk of loss clauses into their contract utilizing the authorization granted by Article 6 of the CISG.

(d) Excuse for Changed Circumstances (Exemptions)

The CISG addresses under the heading of "exemptions" the common law concepts of *force majeure* or "excuse by failure of presupposed conditions". The CISG provides that a party is not liable in damages for failure to perform if the failure was due to an:

> "impediment beyond his control and that he could not reasonably be expected to have taken the impediment into account at the time of the conclusion of the contract or to have avoided or overcome it or its consequences."[94]

If a party's failure is due to the failure by a third person whom it has engaged to perform the whole or a part of the contract, such party is exempt from liability only if the party is exempt under the immediately previously stated exemption rule, and the person whom it has so engaged would be so exempt if the exemption rule were applied to that person.[95]

Like the term "impracticability" used by the UCC in its statement of excuse for non-performance,[96] there is considerable ambiguity about whether the

[93] UCC §2–510.
[94] CISG, *supra* n. 2, art. 79(1).
[95] CISG, *supra* n. 2, art. 79(2).
[96] UCC §2–615 provides:

> "[e]xcept so far as a seller may have assumed a greater obligation and subject to the preceding section on substituted performance:
> (a) Delay in delivery or non-delivery in whole or in part by a seller who complies with paragraphs (b)

term "impediment" includes cases of frustration of purpose of the contract as well as cases of physical impossibility. It is also important to note that excuse for non-performance under the CISG only exempts the non-performing party from liability for damages,[97] thereby entitling the aggrieved party to an action for interest, reduction of the price and, in cases where the delay in performance amounts to a fundamental breach, also a right to avoid the contract. In addition, the aggrieved party would continue to have a right to specific performance after the extinction or termination of the event on which the exemption was based, even though for a period of time failure to perform was due to an unforeseen "impediment beyond its control".

The CISG makes its exemption provisions applicable to both sellers and buyers by stating that "*a party* is not liable for failure to perform" if the required conditions are met.[98] This avoids the problems created by the manner in which Section 2–615 of the UCC is drafted which, if read literally, would make the excuse for non-performance provisions applicable only to sellers and not to buyers. Fortunately, case law interpreting Section 2–615 has not read these provisions literally.[99]

The ambiguities indicated in the CISG "exemption" provisions are further aggravated by the fact that common and civil law lawyers come from systems in which the basis for imposing liability depends on differing strict or fault liability theories. Where the negotiation posture of the parties is such that agreement may be reached on a "*force majeure*-excusable delay" clause, inclusion of such a clause would therefore appear to be desirable in order to avoid uncertainties left unresolved by the CISG provisions.

and (c) is not a breach of his duty under a contract for sale if performance as agreed has been made impracticable by the occurrence of a contingency the non-occurrence of which was a basic assumption on which the contract was made or by compliance in good faith with any applicable foreign or domestic governmental regulation or order whether or not it later proves to be invalid.
(b) Where the causes mentioned in paragraph (a) affect only a part of the seller's capacity to perform, he must allocate production and deliveries among his customers but may at his option include regular customers not then under contract as well as his own requirements for further manufacture. He may so allocate in any manner which is fair and reasonable.
(c) The seller must notify the buyer seasonably that there will be delay or non-delivery and, when allocation is required under paragraph (b), of the estimated quota thus made available for the buyer."

[97] CISG, *supra* n. 2, art. 79(5).

[98] CISG, *supra* n. 2, art. 79(1).

[99] *Tallackson Potato Co., Inc.* v. *MTK Potato Co.*, 278 NW2d 417 (ND 1979); *International Minerals & Chemical Corp.* v. *Llano, Inc.*, 770 F2d 879 (10th Cir. 1985); *Northern Indiana Public Service Co.* v *Carbon County Coal Co.*, 799 F2d 265 (7th Cir. 1986); *Scullin Steel Co.* v. *Paccar, Inc.*, 708 SW2d 756 (Mo. App. Ct. 1986); *Golsen* v. *ONG Western, Inc.*, 756 P2d 1209 (Okla. 1988); *Resources Inv. Cor.* v. *Enron Co.*, 669 F Supp. 1038 (Colo. 1987). *See also* text of UCC §2–615, *supra* n. 188.

VI. NEW CONCEPTS IN BREACH AND REMEDIES

(a) The Preferred Remedy: Specific Performance or Damages Remedies—How to Choose by "Selective Opt-out" or Choice of Forum Clause

A basic assumption of the remedies provisions of the Convention is that the contract of the parties should normally be specifically performed.[100] This is unlike the UCC, pursuant to which damages rather than specific performance are the preferred remedy.[101] However, by providing that in a case involving application of the CISG a court is not bound to enter an order for specific performance if it would not be required to do so under the law of the forum State in which litigation is initiated, the CISG makes it possible to bypass its normally applicable specific performance remedy.[102] Thus, if a US court is selected as the forum for resolution of disputes, award of damages rather than specific performance will be the remedy. However, this approach would require litigation to take place in a US court, involving probable trial by jury, liberal discovery, contingent fees, generally substantially higher levels of liability, etc. Because of such considerations, a US seller's counsel may decide that the appropriate approach might be to use the "opt out" procedure of Article 6[103] by including a clause which excludes application of the CISG specific performance provisions[104] and, if necessary, to litigate in a non-US forum.

It is interesting to note that no cases reported to date raise the issue of specific performance. While the CISG gives the parties the right to choose between specific performance and damages, the limitations placed on the exercise of the specific performance remedy, as well as the infrequency in which aggrieved sellers and buyers opt to exercise it, suggests that this difference in civil and common law systems may not be as substantial as it initially appears.

[100] CISG, *supra* n. 2, arts. 28, 46(1)(i.e. specific performance for buyers), 62 (i.e. specific performance for sellers). *Compare* UCC § 2–716, *infra*.

[101] UCC §2–716 provides:

> "(1) Specific performance may be decreed where the goods are unique or in other proper circumstances.
> (2) The decree for specific performance may include such terms and conditions as to payment of the price, damages, or other relief as the court may deem just.
> (3) The buyer has a right of replevin for goods identified to the contract if after reasonable effort he is unable to effect cover for such goods or the circumstances reasonably indicate that such effort will be unavailing or if the goods have been shipped under reservation and satisfaction of the security interest in them has been made or tendered."

[102] The major concession in the form of a compromise on the applicability of the specific performance doctrine was agreed to by the civil law countries in favor of the common law countries. It was accomplished by inclusion of Article 28 in the Convention which provides:

> "[i]f in accordance with the provisions of this Convention, one party is entitled to require performance of any obligations by the other party, a court is not bound to enter a judgment for specific performance unless the court would do so under its own law in respect of similar contracts of sale not governed by this Convention."

[103] *See* Del Duca and Del Duca, *supra* n. 92 at 346.

[104] *See* CISG, *supra* n. 2, arts. 46(1) and 62.

The CISG specific performance provisions are further softened by their inclusion in a mixed traditional and sometimes innovative set of breach and performance rules addressed in the remainder of this article. These provisions pertain to: (a) requiring buyers to give timely notice of lack of conformity;[105] (b) giving sellers opportunity to cure defects;[106] and (c) utilizing innovative concepts like "fundamental breach",[107] "Nachfrist",[108] and "avoidance",[109] and "reduction in purchase price to the extent of the defect".[110]

(b) Buyer's Duty to Discover and Give Notice of Defects—Estoppel

The CISG requires the buyer to examine the goods, or cause them to be examined within as short a period as is practicable in the circumstances.[111] The buyer loses the right to rely on a lack of conformity of the goods if notice is not given to the seller specifying the nature of the lack of conformity within a reasonable time after buyer has discovered it or ought to have discovered it.[112] The said time in any event is not to exceed two years from the date on which the goods were actually handed over to the buyer, unless this time limit is inconsistent with a contractual period of guarantee.[113]

The difficulty of determining whether a buyer has complied with this "reasonable time" requirement for examining the goods and giving notice of any

105 CISG, *supra* n. 2, art. 38; *see* discussion *infra* at 67.

106 CISG, *supra* n. 2, art. 48; *see* discussion *infra* at 71.

107 CISG, *supra* n. 2, art. 25; *see* discussion *infra* at 72.

108 CISG, *supra* n. 2, arts. 47, 49(1)(i.e. buyer's "Nachfrist") and 63(1)64(1)(b) (i.e. seller's "Nachfrist"); *see* discussion *infra* at 75.

109 CISG, *supra* n. 2, art. 49; see discussion *infra* at 79–80.

110 CISG, *supra* n. 2, art. 50; see discussion *infra* at 82.

111 CISG, *supra* n. 2, art. 38 provides:

> "(1) The buyer must examine the goods, or cause them to be examined, within as short a period as is practicable in the circumstances.
>
> (2) If the contract involves carriage of the goods, examination may be deferred until after the goods have arrived at their destination.
>
> (3) If the goods are redirected in transit or redispatched by the buyer without a reasonable opportunity for examination by him and at the time of the conclusion of the contract the seller knew or ought to have known of the possibility of such redirection or redispatch, examination may be deferred until after the goods have arrived at the new destination."

112 CISG, *supra* n. 2, art. 39 provides:

> "(1) The buyer loses the right to rely on a lack of conformity of the goods if he does not give notice to the seller specifying the nature of the lack of conformity within a reasonable time after he has discovered it or ought to have discovered it.
>
> (2) In any event, the buyer loses the right to rely on a lack of conformity of the goods if he does not give the seller notice thereof at the latest within a period of two years from the date on which the goods were actually handed over to the buyer, unless that time limit is inconsistent with a contractual period of guarantee."

Although the CISG does not define what constitutes a "reasonable" time, the court in one case held that this requirement meant that notice must be given "as soon as possible": *Gruppo IMAR SpA* v. *Protech Horst*, 920159, 6 May 1993 (Netherlands, Arrondissementsrechtbank Roermond) UNILEX.

113 CISG, *supra* n. 2, art. 39. *See also supra* n. 105.

non-conformities has led to considerable litigation and is responsible for twenty-seven[114] of the one hundred and forty-two CISG cases reported to date. This difficulty is primarily due to the factual sensitivity of determining whether the buyer has examined the goods as soon as possible and has given timely notice of any non-conformity to the seller. In reaching these determinations, the court must take into account the circumstances of the case and the opportunities of the parties to the contract to examine the goods.[115]

CISG Article 40 limits the extent to which a seller can rely on the provisions of Articles 38 and 39 "if the lack of conformity relates to facts which he knew or could not have been unaware and which he did not disclose to the buyer".[116] Thus, this section allows the buyer in certain cases to avoid the application of Article 38 or 39 by showing that the seller was aware of the defect and did not disclose it to the buyer.

A Dutch court[117] recently held that a Dutch buyer could not rely on a lack of conformity where the cheese that the Italian seller delivered to the buyer

[114] (Parties not reported), 5713/1989–1989 (ICC, International Chamber of Commerce Court of Arbitration (Paris)) UNILEX, CLOUT (Case 45); (Parties not reported), 17 HKO 3726/89, 3 July 1989 (Germany, Landgericht München I) UNILEX, CLOUT (Case 3); (Parties not reported), 3 KfH 0 97/89, 31 Aug. 1989 (Germany, Landgericht Stuttgart) UNILEX, CLOUT (Case 4); (Parties not reported), 41 O 198/89, 3 Apr. 1990 (Germany, Landgericht Aachen) UNILEX; *EIF SA* v. *Factron BV*, 2762/1989 (Netherlands, Arrondissementsrechtbank Dordrecht) UNILEX; (Parties not reported), 4 O 113/90, 14 Aug. 1991 (Germany, Landgericht Baden-Baden) UNILEX, CLOUT (Case 50); *Fallini Stefano & Co. Snc* v. *Foodic BV*, 900336, 19 Dec. 1991 (Netherlands, Arrondissementsrechtbank Roermond) UNILEX, CLOUT (Case 98); (Parties not reported), 6252, 27 Apr. 1992 (Switzerland, Pretura di Locarno Campagna)UNILEX, CLOUT (Case 56); (Parties not reported), 99 O 29/93, 16 Sept. 1992 (Germany, Landgericht Berlin) UNILEX; (Parties not reported), 3/3 O 37/92, 9 Dec. 1992 (Germany, Landgericht Frankfurt am Main) UNILEX; (Parties not reported), 99 O 123/92, 30 Sept. 1992 (Germany, Landgericht Berlin) UNILEX; (Parties not reported), 17 U 82/92, 8 Jan. 1993 (Germany, Oberlandesgericht Düsseldorf) UNILEX, CLOUT (Case 48); (Parties not reported) HG 930138U/H93, 9 Sept. 1993 (Switzerland, Handelsgericht Zürich) UNILEX; *Gruppo IMAR SpA* v. *Protech Horst*, 920159, 6 May 1993 (Netherlands, Arrondissementsrechtbank Roermond) UNILEX; (Parties not reported), 7660 JK, 23 Aug. 1994 (ICC, International Chamber of Commerce Court of Arbitration (Paris)) UNILEX; (Parties not reported), 6 U 32/93, 10 Feb. 1994 (Germany, Oberlandesgericht Düsseldorf) UNILEX, CLOUT (Case 81); (Parties not reported), SCH–4318 (Arbitral Award, Internationales Schiedgericht der Bundeskammer der gewerblichen Wirtschaft—Wein) UNILEX; (Parties not reported), 31 O 231/94, 23 June 1994 (Germany, Landgericht Düsseldorf) UNILEX; (Parties not reported), 6 O 85/93, 5 July 1994 (Germany, Landgericht Gieben) UNILEX; (Parties not reported), 13/15 O 3/94, 13 July 1994 (Germany, Landgericht Frankfurt am Main) UNILEX; (Parties not reported), 7660/JK, 23 Aug. 1994 (ICC, International Chamber of Commerce Court of Arbitration (Paris)) UNILEX; (Parties not reported), 2 C 395/93, 21 Oct. 1994 (Germany, Amtsgericht Riedlingen) UNILEX; (Parties not reported), 120 674/93, 9 Nov. 1994 (Germany, Landgericht Oldenburg) UNILEX; (Parties not reported), 7 U 3758/94, 8 Feb. 1995 (Germany, Oberlandesgericht München) UNILEX; (Parties not reported), 54 O 644/94, 5 Apr. 1995 (Germany, Landgericht Landshut) UNILEX.

[115] (Parties not reported), 6 U 32/93, 10 Feb. 1994 (Germany, Oberlandesgericht Düsseldorf) UNILEX, CLOUT (Case 81).

[116] CISG, *supra* n. 2, Art. 40 provides:

> "[t]he seller is not entitled to rely on the provisions of article 38 and 39 if the lack of conformity relates to the facts of which he knew or could not have been unaware and which he did not disclose to the buyer."

[117] *Fallini Stefano & Co. Snc* v. *Foodic BV*, 900336, 19 Dec. 1991 (Netherlands, Arrondissementsrechtbank Roermond) UNILEX, CLOUT (Case 98).

was later discovered to contain maggots, since the buyer had failed to comply with the examination and notice requirements of Articles 38 and 39. However, the court noted that, should the buyer succeed in proving that the maggots were in the cheese before carriage, the seller would be prevented by Article 40 from relying on Articles 38 and 39.[118] In another case,[119] an arbitrator held that an Austrian seller was estopped from alleging that the German buyer's notice of non-conformity was untimely. Noting that the question of estoppel is not expressly settled under the CISG, the arbitrator applied Articles 7(2), 16(2)(b) and 29(2)[120] and held, nonetheless that estoppel ("*venire contra factum proprium*") is a general principle underlying the CISG. In this instance, the seller's behavior[121] had led the buyer into believing that the untimely notice defense would not be raised.

(i) Duty to Examine within a Reasonable Time

The Article 38 requirement for discovering a defect within a reasonable time has been litigated in a number of cases. In *Fallini Stefano & Co. Snc* v. *Foodic BV*, the Dutch court held that the buyer bears the burden of proving that the goods were inspected within a reasonable time.[122] Although the cheese ordered by the buyer had been delivered frozen, the buyer was not exempt from the duty to make timely examination. According to the court, the buyer could have defrosted a portion of the cheese and discovered the non-conformity.[123]

[118] *Ibid.*

[119] (Parties not reported), SCH–4318, 15 June 1994 (Arbitral Award, Internationales Schiedsgericht der Bundeskammer der gewerbli) UNILEX.

[120] CISG, *supra* n. 2, art 7(2) provides:

"(2) Questions concerning matters governed by this Convention which are not expressly settled in it are to be settled in conformity with the general principles on which it is based or, in the absence of such principles, in conformity with the law applicable by virtue of the rules of private international law."

CISG, *supra* n. 2, art 16(2)(b) provides:

"(2) However an offer cannot be revoked:

(b) if it was reasonable for the offeree to rely on the offer as being irrevocable and the offeree acted in reliance on the offer."

CISG, *supra* n. 2, art. 29(2) provides:

"(2) A contract in writing which contains a provision requiring any modification or termination by agreement to be in writing may not be otherwise modified or terminated by agreement. However, a party may be precluded by his conduct from asserting such a provision to the extent that the other party has relied on the conduct."

[121] The arbitrator noted that "after receiving the notice [of the buyer], the seller had continued to ask the buyer information on the status of the complaints and had pursued negotiations with a view to reach a settlement agreement": (Parties not reported), SCH–4318, 15 June 1994 (Arbitral Award, Internationales Schiedsgericht der Bundeskammer der gewerbli) UNILEX.

[122] *Fallini Stefano & Co. Snc* v. *Foodic BV*, 90036, 19 Dec. 1991 (Netherlands, Arrondissementsrechtbank Roermond) UNILEX, CLOUT (Case 98).

[123] *Ibid.*

A German court has recently held in a similar case[124] that a German buyer lost the right to rely on lack of conformity by failing promptly to inspect ham delivered by the seller. Since the alleged defect (inadequate seasoning) was easily recognizable, the buyer should have examined the goods within three days. It should be noted that the time period in which to examine goods is very fact-specific. For example, even where a buyer had to install a seller's engines in order to discover possible defects, a German court[125] has held that the duty to examine promptly imposes a duty on the buyer to examine the goods as soon as practicable. In that case, waiting to examine the engines "a full four months" after delivery could not be considered "as short as is practicable under the circumstances".[126]

In transactions between merchants, courts have held that the duty to inspect is an immediate one. For example, a Swiss court held that because both parties were merchants, the buyer should have examined the goods upon delivery.[127] In that case, a Swiss buyer of furniture discovered a defect in the seller's couches only when an unsatisfied consumer complained about the upholstery. The court held that the buyer should have inspected the couches upon delivery instead of doing so only following customer complaints.

In a third case, a German court held that a German buyer had not properly examined the goods received from an Italian seller. Since customers who had purchased shoes under a former order from the same Italian seller had complained of imperfect sewing and discoloration, the buyer had notice of possible defect. The court found that since the buyer had been forewarned by complaints concerning the first delivery, the buyer should have examined all of the shoes from the second order, as opposed to just a few pairs.[128]

(ii) Duty to Give Notice of Non-conformity within a Reasonable Time

Many cases deal with the issue of what constitutes a reasonable time for giving notice of non-conformity under Article 39. For example, the Court of Arbitration of the International Chamber of Commerce has held that notice given within eight days after publication of a report by the buyer's inspector

[124] (Parties not reported), 2 C 395/93, 21 Oct. 1994 (Germany, Amtsgericht Riedlingen) UNILEX.

[125] (Parties not reported), 31 O 231/94, 23 June 1994 (Germany, Landgericht Düsseldorf) UNILEX.

[126] *Ibid.*, *citing* CISG, art. 38. In a recent case dealing with insufficient quantity as a defect, a German court held that the duty to examine the quantity must be immediately complied with at the place of performance of the obligation. According to the court, the Swiss buyer of German clothing should have examined or caused the goods to be examined as soon as they arrived at the agreed destination. Based on witness testimony, the court found that examination of the quantity more than a week after delivery was unreasonable under the circumstances: (Parties not reported), 54 O 644/94, 5 Apr. 1995 (Germany, Landgericht Landshut) UNILEX.

[127] (Parties not reported), 6252, 27 Apr. 1992 (Switzerland, Pretura della giurisdizione di Locarno-Capmagna) UNILEX, CLOUT (Case 56).

[128] (Parties not reported), 3 KfH 0 97/89, 31 Aug. 1989 (Germany, Langericht Stuttgart) UNILEX, CLOUT (Case 4).

who had examined the seller's goods prior to shipment satisfied the Article 39 requirement. Similarly, a German court[129] recently stated that under normal circumstances in a sale of durable non-season-dependent goods, eight days is a reasonable time for giving notice. In that case, however, the Austrian buyer who had entered into a contract with a German seller to deliver goods to a Danish company supplied by the buyer waited two months after the Danish company received delivery before notifying the seller of non-conformity. It is important to note that the buyer bears the burden to show that notice of non-conformity has been given within a reasonable time.[130]

In another recent case,[131] a German court held that the reasonable time for giving notice started to run at the latest at the moment when the buyer had concluded its own examination. Instead of giving notice to the seller of non-conformity following its own inspection of the seller's engines, the buyer sent the engines to a university for further examination.

Courts have also held that one of the elements to be taken into account in determining whether notice has been given in a timely manner is the nature of the goods. For example, in the *Fallini* case[132] a Dutch court found that the period within which the buyer should have given notice was necessarily short, since cheese is a perishable product.[133]

As between merchants, under CISG Article 39, if the defect is apparent, the buyer should give immediate notice of the non-conformity rather than waiting until after a customer complaints are received.[134] Recall the case where the buyer failed to notify the seller of non-conformity until after receiving customer complaints about the upholstery of the seller's couches.

[129] (Parties not reported), 7 U 3758/94, 8 Feb. 1995 (Germany, Oberlandesgericht München) UNILEX.

[130] (Parties not reported), 3/15 O 3/94, 13 July 1994 (Germany, Landgericht Frankfurt am Main) UNILEX.

[131] (Parties not reported), 31 O 231/94, 23 June 1994 (Germany, Landgericht Düsseldorf) UNILEX.

[132] *Fallini Stefano & Co. Snc* v. *Foodic BV*, 900336, 19 Dec. 1993 (Netherlands, Arrondissementsrechtbank Roermond) UNILEX, CLOUT (Case 98).

[133] *Ibid. See also* (Parties not reported), 17 U 82/92, 8 Jan. 1993 (Germany, Oberlandesgericht Düsseldorf) UNILEX, CLOUT (Case 48) (buyer who failed to examine goods before shipment failed to make timely inspection of the goods since the parties had excluded the CISG provision allowing deferred inspection of goods involved in carriage); *EIF SA* v. *Factron BV*, 2762/1989, 21 Nov. 1990 (Netherlands, Arrondissementsrechtbank Dorrecht) UNILEX (the court granted the buyer the opportunity to establish that it had notified the seller of non-conformity immediately and not 15 months after receipt of the goods as alleged by the seller); (Parties not reported), 6252, 27 Apr. 1992 (Switzerland, Pretura di Locarno-Campagna) UNILEX, CLOUT (Case 56) (buyer failed to make timely inspection where both parties were merchants and inspection performed only after customer complaints, not upon delivery). *Cf.* (Parties not reported), 41 O 198/89, 3 Apr. 1990 (Germany, Landgericht Aachen) UNILEX (inspection immediately upon delivery and notice given immediately thereafter satisfactory); (Parties not reported), 5713/1989—1989 (ICC, International Chamber of Commerce Court of Arbitration (Paris)) UNILEX, CLOUT (Case 45) (inspection and notice satisfactory where buyer examined goods before shipment and notified seller of defect 8 days after publication of inspector's report).

[134] (Parties not reported), 6252, 27 Apr. 1992 (Switzerland, Preturea della giurisdizione di Locarno-Capmagna) UNILEX.

Under Article 39, a buyer's notice of non-conformity must also "specify the nature of the lack of conformity".[135] Failure to do so can result in a buyer losing the right to rely on timely notice of non-conformity. For example, under a contract for the sale of shoes between a German buyer and Italian seller,[136] the buyer refused to pay after notifying the seller of non-conformity via the telephone. While the German court noted that notice via telephone is not inherently insufficient, the buyer had not introduced evidence demonstrating that the notice had specified the nature of the non-conformity. Accordingly, the buyer lost the right to rely on Article 39 and was obliged to pay the price of the shoes.

(iii) Ineffective Cure—New Notice Required

When receiving goods that are offered as a cure for non-conforming goods, the buyer must give new notice of any defects should the new goods also be non-conforming. For example, in one case,[137] a German court held that a German buyer which had claimed that the Italian seller's cure was ineffective lost the right to claim a lack of conformity by failing to renew notice of non-conformity upon discovery that the cure was also ineffective. Since the court held that a failed repair represents another non-performance of the contract, the buyer's exercise of remedies for breach of contract by the seller requires another notice.[138]

(iv) Advantage of Clause Providing for Explicit Time for Giving Notice

In order to avoid litigation over whether examination and notice were performed within a reasonable time, the parties may wish to place a clause in their contract to govern the time period when examination and notice should occur. In one case,[139] the parties' agreement provided that any complaints concerning defects in the goods could be raised only within eight days after receipt of the goods. After receiving complaints from its customers about the goods the Italian seller had delivered, the German buyer gave the seller notice of the lack of conformity and refused to pay. The German court held that pursuant to CISG Article 6, parties can derogate from CISG Article 39 regarding time of notice. Because the buyer did not give notice within the agreed period of eight days, the court held that the buyer had lost the right to rely on a non-conformity under CISG Article 39.[140]

135 CISG, *supra* n. 93, art. 39(1).

136 (Parties not reported), 3/15 O 3/94, 13 July 1994 (Germany, Landgericht Frankfurt am Main) UNILEX.

137 (Parties not reported), 12 O 674/93, 9 Nov. 1994 (Germany, Landgericht Oldenburg) UNILEX.

138 *Ibid.*

139 (Parties not reported), 6 O 85/93, 5 July 1994 (Germany, Landgericht Gieben) UNILEX.

140 *Ibid. See also* (Parties not reported), 7660/JK, 23 Aug. 1994 (Arbitral Award, International Chamber of Commerce Court of Arbitration (Paris)) UNILEX (parties fixing of maximum time limit of 18 months for buyer to notify seller of non-conformity validly derogated for Art. 39(2)).

In another case[141] involving a contract for the sale of tiles, an Italian seller and a German buyer had been in an ongoing business relationship. In its acceptance of the buyer's most recent order, the seller had referred to its long-standing general condition that notice of defects would be valid only if given "within 30 days after the date of the invoice". The German court held that, since the thirty-day time limit could not be considered a material modification of the terms of the offer under CISG Article 19(2), the time limit for notice of defects as established in the seller's general conditions had become part of the contract.[142]

The degree of specificity required for proper notice has also been considered in at least one instance.[143] In that case, a German buyer and Italian seller entered into a contract for the sale of fashion goods. The buyer, claiming that the goods were non-conforming and that its inspection and notice of non-conformity were timely, refused to pay the purchase price. The German court held that despite the buyer's timely notice, the buyer had failed to comply with the CISG's notice provisions because notice of "poor workmanship and improper fitting" was not sufficiently specific. The buyer thus lost its right to rely on non-conformity.[144]

Unlike the notice requirements imposed by the UCC on a buyer who has accepted goods,[145] the CISG imposes the notice-giving requirements on the buyer irrespective of whether the goods have been accepted.[146]

Overall, a buyer who fails to give notice of a defect loses his rights under the CISG. However, a buyer who has a reasonable excuse for failure to give notice may still exercise the remedy of reducing the price to the extent of the defect or alternatively may claim damages, except for loss of profit.[147]

141 (Parties not reported), 4 O 113/90, 14 Aug. 1991 (Germany, Landgericht Baden-Baden) UNILEX, CLOUT (Case 50).

142 *Ibid. See also* discussion *supra* at 000.

143 (Parties not reported), 17 HKO 3726/89, 3 July 1989 (Germany, Landgericht München I) UNILEX, CLOUT (Case 3).

144 *Ibid.*

145 UCC § 2–607(3)(a) provides:

> "(3) where tender had been accepted
> (a) the buyer must within a reasonable time after he discovers or should have discovered any breach notify the seller of breach or be barred from any remedy".

146 CISG, *supra* n. 2, art. 39.

147 CISG, *supra* n. 2, art. 44 provides:

> "Notwithstanding the provisions of paragraph (1) of article 39, and paragraph (1) of article 43, the buyer may reduce the price in accordance with article 50 or claim damages, except for loss of profit, if he has a reasonable excuse for his failure to give the required notice."

CISG, *supra* n. 2, art. 50 provides:

> "If the goods do not conform with the contract and whether or not the price has already been paid, the buyer may reduce the price in the same proportion as the value that the goods actually delivered had at the time of the delivery bears to the value that conforming goods would have had at that time. However, if the seller remedies any failure to perform his obligations in accordance with article 37 or article 48 of if the buyer refuses to accept performance by the seller in accordance with those articles, the buyer may not reduce the price."

(c) Seller's Right to Cure

A seller's right under the CISG to cure defective performance is substantially similar to that of a seller under the UCC.[148] Under the CISG, where the seller has delivered goods before the date for delivery, any defective delivery up to the delivery date may be cured by the seller, provided that the exercise of this right does not cause the buyer unreasonable inconvenience or unreasonable expense.[149] The buyer nevertheless retains any right to claim damages provided elsewhere by the Convention.[150] The seller may, even after the date for delivery,[151] remedy a defective tender if this can be done without unreasonable delay and without causing the buyer unreasonable inconvenience or "uncertainty of reimbursement by the seller of expenses advanced by the buyer".[152] Again, the buyer retains any right to claim damages as provided elsewhere in the Convention.

A recent Swiss case discussed above illustrates this right of the seller. Recall the case where the Swiss buyer notified the Italian seller of defects in upholstery after receiving consumer complaints. The seller offered to cure the defect by replacing the upholstery, but the buyer refused. The Swiss court held that the buyer erred in refusing to allow the seller to cure.[153]

In another previously discussed case where a French seller and a Portuguese buyer contracted for the sale and dismantlement of a second-hand airplane hangar,[154] the seller had delivered non-conforming metallic elements. The court held that although the seller had effectively cured the lack of conformity

[148] UCC § 2–508 provides:

"(1) Where any tender or delivery by the seller is rejected because non-conforming and the time for performance has not yet expired, the seller may seasonably notify the buyer of his intention to cure and may then within the contract time make a conforming delivery.

(2) Where the buyer rejects a non-conforming tender which the seller has reasonable grounds to believe would be acceptable with or without money allowance the seller may if he seasonably notifies the buyer have a further reasonable time to substitute a conforming tender."

[149] CISG, *supra* n. 2, art. 37 provides:

"If the seller has delivered goods before the date for delivery, he may, up to that date, deliver any missing part or make up any deficiency in the quantity of the goods delivered, or deliver goods in replacement of any non-conforming goods delivered or remedy any lack of conformity in the goods delivered provided that the exercise of this right does not cause the buyer unreasonable inconvenience or unreasonable expense. However, the buyer retains any right to claim damages as provided for in this Convention."

[150] *Ibid.*

[151] CISG, *supra* n. 2, art. 48(1) provides:

"(1) Subject to article 49, the seller may, even after the date for delivery, remedy at his own expense any failure to perform his obligations, if he can do so without unreasonable delay and without causing the buyer unreasonable inconvenience or uncertainty of reimbursement by the seller of expenses advanced by the buyer. However, the buyer retains any right to claim damages as provided for in this Convention."

[152] *Ibid.*

[153] (Parties not reported), 6252, 27 Apr. 1992 (Switzerland, Pretura della giurisdizione di Locarno-Campagna) UNILEX.

[154] *Marques Roque Joachim* v. *Sàrl La Holding Manin Rivière*, RG 93/4879, 26 Apr. 1995 (France, Cour d'Appel de Grenoble, Chambre Commerciale) UNILEX.

by repair of the elements, the buyer was entitled nonetheless to claim damages since the seller had delayed in delivering the conforming goods requiring the buyer to arrange for transportation of the goods twice. In another case,[155] the arbitrator for International Chamber of Commerce arbitration ruled that where the breach by the seller was of such a substantial character as to constitute a fundamental breach under Article 25,[156] the buyer was entitled to avoid[157] the contract. Furthermore, the seller was not entitled to exercise a right of cure under CISG Article 48(1) apparently because the defect was of such a serious nature in the sole arbitrator's view that the seller only had a right to cure after the due date for delivery if the buyer so consented.

(d) Fundamental Breach

If the seller's failure to cure a defective delivery results in such a detriment to the buyer as substantially to deprive the buyer of what the buyer was entitled to expect according to the contract, such a breach is deemed to be "fundamental" unless the party in breach did not foresee the result, and a reasonable person of the same kind in the same circumstances would not have foreseen such a result.[158] Such a breach gives the buyer the right to avoid (i.e. cancel) the contract.[159]

The concept of fundamental breach has been examined in a number of cases. For example, in one recent case involving a German buyer and Italian seller,[160] the buyer had ordered one hundred and twenty pairs of shoes from the seller through a commercial agent. The contract included a clause which granted the buyer the exclusive right to distribute the shoes in a certain geo-

[155] (Parties not reported), 7531\1994—1994 (Court of Arbitration of the International Chamber of Commerce (Paris)) UNILEX.

[156] CISG, *supra* n. 2, art. 25 provides:

> "A breach of contract committed by one of the parties is fundamental if it results in such detriment to the other party as substantially deprive him of what he is entitled to expect under the contract, unless the party in breach did not foresee and a reasonable person of the same kind in the same circumstances would not have foreseen such a result."

[157] CISG, *supra* n. 2, art. 49(1) provides:

> "(1) The buyer may declare the contract avoided:
> (a) if the failure by the seller to perform any of his obligations under the contract or this Convention amounts to a fundamental breach of contract; or
> (b) in case of non-delivery, if the seller does not deliver the goods within the additional period of time fixed by the buyer in accordance with paragraph (1) of article 47 or declares that he will not deliver within the period so fixed."

[158] CISG, *supra* n. 2, art. 25; *see supra* n. 247.

[159] CISG, *supra* n. 2, art. 49(1)(a) provides:

> "(1) The buyer may declare the contract avoided:
> (a) if the failure by the seller to perform any of his obligations under the contract or this Convention amounts to a fundamental breach of contract;".

[160] (Parties not reported), 3/11 O 3/91, 16 Sept. 1991 (Germany, Landgericht Frankfurt am Main) UNILEX, CLOUT (Case 6).

graphical district. After selling twenty pairs of shoes, the buyer learned that the seller had supplied the identical shoe to a competing local retailer who was offering the shoe at a considerably lower price. The buyer attempted to cancel the remainder of the order and avoid the contract. The German court found no fundamental breach of the exclusive contract by the seller since the seller had no way of knowing that the competing retailer had a branch within the buyer's district and which, in the judgment of the court, the seller could not reasonably have foreseen.[161]

In another case, a German buyer ordered shoes from an Italian seller and provided specifications.[162] The seller produced the shoes, which bore the buyer's trade mark, and subsequently displayed them at a trade fair. When the buyer gave notice of its intention to avoid the contract because of the seller's refusal to remove the shoes from the trade fair, the seller sued to recover the price of the shoes. The German court found that the seller's display of the shoes at the trade fair was a fundamental breach of the contract. It was foreseeable to the seller that its conduct would endanger the buyer's interest in controlling all sales of that shoe under its trade mark to such an extent that the buyer's interest would be virtually non-existent.

The issue of fundamental breach also arose in the previously discussed airplane hangar case.[163] There, the court ruled that since the non-conformity related only to a part of the hangar and the seller had been able to repair the defective parts, the lack of conformity did not constitute a fundamental breach of contract. So ruling, the court reasoned that the buyer had not been substantially deprived of what it was entitled to under the contract and that, therefore, avoidance was not a proper remedy.

Partial delivery of goods as a basis for establishing fundamental breach of contract was recently litigated.[164] In that case, a German buyer had ordered eleven computer component parts from an American seller in order to fulfill its contract with an Austrian company. The buyer faxed its order to the seller and included the price of only five of the parts. The seller, in turn, delivered only five parts and the buyer was forced to obtain substitute goods to cover the remaining six component parts that it needed. The buyer subsequently refused to pay the purchase price of the goods, claiming that the seller's partial delivery constituted a fundamental breach of the contract. The court, however, held for the seller since the seller's partial delivery had not

[161] *Ibid.*

[162] (Parties not reported), 5 U 164/90, 17 Sept. 1991 (Germany, Oberlandesgericht Frankfurt am Main); (1993) 12 J.L. & Com. 261; CLOUT (Case 2).

[163] *Marques Roque Joachim* v. *Sàrl La Holding Manin Rivière*, RG 93/4879, 26 Apr. 1995 (France, Cour d'Appel de Grenoble, Chambre Commerciale) UNILEX.

[164] (Parties not reported), 0 42/92, 3 July 1992 (Germany, Landgericht Heidelberg) UNILEX. *See also* (Parties not reported), 19 U 97/91, 22 Sept. 1992 (Germany, Oberlandesgericht Hamm) UNILEX (buyer's failure to take delivery of more than half of the goods constituted fundamental breach).

substantially deprived the buyer of what it was entitled to expect under the contract because the buyer had been able to obtain substitute goods.[165]

Another recent decision[166] also addressed non-conformity of goods as a basis for establishing fundamental breach in a case where a German buyer and Italian seller entered into a contract for the sale of women's shoes. The buyer refused to pay the purchase price, claiming that delivery had been late and that the goods were non-conforming. The German court held that a contract may be avoided on the basis of non-conforming goods only when that non-conformity constitutes a fundamental breach. Since the buyer failed to establish that the goods could not reasonably be used for their original purpose, the non-conformity of the goods under the contract did not amount to a fundamental breach.

A German court has recently found no fundamental breach of a contract involving a Swiss seller and a German buyer in a contract for the sale of New Zealand mussels.[167] The buyer was not entitled to avoid the contract and refused to pay the purchase price on the ground that the mussels were not completely safe[168] because of the quantity of cadmium they contained. The cadmium concentration admittedly exceeded the threshold level published by the German Federal Health Department. However, the court concluded that the mussels were nonetheless conforming to the contract since they were fit for the purpose for which goods of the same description would ordinarily be used.[169] So ruling, the court reasoned that sellers normally cannot be expected to observe public law, i.e. regulatory, requirements of the buyer's State. A seller could only be expected to do so where the same rules exist in both the seller's and the buyer's countries or where the buyer draws the seller's attention to their existence.

The Cour d'Appel de Grenoble, Chambre Commerciale, in France has held that the buyer's breach of a contract by reselling to a Spanish buyer rather than to a South American buyer constituted a fundamental breach which entitled the seller to declare the contract avoided.[170] The court found that the parties clearly understood that resale was to be in South America and that the seller's expectations under the contract were substantially impaired because

[165] *See also* (Parties not reported), 19 U 97/91, 22 Sept. 1992 (Germany, Oberlandesgericht Hamm) UNILEX (buyer's failure to take delivery of more than half of the goods constituted fundamental breach).

[166] (Parties not reported), 5 U 15/93, 18 Jan. 1994 (Germany, Oberlandesgericht Frankfurt am Main) UNILEX, CLOUT (Case 79).

[167] (Parties not reported), VIII ZR 159/94, 8 Mar. 1995 (Germany, Bundesgerichtshof) UNILEX.

[168] *Ibid.*

[169] CISG, *supra* n. 2, art. 35(2)(a) provides:

> "(2) Except where the parties have agreed otherwise, the goods do not conform with the contract unless they;
>
> (a) are fit for the purposes for which goods of the same description would ordinarily be used."

[170] *Sàrl Bri Production "Bonaventure" v. Société Pan African Export*, 22 Feb. 1995 (France, Cour d'Appel de Grenoble, Chambre Commerciale), UNILEX.

sale of its products in Spain had been seriously hampered by the parallel distribution caused when the buyer resold the goods in Spain rather than in South America.

Deviations from the quality and quantity of the goods originally ordered under a contract have also been litigated as constituting fundamental breaches of contract. For example, a German court has held that a German buyer of coal could not avoid the contract where the quality of the coal actually deviated from the contract, but not sufficiently to amount to a fundamental breach.[171] An Italian court has held that the delay of the seller in delivering goods two months after conclusion of the contract and delivery of only one-third of the goods amounted to a fundamental breach which entitled the buyer to avoid the contract.[172] So ruling, the court noted that the parties had specified in their agreement that the seller was bound to dispatch all of the goods within one week after the contract was concluded.

(e) "Nachfrist"

"Nachfrist" is a procedure[173] taken from German law and incorporated into the CISG.[174] It can be utilized by either a buyer or seller. We first discuss the buyer's "Nachfrist" right.

[171] (Parties not reported), 7 U 4419/93, 2 Mar. 1994 (Germany, Oberlandesgericht München) UNILEX, CLOUT (Case 83).

[172] *Foliopack AG* v. *Daniplast SpA*, 77/89, 24 Nov. 1989 (Italy, Pretura di Parma-Fidenza) UNILEX, CLOUT (Case 90).

[173] The "Nachfrist" procedure is incorporated into the CISG for the buyer in Arts. 47 and 49. CISG art. 47 provides:

> "(1) The buyer may fix an additional period of time of reasonable length for performance by the seller of his obligations. (2) Unless the buyer has received notice from the seller that he will not perform within the period so fixed, the buyer may not, during that period, resort to any remedy for breach of contract. However, the buyer is not deprived thereby of any right he may have to claim damages for delay in performance."

CISG, art. 49(1) provides:

> "The buyer may declare the contract avoided:
> (a) if the failure by the seller to perform any of his obligations under the contract or this Convention amounts to a fundamental breach of contract; or
> (b) in the case of non-delivery, if the seller does not deliver the goods within the additional period of time fixed by the buyer in accordance with paragraph (1) of article 47 or declares that he will not deliver within the period so fixed."

The "Nachfrist" procedure which applies to the seller is incorporated into the CISG in Arts. 63(1) and 64. CISG, art. 63(1) provides:

> "(1) The seller may fix an additional period of time of reasonable length for performance by the buyer of his obligations."

CISG, art. 64 provides:

> "(1) The seller may declare the contract avoided:
> (a) if the failure by the buyer to perform any of his obligations under the contract or this Convention amounts to a fundamental breach of contract; or
> (b) if the buyer does not, within the additional period of time fixed by the seller in accordance with paragraph (1) of article 63, perform his obligation to pay the price or take delivery of the goods, or if he declares that he will not do so within the period so fixed.

cont./

Under the "Nachfrist" concept incorporated into the CISG, a buyer may avoid a contract where performance by the seller has been delayed, even though such delay does not rise to the level of a fundamental breach if:

(1) the buyer gives the seller an additional reasonable period of time for performance, fixing a new deadline beyond the contract delivery date by which the seller must perform; and

(2) the seller does not perform within the additional reasonable period of time.[175]

While the CISG does not provide that expiration of the additional period of time without performance by the seller creates a fundamental breach, it does provide that the buyer may nevertheless avoid the contract after the expiration of such period of time.[176]

Applying the relevant CISG "Nachfrist" provisions, a German court[177] recently held that an Egyptian buyer was entitled to avoid the contract where the German seller failed to deliver goods within an eleven-day additional period fixed by the buyer for performance of the remainder of an installment contract which the seller had only partially performed. So holding, the court found the additional eleven-day period of time was not unreasonable in the context of the particular transaction. It accordingly awarded the buyer the amount by which prepayment exceeded the amount due for the limited amount of goods actually delivered.[178]

(2) However, in cases where the buyer has paid the price, the seller loses the right to declare the contract avoided unless he does so:

(a) in respect of late performance by the buyer, before the seller has become aware that performance has been rendered; or

(b) in respect of any breach other than late performance by the buyer, within a reasonable time:

(i) the seller knew or ought to have known of the breach; or

(ii) after the expiration of any additional period of time fixed by the seller in accordance with paragraph (1) of article 63, or after the buyer has declared that he will not perform his obligation within such an additional period."

[174] The German Civil Code II §326 provides:

"(1) If, in the case of a mutual contract, one party is in default in performing, the other party may give him a reasonable period within which to perform his part with a declaration that he will refuse to accept the performance after the expiration of the period. After the expiration of the period he is entitled to demand compensation for non-performance, or to withdraw from the contract, if the performance has not been made in due time; the claim for performance is barred. If the performance is only partly made before the expiration of the period, the provision of §325(1), sent. 2, applies *mutatis mutandis*.

(2) If, in consequence of the default, the performance of the contract is of no use to the other party, such other party has the rights specified in (1) without giving any period. Ian S. Forrester, Simon L Goren & Hans-Michael Ilgen, THE GERMAN CIVIL CODE, (Fred B. Rothman & Co. 1975)."

[175] CISG, *supra* n. 2, art 47. For full text of the provision, *see supra* n. 264.

[176] CISG, *supra* n. 2, art. 49(1). For full text of the provision, *see supra* n. 264.

[177] (Parties not reported), 20 U 76/94, 24 May 1995 (Germany, Oberlandesgericht Celle), UNILEX.

[178] *See* CISG, *supra* n. 2, art. 81(2) which provides:

"(2) A party who has performed the contract either wholly or in part may claim restitution from the other party of whatever the first party has supplied or paid under the contract. If both parties are bound to make restitution, they must do so concurrently."

See also CISG, art. 84(1) which provides:

"(1) If the seller is bound to refund the price, he must also pay interest on it, from the date on which the price was paid."

Another German case[179] illustrates the consequences of failure to utilize the "Nachfrist" procedure. In this case, a German buyer and Italian seller of fashion goods entered into a contract which explicitly specified that the goods were "to be delivered July, August, September".[180] The seller made the first delivery in September, but the buyer refused the goods, claiming the quoted language required that one third of the goods should have been delivered in July, a third in August and a third in September. The court held that the seller was entitled to the full purchase price, even if the goods had been delivered late, because the buyer had not established fundamental breach by the seller or offered the seller an additional reasonable period of time to perform.

The court reached the same result where a German buyer and Italian seller entered a contract for the sale of women's shoes and the buyer refused to pay the entire purchase price, claiming in part that delivery of the goods had been untimely.[181] The court held that the buyer, in the absence of fundamental breach by the seller, had not validly avoided the contract because it had failed to provide an additional time period for the seller to perform.

Avoidance of the contract either for reasons of fundamental breach or because of compliance with the Nachfrist procedure releases both parties from their obligations under the contract, subject to any damages which may be due.[182]

The CISG also provides "Nachfrist" rights for sellers. Under Article 63,[183] the seller may fix an additional period of time of reasonable length for performance by the buyer of his obligations. Under Article 64,[184] a seller is

[179] (Parties not reported), 5 C 73/89, 24 Apr. 1990 (Germany, Amtsgericht Oldenburg in Holstein) UNILEX, CLOUT (Case 7).

[180] *Ibid.* The "+ or –" is the actual content of the contract clause specifying time for performance.

[181] (Parties not reported), 5 U 15/93, 18 Jan. 1994 (Germany, Oberlandesgericht Frankfurt am Main) UNILEX, CLOUT (Case 79).

[182] *See* CISG, art. 81(1) which provides:

> "(1) Avoidance of the contract releases both parties from their obligations under it, subject to any damages which may be due. Avoidance does not affect any provision of the contract for the settlement of disputes or any other provision of the contract governing the rights and obligations of the parties consequent upon the avoidance of the contract."

[183] CISG, *supra* n. 2, art. 63 provides:

> "(1) The seller may fix an additional period of time of reasonable length for performance by the buyer of his obligations.
>
> (2) Unless the seller had received notice from the buyer that he will not perform within the period so fixed, the seller may not, during that period, resort to any remedy for breach of contract. However, the seller is not deprived thereby of any right he may have to claim damages for delay in performance."

[184] CISG, *supra* n. 2, art. 64 provides:

> "(1) The seller may declare the contract avoided:
>
> (a) if the failure by the buyer to perform any of his obligation under the contract or this Convention amounts to a fundamental breach of contract; or
>
> (b) if the buyer does not, within the additional period of time fixed by the seller in accordance with paragraph (1) of article 63, perform his obligation to pay the price or take delivery of the goods, or if he declares that he will not do so within the period so fixed.
>
> (2) However, in cases where the buyer has paid the price, the seller loses the right to declare the contract avoided unless he does so:

empowered to avoid a contract because of fundamental breach by the buyer or failure of the buyer within the additional period of time fixed by the seller to perform his obligation to pay the contract price or to take delivery of the goods, or if the buyer declares that he will not do so within the period so fixed.

The seller's "Nachfrist" right was recently litigated in a German case[185] where a German seller had given an Italian buyer an additional time period within which to take delivery of acoustic prostheses at the seller's place of business. The court held that the seller was entitled to recover damages for failure of the buyer to perform within the additional period of time which the seller had granted.

A decision of an International Chamber of Commerce arbitration panel[186] awarded damages to an Austrian seller where a Bulgarian buyer had failed to perform its obligation of opening a document of credit for payment within the additional period of time fixed for such performance by the seller. So ruling, the court held that the suspension of payment of foreign debts ordered by the Bulgarian government did not constitute *force majeure* which prevented the buyer from opening the documentary credit.

In another arbitral award by the International Chamber of Commerce Court of Arbitration,[187] while a delay in opening a documentary credit by itself did not amount to a fundamental breach, the Italian seller was nevertheless entitled to avoid the contract. According to the arbitration award, the fact that the seller waited several months before declaring the contract avoided was "equivalent to the fixing of an 'additional period of time' for performance pursuant to Art. 63 CISG", with the result that failure by the Finnish buyer to perform within that period of time entitled the seller to avoid the contract under CISG Article 64(1)(b).[188]

(a) in respect of late performance by the buyer, before the seller has become aware that performance has been rendered; or

(b) in respect of any breach other than late performance by the buyer, within a reasonable time:

(i) after the seller knew or ought to have known of the breach; or

(ii) after the expiration of any additional period of time fixed by the seller in accordance with paragraph (1) of article 63, or after the buyer has declared that he will not perform his obligations within such an additional period."

[185] (Parties not reported), 43 O 136/92, 14 May 1993 (Germany, Landgericht Aachen) UNILEX, CLOUT (Case 47).

[186] (Parties not reported), 7197/1992—1992 (ICC International Chamber of Commerce Court of Arbitration (Paris)) UNILEX, CLOUT (Case 104).

[187] (Parties not reported) 7585/1992—1992 (ICC International Chamber of Commerce Court of Arbitration (Paris)) UNILEX.

[188] CISG, *supra* note 93, art. 61(1)(b) provides:

"(1) The seller may declare the contract avoided:

(b) if the buyer does not, within the additional period of time fixed by the seller in accordance with paragraph (1) of article 63, perform his obligation to pay the price of take delivery of the goods, or it he declares that he will not do so within the period so fixed."

(f) "Adequate Grounds for Insecurity"—"Anticipatory Repudiation"

Under the CISG a party may suspend performance of its obligations if it becomes apparent that the other party will not perform a substantial part of its obligations as a result of:

(1) serious deficiency in its ability to perform or in its creditworthiness; or
(2) because of its conduct in preparing to perform or in performing the contract.

A party suspending performance must immediately give notice of suspension to the other party and must continue with performance if the other party provides adequate assurance of performance.[189] Although this is similar to the UCC provision[190] pertaining to a party's right to adequate assurance where reasonable grounds for insecurity arise, indicating that the other party will not be able to perform the contract, it is not identical, as illustrated by the cases which follow.

The CISG further provides that where the seller has already dispatched the goods before the grounds for insecurity have become evident, the seller may prevent the handing over of the goods to the buyer even though the buyer holds a document which entitles the buyer to obtain them.[191]

The CISG grants the aggrieved party the right to avoid the contract if, prior to the date of performance of the contract, it is clear that one of the parties

[189] CISG, *supra* n. 2, art. 71(1) provides:

"(1) A party may suspend the performance of his obligations if, after the conclusion of the contract, it becomes apparent that the other party will not perform a substantial part of his obligation as a result of:
(a) a serious deficiency in his ability to perform or in his creditworthiness; or
(b) his conduct in preparing to perform or in performing the contract."

CISG, *supra* n. 2, art. 71(3) provides:

"(3) A party suspending performance, whether before or after dispatch of the goods, must immediately give notice of the suspension to the other party and must continue with performance if the other party provides adequate assurance of his performance."

[190] UCC §2–609 provides:

"(1) A contract for sale imposes an obligation on each party that the other's expectation of receiving due performance will not be impaired. When reasonable grounds for insecurity arise with respect to the performance of either party the other may in writing demand adequate assurance of due performance and until he receives such assurance may if commercially reasonable suspend any performance for which he has not already received the agreed return.

(2) Between merchants the reasonableness of grounds for insecurity and the adequacy of any assurance offered shall be determined according to commercial standards.

(3) Acceptance of any improper delivery or payment does not prejudice the aggrieved party's right to demand adequate assurance of future performance.

(4) After receipt of a justified demand failure to provide within a reasonable time not exceeding thirty days such assurance of due performance as is adequate under the circumstances of the particular case is a repudiation of the contract."

[191] CISG, *supra* n. 2, art. 71(2) provides:

"(2) If time allows, the party intending to declare the contract avoided must give reasonable notice to the other party in order to permit him to provide adequate assurance of his performance."

will commit a fundamental breach of contract,[192] or if one of the parties has declared that it will not perform its obligations under the contract.[193] This latter provision in effect explicitly makes anticipatory repudiation a basis for avoidance under the CISG.[194]

A German court[195] found that a German shoe retailer would not be able to pay the purchase price of the shoes ordered and thereby would commit a fundamental breach of contract. The court held that the probability of a future breach of contract was very high and obvious, and that complete certainty or inability of the retailer to pay for the shoes was not necessary. It found that there was reason to believe that the buyer would breach the later contract, based in part on the fact that the buyer had not paid for shoes delivered under two prior contracts.[196] The court rejected the buyer's claim that it had a right to suspend payment on grounds that the goods delivered under the earlier contract were non-conforming. It refused to accept this argument because the buyer had not given notice of such non-conformity within a reasonable time as required by Article 39[197] of the CISG and held the buyer accountable for the purchase price.

[192] CISG, *supra* note 2, art. 72(1) provides:

> "(1) If prior to the date for performance of the contract it is clear that one of the parties will commit a fundamental breach of contract, the other party may declare the contract avoided."

CISG, *supra* n. 2, art. 72(2) provides:

> "(2) If time allows, the party intending to declare the contract avoided must give reasonable notice to the other party in order to permit him to provide adequate assurance of his performance."

[193] CISG, *supra* n. 2, art. 72(3) provides:

> "(3) The requirements of the preceding paragraph do not apply if the other party has declared that he will not perform his obligations."

[194] *Ibid.* The anticipatory repudiation provisions of the UCC are Sections 2–610 and 2–611. Section 2–610 provides:

> "When either party repudiates the contract with respect to a performance not yet due the loss of which will substantially impair the value of the contract to the other, the aggrieved party may:
> (a) for a commercially reasonable time await performance by the repudiating party; or
> (b) resort to any remedy for breach (Section 2–703 or Section 2–711), even though he has notified the repudiating party that he would wait the latter's performance and has urged retraction; and
> (c) in either case suspend his performance or proceed in accordance with the provisions of this Article on the seller's right to identify goods to the contract notwithstanding breach or to salvage unfinished goods" (Section 2–704).

UCC Section 2–611 provides:

> "(1) Until the repudiating party's performance is due he can retract his repudiation the aggrieved party has since the repudiation canceled or materially changed his position or otherwise indicated that he considers the repudiation final.
> (2) Retraction may be by any method which clearly indicates to the aggrieved party that the repudiating party intends to perform, but must include any assurance justifiably demanded under the provisions of this Article (Section 2–609).
> (3) Retraction reinstates the repudiating party's rights under the contract with due excuse and allowance to the aggrieved party for any delay occasioned by the repudiation."

[195] (Parties not reported), 99 O 123/92, 30 Sept. 1992 (Germany, Landgericht Berlin) UNILEX. *Accord* (Parties not reported), 17 U 146/93, 14 Jan. 1994 (Germany, Oberlandesgericht Düsseldorf) UNILEX.

[196] *Ibid.*

[197] *Supra* n. 000.

The possible loss of remedies by an aggrieved party with reasonable grounds for insecurity who fails to give the other party an opportunity to provide adequate assurance of his performance is illustrated by a recent German case.[198] A German buyer and an Italian seller entered into a contract for the sale of shoes, agreeing that the goods should be delivered to the buyer's place of business by the carrier after the buyer had paid 40 per cent of the balance due within sixty days of delivery. The seller ordered the carrier to suspend delivery, which was subsequently resumed five months later after the buyer had paid 40 per cent of the agreed price. Following delivery of the goods, the buyer paid only one-sixth of the balance due and the seller sued to recover the balance of the purchase price. Applying CISG Article 71(3)[199] literally, the court dismissed the seller's claim for the balance of the purchase price on grounds that the CISG requires a party suspending performance based on an assumption that the other party will not be able to perform its contractual obligations to immediately give notice of suspension to the other party and must continue with performance if the other party provides adequate assurance of its performance. Having failed to give the buyer notice of its suspension of performance, the Italian seller not only lost its right to an action for the balance of the purchase price due, but the German court also held that, since the seller had failed to perform its obligation of giving notice of suspension of performance to the buyer, the buyer was entitled to recover damages under CISG Articles 74–77.[200]

[198] (Parties not reported), 32 C 1074/90–91, 31 Jan. 1991 (Germany, Amtsgericht Frankfurt am Main) UNILEX, CLOUT (Case 52).

[199] CISG, *supra* n. 2, art. 71(3) provides:

> "(3) A party suspending performance, whether before or after dispatch of the goods, must immediately give notice of the suspension to the other party and must continue with performance if the other party provides adequate assurance of his performance."

[200] CISG, *supra* n. 2, art. 74 provides:

> "Damages for breach of contract by one party consist of a sum equal to the loss, including loss of profit, suffered by the other party as a consequence of the breach. Such damages may not exceed the loss which the party in breach foresaw or ought to have foreseen at the time of the conclusion of the contract, in the light of the facts and matters of which he then knew or ought to have known, as a possible consequence of the breach of contract."

CISG, *supra* n. 2, art. 75 provides:

> "If the contract is avoided and if, in a reasonable manner and within a reasonable time after avoidance, the buyer has bought goods in replacement or the seller has resold the goods, the party claiming damages may recover the difference between the contract price and the price in the substitute transaction as well as any further damages recoverable under article 74."

CISG, *supra* n. 2, art. 76 provides:

> "(1) If the contract is avoided and there is a current price for the goods, the party claiming damages may, if he has not made a purchase or resale under article 75, recover the difference between the price fixed by the contract and the current price at the time of avoidance as well as any further damages recoverable under article 74. If, however, the party claiming damages has avoided the contract after taking over the goods, the current price at the time of such taking over shall be applied instead of the current price at the time of avoidance.
>
> (2) For the purpose of the preceding paragraph, the current price is the price prevailing at the place where delivery of the goods should have been made or, if there is no current price at that place, the price of such

(g) Buyer's Damages and Reduction of Price

The buyer may claim damages if the seller fails to perform any of the obligations imposed by the Convention.[201] Breach of contract damages consist of a sum equal to the loss, including the loss of profit, suffered as a consequence of the breach.[202] These provisions resemble the direct, incidental and consequential damages provisions of the UCC.[203] The CISG provides a novel "reduction of price" remedy. If the goods do not conform with the contract, the buyer may reduce the price in the same proportion as the value which the

other place as serves as a reasonable substitute, making due allowance for differences in the cost of transporting the goods."

CISG, *supra* n. 2, art. 77 provides:

"A party who relies on a breach of contract must take such measures as are reasonable in the circumstances to mitigate the loss, including loss of profit, resulting from the breach. If he fails to take such measures, the party in breach may claim a reduction in the damages in the amount by which the loss could have been mitigated."

201 CISG, *supra* n. 2, art. 45 provides:

"(1) If the seller fails to perform any of his obligations under the contract or this Convention, the buyer may:

(a) exercise the rights provided in article 46–52.
(b) claim damages as provided in articles 74–77.

(2) The buyer is not deprived of any right he may have to claim damages by exercising his right to other remedies.

(3) No period of grace may be granted to the seller by a court or arbitral tribunal when the buyer resorts to a remedy for breach of contract."

202 CISG, *supra* n. 2, art. 74 provides:

"Damages for breach of contract by one party consist of a sum equal to the loss, including loss of profit, suffered by the other party as a consequence of the breach. Such damages may not exceed the loss which the party in breach foresaw or ought to have foreseen at the time of the conclusion of the contract, in light of the facts and matters of which he then knew or ought to have known, as a possible consequence of the breach of contract."

203 UCC § 2–714 provides:

"(1) Where the buyer has accepted goods and given notification (subsection (3) of Section 2–607) he may recover as damages for any non-conformity of tender the loss resulting in the ordinary course of events from the seller's breach as determined in any manner which is reasonable.

(2) The measure of damages for breach of warranty is the difference at the time and place of acceptance between the value of the goods accepted and the value they would have had if they had been as warranted, unless special circumstances show proximate damages of a different amount.

(3) In a proper case any incidental and consequential damages under the next section may also be recovered."

UCC § 2–715 provides:

"(1) Incidental damages resulting from the seller's breach include expenses reasonably incurred in inspection, receipt, transportation and care and custody of goods rightfully rejected, any commercially reasonable charges, expenses or commissions in connection with effecting cover and any other reasonable expense incident to the delay or other breach.

(2) Consequential damages resulting from the seller's breach include:

(a) any loss resulting from general or particular requirements and needs of which the seller at the time of contracting had reason to know and which could not reasonably be prevented by cover or otherwise; and
(b) injury to person or property proximately resulting from any breach of warranty."

goods actually delivered had at the time of delivery bears to the value that conforming goods would have had at that time.[204]

This remedy was utilized where a German buyer and Italian seller entered into a contract for the sale of shoes.[205] When the buyer paid only half the purchase price, claiming that the goods were non-conforming under the contract, the seller sued for the entire purchase price. The court found that because the buyer had satisfied its *obligations timely* to inspect the goods and notify the seller of defects, it was entitled to a reduction in price of the goods.[206] However, the court noted that the buyer could not arbitrarily reduce the price. The price reduction must reflect the difference between the value of the goods as delivered and the value the goods would have had if they had been in conformity with the contract. Thus, the seller was entitled to recover the difference between the price reduction the buyer actually took and the price reduction the buyer was entitled to take.[207]

In a similar case,[208] an Italian seller and Swiss buyer entered into a contract for the sale of furniture. The buyer claimed that one set of furniture was defective, and when the seller refused to repair the defect, the buyer asked to be reimbursed for its repairs. When the seller sued to collect the entire purchase price, the court found the buyer was entitled to a reduction in price, although the reduction would not necessarily be the equivalent of the buyer's repair expenses. The court held that the price reduction was to reflect the proportion the value of the goods as delivered bore to the value the goods would have had they been free from defect. The court further held that the latter value was to be determined by the price stated in the contract, unless the seller produced evidence to the contrary.[209]

VII. CONCLUSION

The CISG litigation since the CISG entered into effect in January 1988 has generally not produced any unexpected results in terms of the substantive meaning of CISG provisions, although it most certainly has on various occasions surprised parties unaware of its existence. The CISG litigation appears

[204] CISG, *supra* n. 2, art. 50 provides:

"If the goods do not conform with the contract and whether or not the price has already been paid, the buyer may reduce the price in the same proportion as the value that the goods actually delivered had at the time of the delivery bears to the value that conforming goods would have had at that time. However, if the seller remedies any failure to perform his obligations in accordance with article 37 or article 48 or if the buyer refuses to accept performance by the seller in accordance with those articles, the buyer may not reduce the price."

[205] (Parties not reported) 41 O 198/89, 3 Apr. 1990 (Germany, Landgericht Aachen) UNILEX.

[206] *Ibid.*

[207] *Ibid.*

[208] (Parties not reported) 6252, 27 Apr. 1992 (Switzerland, Pretura di Locarno-Campagna) UNILEX.

[209] *Ibid.*

by and large to be producing results that would be broadly consistent with a *lex mercatoria*, a law that traders would wish to have applied to dealings among themselves. The CISG appears to be functioning as its drafters intended, but it remains a serious pitfall for those who have not invested the effort to learn about it.

Those who embrace the CISG to govern their international contracts need to remember that by its terms it does not resolve all issues. The initial body of CISG case law demonstrates this point. Two such areas in particular have already been heavily litigated. Forty-two of the one hundred and forty-two cases reported thus far involve issues as to what interest rate should be applicable to overdue payments or refunds. Twenty-seven of these one hundred and forty-two cases involve issues of what constitutes a reasonable time for a buyer to discover and give notice to the seller of defects in the goods. Such frequently litigated specific issues are perhaps best anticipated by inclusion of special provisions in the contract to resolve them. General use of a supplementary choice of law clause applicable to issues not covered by the CISG may also provide a general umbrella of protection regarding the many unanticipated questions which may become the basis of controversy between contract parties.

When enough States, including the United States, ratified the CISG so that it became operative in 1988, many in the international trading community were hesitant to embrace the CISG and concentrated primarily on acquiring understanding of how effectively to opt out of the CISG. The still small, but growing number of reported CISG cases suggests that this hesitant attitude towards the CISG is evolving. The minimal need of understanding enough about the CISG to avoid being surprised by its applicability remains. However, the reported cases suggest that especially those who would embrace the CISG must understand how it works and also its self defined limitations. It is no longer enough simply to learn how to opt out of the CISG. Any international trader is well advised to understand exactly how the CISG functions as an analog of the UCC's Article 2 and of any other domestic law potentially applicable to international commercial sales of goods.

In our review of the reported cases we have not been able to identify significant conflicts between different fora as to the meaning of the CISG. It thus appears that, at least preliminarily, the CISG's direction to national courts and arbitral bodies to attempt to interpret it uniformly is being respected. As the number of cases grows and as parties to more sophisticated contracts gain sufficient confidence to permit their contracts to be governed by application of the CISG, the nature of the issues litigated may change. Hence, the question of uniform interpretation remains one worthy of monitoring.

Comprehensive legal and management review of procurement and sales procedures to be followed under the new regime by international traders and their legal advisors is desirable as increasing numbers of countries ratify and increasing use is made of the CISG. Such traders need to identify clients and circumstances in which use of the CISG is preferable to use of domestic law. Moreover, the opportunities accidentally and unknowingly to become subject to the CISG remain very real. Failure to think clearly about choice of governing law issues at the time of contracting is quite likely to lead to unpleasant surprises in the event of a dispute. Many similarities between the CISG and the UCC are readily observable, and the litigation involving the CISG thus far reported suggests that the CISG is functioning well. Nonetheless, serious pitfalls may result for those who assume that the differences between the CISG and otherwise appliable law such as the United States' UCC are of no moment.

3

The Case Against Lex Mercatoria

URIEL PROCACCIA*

I. INTRODUCTION

The principles of *Unidroit* are animated by a vision of a unified private law throughout the civilized world. This is a noble dream. Its main protagonists are men and women breaking the yoke of regional distinctions, and bursting into the open domain of a universal legal order. It is with full understanding of this bright prospect, of smoother exchange among liberated equals, that I feel compelled to sound the alarm of dissent. All it takes to remind oneself of a different point of view is to look out of these windows in Jerusalem and in seeing this beautiful, hilly terrain, to engage oneself in telling its ancient tale.

* * *

Approximately two thousand years ago, the troops of mighty Rome quenched a gory rebellion by the Jewish inhabitants of these hills, which you can see if you look through the windows. This event was followed by the destruction of the Second Temple (70 AD), and marked the beginning of a long chapter in the history of the Jewish people, the era of statelessness. A handful of local zealots, led by one Shimon Bar Kokhba, or Bar Koziba, rebelled once again, around 132–135 AD. This rebellion was reduced to ashes by one of the most enlightened of all Roman Caesars, the Emperor Hadrian, who came to be known in Jewish Halachic annals as "Hadrian the Evil".

Hadrian's mission in these parts was not a malevolent one. The Emperor's intentions towards the Jewish people did not set them apart from his intentions towards the rest of the nations under Roman dominion. This was to integrate it within a unified, stable Empire, blissfully enjoying the famous *Pax Romana*, where a single law reigns supreme. He probably failed to understand that it is exactly this spectre of a unified legal order that fired the wrath of the zealots. They had their own law, the law of the Torah, which they wanted to follow, and they were ready to pay with their lives for the attainment of

* Wachtell, Lipton, Rosen and Katz Professor of Corporate Law and Dean, Faculty of Law, Hebrew University, Jerusalem. A fuller version of this short article is currently in preparation and is scheduled to be ready for publication in 1997.

this goal;[1] for, as Rudolf von Ihering once said, many centuries later, each nation that has its own language has its own law. Laws that are foreign to the spiritual soil of a given nation cannot be successfully transplanted there. A unified law is to a national culture what a forced international language (Esperanto) might be to linguistic culture. The realisation of this claim is not less valid even if it entails some inconvenient repercussions. Indeed, the Judean zealots of the First and Second Centuries put themselves to a strikingly unusual inconvenience.

* * *

In this paper I will try to rationalise my ancient ancestors' rebellion by invoking arguments which they could never conceive. While they vibrated to tribal and theological calls, I address the issue in modern behavioural terms. If you deem some of these arguments moderately persuasive, you might join me in reflecting on the rebels' demeanour as being perhaps tragically lacking in worldly savviness, but not altogether devoid of principled merit.

* * *

My argument is not oblivious to the clear benefits that can be obtained by cross-border uniformity or harmonisation of laws. Other things equal, uniformity clearly dominates diversity, given the transaction costs associated with the need to invest in learning the law. This truism is valid for all laws, *a fortiori,* for legal norms falling within the domain of the *lex mercatoria*, where jurisdictions alternate before one's eyes in rapid succession. I refer here both to the unwritten, customary *lex mercatoria* and to mercantile law broadly defined, whether it be statutory, judge-made or customary law.[2] Speaking about this web of commercial law in its entirety, my point is that important social goals may often be better served under diversity than under uniformity; so much so that the transaction costs argument, to wit, the costly imperative to acquaint oneself with numerous legal orders, although valid *per se*, may sometimes be eclipsed by equally important considerations.

My argument proceeds as follows. In the first part of my presentation I show how legal diversity is a necessary environment for statutory and other

[1] This assertion is extremely well documented. For a recent, learned contribution to the literature, see Alfredo M. Rabello, "The Ban on Circumcision as a Cause of Bar Kokhba's Rebellion", 29 *Israel L Rev*. 176 (1995).

[2] The once clear dichotomy between unwritten usages of trade and "formal" law residing in statutes, court opinions and the like is much blurred in modern times, due to the massive infusion of the *lex mercatoria* into formal law. The Uniform Commercial Code, for example, was crafted with the express intention of incorporating the applicable usages of trade, sometimes in the teeth of explicit contractual language. For a clear demonstration and analysis of this phenomenon see, e.g., Lisa Bernstein, "Merchant Law in a Merchant Court: Rethinking the Code's Search for Immanent Business Norms", 144 *U. Pa. L Rev*. 1765 (1996).

normative improvement, whereas uniformity may lead to stagnation and decay. In the second and last part of my presentation I show that private uniform-law givers, such as a committee of experts entrusted with the drafting of cross-border conventions, or even a committee of official commentators, may have an incentive to produce suboptimal statutory products.

II. LEGAL DIVERSITY AS A COMPETITIVE ENVIRONMENT

I should like to begin my argument by invoking a well known insight from the area of American corporate law. This insight is used here as a parable to the general case, and its relevance to the business of the *Unidroit* will become apparent shortly. It is commonly understood that American jurisdictions compete in the implicit market for corporate statutes. In their attempt to mould an attractive statutory product, the States are motivated by a desire to lure companies to incorporate within their jurisdiction, an act that is necessary if a given firm wishes to be governed by the laws of that jurisdiction. If the corporate code is thus bestowed on a given firm, the firm compensates the relevant state for its productive entrepreneurship by paying incorporation taxes and annual fees, by generating business for the local bar and judiciary and so forth.

At this juncture opinions differ as to whether the migration of companies to friendly jurisdictions results in salutary effects, that is whether corporations statutes in the United States have a tendency to improve the law (whether it is a "race to the top") or whether the opposite is true and corporation statutes actually deteriorate (i.e. it is a "race to the bottom"). Race to the bottom advocates point to the fact that the incorporation site decision is reached by management, and that typical managers, bedevilled by principal–agent problems, are prone to choosing a site that turns a blind eye to managerial fraud or incompetence. If firms are, in fact, attracted to such compromising jurisdictions, other States quickly follow in their footsteps, lest they lose their share of the market; hence the race to the bottom.[3] Race to the top theoreticians, in whose ranks I find myself,[4] observe that the investing public will demand a premium for securities of firms incorporated in suboptimal jurisdictions; firms in quest of cheaper capital may be predicted for this reason to shun suboptimal (and from the firm's point of view, more costly) jurisdictions. Moreover, firms which opt to linger on in suboptimal legal environments will eventually go under. Thus, States have an incentive to upgrade, rather than to downgrade, the quality of their statutory products.[5] As it turns out, the

[3] William Cary, "Federalism and Corporate Law: Reflections Upon Delaware", 83 *Yale LJ* 663 (1974).

[4] Uriel Procaccia, *Corporate Law: Rules, Policy and Reform*, (1989) 18 ff.

[5] Ralph Winter, "State Law, Shareholder Protection and the Theory of the Corporation", 6 *J. Leg. Stud.* 251 (1977).

winner in this race for excellence is the tiny State of Delaware, whose corporate law is basically lax, allowing the parties themselves to choose governance moulds that best reflect their (sometimes) idiosyncratic preferences. The moral of this story is, simply, that "lax is beautiful"; the corresponding villain of the story is a heavy handed legislature that mandates particular governance moulds on principled grounds.

Now contrary to what most American scholars believe, the race to the top hypothesis, if it holds water within the United States, is not limited only to federated unions with multiple semi-autonomous jurisdictions. Even in a monistic State like France, Hungary or Israel, a lax approach to corporate law allows firms privately to forge their own governance structures; the equilibrium is expected to reflect moulds that minimize the cost of raising capital. These governance structures are bound to be quality products in every respect. For had there been a better mould not used by a given firm but freely available to its competitors, that firm would have been priced off the market in a Darwinian universe where only the fittest survive. Likewise, had the legislature opted to regulate corporate governance by employing mandatory language, the ensuing monopolisation of the normative structure would have removed the incentive to search for optimal governance alternatives; the cost of capital would have become insensitive to the quality of the legal environment.

So much for the corporate parable. As soon as we turn our attention to some other fields of law it becomes apparent that the corporate example ought to be used with extreme caution. Thus, Liberia and Panama have long ruled the waves as favourite home ports for commercial vessel owners, not because their shipping laws are superior in any meaningful fashion but because they feature laxity in standards of seaworthiness. Switzerland became such a favourite banking haven, not for its competitive interest rates or customer-oriented service but, at least partially, because it acquired a reputation as a tight-lipped guardian of secret deposits, many of which are of a dubious character. Is there any observable common denominator among the types of laws that actually race to the bottom? I think there is one. At a closer look, all inter-jurisdictional competitions that produce sour grapes are characterised by one common feature. They are chosen unilaterally by a given player with the sole purpose of externalising costs to third parties, whether they be seamen or passengers (Liberia and Panama) or, say, fiscal authorities engaged in efforts to collect taxes (Switzerland). Races to the bottom are much less likely to occur when the site is selected jointly by both parties to a given transaction; for in such a case all spillover effects are likely to be internalised. None of the contracting parties would freely agree to share in a shrunken pie without securing for itself a compensatory slice.

The key question to be addressed is whether inter-jurisdictional competition in the private law area, especially in the *lex mercatoria* broadly defined, bears a closer resemblance to the corporate law race, which leads to the top, or to the shipping–banking law race, which crashes at the bottom. Intuitively, the race to the top seems to be the likelier proposition. This is so because in the private law area no one can unilaterally impose inferior patterns of striking a deal on non-consenting parties. But intuition is not enough; this point merits a closer look.

In applying the corporate parable to the private law area two difficulties loom large. The first difficulty stems from the fact that the corporate race to the top argument seems at first blush to be vitally dependent on the existence of active capital markets. To reiterate the argument, managers are presumed to shop for optimal corporate codes, because in doing so they secure cheaper financing for their firms. But is the production of optimal contract laws subject to similar mechanisms? Does any mechanism exist that may properly substitute for a missing capital market in the process of contracting? I submit that the answer to this question is yes. Shortage of space prevents me from developing a full blown argument here. But its core can be captured very succinctly. Players do not transact in goods or in services bereft of their legal attributes. Buying a wedge under an expectation measure of damages for breach or under a broad standard of *bona fides* differs from buying the (otherwise) very same wedge under a reliance rule of damages for breach or under specific rules of prescribed contractual conduct. Since the product is thus differentiated, the supply and demand curves relating thereto are bound to be different as well, and so is the expected economic surplus. Wedges sold in more efficient legal environments generate larger pies to be divided between the parties and provide an incentive for both parties to opt for their attainment. Clearly, then, competition in the products market substitutes beautifully for the missing competition in capital markets. If one legal regime, other things being equal, produces a larger expected benefit from entering into a transaction than another legal regime, it is in the common interest of both parties to opt for the superior regime. They do not necessarily save, like corporate firms, on the cost of financing, but they get more or better consideration for a given monetary outlay or equal consideration for a smaller monetary outlay. Efficiency is efficiency, whether one realises it through the machinations of the capital market, or by measuring directly the costs and benefits emanating from the process of contracting.

The second difficulty in applying the corporate parable to the law of transactions is this. The race to the top hypothesis assumes that jurisdictions can be rewarded for crafting superior corporate codes, by collecting tax revenues from firms incorporated within the jurisdiction. Thus, a third of the revenues of the State of Delaware is derived from incorporation and annual corporate fees. Many a jurisdiction actually tries to emulate the Delaware Code in a (broadly speaking, futile) attempt to capture a part of the Delaware incorporation market. But unlike the rules of private international law applying to corporations, a given contract code can be adopted by mere consent without paying any taxes to the entrepreneurial jurisdiction. Why, then, should any

State take the trouble in crafting a superior, but free, statutory product? One possible explanation is of the softer variety. States may derive satisfaction in spreading their private law gospel far and wide. The Biblical command "For out of Zion shall go forth the law, and the word of the Lord from Jerusalem" was hardly coined by the Prophet Isaiah with the intention of boosting the revenues of the Judean *fiscus*. This softer explanation can easily be supplemented by a more rigorous reasoning.

To see this, let me invoke the Delaware parable once again. Delaware does not generate its sizable income by simply cashing in on past glory, i.e. by collecting taxes from consumers of its code. Had it been possible for any State to use such a passive strategy, it would have become conceivable for other jurisdictions, both within and outside the United States, successfully to compete with Delaware by simply emulating its code and offering a rebate on Delaware's tax rates.[6] Such a strategy is bound to fail because Delaware is uniquely able to provide its own customers with expert advice and interpretation of its own laws, as well as a specialised forum for adjudicating disputes. The local bar joins forces with the local bench in applying a vast stock of precedents, which provide a substratum of certainty for planning ahead. The legal personnel plays centre stage in this game, but it is not an exclusive role. Lawyers are assisted by a host of side characters, such as accountants, economists, MBAs and tradespersons. This complex web of services turns Wilmington, an otherwise dormant provincial town, into a veritable hub of activity. The same holds true of statutes in the area of private law. Even if States cannot collect taxes from parties wishing to consume their legislative products, if consumers opt to be governed by such products this *per se* ensures some revenues for the State of origin. No one in her right mind will turn to, say, a Papuese lawyer for an authoritative interpretation of the BGB, or, for that matter, to a German arbitrator for an adjudication of a fine point under the tribal customs of an African ethnic group. So much for the market for statutory products.

III. THE POLITICAL ECONOMY OF LEGAL UNIFICATION

Unlike the literature on competition among States in the market for statutory products, which is fairly well developed and has reached a certain state of maturity, the literature concerning the political economy of international harmonisation of legal norms is barely in its infancy.[7] All claims made in this area ought to be taken *cum grano salis* and subjected to rigorous scrutiny.

The job of unification or harmonisation is described by Zweigert and Kotz, the leading comparative law experts, in the following words:

[6] I am grateful to Professor Edward Rock for drawing my attention to this argument.

[7] See, for instance, the recent contribution of Alan Schwartz and Robert Scott, "The Political Economy of Private Legislatures", 143 *U.Pa.L Rev.* 595 (1995).

"Where there are areas of difference [among the jurisdictions] one must reconcile them either by adopting the best existing variant, or by finding, through comparative methods, a new solution which is better, and more easily applied than any of the existing ones. Preparatory studies in comparative law are absolutely essential here; without them one cannot . . . decide which of the actual or proposed solutions is the best."[8]

Two tacit assumptions loom large in Zweigert and Kotz's recommendations. They are, first, that there exists a "best" solution to important legal problems on the international scale and that reforming committees, such as *Unidroit*, will not malfunction in their attempt to implement top alternatives. Both claims look to me rather suspect.

Private law is about allocating entitlements and protecting them, in Professors Calabresi and Melamed's phraseology, by either "property rules" or "liability rules".[9] In a world free of transaction costs the choice of any given rule would have been immaterial, at least with regard to its efficiency, because parties have an incentive to contract around any inefficient rule and to substitute it with an efficient one; this is the core of the celebrated Coase Theorem.[10] The need to determine entitlements flows directly from the presence of transaction costs. The role of the lawgiver is to bestow entitlements on parties so that overall societal costs can be minimised and overall welfare maximised. Let us illustrate the point by invoking one of the first achievements of *Unidroit* in the area of private law, the regulation of the status of *bona fide* purchasers without notice in the law of sales. In this scenario two players vie for legislative protection, the original owner and the *bona fide* purchaser. There is a given loss, occasioned by an intervening party (a thief) which can theoretically be prevented, at different cost levels, by either one of the two principal players. In a costly environment (i.e. where the Coasian zero transaction costs assumption is violated) it is a good idea to bestow the entitlement to the disputed good on the party whose prevention costs are higher. The other player, who has to bear the risk of loss, is thus motivated to take prevention measures, which, we assume, are less costly. If the entitlement is reversed, the player with the higher prevention costs is motivated to spend this higher sum, or to engage in a costly negotiation with the other party, to contract around the inefficient outcome.[11]

So it all turns, does it not, on which party has higher prevention costs. But who *is* that party? The key point to be observed here is that the relative level of prevention costs is highly dependent on regional, commercial and even spiritual variables, which may be radically different internationally. Unification does not

[8] Konard Zweigert and Hein Kotz, *Introduction to Comparative Law*, (2d revised ed., Oxford, Clarendon Press, 1987), 23.

[9] Guido Calabresi and Douglas Melamed, "Property Rules, Liability Rules and Inalienability: One View of the Cathedral", 85 *Harv. L Rev.* 1089 (1972).

[10] Ronald Coase, "The Problem of Social Cost", 3 *J.Law & Econ.* 1 (1960).

[11] This is a standard analysis to be found in most sophisticated treatments of the subject. See, e.g., Robert Cooter and Thomas Ulen, *Law and Economics*(1988, 152 ff.).

really make sense here because entitlements need to be customised, to respond to the different cost structures obtaining in different societies. Let me illustrate. Suppose that one system has a reliable registration system with regard to the disputed item and another system does not. Clearly, within the system that has the reliable records, it becomes cheaper for the purchaser to verify title. In such a system the original owner should prevail. In the other system, where records are not easily available, verification of title may become more cumbersome. In that case the *bona fide* purchaser without notice should have the upper hand.

In view of these observations, it appears that the real agenda facing the unifying organisation is not, as in Zweigert and Kotz's naïve observation, "[w]hat is the objectively 'best' alternative within the choice set?", but, rather, "[h]ow to order the different, and often contradictory, preferences of the various members of the international community?". This rephrasing of the issue leads us right to the heart of the political economy angle of the issue.

Given the deep cultural differences among nations and the values that generate their respective preferences and hence laws, any attempt to "reconcile" them, to use once again the Zweigert and Kotz expression, is tantamount to pitting different sets of preferences against one another. A vulgar solution to this problem is simply to opt for sets of norms that fit the preferences of the more powerful nations, which are also likely to be the nations footing the bill of keeping the experts at their jobs.

There is perhaps another, less vulgar but not less damaging, way out. It is to employ such broad standards that would not be likely to conflict with the particular preferences of any nation represented in the lawgiver's general constituency. If, for example, the parties are mandated to act "in good faith", or not "unreasonably" to interfere with the rights of other parties, no nation is likely to raise serious objections.[12] It does not seem unreasonable to expect that unification agencies will indeed be slanted in favour of broad standards. A commonplace assumption in modern political theory is that lawgivers maximise their own utility apart from the attainment of some public agenda. Assume that deep rooted diversity among the member states precludes the adoption of particular rules as the basis for a draft proposal; then the only alternative to adopting broad standards in matters of controversy is to abort the project altogether. Lawgivers may be assumed to resist aborted projects, both because such a strategy implies personal failure and because completed projects enhance their reputation, and conceivably their income, regardless of the broadness of the adopted standards.

The predicted slant in favour of broad standards implies two costly consequences. First, given the costs and benefits of rules and standards, there exists an optimal mix of these two regulatory measures.[13] If a lawgiving agency is

[12] See Schwartz and Scott, n. 7 *supra*.

[13] Thus, standards, being cheaper in production and more costly in application, are preferable when applications are few and far between; and the opposite is true of rules. See Louis Kaplow, "Rules Versus Standards: An Economic Analysis", 42 *Duke LJ* 557 (1992).

constrained towards over-inclusive standards and to adopt under-inclusive rules in its actual product, society is bound to suffer an efficiency loss. Perhaps more importantly, setting a broad standard where particular rules are more appropriate generates an unnecessary vagueness in the law, which hinders the parties' ability to plan ahead. In light of this observation, another central claim of Zweigert and Kotz, that international harmonisation increases the stability of the law and its guiding effect for future transactions, loses much of its intuitive appeal.

VII. CONCLUSION

The sword of Hadrian overwhelmed the shield of Bar Koziba. But Jewish law stood the tide of the sweeping Roman legal order and assisted in formulating a unique national heritage. So did the Common Law of England. So did other diverse, rich and unique legal orders from the four corners of the earth. I surmise that even the legal systems that were based on the Roman paradigm benefited, in the end, by that splendid diversity.

4

Convergence of Contract Law Systems and the Unidroit Principles of International Commercial Contracts: A Search for the Nature of Contract

DONALD B. KING*

I would like to explore today the nature of contract with particular emphasis on what I would term the new "International Restatement of Contract Law". I am referring to the Principles of International Commercial Contracts recently published in Rome in 1994 and prepared by *Unidroit* (The International Institute for the Unification of Private Law). The Principles are beginning to attract considerable attention throughout the world and are an important part of the search for the nature of contract. In effect, the "Principles" constitute a new "International Restatement of Contract Law," a term which will be used throughout this writing.

The search for the nature of contract brings to mind a poem[1] often included in the studies in the high schools and colleges throughout our United States. It concerns the six blind men of Hindustan. In this poem, they discuss the nature of an elephant, which none of them have ever seen. Each goes out to ascertain the nature of the elephant. As the poem describes: one feeling the side describes the elephant as a wall, another feels the tusk and thinks of a spear; another grasping the trunk describes a snake; another putting his arm around the knee feels a tree, another touching the ear talks of a fan, and the last touching the tail describes a rope. Thus, coming back from their respective travels, each describes the elephant quite differently. In reality, the elephant is something different than what each of these has described. This story may in some ways be analogous to the search by legal theorists for the nature of "contract" over a period of many centuries. The ultimate convergence and

* Professor of Law, Saint Louis University School of Law.

[1] "The Blind Men and the Elephant," in *The Political Works of John Godfrey Saxe*, 112 (1887).

end of the search may be in this new International Restatement of Contract Law.

In regard to the nature of contract, there have been many persons who have tried to ascertain and describe it. Let me posit six persons, a mixture of hypothetical and real persons, who have gone out over the span of many centuries to describe contracts.

The first of these we may see as a civil law trained person, perhaps from the early Roman law whose tradition was later carried into the great codes of Europe. Contracts would be seen as a set of promises. This set of promises would have to be in accord with law and public policy. Thus it would be said that the promises must be supported by "causa" or "cause"—meaning that the cause of the contract was one which was devoid of fraud, deceit, or violation of some public policy. There would be no requirement of "consideration", that is the exchange of bargained-for-value or detriment as found in the common law. The great European Codes continue with their enunciations of this description of contracts.

The second person seeking to ascertain the nature of contract we may call Lord Mansfield, who is also known as the father of commercial law in the Anglo-Saxon or common law world. Lord Mansfield described the mercantile contract to be a promise or set of promises made by the merchant; but he did not require consideration as did a number of his common law brethren at the time. In the days of Mansfield the Statute of Frauds was already part of English law and some writing was necessary for many types of contract.

The third person setting forth to view the nature of contract may be said to be from the classical school of contracts within the common law. The classical school required a set of promises, not just to make a contract generally but for it to include a number of the important terms. Indeed there was a type of "ribbon matching" of various terms which was necessary in order to have a binding contract. Some courts even talked in terms of the contract having to be very definite. In addition, in the classic school, there was a firm adherence to the principle that there must be a "bargained-for-exchange" of "value" to constitute legal "consideration". Likewise, a writing was necessary.

The fourth person to view "contracts" we may see as a neoclassicist or the member of a new classical school. This person would see the contract somewhat as a classicist would but in a different sense. There would still be required a set of matching promises; but not all of the major terms needed to be spelled out and some could be implied. Indeed, some were even provided for in the Sale of Goods Act, where they had not been set forth by the parties. This type of legislation was found throughout the British Commonwealth and in the states of the US. Still, a considerable amount of definiteness was required. In addition, "consideration" remained a necessary element and the Statute of Frauds remained an essential component. Even though England abandoned the Statute of Frauds requirement for the sale of goods in 1954, the requirement continues in force in the United States and some other common law jurisdictions.

The fifth person to see the "elephant" of contracts may be said to be a functionalist, a member of the realist school of Karl Llewellyn, who was the Chief Reporter for the Uniform Commercial Code. Under the influence of this school some basic concepts such as the importance of title to determine unrelated questions were abandoned, and the question more often asked was what the was issue and how did business persons approach it? Under this school of thinking, issues were looked at in terms of step-by-step performance and each was determined on the basis of what would be the most realistic outcome. Interestingly, the functionalists who designed the Uniform Commercial Code (perhaps without realizing it fully) were drafting a Code which also supported other schools of contract such as the Relationalist school. The Uniform Commercial Code supports not only that school but also some aspects of the modern "elephant" of contracts as I shall propose later on. I shall point out how these new attributes have been embraced in the new International Restatement of Contract Law.

The sixth person to explore the nature of contract may be said to reflect the more modern schools of jurisprudence. This person has absorbed the teachings of several modern schools, including the Relational and Economic concepts of contract law. The Relationalist school began to develop in the late 1950's and remains well and alive today.[2] The economic law theorists have also been very influenced in modern times, and this was well described by Professor Jacob Ziegel at an earlier Academy conference.[3] Some persons see contracts not in a relational sense but as supporting certain economic values related to economic efficiencies. Sometimes, in seeking those economic efficiencies, they are prone to ignore the plights of vulnerable individuals drawn into unfair contracts and are oblivious to a sense of justice that goes beyond the economic realm. The critical legal studies and feminist movements have focused their criticisms on the influences of vested interests and discriminatory practices in the evolution of modern contract law.

I should now like to offer my own description of the elephant of contracts, with particular reference to this new International Restatement of Contract Law. It is a model or type of animal which I have described in prior articles in the Journal of Contracts Law,[4] but which is well adapted to this new

[2] Macaulay, "Contracts in the Manufacturing Industry" (1963) 9 *Pract Lawyer* 14, 15; King. "New Conceptualism of the Uniform Commercial Code," 10, *St Louis LJ* 30 (Pt 1, 1965); 11, *St Louis LJ* 15 (Pt 2, 1966). MacNeil, "Contracts: Adjustment of Long-term Economic Relations Under Classical Neoclassical, and Relational Contract Law" 72 *NL Rev.* 854, 886–98. MacNeil, "The Many Futures of Contracts" (1974) 47 *S Cal. L Rev.* 691, 695. Goetz and Scott, "Principles of Relational Contracts" (1981) 67 *Va. L Rev.* 1089, 1091. Scott, "Conflict and Cooperation in Long-Term Contracts" (1987) 75 *Calif. L Rev.* 2005; Scott, "A Relational Theory of Default Rules for Commercial Contracts" (1990) 19 *J Leg. Studies* 597. Speidel, "Article 2 and Relational Sales Contracts" (1993) 26 *Loyola Law Rev.* 789.

[3] Ziegel, "What Can The Economic Analysis of Law Teach Commercial and Consumer Law Scholars?", chap. 12, 249 in Cranston and Goode (eds.), *Commercial and Consumer Law: National and International Dimensions*. (Clarendon Press, Oxford, 1993).

[4] King, "Reshaping Contract Theory and Law: Death of Contracts II," 7 *J Contract L* 245 (1994).

International Restatement of Contract Law. It is basically one in which the contract has evolved from resting primarily upon consent to a large number of the terms to a new contract created by an umbrella of generalized consent. (Using U for umbrella, the traditional US abbreviation of K for contract, and the G for generalized, and C for consent, this may be termed an umbrella contract of generalized consent or UKGC). Under this new generalized consent, there is general agreement to the contract without there being an agreement as to many of its terms. For the new generalized consent, only a spark of consent is needed to create the contract. The rest of the UKGC depends upon another factor. That other factor is that many of the terms are implied by law, so that it thus becomes a law-made type of contract.

Still another feature of these umbrella contracts of general consent (UKGC) is that they are contracts which evolve in several stages. (This may be termed K (contracts) I (in) S several, S (stages) or KISS. Since kisses may be in several stages and progressive, this abbreviation too may be most appropriate). Let me now describe what is the nature of contract in our modern times together with the principles of this new International Restatement of Contract Law.

First of all, the UKGC Contract only requires a generalized consent as to its terms, which is sufficient for it to be a contract under the International Restatement of Contract Law.[5] "A contract may be concluded by either acceptance of an offer or by conduct of the parties that is sufficient to show agreement".[6] The comments recognizing that when dealing with complex transactions, it is often difficult to determine if and when a contractual agreement has been reached. All that is necessary is to determine whether there is sufficient evidence of the parties intent for them to be generally bound to the contract. The comments offer the following illustration: "A & B have entered into negotiations, and after some prolonged negotiations, without either a formal offer or acceptance, with some minor points still to be settled, both parties began to perform. The court may find that even though subsequently the parties failed to reach an agreement on these minor points, there is nevertheless a contract."[7]

The comments further note that the proposal of an offer, though needing to have some definiteness and indication of intention to be bound, may omit many of the essential terms. Thus, "a precise description of the goods or services to be delivered or rendered, the price to be paid for them, the time and place of performance, etc., may be left undetermined in the offer without necessarily rendering it insufficiently definite . . .".[8] A further illustration is given of A and B who have renewed a contract for computers and technical assistance over a number of years. After opening a new office, A asks B to provide

[5] Article 2.1.
[6] Comments to Article 2.1.
[7] *Ibid.*
[8] *Ibid.*

assistance for the new computers, and B accepts this undertaking despite the fact that A's offer does not specify many of the terms of the agreement. Nevertheless, the contract has been concluded and "some missing terms can be taken from the previous contract as constituting a practice established between the parties and thus the course of dealing furnishes a basis for finding the other contract principles in that situation".[9]

If there is a contract with a number of the essential terms missing, how are they to be ascertained in most cases? And especially if the parties have not had previous dealings, what can be their source? In the new International Restatement of Contract Law, this is provided for by law. Thus much of the contract may be implied by law: it is not through the consent of the parties to the particular terms that the contract is constituted but rather it is by a law made mechanism. These may be called "implied by law" or "law made" terms.[10] An example of this is found in several of the articles of this New International Restatement of Contract Law. One article[11] points out that implied obligations stem from:

a. the nature and purpose of the contract;
b. practices established between the parties and usages;
c. good faith and fair dealings;
d. reasonableness

Thus the implied obligations or other implied terms of the contract may arise out of the nature or purpose of the obligation or from the conclusion that past practices between the parties, or even trade usages, may be sufficient to fill the gaps or it may be a consequence of the principle of good faith and fair dealing or of reasonableness in contractual relations.

What is the position if the contract does not contain a price or indicate how the price is to be determined? Even then there may be a contract under the New International Restatement of Contract Law. This International Restatement provides that in such a situation the price is the price generally charged at the time the contract was concluded in comparable circumstances in the trade. Even if no such price is available there is still a contract.[12] A reasonable price is determined and becomes part of the contract by operation of law.[13] The reasonable price term is also used where the price is to be fixed by one of the parties whose determination is manifestly unreasonable, or by a third party who will not do so, or by reference to factors that no longer exist.[14] Interestingly, this provision on the effect of a missing price term and its determination is said by the drafters to be "inspired by Article 55 of the Convention on the International Sale of Goods. In the view of the drafters,

9 *Ibid.*
10 See King, *supra* n. 4.
11 Article 5.2.
12 Article 5.7.
13 Article 6.1.
14 Article 11.

these provisions contain the necessary flexibility to meet the needs of international trade.

Because generalized consent forms a contract, even with missing terms, there may also be a missing term as to quality. This is provided that where the quality of performance is not fixed the contract still exists, and the party is bound to "render a performance of a quality that is reasonable and not less than average in the circumstances".[15]

What if the time for the performance of the contract obligations is missing from the generalized consent? In such a situation it is provided that, if such a term is missing, performance shall be within a reasonable period after the conclusion of the contract if the period cannot be determined by other circumstances.[16]

If a contract is to run over a period of time but no definite period has been set within the contract, then it is provided that such a contract may be ended by either party, after giving notice of termination a reasonable time in advance.[17]

What if the place for performance is not included in the terms of the contract? This also may be law-made.[18] If it is a monetary obligation, then it must be performed at the obligee's place of business. If the obligation is of another type, such as providing the goods, then performance is at the obligor's place of business. The general rule is that a party must perform its obligation at its own place of business.

In a number of cases, the law made terms are invoked through the recognition and support of trade usages or course of dealings between the parties. The new International Restatement of Contract Law stipulates that the parties are "bound by any usage to which they have agreed or by any practice which they have established between themselves".[19] In absence of such usage, it provides that the parties are "bound by a usage that is widely known and regularly observed in international trade by parties in a particular trade concerned . . .".[20]

Now, let us turn to the other important aspect of modern contracts—KISS. A contract may develop in stages under the New International Restatement once the umbrella of generalized consent to that contract exists. At this point, under the KISS concept one of several stages may occur. One is that the parties may continue to negotiate and fill in the terms to that contract. But even as they do so, it should be recognized that there is a binding contract between the parties despite the further negotiations taking place on some of the terms.

Another possibility is that the parties simply go ahead and perform the contract. The new International Restatement of Contract Law recognizes that this

[15] Article 5.6.
[16] Article 6.1.
[17] Article 5.8.
[18] Article 6.1.
[19] Article 1.8.
[20] *Ibid.*

is perfectly legitimate. In almost all of these situations there is no legal dispute and the contract is carried out according to its terms and through the parties' conduct. Their conduct furnishes the basis for the missing terms.

Still other possible stages are that the parties will continue to negotiate but not agree upon other terms, or that they may not negotiate but simply carry out part of the contract and later fail to agree on these terms. In such cases, "law-made" terms are again applicable. Thus, all this time a contract has existed under a contractual umbrella but simply awaits the development of these other stages. This evolutionary type of contract is found also in the Uniform Commercial Code. However, in the new International Restatement of Contract Law the umbrella of contract in which these stages occur extends even further than under the Uniform Commercial Code. This is because the umbrella is expanded to take into account some of the earlier negotiation stages, as I will now describe.

There is also a type of contractual liability which exists in the negotiation stage under the new International Restatement of Contract Law. It is made clear that "a party who negotiates or breaks off negotiations in bad faith is liable for the losses caused to the other party".[21] Thus, while recognizing the parties' right to negotiate with each other, the drafters also recognize that right is not unlimited and must not conflict with the principles of good faith and fair dealing. Even if there is no basic contract at this point, there is still a contractual liability which may be viewed as the extension of the contract umbrella. The drafters go on to point out that, in particular, it is wrong for a party to enter into or continue negotiations when intending not to reach agreement with the other party. Also, there is a point in the negotiation process, where a party may no longer break off negotiations abruptly or without justification. At this point, one is committed to KISS! (Contract in several Stages). Whether such a point of "no return" is reached depends, of course, on the circumstances of the case".

One other facet of the new type of contract law is the implanting of the "New Business Ethic". It was pointed out several decades ago that this new business ethic was introduced in the Uniform Commercial Code through the principles of good faith and unconscionability.[22] A new business ethic is also carried into the new International Restatement of Contract Law with their emphasis upon good faith. Indeed, as has just been pointed out, good faith is required even in the early negotiation stages of the contract. As a general requirement, "each party must act in accordance with good faith and fair dealing in international trade".[23] The commentary makes clear that this principle informs many other rules throughout the Restatement. It also states that even in the absence of specific provisions regarding the parties' performance, the good faith duty exists throughout the life of the contract, which includes the

[21] Article 2.15.
[22] See, King, "The New Conceptualism of the Uniform Commercial Code," *supra* n. 2.
[23] Article 1.7.

negotiation process. So important are the duties of good faith and fair dealing that the parties may not contractually exclude or limit it. In addition, it is not limited by standards within any particular national legal system, but rather is good faith and fair dealing in international trade. While the domestic standards may be taken into account, they may not limit scope of this new concept.

All this is part of the new "elephant" of contracts which I am describing to you. It is one in which some of the old views in the "elephant of contracts" must now be rejected. It is an elephant which is concerned with generalized consent in its initiation but consists to a large extent of law implied contract terms. It is also an "elephant" which may grow up in various alternative ways or stages. In its evolution it may consist largely of terms which are later negotiated under an already existing umbrella of contracts or under the already conceived and born "elephant" of contracts. The growing up may also consist of terms implied or read into the contract by operation of the law. It may be largely a law-made "elephant" of contracts or it just may grow haphazardly through conduct and be carried out in that manner. Its nickname may be UKGC or KISS or both.

A final aspect of that elephant of contract which we now see before us is that it is in many ways a better and more ethical animal. It is an animal with a conscience of good faith and fair dealing. It is also an animal that is not limited by national concepts but instead has an international conscience of good faith. In the three-ring circus consisting of national commercial laws like the UCC, the Convention for the International Sale of Goods, and this new International Restatement of Contract Law, this last elephant of contracts should perform well.

PART II

Banking Law, Payment Systems and International Finance

5

Unauthorized Electronic Funds Transfers—Comparative Aspects

BENJAMIN GEVA*

I. INTRODUCTION

Generally speaking, an electronic funds transfer is initiated where a bank customer, acting as a sender, transmits payment instructions to the sending bank's computer[1] from a terminal.[2] Such communication from the customer to the computer of the customer's bank can take place from:

(1) a public-access terminal, usually either an automated teller machine (ATM) or an automated banking machine (ABM);
(2) a point-of-sale (POS) terminal at a retail establishment; or
(3) an exclusive-access terminal used solely by one sender and located at the sender's place of business or home, which could be the sender's own computer or, at the other extreme, a simple telephone or television set.

In fact, the first two types of terminals are both publicly accessed. In practice, they are used for such transactions as cash withdrawals, bill payments, same-person-inter-account transfers, and retail purchases. Terminals falling into the third category may be used for inter-account transfers, whether belonging to the same person, or from an account of one person to an account of another. Usually, the first two categories are associated with consumer card funds transfers. The third category is associated with both consumer home banking and business-to-business payments.

In each case, the sender's instructions are usually authenticated by means of an access device, in the form of a secret code,[3] either alone, or in

* Professor of Law, Osgoode Hall Law School, York University, Toronto, Canada. Financial assistance provided by the Social Sciences and Humanities Research Council of Canada (SSHRCC) and the MAX-Plank Institute, Hamburg, Germany, is acknowledged with great gratitude.

[1] Throughout this paper, "bank" denotes any depository financial institution, and "customer" means an account holder in such an institution.

[2] The customer may also deliver instructions to the bank in writing or in diskettes, in which case input to the computer system may be carried out by the bank itself. The present discussion is however limited to electronic transmission from a terminal, purportedly by the customer or on the customer's behalf. More on the communication flow in an electronic funds transfer see B. Geva, the law of electronic funds transfers §1.03[5] (New York: Matthew Bender, 1992–96).

[3] Instances of unauthenticated electronic instructions are outside the scope of the present discussion.

conjunction with a physical device, such as a card, to be inserted at the terminal. Cards are particularly used, though not necessarily exclusively, in publicly accessed terminals. In each case, authentication is immediately followed by verification by the bank according to its security procedure. Thereafter, the bank proceeds to execute the instructions and carry out the funds transfer.

This paper concerns the initiation of an electronic funds transfer authenticated without the authority of the sending bank's customer but which is nevertheless carried out. The focus is on a card payment transaction as well as on a home banking or business-to-business credit transfer from a sending payer to a receiving payee or beneficiary.[4] The issue to be considered here is the loss allocation between the sending bank and the customer on whose behalf the transfer purported to be initiated.[5] This issue will be explored here under (i) the common law, applicable in England, Canada[6] and other jurisdictions with current or historical connection to the Commonwealth, or its predecessor, the British Empire, such as Australia, (ii) American law, and (iii) Swiss law, with a reference to other civil law jurisdictions.[7]

In the common law, the issue is to be determined under general principles of law, many of which may be derived by analogy to the law governing loss allocation in the case of a forged cheque. Voluntary codes of practice may supplement or supersede such rules in consumer card transactions. In Switzerland the issue is governed by the general provisions of the Code of Obligations. Conversely, in the United States, specific legislation applies to the question. Thus, in the various States, UCC Article 4A[8] governs business-to-business credit transfers. In turn, the federal Electronic Fund Transfer Act[9] and Regulation E[10] that implements it govern the issue in consumer transfers.

Five important preliminary observations ought to be noted. The first relates to the definition of an "unauthorized funds transfer". Thus, circumstances where a transfer is initiated by an agent, or third person entrusted by the

[4] In a credit transfer, the paying party's instructions are transmitted directly to that party's bank so that funds are then "pushed" to the account of the payee or beneficiary. Conversely, in a debit transfer, it is the beneficiary or payee who transmits the message to the beneficiary's or payee's bank, so as to collect or "pull" funds from the payor's account. For more on the distinction, see Geva, above note 2 at s 1.03[3].

[5] The additional issue, that of recovery from the payee or beneficiary, will not be dealt with here.

[6] However, this is not a matter of "banking", nor is it covered by the federal Bills of Exchange Act. Consequently, it is subject to provincial jurisdiction in Canada, so that in the Province of Quebec, civil law, rather than principles of common law, may determine the issue.

[7] Swiss law is not necessarily identical to that of other civil law countries, such as Germany, France, Italy, or Latin American jurisdictions. However, in all such legal systems, the customer-bank relationship is analyzed from the common perspective of the mandate. This ensures substantial degree of similarity of general applicable principles. See further, Part IV below.

[8] UCC Art. 4A was approved in 1989 by the ALI and the NCCUSL. As of March 1996 it was adopted by all 50 states and the District of Columbia, as well as CHIPS, Fedwire, and NACHA. The UNCITRAL Model Law on International Credit Transfers usually follows UCC Article 4A.

[9] 15 USC 1693, enacted in 1978.

[10] 12 CFR Part 205, originally passed in 1981 and most recently simplified and updated in 1996.

customer with an access device, do not give rise to an "unauthorized funds transfer". Rather, they may involve an agent exceeding his[11] actual authority, a case which falls outside our enquiry, and which usually entails the customer's responsibility for the entire amount of the transfers. It is also my view that the same rule ought to apply whenever the customer voluntarily entrusts a third person with the access device, for whatever purpose, and not necessarily with the authority to use it.[12] It follows that an unauthorized transfer must emanate from someone who unlawfully either assumed control of the access device or bypassed it altogether. Such a person may be a member of the customer's household, the customer's employee or associate, or a total stranger.

The second observation relates to the possibility that the customer's fault or negligence may or may not have contributed to an unauthorized funds transfer. That is, a person may unlawfully assume control of the access device, or bypass its use altogether, and initiate an unauthorized transfer, either or not due to the customer's fault, and even in its absence. For example, the customer might not have properly secured the safekeeping of the access device or any pertaining information. Or again, the customer may have been negligent in the choice of the secret access code, where such choice was available to the customer. Thus, the customer could have selected obvious numbers or letters, such as those consisting of the customer's car license plate, birthday or name. Or else, the customer might have failed to advise the bank properly and promptly of the loss or theft of the access device. As well, upon receiving notification from the bank of a transfer, the customer may have failed to act diligently and promptly in discovering the lack of authority. The customer may have thereby precluded prompt recourse by the bank against the wrongdoer, prior to the latter's disappearance or insolvency, and further enabled that wrongdoer to continue drawing on the account without the customer's authority. An alternative scenario is where the customer was quite diligent in the safekeeping as well as in giving required notice to the bank.

The third preliminary point concerns the nature of the electronic authentication and the ensuing process of bank verification. Thus, a handwritten or manual signature is individual to the signer. As such, it *identifies* the signer. Any signature, other than that of the authorized signer, is by definition unauthorized, and may not serve as a valid authentication on the purported signer's behalf. *Prima facie*, it would therefore not justify the bank in debiting the

[11] Throughout this paper, an attempt is made to minimize the use of a gender sensitive language. Otherwise, "he", "his", or "him", denote also "she", "it", "her", and "its", as required.

[12] For cheques, a contrary rule exists in English law under *Smith* v. *Prosser* [1907] 2 KB 735 (CA). Thereunder, a distinction is drawn between the consequences of an unauthorized completion and issue of a blank signed cheque delivered by the signer (i) with authority to issue it, and (ii) for a mere safekeeping. This, however, is an aberration (see e.g. I. Ackermann, "Signature and Liability in the Law of Bills and Notes" (1993), 8 BFLR 295), derived from a particular strict interpretation of a provision in the Bills of Exchange Act, which needs not to be extended to the area of electronic funds transfer.

purported signer's account. Conversely, the electronic authentication is carried out by means of an access device, which can be entered into a terminal by anyone to whom the device, together with access to a terminal, becomes available. Electronic authentication is a means of *legitimizing* the action of that person, but not of identifying him. It is very much like a door key facilitating entry to the system or, better, a seal affixed to an instrument, authenticating it, but not identifying the one who actually placed it. Consequently, any technologically effective entry of the access code, even when it is carried out by an unauthorized person to whom it may have become available unlawfully, appears to the bank as a valid authentication. *Prima facie*, it would thus justify the bank in debiting the customer's account. In this sense, the authentication by means of an access code is not an "electronic signature". Rather, it is more analogous to the placement of an "electronic seal".[13]

This distinguishing feature of the electronic authentication is of tremendous consequence in ascertaining the bank's duties in preventing and detecting unauthorized transfer losses. Indeed, in the case of a manual signature the bank's obligation is in detecting the forgery on each instrument individually. At the same time, in the case of the electronic authentication, the bank is bound to implement a safe system for the distribution of access devices, a safe security procedure for the authentication of payment instructions, as well as an effective system of access blocking upon being advised of loss or theft of the access device.[14] At least historically in English law, banks' liability for payment of forged cheques has been premised on banks being "bound to know the hand-writing of their customers",[15] rather than on a duty of care to detect forgeries. In contrast, in an electronic environment, the banks' duty ought to be premised on negligence. Typically, such negligence is not individual to a bank employee, as where the latter failed to detect the forgery of a manual signature; rather, in the electronic context, we are concerned with "systemic negligence", by the bank organization as a whole, and on the level of implementing satisfactory computer as well as office procedures.[16] Breach of required standards by the bank, while not necessarily attributable to any individual employee, is nonetheless negligence.

The fourth preliminary observation stems from the previous one. In their customer agreements, it is universally common for banks to link their right to debit the customer account to the verification of the proper authentication, purportedly on the customer's behalf, rather than on the instructions being actually authorized by the customer. In light of banks' inability to differenti-

[13] See I. Billotte-Tongue, Aspects Juridiques du Virement Bancaire, 174–175 (Zurich: Schulthess, 1992).

[14] The bank may also be charged with a duty to ensure the safety and security of public-access terminals.

[15] *Smith* v. *Mercer* (1826), 6 Taunt 76, 86, 128 ER 961, 965 , *per* Heath J.

[16] A point well taken by L. Thévenoz, "Le banquier, son client et l'ordinateur— Réflections sur la prestation de services en masse", 1993 la Semaine Judiciaire,17, particularly at 22–23, 42, and 44–45.

ate between an authorized and unauthorized authentication, this is quite understandable.

Finally, the fifth point is that "unauthorized transfers" ought to be distinguished from properly authenticated instructions containing unauthorized or unintended contents. In principle, discrepancies in the contents of properly authenticated payment instructions are at the customer's risk and responsibility. However, subject to some restrictions, UCC Article 4A allows the parties to shift the risk to the bank. Pertinent scenarios can be associated with those of unauthorized transfers; the UCC treatment will thus be analyzed below as part of the discussion on American law.

II. COMMON LAW JURISDICTIONS

American authorities dealing with negotiable instruments have given full effect to corporate resolutions authorizing the use of facsimile signatures to bind corporate entities.[17] This must be correct in English law as well.[18] Case law requiring that the "engraved representation of [a] signature" must be placed on a document "by means of a rubber stamp" by the signatory himself,[19] rather than by somebody acting on his behalf, ought to be narrowly read and is inapplicable. Such case law is limited to situations where a signature requirement is linked by statute to a decision which the signer must have made personally. Accordingly, the agreement to be bound by the electronic authentication must be taken to recognize its sufficiency to establish liability.

There is no case law dealing directly with the bank's responsibilities in carrying out the verification of instructions transmitted to it from a terminal. However, in the USA, prior to UCC Article 4A, *Walker* v. *Texas Commerce Bank*[20] stated that in receiving a payment order from a sender, a receiving bank is under a duty "to implement commercially reasonable internal procedures designed to process [a payment order] in accordance with [the sender's] instructions, to verify the accuracy of, and compliance with, instructions, to detect and minimize inaccuracy, and to act promptly and diligently to remedy errors".[21] This is quite in line with the receiving bank's broad duty to use reasonable care and skill in carrying out a payment order set out in England in *Royal Products* v. *Midland Bank*.[22] In fact, the bank's duty to "use reasonable care and diligence in the discharge of its instructions and the performance of all its banking functions" was characterized as "[t]he most significant implied

[17] See e.g.. *Perini Corp.* v. *First National Bank* 553 F. 2d 398 (5th Cir. 1977).

[18] D.A.L. Smout, Chalmers on bills, 13th ed., 285 (London: Stevens & Sons, 1964).

[19] *Goodman* v. *J. Eban , Ltd.* [1954] 1 QB 550, 557 (CA), per Evershed, MR. See also *Lazarus Estates Ltd.* v. *Beasely* [1956] 1 QB 702, 710 (CA).

[20] 635 F. Supp. 678 (SD Tex. 1986).

[21] *Ibid.*, at 682.

[22] [1981] 2 Ll. Rep. 194,198 (QB).

term" in the banking contract.[23] Accordingly, a bank establishing a reasonable security procedure for verifying electronic authentication has discharged its contractual obligation to the customer and may be justified in debiting the customer's account once the procedure has been pursued.

In practice, a terminal may either be publicly accessed or be in the exclusive possession of the customer. The access device usually consists of a secret code, which must be entered into the terminal with or without a physical device, such as a card. A short secret code, such as one consisting of no more than four digits, may be guessed by an unauthorized user. Particularly in connection with publicly accessed terminals, and even where a physical device is required, a question may then arise as to the reasonableness of this aspect of the bank's security procedure. Indeed, the physical device may be lost, stolen or even be imitated by a technologically sophisticated defrauder. In fact, a sophisticated dishonest observer may also be successful in "spying" on the customer and discover the secret code itself. Furthermore, a sophisticated "electronic thief" or "pirate" may figure out how to bypass the authorized electronic access facility and obtain access without it. This latter case raises the question whether a bank may be required to implement a foolproof security procedure, rather than a mere *commercially* reasonable one.

Where the security procedure is held to be inadequate, and the customer was not negligent, unauthorized transfer loss ought to be allocated to the bank. The question is more complex whenever neither the bank nor the customer was negligent, as well as where the customer was negligent, either alone or together with the bank. An analysis focusing on causality or degree of fault may be hopelessly unpredictable and unsatisfying. The different nature of electronic authentication, as described above, makes the case law dealing with handwritten signature authentication not particularly helpful. Nonetheless, the following rules may emerge:

(1) In principle, a customer is not liable in the absence of a proper authentication according to the security procedure agreed upon with the bank.

(2) The customer may nevertheless be liable even in the absence of such proper authentication where the customer's negligence enabled a sophisticated "electronic thief" or "pirate" to obtain information that facilitated the bypassing of the security procedure in the initiation of the unauthorized payment order.

(3) Where the unauthorized payment order has been properly authenticated, in the absence of fault by the bank, there may be no common law grounds to fasten liability on the bank; the customer is bound by the properly authenticated payment order regardless of whether on not he was negligent.

(4) Nevertheless, the customer's negligence may become relevant in situations where the bank has been negligent as well. In fact, in addition to the

[23] B. Crawford, Crawford and Falconbridge Banking and Bills of Exchange 8th ed, Vol I, 746 (Toronto: Canada Law Book, 1986).

degree of adequacy or reasonableness of the security procedure implemented by the bank (that is, the standard of care the bank is required to meet), the question of the customer's negligence, but only in a situation where the bank was negligent as well, remains uncertain. Thus, even where the unauthorized payment order has been properly authenticated, where both the customer and the bank were at fault, a question arises as to how the loss is to be apportioned. The question is whether loss is to be apportioned between the bank and the customer according to their respective degree of fault, whether the loss is nevertheless allocated to one of the parties, or whether an elusive search for the party primarily responsible, that is, for the proximate or immediate cause to the loss, should be launched. So far, no definite answer has been provided.

The second and fourth rules presuppose the existence of a duty of care owed by the customer to the bank. However, apart from where provided by express contract, the existence of such a duty, so as to give rise to estoppel, liability in tort or liability for breach of an implied contract, is far from certain. In turn, where such a duty exists, its theoretical foundation may resolve, at least on a doctrinal level, the uncertainty involved in the fourth rule. Thus, in the context of the tort of negligence, contributory or comparative negligence is available to apportion the loss according to the degree of fault. In the context of estoppel with respect to forged cheques known to the customer as such, it was held in *Greenwood v. Martin's Bank*,[24] that a negligent bank may nevertheless invoke its customer's estoppel, where available,[25] and shift the entire loss to the estopped customer.[26] In the context of contract, the position may depend on the judicial interpretation of the contractual term.

Nevertheless, in connection with forged cheques, English law provides for a quite narrow duty of the customer to his bank. Indeed, *Young* v. *Grote* dealt with a customer who was "guilty of negligence"[27] by drawing a cheque so as to permit its subsequent unauthorized alteration by the insertion of words and figures without erasures. The court held that under such circumstances, the customer's account may be debited by the bank for the entire raised amount had been paid in good faith by the bank. Subsequently, in *London Joint Stock Bank v. Macmillan*,[28] the House of Lords held that the drawer's duty of care is confined to acts or omissions relating exclusively to the drawing and

[24] [1933] AC 51, 58–59 (HL), *aff'g* [1932] 1 KB 371, 383–384 (CA).

[25] See text at note 31 below.

[26] This may however only be true in connection with cheques whose forgery was not caused by the customer's negligence; namely, where loss occurred due to the customer's failure to advise the bank of the forgeries, a failure which precluded effective recourse from the forger: "while the carelessness of the Bank was a proximate cause of the Bank's loss in paying [such] forged cheques, it was not the proximate cause of the Bank's losing its right of action against the forger" [1932] 1 KB 371, 384, *per* Scrutton LJ. For this interpretation of this aspect of the judgment, and its misapplication in Israel, see A. Barak, "Forgery in Cheque Drawing: Goal and Means in Risk Allocation Between Bank and Customer" (1967–8), 1 mishpatim 134, 142 & n.49 [in Hebrew].

[27] (1827), 4 Bing 253, 258; 130 ER 764, 766 *per* Best CJ.

[28] [1918] AC 777, 789 (HL).

signing of cheques: "the negligence must be in the transaction itself, that is, in the manner in which the cheque is drawn".[29] Consequently, while a customer is liable for material alteration caused by careless drawing of a cheque, no duty is recognized in English case law, even towards the drawee bank, to exercise reasonable care (a) in the safekeeping of cheque books or corporate seals, (b) in the general course of carrying on business, including the selection of employees, so as to detect or prevent forgeries, as well as (c) in relation to the examination of periodic bank statements, so as to discover and report forgeries and prevent their repetition. In all such cases, a customer who was negligent is neither liable in negligence nor estopped by his negligence from asserting the forgeries.[30] Stated otherwise, there is no duty to prevent or detect forgery of one's own signature. There is however estoppel by representation or conduct where the customer fails to advise the bank of actually known or suspected forgery.[31]

The position was well summarized in the South African case *Big Dutchman (South Africa)* v. *Barclays National Bank,* where Philips J stated:

> "A customer's duty to his banker is a limited one. Save in respect of drawing documents to be presented to the bank and in warning of known or suspected forgeries he has no duty to the bank to supervise his employees, to run his business carefully, or to detect frauds."[32]

The position was recently rationalized by Lord Scarman in *Tai Hing Cotton Mill* v. *Liu Chong Hing Bank* on the fact that "the relationship between banker and customer is contractual and that its incidents, in the absence of express agreement, are such as must be implied into the contract because they can be seen to be *obviously necessary*".[33] Accordingly, while the duty to draw cheques carefully and the duty to inform the bank of any known forgery, are "plainly necessary incidents of the relationship" between a bank and its customer,[34] the duty to prevent signature forgery is not, and hence requires express contract.

Arguably however, a stronger case can be made for an implied customer's duty to exercise reasonable care and diligence to prevent unauthorized electronic funds transfers. First, as indicated, the bank is incapable of detecting

[29] *Ibid.*, at 795. An earlier authority holding that negligence must be "in or immediately connected with the transfer itself" is *Bank of Ireland* v. *The Trustees of Evans' Charities* (1855), 5 HLC 389, 410; 10 ER 950, 959, *per* Mr. Baron Parke.

[30] See e.g. *Bank of Ireland* v. *The Trustees of Evans' Charities, ibid.*, at 409–410 (HLC), 959 (ER) by Mr. Baron Parke; *Lewis Sanitary Steam* v. *Barclay* (1906), 95 LT 444 by Kennedy J; and *Kepitigalla Rubber Estates* v. *National Bank of India* [1909] 2 KB 1010, particularly at 1020–1024, by Bray J. See also *Scholfield* v. *Earl of Londesborough* [1896] AC 514, 531. *Arnold* v. *Cheque Bank* (1876) 1 CPD 578; and *Macmillan*, above note 28 at 800.

[31] The leading case on this point, is *Greenwood* v. *Martins Bank,* above note 24.

[32] 1979 (3) SA 267 (WLO), at 283, cited with approval in *Holzman* v. *Standard Bank* 1985 (1) SA 360 (WLD) at 363.

[33] [1985] 3 WLR 317, 327 (PC). Emphasis added.

[34] *Ibid.*, at 329.

unauthorized but properly authenticated electronic instructions. Secondly, it was correctly observed that "the traditional duties which the common law has imposed on both customer and banker in relation to one another are essentially reciprocal and mutual in nature".[35] It may thus follow that, inasmuch as the banker owes the customer a duty of care in maintaining the security of the system, the customer may be charged with a corresponding duty of care to prevent unauthorized initiation of electronic funds transfers. Yet, the point is uncertain, and it may well be that in English law there is no customer's duty to prevent unauthorized electronic funds transfers, just as there is no customer's duty to prevent the forgery of his signature.

In principle, the sender of a payment order ought to be held responsible for the contents of all properly authenticated payment orders, regardless of unauthorized alterations occurring either in the customer's own organization or in a third party communication system employed by the customer. This conclusion is supported by the general law of agency. Obviously, the customer and the bank may agree on a different loss allocation formula. For example, they may agree on identifying codes to indicate varying amounts or specific beneficiaries on a payment order, and may allocate to the bank risks stemming from its overlooking such codes.[36]

It seems quite obvious that apart from express contract, there is no common law duty to examine periodic bank statements in order to discover and promptly report unauthorized electronic funds transfers. No such duty exists with respect to forged cheques,[37] and, on that point, there are no compelling distinguishing features that could be used as grounds for a separate and broader liability rule for electronic transfers.[38] In connection with cheques, and by parity of reasoning this applies also to electronic funds transfers; there is however, disagreement as to the required language in a verification clause which is necessary in order to bind the customer. In Canada, the leading case is *Arrow Transfer* v. *Royal Bank of Canada*.[39] Speaking for the majority, Martland J thought that what is needed to exonerate the bank and to bind the customer is an express undertaking by the latter "to verify the statement of the account, and to accept it as conclusive unless any errors were notified to the bank within a stipulated period".[40] However, such language did not satisfy the Privy Council in *Tai Hing Cotton Mill* v. *Liu Chong Hing Bank*.[41]

[35] M.H. Ogilvie, Canadian Banking Law, 420–421(Toronto: Carswell, 1991). On that point, see Scrutton LJ's judgment in the Court of Appeal in *Greenwood*, above note 24 at 381–382.

[36] As recognized in the American Uniform Commercial Code, and discussed below in text around note 60.

[37] Leading cases are *Tai Hing Cotton Mill* v. *Liu Chong Hing Bank*, above note 33, and *Canadian Pacific Hotels v. Bank of Montreal* (1987), 40 DLR (4th) 385 (SCC).

[38] Conversely, for the case for a narrower liability rule in electronic funds transfers under the American Uniform Commercial Code, see Part III, text around notes 61 62 below.

[39] (1972), 27 DLR (3d) 81 (SCC).

[40] *Ibid.*, at 87.

[41] Above note 33.

Echoing the dissenting opinion of Laskin J in *Arrow Transfer*, Lord Scarman required more specific or "rigorous" language: "[i]f banks wish to impose upon their customers an express obligation to examine their monthly statements and to make those statements, in the absence of query, unchallengeable by the customer after expiry of a time limit, the burden of the objection and of the sanction imposed must be brought home to the customer."[42] A clearer language as to the responsibility for unauthorized payments is thus required.

With respect to forged cheques, there is also no consensus on the ability of a negligent bank to rely on an effective verification clause and allocate the loss on the customer.[43] In principle, this uncertainty ought to be carried over to unauthorized funds transfers as well.

Some uncertainty also exists where a customer actually signs a confirmation or acknowledgment as to the statement balance, containing, not to the customer's knowledge, unauthorized electronic funds transfers. In England, Bray J appears to suggest in *Kepitigalla Rubber Estates* v. *National Bank of India*[44] that such a signed document binds the customer to the entire balance, including the amount of forged cheques included in the statement. This was how Bray J was understood in Canada in *Columbia Graphophone Co* v. *Union Bank of Canada*.[45] In the latter case, *Kepitigalla* was considered to be good law, notwithstanding the contrary authority of *Bank of Montreal* v. *The King*,[46] that was decided earlier, and was not even mentioned in *Columbia Graphophone*. Subsequently in Canada, Martland J purported to reconcile the conflicting authorities, by holding in *Arrow Transfer* that a signed acknowledgment is binding upon the customer only where verification is required from the customer by contract.[47] In England, the question has not been revisited in recent years, and has not been dealt with by the Privy Council in *Tai Hing*. In the absence of any compelling distinguishing feature, this uncertainty is thus imported from forged cheques into unauthorized electronic funds transfers.

Voluntary codes of practice (or conduct) in Australia, Canada and the United Kingdom are unanimous in fastening the entire unauthorized use losses

[42] Above note 39 at 332.

[43] For example, a negligent bank was allowed to invoke the verification clause against the customer in *Le Cercle Universitaire d'Ottawa* v. *National Bank* (1987), 61 OR (2d) 456 (HCJ), as well as in *Don Bodkin Leasing* v. *The Toronto Dominion Bank* (1993), 14 OR (3d) 571 (Gen. Div.). See also *Kelly Funeral Home* v. *CIBC* (1990), 72 DLR (4th) 276 (Ont. HCJ). Cases that went the other way, namely, refused to extend the coverage of verification clauses to protect a negligent payor bank, include *Cavell Developments* v. *Royal Bank of Canada* (1991), 54 BCLR (2d) 1(BC), *239199 Alberta* v. *Patel* (1992), 1 Alta. LR (3d) 215 (QB), and *Armstrong Baum Plumbing & Heating* v. *Toronto-Dominion Bank* (18 February 1994), Toronto 91-CQ-6231 (Ont. Ct. Gen. Div.). The apportionment of loss according to the degree of fault, rather than "an all or nothing solution", is advocated by N. Rafferty, "Account Verification Agreements: When Can a Bank Protect its Own Negligence?" (1993), 8 BFLR 403.

[44] Above note 30 at 1028.

[45] (1916), 34 DLR 743, 745 (Ont. SC).

[46] (1906), 38 SCR 258.

[47] Above note 39 at 87.

on a negligent consumer debit card holder. These codes so provide regardless of the fault of the bank, except for the fact that arguably, in some circumstances, the adequacy of its security procedure may be an important element for the bank's case that the payment order was indeed initiated pursuant to that procedure. However, the code exempts the customer from any substantial responsibility in the absence of fault on his part. Thus, under paragraph 4.14 of the UK Banking Code,[48] irrespective of fault, customers' liability for transactions not authorized by them, and carried out before the card issuer has been notified of the loss or theft of the card, will be limited to a maximum of £50. Evidently, this no-fault limited exposure is designed to encourage customers to be diligent in safekeeping the card and access code. In any event, under paragraph 4.14, the £50 ceiling does not apply where the customer acted fraudulently or with gross negligence. Rather, under paragraph 4.16, customers will be held liable for all losses if they acted fraudulently, and may be held so liable if they acted with gross negligence. Gross negligence may consist of the failure to observe any of the following safeguards, set out in paragraph 4.8, if such failures have caused losses: (a) not to keep the cheque book together with cards, (b) not to permit anyone else to use card and code, (c) to take reasonable steps to keep the card safe and the code secret, (d) not to write down or record the code on the card "or on anything kept with or near it", (e) not to write the code down "without disguising to disguise it", and (f) to destroy any code advice promptly on receipt.

Similarly, section 5.6 of the Australian Electronic Funds Transfer (EFT) Code of Conduct of 1989 deals with such situations as "[w]here the cardholder has contributed to losses resulting from unauthorized transactions by voluntarily disclosing the [code], indicating the [code] on the card, or keeping a record of the [code] (without making any reasonable attempt to disguise the [code]) with any article carried with the card or liable to loss or theft simultaneously with the card". In such cases, the customer's liability is for the entire actual losses, up to the time of notification to the issuer. Unlike under its UK counterpart, a $50 no-fault liability is imposed on the customer under section 5.5 only where it is unclear whether the customer has contributed to losses resulting from unauthorized transactions. No such liability is fastened on a customer where it is evidently clear that he has not contributed to the loss.

No-fault liability does not exist under the Canadian Code of Practice for Consumer Debit Card Services of 1992 (revised February 1996). However, under section 5, a customer is liable for losses incurred "when a [customer] contributes to unauthorized use". Such would be the case where the customer voluntarily discloses the code, writes it on the card, or keeps a poorly disguised record of it in proximity with the card, as well as upon the customer's failure promptly to advise the issuer of the loss, theft or misuse of the card, or the loss of confidentiality as to the code.

[48] Third edition, March 1997.

In connection with all these voluntary codes, difficulties arise in the interpretation of some of the specific requirements giving rise to unlimited customer's liability. For example, under the Australian provision, the circumstances under which a customer will "keep . . . a record of the [code] (without making any reasonable attempt to disguise [it]) with any article carried with the card or liable to a loss or theft simultaneously with the card", are not all that self-evident.[49] As well, difficulties may arise in gathering the evidence establishing the specific requirements. Presumably, the onus is on the bank that purports to prove the customer's fault.

Regardless of these codes of conduct, a most difficult question is that concerning the onus of proof. Generally speaking, in a civil case, the onus is that of a fair preponderance of credible evidence. The question is who, as between the bank and the customer, has to prove what. Presumably, where a customer challenges a debit to his account pleading an unauthorized payment order, a three-stage process may exist:

(1) It is adequate for the bank initially to prove a proper authentication of the payment order by means of the agreed upon security procedure. As part of its case, the bank must *prima facie* prove that the security commercial procedure is adequate. Whether "adequacy" ought to be determined according to "commercial reasonableness" or by reference to a stricter standard has yet to be determined.

(2) At this point, a customer who objects to the debit must (at least) *plead* that the payment order was unauthorized, and *prove* that the security procedure for the authentication of the payment order was not adequate. Alternatively, under codes of conduct, and only where they are applicable, the customer objecting to the debit may prove that the payment order, even though properly authenticated, was not authorized. For example, a customer cardholder may prove that he had lost the card prior to the payment. In the absence of an allegation as to the loss or theft of the card, where the customer simply denied the initiation of the payment instruction and alleged full continuous possession of the card, one American judge was "not prepared to go so far as to rule that where a credible witness is faced with the adverse 'testimony' of a machine, he is as a matter of law faced also with an unmeetable burden of proof".[50] Obviously, it does not follow that the customer's testimony will always be preferred. Furthermore, in accepting the customer's testimony in that case, that judge specifically took into account the fact that the bank's own witness "testified to physical malfunctions of the very system in issue",[51] though not in connection with the specific transaction.

(3) Where the customer meets the burden of proof, the onus shifts back to the

[49] See e.g.. M. Sneddon, "A Review of the Electronic Funds Transfer Code of Conduct" (1995), 6 JBFLP 29, 40–41.

[50] *Judd* v. *Citibank* , 435 NYS 2d 210, 212 (City Civ. Ct. 1980).

[51] *Ibid.*

bank. Where the customer is successful in discrediting the bank's security procedure, the bank may nevertheless be successful in maintaining the debit in the customer's account where it proves that this was in *fact* a properly authenticated or authorized payment order. Alternatively, where the bank is unsuccessful in proving this, as well as in a transaction governed by a code of conduct where the customer successfully proved an unauthorized payment order, it is open to the bank to prove that the customer's fault has caused or contributed to the unauthorized payment order. Where the bank is able to establish it, in the case of a payment order subject to a code of conduct, the customer becomes fully responsible for the entire loss. As indicated, otherwise, that is, in the case of a payment order not subject to a code of conduct, the effect of the customer's negligence, as proven by the bank, is not entirely clear.

A bank may be able to prove that the customer's negligence enabled a sophisticated "electronic thief" or "pirate" to obtain information that facilitated the bypassing of the security procedure in the initiation of the unauthorized payment order. Arguably, this would shift the loss to the customer regardless of the applicability of a code of conduct. Other than under a code, the effect of the inadequacy of the security procedure, as proved by the customer, is again unclear. As indicated, the bank's fault is usually irrelevant under a code of conduct.

III. AMERICAN LAW[52]

In the United States, non-consumer (that is, business-to-business) funds transfers initiated from exclusive access terminals are governed by a different body of law from the one governing consumer transfers initiated from either public access (that is, ATM as well as POS) terminals or exclusive access terminals (namely, home banking). The former is Article 4A of the Uniform Commercial Code, adopted by the various individual States and jurisdictions. The latter is the federal Electronic Fund Transfer Act[53] and Regulation E[54] implementing it.

UCC Article 4A deals with three separate situations involving an unauthorized funds transfer. First, a payment order initiating a funds transfer that reached a receiving bank might not have been sent by the purported sender, namely, the bank customer, or on his behalf. Secondly, a payment order may be issued by the sending customer, containing different instructions from those intended. Finally, before its arrival at the receiving bank, the text of a payment order may be altered in the course of its transmission over a communication system. While the first case is of an unauthorized authentication, the two others are of unauthorized or unintended content.

[52] For unauthorized electronic funds transfers under American law, see Geva, above note 2 §§ 2.05, 2.06, 6.05.

[53] 15 USC 1693, enacted in 1978.

[54] 12 CFR Part 205, originally passed in 1981, as amended effective May 1, 1996.

In principle, a person is responsible for an authorized, and in fact authenticated, payment order sent by himself or on his behalf. The starting point is that one is not responsible without either proper authorization or authentication but is fully responsible for any mistake or discrepancy in the content of a properly authorized or authenticated payment order. This broad principle is further refined and occasionally defied by the provisions of UCC Article 4A.

First, as to authorization or authentication, the starting point of Article 4A is that the customer is liable to his bank for the amount of any authorized payment order[55] for which the customer is bound under the law of agency. Authority can be express, implied or apparent.[56] The customer is also liable for the amount of any payment order, including an unauthorized one, accepted by the bank in good faith, whose authenticity was verified by the bank pursuant to a commercially reasonable security procedure agreed upon between the customer and the bank.[57] A security procedure may require the use of algorithms or other codes, identifying words or numbers, encryptions or call-back procedures. It may not be constituted by a mere comparison between a manual signature and an authorized specimen signature. A verified payment order may not be beyond the scope of any written agreement between the bank and the customer or instruction of the customer, restricting the acceptance of payment orders to be issued in the customer's name. However, in two situations, an unauthorized order does not bind the customer notwithstanding its proper verification. First, where the customer and the bank agreed to allocate the loss, in whole or in part, to the bank. Secondly, where the customer proves that the order was not caused by a person other than an interloper,[58] namely, where the customer in fact puts forward evi-

[55] Jurisprudentially, in honouring an unauthorized (and unauthenticated) payment order, the receiving bank is in breach of contract with the customer. However, the bank is in breach of neither a duty of good faith and fair dealing nor of a fiduciary duty. See *Fernandes* v. *First Bank & Trust Co.* 1993 WL 339826 (ND Ill).

[56] *Quaere* as to whether estoppel, by negligence or conduct, from denying authority, is also included.

[57] According to UCC § 4A–202(c),

"Commercial reasonableness of a security procedure is question of law to be determined by considering the wishes of the customer expressed to the bank, the circumstances of the customer known to the bank, including the size, type, and frequency of payment orders normally issued by the customer to the bank, alternative security procedures offered to the customer, and security procedures in general use by customers and receiving banks similarly situated. A security procedure is deemed to be commercially reasonable if (i) the security procedure was chosen by the customer after the bank offered and the customer refused, a security procedure that was commercially reasonable for the customer, and (ii) the customer expressly agreed in writing to be bound by any payment order, whether or not authorized, issued in its name and accepted by the bank in compliance with the security procedure chosen by the customer."

[58] UCC §§ 4A-201 to 203. Suggestion for revisions are explored by P.S. Turner, "The UCC Drafting Process and Six Questions About Article 4A: Is There a Need for Revisions to the Uniform Funds Transfer Law?" (1994), 28 *Loyola la L Rev*. 351. The author's four out of six questions relate to the unauthorized payment order provisions: (i) Can the 4A–505 statute of repose (discussed below) be shortened by agreement? (ii) May a customer who chooses a security procedure that may not be commercially reasonable waive his right to shift liability to the bank when the customer can prove that fraud was perpetrated by an interloper? (iii) What does the bank have to show in order to prove that it accepted an authorized payment order in good faith? and (iv) Are the rules on unauthorized funds transfers unfair to customers?

dence leading to the conclusion that the order was initiated by an interloper. In effect, under UCC § 4A–203(2), such an interloper is an outsider to the customer's organization, or more specifically, a person other than one:

> "(i) entrusted at any time with duties to act for the customer with respect to payment orders or the security procedure, or (ii) who obtained access to transmitting facilities of the customer or who obtained, from a source controlled by the customer and without authority of the receiving bank, information facilitating breach of the security procedure, regardless of how the information was obtained or whether the customer was at fault. Information includes any access device, computer software, or the like."

The entire scheme can be described as follows: the risk of a payment order, purporting to emanate from the customer but not authenticated with the customer's authority, initially falls on the bank. The risk shifts to the customer if the bank proves its own compliance with an agreed-upon commercially reasonable security procedure. The risk shifts back to the bank where the loss is proved by the customer to be caused by an interloper or is allocated to the bank by agreement. Fault, by itself, other than as part of what constitutes an interloper, is not a factor in the loss allocation. On the other hand, the scope of the customer's liability to transfers initiated by an unauthorized insider is quite broad and is not even stated to be linked to the proximity between access given to the transmitting facilities and the actual misuse of that access. For example, the customer may be held responsible for an unauthorized transfer by a cleaner who was permitted access to the facilities in the course of his employment and who managed to initiate the transfer by means of an access device and code illegally obtained.

Under UCC § 4A–204, a receiving bank that paid a payment order for which the customer is not responsible is liable for interest subject to the customer's duty to notify the bank "within a reasonable time not exceeding 90 days" after being advised of the transfer.

The second and third types of unauthorized payment orders are those with unauthorized or unintended contents. Typical cases of unauthorized or unintended content, irrespective of proper authentication, include the transmittal of a duplicate payment order, an increase in the amount of a payment order (for example, by the addition of zeroes to the sum), or the instruction of payment to an unintended beneficiary (for example, by erring in the account or identification number of the intended beneficiary). In an electronic environment, such deviations from the intended text may result from either error or fraudulent design. UCC §§ 4A–205 and 206 provide for the customer's responsibility towards his bank under such circumstances.

In principle, a sending customer is responsible for the contents of his own payment order. He is also responsible for a discrepancy arising in the course of the transmittal of a payment order through a third party communication system. This means that such an intermediary system is deemed to be an agent of the sender. The sender is then bound by the contents of the payment order as sent to the receiving bank by that communication system.[59]

A sender can nevertheless shift the loss arising from the transmittal (whether by itself or by a third party communication system acting as his agent) of a payment order with unauthorized contents where the receiving bank has failed to comply with an *agreed-upon* security procedure which would have detected the discrepancy. Such a procedure may require a unique code for each payment order (so as to alert the receiving bank in case of a duplicate payment), different codes for different levels of amounts, or identify regular beneficiaries.[60] In order to benefit the sending customer, the security procedure with which the receiving bank failed to comply must have been agreed upon between the customer and the bank in advance.

A customer notified of a payment order with unauthorized contents, who negligently failed to report the discrepancy "within a reasonable time, not exceeding 90 days" of being advised, cannot shift the loss to the receiving bank which did not comply with the agreed-upon security procedure.[61]

Having reimbursed the bank for a payment order, the customer is precluded under UCC § 4A–505 from asserting lack of authority or lack of verification, unless he notifies the bank of any objection within one year from being advised by the bank of the payment order. This is true for a payment order not authenticated with the sending customer's authority as well as for a payment order with an unauthorized or unintended contents.

In connection with forged cheques, UCC § 4–406(c) fastens on a bank customer a specific duty to

> "exercise reasonable promptness in examining [a periodic] statement [of account] or [cancelled cheques] to determine whether any payment was not authorized because of an alteration of [a cheque] or because a purported signature by or on behalf of the customer was not authorized . . . [and] promptly notify the bank of relevant facts."

This indeed, is quite similar to the customer's duty under UCC § 4A–204(a) to "exercise ordinary care to determine" that a payment order with which his account was debited "was not authorized" and "notify the bank of the relevant facts within a reasonable time not exceeding 90 days after the date the customer received notification from the bank" of the payment order or the corresponding debit to his account. It is equally similar to the customer's duty under UCC § 4A–205(b) to "exercise ordinary care" and discover a payment order with unauthorized contents "within a reasonable time, not exceeding 90 days" of being advised. However, in connection with cheques, upon breach of the duty, the customer becomes precluded, under UCC § 4–406(d), from

[59] UCC § 4A–206.

[60] UCC § 4A–205. While the provision is stated to deal with "erroneous" payment orders, it must be read as covering also "errors" fraudulently precipitated.

[61] UCC § 4A–205(b). Liability may however be varied "as provided in an agreement of the bank and the customer". See Official Comment 3 to UCC § 4A–205.

asserting against the bank "the customer's unauthorized signature or any alteration on the [cheque]", provided the bank proves either a resulting loss or recurring forgery by the same wrongdoer. Similarly, under UCC § 4A–205(b), "[i]f the bank proves that the [customer] failed to perform [the] duty" to discover and report a payment order with unauthorized contents, "the [customer] is liable to the bank for the loss the bank proves it incurred as a result of the failure . . .", up to the amount of the customer's order.

Conversely however, under UCC § 4A–204(a), the bank is required to refund the customer with the amount of the unauthorized payment order, even when the customer was in breach of the prompt notification requirement. Under that provision, breach of the customer's prompt notification duty results in loss of interest but not principal. This is so notwithstanding the Official Comment's own admission that "in some cases prompt notification [by the customer] may make it easier for the bank to recover some part of its loss from the culprit".[62] Principal will nevertheless be lost to a breaching customer under UCC § 4A–505, but solely upon the failure to object to the unauthorized debit "within one year after the notification . . .".

In fact, the treatment of the consequences of the customer's failure to discover and report unauthorized funds transfers under UCC § 4A–204 is not all that fundamentally different from the treatment relating to the consequences of the customer's failure to discover and report forged cheques under UCC § 4–406, as might appear at first blush. Thus, preclusion for the full amount of forged or altered cheques by a customer under UCC § 4–406, requires lack of negligence by the bank.[63] In turn, with respect to unauthenticated payment orders, the bank's duty to refund under UCC § 4A–204 is premised on the bank's own breach of duty to the customer. Presumably, however, the bank's duties under UCC § 4A–205 with respect to payment orders with unauthorized contents are less tightly scrutinized, so that their breach by the bank does not preclude recovery from a breaching customer.

The approach for regulating unauthorized consumer transfers under Regulation E is entirely different. The underlying principle is that a consumer is liable for authorized transfers as well for a limited amount of unauthorized transfers, up to the time of notification to the bank. Where such a notification is not given, the customer is liable for the entire amount after the expiry of the notification period. The consumer's negligence contributing to an unauthorized transaction is not a factor's in determining the consumer's exposure.

Regulation E § 205.2(m) defines "[u]nauthorized electronic fund transfer" to mean:

[62] Official Comment 2 to UCC § 4A–204.

[63] UCC § 4–406(e), providing for comparative negligence. This obviously differs from UCC § 4A–204 (as well, in fact, from the pre-1989 Official Text of UCC § 4–406 itself) which effectively precludes the breaching bank from reversing the debit for the unauthorized payment, and does not entail the apportionment of the loss between the two breaching parties.

> "an electronic fund transfer from a consumer's account initiated by a person other than the consumer without actual authority to initiate the transfer and from which the consumer receives no benefit. The term does not include an electronic fund transfer initiated:
>
> (1) By a person who was furnished the access device[64] to the consumer's account by the consumer,[65] unless the consumer has notified the financial institution that transfers by that person are no longer authorized;
>
> (2) With fraudulent intent by the consumer or any person acting in concert with the consumer; or
>
> (3) By the financial institution or its employee."

Transfers thus excluded are evidently deemed authorized to which the consumer is fully responsible.

It was held that "[i]n an action involving a consumer's liability for an electronic fund transfer . . . the burden of going forward to show an 'unauthorized' transfer . . . is on the consumer". However, "[t]o establish full liability on the part of the consumer, the bank must prove that the transfer was authorized".[66] This can be reconciled as follows: to succeed in its action, the bank must initially make a *prima facie* case that the transfer was authorized. To that end, it is adequate for the bank to prove that the transfer was initiated by means of the access device it had issued to the consumer. At that point, the burden of proof shifts to the consumer alleging an unauthorized transfer. Proof of loss or theft of the access device, put forward by the consumer, is adequate to meet this burden. Obviously, notice of loss or theft given by the consumer to the bank is no more than *prima facie* evidence of loss or theft.

Ultimately, however, where loss or theft of the access device is not claimed, in determining the question of "authorized" or "unauthorized" transfer, the court may be forced to choose between the consumer's testimony and the bank's computer printout, often backed by some evidence as to the reliability of its security procedure. A review of case law reveals that a credible witness, usually where his testimony is corroborated, typically by some system

[64] Defined in Reg. E § 205.2(a)(1) to mean "a card, code, or other means of access to a consumer's account, or any combination thereof, that may be used by the consumer to initiate electronic fund transfer".

[65] In "furnishing" the access device, the consumer must have acted voluntarily. Accordingly, where control of the access device is surrendered by the consumer as a result of robbery or fraud, the fund transfer initiated by the robber or the defrauding person is "unauthorized". In contrast, the exception applies so that the transfer is not "unauthorized" where "a consumer furnishes an access device and grants authority to make transfers to a person (such as a family member or co-worker) who exceeds the authority given". Official Staff Commentary to § 205.2(m), as am. effective May 2, 1996. Prior to this interpretation by the Federal Reserve Board, there was some judicial disagreement on the first point (that of *voluntarily* furnishing the access device). See e.g. *Feldman* v. *Citibank*, 443 N.Y.S. 2d 43 (Cfu, Ct., 1981). *Ognibene v. Citibank*, 446 N.Y.S. 2d 845, 847 (Civ. Ct. 1981); and *State* v. *Citibank*, 537 F. Supp. 1192, 1194 (S.D.N.Y. 1982).

[66] *Ognibene, ibid.*, at 847.

[67] See e.g. *Judd* v. *Citibank*, 435 N.Y.S. 2d 210 (Civ. Ct. 1980); *Feldman* v. *Citibank*, 443 N.Y.S. 2d 43 (Civ. Ct. 1981); and *Porter* v. *Citibank* , 472 N.Y.S. 2d 582 (Civ. Ct. 1984).

malfunction, has consistently overcome the machine.[67] Nevertheless, witness credibility may differ from one case to another. Furthermore, relevant case law is from the first half of the 1980s; it is quite possible that, with time, confidence in the reliability of computer systems increases, so that greater weight may be given to evidence generated by them.

The extent of consumer liability for unauthorized transfers is governed by Regulation E § 205.6.[68] Thereunder, and subject to specified ceilings, liability is limited to unauthorized transfers occurring before the consumer advises the bank either of the loss or theft of the access device or of an unauthorized transfer that appears on a periodic statement. Where the consumer is not aware of the loss or theft of the access device, for unauthorized transactions occurring up to sixty days after the transmittal of a periodic statement containing an unauthorized transfer, the consumer is not liable. However, for such transfers, the consumer is liable up to a $50 ceiling where the consumer learns of the loss or theft of the access device and advises the bank of it within two business days. The $50 ceiling does not apply where the consumer learns before the expiration of that sixty-day period of the loss or theft of the access device but fails to advise the bank of the loss or theft within two business days. In such a case, the $50 ceiling applies only until the close of two business days after learning of the loss or theft, and the overall liability for the period ending at the close of the sixty-day period will not exceed $500. Liability beyond the sixty-day period is unlimited, until notice is given to the bank. To be entitled to the $500 as well as the unlimited ceilings, the bank must establish that the consumer's timely notification would have prevented the loss.

Under Regulation E § 205.6(b)(4), time periods for notification may be extended "to a reasonable period" where the consumer delayed notifying the bank "due to extenuating circumstances". However, in *Kruser* v. *Bank of America*,[69] this provision did not assist a consumer who admitted that "she received and reviewed bank statements during her recuperation".[70] In one such a statement, she failed to notice and advise the bank of a $20 unauthorized ATM withdrawal. Almost a year later, the consumer received statements containing close to $10,000 unauthorized ATM withdrawals. The consumer then promptly advised the bank of all unauthorized withdrawals, including the one which was now almost one year old. In the court's view, the consumer

[68] To be entitled to the amounts specified in the provision, the bank must have provided the consumer with certain disclosures as to the extent of the liability, the telephone number and address for providing notices to the bank, and the bank's business days. As well, "[i]f the unauthorized transfer involved an access device, it must be an accepted access device and the financial institution must have provided a means to identify the consumer to whom it was issued". Reg. E s. 205.6(a). An "accepted access device" is generally defined (in § 205.2(a)(2)) as an access device requested and received or used by the consumer. In order to be entitled to *any* amount of unauthorized transfers, the bank must establish the existence of these conditions. See *Ognibene* v. *Citibank*, above note 65 at 847.

[69] 281 Cal. Rptr. 463 (Ct. App. 5 dist. 1991).

[70] *Ibid.*, at 467.

failed to show required "extenuating circumstances". Having delayed the notice for the first $20 unauthorized transaction, the consumer was thus held liable for the entire amount of the unauthorized transfers.

IV. SWITZERLAND AND OTHER CIVIL LAW JURISDICTIONS[71]

Under the Swiss Code of Obligations ("CO"),[72] in carrying out a funds transfer, the bank performs its obligation under a mandate.[73] Accordingly, the bank, as a mandatary, incurs liability to the customer, as a mandator, for the damage it causes in breach of its obligations, under CO Article 398, to carry out the mandate faithfully and diligently.[74] Under CO Article 400(1), the mandatary/bank is further "liable to submit upon demand at any time a proper accounting of the performance of [its] obligations, and to deliver everything which . . . has come into [its] possession in the course of the performance of [its] mandate . . .". In turn, so far as the customer's duties are concerned, under CO Article 402, as a mandator:

> "(1) [he] is obligated to reimburse the [mandatary] for costs and expenses . . . incurred by him in the proper performance of his mandate . . . [and]
> (2) . . . is also liable to the [mandatary] for any and all damages sustained by the [mandatary] in the course of the performance of the mandate, to the extent that the [mandator] is unable to prove that the damage was caused without his fault . . .".

Where the bank carries out authorized payment instructions, it incurs "costs and expenses . . . in the proper performance of [its] mandate", so as to fall squarely within CO Article 402(1), and thus to be entitled to a reimbursement from the customer. Conversely, in connection with unauthorized payment instructions, as long as the bank acted without fault, there is a difference of

[71] This part heavily draws from Billotte-Tongue, above note 13, at 129–210, to which the reader is referred for further detail. See also Thévenoz, above note 16 at 36–48. For information, guidance and feedback I am particularly grateful to jurists in the various jurisdictions. All errors and misunderstandings are mine.

[72] I used the French 1993 official text. Quotes below are taken from the English translation by the Swiss-American Chamber of Commerce. Words in square brackets may reflect disagreement with this translation. Particularly, inasmuch as the civil law "mandate" is not identical with the common law "agency", I prefer the "mandator-mandatary" terminology to that of "principal-agent".

[73] The subject matter of a mandate is effectively defined in CO Art. 394 (1), as "the contractually agreed business transactions or services with which the [mandatary] has been entrusted". Similar definitions appear in the civil codes of France (CC Art. 1984), Italy (CC Art. 1703), Japan (CC Art. 643 in conjunction with Art. 656), Quebec (CC Art. 2130), and Germany (BGB § 662 in conjunction with § 675).

[74] CO Art. 398(1) provides that "[t]he [mandatary] is obligated, in general, to use the same care as the employee under the employment contract". The "faithful and careful" (or in French, "*la bonne et fidèle*") performance of the mandate is required by the mandatary under CO Art. 398(2). An employee is required to perform with care, and is liable to his employer for damage he causes intentionally or by negligence. See CO Arts. 321a(1) and 321e(1), applicable to the mandate on the basis of the referral from CO Art. 398(1).

opinion as to the applicability of the provision. According to a minority view, whether a transfer is carried out in "the proper performance of [the] mandate" is determined subjectively, solely from the mandatary bank's point of view. Hence, where it acted without fault, the bank is entitled to be reimbursed by the customer under CO Article 402(1).

The majority view, however, is that the requirement of CO Article 402(1) is not satisfied merely by the absence of fault by the bank. Whether a transfer is carried out in "the proper performance of [the] mandate" is thus determined objectively, so that an unauthorized transfer is excluded. The bank is thus not entitled to be reimbursed by the customer under CO Article 402(1); a wrongful debit entitles the customer to have the account recredited on the basis of CO Article 400(1).

Nevertheless, a faultless bank may recover from a negligent customer under CO Article 402(2). Indeed, CO Article 402(1) provides for the mandator/customer's obligation to reimburse "costs and expenses . . . incurred by [the mandatary/bank] in the proper performance of [the] mandate". At the same time, CO Article 402(2) sets out the mandator/customer's liability for "all damages sustained by the [mandatary/bank] in the course of the performance of the mandate". "[T]he course of the performance of the mandate" under subsection (2) is thus broader than "the proper performance of [the] mandate" under subsection (1), and may thus cover also unauthorized transfers that are subjectively (and erroneously) determined by the bank, acting diligently, to be authorized. Furthermore, while the purpose of subsection (1) is to compensate the mandatary/bank for a service properly given, subsection (2) is designed to provide the mandatary/bank with a remedy so as to preclude injury to it.

It is however important to stress that by its own terms, CO Article 402(2) limits recovery by the recovering mandatary/bank to circumstances where the mandator/customer "is unable to prove that the damage was caused without his fault". Namely, recovery can be made only from a negligent customer.[75] Accordingly, where the only party at fault is the mandatary/bank, neither the mandator/customer's reimbursement obligation under CO Article 402(1) nor the mandator/customer's liability or damages under CO Article 402(2) arises. Subsection (1) is inapplicable since, as before, carrying out the unauthorized transfer is not a "proper performance of [the] mandate". At the same time, subsection (2) does not apply since the mandator/customer was not at fault. Furthermore, the mandatary/bank is in breach of its diligence obligation under CO Article 398 and is thus liable for damages caused by its negligence to the mandator/customer. In sum, a negligent bank is liable to faultless customer for damage caused by carrying out an unauthorized transfer.

In connection with an unauthorized transfer, in circumstances where neither the mandator/customer nor the mandatary/bank was negligent, neither

[75] To simplify matters, I thus assume that inability to prove lack of fault means fault or negligence on the mandator/customer's part.

CO Article 402, nor CO Article 398 provides for a remedy. The former does not apply for reasons discussed above. The latter is not helpful in the absence of the mandatary/bank's negligence. Nonetheless, in any event, the mandator/customer retains his action, under CO Article 400(1), to have his account recredited with the amount of the unauthorized transfer erroneously debited to the account. It thus follows that the loss falls on the bank. However, according to one view, where the wrongdoer is an insider in the customer's organization or household, the German "theory of spheres" ought to apply. Under this theory, each party is absolutely, namely, irrespective of the lack of his own negligence, responsible to wrongs committed out of his "field of control" or "sphere of influence". This would have placed the loss even on a faultless customer, but only where the wrong emanated from the customer's sphere or "field of control". Overall, however, as applied in this context, this theory is disfavoured in Switzerland, partly because the injury, that is, the unauthorized payment, actually occurred in the sphere of influence of the bank. The prevailing view is thus that where neither the customer nor the bank is negligent, the loss falls on the bank.

Where the mandator/customer and the mandatary/bank were both negligent, both parties have reciprocal claims. The mandator/customer has a claim, under CO Article 400(1), in restitution for the sum erroneously debited to his account, as well as an action for damages, based on the mandatary/bank's negligence, under CO Article 398. In turn, the mandatary/bank has a claim for damages against the negligent mandator/customer under CO Article 402(2). It has been argued that where each party's fault is of equal degree or severity, both reciprocal actions for damages extinguish each other, so that only the customer's contract claim survives. The better view, however, is that where both parties are at fault, the loss is to be apportioned between them according to the degree of fault attributed to each in causing the loss. Doctrinally, this opinion is premised on the view that the customer's negligence claim under CO Article 398 is superseded by his contract claim for reimbursement under CO Article 400(1).

In the final analysis, the loss resulting from an unauthorized transfer is not allocated to a non-negligent customer. In fact, this is consistent with the result under CO Article 1132 providing that in connection with a forged cheque, in the absence of the customer's fault, the loss falls on the drawee bank. Where both the customer and the bank were negligent, unauthorized transfer loss is allocated according to comparative negligence principles. Otherwise, either where only the bank (but not the customer) was negligent, or where neither the customer nor the bank was negligent, loss falls on the bank.

It seems, so far as the onus of proof is concerned, that in order to trigger the customer's reimbursement obligation under CO Article 402(1), the bank must prove that in carrying out a funds transfer, it acted "in the proper performance of [its] mandate". To that end, it is arguably enough for the bank to prove proper legitimation, namely, an authentication pursuant to the agreed upon security procedure.[76] At that point, it is up to the customer to prove that the transfer was unauthorized, thereby taking the case out of CO Article 402(1), and bringing it into the ambit of CO Article 402(2). This however, will not suffice; to preclude the bank from recovering damages under CO Article 402(2), the customer must also prove that "the damage was caused without his fault", namely, that he was not negligent. Stated otherwise, to allocate the loss to the bank, the customer has the formidable task to prove both lack of authority and the absence of negligence.

Where the customer proves that the transfer was not authorized, but fails to prove that he was not negligent, he may still go ahead and prove negligence by the bank, which gives rise to the bank's liability under CO Article 398. In such circumstances, as discussed, loss is shared between the bank and the customer according to the degree of each party's fault. At the same time, where the customer is successful in proving both unauthorized transfer, as well as the absence of negligence on his part, he needs not prove that the bank was negligent; in the absence of negligence on the part of the customer, the entire loss is anyway allocated to the bank, even without any fault on its part.

In their customer contracts, Swiss banks purport to disclaim liability for unauthorized transfers and pass the loss on to their customers. However, under CO Article 100(1), "[a]ny agreement in advance purporting to exclude liability for intentional illegality or gross negligence is void". Furthermore, under CO Article 100(2), at the discretion of the court, a disclaimer clause purporting to exonerate banks from liability even for slight negligence by their *organs*, may be considered void. At the same time, liability for slight negligence for acts or omissions by bank *employees* may contractually be excluded under CO Article 101(3).[77] As previously indicated,[78] inasmuch as in electronic funds transfers bank negligence is typically linked to the overall operation of the computer or office systems, negligence by an organ, rather than that of an employee, facilitating the non-detection of an unauthorized transfer is not all that a remote possibility. Liability for a bank organ's negligence

[76] Obviously, part of the bank's case is that the pertinent security procedure meets the required standard, e.g., "commercial reasonableness".

[77] This is the rule under CO Art. 101(3) with respect to "liability [that] arises from carrying on an officially licensed trade", which is the same as "liability [that] arises from the exercise of an occupation for which a public licence is necessary" under CO Art. 100(2) (that is, both translate the same phrase in the French Official Text, namely, the case where "*la responsabilité result de l'exercice d'une industrie concédée par l'autorité*. While the same phrase was translated differently in both provisions, it should be taken to mean the same thing). Personal negligence, including that of corporate organs (other than employees), even slight, may not be disclaimed at all in respect of such liability. See CO Art. 100(2). Otherwise, namely, not in connection with "liability [that] arises from the exercise of an occupation for which a public licence is necessary", even personal slight negligence, including that of corporate organs, as well as negligence by employees, may be disclaimed altogether. See CO Arts. 100 (2) and 101(3). Since 1986 it is conceded that "banking" is "an officially licensed trade" or "an occupation for which a public licence is necessary", as decided by a Federal Court in ATF 112 II, 450. See Thévenoz above note 16 at 39.

[78] See text at note 16 above.

may thus not be effectively disclaimed altogether; liability for slight, though not gross, negligence by an employee, is however disclaimable.

It follows that under an effective disclaimer clause, a customer who proves lack of negligence on his part may nevertheless be liable, unless he proves either gross negligence (or intentional illegality) by bank employees or even slight negligence by bank organs. That is, where both parties were not negligent, as well as where the customer was not negligent but the bank was only slightly at fault, as long as the slight negligence was attributed to employees and not bank organs, the loss falls on the customer. There are, however, consumer contractual arrangements that allow a non negligent customer to have recourse from a designated reimbursement fund set by banks, usually subject to a deductible.

Notwithstanding an effective disclaimer clause, and due to its limited reach, the loss falls on the bank exclusively where the customer was not at all at fault, and either bank employees were grossly negligent (or committed intentional illegality) or bank organs were even slightly negligent. At the same time, where the customer and the bank were both negligent, the better view seems to be that loss is not to be shouldered by the bank alone. Rather, where the situation involved either gross negligence (or intentional illegality) by bank employees or even slight negligence by bank organs, loss is to be apportioned between the bank and its customer according to the degree of their respective fault. Otherwise, as indicated, the bank is released from liability, so that the customer bears the loss in full. Obviously, where the customer alone was negligent, whether grossly or slightly, the entire loss falls on him.

Swiss standard-form bank agreements invariably require the customer to advise his bank promptly of any complaint he has with respect to a statement or contested transfer for which he was advised. Upon failing to do so within the time period set by the bank, the customer is deemed to have approved all dispositions.[79] This seems to be broad enough to cover unauthorized transfers, advised to the customer, and which he failed to notice and promptly report. Regardless, losses occurring due to unauthorized transfers might have been prevented had the customer not failed to exercise due diligence in discovering and reporting earlier unauthorized transfers by the same wrongdoer. Also losses from such earlier unauthorized transfers might have been precluded, or at least reduced, upon prompt discovery and disclosure by the customer. This is so where prompt discovery and disclosure could have facilitated timely recourse by the bank against the wrongdoer, who in the meantime might have disappeared or become impecunious. Such losses, from the earlier as well as latter undiscovered and hence unreported unauthorized transfers, are then, "damages sustained by the [bank as a mandatary] in the course of the performance of the mandate". For such losses, the customer, as a mandator, is liable under CO Article 402(2), "to the extent that [he] is unable to

[79] See e.g. D. Guggenheim, Les Contrats de la Practique Bancaire Suisse 2eme ed. (Geneva: Librairie de l'Université George et Cie, 1981) at 72.

prove that the damage was caused without his fault". There is thus a duty on a bank customer to discover and promptly report unauthorized transfers. The customer's duty may be absolute under the banking contract and is based on fault under the Code of Obligations. Where the bank effectively disclaims liability for unauthorized transfers, other than for the gross negligence (or intentional illegality) of its employees or even the slight negligence of its organs, this customer's duty is relevant only in assigning the customer's share in the loss, as against the bank's share, attributed to the bank's own negligence, as such bank's negligence is found to exist in that case.

In fastening on the mandatary a duty of care in CO Article 398,[80] the Swiss position follows the current prevailing civilian views,[81] as provided in contemporary civil codes in various jurisdictions.[82] However, as for the mandator's liability, at present, contrary to Swiss CO Article 402(2), the prevailing view is that such liability is not limited to negligence; rather, the mandator's liability extends to all losses and damages incurred by the mandatary in connection with the execution of the mandate,[83] and arises even in the absence of any negligence on the part of the mandator.[84] Nonetheless, in some countries such as France and Germany, notwithstanding the absence of a corresponding provision to Swiss CO Article 402(2), no liability for unauthorized transfers is fastened on a non-negligent customer under general law.[85]

However, the prevailing civilian view is, as in Switzerland, that an effective exemption clause may exonerate the bank from any liability, unless the bank either committed an intentional wrongful act, or acted with gross negligence.[86] Thus, in civil law jurisdictions, under an appropriate exemption clause, a bank, other than one that acted wrongfully either intentionally or gross negligently, is able to fasten unauthorized transfer losses on a customer, even when the latter was not negligent at all.

[80] See note 74 and text, above.

[81] See discussion by R. Zimmermann, The Law of Obligations — Roman Foundations of the Civilian Tradition, 426–430 (Cape Town: Juta, 1990 reprinted in 1992).

[82] See CC Art. 1992 in France; CC Art. 644 in Japan; CC Art. 1710 in Italy; BGG § 276 in Germany (for any debtor in general); and CC Art. 2138 in Quebec.

[83] See CC Art. 2000 in France; CC Art. 1720 in Italy; and CC Art. 2154 in Quebec. In Germany and Japan, the statutory provisions (BGB § 670 and CC Art. 650 respectively) read to entitle the mandatary to claim from the mandator only expenses or outlays (and not losses or damages) incurred by the mandatary in the course of carrying out the mandate. However, at least in Germany, "[these] narrow confines. . . were soon left behind by courts and legal writers. The principle of a liability (not based on fault) for risks arising from and connected with activities undertaken by another person in the debtor's interest, is widely acknowledged today." See Zimmermann above note 81 at 432.

[84] For this development see Zimmermann, *ibid.*, 430–432.

[85] This can be justified either by viewing the unauthorized payment as occurring outside the mandate, even the general mandate generated under the account agreement, or by reference to statutory provisions, such as CC Arts. 1239 and 1937 in France, requiring payment to the true creditor in order to discharge a debt.

[86] See e.g., R. Ben Oliel, "Banker's Liability in the Bank Deposit Relationship" (1979), 14 Israel L. Rev. 164, 174–176.

V. CONCLUSION—OBSERVATIONS AS TO THE DESIRED RULE

Fault plays a significant role in the allocation of losses under the common law as well as in Switzerland and other civil law jurisdictions. In contrast, fault concepts are downplayed in the American statutory schemes. Among the three systems, uncertainty as to existing rules exists, particularly under the common law, mainly with regard to business-to-business transfers. To a large extent, this uncertainty is attributed to the uneasy importation of rules developed in cheque law.

In assessing the current schemes, and determining what ought to be the desired rule, the following observations are noteworthy. First, a rule based on fault is hopelessly complicated, particularly in determining the customer's negligence, its degree, as well as the causal link between it and the actual loss. Secondly, a rule which allocates unlimited loss to the customer, even where he was not at all at fault, is unfair. It overlooks the role of the bank as a depositary for the customer's funds, responsible for their safekeeping. It further does not provide banks with adequate incentives to keep investing in the enhancement of their security systems so as further to reduce losses. It thus follows that both the common law and the Swiss legal system (as other civil law jurisdictions) provide for unsatisfactory solutions.

However, the desired rule ought not to exonerate the customer altogether. Indeed, a scheme allocating the entire loss to the bank may be effective in redistributing losses among all bank customers, as well as in encouraging banks to enhance security measures. However, it fails to encourage customers to take even minimum precautions. An effective rule should provide incentives to the customer to eliminate, or at least reduce, losses. This can be done either by taking fault into account, at least to a specified extent and in relation to well-defined and easily provable events, or by providing for the limited participation of the customer in the amount of the loss, regardless of fault, as if under an insurance scheme providing for a deductible or coinsurance. At the same time, such a rule ought to avoid resorting to complex factual determinations as to the degree of fault and its causal link with the actual loss. The rule should also not ignore the bank's capacity as the best loss absorber and redistributor.

As pointed out by Thévenoz, an optimal system may not be produced by mere market forces.[87] Speaking of Switzerland, he refers to the oglipolistic nature of the payment services market, dominated by large players, as well as to the inherent under-estimation of losses by customers. For example, while the loss of a wallet is limited to the value of the money it contains, the potential loss stemming from the theft of an access device may not be so ascertainable. In general, these observations hold true elsewhere. Here lies the rationale for the need for a specific statutory rule.

[87] Thévenoz above note 16 at 51.

From the three reviewed systems, American law seems to be the most effective in meeting the desired standard. It provides incentives to eliminate or reduce loss, while at the same time it avoids the preoccupation with customer's fault. Thus, for business-to-business transfers, by fastening liability on the customer for unauthorized transfers initiated by an insider, UCC Article 4A effectively implements a "sphere of influence" theory. This rule may be too harsh for consumer unauthorized transfers. Accordingly, for the latter, the Electronic Fund Transfer Act and Regulation E implementing it provide for a deductible, which keeps increasing as the delay in informing the bank of an unauthorized transfer of the delay grows. Both schemes thus avoid the need to determine customer's fault, its degree and causation.[88] In the final analysis, regardless of detail, the American model is worth considering elsewhere.

[88] The absence of a duty under Article 4A to promptly disclose and report unauthorized transfers, as noted in Part III above, is however, quite enigmatic.

6

Standby Rulemaking: A Glimpse at the Elements of Standardization and Harmonization of Banking Practice

JAMES E. BYRNE*

I. INTRODUCTION

Representing an estimated US$ 300 billion in outstanding obligations,[1] standby letters of credit have become the workhorse of commerce and industry, assuring payment and performance and serving as an anchor for fund-raising on the capital markets. As such, they long ago surpassed their progenitor, the commercial letter of credit, in outstanding amount, commercial significance and utility. Nonetheless, standbys are not well understood and, consequently, are under-utilized in major areas of the commercial world.[2] As a result of major efforts now under way involving both law and practice, the regime surrounding standbys is being articulated and the various uses to which they can be placed are being de-mythologized and widely studied

* Professor Byrne is Director of the Institute of International Banking Law & Practice, Inc., Maryland, USA. He chairs the American Bar Association's Letter of Credit Subcommittee and is Chair/Reporter of the International Standby Practices Working Group. He chaired the Joint USCIB/ABA Task Force on the study of UCC Art. 5 (1986–90), chaired the US delegation to the UNCITRAL Working Group on Stand-by Letters of Credit and Independent Guarantees (1988–95), was an advisor to the NCCUSL Drafting Committee to Revise US UCC Art. 5 (Letters of Credit) (1990–5). He is editor-in-chief of *Documentary Credit World*, an international journal of letter of credit law and practice. He teaches at George Mason University School of Law. This article is based on a paper given in August 1996 and revised for publication in mid 1997. In the meantime, the ISP has been finalised and will be effective as of 1st January 1999.

[1] As at 1996, the end of the third quarter of 1995, the top 300 US federally insured banks reported a total of $36,750,994,000.00 outstanding in performance standbys and $120,022,605,000.00 outstanding in financial standbys. It is reasonable to assume that the amount of financial standbys issued by non-federally insured foreign banks in the USA greatly exceeds these amounts, given the recent credit-rating history of U.S banks; however no statistics are available. A conservative estimate of a worldwide total would be US $ 300 billion.

[2] For an excellent explanation of the history and use of standby letters of credit by a leading banker, *see* Vincent M. Maulella, "Standby Letters of Credit" [1996] *Annual Survey of Letter of Credit Law and Practice* 81.

throughout the world. This paper examines one important aspect of that process: formulation of rules for standby letters of credit and attempts to identify in a preliminary fashion the insights which this process may afford into the nature of private rulemaking.

The import of private rulemaking is significantly underestimated in commercial law. Despite the fact that private codes of mercantile conduct not only shape the formal process of rulemaking in positive law and statute but also provide the norms which regulate day-to-day business, there is little appreciation of the role of private rules, their relationship to the law, and—more importantly—what constitutes sound rulemaking and how it can be encouraged. As a result, commercial law is not only weakened in its relevance but rendered far more inefficient.

In part, this failure is due to a certain institutional and philosophical arrogance by which the law is thought to be only what courts or legislatures say it is. In large part, however, it is due to the enormous difficulty of obtaining data and assessing them. Such a task requires empirical research covering decades of effort and, more challengingly, an assessment of its significance.

In this regard, the process of law and practice and reform of letters of credit provide a unique laboratory for commercial jurisprudence. Over the last decade, every aspect affecting the field has been subjected to extensive and ongoing scrutiny at national and international levels in a variety of fora. This has included the revision of US domestic law, UCC Article 5,[3] the United Nations Convention on Independent Guarantees and Stand-by Letters of Credit,[4] and the latest revision of the Uniform Customs and Practice for

[3] A joint product of the American Law Institute and the National Conference of Commissioners on Uniform State Laws, this project was undertaken by the NCCUSL. The formal revision of UCC Art. 5 commenced in late 1990. At that time, a Drafting Committee of the NCCUSL was appointed under the chairmanship of Carlyle C. Ring, Jr. The first meeting of the Drafting Committee was held in January 1991 with 8 subsequent full meetings of the committee and its advisors and observers. Draft UCC Art. 5 Revision (12 Apr. 1991), *reprinted in* 8 *Letter of Credit Update* 44 (Mar. 1992); Draft UCC Art. 5 Revision (16 Sept. 1991); Draft UCC Art. 5 Revision (28 Jan. 1992), *reprinted in* 8 *Letter of Credit Update* 21 (July 1992) and 8 *Letter of Credit Update* 50 (Aug. 1992); Draft UCC Art. 5 Revision (1 Sept. 1992) *reprinted in* 8 *Letter of Credit Update* 29 (Nov. 1992); Draft UCC Art. 5 revision (29 Jan. 1993) *reprinted in* 9 *Letter of Credit Update* 34 (Mar. 1993); Draft UCC Art. 5 Revision (31 Mar. 1993) *reprinted in* 8 *Letter of Credit Update* (May 1993); Draft UCC Art. 5 Revision (15 Dec. 1993) *reprinted in* 10 *Letter of Credit Update* 18 (Jan. 1994); Draft UCC Art. 5 Revision (19 Feb. 1994) *reprinted in* 10 *Letter of Credit Update* 27 (Mar. 1994); Last NCCUSL Reading Draft Art. 5 Revision (29 July 1994) *reprinted in* 10 *Letter of Credit Update* 26 (Sept. 1994). Revised Art. 5 was approved at the August 1994 NCCUSL Annual Meeting. The draft (with one substantive change in Revised § 5–111, various style changes, and revised Official Comments) was approved by the ALI at the ALI's May 1995 Annual Meeting. *See* "Current Draft of the UCC Art. 5, Dated April 6, 1995", 11 *Letter of Credit Update* 27 (Apr. 1995). The one substantive change was approved at the July–August 1995 NCCUSL Annual Meeting. As at 1 Jan. 1997, 14 states had enacted the revision. *See* "Status of Revised UCC Art. 5", 12 *Letter of Credit Update* 9 (Dec. 1996).

[4] In 1988, the UN Commission on International Trade Law (UNCITRAL) formally requested its Working Group on International Contract Practices to report on the desirability and feasibility of an international codification of the law of standby letters of credit and independent bank guarantees. At its XIIth Session (Nov. 1988), the Working Group reported affirmatively on both questions, and in subsequent sessions (1990–5) drafted the proposed law. For the final text of the proposed law *see* United Nations, "UN Convention on Independent Guarantees and Stand-by

Documentary Credits.[5] These efforts, though independent, have been intellectually linked and, in many instances, bridged by the participation of the same people who have shared a common foundational and doctrinal approach. First set forth in a Joint American Bar Association/US Council on International Banking, Inc. Task Force Report,[6] this approach was based on

Letters of Credit", (1996) 35 ILM 735. Notes of the Secretariat and Reports of the Working Group from the earlier sessions are as follows: *Report of the Working Group on International Contract Practices on the Work of Its Twelfth Session*, UN Doc. A/CN.9/316 (1988); *Report of the Working Group on International Contract Practices on the Work of Its Thirteenth Session*, UN Doc. A/CN.9/330 (6 Feb. 1990), *reprinted in* 5 *Letter of Credit Update* 28 (Dec. 1989) and 6 *Letter of Credit Update* 18 (Jan. 1990); *Report of the Working Group on International Contract Practices on the Work of Its Fourteenth Session*, UN Doc. A/CN.9/342 (27 Sept. 1990), *reprinted in* 6 *Letter of Credit Update* 17 (Jan. 1991); *Report of the Working Group on International Contract Practices on the Work of Its Fifteenth Session*, UN Doc. A/CN.9/345 (3 June 1991), *reprinted in* 7 *Letter of Credit Update* 19 (Oct. 1991); *Report of the Working Group on International Contract Practices on the Work of Its Sixteenth Session*, UN Doc. A/CN.9/358 (12 Feb. 1992), *reprinted in* 8 *Letter of Credit Update* 24 (June 1991); *Report of the Working Group on International Contract Practices on the Work of Its Seventeenth Session*, UN Doc. A/CN.9/361 (27 Apr. 1992). *Independent Guarantees and Stand-by Letters of Credit: Revised articles of Draft Convention on International Guaranty Letters*, UN Doc. A/CN.9/WG.II/WP.76 (16 Oct. 1992), *reprinted in* 9 *Letter of Credit Update* 27 (Apr. 1993); *Report of the Working Group on International Contract Practices on the Work of Its Nineteenth Session*, UN Doc. A/CN.9/374 (23 June 1993), *reprinted in* 10 *Letter of Credit Update* 27 (Jan. 1994); *Independent Guarantees and Stand-by Letters of Credit: Further revision of draft Convention: articles 1 to 17*, UN Doc. A/CN.9/WG.II/WP.80 (12 Oct. 1993), *reprinted in* 10 *Letter of Credit Update* 25 (Apr. 1994); *Report of the Working Group on International Contract Practices on the Work of Its Twentieth Session*, UN Doc. A/CN.9/388 (23 Dec. 1993), *reprinted in* 10 *Letter of Credit Update* 27 (May 1994); *Report of the Working Group on International Contract Practices on the Work of Its Twenty-First Session*, UN Doc. A/CN.9/391 (Mar. 1994), *reprinted in* 10 *Letter of Credit Update* 31 (June 1994); *Report of the Working Group on International Contract Practices on the Work of Its Twenty-Second Session*, UN Doc. A/CN.9/405 (16 Nov. 1994), *reprinted in* 11 LETTER OF CREDIT UPDATE 39 (Jan. 1995); *Report of the Working Group on International Contract Practices on the Work of Its Twenty-Third Session*, UN Doc. A/CN.9/408 (15 Feb. 1994), *reprinted in* 11 *Letter of Credit Update* 27 (Mar. 1995); *see also Explanatory note by the UNCITRAL Secretariat on the United Nations Convention on Independent Guarantees and Stand-by Letters of Credit*, UN Doc. A/CN.9/431 (4 July 1996) *reprinted in* 12 *Letter of Credit Update* 32 (Aug. 1996).

[5] The current revision of the UCP, designated as ICC Publication No 500, began in 1989. There were 3 formal drafts, and the final product was submitted to the Commission on Banking Technique and Practice of the International Chamber of Commerce in the fall of 1992 and adopted in 1993, The drafts are: ICC Doc. No 470–37/4 (June 1991); ICC Doc. No 470–37/37 (Nov. 1991); ICC Doc. No 470–37/72 (May 1992). The final product was submitted to the Commission on Banking Technique and Practice of the International Chamber of Commerce at its meeting in the fall of 1992, adopted in 1993, effective 1 Jan. 1994. ICC Doc. No 500 (1993). There has also been a formulation of rules for independent guarantees: *The Uniform Rules for Demand Guarantees*. ICC Publication no 458. This product has benefitted incidentally from the conceptual development described here, but it is not a product of it. The URDG, like its predecessor, the *Uniform Rules for Control Guarantees*, ICC Publication no 325, has so far been rarely used with little indication of any increase in the offing.

[6] J. Byrne (ed.), *An Examination of UCC Art. 5 (Letters of Credit)*, A Report of the Task Force of the Letter of Credit Subcommittee of the UCC Committee, Business Law Section of the American Bar Association XI (1989) (hereinafter Task Force Report). The Report of the Task Force on UCC Art. 5 was presented in 1989 to the Uniform Commercial Code Committee of the Business Law Section of the American Bar Association and to the US Council on International Banking, Inc. The Report appears at 45 *Bus. Law.* 1527 (June 1990) and is available in a bound version for $35.00 from the Institute of International Banking Law and Practice, PO Box 2235, Gaithersburg, MD 20886–2235. The members of the task force were: James E. Byrne, Professor,

the understanding that sound commercial law should be founded on and encourage the reasonable expectations of the merchant community.[7] In the field of letters of credit, the failure to recognize this principle created serious difficulties in the formulation of an earlier statute and resulted in the irrelevance of the statute which emerged.[8] Moreover, it rendered judicial decisions increasingly problematic.[9] The most recent of these efforts, the formulation of rules of practice for standby letters of credit, benefits from the cumulative experience of the preceding efforts and is now well under way. At the midway point in its formulation, it offers commercial jurisprudence a wealth of raw material whose appreciation can only further an understanding of the dynamics of the relationship between law and practice. This paper is a modest attempt to contribute to the process by identifying some of the salient features of the process and to suggest tentative evaluations of their significance and implications.

II. STANDBY LETTERS OF CREDIT

The standby letter of credit has suffered through identification of its legal nature with its function. To some extent, this can be explained by its historical antecedents, as the standby emerged from the commercial letter of credit to back up (or "stand-by") another payment mechanism.[10] In this sense, it

George Mason University School of Law, Arlington, Virginia (Chairman); Michael Evan Avidon, Moses & Singer, New York City; James G. Barnes, Baker & McKenzie, Chicago, Illinois; Alan Bloodgood, Vice President, Morgan Guaranty Trust Co. (ret.), New York City; Charles del Busto, then Senior Vice President, Manufacturers Hanover Trust Co., New York City; Boris Kozolchyk, Professor, University of Arizona College of Law, Tucson, Arizona; Arthur G. Lloyd, then Vice President, Citibank, NA, New York City; Vincent Maulella, then Vice President, Manufacturers Hanover Trust Co., New York City; Janis Penton, Miami Beach, Florida, and Richard Purcell, Senior Vice President, Connell Rice & Sugar Co., Westfield, New Jersey. The linkage of this cooperation has been traced to the efforts of the Task Force and its impact delineated in J. Barnes, "The Impact of Internationalization of Transnational Commercial Law: Internationalization of Revised UCC Art. 5" (Letters of Credit) (1995) 16 *J Int'l L Bus.* 215, *reprinted in* 1997 *Annual Survey of Letter of Credit Law & Practice* 7.

[7] *See* Byrne, "Preamble" to J. Byrne (ed.), "An examination of UCC Art. 5 (Letters of Credit)" 45 *Bus. Law* 1527 (June 1990).

[8] In the creation of the original US letter of credit statute in 1950–65, Art. 5 of the Uniform Commercial Code, New York, the major commercial state (at that time, the center of all US letter of credit practice) adopted a non-conforming version which made the statute non-applicable to most letters of credit—i.e. those which were subject to the UCP. In this it was followed by 3 other states, Alabama, Arizona and Missouri. This process is outlined in James E. Byrne, "The Revision of UCC Art. 5: A Strategy for Success", (1990) 56 *Brook. L Rev.* 13.

[9] In addition to the Task Force Report, the difficulties of UCC Art. 5 were explored in a symposium: "UCC Art. 5 Symposium" (1990) 56 *Brook. L Rev.* 1.

[10] The origins of standbys are lost in the myths of New York money center banking legend. The two likely sources of their origin—or possibly simultaneous emergence—were Citibank, on the one hand, where they were first seen as a means of alternate payment for transactions for the sale of goods in which the buyer intended to make payment directly but the seller wanted assurance of payment from a solvent third party in the event of non-payment. (This information is based on a personal interview by the author with Derek Kennedy, long time employee of

became readily confused with an accessory or suretyship guarantee. Similarly, its character was associated with the occurrence of a default. Strictly speaking, neither characterization is satisfactory or complete.

Standbys are, of course, used in default situations. Classified by the Bank of International Settlements as "performance standbys", default standbys assure performance of various undertakings which run the gamut of human and commercial conduct.[11] In this sense, they are similar in many respects to the uses with which independent guarantees are almost exclusively associated.[12] Another use of standbys has emerged, however, which illustrates the remarkable flexibility of this device and which demonstrates the limitations of a system of classification predicated upon function. Since the mid-1980s, the capital markets have relied heavily on standby letters of credit to assure payment of principal and interest to trustees on behalf of purchasers of bonds and commercial paper.[13] The volume of these issuances exceeds all other uses of standbys. Although these financial standbys provide for payment in the event of default, they also provide for regular payment of interest and principal as the ordinary avenue of payment. As a result, it is incorrect to describe them as "default" instruments.

This so-called "direct pay" feature of a financial standby makes the definition of a standby almost impossible. The only satisfactory definition is that it is an independent undertaking to pay against the presentation of documents

Citibank, 18 June 1993.) On the other hand, they may have emerged first in the practice of Manufacturers Hanover Trust Co. and Irving Trust Co. which saw their possibilities as alternatives to guarantees (interview with Arthur Bardenhagen, 18 June 1993). The early development was fueled by the fact that there was no capital reserve requirement for standbys, making them far more attractive than loans. Initial problems lead to the imposition of lending limits, regulatory constraints and, ultimately, the imposition of capital adequacy requirements. *See* "Regulation of Standby Letters of Credit, 1976: Hearings on S. 2347 Before the Committee on Banking, Housing and Urban Affairs", 94th Cong., 2d Sess. (18 June 1976). For a collection of the regulatory provisions affecting standbys, *see* James E. Byrne (ed.), *Understanding the New OCC Interpretive Rulings* (1996). Copies of this publication are available for $45 from The Institute of International Banking Law and Practice, Inc., PO Box 2235, Gaithersburg, MD 20879.

[11] The BIS characterizations are contained in *International Convergence of Capital Measurement and Capital Standards* reprinted in 4 *Letter of Credit Update* 17 (Sept. 1988) and reflected in the capital adequacy rules adopted by major central banks: see, e.g., 12 CFR § 3 (1996). Colorful stories of the use of standbys abound from assurance of payment in domestic relations disputes to assurance of the shipment of medical supplies in exchange for the Bay of Pigs prisoners.

[12] The differences between standbys and independent guarantees, to the extent that they exist, depend on the degree of independence of the particular guarantee. Because independent guarantee practice has not become as sophisticated as standby practice, there are varying degrees of independence as the instrument emerges from its origins as a suretyship or accessory guarantee.Therefore, in some jurisdictions and with respect to some issuers, there is little difference at the level of law, if any, between the two. Where the jurisdiction or issuer is less clear regarding the independent character of the guarantee undertaking, the differences are significant. The differences between the two may not be reflected so much in law as they are in features of practice, such as "extend or pay" practice or giving notice to the applicant of a drawing so as to facilitate seeking extraordinary judicial relief.

[13] *See* Boris Kozolchyk, "The Financial Standby: A Summary Description of Practice and Related Legal Problems" (1996) 28 *UCC LJ* 327.

which is not predicated upon payment against documents related to the sale of goods. Simply stated, a standby is a letter of credit which is not a commercial letter of credit. Even this attempt at a definition is rendered difficult by the existence of so-called "commercial standbys" which are used as a back-up for payment of commercial transactions and which require the presentation of many of the same documents which would have been expected to be presented under a commercial letter of credit.

While there is no definitive list of the different types of uses to which standbys can be placed and the "types" of standbys which emerge, the following represents the considered opinion of the US Secretary of State's Select Advisory Group:

> "(2) Standby letters of credit are governed by the same principles and rules that govern all letters of credit without regard to differences in their purpose or function. In so far as they serve different purposes of the applicant and beneficiary, they may be identified and categorized to include the following types of standbys:
>
> (a) A financial standby, which provides for honor upon presentation of documents stating that payment is due for money borrowed or advanced, or on account of any mature indebtedness undertaken by the applicant or another person.
>
> (b) A performance standby, which provides for honor upon presentation of documents stating that payment is due because of a default in the performance of a non-financial or commercial obligation.
>
> (c) An advance payment standby, which provides for honor upon presentation of documents stating that an advance payment has been made and that its return is demanded.
>
> (d) A bid standby, which provides for honor upon presentation of documents stating that there has been a failure to tender a bid and/or to execute the award on the bid.
>
> (e) A commercial standby, which provides for honor upon presentation of documents stating that there has been a failure to deliver or to pay for delivery of goods or services under an underlying commercial transaction, supported or not by a commercial letter of credit.
>
> (f) A clean standby, which provides for honor solely upon the presentation of drafts or demands for payment.
>
> (g) A counter standby, which provides for honor upon presentation of documents stating that the beneficiary has honored or is obligated to honor its standby or commercial letter of credit, guarantee or other undertaking."[14]

The existence of these various sub-categories gives rise to disagreement about the extent to which this diversity should be recognized in law or practice. On the one hand, differences in practice seem to exist, although it is doubtful that they are ever material. On the other hand, there is present the legitimate concern that the "balkanization" of letter of credit law or practice will dilute the recognition that the standby is intimately linked with the com-

[14] James E. Byrne, "Standby Letter of Credit Rules: An Exercise in Drafting a Commercial Statute" (1992) 9 *Ariz. J of Int'l & Comp. L.* 366.

mercial letter of credit as an independent undertaking. The reality is, however, that at the abstract level of law all standbys are alike and, more importantly, not materially different from commercial letters of credit or, for that matter, other independent undertakings. This essential unity was recognized recently by the US Comptroller of the Currency in the re-formulation of its influential interpretive ruling on letters of credit whose scope has been broadened to include all "independent undertakings".[15] On the level of practice, this debate is likely to be resolved pragmatically depending upon whether there are functional differences which require distinct treatment in rules of practice. In their present state, the draft rules for standby practices, the International Standby Practices (hereinafter "ISP") only recognizes such differences with respect to default provisions for documents which require payment.

III. STANDBYS AND THEIR REGULATION IN LAW AND PRACTICE

The fundamental reality of letter of credit law is that it has followed letter of credit practice. The history of the legal nature of the letter of credit has been a story of courts and, only recently, legislative bodies deferring to mercantile principles (or refusing to do so). The letter of credit is, in its essence, a mercantile promise. Its enforceability depends only on its issuance and it requires only minimal formalities.[16] It differs radically from traditional bilateral

[15] *See* 12 CFR § 7.1016 (effective 1 Apr. 1996). This ruling is discussed in detail in Byrne, *Understanding the New OCC Interpretive Rulings*, available for $45 from the Institute of International Banking Law & Practice, Inc., P.O. Box 2235, Gaithersburg MD 20879.

[16] These principles are reflected in UN Convention Art. 7 and Revised UCC Art. 5 S. 5–104 and 5–106. They provide:

"Article 7: Issuance, form and irrevocability of undertaking
(1) Issuance of an undertaking occurs when and where the undertaking leaves the sphere of control of the guarantor/issuer concerned.
(2) An undertaking may be issued in any form which preserves a complete record of the text of the undertaking and provides authentication of its source by generally accepted means or by a procedure agreed upon by the guarantor/issuer and the beneficiary.
(3) From the time of issuance of an undertaking, a demand for payment may be made in accordance with the terms and conditions of the undertaking, unless the undertaking stipulates a different time.
(4) An undertaking is irrevocable upon issuance, unless it stipulates that it is revocable."

"SECTION 5–104. FORMAL REQUIREMENTS. A letter of credit, confirmation, advice, transfer, amendment, or cancellation may be issued in any form that is a record and is authenticated (i) by a signature or (ii) in accordance with the agreement of the parties or the standard practice referred to in Section 5–108(e)."

"SECTION 5–106. ISSUANCE, AMENDMENT, CANCELLATION, AND DURATION.
(a) A letter of credit is issued and becomes enforceable according to its terms against the issuer when the issuer sends or otherwise transmits it to the person requested to advise or to the beneficiary. A letter of credit is revocable only if it so provides.
(b) After a letter of credit is issued, rights and obligations of a beneficiary, applicant, confirmer, and issuer are not affected by an amendment or cancellation to which that person has not consented except to the extent the letter of credit provides that it is revocable or that the issuer may amend or cancel the letter of credit without that consent.
(c) If there is no stated expiration date or other provision that determines its duration, a letter of credit expires one year after its stated date of issuance or, if none is stated, after the date on which it is issued.
(d) A letter of credit that states that it is perpetual expires five years after its stated date of issuance, or if none is stated, after the date on which it is issued."

contractual undertakings in that there is no mutuality, no defense based upon the non-existence of *causa* or consideration for its issuance. Indeed, the beneficiary of a letter of credit may be a complete stranger to the issuer.

The so-called "struggle for independence" (from contract law and the underlying transaction) was won for the letter of credit in the mid-nineteenth century in most jurisdictions as courts came to recognize under one theory or another that the letter of credit was enforceable according to its terms and that defenses were not available which might otherwise be asserted were it a contract.

Recently, it has come to be recognized that the independent character of the letter of credit is linked to its documentary nature. Because a credit is payable against conditions which are readily susceptible to determination (documents which do or do not conform to the terms and conditions of the credit), liability can readily be ascertained. This doctrinal evolution is recognized in the recent modern statutory formulations which have emerged during this decade as well as in the UCP.[17]

[17] Arts. 2 and 3 of the UN Convention on Independent Guarantees and Stand-by Letters of Credit provide:

"ARTICLE 2: Undertaking

1. For the purposes of this Convention, an undertaking is an independent commitment, known in international practice as an independent guarantee or as a stand-by letter of credit, given by a bank or other institution or person ('guarantor/issuer') to pay to the beneficiary a certain or determinable amount upon simple demand or upon demand accompanied by other documents, in conformity with the terms and any documentary conditions of the undertaking, indicating, or from which it is to be inferred, that the payment is due because of a default in the performance of an obligation, or because of another contingency, or for money borrowed or advanced, or on account of any mature indebtedness undertaken by the principal/applicant or another person.

2. The undertaking may be given:

(a) At the request or on the instruction of the customer ('principal/applicant') of the guarantor/issuer;

(b) On the instruction of another bank, institution or person ('instructing party') that acts at the request of the customer ('principal/applicant') of that instructing party; or

(c) On behalf of the guarantor/issuer itself.

3. Payment may be stipulated in the undertaking to be made in any form, including:

(a) Payment in a specified currency or unit of account;

(b) Acceptance of a bill of exchange (draft);

(c) Payment on a deferred basis;

(d) Supply of a specified item of value.

4. The undertaking may stipulate that the guarantor/issuer is the beneficiary when acting in favor of another person."

"ARTICLE 3: Independence of Undertaking

For the purpose of this Convention, an undertaking is independent where the guarantor/issuer's obligation to the beneficiary is not:

(a) Dependent upon the existence or validity of any underlying transaction, or upon any other undertaking (including stand-by letters of credit or independent guarantees to which confirmations counter-guarantees relate); or

(b) Subject to any term or condition not appearing in the undertaking, or to any future, uncertain act or event except presentation of documents or another such act or event within a guarantor/issuer's sphere of operations."

Revised UCC Art. 5 provides:

"SECTION 5-102.Definitions

(a) In this article:

(10) 'Letter of Credit' means a definite undertaking that satisfies the requirements of Section 5–104 by an issuer to a beneficiary at the request or for the account of an applicant or, in the case of a financial

iii. authorizes another bank to negotiate, against stipulated document(s), provided that the terms and

The reform of letter of credit law reached an important international junction in the successful completion of the United Nations Convention on Independent Guarantees and Stand-by Letters of Credit and its adoption by the UN General Assembly on 12 December 1996. This project had its origin in the perception of many governments that there was a need to re-affirm the legal character of the independent guarantee. The project coincided with the attempt of the International Chamber of Commerce to formulate rules of practice for independent guarantees, an effort which eventually produced the Uniform Rules for Demand Guarantees (URDG). The goal of this project was to produce rules which would provide uniformity and legitimacy to the independent guarantee in a manner similar to that provided by the universally recognized Uniform Customs and Practice for Documentary Credits (UCP) to the commercial letter of credit. Despite an original effort to link the standby to the URDG—an attempt rejected out of hand by the US banking community—it has remained under the UCP regime which indicates in UCP 500 Article 1 that it shall apply to standbys "to the extent to which they may be applicable".

Due to the perception of some observers that the standby shares characteristics with the independent guarantee and to attract support from countries tied to standby practice rather than guarantee practice, the scope of the project was broadened to encompass both independent guarantees and standby letters of credit. As the sessions began, however, it became readily apparent that the inclusion of the standby would require more than an addition to the name of the Convention. There are significant differences between the typical use to which standby letters of credit is put and the typical use of independent guarantees, and these differences mandate different treatment.

Independent guarantees tend to be used in lieu of bid or performance bonds in situations such as construction projects or projects to develop or install systems relating to infrastructure improvements. Linked to default, they typically require only a demand or a statement of default. Because of regulatory requirements and preferences, there is frequently a requirement that the undertaking be issued by a local bank. These undertakings are often "backed" by a counter-guarantee of which the local bank is the beneficiary, but the two undertakings are only accidentally linked. The impropriety of the drawing on

institution, to itself or for its own account, to honor a documentary presentation by payment or delivery of an item of value."

UCP 500 provides:

"ARTICLE 2: Meaning of Credit

For the purposes of these Art.s, the expressions 'Documentary Credit(s)' and 'Standby Letter(s) of Credit' (hereinafter referred to as 'Credit(s)'), mean any arrangement, however named or described, whereby a bank (the 'Issuing Bank') acting at the request and on the instructions of a customer (the 'Applicant') or on its own behalf.

i. is to make a payment to or to the order of a third party (the 'Beneficiary'), or is to accept and pay bills of exchange (Draft(s) drawn by the Beneficiary, or

ii. authorizes another bank to effect such payment, or to accept and pay such bills of exchange (Draft(s)), or conditions of the Credit are complied with. For the purposes of these Art.s, branches of a bank in different countries are considered another bank."

the local guarantee is not a defense to a drawing on the counter-guarantee. Independent guarantees rarely are advised, confirmed, paid or negotiated by corespondent banks. Drawing rights are almost never transferred and assignment of their proceeds rarely occurs. Of course, there are exceptional situations, but the expectation of the delegates from the countries using independent guarantees was that the Convention would be drafted to accommodate a relatively simple and straightforward instrument.

The standby letter of credit, however, does not fit this pattern. It is not precisely a default instrument because of the widespread use of direct pay provisions. Standbys frequently require multiple documents in addition to a demand. They are regularly confirmed, advised, paid by and occasionally negotiated by correspondent banks. The linkage between these banks is not accidental, as with the counter-guarantee, but intricate. A non-conforming draw on a standby is a defense to payment by any correspondent bank. Drawing rights under standbys are commonly transferred, they are issued in transferable form, and it is not uncommon for proceeds of a drawing to be assigned. As a result, the inclusion of standbys in the project required a broader approach than might have been necessary were its scope limited to independent guarantees.

IV. THE INTERNATIONAL STANDBY PRACTICES[18]

The relationship between the UCP and standbys has long been ambiguous. From the perspective of those familiar with traditional commercial letter of credit practice, the standby was not really a letter of credit. It was often drawn in the context of a dispute, frequently involved litigation and did not usually require the type of documentary judgments in which the traditional document examiner had been trained. Even more problematic, standbys typically involved attorneys in a more active manner than was true with commercial letters of credit. Because of the nature of the transactions for which standbys were used, it was not unusual for them either to be drafted by an attorney or for an attorney to issue an opinion regarding their validity.

[18] The formulation of the International Standby Practices is an ongoing process in which dramatic changes regularly have occurred due, in large part, to the absence of any prior formulation. This paper was written in 1996 based on the version of the ISP circulated internationally early in 1997. Necessarily that version has itself been revised and is undergoing further revision, even as this article is being edited for publication a year later. The fact that the text of many of the provisions referred to in the article has been altered (and that many will be further altered afterwards) does not diminish the value of the insights. The purpose of the article is not to provide a final assessment of the ISP, a task not possible until they are complete, but to examine and assess the methodology by which they are being formulated. For this task, any mature stage of the rules will suffice. The evolution of the rules and their final formulation are the topic for another article. For the current text of the ISP, the reader is advised to contact the Institute of International Banking Law & Practice or its website (www.iiblp.org)

Indeed, the link between standbys and the UCP has been a mixed blessing from the perspective of the standby. On the positive side, by subjecting a standby to the UCP, its character as a letter of credit was affirmed. Furthermore, the issuer was given moral support in resisting attempts by the beneficiary to burden the undertaking with provisions such as perpetual duration or to force extensions by threatening to draw on the undertaking even though there was no proper basis for the drawing. In addition, the UCP was linked to standard international banking practice and articulated this regime in a manner universally followed. Most significantly, the UCP embodied the concept of preclusion for failure to give proper or timely notice of discrepancies regardless of the curability of discrepancies in order to assure finality of the determination.

On the other hand, only the most rudimentary accommodation for standbys has been made in the UCP.[19] It is common for legal practitioners either not to refer to the UCP or to make extensive modifications because of its unsuitability for standby practice.[20] The problems fall into two categories: problematic provisions of the UCP and omissions in UCP coverage.

For example, UCP 500 Articles 17, 42 and 44 place the risk of the closure of the office of an issuer or confirmer on a non-business day which is the last day of presentation on the beneficiary. This allocation has generally been acceptable to most beneficiaries of commercial letters of credit in large part because they have control of the underlying transaction. Knowledgeable standby beneficiaries, however, are not prepared to accept this risk. Unlike the commercial credit, there is little possibility of an accommodation with the applicant: the drawing itself frequently is a result of difficulties experienced with the applicant. As a result, so-called "power" beneficiaries negotiate clauses which provide for an extension of liability after the reopening of the office. These clauses are individually crafted, contain differing time periods and, because of the failure to anticipate various possibilities, work to the disadvantage of all parties in various ways.

The provisions in UCP 500 Article 19 regarding reimbursement shift the charges and costs relating to reimbursement to the applicant in accordance with commercial practice. Standby practice typically regards the intervention of a correspondent bank as designed exclusively for the benefit of the beneficiary who is expected to bear all charges and costs without recourse to the issuer.

[19] The only mention of standbys occurs in UCP 500 Arts. 1 and 2. The enigmatic indication that it is applicable to standbys to the extent to which it may be applicable is indicative of the reluctance with which standbys were embraced. The only other concession to standbys was that the word "drawings" was added to the term "shipments" in several technical sections. This brusque treatment of standbys has reinforced the impression that they have been regarded as unwanted step-children by the leadership of the ICC. *See, e.g.* B. Wheble, " 'Problem Children'—Stand-by Letters of Credit and Simple First Demand Guarantees" (1982) 24 *Ariz. L Rev.* 301.

[20] *See* Michael Evan Avidon, Alan L. Bloodgood and Janis Penton-Soshuk, "Standby Letters of Credit and the UCP" in James Byrne *et al* (eds.), *1995 Annual Survey of Letter of Credit Law & Practice* (1995), available from The Institute of International Banking Law & Practice, P.O. Box 2235, Gaithersburg, MD 20879.

UCP 500 Article 21 provides that the data content of documents presented must be consistent not only with the terms and conditions of the credit but with the other documents as well. This requirement is logical in a commercial letter of credit since the transaction is typically a holistic exercise in which internal consistency can be expected. This expectation does not necessarily follow for standbys. While there may be consistency as to some data, the very *raison d'être* for the drawing may be an inconsistency between two documents, thereby evidencing the default.

The attempt to allude to standbys in UCP 500 Article 41, which deals with instalment shipments and drawings, is a misconceived attempt to accommodate standbys and only introduces greater difficulties. In the setting of a transaction for the sale of goods, the failure to make one of a series of instalment drawings signals a departure from the intention of the parties and renders suspect any further drawings on the credit. Not so with standbys. In the first place, the failure to make a drawing will rarely be regarded as a problem by the applicant for the standby. Even if there is an expectation that such a drawing will be made, its absence does not work a hardship on the applicant. Moreover, the beneficiary expects that it will be able to make drawings in a series without regard to whether it has made prior drawings.

UCP 500 Article 43 provides against stale documents of title by establishing a default rule that they must be presented within twenty-one days of their issuance. In effect, this establishes a second deadline in addition to the expiry date. The concern is that delayed presentation of such documents will expose the applicant to unanticipated potential charges for demurrage or storage. Where a commercial standby requires presentation of transport documents (or copies of them), there has been a failure to obtain payment by another means. Quite typically, the document is not negotiable and the goods have been consigned to the applicant. In such a situation, application of the latest date for presentation rule constitutes a trap for the beneficiary and works contrary to the dynamic of the standby transaction.

Transfer of drawing rights under a commercial letter of credit, where the credit is transferable, is typically expected to involve only one transfer, but that transfer may contain multiple partial transfers in proportionate amounts to any number of second (partial) beneficiaries. This practice reflects the commercial expectation in a contract for the sale of goods that the beneficiary may need to use the letter of credit as a mechanism to assure suppliers of payment and may not have sufficient credit to induce another bank to issue a credit on its behalf. The multiple transfers enable the beneficiary to provide assurance to the suppliers that they are the direct recipients of the obligation of a bank while maintaining control of the entire transaction, and enable the beneficiary to collect the balance due under the credit after the transferred amounts are paid. It is rare, however, for the beneficiary to transfer the entire credit more than once, and such a transfer would be so unusual as to raise questions. In a standby setting, the opposite holds true. The typical standby contemplates multiple whole transfers when the beneficiary assigns its right to draw to others. Since the beneficiary is not expected to perform, there is no disadvantage to the applicant in this arrangement where it has, or the beneficiary is a trustee or agent on behalf of multiple bondholders. agreed to a transferable credit in the first place. It is rare, however, for there to be multiple partial transfers and the ability of multiple second (partial) beneficiaries to make drawings would cause serious difficulties.

The presence of these provisions in the UCP is problematic for standbys. At best, they require additional negotiation and drafting. At worst, they defeat the purpose of the standby and frustrate the parties' expectations. Even more significant, however, are the numerous standby issues which are not even addressed by the UCP.

In the course of the development of standby practice, as might be expected, there has arisen a vocabulary containing terminology which requires definition. Other terms are misleading or ambiguous. Examples include "amendment", "automatic", "evergreen", "clean", "unconditional", "partial drawing" and "multiple presentations". Depending on the context, an amendment may be either a proposal to amend or the operative change in the issuer's obligation. Because of the parties' desire for certainty, there is interest in amendments which are effective automatically, with or without the possibility being open to the issuer to disaffirm its obligation under the credit within a certain time frame.

For example, the standby is issued in a form which contains a definite expiration date but is automatically renewable unless the issuer gives notice of its decision not to renew within a certain period before the expiry date. Because of the inevitable tendency of merchants to resort to shorthand terminology, it is not uncommon that these provisions are loosely referred to by terms such as "automatic", "evergreen" and the like without any precise delineation of the consequences intended. Government beneficiaries, in an excess of caution, often require the standby to state that it is "unconditional", meaning that there is no condition other than a simple demand. The demand itself, however, is a condition and by its nature the letter of credit is conditioned upon the demand being made in a timely fashion. Similar confusion exists regarding whether the term "partial drawing" refers to a drawing for less than the amount available or the making of more than one presentation—i.e. multiple partial drawings. "Clean" has two different meanings in standby practice, signifying a standby or a standby which requires only a draft or demand. These terms and many others are used and require a definitional framework to reduce confusion and conflict.

One of the most significant contributions of the UCP to commercial letters of credit was the detailing of specific minimal requirements for invoices, bills of lading and insurance documents. Not only did these rules reduce confusing verbiage in letters of credit but they worked to standardize the practice of issuers of these documents and often to reshape their practices and forms to accommodate the concerns of the banks. The absence of provisions regarding typical standby documents has hindered this process for standbys and contributed to the inability of banks to standardize standby formats. For example, there is no standard SWIFT format for standbys which guides users in a fashion similar to commercial or "documentary" letters of credit. While some have objected that the complexity of standbys prevents such standardization, anyone familiar with the practice will recognize that commercial credits are inherently more complex than most standbys. The difference is seven decades of pressure from the banking community through the UCP which has resulted in a remarkable degree of standardization. On the other hand, even the most typical standby document, the default statement, lacks standardization.

It is typical that standbys contain statements regarding their truth or the sincerity with which they were made. There exists a plethora of phrases by which these statements are described and there is no system by which their common features are identified.

Standbys commonly contain text within quotation marks or in attached documents. This language is not always drafted with precision. For example, it may contain blank lines or contradictory alternatives (e.g. "[t]his drawing is due because the project has been completed or because the standby has not been renewed"). It is not sensible to think that the exact format be duplicated (e.g. the blanks or words such as "complete"). Filling in language or deleting an alternative, however, requires the document examiner to exercise judgement in determining compliance. Ordinarily, the examiner would do so. The presence of the literal text, however, presents difficulties about which the UCP provides no guidance.

Standbys which are issued to back up local guarantees sometimes contain the text of the local guarantee. At other times, the local guarantor will present not only the documents required under the standby but also those required under the local guarantee. The UCP provides no guidance on whether the bank is to examine the documents relating to the local guarantee in such a situation.

It is not uncommon for a legal successor to the named beneficiary (administrator, bankruptcy trustee or the like) to make a drawing in its own name and not that of the named beneficiary. The UCP makes no provision for such a situation.

Standbys are frequently syndicated or participated out. These terms are not defined, nor are the implications always clear to the applicant and beneficiary. For example, it is often unclear to the applicant that the issuer assumes it has the right to participate out its obligation so as to set it off. To do so, it assumes that it can in confidence reveal confidential information regarding the creditworthiness of the applicant to other banks interested in participating without seeking the applicant's permission or advising the applicant of the issuer's intention. Likewise, it is assumed that any participation has no effect on the beneficiary's rights against the issuer, but the UCP does not provide any guidance on these matters.

Proceeds from a payment under a standby are commonly assigned, but UCP Article 49 completely defers to local law in this matter. Local law regarding assignment, however, often has been shaped in the context of the free assignability of choses in action and is not able easily to adjust to the esoteric terminology of letter of credit practice in which what is meant by assignment of proceeds is not the assignment *per se* but acknowledgment of the assignment by the bank. This abdication of direction by the UCP results in confusion. Even if such an unsettled state is acceptable for commercial letters of credit, it is not acceptable for standbys.

The result of the absence of rules in these common situations is the need to negotiate and draft specific and individual provisions in each situation. Such provisions necessarily utilize different approaches and terminology and, not uncommonly, omit important provisions. They cause confusion, disputes, litigation, and defeat the purpose of the standby as a mechanism for payment. Many of these problems could be reduced or eliminated by standard rules. Even where the parties require unique solutions, the rules would provide a starting point for their negotiations.

No effort was under way to formulate separate standby rules and the ICC Banking Commission had decided not to make any adjustments addressing standby practices in UCP 500, despite requests from the US banks. As a result, the US Department of State requested the US letter of credit community, in conjunction with the US Council on International Banking, Inc. and the Institute of International Banking Law & Practice, Inc., to take the lead in formulating draft standby rules in consultation with letter of credit communities throughout the world. The process which has followed has actively sought the participation of every segment of the letter of credit community including bankers, users, attorneys, regulators, rating agencies, government officials, international agencies and academics.[21] The ICC Banking Commission has been invited to participate and has set up an Ad Hoc Working Group to examine the ISP. The banking associations of the countries where standbys are used extensively have also been asked to comment. In addition, the project has been sponsored by Citibank, NA, The Chase Manhattan Bank, NA ABN AMRO, Baker and McKenzie, and the National Law Center for Inter-American Free Trade.

Its product has been the Draft ISP.[22] The ISP seeks to assure for standby

[21] The drafting exercise involved literally hundreds of individuals, banks and organizations from throughout the USA and around the world. Every effort was made to solicit the involvement of all segments of the standby community. Some organizations chose actively to participate at every meeting, some chose to send in comments and abstained from the meetings and others simply requested to see the progressive drafts as they became available. Those actively involved in the drafting included numerous bankers from major banks, regulators from the NY Fed. and the OCC, the Secretary of UNCITRAL, counsel from the US Department of State, numerous attorneys involved in the field and representatives from user organizations. Meetings of the drafting group were held in Jan., Mar., June, Oct., Nov. and Dec. 1995 and in Jan. and Mar. of 1996.

[22] The Draft ISP can be accessed at www.iiblp.org.

practice the same integrity from these self-standing rules as is provided for commercial credits under the UCP. The rules establish generally accepted norms for standbys which can either be accepted or used as a starting point for negotiations. Where different approaches are common, the ISP follow the most widely accepted approach. The rules are also designed to be compatible with the United Nations Convention and local law.

ISP 98, which will be finalised in April 1998 and available for use from 1st January 1999, is self-contained, is intended to be applied to standbys, is not intended to be applied to accessory or contractual undertakings, and is intended to supplement statutory legal institutions. It contain a specific provision giving its provisions priority over other rules of practice which may be incorporated in standby letters of credit.

V. SELECTED INSTANCES OF STANDARDIZATION AND HARMONIZATION

In the process of drafting, several preliminary insights have been gained about rulemaking which yield meaning about the ISP and the broader issue of determining sound rules. Several examples are given here because of their overarching significance. It needs to be emphasized that these provisions are in draft form and may be altered before the ISP are finalized. Nonetheless, whatever their final form, the process itself is sufficiently mature to permit some general observations.

(a) Instances of Mercantile Obligations: Implications of Preclusion (ISP Rule 5.03)

The preclusion rule of letter of credit practice is a remarkable instance of mercantile rulemaking. It appears to run against the self-interest of banks, in that it prevents a bank which fails to give notice of a discrepancy in a timely fashion from asserting it. It also provides that a bank which fails to hold the documents presented at the disposal of the presenter is precluded from dishonoring the presentation.[23] This rule operates even where the discrepancy is not curable. In part, the rule exists to provide rigor for the system, to assure finality by fixing the position of the bank so that it cannot sit back and wait for market conditions to improve and to avoid the impossible task in many situations of determining whether a discrepancy is curable or not.

[23] UCP 500 Art. 14(e) provides:

"If the Issuing Bank and/or Confirming Bank, if any, fails to act in accordance with the provisions of this Art. and/or fails to hold the documents at the disposal of, or return them to the presenter, the Issuing Bank and/or Confirming Bank, if any, shall be precluded from claiming that the documents are not in compliance with the terms and conditions of the Credit."

While the rule imposes a burden on banks to examine a presentation, it also assures the long-term integrity of the letter of credit. The source of the rule is the clearing banks which are typically on every side of a credit transaction as issuer, confirmer, nominated correspondent bank, beneficiary and, vicariously through their customers, as applicant. Occupying such a position, these banks cannot support a rule which is tilted toward any party and could not maintain their trusted position in the correspondent system if they were seen to be partisan.

An issue which has eluded formulation in the UCP revisions is the application of this rule to re-presentations. The ISP, seeking to strengthen the integrity of the undertaking, has attempted to refine the preclusion rule in this area, in large part because the issue of re-presentations often arises with respect to standbys.

The notice of dishonor does not preclude an attempt to cure discrepancies and re-presentation. This area of banking practice, however, has never been explicitly addressed by the UCP. Nor has the relationship between a given presentation and prior presentations been articulated despite the near unanimity of banking practice on these issues and the necessary inferences which follow from the UCP rules.[24] The drafters of the ISP decided to address these issues in the interest of clarifying the bank's obligation and the rules of practice surrounding it.

The base line for analysis is the nature of the undertaking—an obligation to pay against a conforming presentation and the obligation to examine any presentation in light of standard international banking practice within a reasonable time and to take a position so that the beneficiary may adjust its conduct accordingly.

The first "hidden" issue revolves around the right of the beneficiary to cure a discrepant presentation. If the issuer's undertaking is irrevocable, it would follow that one non-conforming presentation cannot extinguish it. Unless cancelled by the beneficiary, the obligation runs until expiry or payment. It therefore follows that a conforming re-presentation would comply. Other conclusions are, of course, theoretically possible; for example, that the beneficiary, having made one drawing, can make no others. Such a rule would unnecessarily undermine the irrevocability of the undertaking and heighten the technicalities of a device that is, after all, intended to be an assurance of payment and not a litany of excuses. It is, therefore, possible for a beneficiary to cure a discrepant presentation under standard international banking practice. Nonetheless, it must be recognized that the curability of a presentation is secondary to the concerns which led to the preclusion rule. The beneficiary

[24] This issue arose in *Banco General Ruminahui, SA* v. *Citibank International* and was addressed in the *amicus curiae* brief of the US Council on International Banking, Inc., reprinted in Byrne, *1996 Annual Survey of Letter of Credit Law & Practice* at 678. The trial court decision, which turned banking practice on its head, was reversed on appeal: *ibid.*, 97 F.3d 480 (11th Cir. 1996), *1997 Annual Survey of Letter of Credit Law & Practice* 529.

has the responsibility of making a conforming presentation and it is not the duty of the banking system to educate the beneficiary on how to comply.

Having recognized the beneficiary's right to cure and re-present within the terms of the credit, several issues remain to be answered. The first relates to the effect of prior presentations under similar credits or the same credit. The second relates to the effect of the prior presentation where there is a re-presentation of documents under the same presentation. Both issues touch upon the scope of the preclusion rule, an important adjunct to the firm and hard nature of the promise—a feature of its irrevocability.

Under standard banking practice, each presentation is thought to stand on its own. In part, this approach is a result of operational issues; banks do not keep files open on prior presentations. Even if they were to do so, examination of the technicalities of that presentation and the documents presented under it (much less an entire series of presentations under different credits) would turn each examination into the letter of credit equivalent of a title search for real property, which would unduly delay payment and magnify costs—all to no good end. Whatever the bank may have done with regard to similar credit, or the same credit, does not alter the nature of its undertaking. This is to pay against conforming documents and the requirement that the beneficiary present conforming documents.

While there is an important mercantile basis for the requirement that all discrepancies be noted in the event of dishonor, there is no such basis for requiring a delineation of discrepancies when the credit is honored. If a bank, for whatever reason, chooses to honor a presentation despite discrepancies, it does not thereby alter its undertaking. The equitable notion that such notification would alert the beneficiary to future difficulties—a notion predicated on a misunderstanding of the responsibility of the banks in this process—does not justify the penalty of preclusion for "expansive honor" of a discrepant presentation (i.e. honor notwithstanding the presence of discrepancies). Even in terms of efficiency, were such a consequence to follow, it is possible that the practice of expansive honor (salutory by all accounts) would diminish. More importantly, the notion that a bank's role is to educate the beneficiary is founded on an incorrect premise. As a result, the ISP has adhered to the mercantile approach and provide that an issuer's obligation is not affected by prior presentations under the same or similar credits.[25]

Having reached this conclusion, does it also apply to re-presentations? A geometrical sense of consistency would perhaps suggest so. Mercantile practice, however, reaches the opposite conclusion. The scope of the preclusion rule is at stake so far as the same presentation is concerned. Here there is no question of different document checkers, different terms, research of archives

[25] "*5.03 Failure to Give Notice of Dishonor.*

a Failure to give notice of a discrepancy precludes assertion of the same discrepancy in that document upon re-presentation of that document but does not preclude assertion of that discrepancy in any different presentation under that standby or a separate standby."

and the like. More significantly, not applying the preclusion rule would allow a bank to change its position by finding additional discrepancies on later presentations. A bank wilfully seeking to avoid its obligation might even raise only one of several discrepancies at a time in an effort to ride out the life of the credit. Such an approach undermines the integrity of the preclusion rule.

Nonetheless, important qualifications must be recognized. The preclusion rule only applies to the same discrepancy. The re-presentation may introduce new discrepancies which may arise even though the original discrepancy is cured. For example, if the standby contains internal deadlines in addition to the expiry date, a re-presentation after these deadlines would be a new discrepancy. In addition, the attempted cure may itself give rise to a new discrepancy or may introduce a conflict with another term in the standby. These discrepancies would not fall within the scope of the preclusion rule.

Because of the importance of these issues to standby practice, the ISP has expressly articulated this aspect of standby letter of credit practice.[26] It has chosen to follow the mercantile approach which has shaped standby practice. This approach is based on different premises from those which might have influenced attorneys or jurists. Cure is clearly not in the forefront. While permitted, the purpose of notice is not to facilitate cure so much as to fix positions and there is, of course, no duty to expedite examination of a presentation. The beneficiary who presents documents on the verge of expiry or a similar deadline must take care to do so in a conforming manner or bear the risk that the examination (which will occur in the ordinary course of the bank's work) may not be completed in time to permit cure. The result, then, is a rule which provides important protections for the beneficiary and the banks which are obligated on the undertaking. Nevertheless, the rule is shaped not so much by these considerations (and without any regard for balancing or trading them off) but by a concern for the demands of the correspondent system of banking which underlies standby letter of credit practice and the integrity of the standby.

Perhaps the most important lesson, however, lies not in the specific rule itself, but in the process of analysis which led to the choices which shaped the rule. These choices were not accidental. They form part of a broader system readily recognizable to any banker trained in letter of credit practice. In a sense, the result is inevitable because the underlying principles which govern this institution make it so. In addition, the rule flows not simply from principles but is an integral part of an entire system driving the institution. This system replicates the legal system and, to a considerable extent, replaces it. In the absence of a unified international regime of law, such a system is as necessary for the standby letter of credit as for the commercial letter of credit from

[26] The rule is not new but is rarely stated and has not been articulated in the revisions of the UCP. For an expression of the practice, see J. Decker, *Case Studies on Documentary Credits*, (1989) Case No 52, 57.

which it developed to meet the demands of certainty and international uniformity.

The jurisprudential implications of the preclusion rule and its ouster of equitable estoppel are sometimes difficult for trained lawyers to grasp and accept because they go to the essence of what law is and who should be the lawgiver. American common lawyers, in particular, are raised on the fundamental Holmesian notion that the law is what the courts say it is. Influenced by this approach, private rules are an incident to party autonomy or freedom of contract—a theory which dovetails neatly with nineteenth century contract theory based on bilateral contracts.

In this field, as well as other fields of modern commercial law, however, this theory is inadequate to explain the role of private rules in ordering the behavior of the participants. Indeed, it would be no exaggeration to conclude that the UCP has had a far greater influence on letter of credit law than any public rule of law and that it has been the primary source of judicial and legislative law in this area.

Under the typical approach, custom or usage is confined to so-called linguistic custom.[27] The terminology of the parties is affected by the rules of practice. For example, under the Draft ISP, the use of the term "absolute" to describe the undertaking of the parties would signify that the undertaking is irrevocable.[28] The major difficulty with this approach is that it tends to blind the courts and attorneys to the systemic nature of the rules. By focusing on the particular term or phrase, the courts fail to understand that what is at stake is not merely one phrase but an alternative system within which the problem is to be resolved. In addition to providing definitions, the rules provide a complete regime, which includes identifying normative behavior, setting standards against which minimal acceptable behavior must be measured, a remedial system with sanctions and a theory of damages.

This system tends to be self-contained and exclusive. Its universal acceptance suggests that it is more than the attempt of one set of interests to impose self-serving rules on others, but that it contains its own system of checks and balances which have commanded the respect and adherence of the vast majority of participants. Most systems of law have developed similar devices to balance the behavior of the parties and to assure that certain basic notions of fairness are given effect to, if only in situations where there is no specific pro-

[27] The literature on this subject in the USA is not as complete as one might have hoped. Perhaps the most thoughtful piece on the subject is A Wright, "Opposition of the Law to Business Usages" (1926) 26 *Columbia L Rev.* 917. He distinguishes business usages from so-called "trade codes" (rules advanced by trade associations) and standardized forms, concluding that the importance of business usage has diminished considerably—especially in light of the hostility of traditional contract theory. Linguistic custom is the use of shorthand phrases to capture notions with legal significance and to give them that significance. This approach to custom is consonant with the consensual theory of contract since the incorporation of the customary usage into the contract permits the maintenance of the fiction that the parties have agreed to the custom.

[28] ISP Rule 1.22 (Inappropriate Terminology) (a) provides that "[a] standby should not state that it is: . . . (ii) absolute (if it does, it signifies merely that it is irrevocable); . . .".

vision to the contrary. Under US common law, many of these notions derive from equitable jurisprudence and the theoretical constructs upon which the law is based. Thus, in the problem already examined, traditional equity would have predicated its solution upon a notion of detrimental reliance. This theory, in turn, is based on a concept of compensation for damage actually suffered and spends considerable psychic energy attempting to identify that damage. Letter of credit practice has eschewed this approach entirely. It provides instead the remedy of specific performance for wrongful dishonor—the full face amount of the undertaking—without regard to proof of actual damages. As a result, there is little theoretical or practical difficulty in adhering to a theory of preclusion instead of estoppel because the focus is not on whether or not there was justifiable or reasonable reliance. The mercantile notion is that reliance on the integrity of the instrument is sufficient.

(b) Beyond Linguistic Custom: Normalization

Normalization of behavior is one of the primary effects of private rulemaking. As indicated, it can often be achieved in a primitive sense by definition of terms. The ISP, following the UCP's lead, has gone beyond this stage and provides rules which affect the behavior of the entire industry more directly. Four instances will illustrate this approach.

(i) Closure of Issuer on Expiry Date (ISP Rule 3.2)

As indicated, the ISP varys the UCP rule on *force majeure*, requiring the beneficiary to bear the risk of the closure of the bank making the undertaking on the undertaking's expiry date. In addressing this problem, a variety of factors had to be considered. Those beneficiaries who were sophisticated and with sufficient leverage varied the UCP provision, leaving those without such leverage subject to its vagaries. How the problem was addressed, however, varied widely. Typically, the bank was expected to keep open its undertaking for a given number of days after the closure and reopening, sometimes as long as six months. No provision was commonly made for alternative presentation or for a conclusion that the failure to reopen should be deemed to be a repudiation. As a result, the various provisions inserted in standbys often failed to provide an adequate and balanced system.

The circumstances in which this issue can arise include those where the sole place of presentation indicated in the standby is closed because of *force majeure*, but the place will reopen. It can also include circumstances in which the place is closed due to a business decision (i.e. to close a branch or agency) which has nothing to do with *force majeure*. In the latter case, the failure to maintain an office may constitute a repudiation of the undertaking. Where an institution's offices are closed, for example by government action (such as nationalization), the parties' position is not always clear. From the perspective of the beneficiary, can the closure be treated as a repudiation? From the issuer's and applicant's perspective, can it treat its obligation as fixed and not expect to have to perform its obligations years later should circumstances change and the branch reopen?

ISP Draft Rule 3.22 attempts to find a balanced approach to these issues.[29] The central thesis is that a closure on the last business day for presentation is not a risk to be borne by the beneficiary. As to the scope of the rule, two factors were taken into account: (1) its reach should not be confined to situations involving *force majeure* but extend to closure on a business day for any reason; (2) it should apply on the last business day for presentation regardless of whether that was the date of expiry or some other later date created by the internal provisions of the standby. In either event, the closure defeats the beneficiary's expectation that the presentation would comply if conforming documents were presented on the expiration date.

In order to seek a practical solution to these problems so far as possible, the rule permits the issuer effectively to amend the standby by designating an alternative mandatory place for presentation as long as the communication is received by the beneficiary and the alternative place is reasonable. The provision also provides an additional thirty days for presentation where the communication is received less than thirty days before the last day for presentation. This bifurcated approach permits banks to anticipate closing of branches and to provide for an orderly alternative without extending their credit exposure, and also protects the beneficiary where there is no advance notice or the alternative is not reasonable.

The rule also fixes liability by providing that the standby will be deemed to have been repudiated if the beneficiary is unable to make presentation at the authorized place despite its best efforts, thereby entitling it to seek legal relief and fixing the accrual date for the purpose of any statute of limitations or prescription period.

[29] "3.20 CLOSURE ON EXPIRY DATE

3.21 Closure on a Non-Business Day.

If the last day for presentation stated in the standby is not a business day where presentation is to be made, presentation made there on the first following business day shall be deemed timely. An issuer may rely on a nominated person's statement regarding timely presentation under this Rule.

3.22 Closure on a Business Day.

a. If on the last business day for presentation, the sole place for presentation stated in the standby is closed for any reason:

(i) presentation must be made at any reasonable place authorized by the issuer in a communication received by the presenter; and

(ii) if the communication is received fewer than thirty days before the last day for presentation, that day shall be automatically extended thirty days after the communication is received.

b. If presentation is not made at any authorized place despite the presenter's reasonable efforts, the standby shall be deemed to have been repudiated on the last day for presentation."

(ii) Transfer by Operation of Law (Rule 6.0)

Draft Rule 6.21 explains the scope of the provisions on transfer by operation by law. It provides that:

> "Where an heir, trustee, receiver, successor corporation, or similar person who claims to be designated by law to succeed to the interests of the beneficiary presents documents in its own name as if it were the authorized transferee from the beneficiary, these rules on transfer by operation of law apply."

Despite the strict scope of the undertaking involved in a standby, the situation where there is a successor to the named beneficiary is troubling. From the perspective of the beneficiary, this is a situation where an exception based on the parties' intention might be warranted. In all likelihood, had the parties anticipated the problem, they would have agreed that the successor was entitled to draw in its own name. Moreover, in many cases the non-conformity of the drawing is waived or overlooked. The cases which tend to be litigated are situations where the applicant has become insolvent and the issuer raises the defense in order to avoid its obligation. In such a situation, the defense appears to many to be a windfall. Indeed, some bankers themselves regard the assertion of the defense as departing from the notion that the undertaking is firm.

Having recognized the rationale for an exception to the rule of strict compliance, there remain several serious difficulties. The problem was addressed in the USA, in part, in the revision of UCC Article 5. Section 5–113(b) provides a novel solution. It states that:

> "A successor of a beneficiary may consent to amendments, sign and present documents, and receive payments or other items of value in its own name as the disclosed successor of the beneficiary. Except as otherwise provided in subsection (e), an issuer shall recognize a disclosed successor of a beneficiary as beneficiary in full substitution for its predecessor upon compliance with the requirements for recognition by the issuer of a transfer of drawing rights by operation of law under the standard practice referred to in Section 5–108(e) or, in the absence of such a practice, compliance with other reasonable procedures sufficient to protect the issuer."

By looking to standard practice, the provision permits banks to impose reasonable limitations in order to protect themselves and the applicant.[30] ISP Rule 6.22 outlines those provisions.[31] Where an issuer requests information

[30] On this issue, see generally J. Byrne, "Critical issues in the International and Domestic Harmonization of Letter of Credit Law & Practice" in del Duca (ed.), *Commercial Law Annual* 1995.

[31] ISP Rule 6.22 provides:

"*6.22 Conditions to Drawing in Successor's Name.*
A claimed successor may be treated as if it were an authorized transferee of the beneficiary's drawing rights in their entirety if it presents an additional document or documents which appear to be issued by a governmental entity or representative (including a judicial officer) and indicate:

cont./

intended to provide assurance of the succession, ISP Rule 6.23 suspends the issuer's obligation to examine a presentation until it receives that information in a satisfactory manner.[32] Whether the issuer chooses to exercise its right to request information lies within its discretion, and failure to do so cannot be asserted against it by the applicant as an excuse from its obligation to reimburse.

This provision balances the issuer's entitlement to reimbursement with the successor's continued entitlement under the standby in situations where the law would otherwise protect that right. Instead of relying on complex legal formulae to achieve this balance, however, the law looks to standard practice.

(iii) Cover Instructions (ISP Rule 5.08)

It is not uncommon for the beneficiary to submit a transmittal letter with a presentation, which contains various instructions related to payment under a standby. How such instructions should be treated is a matter of some debate. In the first place, such a document might be regarded as extraneous and disregarded. It may provide for truncation of notice or payment and instruct the issuer to communicate directly with a person other than the presenter. Under standard letter of credit practice, all communications are channeled through the same route as they are forwarded, through the presenter. ISP Draft Rule 5.08 permits the issuer to follow instructions that are not inconsistent with the express terms of the standby, but does not require it to do so.[33] This provision clarifies a situation commonly arising in standby practice and provides an acceptable "rule of traffic" to govern of the parties' interaction.

a. merger, consolidation, or similar action of a corporation, limited liability company, or other similar organization;

b. that the claimed successor is authorized or appointed to act on behalf of the named beneficiary or its estate because of an insolvency proceeding;

c. that the claimed successor is authorized or appointed to act on behalf of the named beneficiary because of death or incapacity; or

d. that the name of the named beneficiary has been changed to that of the claimed successor."

32 "*6.23 Suspension of Examination Upon Presentation by Successor.*
An issuer's obligation to examine a successor's presentation is suspended if it requests and until it receives, in a manner satisfactory as to form and substance:

a. a legal opinion;

b. an additional document referred to in Rule 6.22 from a governmental entity;

c. statements, covenants, and indemnities regarding the status of the claimed successor as successor by operation of law;

d. payment of fees reasonably related to these determinations; and

e. anything which may be required for a transfer under Rule 6.03 or an acknowledgement of assignment of proceeds under Rule 6.13.

Failure to request or receive any of the above shall not affect the applicant's obligation to reimburse."

33 "*5.08 Cover Instructions/Transmittal Letter.*

a. Instructions in or accompanying a demand made under a standby may be relied on to the extent that they are not inconsistent with the express terms of the standby, the demand, or these Rules.

b. Notwithstanding receipt of instructions, an issuer or nominated person may pay, give notice, return the documents, or otherwise treat with the presenter directly."

(iv) Applicant Approval (ISP Rule 4.10)

A disturbing trend in recent years has been the appearance of standbys containing provisions requiring a document or signature within the applicant's control. In effect, such a provision gives the applicant an effective veto over payment because the applicant can withhold the necessary signature or document. As a result, what may appear to have been an irrevocable undertaking becomes a revocable undertaking. It is generally agreed that this is sharp practice and should be discouraged. How to do so, however, is less clear.

One approach would be to deny effect to such provisions or to permit the beneficiary to produce the requisite document or signature. This is a radical approach and has met with considerable hesitation since it alters the terms and conditions of the undertaking. Perhaps an additional explanation for the hesitation is that the practice could easily take another form, which could not be policed, by requiring the signature or document from a third person not directly connected with the applicant but under its control.

Another approach which commanded some interest was the requirement that a standby containing such a provision be required to contain a conspicuous notice to the effect that the undertaking may not be irrevocable in practice. This approach draws on the methodology often used in consumer credit regulation in the USA.

The approach finally adopted in ISP Draft Rule 4.10 combines an attempt to discourage such a practice with a statement indicating that the issuer bears no responsibility if the applicant withholds the required signature or document.[34]

VI. CONCLUSION: OBSERVATIONS AND REFLECTIONS REGARDING NORMALIZATION BY RULES OF PRACTICE

These examples illustrate various aspects of the Draft ISP providing operational norms beyond traditional linguistic rules of custom or default rules. They simulate a legal scheme by providing a comprehensive system of regulation for the standby. This system is intended to, and does, displace traditional balancing methods utilized by the courts and the wider legal system with one based on mercantile practice and worked out according to the norms and principles which follow from that practice. It is didactic and far more flexible than formal rules, whether judicial or legislative. The goal is to order practice and to preserve the integrity of the undertaking.

[34] "*4.10 Applicant Approval.*
The standby should not specify that the applicant sign, counter-sign, or originate a required document. However, if the standby includes such a requirement, the issuer is not responsible for the applicant's withholding of the signature or document."

The key to deference to such rules is their soundness. Soundness must be measured not by their acceptability to trained commercial lawyers or to those with a preconceived bias in favor of one position or another or one method of balance or another. The test should be whether the rules are widely accepted and acceptable throughout the entire field and on whether they are based upon rational principles and consistent with those principles.

Where this result is achieved, the courts should defer to the rules. Further, in their interpretation and application, deference should be given to the principles upon which the rules are based. The Draft ISP seek to signal this approach by setting forth in some detail the principles on which the rules are based.[35] They also provide guidelines for their interpretation. Draft Rule 1.04 provides:

> "In the interpretation of these Rules, regard should be had for:
> a. the current practices and terminology of banks and businesses in day-to-day transactions;
> b. their role as mercantile rules and the needs for worldwide uniformity in their application;
> c. integrity of standbys as reliable and efficient undertakings to pay upon a drawing for default or other reasons; and
> d. uniformity of the worldwide system of banking and commerce."

In an environment where there is increasing pressure to standardize because of efficiencies imposed by computerized technology, it is important to recognize the link between rulemaking and standardization. The increasing standardization of commercial practice (and its inevitable effect on law) is unavoidable. The real question is how it will be driven—whether by technical considerations based on the computerized and processing system used or by the inherent characteristics of the given field, taking into account the nature and dynamics of that field. The ISP provide a living laboratory for examining the process of rulemaking and standardization in practice. The process has considerable significance beyond its own narrow scope and merits the serious attention of the commercial law community.

[35] Part 1.10 sets forth the general principles upon which the ISP is based. Rule 1.11 addresses the nature of standbys in the context of their irrevocability, independence, documentary and binding character, terms which it then explains in some detail. It also details the meaning and implications of the mercantile doctrine of strict performance and the limits which are generally understood to issuer responsibility.

7

International Demand Guarantees: The Interaction of the Uncitral Convention and the URDG Rules of the ICC

RAFAEL ILLESCAS-ORTIZ*

I. INTRODUCTION

On December 12 1995, in New York City, the 50th General Assembly of the United Nations adopted, and opened for signature and ratification, the UN Convention on Independent Guarantees and Stand-by Letters of Credit. The adoption of this new instrument was the final act of a long process in which, first, the UNCITRAL Secretariat and, next, the Working Group on International Contract Practices of the Commission, have spent almost eight years. The Commission's decision to examine the feasibility and desirability of a greater universal uniformity in respect of demand guarantees and standby letters of credit was taken at its 21st session in 1988. During this period, the Working Group held eleven meetings and there were lively discussions among the delegates and observers on several points raised by the process of unification of the substantive law applicable to demand guarantees.

Among the observers, the International Chamber of Commerce (ICC) showed a particular interest in the project. For many years, the ICC has become the most globally respected authority in regulating documentary credits and related undertaking. From 1988 to 1995, the ICC drafted two main texts relating to independent undertakings of a type contemplated by the UN Convention: the "ICC Uniform Rules for Demand Guarantees" (URDG) of April 1992 (ICC Publication 458) and the new version of the ICC, "Uniform Customs and Practice for Documentary Credits" of March, 10, 1993 (the UCP 500).

* Professor of Commercial Law and Dean, Faculty of Law, Universidad Carlos III de Madrid. Dean Illescas headed the Spanish delegation to the Working Group which drafted the UN Convention and the session of UNCITRAL at which the Convention was adopted.

The URDG is solely devoted to demand guarantees. Article 1 of UCP 500 states that the Rules ". . . shall apply to all Documentary Credits (including to the extent to which they may be applicable, Standby Letter(s) of Credit . . .". The double and different scope of application of both set of rules reveals that demand guarantees and standbys are undertakings that to the ICC reflect different documents and entities and, in another way, also reveals the lack of uniformity in the regulation of guarantees and standbys. Simultaneously, the historical lack of a basic similarity between the national laws concerning guaranties affected the growth of standbys in lieu of independent guarantees, and this was particularly true in North America.

The UN Convention attempts to address this lack of uniformity in the regulation, terms, regime and character of demand guarantees and standby letters of credit by establishing a set of new rules. The Convention does not intend to alter related national banking regulations in these fields.

UNCITRAL's work has its own unique character, which will initially be compared with the different ICC rules. At a very late stage of the UNCITRAL discussions, a firm decision was reached confirming the Working Group's assumption that the project would take the form of a convention. It is well known that the UCP rules previously referred to are frequently incorporated in the undertaking and that the URDG may also be used. If both the Convention and the ICC rules apply to the same undertaking, this may give rise to conflict. Such conflict would have substantive implications for the applicability—and desirability of the private use by the parties of the UN Convention. The application of the Convention to the parties' agreement depends on the ratification of the Convention by national Parliaments; the incorporation of the Rules in the undertaking depends solely on the parties.

Because of the separate nature of the Convention and the Rules, any conflict between them is not likely to be very serious. Furthermore, the opting-out and opting-in mechanism provided by Article 1 of the Convention gives considerable freedom to the parties to the undertaking to choose whether to submit their undertaking to one or other set of rules in specific cases. In addition, the URDG and UCP clearly and explicitly establish the manner in which the guarantee and standby fall under the jurisdiction of the respective ICC Rules.

There may be some conflict at a superficial level. But it is not easy to foresee substantive conflict in the same sense that the Hague Rules compete with the Hamburg Rules in the field of the carriage of goods by sea because the two are mutually exclusive systems. The reason why there are neither deep nor large differences between the Convention and the Rules is because of the way they both address the basic issues: form and content of the undertaking and the rights, obligations and defences of the parties to the guarantee or standby. These questions are treated along analogous or similar lines. Not only that but in many cases the Convention also totally respects the solutions reached under the Rules with respect to the specific issues addressed in the

Rules. This respect for private rulemaking is expressly stated in various articles of the Convention without, however, specifically mentioning the ICC Rules.

From these introductory considerations, there follows both the impossibility of a serious conflict between these instruments and the possibility of cooperation or interaction between them. From my own point of view, a significant number of explicit manifestations of the positive interactions exist between the UN Convention and the ICC Rules, mainly with the URDG but not exclusively so. Some thoughts about the signs of the positive relations are offered here.

II. THE "GENERALLY ACCEPTED INTERNATIONAL RULES AND USAGES" IN THE UN CONVENTION

In five different contexts the UN Convention makes reference to external sources of the dynamics of the undertaking embodied in a demand guarantee or a standby letter of credit. These situations are:

(1) The accurate determination of all the rights and obligations of the guarantor/issuer and the beneficiary of the undertaking. That determination, as stated by Article 13.(1) of the Convention, must be made by the "terms and conditions set forth in the undertaking, *including any rules, general conditions or usages specifically referred to therein, and by the provisions of this Convention*" [(emphasis added)].

(2) The correct interpretation of the terms and conditions of the undertaking and the settlement of questions not addressed by those terms and conditions must be done with regard to "*generally accepted international rules and usages of independent guarantee or standby letter of credit practice*": Article 13.(2) of the UN Convention [(emphasis added)].

(3) The standard of conduct of the guarantor/issuer in discharging its obligations under the undertaking are good faith and reasonable care. In order to fix the meaning of both standards—the good faith and the reasonable care—"*due regard shall be had to generally accepted standards of international practice of independent guarantees or standby letters of credit*": article 14.(1) of the Convention (emphasis added).

(4) When demand for payment is made by the beneficiary to the guarantor/issuer, Article 16.(1) of the Convention states that "the guarantor/issuer shall examine the demand and any accompanying documents in accordance *with the standard of conduct referred to in paragraph (1) of article 14*" (emphasis added).

(5) Examination of the document mentioned above obligates the guarantor/issuer to honour the promise of payment contained in the

> undertaking if the guarantor/issuer concludes that the beneficiary's demand is a proper demand. As article 16.(1) of the UN Convention requires, in determining whether documents are in facial conformity with the terms and conditions of the undertaking and are consistent with one another,—upon which is based the conformity of the demand of payment—the guarantor/issuer shall have due regard to *the applicable international standard of independent guarantee or standby letter of credit practice*" (emphasis added).

In these five situations the Convention makes express and successive mention, with inconsistent terminology, to "rules, general conditions or usages" [article 13(1)], "generally accepted international rules and usages of independent guarantee or standby letter of credit" [article 13(2)], "generally accepted standards of international practice of independent guarantee or standby letter of credit" [articles 14(1) and 16(1) *ab initio*], and "applicable international standard of independent guarantee or standby letter of credit" [article 16(1) *in fine*].

Obviously, in any of the five cases, the meaning of the words used by the Convention and the references made to the external sources are different. The external source for determining the rights and obligations of the parties in the undertaking—called in this context "rules, general conditions or usages"—must be specifically mentioned in the undertaking. If there is no such reference in the undertaking the outsourcing law will not be applicable in the very large majority of jurisdictions in which the ICC Rules are considered contractual terms and not commercial usages.

On the other hand, in the interpretation of the undertaking, the "generally accepted international rules and usages" will operate independently of their incorporation in the provisions of the undertaking. Also independently of its provisions, the "generally accepted standards of international practice",—whether mentioned or not in the undertaking, will illuminate the good faith conduct of the guarantor/issuer and will have to be applied to determine what amounts to reasonable care in the fulfilment of its obligations, specially the obligation to examine the demand for payment and accompanying documents. To decide about the conformity and consistency of the demand and documents (always independently of the contractual provisions), the guarantor/issuer must have due regard not to "generally accepted standards of international practice" but, in a specific way, to the "applicable international standard of independent guarantee or standby letter of credit".

The five allusions made by the Convention to the international rules, usages and standards certainly includes the formalised works of the ICC on demand guarantees and documentary credits. At present, no other rules exist except the URDG and UCP,—although other sources (such as the International Standby Practices or ISP currently being formulated) may emerge. When they do, they will be included in the panoply of concrete references to international rules and standards. Under that formula, the ICC Rules and the criteria for their interpretation, must or could apply to the undertakings issued in accordance with the UN Convention. Only in the first out of the five cited situations, does the applicability of the ICC rules to the Convention's undertakings depend on their express incorporation in the undertaking or instrument. In fact, the undertaking must refer to the ICC Rules to make them applicable to the parties' rights and obligations. Without such a reference, they cannot affect the parties' rights and obligations. In the other four situations, the international rules and standards apply without the need for an express reference in the undertaking.

No greater deference to private rules of practice can be found in any other formulation uniform international trade law than that which exists in the UN Convention.

III. THE MOMENT AND PLACE OF ISSUANCE OF THE UNDERTAKING: ARTICLE 7(1) OF THE CONVENTION

The reader will not find in the URDG articles any chronological indication about the moment of issuance of the demand guarantees by the issuer bank. The rules are silent on this matter. This gives rise to problems due to the fact that, from the moment of issuance of the guarantee, the beneficiary can demand payment from the guarantor. Payment depends on a proper demand and the demand can only be made if the guarantee exists. The existence of the guarantee and the right of payment by the beneficiary are circumstances definitively linked to the substantive construction of the instrument governed by the ICC Rules but the liaison between guarantee and demand is not clearly established. However, Articles 3.9 and 16 of the URDG suggest this sequence of events. First, the guarantee must stipulate "the terms for demanding payment"; next, "a guarantor is only liable to the beneficiary in accordance with the terms specified in the guarantee". Both rules are evidence of the irrelevance of the relationship between the principal and the guarantor with respect to the rights of the beneficiary. The beneficiary's rights are only based on the guarantee itself.

In this context, the issuance of the guarantee marks the beginning of the guarantor's exposure to a demand for payment. The moment of issuance is the time when the guarantor's liability becomes operative; it cannot be drawn upon by the beneficiary before then. This relevant chronological point is absent from the URDG. None of its articles defines the exact moment of issuance.

A similar lacuna is found regarding the place or location of the issuance of the guarantee. No provision in the ICC Rules requires mention of the place of issuance in the text of the guarantee. No substitute means of determining that place can be found in the Rules. This silence creates several problems related mainly, but not exclusively, to the international character of the guarantee and, perhaps, the applicable law and its determination. No questions about jurisdiction should arise in the URDG. They are addressed specifically in Article 28. In a most accurate way, article 7(1) of the UN Convention states the referred relevant moment and place quite precisely: "Issuance of an undertaking occurs when and where the undertaking leaves the sphere of control of the guarantor/issuer concerned".

This rule fills the gap in URDG and, in so doing, uses a conceptual resource familiar in uniform international trade law. Recent use of the notion of control is also made in article 15 ("Time and place of dispatch and receipt of data messages") in the still new UNCITRAL Model Law on Electronic Commerce of June, 1996. This applies the test of the message leaving the "sphere of control" of the person contractually obliged to the issuance or expedition of documents, goods or messages. The "leaving", as an actual and material activity, has one place and one moment. After it has left, the issuer can no longer recover the document or whatever because it is no longer under this control. Rather, after its departure, the document is controlled by another unrelated person—the beneficiary in our case.

I do not need to emphasize the advantage which these provisions of the UN Convention confer in determining the moment and place of issuance of the guarantee. This is particularly true if we compare Article 7(1) of the Convention with Article 6 of the URDG. The URDG introduces the concept of the "entrance into effect" of the guarantee which, by reason of the discretion which that concept implies in favour of the guarantor/issuer, must be rejected and replaced by the "issuance" concept of the UN Convention. The leaving the sphere of control test of the guarantor is a objective fact; the "entrance into effect" notion is a subjective one.

IV. AMENDMENT OF THE DEMAND GUARANTEE AND ARTICLE 8 OF THE UN CONVENTION

The URDG refers to amendment of the guarantee in several places: at the end of Article 1, which deals with the scope of application of the Rules, and here the Rules are explicit about amendment of the guarantee and its consequences, mainly on the rights and obligations of the guarantor/issuer and beneficiary; in Article 3 on stipulations of the guarantee; in Article 4 on the beneficiary right to assign the demand for payment; in Article 16 on liability of the guarantor; and in Article 23 dealing with cancellation of the guarantee. These are some of the provisions containing specific mention of amendment of the guarantee.

Problems regarding amendments arise if we consider that they modify the contract to issue a guarantee between the guarantor and its principal. The latter is the person engaged in an underlying transaction with the beneficiary and with the guarantor in the guarantee contract. However, the beneficiary remains quite separate from the guarantor before the issuance of the guarantee in the sense of Article 7(1) of the UN Convention. The beneficiary is a third party to the contract between the principal and guarantor until the moment when the guarantee is issued and, consequently, delivered to the beneficiary. As previously noted, immediately after receipt of the guarantee by the beneficiary, the guarantor has the right to demand payment in accordance with the terms specified in the guarantee. This means that any amendment of the guarantee by agreement between the guarantor/issuer and the principal is enough to alter beneficiary's rights. Under these circumstances, it seems opportune to put the question about the fairness of such a modification without the need for previous authorization of the beneficiary.

The URDG contains no provision on the procedure for amendment of the guarantee and the need to obtain the beneficiary's approval. It is therefore possible to conclude that, unless otherwise stipulated in the guarantee, a later amendment can be adopted by the principal and the guarantor/issuer without the beneficiary's approval: for example, with regard to the maximum amount payable, the currency in which it is payable, the expiry date or the expiry event of the guarantee, and the terms for demanding payment are the main points exposed to amendment without beneficiary's consent. Only in a very narrow sense, can Article 8 of the URDG be identified as a provision related to the procedure for amendment of the guarantee. The amendment referred to there certainly does not need the beneficiary's approval but, at least, the beneficiary's previous knowledge is necessary about the amounts and dates involved because of the express provisions in the original guarantee.

Contrary to the ICC amendment system, Article 8 of the UN Convention contains a complete set of rules governing amendment of the guarantee and reinforces the rights of the beneficiary in relation to that modification. As a result, no amendment will be given effect to without the previous approval of the beneficiary. Article 8(3) of the Convention is clear and precise and respects the intention of all the parties involved—the parties to the underlying transaction and the parties to the guarantee agreement. Article 8(3) states that, "Unless otherwise stipulated in the undertaking or elsewhere agreed by the guarantor/issuer and the beneficiary, where any amendment has not previously been authorized by the beneficiary, the undertaking is amended only when the guarantor/issuer receives notice of acceptance of the amendment by the beneficiary in a form referred to in paragraph (2) of Article 7". Also, paragraph 8(2) ends with the rule that, " . . . an undertaking is amended upon issuance of the amendment if the amendment has previously been authorized by the beneficiary".

Article 8(4) not only affirms the principle of defense of the beneficiary's position but also sets forth the provisions on form and other requirements for the modification of the guarantee and on the effects of such modification on the rights of the principal and other persons involved in the contract. In my opinion, the UN Convention's treatment of amendment of the guarantee has the merit of dealing with a frequent issue in guarantee and standby practice more completely and satisfactorily than is true of the URDG.

V. THE *EXCEPTIO DOLI* AND THE EXCEPTION TO THE PAYMENT OBLIGATION OF THE GUARANTOR

Article 19 is the UN Convention's paramount contribution to the law of demand guarantees and standby letters of credit. Nothing similar to it can be found either in the URDG Rules in UCP 500. The juridical and material importance of the set of norms introduced by Article 19 seems to me of great relevance. The article, first, develops the general principle of observance of good faith in the international practice of demand guarantees as stated in Article 5 of the Convention and Articles 11 and 15 of the ICC Rules but with a narrower scope. The article, second, confers on the guarantor the power of a guarantor/issuer—a combination of both is set forth in the Article 19(1) *in fine*—"a right" to withhold payment if it is manifestly clear that the demand for payment is improper. The article indirectly raises the question of the guarantor's *duty* to withhold payment; the answer probably can be found under the applicable national law. Article 19, thirdly, gives appropriate significance to the classical, and always controversial, *exceptio doli* defence to be used by the guarantor not to honour the guarantee. In describing the circumstances in which payment can be withheld, the Convention establishes a higher degree of certainty regarding extension of the *exceptio* defence and the guarantor/issuer's option to withhold payment than can be found under existing national practice.

It is only possible to touch upon the surface of the implications of Article 19 of the UN Convention. But these reflections are an absolute necessity. The new article, as a specific manifestation of the principle of good faith, gives the guarantor/issuer the right to refuse payment. This implies for them a more discretionary type of conduct. Payment, in demand guarantees or standbys, is always an easy and desirable discharge of the liability of the guarantor/issuer. Payment also manifests the guarantor's honouring of its obligation and does not present any additional problem for the guarantor. This is because the equivalent of the payable amount, in fact and through different ways (a deposit, by example), remains at the issuer's disposal from the moment of issuance of the undertaking or even before. In those circumstances, payment is always the most convenient and reputable solution for the guarantor/issuer. The new rule introduces a slight degree of flexibility in this panorama. After the introduction of Article 19 of the UN Convention, guarantors may decide on their own responsibility whether or not an *exceptio doli* defence alleged to exist by the principal can be taken into account. They may therefore exercise their "right to withhold payment" against the beneficiary who introduces an improper and abusive demand.

This rule, with its high level of attribution of freedom and responsibility, can also be inconvenient. The norm interrupts a quiet landscape in which payment on facial conformity of the demand with the guarantor is the general rule and non-payment is the exception. Now, after the Convention, this norm may be altered under the exigencies of the dictates of good faith in international trade; and every alteration of customs is always a hard one.

In contrast, the UN Convention contains a very comprehensive formulation of the rule governing the form of the undertaking by taking into account all the present and future conceivable electronic technologies. Compare in this context, Article 7(2) with the very much limited scope of Article 3.d of the ICC Rules. Also, for the first time in the history of this kind of instrument in international trade law, the Convention contains Article 20 with its provision for a provisional court order requiring withholding of payment by the guarantor at the principal's request. This constitutes an advance on the previous regimes that lacked any provisions for judicial assistance. At the same time, Article 19 may represent an additional difficulty for the ratification of the Convention by many legislatures. Rules of procedure are always perceived as sensitive questions for sovereignty. International instruments which include rules on these kind of matters usually create obstacles for national ratifications.

In any case, the interaction of the URDG and the 1995 UN Convention provides much intellectual challenge for commercial lawyers. It is my hope that the interaction will become a practical and effective tool in the coming years.

8

Guarantees on First Demand: The Chilean Position

RICARDO SANDOVAL LOPEZ*

I. INTRODUCTION

As business relations intensify and transcend the boundaries of States, there is a growing need to establish new structures or mechanisms for their formalisation and perfection. This also applies to security interests and personal guarantees intended to ensure the performance of obligations assumed by debtors to their creditors.

The type of security of security interest and personal guarantees contemplated in general law, such as the mortgage, possessory pledge, pledge where possession is retained by the debtor, and personal guarantees such as joint and several liability, common bonds and joint and several liability bonds, do not meet the needs of efficiency and speed required by business relations for mass transactions. Business law has sought to create guarantees that are simpler and more effective, such as joint and several liabilities and negotiable obligations and the special guarantee or accommodation endorsement (*aval*). These guarantees are effective in negotiable instrument areas where they are well established. They are not useful to secure other types of obligations which are not of the negotiable instrument type such as those arising from the issue of credit instruments.

Chilean law recognises the following types of special pledges (security interests):

(1) pledge of securities in favour of banks, regulated by Law 4.287 of 1928;
(2) pledge of chattels sold on credit, created by Law 4.702 of 1929;
(3) industrial pledge, created by Law 5.687 of 1935; and
(4) pledge of every type of chattel, created by Law 18.112 of 1982.

All these security interests are widely used in Chilean commercial practice because of their common feature that the pledged goods remain in the hands of the pledgor. This represents a considerable economic advantage for the

* Professor of Commercial Law, University of Concepcion, Chile.

pledgor, since he can continue using them in his business or industry, which is why they are known as non-possessory security interests.

However, these types of security interests are only available for particular types of transaction and require the execution of prescribed formalities in the form of either a public instrument (*escritura publica*) or a private instrument attested by a competent notary, and must be registered in summary form in a special pledge register. In addition, these non-possessory security interests are only available for goods or groups of goods which are specified in the laws that regulate them, with the exception of the pledge instituted by Law 18.112 of 1982. This latter type of security interest is perfected by means of a simple public instrument, an extract from which is published in the *Diario Oficial*, and applies to any type of chattel.

Because of this, the special business pledges do not satisfy today's business environment, which requires easily enforceable guarantees independent of the main transaction. Nevertheless, the guarantee on first demand is not systematically dealt with in Chilean private law, although in practice there exists a bank draft guarantee deposit that may be considered a type of guarantee of first demand.

II. THE BANK DRAFT GUARANTEE

(a) General Observations

The first demand guarantee involves a complex bank operation formed by several juridical acts or contracts individually determined, but connected by the common guarantee purpose pursued by them. It is common for banks to issue guarantee drafts to secure obligations that a person contracts on behalf of the third party and the performance of which is guaranteed by the bank by means of the payment of a draft when the drawer does not fulfil its obligations. Bank draft guarantees are generally issued to guarantee the fulfilment of obligations "to do", as in the case of large material works. There are two alternative forms for the creation of this guarantee. The first consists of the drawer making a cash deposit so that the bank can issue the guarantee draft. To have the draft issued in favour of the beneficiary, the drawer makes a stipulation in the third party's favour. In the second alternative, where the drawer lacks the money to make the deposit, the bank makes him a loan to enable him to make it, and after that the draft guarantee is issued. In the latter case, the drawer signs a sight promissory note in favour of the bank for the amount of the loan.

The second alternative, which represents the general practice, does not necessarily imply the disbursement of the value for which the draft is issued if, as is usually the case, the obligations between the drawer and the beneficiary are guaranteed by the draft are fulfilled. In that case, the drawer pays the bank only a commission for carrying out the operation.

(b) Applicable Legislation

In Chilean business law the bank draft guarantee is not systematically regulated. Decree 252 of 4 April 1960, which contains the General Law of Banks, mentions only the bank draft guarantee among the operations commercial banks may conduct with their clients (Article 83, N° 10). Nowhere does the legal text provide specific rules to regulate the bank draft guarantee or the juridical effects with respect to the persons that participate in it. To protect the bank's position and achieve greater legal and economic efficiency, the General Law on Banks prescribes that the deposit and the draft itself cannot be seized in execution by third parties foreign to the contract or the obligations secured by the guarantee (Article 83, N° 10). Exceptionally the drawer can attach the deposit when the payee has not accepted the stipulation made on his behalf. The deposit may be seized by the parties to the obligation secured by means of the guarantee draft and also when the beneficiary issues a draft secured by the earlier guarantee in favour of a third person to secure another obligation.

(c) Descriptive Analysis of the Operation

There are three parties in the operation:

(1) the drawer, who makes the deposit with the bank in the name of a third party to whom he has an obligation that is guaranteed by the draft;
(2) the beneficiary, who is the third party in whose name the deposit in made and in whose favour the draft is drawn by means of a stipulation made by the drawer; and
(3) the bank, which receives the deposit from the drawer or that grants him credit to enable the guarantee document to be issued.

(d) The Effects of the Bank Draft Guarantee

Given that the bank draft guarantee may be issued in two different forms, the juridical effects are also different. It is necessary to distinguish the situation in which the drawer actually deposits money in the bank in order to obtain the bank draft guarantee, from the second alternative in which the bank grants credit to the drawer for the issue of the guarantee. The first case gives rise to the normal consequences of a deposit contract to which are added those of a stipulation in favour of a third party to achieve the objectives of the guarantee with respect to the draft beneficiary. The second case not only honours the juridical consequences of the deposit itself and the stipulation in favour of a third party, but also the rights and obligations derived from the loan contract. Let us look at both situations separately.

(e) Effects Derived from the Deposit

Since there exists a juridical relationship equivalent to a deposit between the bank and the beneficiary of the guarantee, the bank must return to the depositor an amount equivalent to that deposit. In addition, the bank draft guarantee may be classified juridically as a money credit operation, since there exists on the one hand the delivery of money and on the other the obligation to return it at a time different from the time when the contract was performed. According to Law 18.010, the parties may agree on a modification of the amount deposited or loaned because of the effects of inflation. They may also amend the interest rate payable as provided by the Law. Generally speaking, the customer (drawer) must give thirty days' advance notice of the withdrawal of the deposit.

The bank receives a fee for the service rendered by this operation. The bank charges a commission which is paid by the drawer before the draft is issued. The deposit is paid to the beneficiary when the beneficiary has performed the terms of the draft, and is paid to the drawer when the beneficiary has not accepted the terms of the draft.

(f) Effects Derived from the Mutuum

When the client has not deposited money for the issue of the draft, the bank grants him a credit for the amount of the draft. In this case, the drawer must repay the loan and pay the agreed interest. As already mentioned, at the time of the issue of the draft the bank requires the customer to sign a promissory note to the order of the bank. This note is payable at sight so that the bank may collect it at any time, thus covering the amount of the draft it must pay to the beneficiary. The bank may collect on the note when the draft has been honoured or where the customer has been declared bankrupt or is notoriously insolvent. The draft will be collected when the drawer does not fulfil his guarantee to the beneficiary. In practice, it is not common for the bank to pay the draft and collect on the promissory note, because in most cases the drawer fulfils his obligations and the draft is returned by the beneficiary to the drawer. In this case, the drawer returns the draft to the bank and his obligation to pay the *mutuum* is compensated for by the bank's obligation to return the amount deposited. In any case, the drawer must pay the bank interest during the period that the draft guarantees the customer's obligations towards the beneficiary.

(g) Effects of the Draft Between the Drawer and the Beneficiary

Chilean doctrine is not agreed on this question. Some authors believe that the juridical effects produced by the operation between the drawer and the beneficiary are regulated by the contract of pledge, since the guarantee draft represents a pledge of money or pledge of the credit instrument. In contrast, other authors argue that the effects of this operation cannot be regulated by the pledge contract because the drawer and the beneficiary of the draft guarantee have not met the requirements of the pledge contract. This is because there is no delivery of the thing for the perfection of the contract and, in the case of the guarantee mechanism, there is no delivery. In addition, it is argued that to maintain that there is a pledge contract implies a fiction in which there is a hidden act and a real one, but this simulation does not occur in the case of the bank draft guarantee.

Nevertheless, it is pointed out that there is such a simulation with all its juridical consequences, although the parties use this transaction to fulfil a different economic purpose. Thus, the beneficiary may collect at will the amount deposited because of his capacity as a depository. The drawer, when he makes the deposit in the name of the beneficiary for guarantee purposes makes a stipulation in favour of the beneficiary that transforms the beneficiary into a depositor if he accepts the terms of the deposit. Since a fiduciary business presupposes confidence between the parties, what happens if the beneficiary abuses his position and collects the draft without having performed? The answer is that the drawer will then have the right to demand indemnity for damages suffered because the beneficiary has infringed the obligations arising from the fiduciary relationship constituted by the draft guarantee.

In my opinion, the relations between the drawer and the beneficiary are regulated by the pledge contract and there is no simulation at all. The pledge is perfected by the delivery of the document (the draft) drawn in favour of the beneficiary and he receives it exactly as the guarantee of an obligation existing between the parties. The draft is a pledge; the drawer cannot oppose its payment to the beneficiary even if he argues that the beneficiary has not fulfilled his obligations. The bank is not concerned with these defences and they must be resolved between the drawer and the beneficiary. As a consequence, the bank must honour the draft, after giving legal notice of its intention to do so. If it were otherwise, the beneficiary's right to payment under the guarantee would be illusory. On the other hand, by making the deposit and the draft non-attachable by third parties who are foreign to the contract guaranteed by the draft, the law protects the preferred rights of the beneficiary. When the drawer has fulfilled the obligations guaranteed by the draft, he has the right to demand the return of the document and thereupon the pledge is extinguished for the beneficiary's benefit.

(h) Juridical Nature of the Bank Draft Guarantee

It is important to determine the legal nature of the bank's guarantee, because this also affects the applicability of other legal rules. One trend in Chilean doctrine considers the bank draft guarantee to be a fiduciary transaction and, if this is correct, it will also enable us to understand the relationship between the drawer and the beneficiary. In the opinion of other commentators, however, the draft constitutes a unilateral, abstract and unconditional promise by the bank to pay a certain sum to the beneficiary. As between the drawer and the beneficiary, the draft is a guarantee that consists of the pledge of an instrument—the drawer delivers to the beneficiary. This interpretation has been criticised because it does not reflect the reality of the transaction or its origin. I support the prevailing view according to which the bank, the drawer and the beneficiary are bound by an irregular deposit contract and a stipulation in favour of third parties. These contracts are merged by the guarantee purpose of the draft. It signals that we are in the presence of an atypical operation which generates some of the effects of an irregular deposit or *mutuum*, depending on whether the client (drawer) deposits the money or whether the bank grants him a credit for the amount of the draft. On this basis, the relationship between the drawer and the beneficiary can be explained juridically by the contract of pledge.

(i) Formalities of the Bank Draft Guarantee

The formalities differ depending on whether the bank grants the drawer credit for the amount of the draft or whether the drawer deposits money corresponding to the amount of the guarantee. In the first case, as previously noted, the bank grants the loan against a promissory note signed by the drawer in favour of the bank and payable at sight. The bank then issues the draft guarantee in favour of the beneficiary. In the second case, the deposit is made by the issue of a guarantee draft by the bank. The client must also complete an undertaking to make the cash deposit. Juridically, the bank draft guarantee is not a credit instrument; it is simply a voucher or receipt for the deposit, which constitutes proof that the deposit has been made.

The bank draft bears the name and signature of the depository bank, the fact of the deposit having been received for the benefit of the designated person (the beneficiary), the name of the drawer, the obligation guaranteed by the document for the deposited amount, the date after which the bank must return the deposit if unused and the date and place of issuance of the guarantee.

(j) Termination of the Transaction

The termination of the operation depends on the several acts that constitute the transaction. Thus, where there has been a deposit to support the draft, the deposit ends when the beneficiary cashes the draft. On the other hand, when the bank has granted a *mutuum* to its client (the drawer) in order to issue the draft, the fact that the draft is cashed by the beneficiary does not imply that the loan is extinguished; rather, the loan continues as long as it remains unpaid unless it is extinguished by some other legal means. As previously indicated, when the bank grants a loan to its customer to enable the customer to perform its obligation to the beneficiary, the bank requires the signing of a promissory note payable at sight. The bank may decide, in view of the diminishing solvency of the drawer and the possibility of the beneficiary deciding to cash the draft, to collect on the promissory note in advance. In this case, the *mutuum* is extinguished although the guaranteed deposit continues to survive.

In any case, we must bear in mind that the purpose of the transaction being discussed is to guarantee the drawer's obligation arising out of a contract made with the beneficiary. Ordinarily this means that if the contract is performed, the draft will be returned by the beneficiary to the drawer, and by him to the bank, which normally brings the operation to an end. The delivery of the draft to the bank by the drawer extinguishes the deposit, so that the bank must repay the amount deposited. Where there exists a *mutuum*, the return of the draft extinguishes the drawer's obligation to pay the *mutuum* and obliges the bank to return the deposit.

(k) Prescription of Legal Action

The bank's action against the drawer, who has signed the promissory note payable at sight, is considered an act of commerce (Article 3, N° 10 of the Commercial Code) for which there is a one year's prescription after the note's maturity. Since this is a promissory note payable at sight or on presentation, the prescriptive term begins to run from the date of protest for non-payment of the note.

III. THE BANK DRAFT AS A GUARANTEE ON FIRST DEMAND

(a) The Bank Draft and the Conditional Letter of Credit

"Conditional letter of credit" is the Spanish equivalent (*cartas de credico contingente*) for stand-by letter of credit. The Spanish term is new and has the virtue of revealing the sense of the English expression. It refers to a letter of credit issued to meet a particular contingency, which may consist of breach of an underlying obligation by a debtor at whose request the stand-by is being issued. Stand-by letters of credit may be issued to secure the beneficiary against such a breach or even the risk of its happening. The expression "stand-by" means to be ready, to be prepared for the happening of a contingency, so it is indicative of the function fulfilled by this document.

The characterisation of the stand-by letter of credit as a "contingent letter of credit" is unfortunate, since "contingent" implies an event that may or may not occur, and in that sense it is evident that the letter of credit depends on the contingency of other events and does not impose an absolute obligation.

Likewise, it is necessary to establish the difference between commercial letters of credit (*carta de credito commercial*) and stand-by letters of credit, because the first is a formal payment mechanism and the second is a guarantee device. I will return to the different types of commercial letters of credit later on.

(b) Certificates of Deposit and Guarantees at Sight

Autonomous or independent guarantees are those in which the guarantor's obligations are not conditional on the non-fulfilment, duly proved, of the principal obligation. As issuer of the guarantee, the bank or insurance company does not have to decide whether the principal obligor (i.e. its client) has or has not fulfilled the obligations assumed by him in the underlying transaction. Likewise, the issuer of the guarantee does not have to play the role of a judge or arbitrator to determine whether a breach of the principal obligation has occurred, because this is what makes the guarantee autonomous. Contrary to what occurs in an accessory guarantee, the beneficiary of an independent guarantee does not need to prove the non-fulfilment of the main debtor's obligations; he has only to present the demand according to the terms stated in the letter of guarantee.

The independence or autonomy of the letter of guarantee from the underlying transaction, which may be of the most varied nature, reflects itself in a system that does not admit the opposability of exceptions external to the guarantee itself, that is exceptions derived from the underlying contract between the principal and the beneficiary. In other cases, it may derive from the relationship between the obligor and the issuer of the letter of guarantee. There may be an exception to this rule based on *exceptio doli*, but there is much doubt about its operation in concrete cases. To reiterate, when one speaks of independent guarantees, one expects the guarantor's obligations not to be affected or impaired by the vicissitudes of the obligor–guarantor relationship. The letter of guarantee generates its own obligation, the scope of which is determined by the terms of the guarantee and is autonomous with respect to the main debtor's obligations to the beneficiary.

At this point, it becomes necessary to say something about the relationship between an independent guarantee and the inclusion in it of a clause of payment "on first demand" or "on first request". It is pertinent to observe that, although in practice the guarantee on first demand is usually an independent guarantee, from a theoretical point of view it is possible to distinguish these two concepts. Thus the phrase "on first request" is essentially a procedural device since it is governed by the principle of *solve et repete*. This means that the guarantor must pay the promised amount when the creditor demands payment in conformity with the terms of the guarantee, and litigate afterwards if there is a dispute about the beneficiary's entitlement to payment. There is therefore a sort of role inversion, in that the beneficiary does not have to prove the non-fulfilment of the main debtor's obligations. Rather, the burden falls on the debtor to show that the beneficiary was not entitled to receive the payment.

The same autonomy does not exist in the case of the guarantee on first demand. Here, the guarantor, once the demand is satisfied, may claim back from the beneficiary the amount improperly collected by the beneficiary (if that was the case), but basing its claim on the underlying contract. As a consequence, the guarantee "at sight" or "at first demand" has an accessory character and is suspended, in the sense that it only comes into effect after the guarantee has been honoured. In other words, the guarantor waives the right to rely on the underlying relationship to resist payment on the guarantee but reserves the right to invoke the underlying contract to recover the payment if it can be shown that the main debtor had not breached his obligations or that the contract was void or otherwise unenforceable.

In the case of the independent guarantee, the rule "pay first, litigate afterwards" acquires substantial value because, with the possible exception of fraud cases, only the drawer and not the guarantor can recover payment made to the beneficiary, and only the drawer can invoke the underlying contact *vis-à-vis* the beneficiary that binds them together. To allow the guarantor to recover payment based on the underlying contract would contradict the guarantor's implicit promise in the guarantee not to rely on the terms of that contract. On the other hand, where there is an accessory contract with a payment clause on demand, the guarantor can bring an action of recovery against the creditor because the beneficiary has received an improper payment which affects the guarantee relationship because of its accessory character.

Normally, the inclusion of a payment term "on first demand" in a guarantee is considered to be an indication of its independent character, but it is not conclusive. The letter of guarantee has to be interpreted in the light of all of its terms.

The Uniform Rules on Guarantees of the International Chamber of Commerce (hereafter "Uniform Rules" or "ICC Rules") apply only to documentary guarantees, that is guarantees payable upon the presentation of one or more documents. This documentary feature reinforces the independent or autonomous character of the guarantee *vis-à-vis* the underlying relationship. The guarantor never has to concern himself with extrinsic facts; he deals only with documents. The guarantor's obligation is to ensure that the documents which are presented to him correspond with the terms of the guarantee, but he does not have to concern himself with whether the beneficiary's actually fulfils the terms of the underlying contract. The guarantor's obligations cannot be qualified by conditions that are not included in the document.

Thus, the guarantees governed by the ICC Rules are independent guarantees payable on demand, and therefore these also apply to them the rule "pay first and then litigate". They do not necessarily have to be guarantees on "simple demand", by which is meant that the only condition necessary to trigger the payment obligation by the guarantor is the presentation of a written claim by the beneficiary. As explained in the introduction to the ICC Rules, the documents required to invoke payment under the guarantee may vary from a "simple written demand" to a judicial arbitral decision about the non-fulfilment of the guaranteed contract. There may also be intermediate situations, such as those which require the beneficiary to present certificates or written statements from third parties (such as engineers, acknowledged experts and governmental authorities) attesting to the fact that the conditions required by the underlying contract have been fulfilled. The ICC Rules state that, unless otherwise provided in the guarantees, besides any other document specified to the letter of guarantee the payment demand must be accompanied by a written statement of the beneficiary claiming that the principal debtor has not fulfilled the obligation assumed by him in the underlying relationship and the nature and kind of the breach.

PART III

Secured Transactions in Movable Property

9

Modernizing the Secured Financing and Lease Financing Laws of Developing Nations, with Particular Focus on the West Bank and Gaza

R.C.C. CUMING*

I. INTRODUCTION

An unprecedented level of activity directed toward the reform of secured financing and lease financing law of developing nations has occurred in recent years. There is little indication that this will abate in the immediate future. The driving force behind the activity is rarely indigenous; much of it is the product efforts of organizations such as the World Bank, the European Bank for Reconstruction and Development, the National Law Center for Inter-American Free Trade and the IRIS Center at the University of Maryland. Countries and political units which are the intended recipients of the benefits of this reform activity are located principally in Eastern Europe, the Middle East and Latin America. The primary focus of this activity is the development of legal structures within which private sector financing of business activity can expand. These structures would embody approaches to secured financing and leasing that have been used with considerable success in North American and some Western European states.

II. THE CASE FOR REFORM

Economic development in many areas of the world is being unnecessarily hampered by inadequate legal structures for secured financing of businesses and agriculture. Banks supply most of the commercial loans to the private sec-

* Professor of Law, University of Saskatchewan, Saskatoon, Canada.

tor in these countries. For the most part, the banks accept only real estate as collateral for their loans or personal guarantees of persons who own real estate. They do not accept, or only rarely accept, inventory, accounts receivable, livestock or industrial equipment as collateral. These policies make it difficult for anyone without real estate to finance the purchase of equipment, inventory or livestock. They limit access to credit by businesses in rented quarters and by farmers who work rented land or have unclear title. They restrict profitable and socially useful lending by banks as well as credit sales by producers, importers and merchants. They lead to unnecessarily high interest rates and low volumes of lending and investment. The problem is generally not one of excessively conservative lending policies of the banks, lack of interest in making credit available or unduly restrictive banking regulations. The source of the problem is often the secured financing law of the country. The lack of an efficient legal system facilitating secured financing negatively affects the development of the economy of a country.

If a business is to expand, its sales must increase. The higher the volume of business the greater the need for larger inventories. The increased volume of inventory must be financed in one of two ways. The merchant can allocate profits to the purchase of the new inventory. However, the ability to do this will be very seriously limited if the profit margin on the sale of existing inventory is small or the income from the sale of it is needed by the merchant to pay operating and living costs. The alternative method of financing the inventory is through borrowing. If the merchant can obtain borrowed money to acquire more inventory, the ability to increase profits is greatly enhanced. Increased sales may produce sufficient income to repay the inventory loan and provide additional income.

Farm income can be enhanced in the same way. Expanding farm income often involves increasing yields per acre by using more machinery or livestock on a given amount of land. Again, if this expansion is facilitated by the availability of credit, it will occur at a much more rapid rate than if it must be financed out of accumulated savings.

Construction contractors (of buildings, roads and other infrastructure) require equipment. The ability of a contractor to bid on larger and more profitable projects will depend on the contractor having access to the types of equipment that are required in the projects. Without the equipment, the contractor is limited to bidding on projects for which there are many bidders and, consequently, low profit margins. If financing facilities are available to the contractor, the necessary equipment can be obtained and the higher earnings realized.

Most modern manufacturing involves the use of sophisticated manufacturing equipment. Like the contractor, the manufacturer will generally require financing facilities if profitable, large-scale production is to occur. The success of many nascent export industries depend upon acquiring modern manufacturing equipment.

However, in order for loan capital to be available, lenders (including banks, insurance companies, equipment lessors and other credit grantors) must be convinced that the loans they make will be repaid. This involves giving to lenders the ability to take and enforce security interests in marketable assets of their borrowers. The merchant's inventory and the accounts generated by the sale of it, the farmer's equipment, livestock and crops, the construction equipment and accounts of the contractor and the equipment, finished products and accounts of the manufacturer can serve as these marketable assets. What is required is a legal regime that facilitates this. Lenders who can contract for and receive legal protection for rights to seize or have seized contractually specified kinds or items of defaulting debtors' movable property have a much lower risk of loss than will be the case where these rights are not available. As a result there is a direct, inverse relationship between legal risk and the availability of credit facilities: the lower the risk, the greater is the willingness to grant credit.

The preceding generalizations apply to the West Bank and Gaza. As noted later in this paper, most of the current laws of the West Bank and Gaza dealing with secured financing transactions are antiquated, unclear and little understood by most lawyers and lenders. World Bank research, including extensive interviews with representatives of banks and insurance companies carrying on business in the West Bank, confirms the conclusion that the inadequacy of current law dealing with secured financing and equipment leasing has been an important factor inducing the very restrictive lending practices presently employed by lenders in the West Bank and Gaza.

III. THE WEST BANK AND GAZA

(a) Background

When describing the law of any state, it is necessary to distinguish the law in theory from the law in practice. Nowhere is this required more than in the context of the secured financing law of the West Bank and Gaza. This state of affairs is a product of the political history of the region. Because until recently Palestinians did not control these territories, they have not been able to develop an indigenous body of commercial law. Turkish, British, Jordanian (in the case of the West Bank) and, to a much smaller extent, Israeli rulers brought their commercial laws with them when they took political control of the region. Great complexity and considerable uncertainty resulted from the fact that each foreign system was superimposed on the former without necessarily displacing prior law. Consequently, when attempting to describe the existing secured financing law of this area, one must be careful to distinguish between what might fairly be described as the rich, if complex, law that exists in theory and the very minimal and largely primitive practical law in use.

The political strife that has characterized the recent history of the region has played a major role in retarding the development of commercial law. In this environment, commercial activity has been greatly inhibited and, consequently, there has been little need for modern commercial law. There has been little opportunity for courts to clarify and systematize the secured financing law that was brought to Palestine. The problem has been exacerbated by the fact that there has been no institution in the West Bank or Gaza for the education of Palestinian lawyers or for academic contributions to the development of this area of the law.[1] All Palestinian lawyers have had to go elsewhere for their legal education. Since most of them were trained in the law of different foreign States, it is unlikely that their legal education involved study of the commercial law of Palestine. Consequently, they returned to Palestine ill-prepared to play a central role in the further development of an indigenous commercial law.

Somewhat anomalously, the commercial law that was brought to Palestine by the British during the Mandatory period provides an adequate, although fragmented, conceptual basis for most modern secured financing transactions. It is conceptually and structurally quite similar to current English secured financing law. However, as any student of comparative law will attest, English law is not easily understood or assimilated since it is composed of concepts and rules drawn not only from statutory enactments but as well from the judgments of common law courts modified and supplemented by the principles established by the courts of equity. It would be unreasonable to expect Palestinian lawyers trained in countries that do not have strong English common law traditions to look to those features of English law that technically remain the law of their home jurisdiction as a source of practical commercial law.

(b) The Existing Structure

The existing theoretical secured financing law of the West Bank and Gaza is composed of layers of law imposed by the various foreign political rulers of the area. Each layer displaces some, but not all, of the law that preceded it. To complicate matters, not all of the layers are from the same family of law. The Turkish and Jordanian commercial law that is part of the law of the area is conceptually and structurally civilian. It is based on codes of law enacted in countries of continental western Europe. The very significant layer of law that resulted from British rule during the Mandatory period reflects the approach to law-making of a common law jurisdiction.

[1] In 1920 a law school was opened by the British under the name of the "Law Course" which functioned until 1948. The purpose behind it was to accelerate the anglicization of Palestine law. See D. Friedmann, "The Effect of Foreign Law on the Law of Israel: Remnants of the Ottoman Period" (1975) 10 *Israeli Law Review* 192 at 202.

Turkish law still provides what might be described as the "background" commercial law of the West Bank and Gaza. Palestine was part of the Ottoman Empire during the period 1516 to 1917.[2] During the last century Ottoman law underwent a period of codification. The new laws were based in part on Moslem law and in part on civil codes inspired by the *Code Napoléon*. The Ottoman Civil Code, the *Mejelle*, was enacted on an incremental basis beginning in 1867. Portions of other Turkish legislation remain in effect in either Gaza or the West Bank or both. However, a great deal of Ottoman commercial law was displaced or very substantially modified. Most, but not all, features of the Ottoman Commercial Code of 1850 and the Ottoman Code of Civil Procedure of 1879 were displaced by British Mandatory legislation.

The *Mejelle* remains a source of basic contract law applicable to secured financing transactions. While it does not contain a chapter of contracts, it deals in great detail with specific types of contracts used in secured financing such as contracts of sale, hiring (leases of movable property), pledges and guarantees. For example, since there is no modern law of leasing, any attempts to use leasing as a vehicle through which to facilitate an immediate increase in secured equipment financing in the West Bank and Gaza must be undertaken within the limits of the regime set out in the chapter of the *Mejelle* dealing with hiring.

The rules of contract contained in the *Mejelle* were considerably amplified by Articles 106–112 (dealing with damages for breach of contract) and Article 64 of the Ottoman Code of Civil Procedure enacted in 1914, which were clearly intended to modernize the then existing contract law. Of particular significance is Article 64,[3] apparently copied from the French Civil Code,[4] which introduced into the law of Palestine the principle of freedom of

[2] See generally D. Friedmann, "The Effect of Foreign Law on the Law of Israel: Remnants of the Ottoman Period," *supra n.* 1; and "Infusion of the Common Law into the Legal System of Israel" (1975), 10 *Israeli Law Review* 324.

[3] "64.(1) The terms of all contracts and agreements which are not forbidden by special laws and regulations and which are not contrary to morality and which do not disturb public order nor conflict with matters of personal status such as the capacity to contract, and the rules of law relating to inheritance and succession, and to any disposition of money or real property dedicated to pious purposes and immovable property, are valid as regards the contracting parties. Provided, however, that if the subject matter of the contract cannot be produced, such contract may be declared null and void.

(2) Any matter which possesses some special value may be the subject of contract. Any determinate object, interest or right which is generally recognized as being capable of transmission is regarded as possessing some special value. Agreements relating to things to be produced in the future are also valid.

(3) Should the parties have agreed as to the fundamental points of a contract, such contract shall be regarded as being completely concluded, even though subsidiary matters may have been passed over in silence. In cases where the parties have not been able to arrive at an agreement concerning subsidiary matters, the Court shall give a decision thereon, bearing in mind the nature of the business."

[4] See D. Friedmann, "The Effect of Foreign Law on the Law of Israel: Remnants of the Ottoman Period," *supra n.* 1, at 201.

contract allowing parties to make contracts in areas not covered by the *Mejelle*, and making it possible for parties to contracts provided for in the *Mejelle* to agree on questions affecting the execution and performance of their contracts.

The British Mandatory period, while short in duration (1923–48), was one during which a very substantial body of English law (including secured financing law) was imported into Palestine.[5] Indeed, much of what is currently needed for modern secured financing transactions became part of the law of the area during this period.[6] Legislation was passed providing the legal basis for the use of sophisticated secured financing devices such as floating charges and general assignment of debts. Almost as important is the fact that Article 46 of the Palestine Order-in Council,[7] which established the constitutional basis for the legal system during the Mandatory period, provided for the importation of general principles of the common law and equity. This was necessary since very few statutes enacted in a common law system are self-contained codes. They generally assume a background of common law principles and equitable doctrines; their principal role is to extend or otherwise modify these principles and doctrines. For example, the Debts (Assignment) Ordinance of 1928 enacted during the Mandate assumes an extensive body of choses-in-actions law based almost entirely on the system for the recognition and transfer of intangible rights created by the English courts of equity.

The annexation of the West Bank by Jordan in 1949 resulted in the imposition of a third layer of law: Jordanian civil law.[8] During the annexation period (1949–67), several enactments resulted in further diminution in the significance of the Ottoman commercial law and in the displacement of some Mandatory commercial legislation. For example, the Pledge of Non-movable

[5] Professor D. Friedmann notes that since s. 64 of the Ottoman Code of Civil Procedure left a large number of questions unanswered, "the law of contract was imported almost in its entirety from English *via* Art. 46 of the Order-in-Council. Rules absorbed including those regarding mistake in the formation of a contract, misrepresentation, including the requirement of disclosure in contracts *uberrima fidei*, illegality, duress, and even rules regarding undue influence deriving from equity. In the area of remedies for breach of contract, the English distinction between penalty and liquidated damages clauses was imported and, in its wake, equitable remedies, such as specific performance": see D. Friedmann, "Infusion of the Common Law into the Legal System of Israel," *supra* n. 2, at 370–1 (footnotes omitted).

[6] Professor Friedmann points out that it was in the area of commercial law that the British influence was the greatest. The Ottoman commercial law was based largely on French sources, and it was this law that the British were most active in replacing. *ibid.*, at 328.

[7] "The jurisdiction of the Civil Courts shall be exercised in conformity with the Ottoman Law in force in Palestine on November 1st, 1914 . . ." nevertheless "so far as the same shall not extend or apply", the jurisdiction of the courts "shall be exercised in conformity with the substance of the common law, and the doctrines of equity in force in England . . . Provided always that the said common law and doctrines of equity shall be in force in Palestine so far only as the circumstances of Palestine and its inhabitants and the limits of His Majesty's jurisdiction permit and subject to such qualification as local circumstances render necessary."

[8] The Egyptian rule of Gaza during the same period led to very little change in the commercial law. No legislative enactments had any significant effect on secured financing law in the area. The result is that the Mandatory law remains the dominant source.

Assets as Security for Debt Act of 1953 displaced prior Ottoman and British Mandatory law dealing with mortgages. The Jordanian Commercial Code of 1966 displaced British Mandatory legislation dealing with bankruptcy and bills of exchange and the Jordanian Company Law of 1964 displaced the 1929 Mandate Companies Ordinance.

Theoretically, current law provides a range of effective secured financing devices. Book V of the *Mejelle* provides for the pledge without delivery of possession to the debtor. It is technically possible under the law of Gaza and the West Bank law to create a chattel mortgage governed by the rules of the common law and equity. However there are no registration requirements other than those set out in section 127 of the Companies Ordinance of 1929 (applicable in Gaza) and road transportation legislation. A form of "chattel mortgage" that enjoys statutory recognition is presently in use in the West Bank and Gaza. It is quite common to use it to finance the purchase of registered motor vehicles. Its efficacy is based almost entirely on the fact that when registered, the mortgage becomes a bar to any transfer of title by the debtor to a third party.[9] Under Gaza law, a company may give a chattel mortgage over its assets. Section 127 of the Companies Ordinance of 1920 gives specific recognition to mortgages of movable property of a company by requiring them to be registered with the registrar of companies as a prerequisite to their enforceability against a liquidators or creditors of the mortgagor companies. Article 68 of the Jordanian Companies Law of 1964 provides for the mortgage of company shares. The existence of the mortgage is recorded in a registry maintained by the company and on the share document. Since there are few locally incorporated companies in the West Bank that have marketable shares, this device is of little practical significance.

The current law of Gaza theoretically provides for one of the most popular and useful secured financing devices ever devised: the English floating charge. The use of floating charges is specifically recognized in company legislation enacted in Palestine during the Mandatory period. This legislation is still in force in Gaza but may have been displaced by Jordanian company law enacted in 1964 during the period of Jordanian annexation. The Companies Ordinance No. 18 of 1929 contains several provisions dealing with mortgages and charges given by companies. However, it does not prescribe the characteristics of these devices. Its principal role is to provide a public record of their existence so as to protect third parties who deal with companies which have

[9] The Jordanian Road Transportation Act of 1958, which remains the law of the West Bank, provides in Art. 104(B) as follows:

"Transferring ownership of a motorized vehicle or mortgaging it is subject to approval of the main licensing authority. It is forbidden to transfer ownership of a mortgaged machine without the consent of the creditor. A business transaction which was not given approval by the main licensing authority is invalid, and has no legal validity."

The term "vehicle" is defined in Art. 2 as including "any kind of vehicle which has wheels, which is moving by the power of a motor . . . and which is used, or intended to be used for the purpose of transporting goods or people in any way . . .".

charged their assets. Section 125 requires each company to keep at its registered office a register of mortgages and floating charges affecting property of the company. Section 127 provides that mortgages or charges (including floating charges) on shares, land, movable property, book debts, ships, patents, licences, trademarks or copyrights that are not registered with the registrar of companies within twenty-one days of their creation "shall, so far as any security on the company's property or undertaking, be void against the liquidator and any creditor of the Company . . .". Section 134 of the Ordinance recognizes the use of receiverships in the enforcement of corporation mortgages and charges. However, this highly theoretical and administratively elaborate system is of little value in Gaza. The great bulk of businesses are small and unincorporated. Those that are incorporated do not have the range of assets that would justify the expense associated with floating charges. Further, very few Palestinian commercial lawyers know anything about floating charges and, consequently, are unlikely to recommend the use of this device even where the circumstances might warrant it.

The law of Gaza and the West Bank provides for the transfer of debts and other non-documentary intangible rights. However, there is no evidence that assignments of business debts for security purposes or outright sale (factoring) currently occurs. Most of the applicable law originated during the Mandatory period. As is the case with most other British secured financing law, the law regulating assignments is complex, but, for the most part, effective. The Debt (Assignment) Ordinance of 1928 is very similar to section 136 of the English Law of Property Act 1925. The purpose of the legislation is to remove some procedural requirements of equity. However, an assignment that does not meet the requirements of the Ordinance is not invalid; it remains effective according to the rules of equity.

The law governing leases of movable property in Gaza and the West Bank is found in Book II of the *Mejelle*. While the *Mejelle* does not accommodate features common to modern leasing contracts, there appears to be nothing in it that prevents the use of leases of equipment as a financing device, including a lease with an option given to the lessee to purchase the equipment.[10] However, given the fact that its provisions were drafted nearly a hundred years ago, it will be a surprise to no one to find that the *Mejelle* does not address or adequately regulate the various forms of modern leases such as security leases and financing leases. For this reason leases are not currently being used in Gaza or the West Bank as secured financing devices.

[10] Art. 442 provides that "[i]f the person taking the property on hire becomes owner of the hired property in any manner, such as by way of inheritance or gift, such property loses its quality of hired property."

IV. A BLUEPRINT FOR REFORM

(a) Approaches to Reform

A jurisdiction that undertakes to modernize its law dealing with secured financing must choose the approach to be used. One approach is to amend existing law so as to ensure that it minimally meets the current needs of credit grantors and credit consumers. An alternative approach is to undertake a complete reform of this area of the law with the goal of producing a modern, integrated code of secured financing law. The minimalist approach assumes that a generally satisfactory system prevails and that all that is required is some fine-tuning or additional features.[11] The more ambitious approach is generally undertaken in jurisdictions where the then existing law is hopelessly inadequate[12] or where legislators take the view that the law should be completely modernized so as to be a facilitator and not just a regulator of this type of economic activity.[13]

Clearly, more than fine-tuning of the present systems of the West Bank and Gaza dealing with security interests in movable property is required even though, in many respects, these systems provide most of the concepts necessary for modern secured financing transactions. Fine-tuning presupposes an existing, functioning system that requires minor changes. As noted earlier in this paper, British Mandatory ordinances along with the common law and rules of equity imported by Article 46 of the Palestine Order-in-Council provide a range of secured financing devices such as equitable chattel mortgages, floating charges and assignments of debts that meet many of the requirements of a modern secured financing system. However, this law exists, for the most part, in a peculiar state of suspension. It is rarely if ever used in practice and is understood by very few commercial lawyers or judges. Further, it is essentially foreign law—the law of another country. As noted above, in order for practitioners and courts to use it effectively, they must draw on a large body of English case law. None of British Mandatory law is in the form of a code; it is common law legislation that can only be understood fully in the context of concepts and doctrines peculiar to a common law system and set out in

[11] For an example of a proposal of this kind, see Department of Trade and Industry, *Security Over Moveable Property in Scotland, A Consultation Paper,* Nov. 1994.

[12] This was the situation in the Canadian province of Quebec prior to the recent enactment of Book Six, Title Three, Hypothecs, Civil Code of Quebec, *Loi sur l'application de la réforme du Code civil*, S.Q. 1992, c. 57.

[13] This approach has been taken in States of the United Sates and several of the provinces of Canada. See Art. 9, Uniform Commercial Code, 1978 Official text (enacted in all States of the United States); and the following Canadian Personal Property Security Acts: Alberta, S.A. 1988, c.P–4.05 as amended; British Columbia, S.B.C. 1989, c. 36 as amended, Manitoba, S.M. 1993, c. 14; New Brunswick, S.N.B. 1993, c. P–7.1 as amended; Northwest Territories, S.N.W.T. 1994, c. 8; Ontario, R.S.O. 1990, c. P–10 as amended; Saskatchewan, S.S. 1993, c. P–6.1 as amended; Yukon Territory, R.S.Y. 1986, c. 17 as amended. For the balance of this chapter, the Saskatchewan Act will be treated as representative of most of the other Canadian legislation.

judgments of English courts. This is particularly so with respect to the doctrines of equity (which provide the conceptual flexibility that characterizes chattel mortgage, floating charge and assignment law) that are so important to transactions in which the collateral is inventory or future debts.

Any programme of reform of this area of the law must take into account the need to educate the commercial bar and the courts. However, the complexity and uncertainty of existing secured financing law of Gaza and the West Bank would greatly limit the efficacy of legal education measures. The stacking of two systems in the case of Gaza and three systems in the case of the West Bank results in a level of complexity, if not confusion, that makes it almost impossible to determine the current state of the law on any particular issue. Added to this is the general lack of availability of primary sources and analysis of extant law. Statutory materials are not readily accessible and a case reporting system does not exist.

An additional factor that militates against a fine-tuning approach to the reform of existing secured financing law applicable to movables is the fact that, in some important respects, the law of Gaza is different from the law of the West Bank. There can be no basis for the maintenance of two separate systems since, ultimately, they will coalesce into a single economic unit.

All of the factors point to the need for a complete reform of secured financing law applicable to the West Bank and Gaza. This would involve the preparation of a code of law that meets the need of the West Bank and Gaza to have a modern, efficient, accessible system of secured financing law.

(b) Sources of Principles and Structures

As noted in the opening paragraphs of this paper, a great deal of reform activity directed to modernizing the secured financing and leasing law of developing nations has occurred in recent years. Those involved generally seek sources or models which can provide proven concepts and structures to adopt in original or modified form when preparing recommendations for changes to the law of states which are the focus of their attention. The European Bank for Reconstruction and Development has gone further. Not content with what was available, it prepared its own model law on secured transactions[14] that it could offer to interested client States.

Undoubtedly the most significant event in the development in secured financing law during the second half of this century was the publication of Article 9 of the American Uniform Commercial Code.[15] The drafters of UCC Article 9 saw their creation as a model for the reform and harmonization of

[14] European Bank for Reconstruction and Development, *Model Law on Secured Transactions* (1994).

[15] See generally G. Gilmore, *Security in Personal Property* (Boston, Mass., Little Brown & Co., 1965).

secured financing law of the States of the United States. Nevertheless, concepts and approaches to the regulation of secured financing transactions contained in Article 9 are viewed by a growing number of reformers as the basis for modernizing national secured financing law of jurisdictions outside the United States. The first indication of the potential international influence of Article 9 came with the decision of several Canadian common law provinces (which had systems containing many of the features found in the current law of the West Bank and Gaza) to enact entire new regimes[16] for the regulation of secured financing law based on Article 9. Since the Canadian Personal Property Security Acts were developed at a time when computer technology was available, it was possible to design registry systems that are vastly more efficient and accessible than the systems developed two decades earlier for Article 9. Remote access computerized registration systems of the kind found in most Canadian provinces provide convincing evidence to reformers in other jurisdictions that public disclosure of information that is so important to the risk assessment process endemic to secured financing can be effected in a very efficient and inexpensive manner.

It might appear on first impression that the choice of a source or model for reform of secured financing law of a jurisdiction would be dictated by the "family" of law to which the jurisdiction belongs. If it is a civil law jurisdiction, modern secured financing laws of common law jurisdictions would be inappropriate; if it is a common law jurisdiction, civil law approaches would be unacceptable. While, of course, background law cannot be ignored, there is no firewall between civil and common law systems with respect to basic features of modern secured financing law.[17] In any event, as noted above, the current law of the West Bank and Gaza has both civil and common law parentage. Consequently, Palestinian reformers are free to accept principles and approaches from either or both systems.

It is the author's view that a regime based principally on the concepts and structures of Article 9 and a registry system based substantially on the Canadian systems would best serve credit grantors and debtors in the West Bank and Gaza.

[16] See *supra* n. 13.

[17] This was recognized by the drafters of the EBRD Model on Secured Transactions. The following passage appears in the Introduction to the Model Law: "[o]ne principle which has guided the drafting of the Model has been to produce a text which is compatible with the civil law concepts which underlie many central and eastern European legal systems and, at the same time, to draw on common law systems which have developed useful solutions to accommodate modern financing techniques": see *supra* n. 14 at p. v.

(c) North American Law as a Model

(i) The Functional Approach to Scope

A central feature of the North American approach to the regulation of secured financing transactions is to adopt a generic concept for all secured financing devices. The great benefit of this approach is that it facilitates the design of a totally integrated and internally consistent regime. This is often referred to as the functional approach. The core of the functional approach to the identification of transactions that fall within the unifying regime of Article 9[18] is the "security interest". This term is defined in UCC § 1–201(37) as "an interest in personal property or fixtures that secures payment or performance of an obligation".[19] UCC § 9–102(1) provides that the Article 9 regime applies to any transaction (regardless of its form) which is intended to create a security interest in personal property or fixtures. UCC § 9–202 provides that the regime applied "whether title to collateral is in the secured party of in the debtor". These provisions give very few clues as to the nature of a security interest. It is clear that the locus of title to the collateral and the form of the transaction are not to be relied upon to determine whether or not a security interest exists. A security interest is proprietary in nature, in that a secured party who has a valid security interest is not treated as an unsecured creditor.[20]

An Article 9 security interest is a charge conceptually equivalent to the English equitable charge or the hypothec of Roman law. A security agreement results in a hypothecation of the collateral. A security interest does not involve any dealing with the title to or ownership of it. The rights of the secured party are exercisable over *res aliena* and not *res propria* since their only role is to provide an alternative source of compensation should the debtor fail to perform his or her obligations to the secured party.

Since a security interest is a charge or hypothec, it follows that a security agreement in the form of a legal mortgage does not involve transfer of title of the mortgaged goods to the mortgagee, and ownership of goods that are the subject-matter of a security lease or conditional sales contract vest in the buyer or "lessee" upon execution of the agreement. At the same time the seller or "lessor" acquires a charge on those goods.[21] As it applies to conditional

[18] All references to UCC Art. 9 are to Uniform Laws Annotated, Uniform Commercial Code (St Paul, Minn.: West Publishing Co., 1989).

[19] The definition is not limited to this general proposition. It provides amplification of the proposition in the context of several transactions, most notable conditional sales contracts and leases. The definition was substantially amended in 1987 to the extent that it deals with leases.

[20] See UCC § 9–301(1)(b) and (c).

[21] The recharacterization of transactions that is a necessary feature of a UCC Art. 9-type regime should not be confused with another, and clearly subsidiary, feature. As a result of UCC § 9–102(1)(b), Art. 9 applies to "any sale of accounts or chattel paper". The effect of the section is to deem these two transactions to be security agreements for limited purposes but not to view them as transactions that in substance are security agreements.This feature has been expanded significantly in the context of equivalent Canadian legislation.

sale contracts and security leases this conclusion was legislated in the United States.[22] In Canada, the matter has been left to implication and judicial amplification.

The available evidence indicates that the recharacterization of traditional title-based security devices has not been a problem for those who have looked to Article 9 as a model for modern law reform. What has been less acceptable is the recharacterization of transactions that traditionally are not viewed under otherwise applicable law as security agreements, such as title retention sales contracts and leases of movable property. For example, while the "hypothec" of the (new) Quebec Civil Code[23] is the conceptual and functional equivalent of the "security interest" of the PPSAs and Article 9, and while it displaces most types of financing devices used in Quebec prior to the new Code's implementation, it does not encompass title retention sales contracts and leases. These transactions remain separate and are subject to regimes that prescribe different legal relationships between the parties than those applicable to transactions that create hypothecs.[24]

It is the author's view that there should be no difficulty for legislators in the West Bank and Gaza adopting the North American functional approach even to the extent that it encompasses title retention sales contracts and security leases. Very likely, however, it will be necessary to include in the new law a prescribed set of rules to be applied by the courts when faced with the determination as to whether or not a particular transaction is a true lease or a security lease. In this respect, the presumptions set out in UCC § 1–201(37) can be adopted and, where necessary, expanded.

If the Canadian approach is adopted (and, in the opinion of the author, it should be), the need to distinguish between true leases and security leases will arise in far fewer circumstances than is the case under current law in the United States which does not require the registration of true leases. Under several of the Canadian Personal Property Security Acts, leases of goods for a period of more than one year (along with commercial consignments, sales of accounts and sales of chattel paper) are deemed to be security agreements for the purposes of the registration, priorities and private international law

[22] UCC §§ 1–201(37) and 2–401(1) provide that retention or reservation by the seller of the title (property) in goods shipped or delivered to the buyer is limited in effect to a reservation of a security interest. In 1987 further clarification was provided in the context of leases through revision of the "security interest" in UCC § 1–201(37).

[23] LQ 1991, c. 64, Book Six, Title Three. See esp. Arts. 2660, 2666, 2667.

[24] E.g. the seller of movables under a title retention agreement must elect between taking back the movables or bringing action against the buyer for the balance of the purchase price See Arts. 1745–9. However, a sale with a right to redeem which is used to secure a loan is treated as creating a hypothec. See Art. 1756.l. Similar rigidity is applied to leasing arrangements. The Code treats operating leases and financing leases quite separately from hypothecs (see Arts. 1851–91 and 1842–50) and there appears to be no basis on which a Quebec court could conclude that a lease of the kind that would be characterized as a security agreement under UCC Art. 9 or the PPSAs is a hypothec.

provisions of the Acts.[25] The principal reason for including these transactions in the Canadian legislation was to address the potential for third party deception that is endemic to these transactions. The drafters of the Canadian legislation reasoned that the efficient registry systems designed to provide public disclosure of security interests could be used to provide public notice of the fact that lessees and consignees have only possessory interests in goods in their possession. Since these transactions are deemed to be security agreements for this limited purpose, those provisions of the Acts that regulate the respective rights and obligations of secured parties and debtors in the event of default by debtors do not apply to them.[26]

(ii) Inventory Financing

A code of secured financing law for the West Bank and Gaza (and any other nation that seeks to modernize its law in this area) would permit the creation of security interests in any type of property that has commercial value. This includes tangible movable property (goods or chattels) and intangible movable property such as accounts (book debts), securities (shares) and intellectual property (trade marks, copyright, etc.). The code would be designed to facilitate inventory financing (using the term "inventory" in a broad sense to include, for example, agricultural products) and accounts financing by recognizing the possibility of automatic creation of security interests in property acquired by the debtor after the date of execution of the security agreement. The parties to a security agreement must be free to design their arrangement so that only the kinds (and not necessarily the items) of property taken as collateral need be specified in the agreement and that any property falling within the specified kind or kinds of property acquired by the debtor during the currency of the agreement come automatically within the scope of the security agreement. Without this feature, inventory financing becomes administratively and economically prohibitive except in cases where the volume of business of the debtor is very small. Accounts financing (other than factoring) requires the same degree of flexibility. Where a credit grantor seeks to secure advances to a merchant seller through a security interest (assignment) of short term debts being generated by the debtor in his business, it is crucial that the law recognize that the security interest captures debts arising at any time during the currency of the agreement.

Conceptually, these features are not new to the West Bank and Gaza. As noted above, they were a part of the system of law imported into the area during the British Mandate period. However, they should be reintroduced in

[25] *Supra*, n. 13, s. 3(2). The terms "lease for a term of more than one year" and "commercial consignment" are defined in s. 2(1)(h) and s. 2(1)(y) respectively. For a fuller examination of these provisions, see Cuming and Wood, *Saskatchewan and Manitoba Personal Property Security Acts Handbook* (Calgary: Carswell Co., 1994), 49–52.

[26] *Ibid.*, ss. 3(2) and 55.

a more modern form which does not rely on the principles established by the English courts of Equity.

(iii) An Integrated Priority Structure

As is noted elsewhere in the paper, the secured financing laws of the West Bank and Gaza, including the law adopted during the Mandate, developed in a haphazard and unsystematic way. One of the by-products of this development is the lack of symmetry and integration of the various types of secured financing devices that were introduced. In this respect, the law of Palestine was very similar to that of other jurisdictions in which English common law and equity prevailed.

A code of secured financing law based on a North American model would provide a completely integrated and symmetrical priority structure to deal with competing interests in collateral. When this type of structure functions in the context of a readily accessible, efficient registry system, the result is that persons who deal with debtors in possession of collateral are in a much better position to predict the likely outcome of conflict between any interest they acquire in the collateral and prior and subsequent interests in it acquired by others (including the debtor's trustee in bankruptcy). The result is a dramatic increase in the accuracy of legal risk assessment.

(iv) An Efficient Public Disclosure System

A problem endemic to non-possessory security interests is that a dishonest or desperate debtor in possession of collateral may be tempted to offer the property for sale or as security to someone who is unaware of the existence of the security interest in the property. If the third party buys or otherwise acquires an interest in the property, the law is faced with a dilemma: who as between two innocent parties (the secured party and the third party) must suffer the loss? By far the most effective solution to the dilemma is to make public disclosure of the security interest a pre-condition to recognition of the security interest's priority over any subsequent *in rem* interest in the collateral acquired by a third party. In most systems, this public disclosure comes in the form of registration of a notice of the security interest in a registry.

It is not enough that there be a registry, however. A modern secured financing regime will provide a single, central registry for all non-possessory security interests that is readily accessible to both secured parties and other persons who may deal with debtors. Accessibility in this context includes physical as well as financial accessibility. The cost of using the system must be such as to have little or no effect on the parties' decision to engage in a secured financing arrangement. Experience in several jurisdictions has demonstrated that computerization of a registry system can offer the advantages of ready accessibility, efficiency and very low cost.

Under the Canadian systems,[27] all registrations are effected in a single registry system. While there may be regional "registry offices", they are nothing more than entry points for registration information that is transmitted to the registry. It is possible to register a security interest in any type of personal property, including highly negotiable property such as money and negotiable instruments. The effect of registration, however, is not the same in all cases. In some cases, it provides only a minimal priority status.[28] In addition, the systems employ what is often referred to as "notice registration". What is registered is a simple document or computer screen of information (called a "financing statement") setting out some basic information about the secured party and the debtor and their relationship.[29] Clearly, the registry does not give public notice of particular security agreements; it is a registry of existing or potential security interests. A single financing statement can relate to one or more security agreements. Indeed, it is possible for a properly drawn financing statement to meet registration requirements for many security agreements between the same parties entered into over a period of several years. A financing statement can be registered before a security agreement is executed between the parties.

Notice registration works extremely well in the context of computerized registries like those in operation in Canadian provinces. Under these systems, a financing statement is a computer screen (referred to as an "electronic financing statement") provided to the secured party by the registry software. The person registering the financing statement simply enters on it the basic information required by the regulations which is then transmitted to the registry database. What is stored in the database of the registry is the text entered on the financing statement. Most Canadian systems still permit the use of hard copy (paper) financing statements. However, the form of financing statement is prescribed and supplied by the registry. No other form can be used. The way in which the form is to be completed is spelled out in detail in regulations. This control facilitates key edit entry of the data into the registry database. After key editing, the hard copy financing statements are destroyed.

Computerization eliminates any need to limit the length of registrations in order to clean out great volumes of paper security agreements or financing statements. Text data are stored, not hard copy documents. Consequently, it is possible to allow the secured party to choose the duration of a registration to parallel the duration of the security agreement with the debtor or the poten-

[27] The balance of the comments on registration reflect the Canadian system which have been more fully developed than their counterparts in States of the United States.

[28] It is possible for a secured party to take possession of the collateral and have a status as good as or better than a secured party who registers his or her security interest. However, as a practical matter, possession is used only where negotiable property such as negotiable instruments, bills of lading and corporate securities are taken as collateral.

[29] The financing statement contains the names and addresses of the secured party and the debtor, a description (either general or specific) of the property taken as collateral and an indication as to how long the registration is to be effective.

tial duration of the relationship he expects to have with the debtor. Under the computerized Canadian systems, it is possible for the registering party to select the duration of a registration. He can choose any period of years between one and twenty-five; he may also choose infinity registration. The choice of unnecessarily long registrations is controlled in two ways. The registration fees paid by the registering party are calculated on the basis of the length of the registration. In addition, a debtor is given the legal right to require the secured party to discharge a registration when the security agreement to which it relates has been discharged.

Access to a computerized personal property registry for registering financing statements, searching for registrations and amending and discharging registrations is possible through remote computer terminals (simple PC equipment and a modem) which can be located in a remote government office (court house or county office), in the office of a financing institution or in any business premises. In fact, registrations and searches can be effected by remote computer access from any place in the world where long distance telephone communication to the registries is available.

Effective public disclosure of the existence of security interests need not entail replication of all of the features of the Canadian systems. Some of these features may appear too radical for a jurisdiction that currently has only the most rudimentary registry system. Some Palestinian bankers have expressed the view that it is contrary to current Palestinian cultural and business practices to have "private" business matters open to inspection by any person willing to pay for a search fee. Their view is that borrowers will insist on having much more control over who has access to the registry than is required under Canadian law. This could be accomplished by requiring the debtor's consent to a search of the registry by a prospective lender or buyer of property. Such a system, however, will limit the use of the registry as one source of information as to the general credit-worthiness of a debtor.

Central storage of registration data is crucial to the effectiveness of a registry system. Registering parties should not be required to determine the appropriate registry office in which to effect their registrations and third parties seeking information from the registry should not be required to search several registries in order to protect their interests. In a physically divided jurisdiction such as the West Bank and Gaza, it will be necessary to have at least one additional in-put point other than the central registry. However, tender of a registration document at this point should not be treated as registration of an interest until the information on the document is entered into the central registry.

It is inconceivable that the registry database of the West Bank and Gaza under a modern secured financing law would be manual. Computerization of registry data yields too many efficiencies of time, accessibility and cost to ignore it. However, remote direct access to the database is a facility that could await the development of a much large secured financing market. Before implementing remote access facilities, several Canadian systems used financing statements in hard copy form delivered in person or by mail to the registry. Searches were permitted by request in person, by mail, by telephone or by telecopier.

Palestinian bankers have expressed the view that the current system for registration of "mortgages" against registered motor vehicles[30] should be maintained. This system is very effective since it gives complete control to the lender who holds a registered charge against the vehicle. There is no need for a priority structure to apply to competing interests in the vehicles since it is not legally possible for the debtor to create a competing interest. The negative feature of this is that the debtor does not have the ability to use his or her "equity" in the vehicle as collateral to obtain credit from alternative sources. This could be a matter of considerable significance for a business which requires the extensive use of vehicles in its business operations. Even if the proposed code does not deal with registration of interests in registered motor vehicles and competing priority claims to this form of collateral, there is no justification for excluding these transactions entirely from the scope of the proposed code. The post-default enforcement provisions of the code should apply since the current law dealing with enforcement of these charges is at best unclear.

(v) Self-Help Enforcement

A feature of the North American systems that may well be questioned by Palestinian legislators is secured party self-help enforcement of security agreements. Under these systems, seizure of collateral need not, and rarely does, involve any form of public administrative or judicial intervention. While a debtor must be given notice of disposition of collateral after its seizure, there are no requirements for the secured party to obtain the permission of a court to seize tangible collateral or involve a public official in the act of seizing it. Self-help is considered in North American jurisdictions to be factor contributing to the effectiveness of secured financing devices. Significant State involvement in the enforcement process may result in long delays in the enforcement of security agreements and, consequently, affect the ability of the secured party to obtain expeditious repayment of the obligation owing to him from proceeds of the sale of the collateral. It may also involve additional costs of disposition and possible failure to realize the full market value of the property being sold.

Self-help enforcement of security agreements traditionally is not permitted under many systems. This is a feature commonly found in civil law systems. While there are historical reasons for this, the principal policy-based reason is that too much freedom and control given to creditors might result in abuse

[30] See *supra* n. 9 and accompanying text.

in the form of unwillingness on the part of the secured party to recognize and protect the interests of the debtor or subsequent interest-holders in the property subject to the security interest. For example, an improvident sale of the property will not result in the full market value of the property being realized and any surplus over and above what is necessary to discharge the obligation secured would be lost to the debtor. Self-help enforcement is not part of the legal tradition of the West Bank and Gaza. Seizures and sale of property are carried out through a governmental enforcement office. However, this has not been a matter of concern to lenders since they rarely lend on the security of personal property and, consequently, have had little need to rely on it.

In order for a judicially or administratively controlled enforcement system to work properly, it is necessary that the system be efficient. Inefficiency, while often associated with judicial involvement in enforcement of security interests, is not a necessary feature of it. It is possible, in theory at least, to have an expeditious and inexpensive system that provides the necessary protection of debtors' interests without unreasonably affecting secured parties' rights to realize on their security. However, given the fact that the systems for the administration of justice in the West Bank and Gaza will continue to be in the developmental stage over the next few years, it is most unlikely that, for the foreseeable future, they will be able to deliver the necessary levels of efficiency. For this reason, private enforcement of secured creditors' rights to seize and sell movable property will likely be warranted. Of course, it should only be exercisable in situations where breaches of the peace are not likely to result from the actions of creditors. Experience in the United States and Canada (jurisdictions in which the volume of secured business and consumer credit is very large) indicates that private enforcement need not result in widespread or uncontrollable abuse by secured parties. If the law properly punishes creditors for breaches of the peace resulting from the exercise of self-help remedies and debtors are given by law an adequate opportunity to correct minor defaults, a right to invoke court intervention when abuse does occur and a right to full accounting for the sale of collateral, there is little need for *ab initio* official public involvement in the enforcement of security interests.

(vi) Private International Law Rules

It is no longer sufficient for a State to have a modern system for regulating secure financing agreements executed by persons domiciled within its borders and providing for security interests in property located in the State. Many types of collateral are highly mobile, with the result that an item of collateral may be taken temporarily or permanently by the debtor to another State.[31] On the other side of the coin, mobile collateral that is brought into a State by

[31] The immediate need for a common set of conflict of laws rules is lessened, although not eliminated, by the fact that West Bank and Gaza, Jordan and Israel all have "ownership registration" for most motor vehicles.

a debtor may be subject to a security interest created under the laws of another State. Intangible collateral such as debts may be owed to the debtor by persons who do not reside in the State where the debtor is located or where the security interest has been taken. In order to address issues that arise in these contexts, it is necessary to have a set of rules generally accepted by States within a region and prescribing what law is applicable to the validity and priority of security interests taken in any one of the States.

The small geographic size and the ever-increasing degree of integration of the economies of the West Bank and Gaza, Israel and Jordan will result in a dramatic increase in cross-border movement of collateral and financing arrangements involving residents of these jurisdictions. Fortunately, the governments of both Israel and Jordan have indicated interest in modernizing their secured financing law. This presents an opportunity to develop a set of private international law rules that can provide a regime within which the inevitable disputes involving inter-jurisdictional issues can be addressed.

(vii) Balance Between Security Interests and State Claims

A problem that is frequently encountered by designers of modern secured financing regimes is to find the appropriate balance between security interests in business debtors' assets, on the one hand, and, on the other, liens and charges against those assets arising by operation of law. These liens and charges are devised to protect State interests (e.g. taxes owing by the debtor or collected by the debtor on behalf of the State) or interests of employees of the debtor. It is not uncommon for legislation to give priority to the claims secured by these liens and charges over all security interests in the debtor's property, whether the claims arose before or after the security interests arose. It is clear that in these States there is an inverse relationship between the value of the secured party's security interest and the number and amount of claims that have a superior priority status.

There is no universally applicable formula or approach that will provide the appropriate balance between the need to protect interests represented by statutory liens and charges and the need to facilitate secured financing. The decision as to what balance is to be struck will be conditioned by a range of factors many of which will be peculiar to the State in which the decision is being made.

V. CONCLUSION

There is a growing recognition that secured financing provided by private sources can play an important role in the development of emerging economies. While there are many factors that have contributed to the very low level of private lending on the security of movable property, it is clear that failure to modernize secured financing regimes has played an important role. International organizations have undertaken projects designed to encourage and assist nations to modernize their secured financing law.

One of these projects involves the West Bank and Gaza. This area is like many others in the world in that the private savings that are available are not being fully utilized for development purposes since banks are reluctant to take the very considerable risks involved in lending in the context of existing antiquated legal regimes. The area is *sui generis* in some respects, however. Its legal traditions are solely those of neither the civil nor the common law. Part of its existing legal system could support modern secured financing; however, the peculiar history of the region has prevented the development of an indigenous law grounded in concepts and mechanisms that were imported during the British Mandate period.

The author has suggested in this paper that, while most of the concepts and structures that comprise the very successful secured financing regime of the United States and Canada can be employed in the reform of the secured financing law of the West Bank and Gaza, there are features that may not be suitable.

10

The Registration of Company Charges Against Real Property Under Israeli Law

SHALOM LERNER*

I. INTRODUCTION: THE ISRAELI LAW OF CHARGES AGAINST PROPERTY OF COMPANIES AND INDIVIDUALS

The principal Israeli statute that treats of charges is the Pledges Law, 5727–1967. In addition, various specific provisions can be found elsewhere. For example, several provisions of the Companies Ordinance refer to charges against company assets, and certain sections of the Land Law, 5729–1969, deal with encumbrance on land.

In practice, no particular legal system can be singled out as the primary source of the Pledges Law. The committee that prepared the law drew upon several legal systems in making its recommendations.[1] As is characteristic of Israeli civil legislation, the law is not detailed, comprising but twenty-seven sections. Nonetheless, the law deals with a broad range of topics, such as the creation of a pledge, the replacement of pledged property, pledges to secure the obligation of the non-pledging party and termination and realisation of a pledge.

The laws relating to charges on company property, and the legal distinction between charges on the property of a company as opposed to that of an individual, reflects the influence of English law. The Israeli Companies Ordinance, promulgated in 1929 during the British mandate, was copied in its entirety from the English companies law in force at that time. Hence the special provisions for charges on company property.[2] In 1995, a bill was introduced in

* Professor of Law, Faculty of Law, Bar Ilan University, Israel.

[1] See J. Weisman, *Security Interests Law, 1967* (Jerusalem, 1975) 4.

[2] English law influenced most common-law countries, including mandatory Palestine. It should, however, be noted that the same distinction was not adopted in all countries. The United States did not adopt the distinction between the encumbrance of company property as opposed to the property of an individual. Canada originally followed the English approach but since the 1960s the influence of Article 9 of the American Uniform Commercial Code and the adoption of modern Personal Property Security Acts has led to the abandonment of the distinction.

the Knesset for a new companies law.[3] The proposed law introduces significant changes in companies law, but suggests no changes in the area of charges against company property. Reform of the rules governing charges has been set aside for the moment, as it is the legislature's view that such changes should be made in the framework of a comprehensive reform of the law of secured transactions. It is a view that I share.

The relationship between the Pledges Law and the provisions dealing with charges in the Companies Ordinance is that of *lex generalis* and *lex specialis*. In other words, charges against company property are governed by the Pledges Law, unless special provisions of Companies Ordinance deviate from that law.[4] Such provisions are found primarily in two areas: floating charges and registration of charges.

The existence of special security interest laws for companies immediately raises questions. A creditor places a charge on a debtor's property in order to collect the debt by realisation of the charge in a manner not contingent upon the identity of the debtor or upon any change of circumstances in the debtor's financial conditions. It is thus surprising to discover separate security interest rules governing debtors who have a particular legal identity. The rule that a company is a separate legal person and that its creditors do not have recourse against the property of the stockholders often induces a creditor to take a charge in order to reduce the risk of non-payment. It is only proper that such a charge not be governed by companies law. Indeed, in my opinion there is no justification for the existence of separate security interest laws for company property. However, under the current law, various provisions of the Companies Ordinance establish special rules for charges against company property.

Examination of the Pledges Law and the security interest provisions of the Companies Ordinance reveals an interesting fact. The Pledges Law comprises just twenty-seven sections whereas the parallel provisions of the Companies Ordinance, applying special rules for companies, cover thirty-eight sections.[5] This discrepancy may be attributed in part to the different legislative techniques of the Israeli legislature and the mandatory authorities. The Pledges Law does not contain provisions regarding various substantive and technical aspects of registration, whereas numerous sections of the Companies Ordinance are devoted to such matters as modes of registration and filing dates (sec. 179), issuance of a certificate of registration of a charge by the Registrar of Companies (sec. 185), registration at the request of an interested

[3] Companies Law Bill, 5756–1995, *H.H.* 2. The bill is based upon the report of a Select Committee chaired by the president of the Supreme Court, Prof. Aharon Barak. See *Report of the Committee for the Enactment of a New Companies Law* (5755). Prof. U. Procaccia's book, *New Companies Laws for Israel* (Jerusalem, 1989) served as a basis for the committee's work.

[4] See the recent decision *Bank Leumi* v. *Niar Graph (Industries) Ltd. (in liq.)*, (1992) 46(I) P.D. 433.

[5] Chapter Eight of the Ordinance, entitled "Debentures and Charges", comprises sections 164–201.

party (sec. 186), extension of the filing date (sec. 191), and penal sanctions for failure to register a charge (sec. 192). The mandatory legislator included various matters in primary legislation that the Israeli legislature has relegated to secondary legislation. However, an examination of some of the provisions reveals two approaches to the registration of charges. Besides the establishment of a separate registry, the two approaches differ significantly in other ways as well. The primary differences between the two systems are as follows:

(1) The Pledges Law does not impose a duty to register a charge within a particular period of time whereas the Companies Ordinance provides that a charge is void if it is not delivered for registration within 21 days after the date of its creation.

This harsh sanction, established by the Ordinance, has been mitigated by statute and case law. The Ordinance provides a means for extending the filing date. Following that lead, the case law holds that a charge that is submitted for registration after the filing date, and that is subsequently registered by the Registrar, will be valid against regular creditors even if no request for an extension of the filing date was submitted.[6]

(2) Under the Pledges Law, priority between two secured creditors is decided in favour of the pledge first registered. According to the Companies Ordinance, a charge that is registered within the 21 day period will be preferred over any subsequent charge, even if the later charge was registered first.[7]

(3) A charge against real property or against a registered lease held by an unincorporated person is only registrable in the Land Registry. A mortgage against the real property or registered lease of a company must be registered by the Registrar of Companies after it has been registered in the Land Registry.

(4) Under the Companies Ordinance, an error in the records of the Registrar of Companies does not prejudice the rights of a secured creditor who submitted the particulars of the charge. The scope of the charge is defined in accordance with the parties' agreement and not by the erroneous information in the Registry, whether caused by the negligence of the creditor or the Registrar. As opposed to this, it would seem that under the Pledges Law, a mistake will not bind a person who would not have discovered it by reasonable inspection of the register.[8]

(5) Under the Ordinance, a creditor meets the registration requirements if notice of the charge is received by the Registry. As opposed to this, it would seem that under the Pledges Law, if a person examines the

[6] *Iscoor Steel Services Ltd.* v. *Shlomo Nes, Adv. & C.A., Liquidator of Elkol Ltd. (in liq.)*, (1992) 46(4) P.D. 289.

[7] On the retroactive effect of registration of a charge against company property, see: *Bialostuzki Ltd.* v. *Niar Graph (Industries) Ltd. (in liq.)*, (1991) 45(1) P.D. 698.

[8] On this subject from the perspective of registration in the Land Registry, see: *State of Israel* v. *American Israel Bank Ltd*, (1994) 48(3) P.D. 249.

register, finds that there are no charges against the property and acts in reliance upon that examination, his right will prevail against a prior charge that did not appear in the register.

(6) The Companies Ordinance requires that the charge agreement be submitted to the Registry. The Pledges Law only requires the submission of a notice of charge comprising the basic particulars of the agreement.

(7) Under the Pledges Law, an undeposited and unregistered pledge is effective against a creditor who knew or should have known of the pledge. As opposed to this, under the Companies Ordinance, an unregistered charge is not effective even against a person who was actually aware of it.[9]

Elsewhere, I have explained that these distinctions reflect different conceptions of the role of the Registry of Charges.[10] In the context of this paper, I want to examine one of these distinctions—that related to charges on real property belonging to a company. What is distinctive to charges on real property is the existence of an additional registry, the Land Registry. Naturally, this raises the question of the relationship between the two registries in which charges may be recorded—the Land Registry and the office of the Registrar of Companies. The following sections will address three aspects of the relationship between the two registries. Section 2 examines the method of registering a mortgage against the proprietary rights of a company in a particular piece of real estate. Section 3 considers the subject of cautionary notes, and Section 4 describes the treatment of a floating charge on real property in the different registries. In Section 5, I discuss briefly the functions of the Registry of Charges in relation to company property and its influence on the registration of a charge against such property.

II. MORTGAGES OF COMPANY LAND

Under sec. 178(1) of the Companies Ordinance, the following charges must be recorded in the office of the Registrar of Companies:

(1) a charge for the purpose of securing debentures, including a floating charge or a charge upon uncalled share capital, capital called up but not paid, or goodwill; or

(2) a charge on any land, wherever situate, or any interest therein; or

(3) a pledge of any movable property of the Company save where the pledgee is in possession of the property; or

(4) a charge on any book debts of the Company; or

(5) a charge on ships or shares in ships; or

(6) a charge on patents or licences under patents, trademarks or copyrights.

[9] On this comparison, see: *Stuckman* v. *Spitani*, (1974) 28(2) P.D. 182.

[10] S. Lerner, *Company Charges* (Tel Aviv, 1996), chap. 15.

Under subsec. (2), "a charge on any land, wherever situate, or any interest therein," must be registered with the Registrar of Companies as a precondition for its validity against a company's liquidator or creditors. Under sec. 179(a)(2), the date for registering the charge is "within twenty-one days from the day upon which the Registrar of Land approved the transaction for registration, whether executed before him or before an advocate." It is clear from these two provisions that a charge upon a company's land must be registered twice, once in the Land Registry and a second time with the Registrar of Companies.

Actually, the drafter of the Companies Ordinance did not require the registration of a mortgage with the Registrar of Land. Rather, the drafter assumed this to be required by other legislation. Indeed, under sec. 7(b) of the Land Law: "A transaction which has not been completed by registration shall be regarded as an obligation to effect a transaction."[11] A mortgage constitutes "a transaction in immovable property" under the Law and, as stated, if it not be registered it will be viewed merely as an obligation to grant a mortgage. The status of an obligation, as opposed to a proprietary right, does not give the secured creditor priority over other creditors upon liquidation of the company. In the Companies Ordinance, the drafter was not satisfied with a land registration and insisted upon additional registration with the Registrar of Companies, so that the charge would be effective against the company's liquidator.[12] The result under the current law is, therefore, that a creditor who registers a mortgage on company land only in the Land Registry will not be deemed a secured creditor and the charge will not be effective against general creditors upon the company's liquidation.[13]

Section 179 also regulates the order of registration. The section requires that a mortgage must first be registered in the Land Registry, and only thereafter with the Registrar of Companies. The case law has emphasized that a mortgage cannot be registered with the Registrar of Companies in the absence of prior registration in the Land Registry. The Israeli Supreme Court explained the basis of this rule as follows:

"A mortgage deed, when presented to the Registrar of Companies for registration in the company's register of charges, must bear the approval of the Registrar of

[11] When the provisions of sec. 179(a)(2) were adopted, land transactions were governed by the mandatory Land Transfer Ordinance, which was replaced by the Land Law of 1969. Under that Ordinance, an unregistered mortgage lacked legal force even between the secured creditor and the debtor. Today, under sec. 7(b) of the Land Law, an unregistered transaction enjoys relative force. It is valid between the parties themselves, but not against third parties. For a comparison of the Land Law and the pre-existing law, see: J. Weisman, *The Land Law, 1969: A Critical Analysis* (Jerusalem, 1970) 85.

[12] Double registration is statutorily required for other types of property, as well, such as ships and patents. Under sec. 178, charges on ships and patents must be registered with the Registrar of Companies, while specific laws impose a duty of registration with other registrars, See e.g.: Shipping (Vessels) Law, 5720–1960, sec. 65; Patents Law, 5727–1967, sec. 90.

[13] See, e.g.: *Azoulay et al.* v. *Atzma'ut Development and Mortgage Bank Ltd.*, (1978) 32(1) P.D. 365.

Land. This flaw in the process cannot be passed over as a matter of mere procedure, as it is a flaw that goes to the very heart of the matter. The content of a registration so performed, without the prior approval of the Registrar of Land, is wanting and flawed, inasmuch as, in effect, it reflects a security interest that has yet to be created. The 'charge', according to the instrument, in the manner and wording entered in the Register of Charges, does not exist, and this is, therefore, an erroneous, mistaken and misleading entry. . . .

The Register of Charges is a statutory registry, intended to provide a reliable and authoritative reflection of the existence and extent of charges upon a company's assets. The accuracy of this register should not be infringed by excusing substantive mistakes and flaws made therein . . ." [14]

According to the decision, a mortgage cannot first be registered with the Registrar of Companies because no mortgage exists prior to its entry in the Land Register, and the Registrar of Companies must refrain from recording mistaken or inaccurate information. However, in my opinion, it is hard to justify this approach. A mortgage, like any pledge, is created by agreement between the creditor and the debtor.[15] Recording the mortgage in the Land Registry does not create the mortgage but transforms it from an obligation to a property and grants it additional force against third parties.

The decision instructs the Registrar of Companies not to record a mortgage prior to its being recorded by the Registrar of Land. As a result, it is not common for a mortgage on company land to be registered only with the Registrar of Companies and not to appear in the Land Registry. However, if such a situation were to arise, the holder of the charge will not be a secured creditor, inasmuch as under sec. 7(b) of the Land Law, the transaction will only be treated as creating an obligation and not a proprietary right.

Later in this paper I shall express my opposition to the requirement of double registration for mortgages on company land, and will propose making do with registration in the Land Registry. However, even following the double-registration approach, it is hard to understand the motive for strict adherence to the order of registration.[16] If the legislature is of the opinion that a mortgage on company-owned land must be reflected in the records of two registries, it would be sufficient to establish that a creditor who does not record his right in both registries will not be deemed a secured creditor in the event of the company's insolvency.

[14] *United Mizrahi Bank* v. *Adv. Rozovski ("Ytong")*, (1994) 48(2) P.D. 102, 136.

[15] Pledges Law, sec. 3(a).

[16] Sec. 396 of the English Companies Act of 1985 requires that a charge upon a company's land be registered with the Registrar of Companies, but it does not refer to additional registration in the Land Registry or to any order of registration. This accounts for an additional distinction between the English and Israeli legal situations. According to sec. 395 of the English Act, the particulars of the mortgage must be submitted to the Registrar of Companies within twenty-one days from the making of the mortgage agreement, whereas under sec. 179(a)(2) of the Companies Ordinance, the twenty-one days begin to run from the date the mortgage is recorded by the Registrar of Land.

"A charge on any land" that must be submitted to the Registrar of Companies under sec. 178 of the Ordinance is a charge on the ownership of the land. As in other cases, the drafter identifies the property itself, the land, with the right to own it.[17] That the intention is to the encumbrance of the right to ownership and not to other rights pertaining to the land can be inferred from the drafter's presumption that the charge must first be recorded in the Land Registry. When an individual grants a secured creditor a charge on a contractual right relating to land, the subject of the pledge is the right, not the land. The transaction must be recorded only by the Registrar of Pledges and not by the Registrar of Land.[18] Similarly, when such a charge is made by a company, it must be reported only to the Registrar of Companies.[19]

Under the Land Law, if a lessee grants his creditor a charge upon a lease registered in the Land Registry, that charge is deemed a mortgage and it must be recorded by the Registrar of Land.[20] According to the Companies Ordinance, any charge by a company that must be entered in the Land Registry must also be recorded by the Registrar of Companies. In other words, a charge upon a company's registered lease must also be registered twice; by the Registrar of Land and by the Registrar of Companies. However, if the lessee company pledges its right to an unregistered lease, the pledge will only have to be recorded by the Registrar of Companies. It would seem not to matter whether the lease is unregistered because it is a short-term lease that is exempt from registration,[21] or whether it is unregistered because the lessee pledges the right before the parties duly register a long-term lease.[22]

The double-registration requirement for company land would not seem to be consistent with the purpose of registering rights. It is generally accepted that the primary purpose of the existence of a registry is to allow various parties to carry out a quick, reliable examination of all the rights related to specific properties. From this perspective, it would seem preferable to concentrate all the information in one registry.[23] The existence of two registries places a burden on the secured creditor interested in registering a charge as well as upon a person investigating whether or not a particular property is in any way

[17] Cf. J. Weisman, *Property Law—General Part*, (Jerusalem, 1993) 365–367.

[18] *Official Receiver* v. *Bank HaPoalim Ltd.*, (1987) 41(2) P.D. 275.

[19] The charge must be recorded by the Registrar of Companies under sec. 178(a)(2) of the Ordinance, which requires the registration of "a mortgage or charge on any land, wherever situate, or any interest therein." According to the Ytong decision, *supra n.* 14 at 129, the last term is intended to encompass situations in which "the land itself does not belong to the company, but it [the company] has some 'interest' in it, whether proprietary or contractual, and therefore a charge upon such an interest requires registration with the Registrar of Companies."

[20] Land Law, sec. 81(a).

[21] A lease for a period not exceeding ten years does not require registration, see S. Lerner, *The Law of Leases* (Tel Aviv, 1990) 73–77.

[22] See *Mercaz HaArgazim Ltd.* v. *Industrial Development Bank of Israel Ltd.*, (1994), 1994(1) P.M. 68.

[23] On the advantages of concentrating data in the context of rights to motor vehicles, see *State of Israel* v. *Bank HaPoalim Ltd.*, (1990) 44(2) P.D. 726, 730. For a different view concerning fixtures, See e.g Ontario Personal Property Security Act, sec. 34.

encumbered. The need to check the register in two different offices makes the investigatory process more expensive, and may deter potentially interested parties from carrying out a proper search.[24] Additional problems are raised by comparison to another area with double registration, that of charges on the ownership of motor vehicles, which is listed both with the Registrar of Pledges or of Companies and with the Licensing Office.[25] Experience shows that the public tends to attribute decisive weight to one of the registries, and to suffice with an examination of the records of that registry alone. The common practice in Israel is for a buyer to check only the records of the Licensing Office. However, he or she may later discover that a charge is registered against the vehicle in the Pledges Registry or with the Registrar of Companies.[26]

Double registration, by its very nature, raises additional problems. A system that prescribes double registration must stipulate that a right recorded in only one registry will not be deemed perfected and will be unenforceable against various parties. Granting full recognition to a right that has been registered only in one registry would frustrate the legislative intent that the existence of the right be reflected in two registries. Nevertheless, it would seem that recording a right in one registery would suffice to negate the good faith of a person claiming an adverse interest. The courts would be hard pressed to attribute good faith to a party who relied upon the absence of an entry in one registry when the right had been recorded in another. The Israeli legal system attaches much weight to the good-faith principle in resolving a contest between conflicting rights.[27] It would therefore appear that a person who records a charge in one registry will have priority over persons who acquire rights thereafter, due to their lack of good faith.

In the case of *United Mizrahi Bank* v. *Rozovski* (the *Ytong* case mentioned above), D. Levin J. explained the need to record a charge upon a company's land in the Land Registry and with the Registrar of Companies as follows:

> "These entries [in the Land Register], as opposed to the company's register of charges, warn of the existence of charges upon some specific property located in

[24] Cf. Douglas G. Baird, "Notice Filing and the Problem of Ostensible Ownership," 12 *J. of Legal Studies* (1983) 53, 59.

[25] On the registering of charges on motor vehicles with the Licensing Office, see the Motor Vehicle Regulations, 5721–1961, reg. 284(c)(d). However, unlike charges on company land, the practice of registering motor-vehicle charges in two places developed without any legal requirement. According to the Law, the right of the secured creditor is realised upon registering the charge in the Pledges Registry alone. See in this regard, *State of Israel* v. *Bank HaPoalim, supra* n. 23.

[26] See, e.g. *Osama* v. *Bank HaPoalim*, (1991) 1991(2) P.M. 108. In that case, the buyer examined the register in the Licensing Office but not that of the Registrar of Pledges. As a result, the buyer lost the property to the secured creditor who had registered the charge in his favour only with the Registrar of Pledges.

[27] See, e.g. Land Law, secs. 9 and 10; Movable Property Law, sec. 12; Sale Law, sec. 34. The only situation where the legislature does not apply the good-faith factor is in sec. 4 of the Assignment of Rights Law, 5729–1969. On good faith in this context, see S. Lerner, "Assignment of Rights," in D. Friedman, ed., *Law of Obligations—General Part*, (Tel Aviv, 1994) 148–149.

their district. Thus, anyone interested specifically in a particular piece of land owned by the company can turn to the Land Registry in the district in which the property is situated, and enquire as to the charges upon it. However, the company may possess numerous real properties, scattered among various districts throughout the country. A person seeking to evaluate the general condition of the company and to apprise himself of all the charges encumbering its assets will have to trudge from one district office to another, and examine the registers in each and every office, while piecing together all the bits of information to form a whole picture."[28]

On a first reading, especially under the influence of the depiction of a person trudging from one office to another, one gets the impression that establishing a central land registry for all of Israel would alleviate the need for recording charges with the Registrar of Companies.[29] However, it would appear that the Court justified double registration in light of the different systems of registration employed by the two registries. Indeed, as will shortly be seen, there are important differences between the Land Registry and records kept by the Registrar of Companies. The establishment of a central land registry would not cause the supporters of double registration to change their position.

The records of the Land Registry refer to properties. An examination of the register reveals all the rights associated with a particular piece of land, identified by its parcel and section number. The records of the Registrar of Companies and of the Registrar of Pledges record charges alphabetically according to the name of the debtor, and not according to the identity of the pledged property.[30]

The Land Registry records rights whereas the Registrar of Companies records transactions.[31] The land registers profess to reflect all the existing rights associated with any particular parcel of land. Therefore, if a person examines the register and finds that a certain individual is listed as the owner of a given property and that no third-party rights are recorded, and he or she thereupon enters into a transaction involving that property in reliance upon the state of the register, he acquires a free and clear title if he records the transaction in the register. The law prefers the buyer in ordinary course, and the buyer receives a free and clear title even if the transferor did not enjoy such a right.[32]

[28] *Supra* n. 14. at 126. The Court relied upon U. Procaccia, *New Companies Laws for Israel* (Jerusalem, 1989) 157.

[29] This impression is even more forceful in reading Procaccia's book, loc. cit. The author justifies double registration by the effort required to examine the records in all the Land Registries. "If the company has real properties spread throughout the country, an examination of their encumbrances would require visiting the various district Land Registries, inasmuch as there is no single office that centralizes the recording of the transactions on all the land in the country . . ." (This passage is quoted on p. 127 of the decision).

[30] On the new system in regard to motor vehicles, see Pledges Regulations (Registration and Examination Procedures) 5754–1994, reg. 5(b).

[31] On the distinction between a register of rights and a transactions register, see Weisman, *supra* n. 17, at 294–296.

[32] Land Law, sec. 10.

As opposed to this, the records of the Registrar of Companies do not reflect all the rights on a charged property. The register records all the charge transactions, but the registration of a transaction does not of itself impart full validity to the charge. Thus, if a company grants a creditor a pledge against property that it does not own, registration of the pledge will not remedy the flaw and the secured creditor will have to retreat before the true owner of the property. For this reason, a person interested in acquiring a specific interest in a company's real property cannot limit itself to examining the records of the Registrar of Companies but must examine the Land Register.

The Land Registry thus serves those interested in specific information about specific parcels of land belonging to a company, and not in general information about the company. A person interested in purchasing a company's land examines the Land Register in order to ascertain that it actually belongs to the company and whether or not there are any third-party rights. A party interested in using a company's land as security for a loan will have to examine the Land Register. But a party interested in general information about a company, such as a potential creditor, an investor, or a financial analyst, will find what he is looking for only in the records of the Registrar of Companies.[33]

Nevertheless, these distinctions still do not explain the need for double registration. It is instructive to note that a pledge of the land of an individual does not require double registration. Recording the pledge in the Land Registry protects the secured creditor, and his right is good against all third parties without further registration with the Registrar of Pledges.[34] In light of the above, it would seem that no distinction should have been drawn between charges against company property and charges against individual property. Registration in the Pledges Register is in every way identical to registration with the Registrar of Companies, and there is no obvious reason for applying a different rule to individuals in regard to double registration. Registration in the Land Register and in the Pledges Register serve different functions. A person interested in obtaining general information about another's financial state can only find it in the Registry of Pledges, where records are maintained under the debtor's name. As opposed to this, the information in the Land Registry is more accurate, as it is a register of rights and not of transactions. The distinction between an individual and a company points to the existence of another function fulfilled by the registration of charges against a company's assets, a subject which will be examined in Section 5.

As we have seen, the record of charges maintained by the Land Registry and the Registrar of Companies answer different concerns. The Land Register

[33] It should be noted that the Registrar of Companies' records do not provide a complete picture of a company's holdings. The Registrar records only charges on a company's property and does not maintain a record of a company's unencumbered properties.

[34] It is true that the Pledges Law requires that a charge on an individual's property be registered with the Registrar of Pledges, but the Law does not apply when some other law contains special registration provisions, See sec. 4(1) of the Law.

is intended for the use of persons seeking to acquire a specific interest in a company's real estate, such as a buyer or a secured creditor, whereas an unsecured creditor, interested in the company's general status, will make do with an examination of the records of the Registrar of Companies. This distinction should provide the key for deciding various disputes in regard to the company's assets. The statutory requirement that a charge against company land be recorded by the Registrar of Companies only after being entered in the Land Register is, in my view, of consequence only in a conflict between a secured creditor and general creditors. As stated above, the Land Register is not relevant to general creditors, and if they are involved in a dispute, a charge not recorded with the Registrar of Companies will not be deemed perfected. As opposed to this, registration in the Land Registry will decide the fate of a dispute between the secured creditor and a claimant to a specific adverse right in the mortgaged property.

According to the distinction I have suggested, a secured creditor who records a mortgage on a company's property in the Land Registry should be preferred over anyone who acquires a later right to the same property, even if the secured creditor did not register his right with the Registrar of Companies. Registration with the Registrar of Companies is, as stated, irrelevant to the dispute between two or more claimants to a specific interest in a particular piece of real estate. Such a conflict would only be governed by the provisions of the Land Law and not by the provisions of the Companies Ordinance. According to the Land Law, the first to register in the Land Registry takes preference over later rivals.[35] However, such a conflict would not be common because anyone seeking to acquire a specific interest in land is likely first to check the Land Register. Recording a mortgage in the Land Registry will almost certainly prevent any other person from acquiring an adverse right even if such a person discovers that the mortgage was not recorded with the Registrar of Companies.

However, the interests of a secured creditor differs from those of a purchaser. The former purpose is to use the mortgage as a means for collecting his debt. Therefore, if the company is solvent, a secured creditor who loses in the conflict can collect from the company's other assets. As opposed to this, if the company has gone into liquidation, unsecured creditors will be a party to the conflict and a mortgage that was not recorded by the Registrar of Companies will be rendered void.[36] But when the conflict is between two

[35] The owner of a right in real property whose title has not been perfected by registration could lose his right under the conflicting transactions rule, See sec. 9 of the Land Law. However, in my opinion, a mortgage on a company's property that is recorded only in the Land Registry is a completed transaction only in regard to a rival who claims a specific interest in the same property, and not merely an obligation. Therefore, the conflicting transactions rule would not apply to a conflict between the holder of a mortgage and another.

[36] In England, a charge recorded in the Land Registry but not reported to the Registrar of Companies is good against a later purchaser, but it is void against a later secured creditor, who is protected by the English counterpart of sec. 178, see: *Barnsley's Conveyancing Law and Practice*, (3rd ed., 1988) 366.

secured creditors, one of whom recorded his right only in the Land Registry, and the other only in with the Registrar of Companies, the first should prevail.[37]

The proposed interpretation of the current law limits the importance of double registration. According to this approach, double registration is only required where unsecured creditors are party to a conflict. This marks a step in what I believe to be the right direction—cancellation of the double-registration requirement as well in regard to unsecured creditors. I suggest amending sec. 178(a)(2) to repeal the requirement to register a mortgage on company property with the Registrar of Companies.[38] According to the proposed arrangement, a charge of a contractual right in land that cannot be recorded in the Land Register will have to be submitted to the Registrar of Companies, while a transaction that should be entered in the Land Register in accordance with the Land Law will be exempt from additional submission to the Registrar of Companies.

In my opinion, the registration of mortgages against company property in the Land Registry is sufficient because anyone interested in a specific right in a particular property will, inevitably, inspect the records of the Land Registry. As opposed to this, general creditors do not usually enquire as to the charges against the debtor company's assets, not even those listed in the Land Registry. A step in the proposed direction was recently taken by the legislature in regard to cautionary notes, which will be discussed in the following section.

III. CAVEATS

Under secs. 126 and 127 of the Land Law, if the holder of a right in immovable property enters into an obligation to effect a particular transaction, such as a sale or pledge, the obligee may immediately register a caveat to that effect. The obligee under the cautionary note is protected against subsequent liens and the insolvency of the obligor. The caveat is of great practical value, and is quite common in nearly all Israeli real estate transactions. The registration of the actual conveyance takes considerable time and is possible only after various taxes are paid and other requirements have been met. In contrast, the entry of a cautionary note takes immediate effect, and, as stated, the obligee enjoys nearly full protection from the moment the note is recorded.

In the *Ytong* case, which was decided several years ago,[39] the Supreme

[37] The problem with the proposed rule is that the rights of a secured creditor who did not record his mortgage in the Land Registry is less than that of an unsecured creditor. Therefore, it may be said that when the company is insolvent, both of the above secured creditors will be deemed unsecured creditors. In practice, the Land Law tests will only apply in the event of the company's insolvency.

[38] Cf. sec. 262(8) of the Australian Corporations Law under which a pledge on company land is exempt from registration with the Registrar of Companies.

[39] See *supra*, n. 14.

Court held that where the obligor is a company, a caveat recorded in the Land Register must also be recorded with the Registrar of Companies, and that in the absence of such a registration, the obligee under the note will not enjoy priority over other creditors upon liquidation of the company.

In the opinion of the Court, a caveat is deemed a "charge" as defined by sec. 1 of the Companies Ordinance. Like every charge, it must be registered with the Registrar of Companies in accordance with sec. 178. Under the Ordinance, a charge is "a mortgage and any other form of granting property as security". According to the Court, a caveat is not a mortgage, inasmuch as the proprietary stage has not yet been completed in the Land Registry,[40] but it does fall within the scope of "any other form of granting property as security". A caveat has economic value in the event of the winding up of the obligor company, inasmuch as the recording of it places the property that is the subject of that caveat at the disposal of the obligee, and the property is thus not available for distribution among the creditors.[41] "The caveat protects the obligee in cases of insolvency, and therefore, gives him priority over the debtor's other creditors. This substantive advantage is enough to compare the status of the caveat holder to that of a secured creditor."[42] Registration of the cautionary note with the Registrar of Companies is important in order to give notice that a particular property will not be available for distribution among the creditors.[43]

The result of the Supreme Court's decision is that a caveat in regard to real property that a company has undertaken to pledge or sell must be registered within twenty-one days of the conclusion of the agreement or, at the very latest, within twenty-one days of the recording of the note in the Land Registry. Prior to the decision, caveats were not customarily submitted for registration to the Registrar of Companies. The decision thus created a situation in which cautionary notes that had not been registered with the Registrar of Companies were rendered void. In order to protect secured creditors—and, primarily, to ensure that people who had purchased flats from building contractors would not lose their homes in the event of the liquidation of the seller—the legislature immediately reacted by adopting an amendment that changed the rule established by the Court.

Section 2 of the Land Law (Amendment No. 16) 5754–1994,[44] added the following clause to sec. 127 of the Land Law: "A caveat entered in accordance with sec. 126 is not required to be recorded in any other statutory registry or register." In other words, a caveat recorded in the Land Register has full legal force without being additionally recorded by the Registrar of Companies. The

[40] *Ibid.*, at 116.

[41] Land Law, sec. 127(b).

[42] *Supra* n. 39, at 123.

[43] The Court held that not only a note regarding a mortgage but also a note in regard to a company's obligation to sell company-owned property must be registered with the Registrar of Companies. *Ibid.*, at 127 –128.

[44] *S.H.* 1482, at p. 364, enacted by the Knesset on 31 August 1994.

scope of the amendment was extended to include cautionary notes recorded prior to its enactment, and it solved the problem of the many notes that for years had been submitted only to the Land Registry. The Court's decision thus affected only the parties before it.

The amendment did not change the Court's holding that a caveat is deemed a charge but is exempt from registration with the Registrar of Companies. From now on, contrary to the approach of the *Ytong* case, all charges on a company's assets are not concentrated under one roof. A person interested in ascertaining the general state of charges upon a company's assets will be unable to make do with a visit to the Registrar of Companies, because certain charges on the company's real property—cautionary notes—can be found only in the Land Register. As earlier stated, a person interested in acquiring a specific interest in a particular property will in any event examine the Land Register. The Law will affect only those interested in obtaining a general picture of the charges against company assets.

Actually, the amendment to the Land Law makes an illogical distinction between a caveat of a mortgage and an actual mortgage. If a mortgage agreement is in its initial, contractual stage, a secured creditor who records a cautionary note is exempt from further registration. But when the mortgage becomes "stronger" and enters the proprietary stage, it must be registered with the Registrar of Companies. If a company goes into liquidation after only a caveat has been recorded, the beneficiary's right will prevail against regular creditors. But if the mortgage has been duly recorded in the Land Registry but not with the Registrar of Companies, those creditors will have priority over the secured creditor.

I do not mean to criticize the amendment itself but the fact that the legislature only completed half of the job. In my opinion, there is no justification for changing the legal situation in regard to caveats while leaving the law unchanged in regard to mortgages. The *Ytong* decision grounded the double-registration requirement for mortgages in the need to concentrate all the information regarding charges created by a company in a single registry. But after the Land Law amendment an examination of the Land Register is necessary in any event in order to obtain a complete picture, as it is the only place in which cautionary notes are recorded. That being the case, it should also be sufficient to record mortgages only in the Land Registry.

Amending the Land Law in regard to cautionary notes thus supports my suggestion that charges against company property only be registered in the Land Registers. Following this approach, a creditor who records a mortgage on company property in the Land Register will take priority over anyone who subsequently acquires an interest in that property and over the company's general creditors, even if the mortgage is not registered with the Registrar of Companies. In this sense, the rule for mortgages will be the same as that for cautionary notes, and the rule for charges on a company's real property will be the same as that applicable to charges on the property of an individual.

The special case of a floating charge on real property will be considered in the next section.

IV. FLOATING CHARGES

The floating charges customary in Israel generally apply to all the assets of the borrowing company, including its immovable property. Section 169(a) of the Ordinance provides that:

> "Where a debenture or a series of debentures is secured by a floating charge upon assets of the Company not excluding its immovable property such charge shall, whether it is registered in the Land Registry or not, be enforceable against the immovable property of the Company."

On its face, the section states that a floating charge that is also applicable to a company's real property[45] and that is recorded with the Registrar of Companies is completely valid even if not recorded in the Land Registry. The existence of a floating charge on a company's real property is, therefore, not reflected in the Land Registers. Thus, floating charges join the ranks of other property interests that are exempt from the burden of registration, such as an easement by prescription,[46] a short-term lease,[47] as well as others.[48] This exemption from registration could harm a person who acquires a right in the property without knowing of the existence of those adverse interests. But the effect of such rights is relatively limited because they have negligible practical importance or have a limited life span and for other reasons.

The fact that floating charges are not reflected in the Land Registers caused no noticeable problem as long as the Companies Ordinance recognized the classical floating charge that did not restrict the creation of additional pledges or the sale of charged assets. In any event, a floating charge is subordinated to specific interests in the charged property. A person who acquires a specific right in immovable property takes priority over the holder of a floating charge, even if he knew of the existence of the charge.[49] But it is important to ask whether or not the exemption from registration in the Land Registry applies to a floating charge that incorporates a restriction. In accordance with sec. 169(b), a floating charge with a restrictive clause that is registered with the Registrar of Companies takes priority over a subsequent adverse transaction. The question is whether or not this priority applies even if the floating charge on real property is not recorded in the Land Registry but only with the Registrar of Companies.

[45] By its language, the section does not apply to a floating charge limited to a company's immovable property, although I cannot see any justification for the distinction.

[46] Land Law, sec. 94.

[47] See Lerner, *supra* n. 21, at pp. 73–77.

[48] Weisman, *supra* n. 17, at pp. 299–301.

[49] Sec. 169(b) of the Ordinance.

There are two possible interpretations. According to the first, sec. 169(a) applies even to a floating charge with a restriction and even if the charge is registered only with the Registrar of Companies it takes priority over an after-acquired specific right. Accordingly, if a person finds that a particular property is listed in the Land Registry under the name of a company, he would be well advised to enquire of the Registrar of Companies whether there is a floating charge against the company's assets. A buyer or mortgagee who checks only the Land Register and who, finding no recorded adverse interests, completes registration of his right in the Land Register,[50] will be displaced by a floating charge registered only with the Registrar of Companies.

This interpretation of sec. 169(a) would not appear to contradict the provisions of the Land Law. Under sec. 10 of the Land Law, "Where a person acquires a right in settled immovable property for consideration and in bona fide reliance on registration, his right shall be valid even if the registration was not correct." An entry in the Land Register is, therefore, conclusive evidence of its contents,[51] and it would seem that a person who relies on that entry holds all the aces. However, the principle established under sec. 10 applies only to rights that must be recorded in the Land Register, and not to rights that are exempt from registration, or that must be recorded elsewhere.[52] Section 10 places yet another obstacle in the path of a buyer of immovable property or a secured creditor. The section benefits only a person who acquires the right in good faith. There is some doubt as to whether a person will be deemed to have acted in good faith for the purposes of sec. 10 if he refrains from checking the records of the Registrar of Companies after discovering that the property is registered in the Land Register in the name of a company.[53]

According to the second approach, sec. 169(a) applies only to a classical floating charge, whereas a floating charge containing a restrictive clause must be registered in the Land Registry. In this sense, the law is the same for a fixed charge, or mortgage, on a company's real property, and a floating charge with a restrictive clause. Both must be doubly registered. Under this approach, registering a floating charge with the Registrar of Companies will prevent its

[50] The Registrar of Land will record a mortgage on the property of a company without checking to see whether an adverse right is recorded in another Registry.

[51] Land Law, sec. 125(a).

[52] J. Weisman, *supra* n. 17, at 312 and 318.

[53] Similarly, it is doubtful that the conflicting transactions rules in sec. 9 of the Land Law will benefit the holder of a later right. Priority over an earlier right is conditional, inter alia, upon the good faith of the obligee in the second transaction. As stated, in such circumstances it is not clear that a person who examined only the Land Register will be considered to have acted in good faith. Under the proposed interpretation of sec. 169(a), the holder of a floating charge with a restrictive clause who registered the charge and the restriction with the Registrar of Companies will be deemed to have fulfilled all that is required of him by law and his right will have been transformed from an obligation to a proprietary right. Sec. 9 of the Land Law deals with contests between conflicting rights. But where the first right is proprietary, it can be defeated only by a market overt transaction, and as we have seen, this defence will fail for lack of good faith if the records of the Registrar of Companies were not examined.

invalidation under sec. 178 of the Companies Ordinance, and will afford the holder of the charge priority over general creditors in case of liquidation of the company. However, in the absence of registration of his right in the Land Registry, he will not enjoy preference over the holders of specific rights in the charged property.[54] The holder of a floating charge with a restrictive clause who seeks to protect his right against subsequent mortgagees and buyers will thus have to record it as well in the Land Register.[55]

According to this approach, if an examination of the Land Register reveals that a particular property is owned by a company, a buyer or secured creditor interested in the property need not enquire of the Registrar of Companies. A classic floating charge registered with the Registrar of Companies is subordinated to a later transaction in immovable property, and, as a result, a floating charge with a restrictive clause that is only registered with the Registrar of Companies is also subordinated to the holder of an after-acquired specific right that is recorded in the Land Register.

For reasons of policy, I prefer the second interpretation of sec. 169(a) even if it is not as easily reconcilable with a plain-language reading of the text. One of the central purposes of the Land Law is that the Land Register shall reflect all rights in real property to the greatest possible extent. Although there are certain rights that are not recorded in the Register, the aim is to keep such situations to a minimum.[56] Viewing sec. 169(a) of the Companies Ordinance as not applying to a floating charge with a restrictive clause would serve that aim. Following the first approach, the existence of a floating charge would be expressed only in the records of the Registrar of Companies. This would impair the comprehensiveness of the Land Register.

Following the approach I have proposed, a floating charge with a restrictive clause will have to be recorded in the Land Register by virtue of the provisions of the Land Law. According to sec. 7 of that law: "A transaction in immovable property requires registration [and] a transaction which has not been completed by registration shall be regarded as an obligation to effect a transaction." Transaction being defined as the grant of the ownership thereof or of any other right therein.[57] In my opinion, this definition encompasses a floating charge with a restrictive clause. Although the Law contains a list of rights in real property, such as lease, mortgage, and easement, the list is not exhaustive, and a right created by virtue of another law, in this case the Companies Law, can constitute a right in immovable property.[58]

[54] On a similar rule in the western provinces of Canada, see Roderick J. Wood, "The Floating Charge on Land in the Western Provinces," 20 *Can. Bus. L.J.* (1992) 132.

[55] If the real property constitutes part of the business inventory of the company, as in the case of a building contractor, the holder of the floating charge will not have an interest in registering the charge with the Registrar of Land, inasmuch as, in any event, he allows the company to sell the property in the normal course of business.

[56] Cf. *America Israel Bank, supra* n. 8, at 258.

[57] Land Law, sec. 6.

[58] Sec. 161 of the Land Law establishes that "there shall be no right in immovable property save under an enacted Law." This wording rules out the creation of proprietary rights by virtue

As opposed to this, a classic floating charge without a restrictive clause will not require registration in the Land Registry. This result can be justified in one of two ways. The first is that a classic-floating-charge agreement is not a transaction in immovable property because the holder of the charge does not acquire a proprietary right. A transaction under sec. 6 of the Land Law is "the grant of any other right therein," that is, the transfer of a proprietary right in regard to real property and not some other right.[59] Even if a classic floating charge on a company's real property is a grant of a right in immovable property, it can be argued that such a grant is exempt from registration under sec. 169(a) of the Companies Ordinance. In this context, sec. 169(a) is a special law that sets aside the general registration requirement under sec. 7(b) of the Land Law.

Under this interpretation, the Registrar of Land will have to comply with a request to register a floating charge with a restrictive clause. However, even if I am mistaken and a floating charge is not a transaction in immovable property, the holder of the charge will be able to protect itself by recording a caveat. This distinction between the impact of a classic floating charge and a floating charge with a restrictive clause upon the creation of later transactions found expression in a decision by the Haifa District Court.[60] The court upheld the Registrar of Land's refusal to allow the holder of a classic floating charge to record a cautionary note, on the ground that before crystallization, the holder of the charge is not permitted to prevent the sale or pledge of the charged property. Therefore, he cannot be allowed to record a caveat that would restrict such transactions.[61] As opposed to this, the holder of a floating charge with a restrictive clause has a justified interest in bringing the restriction to the public's notice and he should be permitted to do so by means of a cautionary note.

of contract, and recognizes rights created by virtue of another statute, see J. Weisman, supra n. 11, at 40.

Under sec. 91 of the Land Law, "immovable property or a registered lease of immovable property shall not be pledged except by mortgage," but I do not believe that this provision prevents recognising a pledge of property by means of a floating charge. On the ambiguity of sec. 91, cf. J. Weisman, *ibid.*, at 64–65.

[59] *Bikser* v. *"Amidar" The National Corporation for Immigrant Housing Ltd.*, (1978) 32(1) P.D. 73, 77.

[60] *United Mizrahi Bank Ltd.* v. *Registrar of Land* (1992) 1992(1) P.M. 58.

[61] When the debtor company has sold numerous assets and the charge holder suspects that insufficient assets will remain for paying the debt it may attempt to prevent the removal of further assets by recording a caveat in the Land Register. Under sec. 170 of the Ordinance, the holder of the charge may apply to the court to request "an order to restrain the Director of Lands from permitting any further mortgage or sale to be entered in the Register in respect of any land then registered in the name of the Company and not excluded from the security of the debenture holders, save under order of the court: and the court may upon being satisfied that the security of the debenture holders is in jeopardy or that it is otherwise just and equitable to do so, make such Order accordingly upon such conditions as to costs and otherwise as it may think fit." The order will be recorded in the Land Register, and will prevent the recording of an adverse right. Such an order is of a negative nature. It does not make any grant or declaration as to the nature of the right of the holder of the charge but prevents the creation of an adverse right by the debtor, in a manner similar to the recording of a lien in the Land Register.

The court's decision did not distinguish clearly between the recording of a cautionary note and the recording of the floating charge itself, and it is not clear if the registration refers to the charge or only to the restriction. Under sec. 126 of the Land Law, a caveat may be recorded not only in regard to obligation of the owner of a right in real property to effect a particular transaction but also in regard to an obligation "to refrain from effecting a transaction in respect thereof." A similar result can be derived from sec. 128 of the Law.[62] It would appear therefore that a "negative charge" can be recorded in regard to real property by which the owner of the property does not pledge anything but undertakes not to pledge the property to another creditor. In our context, this means that a caveat can be recorded pursuant to a restriction in a floating-charge debenture even if the floating charge itself cannot be registered.

I have previously recommended changing sec. 178 to provide that a charge on company real property will not require registration in the records of the Registrar of Companies but only in the Land Register. However, my recommendation did not relate to a floating charge on real property, because the Registrar of Land is not a suitable substitute for the Registrar of Companies.[63] The reason is that a floating charge also covers the company's after-acquired real property while at the time of the creation of the charge nothing can be recorded in the Land Register. In order to prevail against general creditors upon the company's liquidation, the floating charge must, therefore, be registered with the Registrar of Companies. However, in keeping with my proposed approach, a floating charge with a restrictive clause that has been registered only with the Registrar of Companies will be subordinated to a subsequent mortgagee or a good-faith purchaser of the property.

This result would appear to place a considerable burden upon the holder of the charge. In order to protect himself against a purchaser or mortgagee, the holder of the restrictive floating charge will have to keep track of every real-property acquisition by the company and record the charge or, at least, a cautionary note, against every such property. However, the purchase of real property that is not intended to form part of the company's business inventory is not a common event, and it generally comes to the notice of the holder of the charge.

V. THE ROLE OF THE REGISTRY OF CHARGES

Any registry of rights, the Registry of Charges included, has two primary functions. At present, its main task is to inform outsiders as to the nature of

[62] Under this section: "Where it has been proved to the satisfaction of the Registrar that the completion of a transaction by the owner of immovable property . . . is subject—by virtue of . . . written obligation by the owner—to the consent of a third party, the Registrar shall, upon the application of the third party, enter a note to this effect."

[63] If the floating charge applies to real property and to other assets of the debtor company, it is clear that it is not possible to waive registration with the Registrar of Companies.

the rights in a property. This information is important to persons planning to purchase a particular property or to accept it as security for credit to be extended to a company. Such persons are interested in finding out if the property is subject to any adverse rights for the benefit of others. From this perspective, the record determines priority among holders of competing rights, with the first to register having priority.[64] This aspect of registration is irrelevant to a person providing a company with unsecured credit. The latter relies upon the general financial state of the company and is not interested in the number of charges upon its assets.[65]

The other function of a Registry is evidentiary, testifying to the existence of a right in favour of a particular transferee.[66] Such evidence is of particular importance where a company is insolvent and its assets are insufficient to pay all its debts. In such a case, the company may wish to benefit a particular person and claim that certain of its assets are subject to a charge in his favour. In order to prevent the initial raising of such a claim at the time of insolvency, the law denies an unregistered charge validity against a company liquidator. In this respect, registration plays an important role in the conflict between the secured creditor and unsecured creditors, and is irrelevant to a conflict between secured creditors.

In its decision in *United Mizrahi Bank* v. *Adv. Rozovski (Ytong)*, mentioned earlier,[67] the Court said the following concerning the importance of the Registry:

> "The advantage of the records kept by the Registrar of Companies is in that it allows for the concentration of the relevant information regarding various charges against the company's assets, whatever their composition, such that anyone interested, whether a potential investor, a stockholder, or a company officeholder, can

[64] Cf. Uniform Commercial Code, 9–312(5).

[65] Already at the turn of the century, Buckley J. commented on the negligible value of the Registry of Charges for general creditors, See *In Re Cardiff Workman's Cottage Co. Ltd.*, [1906] 2 Ch. 627, 630 and in general, Douglas G. Baird, "Notice Filing and the Problem of Ostensible Ownership," 12 *J. of Legal Studies* (1983) 53. It would seem that the claim that the Registry of Charges is of no importance from the point of view of unsecured creditors also has empirical support. Various reports show that unsecured creditors do not usually examine the Registry of Charges before granting a company credit, See, re the United States, Allison Dunham, "Inventory and Accounts Receivable Financing," 62 *Harv. L. Rev.* (1949) 588, 609–613.

A similar claim has been made in Canada, see R.C.C. Cuming, "Canadian Bankruptcy Law: A Secured Creditor's Heaven," 24 *Can. Bus. L. J.* (1994) 17, 27 ("There is very little empirical evidence that potential unsecured creditors use information from the personal property registry when assessing the risk involved in granting credit.").

[66] See Roderick J. Wood, "The Floating Charge in Canada," 27 *Alberta L. Rev.* (1989) 191, 213–214. See, in the United States, Carl Felsenfeld, "Knowledge as a Factor in Determining Priorities Under the Uniform Commercial Code," 42 *N.Y. Univ. L. Rev* (1967) 246, 249. The author compares the registration laws that preceded the UCC with those under the Code. ("Most pre-Code filing and recording statutes were designed to exhibit to the world the existence and good faith of the lien transaction.")

[67] See n. 14.

learn of their existence easily and at little expense through a short examination of the company's charge register."[68]

Although unintentionally, this paragraph raises an important question. The Court considers the importance of the Registry of Charges in regard to such persons as stockholders and company officers, but does not mention creditors. The Court perceives the Registry of Charges as a source of information to a person about to invest his time or money in the company. According to this approach, the disclosure of charges against company assets is not an isolated datum, but is part of the company's general financial profile. Providing information about charges is necessary so that a potential investor in the company, or a person about to conclude various transactions with it, can estimate its worth.[69] From this perspective, the recording of charges is like the recording of other data about the company, such as its main area of business and the names of its directors and stockholders. However, the sanction for failure to report the particulars of charges is different from that imposed for failure to report other information. Under section 178 of the Ordinance, an unregistered charge is void "against the liquidator and every creditor of the company." This sanction is special to security interest law and is also found in sec. 4 of the Pledges Law. However, the purpose of registration under the Companies Ordinance is not limited to serving the needs of potential creditors, secured or unsecured as in the case of charges against the property of individuals, but is also intended to supply information to investors, employees, analysts, etc.

The intermingling of the primary functions of the Registry of Charges—establishing the relationship between a secured creditor and other secured and unsecured creditors on the one hand, and comprehensive disclosure of a company's activities, including the charges created by it on the other—led to the imposition of rules inappropriate to the primary function of the Registry. The Companies Ordinance imposes upon the debtor company, and not upon the secured creditor, the duty to notify the Registrar of the particulars of the charge and imposes a daily fine upon the company and every officer of the company who fails to comply with this duty.[70] Such sanctions are out of place in secured transactions law. That law does not require the imposition of fines for failure to register, but makes do with the sufficiently harsh sanction of avoiding an unregistered charge. The ineffectiveness of an unregistered charge against a liquidator and other company creditors is sufficient to induce a secured creditor to register a charge in his favour. Security interest law

[68] *Ibid.*, at 126.

[69] Also see the report of A.L. Diamond, *A Review of Security Interests in Property* (1989) p. 98. ("Today, the registration of charges serves several different purposes. Apart from the general climate of opinion in favour of public disclosure of a company's financial activities, there is the provision of information for persons proposing to deal with the company so that they can assess its creditworthiness; this information is of course particularly relied on by credit agencies. The information may similarly be of use to financial analysts and to persons considering whether to invest in the company.")

[70] Secs. 186 and 192 of the Ordinance respectively.

assumes that a charge will be recorded in a public registry without the need to impose administrative and criminal sanctions. Moreover, the Companies Ordinance requires that the particulars of a charge be submitted to the Registrar within a defined period of time and provides that a charge that is not submitted for registration within that period is void. Such a rule is foreign to security interest law, and is unnecessary. The two purposes of a charges registry considered above—providing information to parties seeking to acquire specific interests in charged property, and providing proof of the perfection of a charge—do not require the charge to be registered within a defined time frame. The need to submit the particulars of a charge within a given time derives from the general duty of disclosure that applies to the company and its transactions. It is foreign to the law of security interests.[71]

In summary, the registration of charges upon company assets became part of the general duty of disclosure imposed upon a company for the benefit of investors, interested parties, analysts, etc. The disclosure duty marginalized the classic purposes of the charges registry and transformed its rules. In this framework, various alien rules infiltrated the field of charges, such as the duty to register a charge, the imposition of a duty upon the debtor company rather than on the creditor, the imposition of administrative and criminal sanctions for non-compliance, and avoidance of a charge not registered within the stipulated time period. This development introduced superfluous distinctions between charges upon company property and charges upon individual property and prevents the consolidation and improvement of security interest law.

In my opinion, even if the list of a company's charged assets is necessary to non-creditors, this information should not be disseminated by means of the charges registry. A charges registry is intended to serve only the company's creditors and not other persons. The attempt to house two purposes under one roof has not succeeded, and has led to a system of rules that is inappropriate to the primary functions of a charges registry. I believe that the focus of the registration of charges against company assets should be on the law of pledges and not on the field of company law. From this perspective, there should be no distinction between the rules applicable to charges upon company assets and those applicable to charges on the property of individuals. I would recommend severing the disclosure duty from the classic functions of a charges registry. Such a separation would permit the consolidation of security interest law for companies and individuals. The existence of a uniform registry for all charges would make it possible to leave the duties of notification and disclosure to the Registrar of Companies.

In accordance with my proposal, registration of a security interest would take place in a general charges registry, common to companies and individuals. Registration in these registers would be governed by the regular rules of security interest law. Registration would not be obligatory, but an unregis-

[71] On various anomalies that derive from the dual function of the companies registry in English Law, see R.M. Goode, *Commercial Law*, (2nd ed., 1995) 703–704.

tered charge would be unenforceable against a liquidator and other company creditors. Registration in these registers would, therefore, be relevant to establishing the relationship between the secured creditor and others. The particulars of the charge would be submitted to the registrar by the secured creditor at whatever time he chose. Section 191 of the Ordinance, dealing with the extension of registration periods, would thus be unnecessary.

Under my proposal, various charges created by a company will continue to be reported to the Registrar of Companies. The purpose of this registration will be to provide comprehensive information about the financial transactions of the company. The records of the Registrar of Companies would not affect conflicts between the holder of a charge and other creditors. In other words, sec. 178 will not apply to the submission of the particulars of a charge to the Registrar of Companies and a charge registered only with the charges registry and not with the Registrar of Companies will have full force in the event of the winding up of the company. A company that fails to report the particulars of charges against its assets to the Registrar of Companies will expose itself to administrative and criminal sanctions. The company will be under a duty to report the particulars of a charge to the Registrar of Companies within a defined period of time, so that the register will accurately reflect the company's transactions.

This proposal will lead to uniform rules for the registration of charges against the real property of individuals and that of companies. As will be recalled, the Companies Ordinance requires double registration of a mortgage on company property, both in the Land Register and with the Registrar of Companies. A charge not registered in one of the two Registries is void against a liquidator. In my opinion, registration in the Land Registry is sufficient to fulfil the two functions of security interest law. It provides information to anyone interested in acquiring a specific right in the property, by examining the Land Register. It also proves that the parties effected a legitimate transaction. Indeed, it was observed that the need for double registration is explained by the broad duty of disclosure applicable to substantive company matters. However, this requirement may raise a variety of difficulties. Under the system proposed here, registration in the Land Register will be relevant only to security interest law, while the registration of a mortgage with the Registrar of Companies will serve the general duty of disclosure.

11

The Case for Worldwide Reform of the Law Governing Secured Transactions in Movable Property

HARRY C. SIGMAN*

Reform of personal property security law, in the form of the creation of a modern practical legal framework for efficiently securing obligations by hypothecation of personal property, responds to the inability of many would-be debtors to obtain credit (particularly from local credit sources). Studies by the World Bank establish that expansion of the universe of available collateral beyond real property would, *ipso facto*, likely have a significant impact on the GNP of many countries where at present security interests can be taken effectively only in real property. Moreover, adoption of a legal structure such as that provided for in UCC Article 9/Canadian Personal Property Security Acts (all of which, though not identical, are sufficiently uniform to be fairly described as providing not only a single conceptual framework but also for the most part the same substantive rules), by virtue of its proven effectiveness and its familiarity to North American credit sources which are presently constrained in their extension of credit in such countries, would doubtless have the further effect of increasing the quantum of credit available to facilitate growth of the local economies. Increased legal certainty and increased competition in the provision of credit (by attracting credit from external sources and by providing for security interests available without distinction to all

* Mr Sigman has been a member of the California Bar for over 30 years, specializing in commercial law. He is a member of the Drafting Committee that is currently revising Art. 9 and is a member of The American Law Institute. He has taught at the Law Schools of the University of Southern California, University of California at Los Angeles and Tilburg in the Netherlands, and will be Visiting Professor of Law at Leuven (Belgium) during winter 1997.

This comment is a written version of remarks made in response to the presentations, including the remarks of other commentators, delivered at the segment on Secured Transactions in Movable Property at the Academy's 8th Biennial Conference. It consists, therefore, not of a straightforward exposition of a single thesis fully developed and documented, but rather of a series of points (somewhat reorganized and expanded) offered with respect to statements made by preceding speakers. There is, however, a thread running through these remarks—my view that worldwide reform in the area of personal property security law is highly desirable, is timely and should be pursued vigorously, with uniformity as a primary goal.

types of credit extenders) should result in an increase in the availability of credit and a decrease in its cost.

It is, of course, not my thesis that the North American framework is better than all other existing or possible systems simply because it is North American. Rather, I base the case for its adoption elsewhere on the pragmatic grounds that it has been proven effective in a sophisticated fast-paced credit market over a period of four decades, it is in place successfully supporting countless billions of credit, it is familiar to major credit sources ready to offer similar credit on a worldwide basis, and it comes not simply as unadorned black-letter language but accompanied by a large body of judicial interpretation and academic and professional analysis.

The goal is not to achieve a magnificent conceptual framework to be admired by philosophers but rather to facilitate credit availability in the real world. Therefore, untested approaches, particularly approaches based on theory rather than business realities, are likely to be counterproductive. Matters of logical completeness and perfect consistency are likely to distract from the economic purpose of this area of the law. The "best" may well be the enemy of the "good" unless reformers keep their eyes firmly fixed on the goal. Indeed, since the goal is to enable business people to conduct their affairs efficiently by providing a legal structure that gives certainty to their conduct and yet at the same time is flexible enough to allow them to develop new patterns as their needs dictate, the object of the draftsman, as Grant Gilmore told us, is "to be accurate [in ascertaining real world practices] and not to be original".[1]

It need hardly be said that uniformity in commercial law generally, and in personal property security law in particular, is highly desirable. The primary function of this body of law is to provide sufficient certainty and predictability that credit can be extended rapidly, with confidence and economically. Elimination of conflict of laws issues, doubts engendered by lack of clarity, the costs of engaging local counsel, etc., strongly argue for uniformity.

By way of specific example relating to today's presentations, we have been told that Israel, Jordan and the Palestinian Authority are all in the early stages of reform in this subject. It would be of obvious advantage to all three were they to adopt the same legal framework, putting all of them on the same competitive footing, facilitating both the internal and the cross-border functioning of domestic institutions (credit extenders, competing creditor interests, and their counsel) in each of the three places, and maximizing in the aggregate their attractiveness to credit suppliers from outside the region. Indeed, adoption of the same substantive law would also facilitate the creation of a single regional filing office, or at least the ability to share information in a single database, making filing and searching efficient and less expensive, minimizing the need for multiple filings and searches and for rules to deal with

[1] Grant Gilmore, "On the Difficulties of Codifying Commercial Law", 57 *Yale LJ* 1341 (1957).

situations where movement of collateral or debtors would otherwise result in the need for refiling in a different office.

Personal property security law for the most part involves the formulation of rules providing certainty, predictability, validation of business practices and facilitation of development of new business practices—shared values—and rarely implicates local cultural mores or traditions indigenous to a particular country. History and tradition play no instructive role here—indeed, rules based on history and tradition are likely to be inefficient and not well-suited for modern sophisticated financing. In the case of the formerly Communist countries and in some of the underdeveloped countries, reformers face the daunting task of creating a legal structure for an economy of a type that does not yet exist. And it seems safe to predict that in ten years, virtually everywhere, economies and the way wealth is embodied and dealt with will be quite different from what they are today. It is certainly true that there are a few discrete areas where truly local and important policy differences might come into play (e.g. remedies upon default), and in these areas a lack of uniformity may well not be particularly harmful. General appeals to local tradition, however, are likely to be counterproductive. Personal property security law is facilitative rather than regulatory, and must be open, flexible and forward-looking. It is certainly not the repository of national identity, and insistence on "local flavor" is likely to sabotage attainment of the ultimate ends.

Absence of demand for law reform in this subject hardly proves the absence of need. After all, existing local financing patterns are based on existing legal structures. Were the business, legal, governmental and academic communities of a country fully aware of the benefits to be reaped from this reform, I have little doubt that the demand would be there. Recent political changes, increasing globalization of commerce and the increasing embodiment of wealth in personal rather than real property, all militate in favor of reform; and the increasing proportion of wealth found in intangibles (ranging from mundane receivables to exotic intellectual property rights) underscores the need for cross-border uniformity as well as modernization.

The question was raised whether law reform in this area should separate personalty from realty (immovables) collateral. Were one writing on a clean slate, one might be tempted to try to integrate all types of collateral into a single security law scheme. However, that is not today's reality. Virtually every country has a long established real property registry, usually forming the basis of ownership (title) claims, with encumbrance claims being incidental. These registries are typically fairly primitive technologically, inefficient because of their vintage, and encrusted with a well-entrenched bureaucracy and supporting cast of notaries. Attempting change involving real property would arouse the opposition of all those interested in maintaining the *status quo*, who would raise, *inter alia*, the specter of social and financial instability that might be caused by change to the highly valued realty ownership registry system.

Moreover, traditional realty-secured lending is long-term, static, single-advance lending, secured by an asset the location of which is always known with certainty and does not change, changes ownership (in many countries) only as the result of an official act on the public record, cannot be stolen, and tends to fluctuate in value only gradually—quite unlike, for example, revolving credit, which involves daily advances secured by daily changing pools of inventory and receivables. The priority rules of a personal property security regime have to provide for vastly different fact-patterns, the filing system is not an ownership registry but simply a notice bulletin board allowing searching parties to discover potentially prior security interests, and remedies upon default are of necessity quite different. Further, realty security law must take into account the inclusion of collateral that may constitute the debtor's residence, a fact that is likely to engender the need for special rules.

This leads to the question of the need for and desirability of a public notice filing system. It is certainly true that countries such as Germany and the Netherlands have sophisticated economies that include a significant amount of personalty-secured debt and do so without a public registry. Such countries, however, traditionally have presented a credit marketplace not only very different from that found in the newly emerging and developing economies but also quite possibly unlikely to be characteristic of the twenty-first century European single market. They presently reflect a highly concentrated lending market dominated by a small number of very powerful banks, which share information about debtors informally amongst themselves, and which typically lend to borrowers with well-established credit histories that are often owned and operated by citizens who have resided locally for generations.

Antipathy toward an Article 9-type public filing system is often based on a concern that it would be an expensive, bureaucratic inefficient set-up similar to the familiar realty registries. This fear is not well-founded. Because the systems serve very different purposes, they can (and do) function very differently. Article 9/PPSA does not involve placing on the record original documents, prepared by notaries, that create "real" rights. All that need be publicly filed is a "financing statement", a simple (if on paper, typically one page) notice setting forth the names and addresses (or other minimal identifying information) of the debtor and secured party and a simple (often general) description of the collateral. The Article 9/PPSA filing system neither creates nor evidences "real" rights in property (the debtor may not even own the collateral described in the filing); it simply provides a warning to potential credit-extenders to get more information from off-record sources (usually from the prospective debtor, other credit-extenders, information services such as Dun & Bradstreet, etc.), and is a tool utilized in deciding certain priority contests.

The details of the financial arrangements between debtor and secured party are private matters and there is no reason to put these on the public record;

the security agreement is not filed. The limited role played by the filing system minimizes the need for formalities and permits efficient operation by removing from filing office administrators any power of review or exercise of discretion with respect to tendered filings. Indeed, given the state of current technology, there need be virtually no human intervention involved and no archiving issues are presented. A handful of employees can handle a database of millions of filings. In fact, even with the relatively inefficient systems currently in place in the United States (where electronic filing is in its infancy; unlike Canada, where electronic filing is so well-entrenched that the PPSA most recently to come into force, in New Brunswick, does not even permit paper filings), typical filing fees are between $5 and $15, and these low fees nevertheless typically generate net revenue for the filing office. Thus, the fears of opponents of filing systems are not well-founded.

Article 9 uses the term "filing system", and, for essentially the same system, the Canadian PPSAs use the term "registry". I use the term "filing system" with respect to the type of public notice system provided under both Article 9 and the PPSAs deliberately in order to emphasize to non-North Americans that these systems are very different from the registries (such as realty registries) with which the rest of the world is familiar.

Opposition to a public filing system is sometimes asserted on privacy grounds. This argument, too, is not well-founded. To begin with, at least in the European Union, companies are required to publish annual statements that, *inter alia*, would reveal secured financing. Thus, this information is already publicly available; it is just not current. Moreover, no company anywhere can in fact get credit without disclosure to its prospective lender; the real issue is how the lender verifies the disclosure and publicizes its claim. Also, in many countries, credit information providers such as Dun & Bradstreet offer extensive financial data concerning would-be borrowers and customers. In any event, to the extent privacy is perceived of as a "human" right, it is hard to argue that it extends to economic persons. And, with respect to individuals, in most of the Western European countries there are long established consumer credit information repositories (such as Schufa in Germany and BKR in the Netherlands). Thus, in fact, consumers in such countries have effectively no privacy at all in their use of credit, and such repositories hold far more revealing detail than is found in financing statements filed under Article 9/PPSA.

One of the speakers at the conference discussed a proposed rule that would involve a twenty-one day retroactivity. Given the available modern technology (particularly electronic filing and remote access searching), there is neither need nor justification for such a rule, which can only delay the extension of credit or increase risk.

Finally, another priority rule discussed was the priority accorded under Article 9 to the party first to file, without regard to the knowledge of the first filer that an unfiled secured party had already extended credit on the strength of the same collateral. The rule is supported on efficiency grounds. An absolute first to file rule eliminates litigation concerning knowledge, maximizes certainty for all concerned and maximizes the reliability of the public record by providing a strong incentive to make the record as complete as possible at the earliest possible time.

PART IV
Conflict of Laws

12

Territoriality and Choice of Law in the Supreme Court of Canada: Applications in Products Liability Claims

CATHERINE WALSH*

"[T]he common idea that the local law should be preferred in cases of doubt, is essentially a corollary of the local policy doctrine; it is evidently a counsel of despair, which should be ignored in formulating the policies of conflicts law . . . [The local law theory] lends comfort to the narrow minded, who may be inclined to deprecate the practical and equitable consequences that should control the adjudication of conflicts cases in favour of exaggerated local policy on the ground that they and the sovereign which they represent can do as they please. This view . . . is at the end a shallow and even brutal philosophy, namely, that law is power.[1]

I. INTRODUCTION

Canadian news continues to be much preoccupied with the Helms-Burton Act[2] signed into law by US President Clinton on 12 March 1996. Entitled the Cuban Liberty and Democratic Solidarity (Libertad) Act of 1995, the aim of the legislation is to force political and economic change in Cuba by

* Professor, Faculty of Law, University of New Brunswick, Fredericton, Canada. This paper has also been published in (1997) 76 *Can. Bar. Rev.* 91. I thank Professors Roy Goode, Mary Hiscock, Walter Stoffel, and Jay Westbrook for their insightful comments on the paper at the Bar Ilan Conference. I am grateful also to Professors Vaughan Black, Patrick Glenn, John McEvoy and Norman Siebrasse for valuable feedback on a later version.

[1] Hessel E. Yntema, "The Objectives of Private International Law" (1957) 35 *Can. Bar Rev.* 721, 721–2, 735. And see Hessel E. Yntema, "The Historical Bases of Private International Law" (1953) 2 *Am.J Comp.L* 297, 316–17.

[2] 110 Stat. 785 (12 Mar. 1996). The Helms-Burton Act was introduced by Sen. Jesse Helms of North Carolina and Rep. Dan Burton of Indiana, both conservative Republicans. It was passed after the downing on 24 Feb. 1996 of two US civilian aircraft flown by anti-Castro Cuban Americans.

penalising foreign nationals who do business in that country.[3] Under Title III, US nationals whose Cuban properties were confiscated by the Castro government in 1959 are authorised to bring suit for compensation against any third party national who "traffics" in those properties.[4] Under Title IV, the State Department is empowered to bar "traffickers" from entry into the United States, with "trafficker" defined broadly to include senior corporate executives, controlling shareholders and their spouses and minor dependents.[5]

Reaction to the US initiative has been sharply critical from the outset. The Act is seen as an excessive extraterritorial assertion of US domestic policy, antithetical to customary international law and violative of the US commitment to its trading partners.[6] Canada has been a particularly outspoken opponent,[7] retaliating with "blocking legislation" barring the enforcement of Helms-Burton judgments in Canada, and "claw-back legislation" entitling Canadians to claim amounts recovered against them under Helms-Burton in the United States in proceedings in Canada against the local subsidiaries of US companies.[8]

[3] A detailed account of the US government's official rationale for the Act is given in Title I. For a critical analysis of the Act, see Andreas F. Lowenfield, "Congress and Cuba: The Helms-Burton Act" (1996) 90 *Am. J of Int'l L* 419. In reply, see Bruce M. Clagett, "A Reply to Professor Lowenfield" (1996) 90 *Am. J of Int'l L* 641. For a descriptive review of the legislation and its background, see Saturnino E. Lucio, II, "The Cuban Liberty and Democratic Solidarity (Libertad) Act of 1995: An Initial Analysis" (1995–6) 27 *U Miami Inter-Am. L Rev.* 325.

[4] Title III was to have taken effect on 1 Aug. 1996, but the Act authorises the US President to suspend its effectiveness for successive periods of up to 6 months by certifying to Congress that the suspension is in the national interest and will expedite a "transition to democracy" in Cuba. President Clinton exercised his suspension power on 16 July 1996 and again on 3 Jan. 1997 for successive 6-month periods. See "Clinton's Cuba move criticized as both too harsh and too soft", CP–AP, Ottawa, 4 Jan. 1997.

[5] Title IV is in effect. Thus far, executives (and their families) of only one Canadian company (Sherritt International) have been advised that they are barred from entry to the US. A Mexican holding company also has been targeted. See Valerie Lawton, "Sherritt Insists It's Taking Moral High Road in Cuba." CP, Toronto, 24 Feb. 1997; Laura Eggertson, "Sherritt Releases Names of VPs that U.S. to Ban", *Globe and Mail*, 18 Mar. 1997.

[6] The Inter-American Juridical Committee has concluded, not unexpectedly, that the Helms-Burton Act "does not conform to international law": see (1996) 35 ILM 1322. See also Lowenfield *supra* n. 3, at 430–2. The US government's official justification for Title III, as stated in the Helms-Burton Act itself, rests on a combination of the controversial "effects" and "passive personality" bases of international prescriptive jurisdiction: "Sec. 301 (9). International law recognizes that a nation has the ability to provide for rules of law with respect to conduct outside its territory that has or is intended to have substantial effect within its territory. (10) the United States Government has an obligation to its citizens to provide protection against wrongful confiscations by foreign nations and their citizens, including the provision of private remedies."

[7] Mexico and the EC also expressed strong initial opposition to the Helms-Burton legislation. Indeed, the EC formally asked the World Trade Organization (WTO) to rule that the measure violates international trade rules. However, in Apr. 1997, the USA and the EC agreed to suspend some provisions of Helms-Burton in exchange for a withdrawal of the WTO complaint: see Robert Russo, "Sign Anti-Cuba Agreement or Else, U.S. Official Warns Canada" CP, Washington, 16 Apr. 1997.

[8] An Act to Amend the Foreign Extraterritorial Measures Act, S.C. 1996, c. 28 (Bill C–54 1996) (amending RSC 1985, c. F–29), royal assent 28 Nov. 1996, proclaimed in force 1 Jan. 1997. A challenge under NAFTA (North American Free Trade Agreement) would be a more effective counter-measure but it also would be a more politically provocative one. Although Canada has

The Helms-Burton controversy affords a dramatic example of an issue germane to this paper: the appropriate allocation of law-making authority among sovereign States. The resolution of that problem is a function of time and context. But the strong condemnation of Helms-Burton suggests that there continues to be little tolerance in today's world for the aggressive extraterritorial assertion of domestic policy. With global economic integration proceeding apace, such opposition may seem paradoxical. After all, economic integration is thought to be transforming classical notions of the inviolability of State sovereignty and territorial jurisdiction.[9] But the modern pooling and transfer of sovereign power has occurred volitionally, through the conclusion of rules-based bilateral and multilateral conventions. Because the unilateral assertion of extraterritorial authority threatens to undermine confidence in the always fragile process of consensus-building, it must attract opposition.

The Supreme Court's recent revolutionary jurisprudence in the private international law field reflects a like commitment to traditional principles of sovereign equality and territorially-restrained jurisdiction.[10] The Court's reform initiatives began with a liberalisation of the protectionist nineteenth-century common law rules on the recognition of extra-provincial judgments.[11] Writing for the Court in *Morguard Investments Ltd.* v. *De Savoye* and *Hunt* v. *T&N Plc*,[12] La Forest J ruled that Canadian courts were constitutionally

not ruled out that possibility, neither has it proceeded. See Marty Logan, "Canadian Law to Counter Possible U.S. Court Action Ineffective: Experts," CP, Ottawa, 4 Jan. 1997.

[9] See, e.g., Joel P. Trachtman, "The International Economic Law Revolution" (1996) 17 *U Pa. J Int'l Bus. L* 33, 47–8.

[10] *Morguard Investments Ltd* v. *De Savoye* [1990] 3 S.C.R. 1077; *Hunt* v. *T & N Plc* [1993] 4 S.C.R. 289; *Tolofson* v. *Jensen, Gagnon* v. *Lucas* [1994] 3 S.C.R. 1022. The themes developed in these three cases were presaged by the Court's earlier decision in *R.* v. *Libman* [1985] 2 S.C.R. 178 on the territorial limits of Canadian criminal law jurisdiction. All four decisions were the product of one justice, La Forest J, and some question the stability of a line of Supreme Court jurisprudence uttered in so singular a voice. Certainly, Sopinka J's reasoning on behalf of the Court in *Amchem Products Inc* v. *British Columbia (Workers' Compensation Board)* [1993] 1 S.C.R. 897 does not fit comfortably within the *Morguard/Hunt/Tolofson* trilogy. In that case, Sopinka J addressed the availability of anti-suit injunctions to restrain litigation abroad, and the relationship between the exercise of that power and the doctrine of *forum non conveniens*. In relation to the latter doctrine, Sopinka J used the terminology of "real and substantial connection", the test adopted by La Forest J in *Morguard* to delineate the territorial basis of subject-matter jurisdiction over a foreign defendant. In so doing, he may have contributed to the continuing doctrinal confusion seen in some of the lower court decisions (*infra* n. 17) between the question whether jurisdiction is available in the first instance, and the second-level question whether, if jurisdiction exists, the court should exercise its discretion to decline jurisdiction on the basis of *forum non conveniens*.

[11] English common law accepts only two bases of "international" jurisdiction for the purposes of enforcing a foreign judgment: (1) residence and possibly physical presence of the defendant within the territorial limits of the foreign jurisdiction at the time process is served; (2) the defendant's consent or submission to the exercise of jurisdiction by the foreign court: see P. M. North and J. J. Fawcett, *Cheshire and North's Private International Law* (12th edn., London/Dublin/Edinburgh, Butterworths, 1992), at 348 ff. Prior to *Morguard and Hunt*, *supra* n. 10, these rules were applied by the courts in common law Canada to both sister-province and foreign-country judgments.

[12] *Supra* n. 10.

obligated to give "full faith and credit" to sister-province default judgments where there is a "real and substantial connection" between the subject matter of the litigation and the judgment forum.[13] At the international level, comity compelled a similar expansion, albeit as a matter of common law doctrine rather than constitutional imperative.[14]

The Court's decisions in *Morguard* and *Hunt* are equally significant for the territorial limits they recognise on the adjudicatory jurisdiction of Canadian courts. Over the last several decades, the statutory service *ex juris* rules in the common law provinces have been expanded to the point where no connection with the forum, or only the most tenuous connection, is sufficient.[15] In *Morguard* and *Hunt*, La Forest J confirmed that the exercise of 'long-arm jurisdiction' under these rules is subject to the territorial limits imposed on provincial legislative authority by the Canadian Constitution.[16] Although there had been some prior recognition of this, no general standard for territorially-competent adjudicatory jurisdiction had been articulated. In the wake of *Morguard* and *Hunt*, it is clear that "[i]n Canada, a court may exercise jurisdiction only if it has a 'real and substantial connection' (a term not yet fully defined) with the subject matter of the litigation".[17] The territorial lim-

[13] The use of the term "full faith and credit" in this context will be familiar to Australian and US lawyers whose Constitutions contain an express full faith and credit clause. See s. 118 of the Australian Constitution and art. IV. s. 1 of the US Constitution. But Canadian constitutional documents lack any comparable written directive. This did not deter La Forest J. He regarded the obligation as inherent in the very nature of Canadian federalism, in the intention to create a national market for the free flow of persons, goods and, by implication, judgments. On the origin of the term "real and substantial connection", see *infra* n. 17.

[14] In the wake of *Morguard* and *Hunt*, Canadian courts have shown no hesitation in extending the new recognition rules to foreign-country judgments: see Catherine Walsh, "Conflict of Laws—Enforcement of Extraprovincial Judgments and *In Personam* Jurisdiction of Canadian Courts: *Hunt* v. *T & N Plc*" (1994) 73 *Can. Bar Rev.* 394, 401–4; and see Joost Blom, "The Enforcement of Foreign Judgments: *Morguard* goes forth into the World" (1997) 28 *CBLJ* 373.

[15] For instance, the Rules of Court in several provinces authorise service *ex juris* in the case of a claim for damage sustained in the province arising from a tort "wherever committed" (e.g., Ontario Rule 17.02(h), New Brunswick Rule 19.01(i), Manitoba Rule 17(02)(h)). This wording has been interpreted to support the exercise of jurisdiction by the courts in the plaintiff's home province over an out-of-province defendant in respect of an out-of-province accident on the theory that an accident victim continues to suffer pain, suffering and fiscal loss on returning home. The seminal decision in this unhappy line of authority is *Vile* v. *Von Wendt* (1979), 103 DLR (3d) 356 (Ont. Div. Ct.). This is equivalent to saying that the plaintiff's residence in the forum is a sufficient basis for the exercise of jurisdiction over a foreign defendant, a proposition that cannot stand in the wake of *Morguard* and *Hunt*: see further *infra* n. 17.

[16] The territorial limit on the reach of provincial legislative power over property and civil rights is reflected in the use of the attenuating words "in the Province" in s. 92(13) of *The Constitution Act, 1867*. See Peter W. Hogg, *Constitutional Law of Canada* (3rd edn., Toronto, Carswell, 1992), at 13–14: "[I]n a federal system it is obvious that a province, whose government is elected by and responsible to only those people within its territory, should not have extensive powers outside its territory where other provincial governments have a better claim to govern. It is not surprising to find, therefore, that the Constitution Act, 1867 couches provincial legislative power in terms which rather plainly impose a territorial limitation on the scope of the power."

[17] *Tolofson supra* n. 10, at 1049. For a recent application, see *Cook* v. *Parcel, Mauro, Nultin & Spaanstra P.C.* (1997), 143 DLR (4th) 213 (BCCA). The "real and substantial connection" test originated in the decision of the House of Lords in *Indyka* v. *Indyka* [1969] 1 AC 33 in relation

its of domestic and foreign court jurisdiction, in other words, are now seen as coterminous.

In its 1994 decision in *Tolofson* v. *Jensen*,[18] the Court turned its attention to the controversial question of choice of law in tort, the focus of this article. The prevailing doctrine in common law Canada rested on what easily qualifies as the most criticised choice of law rule ever to have been devised in private international law.[19] Under the rule in *Phillips* v. *Eyre*,[20] formulated by Willes J in England in 1870, the substantive law to be applied was the *lex fori* provided that the defendant's act was non-justifiable where it was done.[21]

In *Tolofson*, the Court decisively rejected the *lex fori* orientation of the traditional approach, replacing it with a forum-neutral choice of law rule in which territorial contacts dominate. Indeed, in the interprovincial context, the law of the place of the tort now applies exclusively.[22] And while some room

to the jurisdiction of courts to render an internationally-recognised divorce order. The use of the concept to delineate the scope of territorial jurisdiction in Canadian law first surfaced in the Supreme Court's public law jurisprudence, specifically in determining the reach of Canadian criminal law authority: see *R.* v. *Libman*, *supra* n. 10. Although the meaning of "real and substantial connection" is not yet fully defined, one thing is clear. Plaintiff connections to the litigation forum standing alone are insufficient. See e.g. *Wilson* v. *Moyes* (1993), 13 OR (3d) 302 (Gen. Div.). Consequently, the authority of cases in the *Vile* v. *Von Wendt* line of authority (*supra* n. 15) is suspect: see *MacDonald* v. *Lasnier* (1994), 21 OR (3d) 177 (Gen. Div.); *National Bank of Canada* v. *Chance* (1996), 30 OR (3d) 747 (Gen. Div.); and see Walsh *supra* n. 14 at 410. This point continues to be under-appreciated in the case law: see e.g. *Sto. Domingo Estate* v. *Kenora (Town)* (1996), 111 Man. R (2d) 124 (QB); *Dunlop* v. *Connecticut College* (1996), 50 CPC (3d) 109 (Ont. Gen. Div.).

18 *Supra* n. 10.

19 E.g. Moffatt Hancock, "Case Comment on *McLean* v. *Pettigrew*" (1945) 23 *Can. Bar Rev.* 348.

20 (1870), LR 6 QB 1. Until the recent enactment of a new civil code, the rule in *Phillips* v. *Eyre* also formed part of Quebec civil law: *McLean* v. *Pettigrew* [1945] SCR 62. See now *Civil Code of Quebec* SQ 1991, c. 64, art. 3126, adopting the *lex loci delicti* as the general choice of law rule, subject to exceptions, including a common residence exception (proviso to art. 3126, *infra* n. 90) and an alternative reference rule in products liability claims (art. 3128, *infra* n. 119).

21 Under the first part of the rule, in order to sue for a tort committed abroad, the plaintiff had to show that the "wrong" was "of such a character that it would have been actionable if committed" within the forum: *Phillips* v. *Eyre*, *supra* n. 20 at 28–9. Under the second part of the rule, the law of the place where the defendant acted also had a role to play: the defendant's "act must not have been justifiable where it was done": *ibid*. However, that role was interpreted so as to make the *lex fori* the governing law once non-justifiability under the place of acting was shown: *McLean* v. *Pettigrew*, *supra* n. 20 (adopting the reasoning in *Machado* v. *Fontes* [1897] 2 WB 231 (CA)). The facts of *McLean* v. *Pettigrew* demonstrate the ease with which the requirement for non-justifiability under the *lex loci delicti* could be satisfied in motor vehicle accident claims. A Quebec plaintiff sued a Quebec defendant in the Quebec courts for personal injury suffered in an accident that occurred in Ontario. The plaintiff had been riding as a gratuitous passenger in the defendant's vehicle at the time of the accident and Ontario's notorious "guest-host" statute barred recovery. However, under the Ontario Highway Traffic Act, RSO 1937, c. 288, s. 47, careless driving constituted a punishable offence. For the Supreme Court, this was enough to say that the defendant's conduct was non-justifiable under the *lex loci delicti*, notwithstanding that the defendant had been charged and acquitted of an offence under the Ontario Act.

22 Of the 7 justices who decided *Tolofson*, only 2—Sopinka and Major JJ—would have left open the possibility of an exception to the *lex loci delicti* for intracountry torts: *Tolofson*, *supra* n. 10, at 1078. For post-*Tolofson* confirmation of the unqualified application of the *lex loci delicti* rule in interprovincial motor vehicle accident claims, see *Leonard* v. *Houle*, (1996), 21 MVR (3d) 212 (Ont. Gen. Div.); *Stewart* v. *Stewart Estate* [1996] 8 WWR 624 (NWT SC).

was conceded for the operation of a public-policy exception to the *lex loci delicti* rule at the international level, it was thought that such cases would be rare.

As in *Morguard* and *Hunt*, traditional public and private international law values dominated La Forest J's reasoning.[23] In resolving choice of law problems, he stressed, a court is not concerned with "interest balancing" in the substantive tort law sense, but with the "structural problem" of allocating law making authority among territorially-defined sovereigns.[24] From the general international law principle that a State has exclusive law-making authority within its own territory, La Forest J regarded it as axiomatic "that, at least as a general rule, the law to be applied in torts is the law of the place where the activity occurred, i.e., the *lex loci delicti*".[25] The theoretical arguments favouring a territorial principle also responded to traditional conflicts values ("certainty", "predictability", interjurisdictional "harmony" of result, the facilitation of transnational commerce, respect for "well grounded legal expectations"), values which he thought should be given primary emphasis in a global economic order if chaos were to be avoided.[26] Within the Canadian federal system, La Forest J thought that much the same approach should apply, with one significant caveat. In the case of an interprovincial tort claim, "constitutional imperatives and other structural elements" made interjurisdictional harmony of result more desirable and more feasible so as to justify an exclusive *lex loci delicti* rule.[27]

Although no one questions that reform was overdue, the general reaction of Canadian commentators to the new centrality of territorial connections in choice of law for tort has been largely critical.[28] The focus of the criticism is La Forest J's methodology, his avowed preference for classic "one-law-selecting" choice of law rules directed at the identification of a single comprehensive governing law and premised on a philosophy of co-equal territorial sovereignty.[29] For his critics, La Forest J's approach is reminiscent of

[23] The connection to the Court's prior jurisprudence was acknowledged by La Forest J: "All of this is simply an application to 'choice of law' of the principles enunciated in relation to recognition and enforcement of judgments in *Morguard* . . ." (*Tolofson*, *supra* n. 10, at 1048).

[24] *Ibid*., at 1046–7.

[25] *Ibid*., at 1049–50.

[26] *Ibid*., at 1050–1. And see *infra* n. 29.

[27] *Ibid*., at 1048. And see *supra* n. 22.

[28] John Swan, "Federalism and the Conflict of Laws: The Curious Position of the Supreme Court of Canada" (1995) 46 *South Carolina L Rev*. 923; Jean-Gabriel Castel, "Back to the Future! Is the 'New' Rigid Choice of Law Rule for Interprovincial Torts Constitutionally Mandated?" (1995) 33 *Osgoode Hall LJ* 35; John P. McEvoy, "Torts and Choice of Law" (unpublished manuscript on file with author). The reaction of an Australian commentator was more positive: Peter Kincaid, "*Jensen* v. *Tolofson* and the Revolution in Tort Choice of Law" (1995) 74 *Can. Bar Rev*. 538.

[29] By a "one-law-selecting" choice of law rule, I mean a classic multilateral choice of law rule that seeks to identify one particular set of provincial or State laws to apply to an actor's conduct. Westbrook uses the term "one-law" values to denote the values that traditional conflicts doctrine, by generating rules that create a reliable expectation about the applicable law, seeks to vindicate: (1) fairness to regulatees who might otherwise feel required to conform their conduct to more

mechanical "vested rights" thinking, long ago discredited by "local law" theorists in favour of a unilateralist perspective in which the overriding goal is the achievement of substantive tort justice between the litigants, not the abstract allocation of law-making power among sovereigns.[30]

A related line of criticism accepts the Court's premise that choice of law engages issues of State sovereignty as well as private justice. But it is argued that State sovereignty requires tolerance for diversity as much in conflicts cases as in wholly domestic cases and as much within federations as internationally. From this perspective, La Forest J's emphasis on forum-neutral adjudication and deference to foreign territorial sovereignty is seen as negating the values of pluralism and diversity on which sovereignty is premised.

Conflicts theories are essentially cyclical[31] and the fact that a once pervasive way of thinking has lost intellectual currency over time is not enough to condemn its revival. It may simply signal the end of one era and the beginning of another with the bright-line distinctions that typify such transition points. *Tolofson* represents precisely such a transition point,[32] and it is the thesis of this article that it is a welcome one.

Part I begins with a review of the reasons for the extraordinary tenacity of the traditional *lex fori* rule in Canadian law and the changes in the surrounding tort law environment that eventually created pressure for reform. I then analyse the criticisms advanced against *Tolofson* in light of developments

than one set of possibly inconsistent laws; (2) the production of conduct that is lawful by the laws of at least one State; (3) the facilitation of transnational commerce and enterprise and the lowering of the transactions costs of such activities: see Jay Westbrook, "Extraterritoriality, Conflict of Laws, and the Regulation of Transnational Business" (1990) 25 *Texas Int'l LJ* 72, 79–81.

[30] The vested rights theorists believed that a legal right "vests" when and where the last event necessary to create the right occurs. In tort cases, the theory yielded a strict place of injury rule. In *Tolofson*, La Forest J endorsed a passage from *Phillips* v. *Eyre* (*supra* n. 20) that has always been accepted as a classic expression of the vested rights theory: "[C]ivil liability arising out of the wrong derives its birth from the law of the place [where it occurred], and its character is determined by that law." La Forest then went on to say: "In short, the wrong is governed by that law. It is in that law that we must seek its defining character; it is that law, too, that defines its legal consequences" (*supra* n. 10 at 1050). Such is the thoroughness with which the territorial principle that underpinned vested rights thinking is thought to have been discredited over the last 60 years that critics of *Tolofson* regard its territorial approach as a sufficient ground of criticism in itself. The point is captured in John Swan's comment: "A judgment written in 1994 that adopts so unequivocally the vested rights theory of conflict is so unexpected that one could not be more surprised than if we had come across a practising alchemist: What can one possibly say?" (*supra* n. 28, at 948). Legal realism is widely acknowledged to be the impetus behind the rejection of vested rights theory in favour of a result-oriented jurisprudence under which the advancement of local policies and local concepts of justice guides choice of law adjudication in the same way as it does other categories of domestic adjudication. For a recent re-evaluation of the logical entailments of the realist vision for choice of law, see Michael S. Green, "Legal Realism, Lex Fori and the Choice-of-Law Revolution" (1995) 104 *Yale LJ* 967.

[31] For 2 recent works that emphasise the cyclical nature of conflicts theories, see Friedrich K. Juenger, *Choice of Law and Multistate Justice* (Dordrecht, Martinus Nijhoff, 1993) and Lea Brilmayer, *Conflict of Laws: Foundations and Future Directions* (Boston, Mass., Little, Brown, 1991).

[32] The reader will be appreciative that I have avoided the term "paradigm shift" (although this is in fact what *Tolofson* represents).

in other common law jurisdictions, concluding that the Supreme Court's territorial orientation is consonant with significant currents of reformist thinking in the United States and Australia. Part II takes the analysis to a more concrete level and examines the implications of the Court's *lex loci delicti* rule in products liability claims, a particularly fertile source of choice of law problems.[33]

II. THE RESURGENCE OF TERRITORIAL ANALYSIS IN CHOICE OF LAW IN TORT

(a) Explaining the Tenacity of the Traditional *Lex Fori* Rule

A choice of law rule that directs the court to apply its own law is a choice of law rule in name only. Therein lies the principal source of the criticisms of *Phillips* v. *Eyre*.[34] In giving a controlling effect to the *lex fori*, the rule not only reflected a parochial attitude; it abdicated the choice of law decision to the plaintiff with whom the choice of forum rests.

Legal rules that lack widespread respect rarely survive long. How then did *Phillips* v. *Eyre* endure so long in Canadian law? A large part of the reason must be attributed to the fact that most of the tort cases in which the potential for choice of law issues arose involved personal injury claims arising out of motor vehicle accidents. This is an area in which, until recently, the legal regimes governing liability and compensation were largely uniform throughout Canada and, indeed, North America. Where substantive differences existed, the conflict typically involved an "anachronistic" rule, e.g., a drastically attenuated limitations period or a statute barring recovery or raising the standard of care in actions by a gratuitous passenger against the "host" driver. In a climate in which the compensation and loss-distribution functions of tort law increasingly dominated, the pro-plaintiff pro-recovery bias inherent in the traditional choice of law rule was consonant with prevailing standards of substantive tort justice. The "better" more "progressive" law could be applied.

Insurance considerations also played a significant role. The defendant's fiscal interests were protected by the near universal enactment of compulsory liability insurance laws covering automobile accidents anywhere in the United States or Canada. The pro-recovery bias inherent in the application of the *lex*

[33] Substantial variations in theories of enterprise liability in tort and delict from one State to the next have prevented the emergence of international or even national agreement on the optimal products liability regime. Notable exceptions are the European Directive on Products Liability (Strasbourg, 1973) and the federal products liability regime recently incorporated into Australian law as Part VA (ss. 75AA–75AS) of the Trade Practices Act 1974 (Cth.) (commenced 9 July 1992). Even in these 2 cases, however, member State variations have not been eliminated entirely.

[34] *Supra* n. 20.

fori thus also served to further the loss-distribution objectives of compulsory insurance without inflicting any practical hardship on the defendant against whose interests it operated.

No doubt for these same ultimately pragmatic reasons, the *lex fori* orientation of the traditional Canadian rule was also compatible with the results reached under the "modern" conflicts theories in ascendance in the United States. True, the US courts had early on rejected the rule in *Phillips* v. *Eyre* as parochial in the extreme, replacing it with a strict *lex loci delicti* rule.[35] But the vested rights theory on which the *lex loci delicti* rule was based eventually gave way in the scholarship, and then in the decisional law of the leading States, to a variety of realist-inspired result-sensitive approaches in which traditional conflicts values were subordinated to the forum policy of compensation for injury.[36] While the new theories varied in their intellectual orientation, the results achieved reflected the same "homeward trend" as the *Phillips* v. *Eyre* formula.[37]

Indeed, one might argue that the "mechanical jurisprudence" produced by the Canadian courts under *Phillips* v. *Eyre* was to be preferred for its efficiency advantages. The new US approaches shared a common antipathy to broad-brush "one-law-selecting"[38] choice of law rules and a common preference for open-ended instrumentalist analysis. As such, they tended to be labour-intensive, requiring detailed *ad hoc* issue-by-issue justification for the choice of law resolution in each case.[39]

[35] E.g. *Alabama Great Southern Railroad* v. *Carroll*, 97 Ala. 126, 11 So. 803 (1892). The *lex loci delicti* rule was incorporated into §378 of the (first) *Restatement of the Law of Conflict of Laws* (1934).

[36] E.g. Westbrook *supra* n. 29, at 78. And see *supra* n. 30. For 2 highly readable and comprehensive accounts of the US "conflicts revolution" against the perceived rigidity and injustice of vested rights thinking, see the recent monographs by Brilmayer and Juenger, *supra* n. 31.

[37] See e.g. Frederick K. Juenger, "An International Transaction in the American Conflict of Laws" (1992) 7 *Fla. J Int'l L* 383, 396–7 (footnotes omitted): "[T]he large majority [of state supreme courts have] adopted one of three modern methodologies, or a mixture thereof: 1. Interest analysis; 2. The Second Restatement; 3. Leflar's choice influencing considerations. As a statistical analysis has demonstrated, in practised application the differences between these approaches are not great. All three of them favour application of the lex fori, and since counsel who charge contingent fees rarely sue in a jurisdiction whose law is unfavourable to their clients' causes, the plaintiff tends to win. In a few instances when courts do apply foreign law, they usually opt for a sounder sister state rule in preference to a substandard lex fori. Since most of the substantive rules that used to cause conflicts problems—guest statutes, intrafamily immunities and arbitrary monetary ceilings on wrongful death recovery—were substandard, the better foreign rule, again, usually favoured the victim."

[38] This term is defined *supra* n. 29.

[39] *Ad hoc* result-oriented analysis, by its very nature, is also particularly resistant to accommodating concerns with "comity": see Joel P. Trachtman, "Reflections on the Nature of the State: Sovereignty, Power and Responsibility" (1994) 20 *Canada-United States LJ* 399, 410–11 (arguing that if the rules allocating prescriptive jurisdiction are predictable, transparent and easily administered, they minimise transactions costs by facilitating "market agreements" that reallocate authority to another State, with "market agreements" conceived to include other-sensitive practices such as "comity"; conversely, unpredictable, result-oriented rules, or those that depend on an analysis of forum policy that has not yet been undertaken, by reducing the ability of states to predict what other states will do, also reduce the ability of states to arrive at such "exchanges").

(b) Pressures for Reform

The substantial uniformity in tort legal policy among the Canadian provinces on which the stability of the traditional *lex fori* rule was premised changed radically with the emergence of statutory no-fault compensation regimes for personal injury suffered in automobile accidents. In most provinces, these took the form of "partial" or "add-on" schemes in which first-party insurance benefits were made available to accident victims complementary to the tort liability "system". But in 1978, the province of Quebec instituted a "pure" no-fault regime displacing civil recovery and liability altogether for accidents occurring within the province.[40] Visitors and residents alike were instead limited to a tariff of statutorily-prescribed benefits. The level of compensation available was more limited than what would be recoverable in an action in tort, particularly in the realms of general damages for pain and suffering and pecuniary damages for future loss of wages. Quebec motorists were still required to carry liability coverage for out-of-province travel and could sue and be sued before the courts in the jurisdiction where the accident occurred. But within Quebec "first party" insurance principles prevailed.

In this new climate, it was no longer possible for the courts to maintain a plaintiff and forum bias in choice of law in tort.[41] Two different reparations philosophies were now potentially in direct conflict, and one could not be said to constitute the "better", more "progressive" law. Minimally, this required the exercise of greater self-restraint in the application of the *lex fori* and a correspondingly more respectful stance towards territorial connections.

(c) Territoriality, Federalism and Concepts of State Sovereignty

In speculating about the outcome in *Tolofson*,[42] some Canadian conflicts scholars predicted that the law of the place of the tort would play a larger

[40] Automobile Insurance Act, SQ 1977, c. 68, RSQ 1977, c. A–25. For a review and analysis of the conflicts features and implications of the Quebec plan, see Catherine Walsh, "A Stranger in the Promised Land: The Non-Resident Accident Victim and the Quebec No-Fault Plan" (1988) 37 *UNBLJ* 173. The Ontario legislature subsequently introduced a modified no-fault insurance plan, under which insured victims lost their right to sue civilly for personal injury suffered in an automobile accident in exchange for first-party benefits from their own insurers regardless of fault unless their injuries surpassed the statutory threshold established by the Act. See *Insurance Act* RSO 1990, c. I.8, s. 266. Pure no-fault regimes were introduced in Manitoba and Saskatchewan, effective from 1 Mar. 1994. The majority of other Canadian jurisdictions (the exceptions are Alberta, one or two Atlantic provinces, and the Territories) are expected to implement no-fault in the near future or already have enacted significant tort reforms: see Barry L. Gorlick, "No-Fault Insurance Update" (1997) 13.2 *Solicitor's Journal* 21.

[41] As La Forest J observed in *Tolofson* (*supra* n. 10, at 1044), the "fundamental weaknesses" in the *Phillips* v. *Eyre* formula began to be revealed in a series of Ontario cases beginning in the 1980s, in which the victims of Quebec accidents attempted to "top up" their "no-fault" benefits by bringing a tort action in Ontario.

[42] *Tolofson* v. *Jensen, Lucas* v. *Gagnon, supra* n. 10. *Tolofson* involved an action in British

role; indeed that it might become the general rule if only "to retain at least the appearance of reasonable predictability".[43] What nobody anticipated was that the new predominance of territorial over personal contacts would not be tempered by some sort of "flexible exception".[44] Thus, there was widespread surprise, even shock, when the Court ruled that the *lex loci delicti* governed exclusively in the case of interprovincial torts.[45]

La Forest J justified an unqualified *lex loci delicti* rule for interprovincial conflicts on the heightened significance within federal systems of the classic conflicts values of certainty and interjurisdictional harmony of result:

> "The nature of our constitutional arrangements—a single country with different provinces exercising territorial jurisdiction—would seem to me to support a rule that is certain and that ensures that an act committed in one part of the country will be given the same legal effect throughout the country. This militates strongly in favour of the *lex loci delicti* rule."[46]

A territorial approach to choice of law in tort also had the advantage of "unquestionable conformity"[47] with the territorial limits on provincial legislative power over property and civil rights imposed by the Canadian Constitution.[48] Assuming that the constitution limits the extraterritorial application of forum law via forum choice of law rules,[49] it followed that an

Columbia arising out of a two-vehicle accident in Saskatchewan. The plaintiff was a resident of British Columbia. So was the first defendant, his father, the driver of the vehicle in which the plaintiff was a passenger when injured. The second defendant, the driver of the other vehicle, was from Saskatchewan. Saskatchewan tort law imposed 2 limits on recovery: (1) in guest–host situations, the passenger had to establish "wilful or wanton negligence" on the part of the driver; (2) a one-year limitation period for motor vehicle accidents. *Lucas* raised a more "modern" conflicts dilemma. An Ontario passenger sued his driver, also an Ontario resident, for injuries sustained in an accident in Quebec. The Ontario defendant cross-claimed for contribution and indemnity against the Quebec driver of the other vehicle involved in the accident. At issue was whether Quebec's no-fault law (*supra* n. 40) precluded recovery by the plaintiff against the defendant, and by the Ontario defendant against the Quebec respondent on the cross-claim, under Ontario tort and contribution principles respectively.

[43] Joost Blom, "An International Transaction in the Canadian Conflict of Laws" (1992) 7 *Fla. J Int'l L* 403, 416. Cf. Swan, "Choice of Law in Torts—A Renvoi: *Gagnon* v. *Gagon*, *Williams* v. *Osei-Twum*" (1993) 15 *Advoc. Q* 356; Black and Flack, "Choosing the Applicable Law for Cross-Border Accidents" (Annotation) (1993) 14 *CCLT (2d)* 73.

[44] Blom, *supra* n. 43.

[45] *Supra* n. 22.

[46] *Tolofson, supra* n. 10, at 1064.

[47] *Ibid.*, at 1065.

[48] On the constitutional basis for the territorial limits on provincial legislative authority, see *supra* n. 16.

[49] La Forest J was clearly sympathetic to the proposition that the constitution imposes territorial limits on the authority of Canadian courts to select forum law as the *lex causae* under forum choice of law rules. In their prior writings, Swan and Castel have expressed agreement with that proposition, notwithstanding their criticisms of La Forest J's territorial analysis in *Tolofson* (*supra* n. 28): see John Swan, "The Canadian Constitution, Federalism and the Conflict of Laws" (1985) 63 *Can. Bar Rev.* 271, 313; Jean-Gabriel Castel, *Canadian Conflict of Laws* (3rd edn., Markham, Butterworths, 1994), 6–7: " [T]he Judicial Committee of the Privy Council and the Supreme Court of Canada have interpreted the Constitution Act so as to strike down unreasonable attempts by one province to disregard the interests of other provinces or the general

attempt by the courts in one province to impose liability under forum tort law in relation to activities taking place wholly in another province and involving out-of-province parties would give rise to "serious constitutional concerns".[50] A *lex fori* exception to the application of the *lex loci delicti* premised on the common residence of the parties within the forum had some "promise" of constitutional validity.[51] However, if both the *lex loci delicti* and the law of the common residence of the parties were capable as a constitutional matter of applying in such cases, this would "open the possibility of conflicting rules in respect of the same incident".[52] In the result, La Forest J thought it best not to devise a judical rule that might raise "intractable constitutional problems" and to leave any exceptions to the application of the *lex loci delicti* to the legislatures to articulate.[53]

La Forest regarded a territorially-based approach to choice of law as equally applicable in the international context. However, deference to a foreign country's territorial sovereignty is premised on "comity," not "constitutional imperatives" and other federal "structural elements."[54] This difference allowed for greater discretion in the operation of the territoriality principle, a discretion which La Forest J conceded might be needed to "to avoid injustice" in cases where the substantive content of a foreign lex *loci delicti* was so radically at odds with the *lex fori* as to implicate fundamental forum public policy.[55] Consequently, he was prepared to retain a discretion in the court to apply forum law in the international context though he thought that the occasions where this would become necessary would be rare.[56]

La Forest J's willingness to infuse federal and public international law values into his choice of law analysis contrasts sharply with the prevailing judicial doctrine in the United States and Australia. In both countries, the

interests of Canada at the international level . . . Since Canadian provinces lack the power to legislate extraterritorially, territoriality can be used as an instrument of constitutional control over provincial conflict of laws rules."

[50] *Tolofson*, *supra* n. 10, at 1065–6.

[51] *Ibid.*, at 1066. The Quebec legislature enacted a common residence exception in its new Civil Code (art. 3126, *infra* n. 89), a fact noted by La Forest J in *Tolofson*. The common residence exception is discussed *infra* in part I(e) of this article.

[52] *Ibid.*

[53] *Ibid.*

[54] *Ibid., at* 1048.

[55] *Ibid.*, at 1054. La Forest J saw little place for a forum public policy exception to the *lex loci delicti* rule in the interprovincial context: "Certainly, where the place of the wrong and the forum are both in Canada, I am convinced that the application of the *forum non conveniens* rules should be sufficient [to deal with cases where the alleged wrong is not actionable as a tort under the *lex fori*]. I add that I see a limited role, if any, for considerations of public policy in actions that take place wholly within Canada" (*ibid.*, at 1054–5). That greater tolerance for decisional non-uniformity may be necessary at the international rather than the federal level is accepted by even the most committed territorialists: see Douglas Laycock, "Equal Citizens of Equal and Territorial States: The Constitutional Foundations of Choice of Law" (1992) 92 *Columbia L Rev*. 249, 260: "Domestic choice of law need not be flexible enough to deal with totalitarian states, revolutionary states, legally unsophisticated states, or states with legal and cultural traditions fundamentally different from our own."

[56] *Tolofson*, at 1054–5.

starting point in analysing the relationship between federalism and choice of law is the full faith and credit clause in their respective constitutions.[57] That clause obligates each state to give full faith and credit to the laws, as well as the judgments, of sister states. Taken literally, the clause sets up an infeasible task. "To simultaneously apply the conflicting laws of two states is impossible; to require each state to apply the law of the other is absurd; and to let each state apply its own law repeals the Clause.[58] The full faith and credit clause thus makes sense only on the assumption that there exist choice of law rules to identify when sister state law applies and when it does not. But while the clause "assumes the existence of choice-of-law rules, it does not specify what those rules are."[59] Does this mean that states are obligated to apply sister state law only when directed to do so by their own choice of law rules? Or does the full faith and credit obligation assume the influence of constitutional values on the development of state choice of law rules in the first instance?[60]

In Australia, the problem has been the subject of conflicting majority decisions in the High Court in recent years.[61] In 1988, in *Breavington* v. *Godleman*,[62] a bare majority of the Court endorsed an unqualified *lex loci delicti* rule for interstate torts. Deane J's territorial analysis bears a marked similarity to that of La Forest J His starting point was not the full faith and credit clause as such. Rather he saw that clause as reflecting a more general

[57] *Supra* n. 13.

[58] Laycock, *supra* n. 55, at 297.

[59] *Ibid.*

[60] In Canada, the Supreme Court's decision in *Hunt* v. *T & N Plc*, *supra* n. 10, supports the latter approach in the context of the implied "full faith and credit" obligation in the Canadian constitution. At issue in that case was whether the Quebec corporate defendants in a British Columbia tort action were required to comply with a demand for discovery of certain corporate documents which they had been prohibited from removing from the province of Quebec by the order of a judge of the Quebec Provincial Court issued under that province's *Business Concerns Record Act*. The British Columbia courts were thus faced with a "full faith and credit" dilemma: should they compel production pursuant to forum law or yield to the laws of a sister province? On the assumption that the Quebec Act was constitutionally valid, the British Columbia courts yielded: "interprovincial comity" compelled "the recognition of, and deference to the validly enacted legislation of a province by the courts of another province": *Hunt* v. *T&N Plc* (1991), 81 DLR (4th) 763, 767 (BCCA). Writing for the Supreme Court, La Forest J ruled that the Quebec courts were obligated by the full faith and credit doctrine to respect pre-judgment discovery orders issued by the British Columbia courts. The contrary rule would allow the courts in one province to engage in a "pre-emptive strike" against the constitutionally competent exercise of jurisdiction by the courts in another province. In the course of his reasoning, La Forest J confirmed a significant additional point: that full faith and credit does not require a court in one province to yield to sister-province laws which purport to extend their spatial reach to cover the same ground as forum law. Rather, the provincially-constituted courts have full authority to rule on the constitutionality of legislation of a province that has extraprovincial effects in the forum. With this statement, *Hunt* laid the seeds for a transplantation of a full faith and credit doctrine premised on the territoriality principle to the choice of law context.

[61] Generally, see W. M. C. Gummow, "Full Faith and Credit in Three Federations" (1995) 46 *South Carolina L Rev*. 979; Peter Nygh, "Choice of Law and Forum Shopping in Australia" (1995) 46 *South Carolina L Rev*. 899.

[62] 169 CLR 41 (1988).

feature of Australian federalism: the idea that the same legal consequences should attach to an act or omission occurring anywhere within the Australian national territory regardless of where within that territory the matter was litigated.[63] To achieve interstate decisional harmony, it was necessary that the same connecting factor—predominant territorial connection—operate both to identify the applicable sister state law in conflicts cases and to limit state legislative authority *vis-à-vis* other states.[64]

In an Australian constitutional context, however, there is a serious obstacle to Deane J's operative assumption that state legislative competence is subject to significant territorial constraints.[65] Under the prevailing doctrine, the states are free to extend the reach of their legislation to interstate activities and conduct even if the subject-matter nexus is a "remote and general" one and even if the result is to subject persons to the conflicting laws of more than one state.[66] If territoriality does not significantly limit the exercise of state legislative power *vis à vis* other states, it is difficult to see on what constitutional basis the courts are compelled to adopt a territorial approach to choice of law for interstate torts.

It is this reasoning that persuaded a differently-constituted majority of the High Court to later abandon the *lex loci delicti* rule. In *McKain* v. *Miller*,[67] decided just three years after *Breavington*, the Court reinstated the *Phillips* v. *Eyre* formula for interstate torts (it had never abandoned it at the international level), and along the way rejected any role for s. 118 of the Constitution in limiting choice of law.[68] Rather, s. 118 enters the picture only after the com-

[63] *Ibid.*, at 121.

[64] *Ibid.*, at 129–30: "[T]he constitutional solution of competition and inconsistency between purported laws of different states as part of a national law must, where the necessary nexus for prima facie validity exists, be found either in the territorial confinement of their application or, in the case of multi-state circumstances, in the determination of predominant territorial nexus."

[65] *Ibid.*

[66] Gummow, *supra* n. 61, at 1013.

[67] *McKain* v. *R.W. Miller & Co. (South Australia) Pty. Ltd.*, 174 CLR 1 (1991). The majority in *Breavington* was composed of Mason CJ, Dean, Wilson and Gaudron JJ. The minority comprised Brennan, Dawson and Toohey JJ. In the interval between *Breavington* and *McKain*, Wilson J retired and was replaced by McHugh J In *Tolofson*, La Forest J cited the majority position in *Breavington* as reflecting the Australian position, even though *McKain* had been decided by the time *Tolfoson* was argued.

[68] *Ibid.*, at 36–7: "The laws of the States, though recognized throughout Australia, are therefore capable of creating disparities in the legal consequences attached in the respective States to the same set of facts unless a valid law of the Commonwealth overrides the relevant State laws and prescribes a uniform legal consequence. This may or may not be thought to be desirable, but it is the hallmark of a federation as distinct from a union. Far from eliminating the differential operation of State laws, section 118 commands that all the laws of all the states be given full faith and credit: the laws of the forum are to be recognized as fully as the law of the place where the set of facts occurred. Section 118 would not be obeyed by refusing recognition to the laws of a forum State and by applying only the laws of the part of Australia to which the facts occurred. A disparity in legal consequences attached to a set of facts cannot be eliminated by refusing recognition to laws of the forum which create the disparity. In our respectful opinion, section 118 does not prescribe the selection of the lex loci delicti or other extraterritorial body of law as the exclusive body of law governing liability for extraterritorial torts. The selection of the applicable rules governing liability is the function of the common law; section 118 provides for recognition by the

mon law choice of law rules point to the application of the law of a sister state, and those choice of law rules are not themselves required to conform to the Constitution. As Deane J later commented, the approach adopted by the current majority "goes a long way towards converting the Australian legal system into a national market in which forum shoppers are encouraged to select between competing laws imposing different legal consequences in respect of a single occurrence."[69]

The United States Supreme Court has arrived at much the same position as its Australian counterpart. Although initially sympathetic to the idea that the full faith and credit clause obligates the states to apply one and only one state law in conflicts cases,[70] the United States Supreme Court has since all but reversed its position. Today, a state is free to apply its own law even if this conflicts with the law of a sister state so long as some factual connection exists with the forum, and even if that connection does not relate to the subject matter of the litigation. The high point of this reasoning came in 1988 in *Allstate Insurance* v. *Hague*.[71] Justice Brennan conceded that, in theory, full faith and credit requires each state "when acting as a forum for litigation having multi state aspects or implications, [to] respect the legitimate interests of the other states and avoid infringement upon their sovereignty."[72] In practice, however, the clause was interpreted so as make the forum state's interest in the fiscal welfare of its residents *qua* plaintiffs a sufficient nexus to justify recovery under forum law in relation to out-of-state activity involving only out-of-state parties. The decision was widely interpreted as signalling the end of any meaningful limits on the right of state courts to prefer local law and local plaintiffs in conflicts cases.[73]

The very different position taken by the Supreme Court of Canada in *Tolofson* from its Australian and US counterparts reflects their fundamentally different concepts of the implications of State sovereignty. For "territorialists" like La Forest J, the stability of a federal and international legal order premised on a system of territorially-defined sovereign provinces and States requires that greater weight be given to private and public international law values than local substantive legal policy in the choice of law equation. For extraterritorial "regulators" like the majority in *McKain* and the justices who decided *Hague*, sovereignty implicates the value of diversity and the

courts of the forum of the rules so selected." For a detailed critique of this passage, see Gummow (recently appointed to the High Court), *supra* n. 61 at 1002–5.

[69] *Stevens* v. *Head* (1993), 176 CLR 433, 462, quoted by Nygh, *supra* n. 61 at 913.

[70] It has been argued that this was the original intent of the drafters: W. Crosskey, *Politics and the Constitution in the History of the United States* (1953), 553–5.

[71] 101 S.Ct. 633 (1981).

[72] *Ibid.*, at 640.

[73] This was the consensus of the majority of the commentators who participated in a subsequent symposium on the Court's decision: "Symposium, Choice of Law Theory after *Allstate Insurance* Co. v. *Hague*" (1981) 10 *Hofstra L Rev. 1*. And see Gene R. Sheve, "Choice of Law and the Forgiving Constitution" (1996) 71 *Ind. LJ* 271. But see *Phillips Petroleum Co.* v. *Shutts*, *infra* n. 154.

correlative right of States to extend their local policy to interstate and international conduct that has effects within their territorial boundaries even if this conflicts with the territorially-competent laws of other sovereigns.[74] The only constraints are pragmatic: self-interest and practical enforceability.

(d) The Resurgence of Territoriality in Choice of Law in Tort

The primary weight placed by the extraterritorial "regulators" on the advancement of local policy can obscure their common ground with the territorialists.[75] Local policy need not be conceived purely in terms of local concepts of substantive justice. It can also encompass communitarian values associated with the federal and international legal order, including the avoidance of conflict with other States, the promotion of reciprocity and the facilitation of transjurisdictional economic and other activities.[76] There is, in fact, increasing recognition of the importance of these values in the contemporary scholarship and reformist literature in the United States and Australia.

In a study published in 1992,[77] the Australian Law Reform Commission endorsed the majority's premise in *Breavington*[78] that within the interstate context the same conduct or activities should carry the same legal consequences regardless of the forum of litigation. To that end, the Commission recommended the enactment by all States of uniform forum-neutral choice of law rules, including a *lex loci delicti* rule for interstate tort claims. Of course, uniformity at the choice of law level does not ensure interstate decisional harmony if the forum is free to interpret local legislative policy so as to give it wide extraterritorial scope. Consequently, the Commission also recommended the enactment of a presumption making the territorial scope of State legislation co-extensive with the connecting factor for choice of law in the relevant substantive area in the absence of an express indication of a contrary intent.

In the United States, the conflicts scholarship evidences renewed support for the infusion of constitutional considerations into interstate choice of law analysis. The recommendations range from the imposition of more potent limits on the extraterritorial application of forum law in interstate settings[79] to the

[74] In discussing the differences between "territorialists" and extraterritorial "regulators", Westbrook (a confessed "regulator") writes: "[T]erritorialists give much greater weight to the traditional international values and much less weight to local policies. That explains why the two views are so far apart, even though both of them purport to rest upon a respect for sovereignty. The territorialists' view is based on a greater commitment to the *system* of sovereign states, and the deference that system requires, while the regulators' opposing view emphasizes the rights of each individual sovereign considered as such" (*supra* n. 29 at 89).

[75] *Ibid.*, at 91–2.

[76] *Ibid.*, at 81.

[77] Australian Law Reform Commission, *Choice of Law*, Report No. 58, Mar. 1992.

[78] *Supra* n. 62.

[79] Gary J Simson, "State Autonomy in Choice of Law: A Suggested Approach" (1978) 52 *S Cal. L Rev.* 61; Linda Silberman, "Can the State of Minnesota bind the Nation?: Federal Choice of

creation on the *Tolofson* model of territorially-oriented choice of law rules premised on the values of co-equal State sovereignty.[80]

The developments on the constitutional front reflect a more general "counter-revolution" (or at least a "resistance movement") against the "modern" consequentialist choice of law approaches that replaced the territorial orientation of the vested rights theorists.[81] There is a growing consensus that the abandonment of territorial constraints on choice of law, whether constitutionally or common law ordained, rather than heralding a brave new world of communitarian values, has resulted only in a parochial and unjust emphasis on local law and the interests of local litigants.[82] A territorial choice of law is no longer seen as inherently incompatible with the achievement of substantive justice in conflicts cases. On the contrary, because it is a forum-neutral connecting factor, it contains the promise of more even-handed justice for both parties. Globalisation has also influenced the change in thinking. In an age of high personal and professional mobility, the significance attached to the concept of the personal law is in decline; activity-related connections are increasingly thought to offer a more stable and predictable criterion for choice of law.

Even those who remain committed to interest analysis or advocate new alternative methodologies no longer urge the automatic application of the *lex fori* or the equally subjective "better law" in cases where more than one State

Law Constraints after *Allstate Insurance Co.* v. *Hague*" (1981) 10 *Hofstra L Rev.* 103; James A. Martin, "The Constitution and Legislative Jurisdiction" (1981) 10 *Hofstra L Rev.* 133; Arthur T. von Mehren and Donald T. Trautman, "Constitutional Control of Choice of Law: Some Reflections on *Hague*" (1981) 10 *Hofstra L Rev.* 35; Willis L. M. Reese, "The '*Hague*' Case: An Opportunity Lost" (1981) 10 *Hofstra L Rev.* 195. Cf. Linda J Silberman, "*Cooney* v. *Osgood Machinery, Inc.*: A Less than Complete 'Contribution' " (1994) 59 *Brook. L Rev.* 1367. And see Sheve, *supra* n. 73.

[80] Laycock, *supra* n. 55. See also Aaron D. Twerski, "On Territoriality and Sovereignty: System Shock and Constitutional Choice of Law" (1981) 10 *Hofstra L Rev.* 149.

[81] Lea Brilmayer, *Conflict of Laws: Cases and Materials* (4th edn., Boston, Mass., Little, Brown, 1995), at 1, and see generally at 355–9. For summary discussions of the "resistance movement" and references to the burgeoning literature, see Laycock, *supra* n. 55, at 252–6; Larry Kramer, "Rethinking Choice of Law" (1990) 90 *Col. L Rev.* 277, 279; P. John Kozyris, "Values and Methods in Choice of Law for Products Liability: A Comparative Comment on Statutory Solutions" (1990) 38 *Am. J Comp. Law* 475, 482–9. For a more comprehensive treatment, see the recent monographs by Juenger and Brilamayer, *supra* n. 31.

[82] For the insight that territorial choice of law methodologies are linked to the values of liberalism, and personal law methodologies to a more communitarian philosophy, see Lea Brilmayer, "Liberalism, Community and State Borders" (1991) 41 *Duke LJ* 1, 3. In a somewhat similar vein, Westbrook views the attitude of deference to foreign territorial sovereignty associated with the territorialists as indicative of a *laissez-faire* attitude to the regulation of transnational economic activity (*supra* n. 29 at 93–4). But, as Westbrook acknowledges, these arguments can be turned on their head. Thus, it can be argued that the territoriality principle in choice of law advances communitarian values because it pays maximum respect to the principle of self-determination that underpins the division of States into territorially-defined units. Similarly, adherence to the principle of co-equal territorial sovereignty can be said to maximise the effectiveness of transnational regulation because it better ensures that other States will respect the regulatory efforts of the State having the predominant territorial connection with the particular subject matter.

is found to have an "interest" in having its laws applied. The focus is now on achieving a maximum accommodation of the purposes or policies underlying the laws of *all* the implicated States with any policy clashes to be resolved in a manner that "a *neutral* observer will regard as fair and reasonable".[83] Although there "has not been a wholesale return to the old rules, there has been increased emphasis on the territorial principles that underlie the old rules".[84] After all, whatever its other deficiencies, it is generally acknowledged that vested rights theory at least tended to avoid the parochialism and systematic unfairness to defendants associated with classic interest analysis in the United States.[85]

The United States is not the only common law jurisdiction to have retreated from excessive *lex foriism*. In its 1969 decision in *Chaplin* v. *Boys*,[86] the House of Lords recast the *Phillips* v. *Eyre* formula to require civil actionability of the defendant's conduct under both the *lex fori* and the *lex loci delicti*. The enlarged role of the *lex loci delicti* under the new rule was subject to a "flexible" exception allowing the exclusive application of forum law in relation to particular issues in the interests of "justice" to the parties. However, a recent Privy Council decision gives increased prominence to both the *lex loci delicti* and classic choice of law methodologies.[87] It is now clear that the "flexible

[83] Russell Weintraub, "A Proposed Choice of Law Standard for International Products Liability" (1990) 16 *Brook. J Int'l L* 225, 227. See also Russel J Weintraub, "An Approach to Choice of Law that Focuses on Consequences" (1993) 56 *Alb. L Rev.* 701; Kramer, *supra* n. 81.

[84] Brilmayer, *supra* n. 81, at 1. According to one recent analysis, the *lex loci delicti* is the presumptive choice of law rule in a majority of the USA today: Symeon C. Symeonides, "Choice of Law in the American Courts in 1993 (and in the Six Previous Years)" (1994) 42 *Am J Comp. L* 599, 608. David Cavers was an early advocate of recourse to a territorial principle to resolve the "true conflicts" revealed by interest analysis. See his "Principles of Preference" in *The Choice of Law Process* (1965); and see David Cavers, "Cipolla and Conflicts Justice" (1961) 9 *Duq. L Rev.* 360. See also Aaron Twerski, "A Sheep in Wolf's Clothing: Territorialism in the Guise of Interest Analysis in *Cooney* v. *Osgood Machinery*" (1994) 59 *Brooklyn L Rev.* 1351, 1361, commenting as follows on the choice of law rules articulated by the New York Court of Appeals in *Neumeier* v. *Kuehner*, 31 NY 2d 121 (1972): "Although *Neumeier* was developed through interest analysis reasoning, in practice it represents a territorial approach. Except where both parties are from the same state (Rule 1), every conflicts case is resolved by applying the law of the place of injury, unless the difficult out-clause of Rule 3 is met. [i.e. unless application of a different law 'will advance the relevant substantive law purposes without impairing the smooth working of the multi-state system or producing great uncertainty for citizens']." See also Thomas M. Rearley and Jerome W. Wesevich, "An Old Rule for New Reasons: Place of Injury as a Federal Solution to Choice of Law in Single-Accident Mass-Tort Cases" (1992) 71 *Texas L Rev.* 1, 43 (proposing "a strict place-of-injury rule for single accident mass-tort cases because it best fosters uniformity, neutrality, determinacy and efficiency in the resolution of these difficulties").

[85] P. M. North and J. J. Fawcett, *Cheshire and North's Private International Law* (12th edn., Butterworths: London, 1992), at 29–30: "[the vested rights] theory stresses one of the primary objectives of private international law. It serves to emphasize the need to find solutions with international flavour. The notion that a foreign right is vested and as such requires respect, although analytically a fiction, tends to introduce the correct psychological background for the formulation of choice of law rules. The fiction of vested rights is a fiction inimical to insular prejudices."

[86] [1969] 2 All ER 1085 (HL).

[87] *Red Sea Insurance Co. Ltd* v. *Bouygues SA* [1995] 1 AC 190, noted by Andrew Dickinson, "Further Thoughts on Foreign Torts: *Boys* v. *Chaplin* Explained?" [1994] LMCLQ 463. In the wake of *Red Sea Insurance*, Dickinson questions the logic of retaining the requirement for

exception" supports the exclusive application of the *lex loci delicti*, not just the *lex fori.* Moreover, the exception can operate as a "one-law-selecting" choice of law rule,[88] that is, a rule allowing the whole cause of action, not just particular issues, to be governed by the *lex loci delicti* (or the *lex fori* as the case may be). More recently again, the whole area has been overtaken by statutory reform endorsing the *lex loci delicti* as the general rule for choice of law in tort.[89]

(e) The Common Residence Exception and Localising "Relational" Torts

Today, there is really only one situation in which there exists significant support for applying the parties' personal law in preference to the law of the place of tort in motor vehicle accident claims. This is where the parties are both residents or nationals of the forum (or are both resident in a jurisdiction with substantially identical tort law policies).[90] Even here, however, the appropriateness

actionability by the *lex fori.* As he points out, the only justifications for the requirement are certainty, simplicity and predictability, i.e. the requirement acts as a filter to keep out controversial torts not recognised by English law. The admission of an exception effectively eliminates those justifications.

[88] This term is defined *supra* n. 29.

[89] *Private International Law (Miscellaneous Provisions) Act*, 1995, c. 42. Part III of the Act replaces the common law rules applicable to choice of law in tort (with the exception of defamation, which continues to be governed by the common law). The new statutory rules give dominant effect to the law of the place where the events constituting the tort or delict occur, subject to a "proper law" exception. Where the events constituting the tort occur in different countries, the place of the tort is defined to mean: (1) in claims for personal injury or property damage, the place where the individual or property was located when the injury or damage was sustained; (2) otherwise, the place where the most significant elements of the events constituting the tort occurred. The proper law exception can be invoked whenever it would be "substantially more appropriate" for the issues or a single issue to be resolved by another law. The Act originated in an English Law Commission report (*Private International Law: Choice of Law in Tort and Delict*, Law Comm. No 193, 1990) but departs sufficiently from the Commission's model to make the report of "limited use as an aid to interpretation": see Adrian Briggs, "Choice of Law in Tort and Delict," [1995] LMCLQ 519, 520. Briggs is highly critical of the new statutory regime as unnecessarily complex and too "open-ended" in its language to be of much concrete guidance to courts.

[90] Symeon C. Symeonides, "Louisiana's New Law of Choice of Law for Tort Conflicts: An Exegesis" 66 *Tul. L Rev.* 677, 716. The existence of judicial and legislative support for a common residence exception was acknowledged by La Forest J in *Tolofson supra* n. 10, at 1052 and 1057 ff. He listed the following well-known examples: in the USA, *Babcock* v. *Jackson* (1963), 12 NY 2d 473 and *Neumeier* v. *Kuehner, supra* n. 84; in England, *Chaplin* v. *Boys*, *supra* n. 86; and in Quebec, art. 3126 of the new *Civil Code of Quebec*, *supra* n. 20, which reads: "The obligation to make reparation for injury caused to another is governed by the law of the country where the injurious act occurred . . . [But i]n any case where the person who committed the injurious act and the victim have their domiciles or residences in the same country, the law of that country applies." (This exception does not apply to motor vehicle accidents because of Quebec's adoption of a no-fault system *supra* n. 40.) As La Forest J also observed, the Court's own decision in *McLean* v. *Pettigrew*, *supra* n. 20, overruled in *Tolofson*, itself lends supports to the common residence exception in its factual result, though not of course in its reasoning.

of an exception has not gone unchallenged.[91] In *Tolofson*, La Forest J joined the ranks of the sceptics.

First, a common residence exception is typically rationalised on the basis that it is somehow "unjust" to the accident victim to apply the lower liability or compensation standards of the *lex loci delicti* in cases where the common personal law of both parties supports recovery. Viewed from a larger loss distribution perspective, however, where is the "justice" in a choice of law rule under which the compensation rights of forum residents injured in an out-of-province accident turns on whether or not they have the "good fortune" to be injured by a fellow visitor to the accident State.[92]

Secondly, the arguments in favour of the exception rest on a simple two-party litigation model. In multi-party actions, however, a personal law exception can raise intractable problems of contribution and indemnity.[93] Indeed, as La Forest J observed in *Tolofson*, a common residence exception is apt to exacerbate these problems by encouraging frivolous cross-claims and joinders.[94]

Perhaps most significantly, the common residence exception was developed in an era when the tort system comprised the main compensatory vehicle for personal injury inflicted in motor vehicle accidents. The emergence of statutory no-fault insurance regimes puts into question the ubiquity of liability insurance on which the common residence rule is premised. Under these new regimes first-party, not third-party, insurance principles prevail.[95] With the liability insurance factor removed, it is no longer so obvious that there is no unfair surprise to the parties, specifically the defendant, in applying the personal law of the parties in preference to the law of the place where all elements of the tortious conduct and its consequences are centred, especially if the parties are strangers meeting for the first time on foreign soil.[96]

The insurance backdrop to the resolution of interprovincial motor vehicle accident claims figured prominently in La Forest J's reasoning in *Tolofson*.

[91] Twerski, *supra* n. 84, especially at 1359 ff; Martin, *supra* n. 79, at 144–6.

[92] *Tolofson supra* n. 10, at 1058.

[93] For a post-*Tolofson* case emphasising this point, see *Stewart* v. *Stewart Estate*, *supra* n. 22, para. 43. A strict *lex loci delicti* rule will not, however, necessarily solve all the choice of law difficulties presented by contribution claims in multi-party tort cases. See Silberman (1994), *supra* n. 79.

[94] *Supra* n. 10, at 1061: "If it is known that the *lex fori* will apply, when residents of the forum are the only parties involved in an accident, but that the *lex loci delicti* will apply the moment any non-forum natural or legal person is joined to the action, are we not encouraging those who wish to be governed by the latter rule to dig up third parties from the *locus delicti*.?"

[95] *Supra* n. 40.

[96] *Supra* nn. 91, 92. The *Hague Convention on the Law Applicable to Traffic Accidents* links the availability of its exception to the exclusive application of the *lex loci delicti* to the presumed availability of liability insurance: under art. 4, the *lex loci delicti* is displaced, not in favour of the common residence of the parties at large, but in favour of the law of the State of the registration of the vehicle in the case of a one-vehicle accident, or where both vehicles are registered in the same State, or where a defendant from outside the vehicle is habitually resident in the State of registration.

On the international plane, he was prepared to concede some room for a common residence exception, if only because the law suit was likely to take place in the parties' home jurisdiction, and there was some merit, in the interests of efficiency and administrative convenience, in allowing the forum court to apply its own law.[97] However, he cautioned that, unless "narrowed to situations that involve some timely and close relationship between the parties, an exception could lead to injustice" to a defendant who had insured his or her vehicle on the basis of the liability laws of the *locus delicti*.[98]

Insurance considerations also explain why La Forest J rejected a judicially created common residence exception in the interprovincial context.[99] As he observed, the "biggest difference between provinces now is in insurance schemes, and this creates problems of quantum, not of liability".[100] Loss-distribution inequities generated by conflicts in insurance structures are capable of being resolved efficiently and fairly only through legislative intervention.[101] In this connection, it is important to stress again that La Forest J did *not* establish a constitutionally-mandated *lex loci delicti* choice of law rule for torts. Rather, he cited concerns with unconstitutional overreaching by the *lex fori* as a reason to adopt a cautious territorially-based choice of law methodology. In other words, constitutional concerns informed the choice of law exercise, but they did not dictate the resulting rule.

Outside the motor vehicle accident context, a common residence exception is unlikely to be needed. The desired flexibility may be found instead within the concept of the *locus delicti* itself, a solution that preserves the public and private international law values implicit in a territorial choice of law approach. As a prominent US "territorialist" has observed, a "sophisticated territorialism would often recognize that the law's purpose is to regulate a relationship between a group of people", in which event it may be perfectly sound to "reify the relationship" for the purposes of localising the tort.[102] Reasoning along these lines has appeared already in the post-*Tolofson* jurisprudence relating to liability for negligent misrepresentation between parties in a quasi-contractual relationship.[103]

[97] *Tolofson, supra* n. 10, at 1060.
[98] *Ibid.*, at 1062.
[99] *Ibid.*, at 1062.
[100] *Ibid.*, at 1059.
[101] For a detailed discussion of the superiority of a legislated solution in the context of no-fault, see Walsh, *supra* n. 40.
[102] Laycock, *supra* n. 55, at 323.
[103] *National Bank of Canada* v. *Chance, supra* n. 17.

III. CHOICE OF LAW IN PRODUCTS LIABILITY CLAIMS

(a) Localising the Tort in Products Liability Claims: Place of Distribution of the Product and Resulting Injury

In motor vehicle accident cases, determining the place of the tort for purposes of choice of law is straightforward: both the wrongful act and the immediate injury are readily localised within the territorial borders of a single province or State. But in other fact patterns, the relevant connections may be more geographically dispersed. La Forest J's reasoning in *Tolofson* indicates that he was alert to the potential difficulties with applying the *lex loci delicti* rule in such cases. Where a tort claim arises out of some truly transnational or interprovincial activity, he stated, "territorial considerations may become muted" and "other considerations may play a determining role".[104] The post-*Tolofson* jurisprudence indicates that territorial analysis in such cases is effectively synonymous with a flexible "real and substantial connection" analysis,[105] a point presaged by the 1985 decision of the Court in *R.* v. *Libman*,[106] in which La Forest J endorsed precisely this approach in determining the locus of a crime for the purposes of delineating the territorial reach of Canadian criminal law.[107]

Even in less territorially diverse fact patterns, localising the tort can present "thorny" problems.[108] Where the place of the defendant's wrongful activity and the place of its injurious consequences do not coincide, La Forest J indicated that "it may well be that the consequences would be held to consti-

[104] *Supra* n. 10, at 1050. For an example of the kind of multi-jurisdictional fact situation in which a strong case can be made for displacement of a strict territorial approach to choice of law in tort, see Linda J Silberman (1994), *supra* n. 79. As she concludes: "[the vested rights] orthodoxy of Joseph Beale came undone for quite good reasons the first time around; attempts to resurrect similar presumptive rules for particular kinds of cases . . . are helpful but do not fit all cases. Concerns for expectations and fairness to define the legitimate reach of legislative authority must also play a role."

[105] For a recent judicial endorsement of this interpretation, see *National Bank of Canada* v. *Chance*, *supra* n. 103.

[106] *Supra* n. 10.

[107] In *R* v. *Libman*, *ibid*. La Forest J endorsed a jurisdictional rule that gives Canadian courts authority under s. 5(2) of the Criminal Code over any crime that bears a "real and substantial connection" to this country, regardless of whether territorial jurisdiction is also available in another State. Since jurisdiction and choice of law are synonymous in the criminal area, his reasoning has obvious application to private law choice of law analysis: "I might summarize my approach to the limits of territoriality in this way. As I see it, all that is necessary to make an offence subject to the jurisdiction of our courts is that a significant portion of the activities constituting that offence took place in Canada. As it is put by modern academics, it is sufficient that there be a 'real and substantial link' between an offence and this country, a test well known in public and private international law. [T]his does not require legislation. It was the courts after all that defined the manner in which the doctrine of territoriality applied, and the test proposed simply amounts to a revival of the earlier way of formulating the principle. It is in fact the test that best reconciles all the cases."

[108] *Tolofson*, *supra* n. 10, at 1050.

tute the wrong".[109] In making this statement, he no doubt had in mind the Court's prior decision in *Moran* v. *Pyle National (Canada) Ltd.*,[110] the leading Canadian authority on localising a tort in products liability claims.

Moran involved a wrongful death action under the Saskatchewan Fatal Accidents Act[111] by the widow and children of an electrician employed by a Saskatchewan company who was fatally electrocuted in Saskatchewan in the course of removing a spent light bulb. His family alleged negligence on the part of the manufacturer of the bulb. The defendant's manufacturing operations were located in Ontario and the United States and it had no business presence in Saskatchewan, marketing its products there through distributors. The assertion of jurisdiction by the Saskatchewan courts over the Ontario manufacturer therefore depended on whether the tort had been committed in Ontario, where the manufacturer had "acted", or Saskatchewan, where the defective product was distributed and the injurious consequences of the defendant's actions were experienced.[112]

Canadian (and English) authority was divided on the question. Some cases favoured the place of acting, others the place of injury. Dickson J concluded that the place of acting had little to commend it. The production of a defective product does not in itself constitute a wrong. It is the act of distributing that defective product into the market-place and the resulting harm to users that engages tort liability. Nonetheless, Dickson J was unwilling to accept injury *per se* as a sufficient localising event. To do so might lead to fortuitous or arbitrary results. What was needed was a test that would reflect the significant interest of the jurisdiction where the consequences of the manufacturer's activities were experienced *and* the law of which was likely to have been in the reasonable contemplation of *both* parties. Thus, he formulated the following test:

> "[W]here a foreign manufacturer carelessly manufactures a product in a foreign jurisdiction which enters into the normal channels of trade and he knows or ought to know both that as a result of his carelessness a consumer may well be injured and it is reasonably forseeable that the product would be used or consumed where the plaintiff used or consumed it, then the forum in which the plaintiff suffered

[109] *Ibid.* And see also at 1042 where La Forest J indicated that the same approach might be appropriate in defamation cases.

[110] [1975] 1 SCR 393.

[111] R.S.S. 1965, c. 109.

[112] In Dickson J's view, localising the tort within Saskatchewan was necessary to found jurisdiction for two reasons. First, while the presence of the defendant within the forum was normally required for *in personam* jurisdiction, the occurrence of a tort within the territorial limits of the court's jurisdiction constituted a well-established exception to that requirement, as recognised in the Saskatchewan rules governing service *ex juris*. Secondly, it followed from the territorial limits on provincial legislative authority that the Fatal Accidents Act should be interpreted as limited to actions arising out of a wrong occurring within the province. The latter point lends support to La Forest J's equation of the territorial limits on provincial legislative authority with the territorial location of a tort for choice of law purposes, *supra* text at nn. 47–50. On the impact of the Court's recent conflicts jurisprudence on the *in personam* jurisdiction of Canadian courts, see *supra* text at nn. 15–17.

damage is entitled to exercise judicial jurisdiction over the foreign defendant. This rule recognizes the important interest a state has in injuries suffered by persons within its territory. It recognizes that the purpose of negligence as a tort is to protect against carelessly inflicted injury and thus that the predominating element is damage suffered. By tendering his products in the market place directly or through normal distributive channels, a manufacturer ought to assume the burden of defending those products wherever they cause harm as long as the forum into which the manufacturer is taken is one that he reasonably ought to have in his contemplation when he tendered his goods. This is particularly true of dangerously defective goods placed in the interprovincial flow of commerce."[113]

Dickson J's reasoning demonstrates that territorial analysis does not necessarily lead to the mechanical jurisprudence associated with "vested rights" thinking. As incorporated in the first *Restatement* in the United States, the vested rights theory required application of the *lex injurii* as the law of the place where the "last event" necessary to vest liability occurred.[114] But standing alone, the occurrence of injury within a jurisdiction, essentially a *plaintiff* nexus, does not seem to be a sufficient choice of law connection from the standpoint of the "coerced" foreign manufacturer.[115] In contrast, the *Moran* test requires substantial connections between the *defendant's activities* and the place of injury. That approach respects both territorial and fairness concerns. If the place of injury is a jurisdiction in which the manufacturer's products are purposefully or foreseeably distributed, the foreign manufacturer in effect has assented to be regulated according to that jurisdiction's standards of liability and compensation. After all, if manufacturers want to participate in global trade, they must be willing to operate in the target markets on equal terms with local firms. The contrary rule would effectively license the manufacturer's home jurisdiction to set the global liability standard for injury caused abroad by products exported beyond its borders.[116]

[113] *Supra* n. 110, at 408–9. As Swan has observed, the language of Dickson J's test almost exactly parallels that used by the US Supreme Court in *World-Wide Volkswagen Corp.* v. *Woodson*, 444 US 286 (1980): Swan, *supra* n. 28, at 930.

[114] *Restatement of the Law of Conflict of Laws* (1934), §377. The *Restatement (Second) Conflict of Laws* (1969) does not completely dispense with vested rights thinking in products liability actions. While §145 employs a "most significant relationship" test as the general rule for choice of law in tort, §146 creates a presumption in actions for personal injury that this is law of the place where the injury occurred.

[115] See Brilmayer, *supra* n. 82, at 23–4: "Where the parties to a dispute are from different communities, it does not seem fair to resolve the controversy solely according to the norms of one community or the other. The defendant should not be subject to state authority without a showing that he or she has somehow assented to state power."

[116] See, e.g. Michael H. Gottesman, "Draining the Dismal Swamp: The Case for Federal Choice of Law Statutes" (1991) 80 *Geo. LJ* 1, 35: "A rule that declared that the actionability of conduct is to be judged by the law of the state where the conduct occurs would stimulate a 'race to the bottom,' in which states courted manufacturers by proffering ever narrowing theories of liability for product defect." And see Stuart Dutson, "International Product Liability Litigation: The Territorial Application of Part VA of the *Trade Practices Act* 1974 (Cth) and Part 1 of the *Consumer Protection Act* (1987) (U.K.)" (1996) 22 *Monash UL Rev*. 244, concluding that the strict products liability regime in Part VA of the Australian Trade Practices Act, *supra* n. 33, applies

(b) An Alternative Reference to the Manufacturer's Home Law?

Although *Moran* was concerned with localising the tort for the purposes only of establishing jurisdiction, choice of law tests similar to that articulated by Dickson J in *Moran* have strong scholarly and legislative support.[117] His reasoning, in other words, is readily translatable to the choice of law context, a point confirmed in the post-*Tolofson* case law.[118] But what if the law of the jurisdiction where the product is distributed and causes injury limits or even precludes recovery? Should the victim then be able to invoke the manufacturer's home law to support recovery? In fact, while the details vary considerably, there is a surprising level of support for this idea in contemporary codifications[119] and in the scholarship.[120] I say "surprising" because a choice of law rule that systematically advantages plaintiffs and systematically burdens defendants *prima facie* raises problems of fairness. After all, *nobody*

to foreign manufacturers whose products are imported into Australia and cause injury or damage there, notwithstanding that the Act directly implicates only the importer. As Dutson observes, the contrary rule would permit manufacturers deliberately to evade the Australian regime simply by removing their operations to a jurisdiction with less stringent standards and then exporting to Australia through a subsidiary importer with nominal capital and no assets. For a Canadian example of an explicit statutory directive bringing out-of-province manufacturers within the scope of application of a strict products liability regime where the forum is the target market and injury occurs there, see s. 27 of the New Brunswick *Consumer Product Warranty and Liability Act* SNB 1978, c. C–18.1, as amended 1980, c. 12.

[117] All recent scholarly and legislative proposals tend to require substantial affiliations between both parties or their activities and the applicable *lex causae*. Plaintiff-related connections (habitual residence, place of injury) standing alone, even if cumulated, are insufficient. See Kozyris, *supra* n. 81, at 497–8.

[118] *Ostroski* v. *Global Upholstery Co.* [1995] OJ 4211(QL) (Ont. Gen. Div.).

[119] See e.g. art. 3128 of the new *Civil Code of Quebec*, *supra* n. 20: "The liability of the manufacturer of a movable, whatever the source thereof, is governed, at the choice of the victim, (1) by the law of the country where the manufacturer has his establishment or, failing that, his residence, or (2) by the law of the country where the movable was acquired." This approach is nearly identical to that adopted in Swiss law, on which the Quebec rule is likely modelled. On the Swiss rule, see Kozyris, *supra* n. 81, at 492, n. 36. The plaintiff's choice is more limited under the Hague Convention on the Law Applicable to Products Liability (1972) 11 ILM 1283. Under art. 6, the plaintiff can elect between application of the law of the manufacturer's place of business or the law of the place of injury only if neither place coincides with the victim's habitual residence or the place where the product was acquired.

[120] Extrapolating from his theory of "principles of preference", David Cavers would allow the plaintiff to choose the most favourable among the law of the place of manufacture or design of the defective product, the law of the place where the product was acquired and caused injury or the law of the victim's habitual residence. In all three cases, choice is conditioned on the requirement that the defendant could "reasonably have foreseen the presence in that [S]tate of the product". See David Cavers, "The Proper Law of Producer's Liability" (1977) 26 *Int'l & Comp. LQ* 703. Applying a "functional" interest analysis approach, Weintraub advocates application of the plaintiff-favouring law of the defendant's state where it is desirable to punish and deter the defendant's conduct. See Weintraub (1990), *supra* n. 83, at 229–30. He would also allow the plaintiff to choose either the law of the place of manufacture/design of the product or the law of the manufacturer's principal place of business as the default law in cases where the law of the plaintiff's habitual residence is not applicable under his general rule (*viz.* because the defective product or similar products was not distributed there). See Russell J Weintraub, "Methods for Resolving Conflict-of-Laws Problems in Mass Tort Litigation" (1989) *U. Ill. L Rev.* 129.

advocates giving primacy to the manufacturer's home law (whether defined as the place of manufacture/design of the relevant product or the place where the manufacturer has its principal establishment) in cases where that law imposes a *lower* standard of liability or recovery than the law of the place where the product was distributed and caused injury.[121] It is only where application of the manufacturer's home law *advantages* the plaintiff that it is accepted as relevant in the choice of law balance.

In questioning the legitimacy of a plaintiff-favouring alternative reference to the manufacturer's home law, I do not mean to say that a State is precluded in international law from *unilaterally* imposing the *burden* of its laws on its citizens or residents, including local manufacturers, even when the harmful consequences of their misconduct or negligence are wholly extraterritorial.[122] A jurisdiction may wish to do this because it abhors the particular misconduct or it wants to lend its aid to a global attack on the problem or it is concerned with the potential injury to its international reputation from a failure to regulate. A topical example is the increasing tendency of States to extend the reach of their domestic criminal laws governing sexual misconduct with minors to its citizens even when they travel outside the country and even when the victim of the crime is a foreign citizen.

The exercise of this form of regulatory authority, however, is grounded in a personal, not a territorial, theory of international prescriptive (i.e. law-making) jurisdiction.[123] As such, it is an appropriate connecting factor for the purposes of a *unilateral* choice of law rule articulated by the manufacturer's home State, as the only State possessing "personal jurisdiction" over the extraterritorial conduct of the manufacturer.[124] But the alternative reference

[121] *Supra* n. 116, 117.

[122] See e.g. *Restatement (Revised) of Foreign Relations Law*, §402: "a state has jurisdiction to prescribe law with respect to . . . (2) the activities, interests, status, or relations of its nationals outside as well within its territory."

[123] Rosalyn Higgins, "The Legal Bases of Jurisdiction" in C. J. Olmstead (ed.), *Extraterritorial Application of Laws and Responses Thereto* (Oxford, ILS & ESC Publishing, 1984), at 3 ff.

[124] However, if the domestic products liability law is silent on its territorial scope, the presumption against extraterritoriality militates against its application to domestic manufacturers in relation to exported products that inflict injury abroad. In the USA, the argument that domestic products liability laws do not apply extraterritorially is typically advanced at the jurisdictional stage, in the context of an application by a US manufacturer to dismiss an action by a foreign plaintiff for harm caused abroad by a defective product on the basis of *forum non conveniens*. In this context, the federal courts and the majority of state courts have decided that it is the country where the product is distributed and causes injury, not the State where the product is manufactured, that has the greatest interest in setting the appropriate standard of enterprise liability: see Sheila W. Birnbaum and Douglas W. Dunham, "Foreign Plaintiffs and Forum Non Conveniens." (1990) 16 *Brooklyn J Int'l L* 241; Linda J Silberman, "Developments in Jurisdiction and Forum Non Conveniens in International Litigation: Thoughts on Reform and a Proposal for a Uniform Standard" (1993) 28 *Texas Int'l LJ* 501. The US courts traditionally have been attractive to foreign plaintiffs owing to a combination of plaintiff-generous products liability laws, procedural advantages and the *lex fori* bias in choice of law. It is this state of affairs that prompted Lord Denning's famous dictum: "[a]s a moth is drawn to the light so is a litigant drawn to the United States. If he can only get his case into their courts, he stands to win a fortune": *Smith Kline & French Laboratories Ltd* v. *Bloch* [1983] 1 WLR 730, 733–4 (CA). However, the

rule typically is cast in the form of a *multilateral* choice of law rule,[125] i.e. one equally capable of being invoked in any forum, including the State where the product is distributed and causes injury. But that State has neither personal prescriptive jurisdiction over the defendant nor a territorial nexus to the defendant's activities. Although the defendant's activities have created a risk of harm within the forum's territory, that fact gives the forum a sufficient territorial nexus only to apply its own products liability laws, not to prescribe application of the manufacturer's home law via forum choice of law rules. Indeed, imposing the burden of their more onerous home laws on foreign manufacturers is suspect on equal protection as well as territorial grounds, since it amounts to imposing a tariff on foreign manufacturers competing in the local market with local manufacturers.[126]

Not surprisingly, those who advocate the application of the manufacturer's home law where it imposes a stricter standard of liability or a more generous level of compensation do not base themselves on a territorial theory of choice of law but on substantive tort considerations, that that approach better advances the compensation and deterrence goals underpinning products liability regimes at large. This was the reasoning in *Kozoway* v. *Massey-Ferguson, Inc.*[127] An Alberta farmer suffered extensive injuries in the course of operating a hay baler on his family's farm in Alberta. The baler had been manufactured for the defendant in Iowa on order by its Canadian subsidiary and shipped directly to an Alberta dealership for sale in Alberta, where it was purchased by the victim's father. The farmer brought suit in the US District Court in Denver against the US manufacturer.[128] Purporting to apply the "most significant relationship" test in the *Second Restatement*,[129] the Court resolved the

attractiveness of US products liability laws is being steadily diminished by the state legislature-driven "tort reform" movement aimed at lessening "enterprise liability" through such measures as: shorter time limitations on suit, statutory caps on damages, instalment in lieu of lump sum damage awards; stricter judicial scrutiny of the quantum of awards; sanctions on frivolous litigation; reduction of awards through apportionment, contribution and changes in the relevance of collateral sources of compensation; limitations on contingency agreements: see e.g. Weintraub, *supra* n. 83, at 225 n. 6.

[125] E.g. Quebec Civil Code, art. 3128, *supra* n. 119.

[126] *Infra* n. 138.

[127] 722 F Supp. 641 (D Colo. 1989), criticised extensively by Mark B. Rockwell, "Choice of Law in International Products Liability: Internationalizing the Choice" (1992) 16 *Suffolk Transnat'l L Rev*. 69. It was through his article that this case came to my attention.

[128] Technically, the manufacturer was Vermeer Manufacturing Company, which produced farm implements for the defendant Massey-Ferguson, with both companies having their principal place of business in Iowa: *Kozoway*, *supra* n. 127, 642.

[129] Since federal jurisdiction was based on diversity of citizenship, the applicable choice of law rules were those of Colorado, the state in which the District Court was sitting. And since the Supreme Court of that state applies the choice of law rules in the *Restatement (Second) of the Conflict of Laws* (1969), §145, the "most significant relationship" approach governed choice of law. Colorado case law also requires application of the *Restatement's* rules governing specific torts; consequently the presumption in s. 146 in favour of the place of injury in personal injury actions was applicable. However, the Colorado Supreme Court had never adopted a choice of law rule for personal injury claims of the particular type in issue. Consequently, the District Court was not bound by prior Colorado precedent to apply the place of harm theory if, as it

choice of law issue in favour of the law of the "place of acting", the law of Iowa, where the implement had been manufactured and where the defendant had its principal place of business.

In concluding that Iowa law had the most significant relationship with the litigation, the court focussed on Iowa's policy, reflected primarily in the availability of unlimited punitive and exemplary damages, "to deter, punish and make an example of certain dangerous corporate conduct".[130] The court conceded that Alberta also had an interest in "regulating conduct and commerce within its territory to see that its citizens are fully compensated for their injuries".[131] However, Alberta's tort-recovery laws were more restrictive than those of Iowa.[132] Consequently, "Canada's interest in protecting its citizens in the position of this plaintiff would be better served by applying Iowa law".[133] Further, since Iowa law was more favourable to recovery, "Canada can complain of no harm if its citizen's claim is tried under Iowa law".[134]

This is boot-strap reasoning. It is self-contradictory to decide that the importing jurisdiction has a legitimate interest in regulating the misconduct of foreign manufacturers that causes injury within its borders and then to conclude that that interest is better served by applying the law of the defendant's home State. Moreover, the implicit arrogance is startling. While Alberta is not about to claim a violation of its sovereign integrity because its residents are able to forum shop to personal advantage in the United States, it might justifiably take issue with the court's assumption that Iowa rather than Alberta law represents the optimal tort regime applicable to defective products that are distributed and cause injury within Alberta's territorial limits.[135] Although

considered to be the case, the presumption was rebutted by the existence of a more significant relationship to Iowa law: *Ibid.*, at 642–4).

[130] *Ibid.*, at 644. In cases where the exported product is also sold at home, it is sometimes argued that the application of the products liability laws of the forum will incrementally enhance domestic deterrence goals. In the USA, the "incremental deterrence" argument has been rejected in the decisional law as factually questionable: see *Piper Aircraft* v. *Reyno*, 454 US 235, 260 (1981). And see Birnbaum and Dunham, *supra* n. 124, at 248.

[131] *Ibid.*, at 644.

[132] *Ibid.* The Court identified 3 points of difference: (1) while Alberta law required proof of negligence in products liability actions, Iowa law provided for strict liability; (2) while both laws allowed recovery of punitive and exemplary damages, Alberta had a cap on such damages; and (3) while Alberta recognised assumption of risk as an absolute defence to tort liability, Iowa law regarded it merely as an element to be weighed in the comparative fault equation. In support of the second proposition, the Court referred to a 1978 trilogy of Supreme Court of Canada decisions, the main objective of which was to impose a cap on *compensatory* damages for non-economic losses, *not* exemplary and punitive damages. This minor point aside, it is undoubtedly the case that punitive damages are less widely available and lower in quantum in Canadian law. In relation to the third proposition, it bears noting that Canadian courts rarely allow the assumption of risk defence and products liability actions do not typically engage the defence. Moreover, in Canadian law, both common and civil, causal fault reduces the plaintiff's recovery proportionate to fault whereas Iowa law, as the court acknowledged (*ibid.*, at 643), bars recovery if the plaintiff's proportionate fault exceeds 50%.

[133] *Ibid.*

[134] *Ibid.*

[135] Compare *Harrison* v. *Wyeth Lab.*, 510 F Supp. 1, 5 (ED Pa. 1980), aff'd 676 F 2d 685 (3d Cir. 1982): "It is manifestly unfair to the defendant, as well as an inappropriate usurpation of a

all tort regimes may share a common concern with compensation, deterrence and corrective justice, the relative importance attached to these elements turns on the level of enterprise liability each jurisdiction considers appropriate in light of its own political, economic and moral values. Concepts of substantive tort justice, in other words, are time-and context-sensitive.[136]

The court's reasoning also fails to appreciate that substantive tort justice includes substantive justice for defendants as well as plaintiffs.[137] The extraterritorial extension of domestic products liability laws to domestic manufacturers operating in foreign markets imposes a competitive disadvantage on them relative to local manufacturers in the target markets.[138] As such, the rule also undermines the classic conflicts values associated with "one-law-selecting" choice of law rules, particularly the promotion of reliable expecta-

foreign court's proper authority to decide a matter of local interest, for a court in this country to set a higher standard of care than is required by the government of the country in which the product is sold and used."

[136] See e.g. Kramer, *supra* n. 81, at 339–40 (footnotes omitted):"states are co-equal sovereigns, entitled to make their own value judgments. Each state is free to define its own version of the 'just' result, and it is axiomatic that there is no perspective from which to judge one version 'better' or more 'just.' True conflicts present competing but equal versions of what is just in a particular case."

[137] *Supra* n. 135. And see Shimon A. Rosenfeld, "Conflicts of Law in Products Liability Suits: Joint Maximization of States' Interests" (1986) 15 *Hofstra L Rev*. 139, 157 (footnotes omitted): "The thesis of the pro-plaintiff approach [to choice of law] does not comport with the present state of product liability law. When the courts first shifted from negligence to strict liability, the policy underlying product liability rules was pro-plaintiff. Today, however, courts handling product liability issues are more concerned with the limits to which they will stretch strict liability . . . As a result, many legislators [in the United States] have already passed new product liability rules designed to limit the liability of manufacturers. The basic flaw in [the approach taken by] proponents of pro-plaintiff [choice of law] rules is that manufacturer protection can no longer be considered a secondary concern. Today, an equal concern exists for both manufacturer and consumer protection, necessitating choice of law rules that further both policies."

[138] See e.g. Russell J. Weintraub, "Choosing Law with an Eye on the Prize" (1994) 15 *Mich. J Int'l L* 705, 720 (footnotes omitted): "It may make . . . sense to give each user the protection of his or her own home state law, such as it is, if this is fair to the manufacturer because the product is distributed there. If the user's law is favorable to consumers, fine. If not, some courts have placed their own manufacturers at a worldwide competitive disadvantage by applying law more favorable to the consumer than the consumer's own law, but most courts have had better sense." Competitive disadvantage was among the concerns that motivated a Committee of the Australian Senate to reject a proposal to extend the strict products liability regime in the federal Trade Practices Act (*supra* n. 33) to expressly cover non-residents injured abroad by Australian-manufactured defective products: see Australian Parliament Standing Committee on Legal and Constitutional Affairs, "Product Liability: Where Should the Loss Fall?" (the "Cooney Report") (Canberra, Australian Government Publishing Service, 1992). The Report was tabled in the Senate on 4 May 1993. The Government Response, accepting the Committee's recommendations was tabled in the Senate on 1 June 1994. I do not, however, want to over-emphasise the competitive disadvantage argument. Rather, I agree with Professor Silberman that even if the argument has validity, the real issue here is one of international (and intranational) relations, the appropriate allocation of each country's (and province's) substantive regulatory authority within the international (and federal) order, a consideration that independently favours the application of the law of the place where the product was distributed and caused injury: see Linda J. Silberman, "Developments in Jurisdiction and *Forum Non Conveniens* in International Litigation: Thoughts on Reform and a Proposal for a Uniform Standard" (1993) 28 *Texas Int'l LJ* 501, 526.

tions about the applicable law in the interests of facilitating transnational commerce and lowering transaction costs.[139]

An Ontario judge got it right in a recent post-*Tolofson* Ontario case.[140] A Pennsylvania resident alleged that she had suffered injuries when the chair in which she was sitting in the course of her work at a Pennsylvania hospital tipped forward, causing her to fall. The limitation period for suit in Pennsylvania having expired, the plaintiff brought a tort action in Ontario against the Ontario manufacturer of the chair and its Pennsylvania distributor. The court had no difficulty in dismissing the action. Applying the localising test in *Moran* v. *Pyle*,[141] Pennsylvania was found to be the *locus delicti*; consequently the suit was statute-barred.[142] In light of the Supreme Court's emphasis on the value of certainty in *Tolofson*, the courts could no longer, as they might once have done, apply the *lex fori* to get around any "perceived injustice or unfairness" under the *lex loci delicti*.[143] In any event there was nothing "inherently unfair" about the result, since it was brought about by "the application of the law in which the plaintiff resides, in which she sustained injury and suffered the financial consequences of the injury".[144]

(c) A Public Policy Exception for Dangerously Defective Products?

Is there room for a public policy-based exception "when the defendant manufacturer has acted outrageously by, for example, exporting a dangerously defective product to the victim's state, the use of which is banned in the manufacturer's state"?[145] Weintraub regards this as an "easy case" for recognising an exception.[146] Since "both the manufacturer's and the victim's state would wish to punish and deter this kind of conduct", applying the enterprise liability law of the defendant's State "advances the policies of both states" and consequently is the "preferred result".[147]

Weintraub's assumptions are inherently problematic. If the manufacturer's home State authorises the domestic production for export of banned products, how can the defendant's conduct be said to be contrary to that State's policy? Equally, if the victim's home State allows the import and sale of defective

139 On "one-law selecting" choice of law values, see Westbrook, *supra* n. 29.

140 *Ostroski* v. *Global Upholstery Co.*, *supra* n. 118.

141 *Supra* n. 110.

142 In *Tolofson*, *supra* n. 10, the Supreme Court reversed the long-established common law rule that limitation periods are procedural and therefore governed by the *lex fori* rather than the otherwise applicable substantive *lex causae*.

143 *Supra* n. 140, para. 12.

144 *Ibid*., para. 15.

145 Weintraub (1990), *supra* n. 83, at 230. And see *infra* n. 150.

146 Weintraub does not favour giving the plaintiff the option to claim under the manufacturer's home law as a general rule: *supra* n. 120.

147 *Supra* n. 145.

products without sanction, how can it be said that it wishes to punish and deter the manufacturer's conduct?

Those who advocate the extraterritorial application of domestic products liability laws to cover injuries caused abroad by exported products sometimes base themselves on justice considerations, specifically that it is wrong to apply a lower standard of liability and compensation to foreign plaintiffs relative to citizens of the manufacturer's home State.[148] However, unjustifiable discrimination exists only when there is differential treatment of persons who are similarly situated. To equate the position of domestic plaintiffs injured within the forum and foreign plaintiffs injured abroad ignores the plenary territorial authority of the State of distribution and injury of the product to regulate the defendant's conduct.[149] If the victim has cause for complaint, the complaint is with his or her home law.

To challenge the logic in recognising a public policy exception here is not to defend the practice of dumping hazardous products in investment-hungry developing countries or to underestimate the obstacles they face in implementing a more rigorous regulatory regime.[150] But the problem is not created by and cannot be resolved by a wave of the judicial choice of law wand. If the manufacturer's home jurisdiction wishes to regulate and deter extraterritorial "misconduct", it has the legislative power to do so[151] (although this

[148] Arguments along these lines have typically been raised at the jurisdictional level in the context of applications by US manufacturers to dismiss tort actions brought against them in the US by foreign plaintiffs for personal injury suffered abroad on the basis of *forum non conveniens*. Most courts have concluded that they do not have a significant interest in regulating the sale of products beyond their borders and the general tenor of current judicial opinion is against opening the doors to such suits. For a comprehensive review of the issues and cases, see Birnbaum and Dunham, *supra* n. 124.

[149] *Supra* nn. 116, 117.

[150] See *Dow Chemical Co.* v. *Castro Alfaro*, 786 SW 2d 674 (Tex. 1990), cert. denied 498 US 1024, in which a divided (5/4)Texas Supreme Court upheld the Texas appeal court which had reversed the trial court's decision to dismiss for *forum non conveniens*. That case involved an action in Texas by a group of Costa Rican plantation workers who alleged that they were sterilised as a result of their exposure to pesticide. The workers were employed by the Standard Fruit Company, a US subsidiary of the Dole Fresh Fruit Company. Standard was supplied with the pesticide by Dow Chemical Company and Shell Oil Company which manufactured and shipped it, even though it had been banned by the US Environmental Protection Agency for use in the USA. In his concurring majority opinion, Doggatt J regarded the extraterritorial application of US tort law as necessary to impose an effective restraint on multinational corporate misbehaviour because the "tort laws of many developing countries are not yet developed" (at 688–9). But see: Birnbaum and Dunham, *supra* n. 124, at 261–2 (arguing that to allow foreign plaintiffs to sue US manufacturers in the USA for product injury inflicted abroad impedes the opportunity for other states to develop domestic solutions); Peter J Carney, "International *Forum Non Conveniens*: 'Section 1404.5'—A Proposal in the Interests of Sovereignty, Comity and Individual Justice" (1995) 45 *Am. UL Rev*. 415 (can and should the USA be courtroom and legislator for the world?); William L. Reynolds, "The Proper Forum for a Suit: Transnational *Forum Non Conveniens* and Counter-Suit Injunctions in the Federal Courts" (1992) 70 *Texas L Rev*. 1663 at 1708 (arguing that the imposition of US liability and compensation standards for injury abroad is disruptive of the policies of developing countries who have presumably decided that the risk of injury is an acceptable price to pay for stimulating investment). And see Silberman, *supra* n. 124, at 524.

[151] *Supra* text at n. 122.

might more effectively be expressed in the form of restrictions on export[152] than through the extraterritorial application of domestic products liability laws). In the absence of an express legislative directive to this effect, there is no ground to assume a public will to regulate.

(d) Choice of Law in Geographically-dispersed Fact Patterns: Contact-counting, Plaintiff-choice or "Real and Substantial Connection"?

In the cases examined so far, there was a coincidence of the place of injury, the habitual residence of the victim and the place of the initial acquisition of the product. If it is accepted that the manufacturer's nationality or residence standing alone is insufficient as a choice of law connection, then these types of cases are not really conflicts cases at all. They are essentially domestic cases within the natural territorial scope of application of the products liability laws of the State of distribution and injury.[153]

In cases involving more dispersed factual connections, is it still possible to identify a predominant territorial nexus for the purposes of choice of law? Is it even possible to analyse choice of law according to a territorial methodology? Or is this the type of situation which La Forest J had in mind when he stated in *Tolofson* that in cases arising out of truly transnational or interprovincial activities and events, territorial considerations may become muted and other considerations may have to take centre stage?[154]

Some analysts would have us altogether abandon a conventional choice of law approach in multi-jurisdictional products liability cases. The court should instead take into account the substantive laws of all of the places to which the events and the parties are connected—the place of injury, the place where the negligent conduct causing the injury occurred, the place where the product was acquired and the home States of the parties (residence, place of incorporation or principal place of business). As to each issue, the court should then

[152] Kozyris, *supra* n. 81, at 501.

[153] *Supra* n. 116.

[154] *Supra* footnote 104. In class action product liability claims involving widely dispersed injuries, victims and defendants, it has been suggested that the exclusive application of the forum's substantive law would ease judicial administration of the claims. This kind of artificial simplification of the choice of law process has been rejected in the USA as contrary to the constitutional requirement that a State have a significant contact or aggregate of contacts to apply its own substantive law: *Phillips Petroleum Co.* v. *Shutts*, 472 US 797 (1995). And see Linda S. Mullinex, "Mass Tort Litigation and the Dilemma of Federalization" (1995) 44 *DePaul L Rev.* 755, 788. In Canada, as well, the courts have not seen the administrative complexities posed by class actions as justification for by-passing the normal choice of law rules. However, they have been prepared to be flexible at the jurisdictional level. Thus, the existence of a common factual basis for all claims has been held to constitute a sufficiently "real and substantial connection" to found jurisdiction, notwithstanding that the claims of some members of the class, if assessed independently, would be outside the court's jurisdiction: see *Harrington* v. *Dow Corning Corp.* [1997] BCJ 400 (QL) (SC), applying *Nantais* v. *Teleelectronics Proprietary (Canada) Ltd.* (1995), 127 DLR (4th) 552 (Ont. Gen. Div.).

select from the laws of these jurisdictions "the rule of decision which most closely accords with modern products liability standards".[155]

This kind of *ad hoc* anational methodology suffers from the deficiencies of any substantive tort choice of law rule. Concepts of tort justice are time- and place-sensitive. There is no such thing as an optimal tort regime in the abstract.[156] Lacking an ideal standard, the forum is likely to turn to the law "that most closely resembles its own unless the forum considers its own law to be outmoded or inferior, an unlikely outcome".[157] Even if a more neutral stance is attempted, the outcome is still unpredictable, since the choice of the substantive law to govern each issue is premised on each forum's necessarily subjective ideas about the best approach to products liability.[158]

In any event, those who urge the abandonment of a classic choice of law approach in geographically-dispersed products liability cases may be overestimating the difficulties. Once the manufacturer's home law is removed from the equation, there is a surprising level of common ground among commentators and legislators on the appropriate choice of law resolution. The debate is then centred principally between the place of acquisition of the product[159] and the habitual residence of the victim[160]—with the place of injury given second-level significance as a default connection to habitual residence.[161]

The rationale for placing the emphasis on the habitual residence of the victim (or the place of injury in default) is plaintiff-oriented: it is that jurisdiction which will "experience consequences its laws is designed to prevent if what the residence considers proper compensation is not available".[162] The rationale for focussing on the place of distribution of the product is defendant- and territorially-oriented. As we have seen, marketing a product within a State's boundaries gives that State a sufficient territorial nexus with the defendant's conduct and its consequences to support the application of its substantive products liability laws.[163]

The ground of difference between the two solutions is not as large as might be thought. Those who advocate giving primary emphasis to the habitual

[155] Juenger, *supra* n. 32 at 196–7. And see Friedrich K. Juenger, "Mass Torts and the Conflict of Laws" (1989) *U Ill L Rev*. 105. In a similar vein, see Luther L. McDougal III, "Private International Law: *Ius Gentium* versus choice of law rules or approaches" (1990) 38 *Am. J Comp. L* 521; Rosenfeld, *supra* n. ?

[156] Kramer, *supra* n. 136, Rosenfeld, *supra* n. 137.

[157] Rockwell, *supra* n. 127, at 84.

[158] *Ibid*. And *supra* n. 156.

[159] Kozyris, *supra* n. 81, at 501 ff.

[160] The *Hague Convention* favours application of the law of the habitual residence of the victim if it coincides with any one of 3 factors: place of injury, the place the product was acquired or the place of the defendant's principal place of business: *supra* n. 119, art. 4, 5. Otherwise, the law of the place of injury applies if it coincides with either the defendant's place of business or the place the product was acquired.

[161] *Ibid*.

[162] Weintraub, *supra* n. 83 at 228–9. For this reason, he argues that the fact that the injury happened abroad, e.g. while travelling, should not displace the law of the habitual residence of the victim: *ibid*., at 229.

[163] *Supra* nn. 116, 117.

residence of the victim nonetheless concede that it is an insufficient connection, standing alone, to justify the application of that law. There must also exist a volitional nexus between the defendant's marketing activities and the applicable law. It is argued, however, that this should not limit the choice to the law of the place where the actual defective product was acquired. It is enough if the "same or similar products" are distributed by the relevant manufacturer in the victim's home market through "ordinary commercial channels".[164] In these circumstances, it is not "unfair" to subject the defendant to the victim's home law, since "it is fortuitous if a product that the victim might have purchased at home is in fact purchased elsewhere".[165] Some would even liberalise the defendant nexus requirement to the point that "foreseeability" of use or consumption of the product in the place of habitual residence or injury would be enough even if neither the particular product nor products of that type were marketed there in the ordinary channels of trade.[166]

The considerations that favour application of the law of the place where the product was initially distributed respond to many of the classic conflicts values emphasised by La Forest J in *Tolofson*,[167] including decisional uniformity, forum-neutrality and facilitation of interprovincial and international commerce.[168] Predictability would be enhanced because the rule avoids the uncertainties that would inevitably be encountered in interpreting more open-ended defendant nexus tests ("same or similar products", "ordinary commercial channels" and the notoriously slippery "forseeability" of consumption or use). National legislatures would have a greater incentive to create an optimal tort liability regime directed at local market goals, while manufacturers would be better placed to incorporate their potential products liability exposure into their pricing for particular markets.[169]

How well does the suggested rule—the presumptive application of the law of the place of distribution of the product—respond to territoriality and justice principles? The defendant cannot claim unfair surprise in being subjected

[164] In Weintraub's proposal, a sufficient nexus exists "if the defendant should have foreseen that the product that caused the harm or the defendant's *products of the same type* would be available in the victim's habitual residence through commercial channels": *ibid.*, at 228. The test under the Hague Convention is very similar: the law of the habitual residence of the victim or the place of injury, as the case may be, is inapplicable if the defendant "could not reasonably have foreseen that the product or *[its] own products of the same type* would be made available in that state through commercial channels": *Supra* n. 119, art. 7. Cavers goes even further. He advocates application of the law of any State, at the plaintiff's option, where the defendant's products might foreseeably be present regardless of whether they are distributed in that market: *supra* n. 120.

[165] Weintraub, *ibid.*, at 229.

[166] Cavers, *supra* n. 164. Dickson J's language in *Moran* v. *Pyle*, *supra* n. 113, is arguably open to this interpretation.

[167] *Supra* nn. 29, 26.

[168] Generally, see Kozyris, *supra* n. 81, at 501–7. As he notes, "the centrality of the state of distribution in the products liability context is beginning also to attract the attention of conflicts commentators." For a collection of relevant quotations, see at 504–5, n. 56.

[169] McConnell, "A Choice of Law Approach to Products-Liability Reform," in Walter Olson (ed.), *New Directions in Products Liability Law* (1988), at 98, quoted by Kozyris, *supra* n. 81, at 504–5, n. 56.

to the products liability regime in force in the law of the State in which it has placed its products into circulation. If the plaintiff is the initial consumer or user of the product, application of the law of the place of acquisition reflects normal consumer expectations. The same is true if the plaintiff is connected directly or indirectly with the transaction under which the product was acquired (e.g., through a family or employment relationship). In both cases, the transactional or relational connections between the plaintiff and the manufacturer's marketing activities can be seen as sufficiently localising the issues within the State where the product was acquired to support the application of its laws to risks of harm arising out of the consumption of use of the product, even if those risks happen to materialise beyond its borders.[170]

However, the victim of the product defect may be an "innocent bystander" with no *a priori* connection to the transaction in which the product was acquired.[171] In this instance, the relational theory is unavailable to "reify" the tort so as to localise it within the jurisdiction where the product was acquired.[172] Other jurisdictions may have an equally significant territorial connection to the parties or the activities. In such cases, two choice of law approaches are possible. One is to establish a set of *a priori* rules covering the choice of law resolution for each possible combination of relevant connections.[173] Such proposals, however, reflect a mechanical contact-counting approach to choice of law. Because the connections have presumptive equal weight, there is no obvious default rule available in the event that they are widely dispersed. One is driven to plaintiff choice as the tie-breaker,[174] with the uncertainties and potential unfairness to the defendant inherent in any pro-plaintiff alternative reference rule.

The second possibility is to apply an open-ended "real and substantial connection" analysis,[175] in which the identification of the relevant *lex loci delicti* would depend on how the aggregation of relevant connections came together in each particular case, tested against the principles and values identified by Dickson J in *Moran* v. *Pyle*.[176] This solution is the more responsive of the two to territorial and justice principles. "One-law selecting" conflicts values are preserved.[177] There is no plaintiff or defendant bias inherent in the test. And because the element of plaintiff choice is eliminated, there is greater certainty and predictability despite the open ended language of the test.

[170] Kozyris, *supra* n. 81. And see text at nn. 102, 103.

[171] Kozyris, *ibid*., at 506.

[172] *Supra* n. 102.

[173] *Supra* nn. 119, 120, 160, 164.

[174] *Supra* nn. 119, 120, 164.

[175] On the idea that territorial analysis is synonymous with a real and substantial connection test in choice of law cases arising out of truly interprovincial or transnational activities, see *supra* text at n. 105.

[176] *Supra* part II(a) of this article.

[177] This term is defined *supra* at n. 29.

IV. CONCLUSION

At the close of the last century, territorial analysis dominated conflict of laws thinking. Private international law was seen as a branch of public international law, sharing a common concern with the values of comity and a common commitment to preserving the co-equal territorial sovereignty of countries and States. In the intervening years, this way of thinking has fallen into decline in common law jurisdictions. There is no "superlaw" vesting exclusive prescriptive authority in particular States over particular classes of interjurisdictional activities or events. Choice of law decisions are merely another form of expression of local policy and local standards of justice, unconstrained by external limits.

Today, territorial analysis is once again in ascendance in the area of choice of law in tort. Driven by a sense of dismay at the excessive bias towards local law solutions favouring local interests reflected in common law thinking everywhere, scholars, courts and legislators are once again looking outward for external limits on the territorial reach of local law, finding potential for them within federal systems in the constitution, and in the international realm in the old idea of comity as an expression of the principle of co-equal territorial sovereignty.

This "neo-territorialism" differs, however, from the territorial approach to choice of law associated with traditional vested rights thinking. Rather than *commanding* immutable and mechanistic solutions to choice of law problems, territorial values *inform* the choice of law process, acting as an outer limit on the assertion of domestic legal policy and providing a more solid foundation for the development of choice of law rules that strive for greater neutrality in balancing the interests of the parties and connected States.

In the area of products liability, territorial analysis succeeds in eliminating the single most complicating element from the choice of law equation—the reference to the manufacturer's home law—without impinging on substantive justice principles. The remaining choice of law issues are identifiable and finite, and for that reason manageable, even if there may remain room for reasonable disagreement in the details of their resolution. The fact that some areas of uncertainty necessarily remain should not lead us to reject the methodology. Instead we should see it as evidence of the flexibility of the new territorialism. After all, with global economic integration proceeding apace, manageable uncertainty is surely preferable to the state of anarchy inherent in the old *lex fori* rule.

PART V

International Trade Law

13

First Approach to Competition Law and Sanctioning of Disloyal Practices in Mercosur

RAUL ANIBAL ETCHEVERRY*

I. GENERAL BACKGROUND

In today's world organisation, economic principles directed towards a globalised economy have determined the adoption of similar market oriented systems. Their aim is to gain free access for goods and services to national or common markets, thus eliminating tariff barriers and other indirect restrictions that constitute an obstacle to the free circulation of goods and services. Recent papers by Professor Donald King have shown that, together with changes in the world order and the effects of globalisation, corresponding changes have also emerged in the legal sphere. As the Italian jurist Ascarelli has pointed out,[1] "[w]hen market access is free, legal competition in broad terms acquires a new dimension while at the same time transport development tends to unify the various markets, and industrial mass production (a source of transport development, that in turn, leads back to mass production) gives competition a central role."

It was the French Law of 2 March 1791 that first stated the principle that all persons are free to do business and to practise any profession, art or craft; this Law was later complemented by the *Le Chapellier Law* of 17 June 1791, which abolished guilds and, consequently, the restrictions on free trade and free enterprise. As I have described elsewhere,[2] it is in nations where a capitalist economy develops—where the means of production remain in private hands—that the need to create and protect a competitive market with fair rules has arisen. These principles are basically aimed at protecting the

* Professor of Economics and Business Law, School of Law and Social Sciences, University of Buenos Aires, Argentina.

[1] Tullio Ascarelli, *Teoría de la concurrencia y de los bienes inmateriales* (Barcelona, Bosch, 1970), 20 (translation provided by the author of this paper).

[2] Raúl Aníbal Etcheverry, *Derecho Comercial y Económico. Parte General* (Buenos Aires, Astrea, 1987), 192, para. 65.

consumer, who will both gain access to cheaper products and choose the ones he considers most appropriate for his needs.[3]

Since 1976, the European Union (EU) has been applying three directives that tend to protect free competition within the Common Market.[4] The German Law outlawing economic cartels was passed in 1958; but the German Unfair Competition Law of 1909 had already penalized unfair practices of corporations (e.g. false or misleading publicity). Thereafter, State regulation of unfair practices continued until the concept of a market economy was firmly established. Starting with the German Law of 1980 on cartels, this concept gave rise to a series of common market provisions that constitute the foundations of modern competition law in the European Union.

Four different stages can be noted in the evolution of competition law: the first ensures and protects private company initiative (this promotes progress and multi-level changes, especially technological ones). The second facilitates and ensures access to markets. The third stage makes the market competitive so that variety, price and quality of products are offered by many competing enterprises. The fourth stage seeks to maintain a free and competitive market and penalises individual and collective distortions and unfair competitive practices.

In developing countries, the right to compete is often hindered by the State itself. In developed countries or common markets, the right to compete is distorted when it goes beyond its proper boundaries or when businesses are expanded abroad. It is necessary then to reach a fairer balance within the new international economic order in which the rights and obligations of industrialised countries will be maintained as a priority for the benefit of developing countries.[5]

Once accepted, competition rules must be observed in good faith and grant equal rights to all persons—a basic principle in democratic systems.[6] Although it is true that it is not easy to find a genuinely unbiased market, it is also reasonable to claim that competition is one of the essential prerequisites for man's welfare and the natural goal of a modern legal system. This relates to the basic task of governments led by politicians: to protect the individual as well as the public interest.

Individual interests and enterprise activities share a common objective. This is to protect the consumer's rights, the counterpart of these legal regulations.

[3] This is a simplified description of the impact of a free market economy since this paper addresses different topics. Also, Norbert Reich's important contribution must not be overlooked when he points out the two roles of law in the market: see Norbert Reich, *Mercado y Derecho* (Barcelona, Ariel, 1985), 61 ff.

[4] Alberto Trabucchi, "Sviluppo della giurisprudenza e suo significato nella disciplina comunitaria della concorrenza" in *Studi in memoria di Roberto Bracco* (Padova, Cedam, 1976), 561 and ff.

[5] Norbert Reich, "Introducción a la edición española del libro Mercado y Derecho" (1985) 178 *Revista de Derecho Mercantil* 758 and ff.

[6] In this sense see, as a general principle, the concept of "decent and reasonable trader" referred to by Boris Kozolchyk, *El Derecho comercial ante el libre comercio y el desarrollo económico* (Mexico, Mc Graw Hill, 1996), 219 ff.

The consumer performs the so-called "act of consuming",[7] in which civil and commercial norms converge (in countries which distinguish between commercial and civil law) with rules of public law (such as administrative law).[8] In many countries, the State itself controls, directly or indirectly, many enterprises and, although not always justified, those often constitute real monopolies. We consider these situations the exception to the rule, and they should be reversed as soon as possible. In other economic areas, the activity is managed, regulated or controlled by the State, allegedly based on the public interest or the interest of the community, where macro-economic transactions (trade, exchange, currency) or other sensitive activities (banking, securities markets, insurance, intellectual or industrial property among others) take place.

It is instructive to analyse competition law from the perspective of international business, although the concept may also be applied to domestic transactions. Frignani quotes Reese[9] when stating that a contract is international when it shares common features with more than one jurisdiction. Frignani also quotes Carbone and Luzzato,[10] who take into account international trade reality and argue that such contracts should not be governed exclusively by national domestic law in their objective and subjective elements.

II. GATT–WTO AGREEMENTS

Consistently with the international consensus achieved by the GATT round of negotiations and the creation of a new organisation to develop free world trade, the World Trade Organization (WTO) becomes the means of promoting world globalisation. Its rules, aimed at facilitating the application of international norms to liberalise international trade, should be briefly recalled. The GATT, which was signed by or has been extended to more than a hundred countries, came into being with thirty-eight articles. Today, it is a complex Code of agreements dealing with a diversity of subjects. Its two fundamental principles are: (a) the most favoured nation clause, through which any benefit or concession granted by one member country to another must be extended to all other member States; and (b) non-discrimination among member States. Both are part of a gradual expansionist trade policy that has so far proved to

[7] Eva Holz, *Mercado y Derecho* (Montevideo, Fundación de Cultura Universitaria), 20 and ff. We believe that, taking into account the integration of the civil and commercial branches in the interpretation and application of code law (although they are formally separate branches), it is of no importance to determine whether the act of consuming is civil or commercial. In this sense, we implicitly declare our position in my book *supra* n. 2.

[8] Compare my *Derecho Comercial y Económico*, Parte General, *supra* n. 2, 197.

[9] Aldo Frignani, "Il contratto internazionale" in Francesco Galgano (ed.), *Trattato di Diritto Commerciale e di Diritto Pubblico della Economía* (Padova, Cedam, 1990), vol.12, 122, and Wm. Reese, "The Law Governing International Contracts" in *International Contracts*, 4., [000]

[10] *Ibid.*, 123.

be very beneficial. Nevertheless, the simplicity of the principles is not fully reflected in practice, but is distorted by a complex network of private-sector and State interests.

From the beginning, two, I believe justifiable, exceptions to the principles were accepted: the existence of a well-established regional common market (the former EEC, now the European Union) and the position of a country that needs to protect a developing domestic industry. In certain cases, obligatory compensation is provided for. In spite of the reservations expressed below, the GATT's success is unquestionable since world trade has grown greatly and has prospered under its rules. Today, a country wishing to participate in world trade cannot ignore or refuse to adhere to its rules. Each negotiating round has been a step forward, but the decisive move took place at the Uruguay Round whose participants met for the first time in September 1986 in Punta del Este, in South America. Thereafter, progress was made in respect of the regulation of services, high technology, industrial and intellectual property rights and agricultural products.

As tariff barriers were abolished, protectionism and the defence of individual interest have created new indirect non-tariff barriers from which, among others, theories of organised markets or managed trade[11] and market sharing have emerged. This was the case with the agreements on the iron and steel industry, motor vehicles, television sets, video players and semiconductors, signed between the USA and Japan in [00] or the EU and Japan in [00].[12] If true free trade is to be achieved, these practices must be abandoned. Gradually, by pressuring the parties and negotiating, the GATT has managed to bring about a reduction in many import duties, resorting to negotiation in the first place and denouncing restrictions (quotas), subsidies, unfair practices or discrimination if persuasion did not work. Negotiation has been carried out through the method known as "claims and offers" advanced by countries or groups of countries with a view to liberalising trade in a concrete area. By applying the most favoured nation principle, agreements reached by the GATT member countries have become universal.

The restrictions discussed or negotiated may be based on tariffs (concessions or quantitative or qualitative restrictions); limitations on trading certain products (setting up maximum amounts or values); import or export licence regulations where a procedure to approve the licence is established; dumping, a discriminatory strategy that allows a product to enter the market at a lower price than that in the market of origin (anti-dumping rights are set up here); the limitation on exports agreed upon among enterprises or with the participation of governments; State subsidies or forms of State economic support to

[11] Ileana Di Giovan de Battista, *Derecho Internacional Económico* (Buenos Aires, Abeledo-Perrot, 1992), 124.

[12] *Ibid.*, 125. This Argentine author also mentions the Acuerdo Multifibra (Multifibre Accord), which covers 80% of the textile world trade.

help develop exports (this can be controlled by establishing compensation or countervailing duties).

We can assert that the principles of the WTO—in spite of the fact that they do not contain rules about competition law—are reaching the category of a new substantive international law about unfair practices, accepted by the most important nations of the world. Nevertheless, much still needs to be done and it is necessary that the developed countries set the example of free trade.[13]

As is well known, the GATT provides a mechanism, similar to arbitration, establishing panels for the analysis and resolution of disputes when violations of the agreement have been denounced by countries or groups of countries.

III. THE INTERNATIONAL SYSTEM

The principles stated above allow us to anticipate some of the "rules of the game" of international trade by the end of the second millennium. We cannot enumerate them in detail, but we observe a comprehensive "competition law" of great importance for the future of the world economy. Linked to it, other rules will emerge to allow enterprises and enterpreneurs to exercise economic freedom in national and international markets.[14] Within the framework of the international order already described,[15] enterprises competing in national and international markets will gradually abandon the status of guided and State-controlled companies to become free agents; State-owned corporations are being privatised and monopolies or oligopolies begin to disappear.

Since free market access is an unquestionable asset in modern market economies, State subsidies, regarded as unfair competition, and dumping, widely regarded with equal hostility, become among the most debated subjects. In the United States,[16] the doctrine has established the similarities and differences between the American anti-dumping legislation and that of the Uruguay Round, mainly in respect of start-up costs, captive production, price

[13] A paradigmatic case is the reticence of the EU to make concessions in its agricultural policy (PAC) in view of the claims of the meat and grain producing countries (e.g. the Cairns group, of which Argentina is a member).

[14] The topics can be determined in light of the principle of economic freedom, which allows economic agents to enter, leave or stay in the markets and ensures that they shall not be exposed to practices or conditions that may distort that freedom, whether imposed by another enterprise or group of enterprises. As examples I mention unfair practices (misleading publicity, price agreements, market allocations), abuse of dominant positions as a consequence of unfair practices (e.g. contracts with "binding provisions"), unfair penetration of foreign markets through dumping and subsidies. For a very clear and up-to-date treatment of the subject see Carias *et al.*, *Ley para promover y proteger el ejercicio de la libre competencia* (Caracas, Editorial Jurídica Venezolana, 1996).

[15] Raúl Aníbal Etcheverry, "El Derecho Comercial Internacional. Nuevas Fuentes" in La Ley 7/10/92, vol. LVI, nr. 193.

[16] See Alan F. Holmer, Gary N. Horlick and Terence P. Stewart, "Enacted and Rejected Amendments to the Antidumping Law: An Implementation or Contravention of the Antidumping Agreement?" (1995) 29 *Internat. Lawyer* 483.

averaging, export prices and adjustment for profit, anti-circumvention, cost recoveries, no or short supply and duties as a cost and compensation. In the European Union, there are two new anti-dumping directives of December 1994 and February 1995 that try to devise a system closer to what the GATT tried to achieve before the Uruguay Round. The Uruguay Round created a new international order. It reformed the trade remedies available against prohibited subsidies and introduced a new form of legal control of dumping.

The new Anti-dumping Code, as Estoup[17] calls it, seeks to implement measures with the following characteristics:

(1) clarity;
(2) speed;
(3) longer periods for dumping complaints;
(4) direct countervailing solutions;
(5) appropriate countervailing solutions;
(6) discouragement of frivolous dumping reports.

As Estoup[18] says, it is necessary to know and establish the limits of free competition. In a market which endeavours to be free, monopolies and other interests may be beneficial or harmful to the consumer interest. The fact that a product sold at a low price may benefit the consumer does not always imply licit and fair trade. At the international level, it is often difficult to establish the cost of a product for the purpose of the trading regime. This is so where the product has been manufactured in a third country and the product has passed through several hands before being exported. Another issue requiring analysis is the concept of injury, a concept that lacks precision and uniformity among the different domestic trade regimes.

Before turning to an analysis of the trade laws in each of the Mercosur countries, it will be useful to distinguish between the following aspects of competition law:

(1) unfair practices and monopolies;
(2) subsidies;
(3) dumping;
(4) safeguarding of national interests; and
(5) consumer law

Competition is a concept that must soon be unified around the world. It implies a consolidation movement in law that, going beyond harmonisation, leads to material unification. These perceptions differ from Professor King's,[19] who sees in modern commercial law a new trend dominated by change and diversity.

[17] Luis Alejandro Estoup, "La reglamentación moderna del antidumping", La Ley of December 21, 1995, vol. LIX, nr. 245.

[18] *Ibid.*

[19] Donald B. King, "Commercial Law: Times of Change and Expansion" in R. M. Goode and R. Cranston (eds.), *Commercial and Consumer Law* (Clarendon Press, Oxford, 1993), 128.

IV. ARGENTINA

In Argentina, there is a relatively new law on competition and remedies for unfair trade. The legislation begins by dealing with constitutional principles and then branches off into three large groups of provisions: (a) those establishing a competition right, that is, free access to the market; (b) the right to compete in the market without being exposed to unfair practices; and (c) protection of the consumer.

(a) Defence of Free Markets

The Economic Criminal Court of Buenos Aires[20] has stated that the competition law tries to ensure free access to the market for all competitive enterprises, and prohibits and penalises unfair production or exchange of goods and services that may limit or distort competition.

The National Constitution, as amended in 1994, states that consumers of goods and services have the right to adequate and accurate information, freedom of choice and proper and fair treatment (Article 42, first paragraph). In Article 42, the Constitution provides that "the authorities shall protect those rights and in addition provide consumer education, competition against market distortions and natural and legal monopolies, and will ensure the quality and efficiency of public services and the creation of consumers and users' associations". Article 43 guarantees expedited legal action to protect these civil rights in the absence of a more suitable judicial procedure. In particular, the Article refers to rights related to the environment, competition and users and consumers.

Law 22.262,[21] in accordance with the UN rules of 1980 and the European legislation on the subject, protects competition when establishing that acts and conduct related to production or exchange of goods and services that limit or distort competition or that may be considered an abuse of a dominant position[22] in the market and damaging to the general economic interest "are forbidden and shall be penalized". The Law clearly refers to the general economic interest that is protected by the legislation, and does not penalize a corporation for its dominant position, but only if the corporation abuses its position. In Article 41, the legislation enumerates the conduct to be penalized when it damages the legal interests described in Article 1, and they are the following:

(1) to fix, determine or vary market prices directly or indirectly by agreement among competitors;

[20] See the judicial decision cited in Etcheverry, *supra* n. 15, 194, n. 214.

[21] In force as from 6 August 1980.

[22] For debates on the Argentine case law and doctrine on abuse of dominant position, see Etcheverry, *supra* n. 15, 194 and nn.

(2) to limit or control by agreement, technical developments or investments for production of goods or services or their production, distribution or marketing;
(3) to establish, by means of agreement, the terms of sales and marketing of goods, minimum quantities, discounts and other aspects regarding sales and marketing;
(4) to require a buyer to accept additional goods or services that, due to their nature and according to commercial practices, bear no relationship to the object of the contracts;
(5) to conclude or enter into collusive agreements for the allocation of zones, markets, clients or suppliers among the parties;
(6) to prevent or hinder by agreement or concerted actions market access to one or more competitors;
(7) to refuse, as part of an agreement and without reasons based on commercial practices, to accept firm orders for the purchase or sale of goods or services on terms and conditions normal in the market;
(8) to impose by agreement, discriminatory purchase sales terms for goods or services that are not supported by commercial practices;
(9) to destroy goods as part of an agreement at any stage of the manufacturing process or the means used to extract, manufacture or transport them;
(10) to abandon crops or cultivated lands, plantations, agricultural and farming products, or to hinder or prevent operations on industrial premises and in mining fields as part of a concerted action;
(11) as part of an agreement among competing enterprises to fix prices, purchase, sales or marketing.

The Law defines a "dominant position" in the following terms:

> "(a) A party enjoys a dominant position in a market when it is the only supplier within the national market for a certain type of product or service or when, without being the only supplier, it is not exposed to substantial competition; or
>
> (b) Two or more parties enjoy a dominant position in a market when, in respect of a certain type of product or service, there is no real competition between them or a substantial competition from third parties, in the national market or part of it."

Unlike Brazil's, Argentina's competition law has no provisions on economic concentration. Article 4 and its accompanying sections establish the administrative procedure with a prescriptive term of two years for filing an action and the ensuing claim as well as the subsidiary civil action for damages subsequent to the claim.

The National Commission for the Defence of Competition, created by the Law as part of the State Secretariat for Commerce and International Negotiations, is chaired by the Under-Secretary, and consists of two attorneys and two economists with no less than four years of professional practice.

The procedure described in Article 17 is initiated by a private action or by the National Commission itself. The novelty of this administrative procedure is that it allows the defendant to enter into a voluntary agreement with the Commission to provide an "assurance of voluntary compliance" to comply with the Law and to cease and desist from any further violations of the Law.

The Commission may issue a cease and desist order against violators, impose heavy fines or ask the judge for economic crimes or the federal judge to dissolve the offending corporation. All these penalties are to be published in the Official Bulletin.

Apart from the compulsory administrative procedure, there is also the possibility of starting judicial proceedings.

(b) Unfair Practices

Once the enterprises are established in the market, care should be taken to ensure that they are not driven from the market by unfair competition. This is an issue with many aspects, since its object is both to discipline the enterprise's behaviour in the market in relation to other enterprises, whether competitors or not, and also with respect to consumers. There are many types of unfair trade practices. They range from misleading publicity[23] to practices that may damage other enterprises. This applies to both domestic and international trade laws, free trade areas and other areas where dumping, subsidies and other market distortions are penalised. Although it is true that in many countries or regions protective policies are applied to promote or develop various enterprises or whole production areas,[24] it is also true that these policies can only be tolerated when they are of a transitional character.

In May 1983, Argentina enacted Law 22.802 on fair competition. This Law should be interpreted in harmony with other legal norms, such as the Law on trade marks, patents, and identification of goods. I will refer now to some of the relevant features of the Law.

Competition is a struggle for customers. But in this struggle means and practices that are unfair, based on fraud, or that may damage or destroy commercial competitors are not permitted.[25] Law 22.802 on identification of goods states that the following information must be clearly disclosed on the container, label or other form of packaging of the product: the nature of the product, the country of origin, its quality, composition and the net weight of

[23] Rodríguez Carlos Juan Zabala, *Publicidad comercial. Su régimen legal* (Buenos Aires, 1947), 383, num. 338. See also ch. XIV.

[24] E.g. the EU supports a common agricultural policy (CAP) for the protection of its agricultural and farming industries. Argentina supports a private monopoly for telephone services and domestic air transportation. However, these restrictions must be temporary and will gradually be removed by the World Trade Organization and the countries and regions involved, who must understand that the full development of the world economy can only occur where competition is accepted as a norm among trading nations.

[25] Joaquín Garrigues, *Temas de derecho vivo* (Madrid, Tecnos, 1978), 199.

the contents. The other provisions of the Law penalize any inscription or description that may lead to deception, error or confusion as regards the origin of the product or its nature, quality, composition, purity, quantity, uses, marketing conditions or production techniques.

This Law also deals with disclosure of the country of origin. This is a new issue in Mercosur because the Mercosur members have already agreed on a common external tariff and are now seeking fairness in commercial practices and in the statements by manufacturers or traders who distribute or sell the products. Publicity is also briefly regulated by this Law, which penalizes misleading, false or confusing advertising. The Law determines the identity of the enforcement authority during the first administrative stage of the proceedings and the sanctions to be applied. After the administrative review, access to judicial procedure continues to be guaranteed, as was true of previous laws.

(c) Protection of the Consumer

In October, 1993, Argentina enacted Law 24.240, amended by Decree 2089 of the same year, that limits the scope of the earlier Law in certain respects. The Law aims at defending consumers or users, who are defined as "physical or juridical persons who enter into onerous contracts of consumption for their own benefit or for the benefit of their family or a social group, or for the purchase or lease of movable assets, services, and the purchase of new homes, including plots of land, when the offer is made to the public and directed to designated persons" (Article 1). The legal norm ensures proper disclosure of information and health protection for the consumer. It also regulates the conditions of offer and sale, the effects of publicity, the condition of the goods, the contents of the sales contract, warranties, technical services, home sales and sales in instalments. Services both inside and outside the home are also regulated.

Chapter IX of the Law deals with contract provisions. The enforcement authorities are defined as is the procedure to be followed which starts with the administrative stage and ends with the possibility of eventual judicial review. The original Law imposed strict joint liability for damages on producers, manufacturers, importers, distributors, suppliers, vendors and those whose names appear on the product. The Argentine Government vetoed this section by Decree 2089. Only the issue of pharmaceutical patents remains to be regulated. Such patents were prohibited by the previous legislation, but a new law is likely to be passed soon in accordance with the GATT–WTO provisions and the new Brazilian legislation.

(d) Dumping and Subsidies

With respect to dumping and subsidies, the Argentine Government has opted for freedom of commerce, and consequently believes that product competitiveness is more important than producer protection, which only leads to hidden subsidies. Because it is aware of the great world-wide technological changes, Argentina wants its industry to be competitive and efficient and have to play a significant role in international commerce.

Decree 2121 establishes the procedure to determine dumping based on the GATT regulations. New legislation to update the procedure and to adapt it to the Uruguay Round is being analysed. Apart from the proof of dumping or the existence of subsidies, there must also be evidence of injury or threat of injury to the domestic industry. Threat of injury is often invoked but is difficult to establish in practice. An example is the case of the Argentine dairy industry that was threatened in 1992 by subsidied EEC exports. The direct and indirect economic support made the price of the EEC products 40 per cent lower than the domestic Argentine price. In this case, injury had not yet occurred, but the potential harm was obvious. If the injury had occurred, the national dairy industry would have been faced with total destruction. Argentina has also been exposed to dumping from countries with surplus inventory—corn, for example—where the inventory is exported to Argentina at below the market price.

When there are complaints about dumping or subsidies that have caused or may cause injury, different governmental agencies participate in the proceedings: the Ministry of the Economy, the Secretariat for Industry, Commerce and Mining, and the Under-Secretariat for Foreign Trade. In the Mercosur regime, dumping and subsidy claims are studied by the Trade Commission through its National Section.

Since Argentina is a signatory to the GATT and Uruguay Round, unfair practices must be dealt with within the framework of those agreements. Speedy reports and solutions are desirable, but the juridical interests of the respondent exporter accused of dumping must also be respected, since dumping may not in fact have occurred or may not have reached the legally cognizable levels. Law 24.425 and Decrees 2121/94, 766/94 and 704/95 apply. The procedure has shortcomings and produces practical problems. The first is the concept of "like product" and its classification within the tariff list (at times, the list has "package tariff positions" where a great number of products are grouped together). The second problem is to determine the "normal value" of a product. In centrally planned economies, as in China, it is difficult to determine the normal value of a product. This lack of data is remedied in Argentina by adopting the US, EU and other countries' approach. This is to use the best information possible where the exporting country does not provide information or the information is not otherwise available. Where the exporter is located in a country with a planned economy, the missing information may be taken from countries with similar economies.

Argentina did not have many dumping and subsidy complaints between July 1995 and June 1996. Nevertheless, there were some qualitatively significant cases. 20 per cent of the reports on unfair competition involved China and 11 per cent Brazil. These were followed by complaints about exports from the Netherlands, the United States and Germany.

V. BRAZIL

(a) Consumer Protection

Brazil has a very comprehensive consumer protection law based on its Law 8078 of 11 September 1990. It sets up a detailed system imposing strict liability, independent of fault, on the manufacturer, producer, builder (national or foreign) or the importer of a defective product for damage caused by the product as well as for damage caused by product defects, and defects of manufacturing, construction, assembly, formulae, management, presentation or packaging or inadequate information regarding the use and risks of a product (Article 12). Article 12 also describes when a product is considered defective. It also renders traders responsible for a defective product where the manufacturer, builder, producer or importer cannot be identified, where the product is sold without identification or where the product is not properly stored by the trader.

The service supplier is also rendered liable and the law defines the circumstances in which the service is considered defective. The liability of professionals is also dealt with. Their liability is based on fault. The Law is a true consumer code in the civilian sense. It defines the meaning of consumer,[26] supplier or delivery agent ("*fornecedor*"),[27] product[28] and service.[29] It also sets out the national policy governing consumers, establishes basic rights of the consumer (Chapter III), the quality of products and services and the supplier's duty to prevent injury and, where injury occurs, to pay compensation (Chapter IV), commercial practices, contractual protection, administrative sanctions, criminal violations and assistance for the consumer in legal proceedings. An innovation is also the introduction of class actions for the protection of individuals with common interests (Article 91 ff).In light of these provisions, we may conclude that the Brazilian system of consumer protection, as well as in respect of the other issues analysed hereafter, is much more rigorous than the Argentine system.

[26] Art. 2 defines "consumer" as "any physical or legal person who purchases or uses goods or services for his own use or consumption or groups of indeterminable persons who participate in the consumption relationship".

[27] Defined as "any physical or legal person, public or private, national or foreign, who performs activities related to production, assembly, creation, construction, transformation, import, export, distribution or marketing of products or services" (Art. 3, sect. 1).

[28] Defined as "any movable or immovable good, whether corporeal or incorporeal" (Art. 3).

[29] Defined as "any activity offered in to the consumer market for a price, including activities related to banking, finance, credit and insurance, other than labour relationships" (Art. 3, sect. 1).

(b) Competition Law

Brazil has comprehensive legislation governing free competition, abuse of economic power and remedies for unfair practices. Law 4.137 of 1962 and Decree 92.323 of 1986 create a system that outlaws various forms of abuse of economic power by establishing the following criteria of what constitutes an abuse: the monopolisation of the national market, the elimination of competition, wholly or in part, the raising of prices without reasonable cause; the creation of monopolistic conditions, entering into exclusive agreements to the detriment of buyers or sellers and generally practising unfair competition.

In 1962, an Administrative Council for Economic Defence and a Public Prosecution Board were established. They are authorised to impose the sanctions established by the regulatory Decree of 1986. These sanctions may range from a simple fine to judicial intervention, and even the liquidation of a company. Company officials may also be held personally liable as provided in the corresponding Law (Article 159 and Law 6404 of 15 December 1976).

Dumping is regulated by Decree 93.941 of January 1987. The legal text establishes a true anti-dumping code which defines dumping and the concepts of "like product", regulates how injury is to be determined, establishes anti-dumping duties, and deals with the settlement of disputes and other issues. The Law is also linked to the GATT norms.

Law 8137 of 1990 defines tax offences, economic offences and consumer offences and imposes different penalties. Fair competition is regulated by Law 8158 of 1991 and Decree 36 of the same year. These norms grant power to the Ministry of Justice, through the National Secretariat for Economic Law, to propose measures aimed at "correcting the conduct of economic sectors, enterprises or other businesses that may directly or indirectly distort or affect the mechanisms for the establishment of prices, free competition, free initiative or constitutional economic principles".

The Law envisages direct intervention by the agencies to correct the anomalies mentioned before and describes the various types of conduct deemed to amount to unfair competition. The penalties are less rigorous than the previous penalties because a violator is registered in a special register, he is disqualified from participating in public bids for government contracts and he does not enjoy the benefit of deferred tax payments.

Antitrust Law 8884 of June 1994 establishes the prevention and suppression of infringements against the economic order, violating free initiatives and free competition, the protection of the social uses of property, protection of the consumer and suppression of abuse of economic power. The Law modifies the status of the Council for Economic Defence (CADE) by granting it federal autonomy. New rules have also been adopted for its formation, functions and jurisdiction.

In Chapter II of Law 8884, a long list of violations is enumerated (Articles 20 and 21) and Chapter III states the penalties that may be imposed on corporate managers found guilty of violations. It also imposes fines, requires publication of sanctions, outlaws contracts or bids with and on behalf of the State and requires registration of violators and their disqualification for deferred tax benefits. The Law establishes a detailed administrative procedure.

In Title VII, Chapter I, a mechanism is created for the control of acts and contracts by means of which an interested party may consult and receive the approval of the CADE, and thereafter a "performance commitment" may be signed if the acts are included among those otherwise not permissible but which tend to increase productivity and improve the quality of products or the level of efficiency or the rate of technological development. The administrative authorisation will be temporary and must not endanger competition in a substantial sector of the relevant market for goods and services. Finally, we should point out that at the present time Brazil is making vigorous efforts to abandon its traditional State protectionist policy, inspired by the CEPAL Doctrines of the 1960s and 1970s.

VI. CHILE

Chile adopted the common rules of the free trade area of this South American region when it signed the Chile–Mercosur agreement in June 1996. Alvarez Zenteno[30] states that competition law in Chile has now greatly developed. It applies to contracts, joint agreements and foreign or domestic investments, takeover bids, and also to consulting and litigation. The most important Chilean text on the subject is Decree–Law 211 of 22 December 1973 aimed at ensuring a competitive market. However, because of the great economic transformation undergone by Chile in recent years the legislation has become obsolete. In particular, Alvarez Zenteno criticises the penal sections of the Decree for being too broad and therefore likely to lead to the violation of various constitutional principles.

To avoid this, Chile mainly applies civil or administrative sanctions through judges and anti-trust commissions. He says his country, like the United States and Europe, has shifted from a simple prohibition of practices to the application of the rule of reason by means of which the defendant's conduct is measured, taking into account the defendant's motive and impact of the conduct on the market. Together with this juridical technique, Alvarez Zenteno analyses monopolistic practices from the perspective of abuse of a dominant position, which does not penalize monopolies *per se* (because a monopoly may reflect greater efficiency obtained by legal means) but is only concerned with its abuse.

[30] Rodrigo Alvarez Zenteno, "Una visión de nuestro derecho de la competencia", *Revista del Abogado, Santiago*, April 1996, no. 6 24. What follows in the text is based on Prof. Alvarez Zenteno's summary of the Chilean regime.

VII. URUGUAY

(a) Unfair Competition

Xavier de Mello points out[31] that in Uruguay there is no formal legislation on unfair competition. Nevertheless, its constitutional norms, following the liberal tradition, guarantee freedom of work, commerce and industry as well as protection of property rights and bank secrecy. In Uruguay an action alleging unfair competition and seeking a cease and desist order may be filed under the ordinary rules of civil procedure. If the order is not complied with the defendant may be subject to contempt proceedings. The plaintiff is also entitled to seek compensation in the form of damages. According to some authors and pursuant to Law 16.011 on the Protection of Individual Rights, summary proceedings can be applied to stop unfair competitive acts occurring in the domestic market.

(b) Unfair Trade: Dumping

Uruguay adopted anti-dumping legislation by Decree 142 of 8 May 1996, published in the Official Bulletin. The Decree is based on the Uruguay Round agreements and the Final Document of Marrakech, 15 April 1994, which authorise countervailing dumping measures. The Decree allows the imposition of antidumping duties against the import of dumped basic and non-basic products causing injury to the domestic industries. Article 4 includes the GATT definition of dumping, under which dumping occurs when a product is imported, even temporarily, at an export price lower than the normal value. "Normal value" is defined as a comparative price of a similar product manufactured for consumption in the exporter's country in the course of ordinary trade (Article 5). The Decree is very comprehensive and establishes the procedure for determining the normal value of the export price to establish the dumping margin and existence of injury. It also prescribes the investigation procedure and application and collection of anti-dumping duties. Section IV of the Decree authorises the provisional countervailing measures following a preliminary assessment of dumping and after a period of no fewer than sixty days from the beginning of the investigation.

VIII. MERCOSUR

Mercosur is also going through a process designed to lead to the convergence of the member country trading systems, although bilateral agreements are also

[31] Eugenio Xavier de Mellos, *Competencia internacional desleal, in Primeras Jornadas Nacionales de Derecho del Comercio Exterior* (Montevideo, 1991), 84.

being promoted, together with the existing legal norms of the GATT–WTO system (to which the Mercosur countries all belong), unification is sought to establish a common market to enable national and foreign investors to acquire easier familiarity with the legal norms. In addition to the "Protocol on harmonization of rules on intellectual property in Mercosur, in respect of trademarks, origins and names of origin", sanctioned by Decision 8/95 of the Mercosur Common Market Council, that indirectly refers to issues of competition, Mercosur is also drafting a common regulatory regime on competition and unfair practices.

The first step was to approve the Basic Guidelines for the Harmonization of Competition Rules in Mercosur, by virtue of the decision of the Common Market Council. The Guidelines refer to the need to outlaw persisting monopolistic practices and the abuse of a dominant position. Technical Committee 5 for Competition Rules, which is part of the Trade Commission of Mercosur (a new body created by the Ouro Preto Protocol 1995) is working at present on a document aimed at co-ordinating Brazilian and Argentine law with the laws of Uruguay and Paraguay, whose laws contain few and only scattered provisions on competition. As indicated earlier, the Argentine and Brazilian rules are quite developed in both countries as signatories to the GATT–WTO regime.

One of the problems to be addressed is the enforcement of legal rules, since Mercosur does not have a supranational court and the procedure for settlement of disputes is slow and difficult. Disputes cannot be settled under the domestic legislation of the participating countries since two of the Mercosur members do not have any legislation in this area. Paraguay, which has a very small domestic industry, has adopted the Committee 5 proposals.

Decision 21, previously referred to, establishes the basis for future common competition legislation. It will be based on a comparative study of existing legislation and the analysis of general guidelines on harmonisation.[32] Meanwhile, the Mercosur Trade Commission is responsible for investigating complaints in the trade area. The Annex to Decision 21 contains detailed proposals on free competition and access to markets as the two main components on Mercosur trading regime.

Within this framework, the following practices are prohibited: collusive agreements and actions among economic agents; decisions of trade associations aimed at impeding, limiting or distorting competition or free market access relating to the production, processing, distribution and marketing of goods and services in all or in part of Mercosur, or that may affect trade between the Member States, such as: (1) directly or indirectly fixing prices or other terms for the production or marketing of goods and services; (2) limiting or controlling the production, distribution, technological development or investments in goods; (3) allocating shares for markets of goods or services or

[32] The author of this paper is chair of a research group on the subject that co-operates with the Argentine Ministry of Foreign Affairs in drafting a statute on the protection of free competition.

sources of raw materials or basic products; (4) agreeing to co-ordinate actions that affect competitive actions or tenders for public contracts; (5) adopting, in respect of contracts with third parties, disparate conditions for similar services that may place third parties at a competitive disadvantage; (6) requiring buyers to agree to purchase additional goods or services that are not naturally related to the main contract; (7) wrongfully exerting pressure on a customer with the object of dissuading the customer from a course of conduct or applying reprisals or other forms of coercion.

The abuse of a dominant position is also prohibited. This may consist, among others, of the following types of conduct: (a) directly or indirectly imposing buying or selling prices or other unfair terms; (b) limiting, without justification, the production, distribution or technological development of goods and services to the prejudice of enterprises or consumers; (c) imposing unequal conditions on contracting parties for equivalent services, thus placing them in a disadvantageous competitive position; (d) requiring buyers to agree to purchase additional goods or services that are not naturally related to the main contract; (e) improperly refusing to supply goods or services; (f) wrongfully imposing conditions on transactions, without justification and not based on usage, custom or commercial practices, for the use, purchase, sale, distribution or provision of goods or services produced, processed, distributed or marketed by a third party; (g) selling goods or services at predatory prices with the object of eliminating competition in the market.

In addition, Decision 21/94 states that the member States will control economic concentration among enterprises or groups of enterprises involving 20 per cent or more of the relevant market and giving rise to anti-competitive effects in Mercosur. The last part of the Decision provides that member States shall co-operate among themselves directly or through the Trade Commission to ensure due fulfilment of norms, procedures and actions that may be agreed upon as regards competition and free market access. The mechanism will consist of exchanging information and proposals, providing advice and technical co-operation and such other activities as may be deemed appropriate. The Trade Commission must establish co-ordinating mechanisms among the enforcement authorities about domestic competition laws. The Commission is responsible for the enforcement of the regulations for the protection of free competition in Mercosur. On the other hand, dumping, safeguard measures and subsidies have been regulated only by the Mercosur member countries within the framework of the WTO system.

Although free competition and the need to act in good faith without deceiving and without unfair practices may appear to be of only economic significance, they also reflect an important moral value: the common citizens' welfare. We may consider good faith to be one of the major contributions made by the law to commercial activity[33] and, through it, as pointed out by

[33] I thus add this topic to the examples provided by Ross Cranston in "Commercial Law and Commercial Activity" in Goode and Cranston, *supra* n. 19, 286.

Biondi,[34] the law fulfils the function of disciplining the activities of the individual in the general interest of the community, not in the philosopher's abstract sense but in a tangible and realistic way. Mercosur's search for a uniform competition law and the other issues related to it is being studied by the following technical commissions ("*Comisiones técnicas*" (CT), CT4: Public policies that distort competition; CT6: Unfair practices and safeguards, and CT7: Consumer Protection).

At the Fortaleza Mercosur meeting in December 1996, the parties approved a transitional system about unfair competition and postponed until the year 2001 the adoption of a comprehensive system, including the control of monopolies.

[34] Biondi Biondo, *Arte y ciencia del derecho* (Barcelona, Ariel, 1953), 125.

14

State Contracts, State Interests and International Commercial Arbitration: A Third World Perspective

PATRICK C. OSODE*

I. INTRODUCTION

An unmistakable feature of international commerce as carried on over the last four decades is the active participation of developing countries, usually in the form of contractual relationships with foreign private parties.[1] Development economists believe that many developing countries do not have, nor can they generate, enough savings to allow them to carry out industrialization on their own.[2] The direct result is their inability to effectively pursue their development aspirations without seeking, obtaining and relying on foreign investment.[3]

Knowing fully well that doing business with a developing State is tantamount to dealing with a partner whose legal rights, prerogatives and competence in the domestic and international legal orders may be vastly superior to those of the foreign investor, the foreign investor has consistently demonstrated an "almost omnivorous desire for protection of his investment".[4]

* LL.B., LL.M., SJD (Toronto), Senior Lecturer, Mercantile Law, University of Fort Hare, Eastern Cape, South Africa. A slightly different version of this paper has also appeared in (1997) 30 CILSA 37–59.

[1] The most common examples of contractual relationships constituted between States and State entities and private persons of foreign origin, (referred to throughout this paper as "State contracts"), are oil and mineral concessions, joint ventures, production sharing contracts, technical assistance contracts, agriculture and manufacturing concessions, turnkey contracts, transfer of technology and licensing contracts, engineering, construction and building contracts, loan and other financing agreements as well as contracts for the construction and operation of public utilities.

[2] E. Snyder, "Protection of Private Foreign Investment: Examination and Appraisal", (1961) 10 *ICLQ* 469 at 470.

[3] *Ibid.*

[4] *Ibid.* The fact that some developing countries foster a climate of economic nationalism in which multinational corporations are seen as "enterprises committed to the perpetuation of an

Hence, State contracts with foreign private parties, the subject of this paper, regularly contain provisions for the settlement of disputes by arbitration[5] and for the regulation of the contracts by a body of law acceptable to the investor.

State contracts necessarily give rise to significant tension between the interests of the foreign investor as a private party interested in, and committed only to the goal of, profit maximization and, on the other hand, those of the host "developing" contracting States, who enter into the contractual relationship in response to the urgent need for development facing their countries and for the purpose of resisting the entrenchment of poverty and misery among their peoples. One result of this irreconcilable divergence of interest is that while the State contractor frequently desires "flexibility" in the performance of the obligations created, the foreign investor is usually content with nothing short of "stability" and "certainty".

Past experience has shown the readiness of State contractors to exercise their competence, prerogatives or rights in ways fundamentally incompatible with the contractual rights and expectations of foreign investors. This is especially common and likely where those contractors seek an escape from contracts whose terms in the end prove too onerous or injurious to their development aspirations.

This paper examines a number of contemporary developments and trends in the law and legal framework relevant to international arbitration of State contract disputes and the manner in which the "international community" has responded to the tendency of developing State contractors to "abuse" their position in the domestic and international legal orders. The developments and trends in question range from the radical movement away from the absolute version of the doctrine of sovereign immunity and the expressed belief among certain arbitrators and eminent scholars that it is now possible for parties to State contracts to "internationalize" their agreements, to the establishment of the International Centre for the Settlement of Investment Disputes (ICSID) under the auspices of the World Bank.

The discussion proceeds on the premise that it is fundamentally inadequate to explain away these developments and trends as being merely the results of the evolutionary process which international economic law must go through; nor is it sufficient to say that they result from a search, by all the parties whose interests are involved in international commercial arbitrations, for the

inequitable international division of labour" has certainly not helped to persuade foreign investors that greater legal protection of their investments are not absolutely necessary. See B. H. Weston, "The Charter of Economic Rights and Duties of States and the Deprivation of Foreign-owned Wealth" (1985) 75 *AJIL* 437 at 461.

[5] Arbitration, as a dispute resolution mechanism, is preferred because in contrast with judicial settlement of disputes, it allows foreign investors to overcome difficulties resulting from the differing juridical status of the parties, one being a sovereign and the other a private individual or corporation. See I. Dore, *Arbitration and Conciliation Under the UNCITRAL Rules: A Textual Analysis* (Boston: Martinus Nijhoff Publishers, 1986) at 4 *et.seq.*; and H. Horen, "Commercial Disputes and their Settlement: A Factor in Business Planning" in *International Arbitration: 60 Years of ICC Arbitration—A Look at the Future* (Paris: ICC Publishing, 1984) at 35 *et.seq.*

most efficient body of rules and institutional frameworks consistent with the objectives of promoting foreign investment in particular and international commerce in general.

The theses of this paper are as follows. Firstly, each one of the developments and trends examined reveal both a resounding victory for the foreign investor in its search for stability and, rather sadly, an indication that with respect to reforms in the international legal order, "they that have the power of the purse dictate the tune".

Secondly, there is a definite sense in which the international legal and institutional responses under review appear lopsided in that they focus solely upon providing the quality of stability to the contractual relationship between the parties to State contracts. In the absence of any parallel responses aimed at providing the character of flexibility to the said relationship, the conclusion that the former responses are patently partisan appears both compelling and inescapable.

Thirdly, and perhaps more importantly, the developments and trends give birth to a legal regime of foreign investment which, in resolving the unique problems presented by State contracts, follows an approach that does not permit arbitrators and the national courts of the major centres of international commercial arbitration to effectively recognize and accommodate the national interests and the "right to development" of State parties wherever possible. In adopting this approach, the international regime significantly discounts those national interests and fails woefully to recognize the "right to development" in the critical context of State contracting and investment dispute resolution.

The academic enterprise of demonstrating the theses of this paper must, of absolute necessity, entail a confrontation with the twin questions as to the extent to which party autonomy should be respected in the conduct of international arbitrations of foreign investment disputes and the extent to which the law and practice of international commercial arbitration should accord recognition and deference to the national interests and "right to development" of the countries of the Third World. In critically exploring the developments and trends which are the subject of this paper and which effectively constitute the answers that have thus far been provided by the governments of capital-exporting countries, international commercial arbitrators and the World Bank, it is hoped that the closely related theses of this paper will be demonstrated.

II. CHANGES IN THE CONCEPTION AND APPLICATION OF THE SOVEREIGN IMMUNITY DOCTRINE

Access to municipal courts is important in international commercial arbitrations, especially those of a non-institutional character, with particular respect to conduct of the arbitral process. This is essentially due to the fact that judicial assistance may be required for, inter alia, securing interim or provisional measures of protection, subpoenaing witnesses and obtaining discovery of documents. The manner in which the courts of the forum state treat sovereign parties is, therefore, frequently material during such proceedings. More importantly, reference to municipal courts will remain unavoidable as long as arbitrators continue to lack sovereign powers equivalent to those of States as well as the powers necessary to ensure the proper conduct of the arbitration proceedings.[6]

Sovereign immunity is a hallowed principle of international law under which a State is essentially exempted from the jurisdiction of the courts of foreign states. As originally formulated and applied, the doctrine was tantamount to a legal stipulation that a sovereign State could not be made a party to proceedings before the municipal courts of another State unless it had attorned to the jurisdiction. In the common law jurisdictions, the doctrine had its origins in the acknowledgment of the need for international comity and the evolution of the concept of national sovereignty. It was thought that the "assumption of jurisdiction over a sovereign State without its consent constituted an erosion of the principle of sovereign equality of nations and an affront to its dignity".[7] The honour of being the first to apply the sovereign immunity doctrine in its absolute formulation belongs to the United States[8] and it was later followed by the United Kingdom.[9] As if to give the doctrine of sovereign immunity a sense of logical completeness, absolute immunity from execution was also accorded to States by the courts of the United States and the United Kingdom.[10]

The sovereign immunity doctrine attracted judicial hostility in the developed countries in the years immediately following the end of the second world war which saw the increased participation of States in commercial activities. Increasingly, judges became favourably disposed to applying the doctrine only in cases of a non-commercial character, which resulted both in the demise of the doctrine in its absolute formulation and in the birth of the "restrictive doctrine" of sovereign immunity.[11] Essentially, the latter doctrine postulates that a State loses its immunity from suit where the underlying judicial or arbitral proceedings originate from a commercial transaction to which the State or one of its agencies was a party.

[6] A. Redfern and M. Hunter, *Law and Practice of International Commercial Arbitration* (London: Sweet and Maxwell, 1991) at 306–7.

[7] O. Chukwumerije, "ICSID Arbitration and Sovereign Immunity" (1990) 19 *Anglo-American LR* 166 at 169.

[8] See *Schooner Exchange* v. *MacFadden* 7 Cranch 116 (1812).

[9] See *The Parliament Belge* (1880) 5 PD 197.

[10] See O. Chukwumerije, *supra* n. 8, at 170.

[11] See the English cases of *Baccus SRL* v. *Servicio del Trigo* (1958) 1 QB 438; *The Philippine Admiral Case* (1976) 2 WLR 214; and *Trendtex Corporation Ltd.* v. *The Central Bank of Nigeria* (1977) QB 529. As to the abandonment of the absolute version of the sovereign immunity doctrine by the United States of America, Canada and the Italy, see O. Chukwumerije, *supra* n. 8, at 171 *et seq.*

With respect to the particular context of international commercial arbitrations, there is now an overwhelming weight of authority for the view that a State party to an arbitration agreement is precluded from asserting its immunity in order to frustrate the purpose of the agreement. The relevant authorities consist of decisions of arbitral tribunals,[12] provisions found in the European Immunity Convention, the 1978 State Immunity Act of the United Kingdom, the Federal State Immunity Act of the United States of America, and the pronouncements of some English and American courts. The effect of the above-mentioned statutory provisions is that once a sovereign had agreed in writing to submit a dispute to arbitration, it is estopped from asserting his immunity whenever an issue pertaining to such arbitration arises before the municipal courts of either the United States or the United Kingdom irrespective of where the seat of the arbitration was located.[13]

These developments, which owe their genesis to the governments of the major capital-exporting States, must be evaluated keeping in view the interests that they were intended to serve. Without doubt, they are aimed at strengthening the protection available to foreign investors by shielding the arbitration agreement from unilateral State action aimed at frustrating it. These developments seek to eliminate, from the context of international commercial arbitrations, the principle of sovereign immunity from suit which, in the absence of these developments, would have been protective of State contracting parties seeking to escape from their prior commitments to arbitrate.

However, a plausible argument can be made for exempting developing countries from a general application of the restrictive doctrine of sovereign immunity.[14] It is widely acknowledged that the birth of the doctrine was informed by the increase in State participation in transnational commerce and the conviction of the lawmakers of the developed world that when a State steps into the commercial arena it must be seen as doing a "private act" and, therefore, is disentitled to the protection ordinarily available to it when engaged in acts having a public character. While the public/private act distinction is entirely appropriate for the developed countries, given the

[12] See the now famous Libyan nationalization cases, namely: *Texaco Overseas Petroleum Co et al* v. *The Government of the Libyan Arab Republic* (1978) 17 *ILM* 3; *BP Exploration Co. (Libya) Ltd.* v. *The Government of the Libyan Arab Republic* (1979) *Int'L Law Rep.* 297; and *Libyan American Oil Co.* v. *The Government of the Libyan Arab Republic* (1981) 20 *ILM* 1.

[13] See *Verlinden BV* v. *Central Bank of Nigeria* 488 *F.Supp*.1284 (SDNY 1980), aff'd, 647 F2d 320 (2d Cir.1981); s. 9(1) of the State Immunity Act (UK); and G. R. Delaume, "State Contracts and Transnational Arbitration", (1981) 75 *AJIL* 784 at 787–8.

[14] Differential treatment of Third World countries recognizing their right to development is nothing novel. For over three decades now, they have been the beneficiaries of the famous Generalized Preferences (GP) established within the international trading system regulated by the General Agreement on Tariffs and Trade. According to one commentator, the principle of differential treatment "constitutes a statement of the right of underdeveloped States to improve their lot, and, at the same time, implies a duty for the industrialized countries to contribute to the realization of that right. See A. A. Yusuf, "Differential Treatment as a Dimension of the Right to Development", in R. J. Dupuy (ed), *The Right to Development at the International Level* (The Netherlands: Sijthoff and Noordhoff, 1980) at 234.

economic history and structure of their societies, the application of a doctrine founded on that distinction to developing countries is indefensible for a number of reasons.

Firstly, the developing countries have, since their emergence onto the international scene, struggled with economic and social conditions to which the populations of the developed countries can barely relate. Secondly, because of the involuntary contact with Europe dating back to the sixteenth century and the colonial experience that followed, developing countries suffer from an underdeveloped entrepreneurial class lacking in the skills and experience for the manufacture of goods or supply of services and the exploitation of natural resources. Accordingly, engaging in acts of a commercial character, traditionally regarded as private in Western society, is something with respect to which third world governments have no choice. In other words, State involvement in the economy not only as a regulator but also as a trader is a necessity in many developing countries. It is, therefore, submitted that such governments cannot be fairly said to be engaged in acts of a private nature when they enter into transactions having an underlying commercial content in the pursuit of national objectives and aspirations.[15]

There is a further reason why a general application of the restrictive doctrine of sovereign immunity is questionable. It consists of the fact that while the reasoning that informed the absolute doctrine of sovereign immunity can be properly said to have been universal in terms of being common to all the State actors at the time of its birth, this is not true of the restrictive version of the doctrine. The best illustration of that lack of consensus is the position of the former and present socialist States that a State does not cease to be sovereign merely because it performed functions traditionally reserved for private persons in non-socialist legal systems.[16] There is also no evidence indicating that the countries of the Third World have accepted the restrictive doctrine as representing contemporary international law.[17]

III. ARBITRATION AGREEMENTS IN STATE CONTRACTS

The competence of contracting parties to determine what law or laws should govern their relationship as well as the arbitration of any disputes arising therefrom has a long history. Such competence is an all-important part of the

[15] See A. O. Adede, "Loan Agreements with Foreign Sovereign Borrowers: Issues of Sovereign Immunity, Applicable Law and Settlement of Disputes", (1987) 3 *Lesotho LJ* 101 at 119.

[16] That position was best expressed in the rejection of the restrictive doctrine of sovereign immunity by Soviet legal theory on the grounds that a distinction cannot be made between the acts of a socialist State which are of a public nature and those which are of a private nature. See C.Osakwe, "A Soviet Perspective on Foreign Sovereign Immunity: Law and Practice", (1983) 23 *Va.J Int'l L* 13; and E. Morgan, "Foreign State Debtors in Domestic Courts: A Theory of Sovereign Immunity", (1989) 3 *BFLR* 287.

[17] A. O. Adede, *supra* n. 16, at 108 *et.seq*.

parties' "autonomy of will". Accordingly, for the this purpose, the parties may choose the national law of the State contracting party, the general principles of law, the "lex mercatoria", public international law or a combination of those sources of law.[18] Over the past thirty years, however, the trend in State contracts has been to make stipulations of governing law that seek to avoid the application of the municipal law of the contracting State or attempt to keep that law frozen for the duration of the particular contract. This trend results from the foreign investors' distrust of State contracting parties and their power, by virtue of their sovereign status, to make changes in their municipal law without the foreign investor's consent.

In this part of the paper, an attempt is made to evaluate the efficacy and appropriateness of the legal devices adopted by foreign investors to put their disputes and the ensuing arbitral process beyond the reach of the sovereign party's national law and beyond any unilateral changes therein.

(a) **The Law Governing the Arbitral Process** (Lex Arbitri)

The advocates of the "delocalization" theory of arbitration, consisting of both scholars and practitioners, see the law of an arbitration as consisting of a set of procedural rules which, in the case of an international commercial arbitration, is made by the parties or by the arbitral tribunal on their behalf.[19] They suggest, therefore, that arbitral awards may be detached from the law of the country where the proceedings take place and yet remain enforceable.[20] This recent and radical thinking would clearly support the efforts of foreign investors to ensure that the conduct and validity of arbitrations to which they are parties does not dependent on the law and public policy sensitivities of national legal systems, including those of State contracting parties.

However, the "delocalization" theory is not representative of mainstream thinking, which remains inclined to the traditional view that the mandatory provisions of the *lex loci arbitri* (the law of the place of arbitration) govern the validity of an arbitration.[21] The fact, therefore, is that irrespective of the contracting parties' stipulation to the contrary, the law of the arbitration includes the mandatory norms of the seat of arbitration, subject to the caveat

[18] See AnnIDI, vol. 58, tome 2, at 195 (1979).

[19] A. Redfern and M. Hunter, *supra* n. 7, at 82. See also, *Award of the Arbitration Tribunal in the arbitration between Saudi Arabia and the Arabia American Oil Co. (ARAMCO)*, (1963) 27 *Int'L Rep.* 117 at 155–6.

[20] See, for example, J. Paulsson, "Delocalization of International Commercial Arbitration: When and Why it Matters", (1983) 32 *ICLQ* 53 at 57.

[21] F. A. Mann forcefully articulated the position thus: "Every right or power a private person enjoys is inexorably conferred by or derived from a system of municipal law which may conveniently and in accordance with tradition be called lex fori, though it would be more exact (but also less familiar) to speak of the *lex arbitri*". Mann, "Lex Facit Arbitrum", in P. Sanders (ed.), *International Arbitration: Liber Amicorium for Martin Domke* at 157. See also, Hirsh, "The Place of Arbitration and the Lex Arbitri", (1979) 34 *Arb.J* 43.

that those mandatory norms must not be inconsistent with transnational minimum standards of justice.[22] Thus, while parties may choose the law governing their contract and even choose some of the procedural rules applied by arbitrators, they cannot effectively choose the entire body of law governing the arbitration, except indirectly through the choice of its *situs*.[23]

So long as foreign investors ensure that any arbitration with a State contracting party does not take place within that State's territory, the above-stated position does not, prima facie, make ineffective the devices frequently employed by the investors to shield their interests from the municipal law and public policy of the sovereign contractor. It is important to note, however, that many national legal systems prohibit arbitration of disputes involving sensitive public interests, such as contracts with State agencies.[24] On the other hand, where the arbitration is international—in which case the public interests, implicated are not those of the forum State—the *lex loci arbitri* will show no deference to the State contractor but will treat the parties to the arbitration as two private parties who contracted at arm's length.[25]

Accordingly, it must be conceded that the practice of taking arbitrations of investment disputes outside the territories of the State parties is an effective way of placing them beyond the reach of the State's national law and public policy, thereby enhancing the prospect of putting the disputing parties on an equal footing in proceedings before the arbitrator. It is however disturbing that while the municipal laws of the developed countries[26] recognize the non-arbitrability of commercial disputes implicating sensitive public interests of the "forum" State, those laws are indifferent where the public interests involved are those of developing countries who have contracted with foreign investors. If there is indeed something about national interests that entitles them to differential treatment and, if indeed all States are equal in international law and relations, then the principles and demands of international comity argue for a modification in the municipal laws of the major arbitration centres to accommodate the national interests and aspirations of State contractors.[27]

22 See O. Chukwumerije, *Choice of Law in International Commercial Arbitration* (Westport, Connecticut: Quorum Books, 1994) at 88 *et.seq*; and J. Paulsson, "Arbitration Unbound: Award Detached from the Law of its Country of Origin", (1981) 30 *ICLQ* 358 at 369 *et.seq*.

23 William W. Park, "The Lex Loci Arbitri and International Commercial Arbitration", (1983) 32 *ICLQ* 21.

24 For the French position, see T. Carbonneau, "The Elaboration of a French Doctrine on International Commercial Arbitration: A Study in Liberal Civilian Creativity", (1980) 55 *Tulane L Rev*. 1 at 29–30.

25 W. Park, *supra* n. 24, at 29–30.

26 The best known centres of international commercial arbitration are located in these countries. See A. Redfern and M. Hunter, *supra* n. 7, at xiii.

27 Professor William Park, after stating that the courts in a forum state should exercise significantly greater control over those arbitrations in which national policies are implicated, asserts that international commercial arbitration is less likely than domestic arbitration to involve such policies. He further submits that even if an international arbitration touches upon some national interest or policy, "a national legal system still may accommodate the needs of international trade

Even more disturbing is the fact that some countries are now "receptive to the idea of freeing international arbitrations from control of national arbitration laws of the place of arbitration.[28] A good example of that trend is provided by Belgian law where Article 1717 of the *Code Judiciare* excludes some international arbitrations conducted in that country from the supervisory control of Belgian courts by providing that:

> "The courts of Belgium may be seized of a request for annulment only if at least one of the parties to the dispute decided by the arbitral award is either a physical person having Belgian nationality or residence, or a legal entity created in Belgium or having a branch or any other establishment in Belgium".

The effect of this provision is that judicial review of an award resulting from an international arbitration which took place in Belgium is not available in that country.[29] Similarly, recent French judicial practice reveals support for the elimination of national restrictions on the international arbitration process.[30] And of course there is no better illustration of the practice of delocalization than the conduct of arbitrations under the auspices of the International Centre for the Settlement of Investment Disputes (ICSID).[31]

(b) **The Law Governing the Contract** (Lex Contractus)

It should be pointed out at the outset that the governing law of the contract, which regulates the determination of the dispute on its merits is distinct from, and independent of, the law regulating the arbitral process (*lex arbitri*).[32] Mention has also been made of foreign investors' anxiety to shield their contract from the municipal law of the State party even if the net result is uncertainty.[33] On the question of governing law, arbitration clauses are of different types and thus present different scenarios.

(i) Where There is no Stipulation of Governing Law

The first scenario worthy of consideration is where the contracting parties omit a definite statement as to what law should govern their contract in the

and investment by refraining from exercising supervision over the legal merits of the arbitration". Accordingly, he does not subscribe to the accommodation of national interests by a municipal order in dealing with international commercial arbitrations. W. Park, *supra* n. 24, at 30. If his position emerges as the dominant view, the implications for those States frequently involved in international commercial arbitrations are obvious.

[28] O. Chukwumerije, *supra* n. 23, at 92.

[29] *Ibid.*

[30] See T. Carbonneau, Book Review (1984) 24 *Va.J Int'l L* 527, at 530.

[31] See discussion of the origin and nature of ICSID arbitrations at 35–40 *infra.*

[32] See Award of the Tribunal in the *ARAMCO Arbitration*, *supra* n. 20.

[33] See discussion of the now famous "internalization theory", *infra* notes 41–9, and accompanying text.

event of a dispute. A good example of this scenario is presented by a model arbitration clause presently used in the Nigerian oil industry. The particular contract is the 55 per cent participation agreement between the Nigeria National Petroleum Corporation (NNPC), Texaco Overseas Petroleum Co. (Nigeria) Ltd. and Chevron Oil Co. (Nigeria) Ltd.[34] The arbitration clause in the contract fails to make any stipulation about the governing law of the agreement. This is surprising considering that a common feature of contemporary economic development agreements, especially those relating to the exploitation of natural resources, is the stipulation of the municipal law of the contracting State as the *lex contractus*. The question then is which law governs a State contract that contains such an omission.

There is no apparent consensus as to what law is applicable by arbitrators where there is no stipulation of the law applicable to the agreement. In the 1978 dispute between *Revere Copper & Brass Inc.* v. *Overseas Private Investment Corp (OPIC)*,[35] the members of the arbitral tribunal were divided on the point. While the majority decided that the principles of public international law applied to the agreement in so far as the government party was concerned, the minority took the view that the two parties to the dispute being corporations incorporated in the state of Maryland, were governed by the law of the United States of America.

Closely analogous to the position of the majority in this case is that taken by Professor Réné Dupuy, acting as sole arbitrator, in the first of the Libyan trilogy, *Texaco* v. *Libya*.[36] This was to the effect that the mere submission of contracting parties to arbitration is indicative of an intention to "delocalize" or "internationalize" their relationship in terms of having it governed by international law rather than by municipal law.[37] In reaching this conclusion, Professor Réné Dupuy relied on that part of the arbitration agreement which

[34] The contract is dated January 6th, 1978. The arbitration clause reads as follows: "*A*. The NNPC and the companies agree that if a difference or dispute arises between the NNPC on the one hand and the companies or either of them on the other hand, or between any of them and the operator, concerning the interpretation or performance of this agreement, and if the parties hereto fail to settle such difference or dispute by amicable agreement, then either party may serve on the other a demand for arbitration. Within 45 days of such demand being served, each party shall appoint an arbitrator and the two arbitrators thus appointed shall within a further ten days appoint a third arbitrator who shall be of a nationality different from that of either of the parties or the arbitrators . . . and if the arbitrators do not agree on the appointment of such third arbitrator, or if either party fails to appoint the arbitrator to be appointed by it, such arbitrator shall be appointed by the President or Vice-President of the International Court of Justice on the application of either party . . . and when appointed, the third arbitrator shall convene meetings and act as chairman thereat. . . . The arbitration rules and procedures and the award of the arbitrators shall be determined by a majority of the arbitrators, or in the absence of the agreement of any two arbitrators, by the chairman alone. The arbitration award shall be binding upon the parties and the expenses of the arbitration shall be borne by the parties in such proportion and manner as may be provided in the award. *B*. Save as aforesaid, the Nigerian Arbitration Act shall apply.

[35] (1978) ILM 1321.

[36] *Supra* n. 13.

[37] See paras. 40–5.

provided for the appointment of a sole arbitrator by the President of the International Court of Justice where the parties failed to appoint the arbitrators themselves. He also held further that "internalization" would result in cases of absence of choice of "substantive" law if the contract in question is an economic development agreement.[38] This was also the view followed in the *Revere Copper Arbitration*[39] where the majority found it plausible to hold that a State contract was internationalized even in the absence of either a reference to international law or to general principles of law, if it involved the exploitation of natural wealth and resources.[40]

It has been observed that the classification of certain State contracts as economic development agreements and the attribution to them of an internationalizing effect appears designed specifically for contracts to which developing countries are parties.[41] In a scathing critique of the internationalization theory, O. Chukwumerije has noted that:

> "It appears that only contracts involving developing countries would satisfy the test for designating a contract as an economic development agreement. More instructive, the term is usually defined to exclude contracts involving developed countries. This yields the absurd result whereby the legal implication of a contract would vary depending on whether the contract was entered into with a developed or developing country. This discriminatory effect of the theory renders it objectionable."[42]

To the advantage of foreign private contracting parties and the detriment of developing countries, the internationalization theory espoused by Professor Dupuy[43] and the majority in the *Revere Copper Arbitration*[44] disregards the public international law presumption against limiting the sovereign authority of States. While A. A. Fatouros has wondered "why that presumption, which is fundamental in international law, can be so easily reversed in favour of inferences supporting internalization to the benefit of foreign investors",[45] O. Chukwumerije has pointed that "given the restriction that the international standards imported by internationalization would have on the sovereign powers of a State, the existence of a clear and unequivocal evidence of an intention to internationalize is necessary before international law could be

[38] *Ibid.*
[39] *Supra* n. 36.
[40] It is relevant to note here that Rene Dupuy's decision in *Texaco* v. *Libya*, accepting the possibility of regulating State contract relations by a body of international law, was entirely novel. Prior to that decision, the dominant view was that "the system of international law was purely an inter-State system in which an individual or a company has no legal personality". See E. Paasivirta, "Internationalization and Stabilization of Contracts Versus State Sovereignty", (1989) 60 *BYIL* 315 at 321 *et.seq.*
[41] O. Chukwumerije, *supra* n. 23, at 157.
[42] *Ibid.*
[43] *Supra* n. 13.
[44] *Supra* n. 34.
[45] See A. Fatouros, "International Law and the Internationalized Contract", (1980) 74 *AJIL* 134 at 136.

applied to a State contract".[46] This evidence was absent in those cases which currently stand as authority for the internalization theory. Yet almost all the modern text writers continue to express the opinion that State contracts can be internationalized in specified circumstances.[47] Even O.Chukwumerije, in his critique of Dupuy's award, assumes the possibility of effectively internationalizing such a contract.[48]

Furthermore, the theory also disregards a presumption of contemporary international law in favour of the application of the domestic law of the contracting State in the absence of an express stipulation to the contrary. This argument is fortified by the United Nations resolutions on permanent sovereignty over natural resources and the establishment of a New International Economic Order[49] and by the decision of the Permanent Court of International Justice in the *Serbian Loans Case*[50] This argument is not adequately confronted by the submission of Georges R. Delaume that "the presumption that in the absence of a choice of law, State contracts should be governed by the law of the State involved produces a rigidity of results and does not correspond to reality".[51] For this writer, it is sufficiently gratifying that implicit in Delaume's submission is the admission that until recently a presumption *did* arise in favour of the application of the municipal law of State contracting parties in the particular scenario under discussion.

(ii) Where International Law is the Designated Governing Law

There is now a consensus of academic opinion that the parties to State contracts can properly and effectively provide that their contract be governed by international law.[52] However, the debate rages on as to the effectiveness of the various means by which proponents of the internalization theory believed that result could be achieved.[53] In light of the said consensus, the material question is whether international law has a body of rules designed for the

[46] O. Chukwumerije, *supra* n. 23, at 157.

[47] The only exception seems to be Professor Ian Brownlie. See I. Brownlie, *Principles of Public International Law* (Oxford: Clarendon Press, 1990) at 550–1.

[48] O. Chukwumerije, *supra* n. 23 at 155 *et.seq.*

[49] See General Assembly Resolutions 523 (VI) of January 1952; 626 (VII) of December 1952; 1314 (XIII) of December 1958; 1803 (XV) of 1960; 2158 (XXI) of 1966; 2386 (XXIII) of 1968; 2692 (XXV) of 1970; 3016 (XXVII) of 1972; 3171 (XXVIII) of 1973; 3201 (S-VI) of 1974; 3281 (XXIX) of 1974; and 3362 of 1974.

[50] PCLJ Series A, Nos. 20/1, Judgment No.14, July 12, 1929. In that case, the court took the position that a State could not have intended to make the validity of its obligations subject to any law other than its own.

[51] G. R. Delaume, *supra* n. 14, at 798.

[52] See, for example, O. Chukwumerije, *supra* n. 23, at 154; A. Redfern and M. Hunter, *supra* n. 7 at 106; C. Greenwood, "State Contracts in International Law—The Libyan Oil Arbitration", (1982) 53 *BYIL* 27 at 48–53; L. Sohn and R. Baxter, Responsibility of States for Injuries to Economic Interests of Aliens", (1961) 55 *AJIL5* 45; R. Jennings, "State Contracts in International Law", (1961) 37 *BYIL* 156 at 181.

[53] See O. Chukwumerije, *supra* n. 23, at 155 *et.seq.*

regulation of commercial relations between States and individuals or between individuals of different nationalities. If the compelling answer to this question is no, then foreign investors inevitably obtain inadequate protection under the aegis of international law.

In his unusually zealous articulation of the internationalization theory, Professor Dupuy clearly saw in the corpus of international law a collection of substantive rules to which parties to State contracts may submit their disputes. According to him:

> "Treaties are not the only type of agreements governed by international law . . . Contracts between States and private persons, under certain conditions, come within the ambit of a particular and new branch of international law: the international law of contracts."[54]

Unfortunately, the only substantive rule the award seems to have located was the principle of *pacta sunt servanda* (the sanctity of contracts). According to A. A. Fatouros, this singular deduction is of little assistance because any law of contracts, whether national or international, is bound to start with this principle but it cannot legitimately stop there.[55] To the extent that Professor Dupuy did stop there, his award cannot be accepted as a correct elaboration of the legal position with respect to the choice of law question where parties to State contracts resort to international law.[56] More pertinent to the present inquiry is the observation of Ian Brownlie that there is no such body of law in existence as an "international law of contracts".[57] Furthermore, while the need for an international law of contracts or a *lex mercatoria* is now almost generally accepted, it is similarly admitted that the idea of such a law is very clearly only a vision of the future. As F. A. Mann put it:

> "What this so called law is or should be is a complete mystery. It is usually said that it comprises uniform law embodied in or derived from international conventions, trade usages, custom and ideas of business fairness, efficacy or reasonableness. The object frequently is to dispense with the conflict of laws, which is said to create insoluble problems and to lead to artificial and unrealistic results. It is hardly necessary to emphasize that no such body of law exists."[58]

[54] *Texaco* v. *Libya Arbitration supra* n. 13, at para. 32.

[55] A. A. Fatouros, *supra* n. 46, at 135.

[56] Professor D. W. Bowett has also observed that the recurring recourse to the maxim *pacta sunt servanda* is unsatisfactory. In his view, the maxim is at such a level of generality as to be misleading (since all legal systems recognize exceptions to the rule when termination is justified) and even erroneous in that, so expressed, the maxim fails to take account of the fundamental distinction between private and public (or State) contracts. Bowett, "State Contracts with Aliens: Contemporary Developments on Compensation for Termination or Breach", (1988) 59 *BYIL* 49 at 55.

[57] I. Brownlie, *supra* n. 48, at 548–9.

[58] F. A. Mann, "Private Arbitration and Public Policy", (1985) 4 *Civil Justice Quarterly* 257 at 264. See also, M. Bartels, *Contractual Adaptation and Conflict Resolution* (Deventer, The Netherlands: Kluwer Law and Taxation Publishers, 1985) at 110.

It is arguable, therefore, that where parties to a State contract specify international law as the governing law of their contract, this provision should, if an arbitration arises from the contract, be treated as a nullity given its reference to a non-existent body of rules. The contract thus yields itself to treatment in the same way as an agreement that omits to state the *lex contractus*. It follows that the municipal law of the contracting State should be applied by the arbitrators in accordance with the earlier mentioned principle of contemporary international law.[59]

It cannot be denied that the attempts to appeal to an international body of rules in the settlement of foreign investment disputes is a response to the orthodox mode of determining the *lex contractus* which essentially consisted of selecting a national system of law by applying the conflict rules of private international law.[60] That orthodox mode has been the subject of scathing criticisms, Redfern and Hunter have summed it up by suggesting that the "search for the proper law is out of touch with the realities of modern international trade; and that what is needed is not a particular national system of law, but a modern law merchant", which has been variously described as "international law of contracts", "international lex mercatoria", and international trade law".[61]

In seeking the recognition and accommodation of the peculiar position and interests of State contracting parties, I am not averse to the idea of developing an international *lex mercatoria*.[62] This is because of the fact, ignored by many commentators that a modern law merchant is quite capable of accommodating the national interests and right to development of developing countries—the case which this paper seeks to advance. This view is firmly and plausibly founded on the truism that the principal legal systems of the modern world effectively recognize a State party's broad, sovereign or prerogative powers to vary or terminate its contractual obligations in the public interest.[63]

[59] See n. 51 and accompanying text. A limitation in the reasoning of both Rene Dupuy and A.A. Fatouros should be pointed out here. As earlier indicated in this paper, Dupuy failed to elaborate what norms constitute the international law of contracts which he held applicable to internationalized State contracts. In the same vein, Fatouros, in his critique of the internalization theory as espoused by Dupuy, did not mention, let alone discuss, what substantive rules apply to State contracts not specifically governed by the State party's municipal law but by some type of international law. There is therefore an urgent need for a clear elaboration of the substantive rules applicable to "delocalized agreements".

[60] A. Redfern and M. Hunter, *supra* n. 7, at 117 *et.seq.*

[61] *Ibid.*

[62] This is notwithstanding that the employment of the *lex mercatoria*, in the arbitration of State contract disputes, must be treated with caution given that, in its present state, it offers few predictable rules and confers wide discretion on arbitrators. See D. W. Bowett, *supra* n. 57, at 52.

[63] The *International Encyclopedia of Comparative Law*, based on a review of the legal systems of the United Kingdom, United States of America, France, West Germany and Italy, puts the matter thus: "The most radical of special prerogatives enjoyed by the administration is the right to terminate the contract unilaterally, when the public interest so requires. This drastic power is a widespread feature of national systems of procurement, and is evidently considered necessary in order to maintain the freedom of action of public authorities". See *ibid*, vol. 2, at 40.

Accordingly, if, as may be expected, the emerging international *lex mercatoria* is to be built up from the "principles of law common to civilized nations", then the optimism that State interests can be properly and effectively accommodated within such a body of rules is far from being misplaced.

(iii) Where the State Party's Municipal Law is the Specified Governing Law

With respect to agreements for the exploitation of natural resources and other economic development agreements, the contemporary practice is for the agreements expressly to specify the State party's municipal law as the *lex contractus*. This practice brings to the fore the important question of the legal effect of changes in the applicable law subsequent to the parties' execution of their contract. The issue is particularly important in the context of foreign investment dispute resolution because an indisputable attribute of the territorial sovereign is the competence to legislate for the general good.

The general rule applicable to State contract arbitration is that the *lex contractus* is the specified law as it stands at the time of the arbitration, not merely as it was at the time the contract was made. The continued attempts by foreign investors to put their contracts beyond the reach of the national law of State contracting parties in an implicit recognition by the investors and their legal advisers, of both the legislative competence of the State party and the existence of the general rule.

In those cases where the foreign investors have been unsuccessful in securing the incorporation of a choice of law provision that could have the effect of "internationalizing" the contract, they have resorted to specially drafted clauses intended to insulate the contracts from changes in the law of the State party that may be, at least prima facie, unfavourable to the investors' interests.[64] Those clauses, now popularly referred to as "stabilization clauses", are the focus of the discussion that follows.

(iv) Stabilization Clauses[65]

A good example of these clauses, which are most commonly found in economic development agreements, can be seen in the contract between the government of Libya and Texaco Overseas Petroleum and California Oil Company. Clause 16 of that contract provided that "the contractual rights

[64] According to O. Chukwumerije, "stabilization clauses . . . are designed to freeze the essential provisions of State contracts by prohibiting any legislative or administrative act that derogates from, or is otherwise inconsistent with, the provisions of the contract or the legal environment of the transaction". O. Chukwumerije, *supra* n. 23, at 144.

[65] Dr. S. K. B. Asante has pointed out that stabilization clauses are aimed at, inter alia, (1) expropriation, nationalization and any other form of State intervention in the enterprise; and (2) the imposition of any fiscal changes in the general industrial or commercial sectors in excess of the fiscal charges provided in the contract. Asante. Asante, "Stability of Contractual Relations in the Transnational Investment Process", (1979) 28 *ICLQ* 401 at 409.

shall not be altered except by mutual consent of the parties". The final part of the same clause then stipulated that:

> "This concession shall throughout the period of its validity be construed in accordance with the Petroleum Law and the Regulations in force on the date of execution of the agreement or amendment . . . Any amendment to or repeal of such Regulations shall not affect the contractual rights of the company without its consent."

It therefore appears that within the context of State contracts which specifically provide for the application of the State party's municipal law, while also incorporating a stabilization clause, the classical question is whether the State party would be within its rights if it changes of its domestic law so as to change a foreign investor's position without the latter's consent.

In confronting that question, Ian Brownlie took what may be said to be a middle ground when he said:

> "The legal significance of such clauses [stabilization clauses] is inevitably controversial, since the clause involves a tension between the legislative sovereignty and public interest of the State party and the long term viability of the contractual relationship."[66]

This intermediate position only begs the question, probably in its attempt to avoid either one of two seemingly extreme but more definite alternatives. The first of those alternatives is the position taken by the proponents of foreign investment protection who contend that the State contract, including the agreement to arbitrate, must of necessity be sustained by the universally accepted principles of *pacta sunt servanda*, estoppel and good faith.[67] The logical conclusion which the proponents' would have us draw from their argument is that a State contract which incorporates both an arbitration agreement and a stabilization clause is, in effect, immune from interference by a competent legislator.[68]

At the other extreme is the position with which the capital-importing States naturally identify. In simple terms, it consists of the claim that stabilization clauses are invalid as being repugnant to, or inconsistent with, either the contemporary principle of permanent sovereignty over natural resources[69] or the

[66] I. Brownlie, *supra* n. 48, at 551.

[67] See e.g., Martin Domke, "Foreign Nationalizations", (1961) 55 *AJIL* 585. P. Weil articulated the position even more bluntly when he stated that: "In subscribing to a protection clause, the host government has thus created to the benefit of the other contracting party a legitimate expectation, which the government may not subsequently frustrate without infringing the principle of good faith". P. Weil, quoted in W. Peter, *Arbitration and Renegotiation of International Investment Agreements* (Dordrecht, the Netherlands: Martinus Nijhoff, 1986) at 144. See further, Hans Wehberg, "Pacta Sunt Servanda", (1959) 53 *AJIL* 775 at 786; F. Sheikh, *The Legal Regime of Foreign Investment in the Sudan and Saudi Arabia: A Case Study of Developing Countries* (Cambridge: Cambridge University Press, 1986) at 257; Z. Kronfol, *Protection of Foreign Investment* (Leiden, the Netherlands: A. W. Sijthoff, 1972) at 85.

[68] See E. Paasivirta, *supra* n. 41, at 329.

[69] See n. 50, *supra*.

truism that beyond considering the immediate pecuniary benefits of an agreement as a foreign investor would, a State contracting party must regularly reappraise the repercussions of the agreement on the general well-being of the people.[70]

But what is the proper legal position for an international commercial arbitrator to take when confronted with a stabilization clause? A definite answer is needed because a middle ground, such as that taken by Ian Brownlie, does not assist an arbitrator in any meaningful way. It is submitted that the critical issue is whether the principle of *pacta sunt servanda* properly applies to State contracts. The relatively inflexible application of the principle in the public international law of treaties and in the private law of contracts (involving private citizens) is defensible on the bases of fundamental fairness, good sense and justice. This is largely because, while the State parties to treaties have the same obligations towards each other under international law and usually have similar objectives, private contracting parties also contract for the common purpose of profit maximization, represent similar interests, and bear similar burdens in municipal legal orders.[71]

However, the same affinity of purpose, interests and legal burdens is absent in the realm of State contracting.[72] At a minimum, this argues for the view that with respect to State contracts, the principle of *pacta sunt servanda* can only be properly applied subject to far-reaching qualifications. Supporting this view, F. A. Mann has pointed out that the arguments seeking to subject State contracts to the principle "are opposed to the daily and universal experience of mankind and to the requirement of good sense and justice".[73]

It is noteworthy that it is settled law in the United States, the United Kingdom and other developed countries that stabilization clauses are, at a minimum, unenforceable.[74] The American position is best exemplified by the US Supreme Court's judgment in *Georgia* v. *City of Chattanooga*[75] where the Court bluntly stated that:

[70] See E. Arechaga, "Application of the Rules of State Responsibility to the Nationalization of Foreign-Owned Property", in K. Hossain (ed.) *Legal Aspects of the New International Economic Order* (New York: Nichols Publishing Company, 1980) 220 at 230; S. Asante, "Stability of Contractual Relations in the Transnational Investment Process", (1979) 28 *ICLQ* 401 at 403; M. Sornarajah, *The Pursuit of Nationalized Property* (Dordrecht, The Netherlands: Martinus Nijhoff, 1986) at 94; and R. Geiger, "The Unilateral Change of Economic Development Agreements", (1974) 23 *ICLQ* 73 at 77.

[71] See O. Chukwumerije, *supra* n. 23, at 145–6; and C. Njenga, "Legal Regime of Concession Agreements", (1967) *East Afr. LJ* 100.

[72] See Dickinson, "Analogy Between Natural Persons and International Persons in the Law of Nations", (1916) 26 *Yale LJ* 572 at 588.

[73] Mann, "State Contracts and State Responsibility", (1960) 54 *AJIL* 572 at 588.

[74] D. W. Bowett, *supra* n. 57, at 57. Writing along the same lines, Esa Paasivirta has recently noted that "it will have become clear to oil companies that the UK and Norwegian Governments are no more willing than their OPEC counterparts to stick rigidly to contracts that they deem unreasonably disadvantageous and that there is no absolute constitutional protection in either country for the principle of *pacta sunt servanda*". See E. Paasivirta, *supra* n. 41, at 329–30.

[75] 464 US472.

> "The taking of private property for public use upon just compensation is so often necessary for the proper performance of governmental functions that the power is deemed essential to the life of the State. It cannot be surrendered, and, if attempted to be contracted away, it may be resumed at will."[76]

Under the English common law, the absolute power of the State unilaterally to interfere in contracts with private individuals is enshrined in the twin concepts of power of eminent domain and police powers. On their part, the English courts have been consistent in upholding that power without any significant qualifications. For example, in *Czarnikow* v. *Rolimpex*,[77] the Court of Appeal remarked that:

> ". . . a government cannot fetter its duty to act for the public good. It cannot bind itself—by an implication in the contract—not to perform its public duties."[78]

It is particularly striking that in spite of these precedents, no commentator has suggested that the legal systems of the developed countries are unsuitable for the needs of local and international commerce or hostile to foreign investments.

The compelling conclusion therefore is that stabilization clauses in State contracts are invalid as a matter of private and public international law to the extent that they seek to significantly restrict the competence of a territorial sovereign to either legislate or otherwise act for the public good. Inherent in that conclusion is a tacit recognition and acceptance of the fact that "the State has always to take the public welfare into consideration for it only contracts as the guardian of the nation's welfare".[79] Furthermore, given that "foreign investors in their home countries contract with their home governments on a relatively insecure basis",[80] the position articulated here on the legal status of stabilization clauses is not, and ought not to be perceived as, inconsistent with the objective of promoting foreign investments in particular and transnational commerce in general.

Sadly, international arbitral jurisprudence does not show a willingness on the part of international arbitrators to construe stabilization clauses as being invalid for the purposes of accomplishing the objectives intended by those foreign investors successful in procuring the incorporation of those clauses into State contracts. That unwillingness is best illustrated by Professor Rene Dupuy's interpretation of the choice of law provisions in the famous *Texaco Arbitration*.[81] In determining the rights and obligations flowing out of Libya's nationalization of Texaco's assets, Dupuy concluded that the nationalization was an illegal act under international law, whether or not it was accompanied

[76] 464 US472 at 480.
[77] (1977) 3 WLR 686.
[78] *Ibid.*
[79] D. W. Bowett, *supra* n. 57 at 59.
[80] *Ibid.*
[81] *Supra* n. 13.

with appropriate compensation, solely because it was directly inconsistent with the stabilization clause. That conclusion paved the way for his order of *restitutio in integrum*. Although there is an emerging academic consensus that Dupuy's conclusion and accompanying order was in error in that it went too far,[82] there is some recent indication that international arbitrators support Dupuy's position. For example, the Iran-US Claims Tribunal, like Rene Dupuy, took the view that stabilization clauses "preclude a sovereign during the stated period from exercising the rights it otherwise possesses under international law to take an alien's property for a public purpose, and without discrimination and for a just compensation".[83]

One is left to wonder why international commercial arbitrators seem to favour a legal position on the effect of stabilization clauses that is inconsistent with good sense, with the accepted interpretation of contemporary public international law, and even with the law relating to public contracts in the developed countries. Even more disturbing is the fact that the Dupuy position fails to acknowledge the predicament of many developing countries facing a continuing crisis of poverty and underdevelopment.[84]

IV. ARBITRATION UNDER THE AUSPICES OF THE ICSID

This paper would be incomplete without a critical review of the Convention on the Settlement of Investment Disputes between States and Nationals of other States.[85] The Convention resulted from the efforts of the World Bank and it is the only Convention which deals exclusively with issues relating to State contract arbitrations. The Convention establishes an International Centre for the Settlement of Investment Disputes (ICSID). It appears that the Centre was created to fill a gap in the mechanism for settling international disputes—a gap that made it difficult for a government and a foreign investor to find a mutually acceptable forum to settle disputes that might arise between them".[86] Undoubtedly too, it was intended to depoliticize investment disputes and thereby facilitate capital flows across national boundaries to the ultimate benefit of the capital-importing States of the third world.[87] The Centre provides arbitration and conciliation facilities to qualifying contracting parties.

[82] See O. Chukwumerije, *supra* n. 23, at 147; and A. Redfern and M. Hunter, *supra* n. 7, at 105.

[83] (1987) Iran-USCTR 3 at 65.

[84] One plausible explanation may be found in a statement recently made by Dr. Ibrahim Shihata of the World Bank in which he conceded that international commercial arbitration "is still largely dominated by individuals whose cultural backgrounds and values may bring them closer to foreign enterprises [from developed countries] than to host governments in developing countries". I. Shihata, "The Institute of International Law's Resolution on Arbitration between States and Foreign Enterprises—A Comment", (1990) 5 *ICSID Review* 60 at 68.

[85] See (1966) 575 *United Nations Treaty Series* at 160, No. 8359.

[86] G. R. Delaume, *Transnational Contracts: Applicable Law and Settlement of Disputes. Law and Practice* (Dobbs Ferry, N.Y.: Oceana Publications) Booklet I, at 133.

[87] I. Shihata, "Towards a Greater Depoliticization of Investment Disputes: The Role of ICSID and MIGA", (1986) I *ICSID Review* 1; and O. Chukwumerije, *supra* n. 7, at 167.

Several of the Convention provisions deserve specific examination in order to demonstrate the theme of this paper. By virtue of Article 25(1), the Centre's jurisdiction derives solely from the consent of contracting parties. That consent, which must be in writing, may be based on an arbitration clause or a written agreement of parties to submit a dispute to the Centre. Most importantly, the same article stipulates that once consent to ICSID arbitration has been given, none of the parties can unilaterally withdraw its consent. The logical result is that a State contracting party cannot frustrate arbitration as agreed to by the parties by making changes in its municipal law. A contractual stipulation designating the contracting state's municipal law as the proper law of the contract will not change the position. In effect, what foreign investors could not effectively do through the device of stabilization clauses can now, at least to some extent, be accomplished by the submission of investment disputes to ICSID arbitration.

Furthermore, within the context of arbitration under the auspices of the ICSID, there is no place for assertions of sovereign immunity from suit. This is because notwithstanding the consensus of academic and judicial opinion that the effectiveness of the arbitral process is facilitated by municipal courts' assistance,[88] Article 26 of the Convention precludes municipal courts in ratifying states from assuming jurisdiction over a dispute subject to an ICSID clause unless the contracting parties provide otherwise.[89] The only jurisdiction or role left to municipal courts relates to the recognition, enforcement and execution of ICSID arbitral awards.[90] Even at this latter stage of the arbitral process, a State party cannot plead jurisdictional immunity since "every State party to an ICSID arbitration must contemplate the involvement of fellow contracting states in enforcing any attendant award".[91]

Without a doubt, therefore, ICSID arbitration provides the finest example of delocalized arbitration to the extent that it effectively shuts out the courts of the *arbitral situs* as well as those of contracting States from participation in the most critical phases of the arbitral process.[92] For the purposes of this paper's theme, the critical question is what delocalization does for the parties to State contracts. The main postulate of the delocalization theory of arbitration is that an arbitration proceeding is not rendered invalid because it was conducted independently of both the laws and the courts of the place of arbitration so long as transnational minimum standards were observed by the arbitrators.[93] More

88 See A. Redfern and M. Hunter, *supra* n. 7, at 306; and O. Chukwumerije, *supra* n. 8, at 91.

89 O. Chukwumerije, *supra* note at 174.

90 *Ibid.*

91 O. Chukwumerije, *supra* n. 7, at 176–7.

92 O. Chukwumerije, *supra* n. 23, at 93. See also, P. Szasz, "Using the New International Centre for Settlement of Investment Disputes", (1971) 7 *East Afr. LJ* 128 at 140–1.

93 O. Chukwumerije, *supra* n. 23, at 88 *et.seq*; J. Paulsson, "Delocalization of International Commercial Arbitration: When and Why it Matters", (1983) 32 *ICLQ* 53; and J. Paulsson, "The Extent of Independence of International Arbitration from the Law of the Situs", in J. Lew (ed.) *Contemporary Problems in International Arbitration* (London: Centre for Commercial Law Studies, 1986) at 140.

specifically, a delocalized arbitration is not subject to mandatory rules unique to the arbitral situs.[94]

It is a well known fact that the arbitral laws and practice of most countries are replete with provisions giving some form of deferential treatment to State parties. Similarly, some of their courts have been loathe to equate the interests of private investors with those of sovereign entities. Herein lies the special attraction of the delocalized ICSID arbitration machinery to the foreign private contracting parties. It cannot be denied that in providing that additional protection to the private contracting parties, ICSID arbitration, like the other developments and trends examined in this paper, responds vigorously to the private parties' pursuit of stability in the contractual relations with capital-importing States.

Regarding the law applicable to the merits of a dispute, Article 42(1) of the Convention adopts what has been referred to as the "concurrent law" approach.[95] This directs an ICSID tribunal, in the absence of an express choice of governing law by the parties, to apply the law of the host State (including its conflict of law rules) and such rules of international law as may be applicable. The effect of this is to allow the law of the host State being applied, but only to the extent that it is consistent with international law. According to Redfern and Hunter, public international law is thereby made "a regulator of the national law, ensuring that it does not fall below a minimum standard in its treatment of foreign investors and others".[96]

Article 42(1) of the Convention, neutral as it may appear, militates against the interests of State contracting parties to the extent that such a party cannot rely on those parts of its municipal law that may be perceived as falling below international minimum standards. In effect, the power of such parties to legislate and, thereby, affect State contracts is significantly restricted. Worse still, the convention tacitly recognizes the existence of a body of international rules capable of regulating international commercial intercourse and by which the validity or effectiveness of relevant municipal law rules can be judged. One is entitled to wonder whether this is a balanced, non-partisan approach for such an important Convention to take in light of the notorious uncertainties now surrounding the existence of such a body of international rules.[97]

[94] O. Chukwumerije, *supra* n. 23, at 89.

[95] A. Redfern and M. Hunter, *supra* n. 7, at 114 *et.seq.*

[96] *Ibid.* See also, A. Broches, "Settlement of Disputes arising out of Investment in Developing Countries", (1983) 11 *International Business Lawyer* 206.

[97] See discussion of the internalization theory, *supra* notes 41–9 and accompanying text. It should also be noted here that just as there is uncertainty as to the existence of an international law of contract, it is very doubtful whether there is any such thing as an international minimum standard to which one could look in determining the legality of a developing country's legislation affecting the interest of foreign investors. Louis Henkin, Emeritus Professor of International Law at the Columbia University School of Law observed that "in order to determine whether an alien was mistreated, there had to be some standard of treatment, and traditional international law, at least as seen in the West, developed the idea of an international standard of justice". He then continued: "I know of no philosophical foundation for this international standard and no

V. CONCLUSION

This paper has attempted to examine most of the difficult issues that attend the arbitration of investment disputes from a third world perspective. As with the general area of international trade, the conflicting interests pit nations and indeed trading blocs against each other. The reality of this fact is revealed in the continual tightening of the legal framework for international commercial arbitration to strengthen the protection available to foreign investors—a tightening effected by the investors themselves through the employment of various legal devices, by international arbitrators through unbalanced rulings and decisions, by the home governments of the foreign investors through changes in their municipal legal orders, and by international institutions such as the World Bank. What emerges from the efforts of all these agencies is an unwillingness to allow State contractors any privileges not bargained for.

There is little doubt that the legal regime of foreign investments impacts significantly on the development effort of third world countries. To the extent that this regime follows an approach that does not permit arbitrators and the national courts of the major international commercial arbitration centres to effectively recognize and promote the national interests of State parties, it aggravates development problems in at least two ways. In the first place, the regime cloaks and formalizes the unfairness that flows from the basic inequality of bargaining power between the foreign investors and Third World nations.[98] Secondly, one must place foreign investment as part of the economic strategy of the Third World in its proper perspective. Foreign investment in classical economic thinking is meant to fill the gap in domestic saving and investment and the benefits of the resulting accelerated economic growth are expected to trickle down to the population. It is not at all obvious, however, that there has been any improvement in the living conditions of the people of the Third World after decades of experimentation with this economic development strategy. What is clear is the increasing entrenchment of poverty and misery in these countries. A legal regime of foreign investment that consistently prefers the interests and objectives of foreign private foreign contracting parties while disregarding the national interests and right to development of State contractors must at least take some of the blame for the dismal failure of the economic strategy.

One may understandably be reluctant to give a negative characterization to the foreign investors' response to the problems which frequently plague the arbitration of investment disputes because the foreign investors seek to maximize profits for their shareholders. However, the same cannot be said of the

agreed legal definition of its contents, nor are there enough cases from which one might derive a clear sense of what it imports". See L. Henkin, R. C. Pugh, O. Schachter, and H. Smit, *International Law: Cases and Materials* (St. Paul, Minn: West Publishing, 1993) at 596.

[98] See S. K. B. Asante, "Traditional Concepts Versus Developmental Imperatives in Transnational Investment Law", in R. J. Dupuy (ed.) *supra* n. 66, at 368.

governmental and institutional responses discussed in this paper. It is unfair for international commercial arbitrators as well as the governments and institutions in developed countries continually to discount the right to development, the importance of national interests, and the urgency of development specially characteristic of the domestic conditions of the developing countries. This is particularly so since it can be easily shown historically that when the now developed nations were at the same developmental stage, any attempt to tie the hands of the State in regulating foreign investments for the public welfare or otherwise to curtail its regulatory powers and prerogatives was not tolerated.

The critical reader may conclude that the thesis of this paper leads to the submission that effective recognition of the right to development and the development needs of Third World countries requires the reinvention of the legal rules, practices, and institutions of international commercial arbitration with particular reference to the treatment of State contract disputes. However, such a drastic solution is not necessary. This is because, with the exception of the International Convention for the Settlement of Investment Disputes (which may require an elaborate and radical review), the imbalance presented by the examined legislative, interpretive and institutional responses examined earlier can be answered by less drastic solutions.[99] One example of such a solution would consist of a change towards excluding the restrictive doctrine of sovereign immunity where the State contracting party is a Third World country. Another example is represented by a change of attitude by international arbitrators making them less willing to adopt legal reasoning and solutions designed solely to vindicate the interests and expectations of foreign investors.[100] What is certain is that without a new approach to solving the problems unique to the settlement of State contract disputes the institution of international commercial arbitration may lose its legitimacy from the point of view of Third World countries and their academic sympathizers.

[99] An elaborate investigation of the possible and plausible responses to the essentially pro-investor bias of the examined legislative, interpretive and institutional responses is not within the scope of this one paper.

[100] In this respect, international arbitrators, in addition to recognizing the fundamental conflict between the customary values and concepts of international economic law and the development needs of Third World countries, will need to realize that no body of rules can "pretend to be an international system if it merely represents the traditional preoccupation with the protection of foreign private property". See S. K. B. Asante, *supra* n. 66, at 370.

15

The New GATT Agreement on Government Procurement: Impressive Achievements but a Setback for Multilateralism

DARIE REICH*

I. INTRODUCTION

On 15 April 1994, at the same time as the comprehensive Uruguay Round package of new multilateral trade agreements was signed in Marakesh,[1] a new agreement on government procurement was also signed. The Agreement on Government Procurement (GPA),[2] which aims to open up the important public procurement sector to international competition, came into effect in January 1996. The GPA has been hailed as one of the more important achievements of the Uruguay Round, placing a wide range of public contracts under a new regime of international tendering. The official publications on this new agreement,[3] as well as a few independent evaluations,[4] have all stressed its

* Arie Reich, LLB (Bar Ilan University); LLM; SJD (University of Toronto). Dr Reich is a member of the Faculty of Law Bar Ilan University, Israel, where he teaches torts and international trade law. He also serves as the Chairman of the Trade Charges Commission, Israel's Anti-Dumping and Countervailing Duty Tribunal. Thanks are due to Ms Annet Blank of the World Trade Organization for her assistance, and to Professor Jonathan Carlson of the University of Iowa for his valuable comments. An extended version of this paper also published in the Journal of World Trade, vol. 31, p. 125 (April 1997).

[1] See the Final Act Embodying the Results of the Uruguay Round of Multilateral Trade Negotiations (Geneva, GATT Secretariat, 1994); (1994) 33 ILM 1. This Act includes the agreement establishing the World Trade Organization ("WTO Agreement"). On the history of the negotiations leading up to the conclusion of this agreement, see John Croome, *Reshaping the World Trading System: A History of the Uruguay Round* (Geneva, World Trade Organization, 1995).

[2] Agreement on Government Procurement, Annex 4(b) of the WTO Agreement, reprinted in *Uruguay Round of Multilateral Trade Negotiations: Legal Instruments Embodying the Results of the Uruguay Round* (Geneva, GATT Secretariat, 1994) Vol. 31.

[3] See, e.g. *News of the Uruguay Round* No. 084, 5 Apr. 1994, 32; and US "Statement of Administrative Action", regarding The Uruguay Round Agreements Act, House Document 103–316, Vol. 1, 368.

[4] See Patrick A. Messerlin, "Agreement on Government Procurement" in *The New World Trading System: Readings* (Paris, Organization for Economic Co-operation and Development (OECD), 1994), 65.

important achievements, in particular, in broadening significantly the scope of the old agreement of 1979 (the "Tokyo Code")[5] to include important sectors with a great potential for international trade. In this paper, I would like to show not only the achievements but also the defects of the agreement, which may be summarised as a departure from the principle of multilateralism.

I will argue that notwithstanding its apparent achievements, and despite its multilateral setting, the GPA is not a multilateral agreement in the classical GATT sense. The Agreement, as it stands today, in fact violates every possible notion of non-discriminatory multilateralism.[6] It could quite accurately be described as an accumulation of preferential bilateral agreements between a limited number of WTO members somehow brought together under one shaky roof. As a result, the GPA may turn out to generate trade-diversion with negative welfare implications, instead of pure efficiency-enhancing trade creation. In addition, implementation of the Agreement has become extremely complicated due to the drastic differences in coverage in relation to different suppliers, purchasers, types of goods and services, and contract values. The uncertainty caused by these complications, both among suppliers and procuring entities, is likely to seriously impair the potential benefits of the GPA.

The paper will analyse the GPA, its provisions and its coverage annexes and demonstrate the problems indicated above. It will also examine the ways various signatories have chosen to implement the Code and the difficulties this has caused. A different interpretive approach will be suggested which may help to overcome some of the problems. In the end, however, the major remedies lie with the Parties themselves, and I will argue for a different approach to the coverage negotiations, which may provide a solution to the current GPA problems.

[5] The Agreement on Government Procurement, published in *GATT Basic Instruments, Supplements and Documents* ("BISD"), 26th Supp., 33; and in (1979) 18 ILM 10523. The Agreement was amended in 1987. See BISD, 34th Supp., 12. The Agreement, as amended, is hereafter referred to as the "Tokyo Code".

[6] One of the most central principles of the GATT multilateral regime is the principle of non-discrimination embodied in Art. I of the General Agreement on Tariffs and Trade (GATT) opened for signature on 30 Oct. 1947, (1950) 55 UNTS 194; TIAS No. 1700. According to this provision, the "most favoured nation" clause (MFN), GATT parties are not permitted to favour any foreign country over another foreign country, who is a GATT party. Rather, all ought to be on an equal basis and share the benefits of any move toward liberalised trade. See e.g. GATT Information Service, *GATT 30 Years, 1947–1977: What it Is, What it Does* (Geneva, GATT, 1979): "the first principle". On GATT in general, see Kenneth Dam, *The GATT: Law and International Organization* (Chicago, Ill., University of Chicago Press, 1970).

II. THE ACHIEVEMENTS

(a) What is the Government Procurement Agreement?

Before proceeding to evaluate the Agreement, a few words of introduction are warranted about the problems it is meant to solve. Most governments practice some kind of domestic preference policies in their procurement practices whereby locally made supplies are preferred over foreign ones, even at the expense of higher prices and inferior quality.[7] These policies create an enormous barrier to international trade, causing suboptimal allocation of resources and significant efficiency losses.[8] In order to grapple with this problem, an agreement was reached in the previous round of trade negotiations completed in 1979, the Tokyo Round, between some of the participating countries. This was the Agreement on Government Procurement.[9] The current GPA is a new version of the Tokyo Round agreement,[10] intended to improve the provisions of the old agreement and to broaden its scope significantly.

The aim of the GPA is to open up public procurement contracts to international competition under equal commercial conditions free of any national preferences. The GPA therefore prohibits any discrimination against products and suppliers originating from any of the signatories of the Agreement and requires all procuring agencies subject to the Agreement to extend "national treatment" to all such suppliers.[11] In addition to this substantive rule, the GPA

[7] See Organization for Economic Co-operation and Development, *Government Purchasing in Europe, North America and Japan* (Paris, OECD, 1966); and US General Accounting Office, *Governmental Buy-national Practices of the United States and Other Countries—An Assessment* (1976), 7. See also Robert E. Baldwin, *Non-Tariff Distortions of International Trade* (Washington, DC, The Brookings Institute, 1970), 58; and E. McGovern, *International Trade Regulation* (Exeter, Globefield Press, 1986), 204.

[8] For empirical studies on the costs of protection in the government procurement sector, see: W. S. Atkins Management Consultants in association with Eurequip SA-Roland Berger & Partner-Eurequip Italia, *The "Cost of Non-Europe" in Public-Sector Procurement*, Research on the "Cost of Non-Europe", Basic Findings, Vol. 5 (Brussels, EC Commission, 1988); and US Department of Defense, *The Impact of Buy American Restrictions Affecting Defense Procurement*, Report to the Congress by the Office of the Secretary of Defense, 1989. This and other evidence is reviewed and discussed in Arie Reich, *Toward Free Trade in the Public Sector: A Comparative Study of International Agreements on Government Procurement* (Doctoral Thesis, University of Toronto, 1994), 91–103.

[9] See *supra* note 5.

[10] The new GPA is therefore legally distinct from the previous Tokyo Code and supersedes it. See Art. XXIV:3(c) of the GPA. The parties to the Tokyo Code that did not join the new GPA (Hong Kong and Singapore) did thus only have rights under the Tokyo Code. Since all the other parties have terminated their participation in that code (see e.g. US Statement of Administrative Action, House Document 103–316, Vol. 1, 368), in effect it left them with no rights at all. Both Hong Kong and Singapore decided therefore, at a later stage to join the new GPA. Hong Kong deposited its act of accession in May 1997, and Singapore in September 1997. See Committee on Government Procurement, "Report (1997) of the Committee" (29.10.97), paras.[12]–[13], available at: http://www.wto.org/wto/govt/repgp.htm.

[11] See Art. III of the GPA, *supra* note 2. ("National Treatment and Non-Discrimination"). "National Treatment" is a term used in international trade agreements referrring to the obligation to afford to goods and suppliers of the other party treatment no less favourable than that afforded to domestic products and suppliers. See J. Jackson, *The World Trading System* (Cambridge, Mass., MIT Press, 1991), 189.

also prescribes very detailed tendering procedures which are to apply to all purchases subject to the Agreement. The procedures are designed to guarantee true competitive conditions for all potential suppliers and to prevent discrimination against foreigners. They require, for instance, that a tendering notice for every intended procurement is published in a previously determined publication inviting suppliers from all GPA countries to bid for the contract on equal terms.[12] Such notice must be published, at least in a summary form, in one of the official languages of the WTO (English, French and Spanish).[13] The Agreement also requires that the technical specifications for the product in question be based on international standards, if they exist,[14] as opposed to national standards, which may give local producers an unfair advantage. There are also detailed provisions on all other facets of the procurement process, such as the technical qualification procedures,[15] the bid-opening procedures,[16] the contract award criteria[17] and post-award information.[18]

(b) Extended Coverage

The central problem of the previous agreement was its limited coverage, as a result of which the economic impact of the agreement was very limited.[19] Instead of a general coverage with specifically defined limitations, the Tokyo Code was confined to those procurements expressly specified in the annexes,[20] and arrived at through tit for tat negotiations between the parties. These covered procurements were defined by means of four basic parameters:

(1) The contract value;[21]

[12] GPA, Art. IX.
[13] *Ibid.*, Art. IX:8.
[14] *Ibid.*, Art. VI:2(b).
[15] *Ibid.*, Art. VIII.
[16] *Ibid.*, Art. XIII:3.
[17] *Ibid.*, Art. XIII:4.
[18] *Ibid.*, Art. XVIII. Procuring entities are required to publish post-award information notices, specifying, *inter alia*, the name and address of the winning tenderer as well as the value of the winning award, or at least "the highest and lowest offer taken into account in the award of the contract" (*ibid.*, para. 1(d) and (e)). In addition, an unsuccessful tenderer may request information concerning the reason why its tender was not selected and on the characteristics and relative advantages of the tender selected (*ibid.*, para. 2(c)).
[19] See Report by the US Accounting Office, *The International Agreement on Government Procurement: An Assessment of Its Commercial Value and US Government Implementation*, GAO/NSIAD–84–117 (16 July 1984). This study estimates the total value of government purchases covered by the Tokyo Code at around US $20 billion annually. This is only a fraction of the world-wide government procurement market, involving several hundred billion dollars. See also the *Report of the International Chamber of Commerce Working Group on the GATT Government Procurement Code* (ICC Document 103–28), as summarised in A. Frignani, "The GATT Agreement on Government Procurement—ICC Symposium", (1986) 20 *J World Trade L* 567.
[20] See the Tokyo Code, *supra* note 000, Art. I:1 ("Scope and Coverage").
[21] The Tokyo Code applied only to procurement contracts with a value of SDR 130,000 (approximately US $170,000) or more (*ibid.*, Art. I:1(b)).

(2) The type of goods;[22]
(3) The origin of the goods;[23]
(4) The procuring entities.[24]

Unfortunately, the Uruguay Code negotiators did not abandon this approach and the coverage of the new GPA is therefore still defined by reference to the same four parameters. However, the coverage under the second and fourth parameters (type of goods and procuring entities) was significantly extended. Contracts for the supply of services were added[25] and, in particular, construction contracts (buildings, roads, bridges etc.—so-called "public works").[26] Also, instead of being confined to central government agencies (such as federal governments), the new GPA is meant to apply to three categories of agencies:

(1) Central government entities;[27]
(2) Sub-central government entities (State governments, provincial governments, municipalities etc.);[28]
(3) Public enterprises (such as State-owned or State-controlled corporations);[29]

The new Agreement was thus extended to entities operating in important sectors which previously had been excluded from the Code regime. Sub-central governments, especially in federal States, account for a very large share of government procurements,[30] and their addition to the GPA regime has opened up significant new contract opportunities for foreign suppliers. Likewise, under Category C, we find entities operating in the important

[22] The Tokyo Code applied only to contracts for non-defence goods, as military purchases were effectively excluded by the National Security exception. It did not apply to service contracts *per se*, only to services incidental to the supply of products, such as instalment and maintenance (*ibid.*, Art. I:1(a)).

[23] Only goods from Code signatories are eligible for rights under the Code.

[24] The Code only applied to those entities specified by each party in their coverage annexes. These annexes contained mainly central government agencies and not State or provincial governments or government-controlled corporations or agencies.

[25] See the 6th preamble to the GPA: ". . . and to expand the coverage of the Agreement to include service contracts;", and Art. III:1. See also Annex 4 of each party, specifying the services subject to the agreement.

[26] Specified in Annex 5 of each party.

[27] Specified in Annex 1 of each party.

[28] Specified in Annex 2 of each party.

[29] Specified in Annex 3 of each party.

[30] In the USA alone, the market for State and local government procurement is estimated at US $200 billion annually, which amounts to some 45% of the total procurement of US government agencies at all levels. See US Department of Commerce, Economics and Statistics Administration, Bureau of Economic Analysis, *Survey of Current Business*, Sept. 1992, tab. 3.7(b), at 11, quoted in K. J. Cooper, "To Compel or Encourage: Seeking Compliance with International Trade Agreements at the State Level" (1993) 2 *Minn. J Global Trade* 143, in note 102. An official EC report claims the proportion to be as high as 70%. See Services of the Commission of the European Communities: *Report on United States Trade Barriers and Unfair Practices 1990: Problems of Doing Business with the US* (Brussels, EC Commission, 1991) 57.

public utility sectors, providing energy, transportation and water to the public, often enjoying monopoly status or similar dominant positions. These include public corporations operating in the water, airport and port sectors, as well as entities in the electricity and public transport sectors.[31] However, attempts to include the telecommunication sector under the GPA have so far been unsuccessful.[32] Nevertheless, as will be seen, the scope of the Category B and Category C entities is seriously restricted as a result of all the derogations and strict reciprocity requirements imposed by the parties.

(c) **Bid Challenge Procedures**

Another important innovation of the GPA is the introduction of mandatory bid-challenge procedures. The previous Tokyo Code had followed the GATT tradition of excluding private parties from all dispute resolution procedures.[33] Any alleged violation of the Code could be raised only by a government party to the Code and the disputes had to be resolved through bilateral GATT procedures (consultation, arbitration panel, etc.).[34] This system could not by any measure respond to the enforcement needs of the GPA, where violations mostly occur at the individual level and involve a specific contract and a specific supplier. By the time a GATT panel has been established and the hearing procedures have been completed, the contract will usually have been awarded and performed a long time ago, thus making the panel's decision irrelevant. Since the customary practice under the GATT system has not usually included restitutionary remedies, panels have seen themselves unable to recommend annulment of a contract and recommencement of the procurement process, or even to award compensation to an aggrieved bidder.

The new GPA remedies this situation by introducing a private right of action to aggrieved suppliers. Parties are required under the Agreement to establish bid-challenge procedures that are "non-discriminatory, timely, transparent and effective".[35] Any supplier may thus challenge alleged breaches of the GPA arising in the context of procurements in which they have, or have had, an interest, before a court or an impartial and independent review body.

[31] See e.g. Annex 3 to the European Community: "Entities in the water, electricity, urban transport, port and airport sectors". However, the application to these entities is severely limited by the various derogations and exceptions found in the "General Notes and Derogations From the Provisions of Article III", attached to the EC coverage appendix to the GPA.

[32] For an extensive account of the coverage negotiations and the difficulties faced by the parties (albeit from a European perspective), see G. de Graaf and M. King, "Towards a More Global Government Procurement Market: The Expansion of the GATT Government Procurement Agreement in the Context of the Uruguay Round" (1995) 29 *Int'l Lawyer* 435, at 441–52.

[33] See E. U. Petersmann, "The Dispute Settlement System of the World Trade Organization and the Evolution of the GATT Dispute Settlement System Since 1948" (1994) 31 *CML Rev.* 1157, 1169.

[34] See Tokyo Code, *supra* note 5, Art. VII ("Enforcement of Obligations").

[35] The GPA, *supra* note 2, Art. XX:2.

The tribunal in question must be authorised to grant rapid interim measures to correct breaches of the Agreement and to preserve commercial opportunities.[36] Thus, a supplier will be able to petition a tribunal directly as soon as a breach is discovered, and request a stay of the procurement procedures until the procuring entity's acts and decisions can be scrutinised.

If the complaint is proven to be justified, the tribunal must have the authority to correct the breach.[37] This would seem to imply that the review body must be authorised not just to order recommencement of tendering procedures not yet completed but also to order the termination of a contract that has already been awarded.[38] The tribunal could use this authority whenever it has determined that the award was in conflict with the Code and that its termination is feasible and required in order to correct the breach. This would amount to a significant improvement in relation to both the Canada–US FTA and the EC Review Directive, neither of which required such authority.[39]

As an alternative to an injunction, the review body could award compensation to the supplier for the loss or damage suffered, which may be limited to costs for tender preparation or for filing the protest.[40] In other words, the GPA Parties may prevent their bid challenge tribunals from awarding expectation damages, calculated as the profits lost from a contract that ought to have been awarded to the plaintiff. They may also prevent them from awarding punitive damages, aimed to deter violations of the GPA. This may prove to be a problem in the future if these restrictions on the powers of the tribunals are abused by procuring entities.

III. THE SETBACK FOR MULTILATERALISM

(a) A Non-multilateral Agreement: "Plurilateralism"

Despite common perceptions to the contrary, the negotiations that led up to the new GPA were not a part of the Uruguay Round. The Uruguay Round

[36] *Ibid.*, Art. XX:7(a).

[37] *Ibid.*, Art. XX:7(c).

[38] Only this would amount to a correction of the breach. Considering that even as a preliminary measure the tribunal must be authorised to "correct the breach and to preserve commercial opportunities", then, it must be deemed to have at least this much authority in issuing its final corrective measures. Only if such termination would involve serious prejudice to both the procuring entity and the present contractor would the tribunal be entitled to withhold termination and award damages instead.

[39] See e.g. the Canada–US Free Trade Agreement (1988) 27 *ILM* 281, Annex 1305.3, para. (f), which does not require such authority. Indeed, the Canadian review body does not have it. See Arie Reich, "Government Procurement and Bid Challenging in Canada After the Free Trade Agreement" (1991) 18 *Can.Bus.LJ* 195, 220. Likewise, Art. 2(6) of the EC Remedies Directive (Council Directive 89/665/EEC, [1989] OJ L395/33) permits Member States to limit the authority of the review body so that after the conclusion of a contract, following its award, its powers are limited to awarding damages.

[40] The GPA, *supra* note 2, Art. XX:7(c).

was launched with a declaration by the ministers of the GATT Contracting Parties at Punta del Este, Uruguay, in September 1987.[41] The negotiations within the Round were conducted within fifteen negotiating groups on various subjects,[42] in which all interested GATT parties were permitted to participate.[43] The new Code, in contrast, was negotiated mainly within the Committee of Government Procurement (a body established by the Tokyo Code), and pursuant to the authorisation of the Tokyo Code, not the ministerial declaration.[44] Thus, only contemporary signatories could participate in the drafting procedure of the new GPA.

To be sure, many of its participants considered the GPA negotiations to be part of the new "GATT package" and one of the most important aspects of the Uruguay Round.[45] The fact that the GPA was concluded and signed on the same dates as the rest of the package (15 December 1993 and 15 April 1994) also contributed to this perception. Nevertheless, by assigning the substantive negotiations to the Committee, the negotiators had in effect decided that the new Agreement would only apply to its current signatories and that it would continue to serve as a "members only" club. Non-members may apply for membership to the club, but their application will be accepted only if a sufficient "membership fee", i.e. entity coverage, is being offered.[46]

In this respect, the fate of the GPA was very different from that of the other multilateral trade agreements (the so-called "codes") reached in the Tokyo Round and also assigned to the Uruguay Round negotiating group on "MTN Agreements and Arrangements". The other five MTN Agreements[47] under-

[41] The declaration is reprinted in *GATT Focus* (8 Oct. 1986), 1.

[42] See Croome, *supra* note 1, p. 36.

[43] See Decision of the GATT Trade Negotiations Committee of 21 May 1987, reprinted in *News of the Uruguay Round* No. 005.

[44] Art. IX:9 of the Tokyo Code, *supra* note 5. This provision foresaw the need to conduct periodical reviews and negotiations "with a view to broadening and improving [the] Agreement on the basis of mutual reciprocity". The GPA was discussed only marginally in one of the 15 negotiating groups, namely the "Group on MTN Agreements and Arrangements", whose task it was to discuss some of the multilateral trade agreements reached in the Tokyo Round. The issue discussed in this group mainly involved the question of accession to the GPA by new members. See *GATT Activities: An Annual Review of the Work of the GATT* (June 1989), 42–4. South Korea, in particular, had complained that its efforts to accede had been rejected by the other signatories, who had found Korea's entity offer unacceptable. This was an issue fit for discussion within a general forum of GATT parties, and not only in the Committee on Government Procurement, which was the subject of the criticism. Indeed, the final Uruguay Round package includes a Ministerial Decision "inviting" the Committee to "clarify" that accession to the GPA will be made possible in accordance with certain specified procedures (Ministerial Decisions and Declarations adopted by the Trade Negotiations Committee on 15 Dec. 1993, reprinted in *The Results of the Uruguay Round of Multilateral Trade Negotiations: The Legal Texts* (Geneva, GATT Secretariat, 1994), 464).

[45] See e.g. *News of the Uruguay Round* No. 084, 5 Apr. 1994, 32.

[46] The coverage offer made by such a country will be examined by a working party established by the Committee in light of two main parameters: (1) the export opportunities for Code signatories in the public market of the applicant member; (2) the export potential of the applicant member to the public markets of the Code signatories. See "Decision on Accession to the Agreement on Government Procurement", para. 1(d).

[47] The Anti-Dumping Code, the Subsidies Code, the Standards Code, the Custom Valuation Code and the Import Licensing Code.

went a status change as a result of the Uruguay Round. From being "voluntary" agreements, in the sense that GATT Members were free to decide whether to accede to them and to assume their obligations, they became part of a "single undertaking" which all States were required to assume as a condition of becoming members of the new World Trade Organization (WTO) and the new GATT.[48] Thus, all the rights and obligations under these agreements, as well as of the new codes negotiated in the Uruguay Round,[49] were in effect extended to all GATT Members.[50] With the exception of three sectoral agreements,[51] only the GPA was left outside the "single undertaking", and thus remained a voluntary agreement. Indeed, in the new package, the GPA is no longer described as a "multilateral", but rather as a "plurilateral"[52] trade agreement.[53]

As a result, only twenty-three countries, most of them developed countries, are currently signatories to the new GPA.[54] The Agreement therefore remains a "rich man's club", of which the rich countries are the main members, after

[48] Art. II:2 of the WTO Agreement, *supra* note 1, provides that all the multilateral trade agreements are an integral part of the WTO Agreement and are binding on all Members. See also *News of the Uruguay Round* No. 055.

[49] An additional 8 new codes were concluded in the Uruguay Round and were integrated in the final binding act together with two new general agreements on trade in services and intellectual property rights. For a general overview of the results of the Uruguay Round, see OECD Documents, *The New World Trading System: Readings* (Paris, OECD, 1994); and J. Schott and J. W. Buurman, *The Uruguay Round: An Assessment* (Washington, DC, Institute for International Economics, 1994).

[50] See *The New World Trading System*, *supra* n. 49, 28.

[51] The agreements are: Agreement on Trade in Civil Aircraft, International Dairy Agreement, and International Bovine Meat Agreement. See Annex 4 of the WTO Agreement, *supra*, note 1. These agreements, dealing with specific commodities or products, are naturally only of interest to a limited number of exporters and importers and were therefore left outside the single undertaking.

[52] The term "plurilateral" infers that the agreement is of interest to a limited number of States, whereas "multilateral" agreements are of interest to all States. This distinction was first made by Sir Humphrey Waldock in the first report prepared by him in 1962 in connection with the preparation of the Vienna Treaty on the Interpretation of Treaties of 1969. See [1962] *UN Int'l Law Com. Yearbook* 77. See also G. Tunkin, "Is General International Law Customary Law Only?" (1993) 4 *European J Int'l L* 534, at 537.

[53] See Annex 4 of the WTO Agreement, *supra* note 1, titled: "Plurilateral Trade Agreements".

[54] The 23 countries are the following: Canada, the 15 Member States of the European Union (Austria, Belgium, Denmark, Finland, France, Germany, Greece, Ireland, Italy, Luxembourg, The Netherlands, Portugal, Spain, Sweden, United Kingdom), Israel, Korea, Aruba (part of the Kingdom of The Netherlands), Norway, Switzerland, Japan and the United States. This list differs only slightly from the original list of signatories to the Tokyo Round Code. Korea and Aruba are new signatories, whereas Singapore, which was an original signatory, decided not to sign the new Code. Hong Kong participated in all the negotiations preceding the new Code but decided at the last minute not to sign because it felt that some provisions of the agreement were too far removed from the GATT standards of most-favoured nation and national treatment and that "sectoral reciprocity" prevailed too much in the exchange of concessions (see *infra*, paras. 2 and 3). Eventually, both Hong Kong and Singapore decided to join, and their membership came into effect in late 1997 (see *supra* note 10). The principality of Liechtenstein also acceeded in 1997. There are therefore now 26 signatories to the GPA. Countries that currently are in the process of joining are Chinese Taipei and Paraguay.

having paid their dues in the form of the GPA's obligations. All the other WTO members, over one hundred, are not bound by the GPA and are therefore free to practise protectionist procurement policies, since government purchasing was explicitly made an exception to the GATT 1947 obligation of "national treatment".[55] In addition, as we will see, even GPA signatories may practise protection against any country not subscribing to the GPA or in any other case not falling within the GPA coverage.[56]

This situation, where a major trade barrier is allowed to continue and flourish and to distort so much trade between WTO members,[57] is obviously in conflict with the GATT principle of trade liberalisation and open markets. The fact that this has occurred, and the fact that protectionist procurement policies are the only major non-tariff barrier not regulated on the multilateral level by the comprehensive Uruguay Round package, serve as a baffling testimony to the immense domestic interests at stake in this field and the powerful political forces opposing liberalisation of government purchasing. These interests are both internal and within the political establishment, whose members are eager to hold on to the power connected with the granting of government contracts, whether for legitimate or illegitimate purposes, as well as external—coming from those sectors of the domestic industry that depend on such contracts. It is no coincidence that the sectors still completely or partially excluded from the GPA regime are those with the greatest dependency on governmental contracts.[58] The problem, therefore, just as with many other so-called "international trade problems",[59] is both one of governmental probity and domestic distributive policy as well as an issue of foreign trade policy. A multilateral subscription to the GPA, considering its detailed tendering rules

[55] The General Agreement on Tariffs and Trade, *supra* note 1, Art. III:8(a). This exception applies to all procurement by governmental agencies of products purchased for governmental purposes and not with a view to commercial resale or to use in the production of goods for commercial sale. This exception will be further discussed below in Sect. III, subsect. 5 of this paper. A similar exception is found in the new General Agreement on Trade in Services (GATS), (WTO Agreement, *supra* note 1, Annex 1B, at 325), excluding governmental procurement of services from all MFN, National Treatment and Market Access commitments under GATS. See Art. XIII of GATS.

[56] The GPA only applies to government procurements covered by the Agreement, and it requires national treatment and non-discrimination only to products, services and suppliers of other parties to the GPA. See Articles. I:1 and III:1 of the GPA, *supra*, note 2.

[57] Total world government procurement has been estimated at some US $400 billion annually (see Messerlin, *supra* note 4, p. 65). Only a part of that volume is covered by the new GPA (some estimates talk about $200 billion). As we will see, even those procurements are closed to non-signatories of the GPA and partly closed to some signatories. The potential distortion of the international trade in this sector is therefore great.

[58] For instance, the telecommunication sector, where no agreement could be reached, as well as all the other utility sectors, where wide-ranging exceptions and derogations are prevailing. Other conspicuous examples of successful industry lobbying are the US exclusion of hand tools, measuring tools, cutlery and flatware, and Israel's exclusion of cables, electro-mechanic meters, transformers, disconnectors, switchers, and electric motors.

[59] On these aspects, see E. U. Petersmann, *Constitutional Functions and Constitutional Problems of International Economic Law* (1991), particularly chs. V and VI.

and standards of transparency in government contracting, would therefore provide solutions to both problems.

Nevertheless, there have been international attempts to separate the domestic aspects of the problems from the international ones, and to provide at least temporary solutions to the former. These include initiatives by the World Bank, demanding transparent procurement procedures as a condition for its financial assistance to developing countries,[60] and by the United Nations which has promulgated a Model Law on Procurement[61] in the hope that it will be adopted by national legislators. Recently, there have also been talks on an interim agreement within the WTO aimed at introducing basic standards of transparency and probity in government procurement.[62] However, these initiatives have so far not been very successful, and in any case they are only "second-best" and partial solutions. A comprehensive and fully satisfactory regulation of government procurement policies can only be achieved through a multilateral subscription to a GPA-type agreement.

(b) An Intra-discriminatory Trade Regime

As mentioned, the main goal of the new GPA was to extend coverage to the economically important sectors: procurements of public utilities and subcentral governments. In the official press releases on the new Agreement the claim is made that this goal was achieved and a quick glance at the coverage annexes may give the impression that this is indeed the case. However, a more thorough examination will show that the claimed expanded coverage is qualified by a myriad of derogations *vis-à-vis* the various signatories. Instead of a uniform opening of all listed procurement opportunities to all the GPA signatories (such as found in the Tokyo Code) we find different openings for different signatories. The consequences of this approach are not only a coverage significantly more limited than expected but, more importantly, that the GPA in fact harbours an intra-discriminatory trade regime between its members.

[60] See *Guidelines: Procurement under IBRD Loans and IDA Credits* (Washington DC, The World Bank, 1995), Sect. II: "International Competitive Bidding". However, in certain cases, the Bank may allow the borrower to apply domestic preferences (*ibid.*, para. 2.54).

[61] See United Nations Commission on International Trade Law (UNCITRAL), *Yearbook* Vol. XXIII: 1992 (New York, United Nations, 1994), 197–290.

[62] In the informal meetings of WTO mission chiefs leading up to the Singapore Ministerial Conference, such a proposal was tabled by the USA. The proposal was to negotiate an interim multilateral agreement setting basic standards of transparency in government procurement in order to promote openness and predictability and to combat corruption. See *Inside US Trade*, 22 Mar. 1996 ("US Proposes Interim WTO Procurement Deal to Combat Corruption"). During the conference, no agreement could be reached to commence negotiations towards such a deal. However, it was decided to establish a working group in order to "conduct a study on transparency in government procurement practices, taking into account national policies, and, based on this study, to develop elements for inclusion in an appropriate agreement". See WTO, Ministerial Conference, "Singapore Ministerial Declaration", 13 Dec. 1996, para. 21.

The USA, for instance, originally denied access to its Category B and C procurements (i.e. procurements by its State governments and electric utilities) to suppliers from the EC, Canada, Austria, Switzerland, Norway, Sweden, Finland and Japan.[63] Thus the only signatories left to which the GPA would apply were Israel and South Korea. Only in April 1994 was a bilateral agreement reached between the USA and the EC to extend mutual coverage to these categories,[64] and the EC States (including Austria, Finland and Sweden) were taken off the non-application list.[65] Likewise, the EC denied access for US and Canadian suppliers to its Category B procurements,[66] and only changed its position, following the bilateral agreement, with regard to US suppliers of products and not services.[67] In addition, the EC has a long and complicated list of derogations in relation to its Category C procurements. Procurements by entities in the urban transport sector, for instance, are not open under the GPA to suppliers from Canada, Israel, Japan, Korea and the USA.[68] Only Norway and Switzerland are thus allowed to enjoy benefits in this sector. In the airport sector, access is denied to suppliers of Canada, Korea and the USA, and so on.[69] Similar derogations of varying magnitudes can be found in the other GPA signatories' appendices.

These derogations are all accompanied by the declaration that they will only be withdrawn when the signatory is satisfied that comparable access has been given to its suppliers by the other parties.[70] Parties are thus in effect invited to conclude bilateral deals between each other and the GPA only serves as a suggested framework within which to conclude such deals. Sometimes not even this is done, and bilateral arrangements are kept completely outside the domain of the GPA.[71]

[63] See para. 5 of the "General Notes" to the US coverage appendix to the GPA.

[64] The Agreement was ratified by EC Council Decision of 29 May 1995, 95/215/EC [1995] OJ L134/25.

[65] See para. 5 of the amended version of the General Notes. The States still listed are: Canada, Switzerland, Norway and Japan.

[66] See para. 1 of the "General Notes and Derogations from the Provisions of Article III" to the EC coverage appendix to the GPA.

[67] See amended version of para. 1 of the above General Notes, *supra* note 63. Thus, Canadian product and service suppliers are still completely denied rights under the GPA with regards to EC Category B procurements. As for the USA, only its service providers are denied rights.

[68] *Ibid.*.

[69] Contracts of entities in the electricity sectors are not open to suppliers from Canada, Japan and Hong Kong. Contracts of entities in the water sector are not open to suppliers from Canada and the USA. Ports remain closed for Canadian suppliers. Furthermore, several products and services are excluded from coverage in relation to suppliers from various Parties, while included only for others. Additional bilateral "sanctions" are applied to a number of Parties (USA, Japan, Korea, Switzerland, Israel), by barring their suppliers from access to the bid-challenge procedures. Almost identical derogations are found in the coverage annexes of Austria, Finland, Norway and Sweden.

[70] See e.g. the EC declaration, *ibid.*.

[71] For instance, the EC–US bilateral agreement mentioned above, *supra* note 64, contained agreements which were kept purely bilateral and not incorporated in the GPA annexes. This included the US commitment to extend national treatment to EC suppliers in the procurements of the Massachusetts Port Authority. Likewise, an agreement was reached in 1996 between the

Likewise, the actual opening of the service sector is much more limited than may appear at first glance. Not only is application limited exclusively to certain listed types of services,[72] but most signatories have also made their service offers subject to a "strict reciprocity" clause.[73] Under this clause, access will not be extended to service providers of parties which do not themselves include the specific service category in question in their coverage. For instance, procurement of legal services[74] and hotel and catering services, which nominally are opened up by Canada to all GPA signatories,[75] are in effect closed to all of them except for the USA, as a result of the strict reciprocity clause,[76] since these specific services are not included in any of the other GPA signatories' service offers. This restriction disregards the fact that the other party may have included alternative services of equivalent, or even greater, importance than the services included by Canada.

(c) The Problems with Strict Reciprocity

There are several problems with this strict tit-for-tat approach taken by the parties, which results from a preoccupation with the idea of "fair trade" instead of "free trade". First of all, as noted above, a significant number of important public contracts remain closed to suppliers from most countries, including GPA members. Many economists have noted that reciprocity has no intrinsic economic rationale, since trade liberalisation ought to be carried out even on a unilateral basis.[77] Demands for reciprocity are clearly detrimental if they fail to bring about greater liberalisation, but instead stifle the progress of multi-lateral trade negotiations and generate new trade barriers. In addition, the strict reciprocity approach taken, for instance, in relation to services defeats the possibility of cross-sector swaps which often has induced significant reduction of barriers in GATT.[78]

EC and Israel to open up bilaterally to their respective suppliers the procurements of the telecommunication sector. This agreement, unlike other agreements reached concurrently between the two parties, was not incorporated to the GPA. The USA and Japan have also concluded several bilateral procurement agreements outside the scope of the GPA, such as the agreement on procurements in the telecommunication sector.

[72] These services are listed in each signatory's Annex 4. All signatories, except for the USA, chose the "positive list" approach, meaning that the Agreement only applies to those services expressly listed. The USA, in contrast, chose the "negative" list approach, similar to the approach taken by all signatories with regard to their goods commitments, whereby all services are in principle included, except those few services expressly excluded.

[73] See e.g. para. 8 of the US General Notes: "[a] service listed in Annex 4 is covered with respect to a particular Party only to the extent that such Party has included that service in its Annex 4". A similar, and even more restrictive clause can be found in the EC General Notes (para. 1, last sentence).

[74] This refers only to advisory services on foreign and international law.

[75] See Annex 4 of Canada's coverage appendix.

[76] The clause is found in para. 4 of Canada's General Notes.

[77] See e.g. Peter Kenan, *The International Economy* (Englewood Cliffs, NJ, Prentice Hall, 1985), sect. 2.2.

[78] J. Jackson, *The World Trading System* (Cambridge, Mass., MIT Press, 1991), 125.

Secondly, because the derogations are so detailed it is extremely hard to know if a particular procurement is covered under the GPA or not, and whether it is open to all GPA suppliers or only to some. This seriously impairs the commercial predictability of the procurement regime set up by the GPA. It also makes the agreement vary hard to implement. In Israel, for instance, it has led the authorities to decide not to implement the GPA by legislation, because it would be too complicated to set out the coverage rules.[79] This, in turn, has added to the uncertainty and reduced awareness of the Agreement's existence.

In particular, the many country-specific derogations cause serious difficulties of implementation in connection with the determination of origin of the products or services offered. It obliges procuring entities to determine the exact origin of the goods or services in order to ascertain their position under the GPA.[80] To further complicate the situation, the GPA does not provide uniform rules of origin to be applied in this regard. Rather, it provides that Parties must apply rules of origin that are not different from the rules of origin "applied in the normal course of trade and at the time of the transaction in question to imports or supplies of the same products or services from the same Parties".[81] As a result, different rules of origin may be applied to different countries. On the other hand, most countries have rules of origin depending on the international arrangement under which the goods are imported. For instance: goods imported to Country A from Country B may enjoy duty-free treatment under a preferential trade arrangement (such as a Free Trade Agreement) if they meet the rules of origin of that arrangement. If they do not, they may still be entitled to the most-favoured nation (MFN) tariffs rate if they meet the GATT rules of origin.

Which of these rules should be applied to government procurements under the GPA? How can procurement officers be expected to have expertise in such a complex area as rules of origin, which are usually administered by customs officials? How can the officials be expected to apply different sets of rules of origin to different products within a single procurement? And which rules of origin should they apply to services? Most countries do not yet have any such rules that are applied "in the normal course of trade" since usually there are no customs duties on the import of services. Should the origin of the service be determined according to the country where the service supplier is incorporated, or should it be based on the nationality of the owners of the enterprise or of the workers who provide the service? These are all open questions, which demonstrate the immense problems connected with implementing such a complex procurement regime based on the principle of strict reciprocity.

[79] This information is based on talks with Israeli officials.

[80] The GPA National Treatment and MFN obligation apply only to "the products, services and suppliers of other Parties offering products or services *of the Parties*" (Art. III:1).

[81] The GPA, *supra* note 2, Art. IV:1. This provision may be amended following the work programme for the harmonisation of rules of origin for goods to be undertaken under the Agreement on Rules of Origin (in Annex 1A of the WTO Agreement); *ibid.*, Art. IV:2.

Finally, the idea of multilateralism has important rationales, both political and economic,[82] and the GPA's departure from them has negative consequences. A discriminatory trade regime causes political tension between States. It divides the world into trading blocs, which may deteriorate into strategic-military blocs of the type witnessed during the two World Wars in this century. From the economic perspective, discriminatory arrangements result in trade diversion, with negative welfare implications.[83] Several examples of this phenomenon will be discussed below. In the procurement context, it causes waste of public resources and increases the cost of government programmes.[84] A non-multilateral approach also raises the cost of rule formation significantly, given the difficulty of negotiating a multitude of bilateral agreements. Multilateralism, in contrast, leads to generalisation of liberalising trade policies, so that overall more trade liberalisation occurs (the multiplier effect of the MFN clause).[85]

(d) Trade Discrimination Resulting from the GPA

As declared in its preamble, the official objective of the GPA is to "achiev[e] greater liberalization and expansion of world trade".[86] The preamble also states that "laws, regulations, procedures and practices regarding government procurement . . . should not discriminate among foreign products or services or among foreign suppliers".[87] Nevertheless, one can point to several instances where the regime set up by the GPA will result in discrimination among foreign suppliers, and in trade diversion instead of liberalisation.

One prominent example is provided by the United States, which in its implementation of the GPA has essentially barred all countries which have not joined the Agreement from participating in tenders for US Government contracts subject to the GPA.[88] The same was done in the US implementation of the Tokyo Code.[89] As a result, the position of foreign non-GPA suppliers has been significantly worsened compared to the situation prior to the Code. Before the Code, they were allowed to compete for US government contracts

[82] For a survey of the policy arguments in favour of MFN, see Jackson, *supra* note 78, 134–5.

[83] See Jacob Viner, *The Customs Union Issue* (New York, Carnegie Endowment for Int'l Peace, 1950).

[84] For an extensive survey and discussion of the economic evidence on the cost of discriminatory procurement policies, see Arie Reich, *supra* note 39, 91–103.

[85] Jackson, *supra* note 78, 134.

[86] The Preamble to the GPA, *supra* note 2, first para.

[87] *Ibid.*, second para.

[88] See 19 USC 2512(a), entitled "Authority to Bar Procurement From Non-Designated Countries", which requires the President to prohibit the procurement of products originating from countries not Parties to the GPA or other reciprocal trade agreements. The prohibition does not apply to certain less developed countries. An exception to the prohibition may apply when there are no offers of products from the USA or from GPA countries, or when such offers are insufficient.

[89] Trade Agreements Act 1979, s. 302(a)(1), Public Law 96–39, 93 Stat. 236–42.

and were only subject to the 6 per cent or 12 per cent Buy American Act price differential.[90] Thus, if their bid was lower than the comparable US bid by more than the differential, they could still win the contract. Now, however, they are not allowed to participate at all except in cases where the product cannot be obtained from US or GPA sources.

The objective of these exclusions is, of course, to create an incentive for countries to join the Agreement,[91] but as a result we may have serious cases both of trade contraction and trade diversion. Trade contraction will occur when contracts that previously would have gone to foreign suppliers, offering lower bids, now go to potentially more expensive US suppliers; and trade diversion will occur when contracts that previously would have gone to foreign non-GPA suppliers now go to potentially more expensive foreign GPA-suppliers. This, in turn, not only diminishes global efficiency but also serves as a drain on the public purse.

A similar example of such a distortion can be found in Canada's implementation of the Tokyo Code. In purchases not subject to international agreements, the Canadian Content Premium Policy provides that a premium of up to 10 per cent will be granted to the local content of any bid.[92] Consequently, any foreign content in the product or service offered will be evaluated as 10 per cent more expensive than its actual price.[93] Following the entry into force of the Tokyo Code, the Canadian rules provided that such handicaps will not apply to goods originating from a signatory country.[94] They continue, however, to apply to goods originating from non-signatory countries. Such goods may consequently be evaluated as more expensive than goods from Code-signatories and be rejected in favour of the latter type goods when in reality they are less expensive and ought to have won the contract. This is not only a clear case of trade-diversion but also an example of bureaucratic folly, where a policy originally designed to promote domestic industry ends up promoting one foreign industry over another at the expense of domestic taxpayers.

The same result may occur in the employment of selective tendering procedures under the GPA. Under such procedures, which are fully permitted under the Agreement, procuring entities invite only a limited number of suppliers to submit a tender.[95] The GPA provides:[96]

[90] See US Federal Acquisition Regulation, para. 25.105. If the domestic offer is from a small business concern or any labour surplus area concern, the applicable differential is 12%.

[91] See 19 USC 2512(a)(1): "in order to encourage additional countries to become Parties to the Agreement and to provide reciprocal competitive government procurement opportunities to United States products and suppliers".

[92] Deputy Minister of Supply and Services Directive 637 ("Canadian Content Premium Policy") (10/02/89). On Canada's policies in this field, see Arie Reich, *supra* note 39, at 199–205.

[93] See *ibid.*, Annex A–1.

[94] Supply Policy Manual, Directive 3004 ("GATT Agreement on Government Procurement"), 30 Dec. 1988.

[95] See Art. VII:3(b) of the GPA, *supra* note 2.

[96] *Ibid.*, Art. X:1.

> "To ensure optimum effective international competition under selective tendering procedures, entities shall, for each intended procurement, invite tenders from the maximum number of *domestic suppliers and suppliers from other Parties*, consistent with the efficient operation of the procurement system" (emphasis added).

The entities are therefore only required to invite tenders from domestic or GPA suppliers but are free to ignore the existence of non-GPA suppliers. Even though a government may have no official policy of barring countries that have not joined the GPA, government entities will henceforth be free effectively to shut out suppliers and products of such countries from their contract opportunities.

(e) Is Trade Discrimination in Government Procurement Permitted under GATT?

The examples of trade discrimination given above all result from the Parties' implementation of the GPA under their respective legal systems. The question arises, however, what the position of public international law is in relation to such discrimination. *A priori*, there are three possibilities:

(1) The discrimination is prohibited by the GPA or the GATT;
(2) It is permitted by them;
(3) It is required under the GPA.

I have already noted earlier that the GPA, as a plurilateral agreement, grants rights exclusively to its own Parties. Its national treatment obligation applies only to products, services and suppliers of GPA Parties and likewise its MFN obligation only prohibits discrimination as between such Parties.[97] As for the GATT, its national treatment provision includes an express exception, which reads as follows:[98]

> "The provisions of this Article shall not apply to laws, regulations or requirements governing the procurement by governmental agencies of products purchased for governmental purposes and not with a view to commercial resale or with a view to use in the production of goods for commercial sale."

Consequently, GPA Parties, as well as all other WTO Members, are free to give preference to domestic products over products originating in non-GPA countries in the context of procurements by governmental agencies for governmental purposes.

But what about giving preference to one WTO member over another? The exception quoted above only applies to "the provisions of this Article", i.e. Article III. The general MFN obligation is found in Article I of GATT, which does not include a similar exception. Article I provides that "any advantage,

[97] See *ibid.*, Art. III:1.
[98] Art. III:8(a) of the GATT, *supra* note 55.

favour, privilege or immunity granted by any contracting party to any product originating in . . . any other country, shall be accorded immediately and unconditionally to the like product originating in . . . all other contracting parties".[99] In defining the application of this obligation, the provision refers expressly to "all matters referred to in paragraphs 2 and 4 of Article III", which in turn includes "all laws, regulations and requirements affecting [the] internal sale, offering for sale, purchase etc." of such products. This wording clearly includes discriminatory government procurement rules, which certainly affect the internal sale, offering for sale and purchase of imported products. If it did not, there would have been no need to include the special provision found in paragraph 8 of the same Article, in order to exclude government procurement rules from the national treatment obligation. The MFN obligation therefore also applies to government procurement policies and, therefore, discrimination between the products of two foreign countries would appear to violate GATT Article I.

Further support for this conclusion is provided by the fact that, unlike GATT, in GATS the exclusion of government procurement policies refers explicitly to both the national treatment and the MFN obligation.[100] Moreover, the exception in Article III:8(a) of GATT could hardly have been considered as applying to the entire agreement since in Article XVII, which applies to State trading enterprises, the text again expressly specifies the exception of government procurement from "the provisions of paragraph 1 of this Article". One could thus clearly infer that the exception only applies to those specific provisions, and not to any other obligation, such as the MFN. In light of these circumstances, the opposite view expressed by Professor Jackson,[101] according to which the MFN obligation does not apply to government purchases, would seem to contradict the clear wording of the Agreement.[102] It would also conflict with the declared object and purpose of GATT of "elimination of discriminatory treatment in international commerce".[103]

Several GATT authorities have already determined[104] that both the General Agreement and all other components of the WTO Agreement should be inter-

[99] *Ibid.*, Art. I:1.

[100] GATS, Art. XIII, refers to both Art. II, which is the MFN commitment, and to Art. XVII, which is the specific National Treatment commitment.

[101] J. H. Jackson, *World Trade and the Law of GATT* (Bobbs-Merrill Co., 1969), 290; J. H. Jackson, W. Davey, and A. Sykes, *Legal Problems of International Relations* (3rd edn., St Paul, West Publ. Co., 1995), 550. See also GATT, *Analytical Index: Guide to GATT Law and Practice* (6th edn., Geneva, GATT, 1994), 174.

[102] Prof. Jackson agrees, however, that "a modest constraint" on purchases by State enterprises emanates from Art. XVII, which requires such enterprises to accord to the trade of the other contracting parties "fair and equitable" treatment (para. 2). He concedes that this may mean MFN treatment. State trading enterprises, such as many of the Category C entities under the GPA, would therefore in any case be bound by the MFN requirements.

[103] See the Preamble to the GATT, *supra* note 1, last sentence.

[104] Most recently in WTO Appellate Body Reports: *Japan—Taxes on Alcoholic Beverages*, WT/DS8/AB/R, 10; and *United States—Standards for Reformulated and Conventional Gasoline*, WT/DS2/9, p. 17.

preted in accordance with the Vienna Convention on the Law of Treaties,[105] which has attained the status of customary and general international law.[106] Thus, employing the Convention's General Rule of Interpretation to interpret GATT "in good faith in accordance with the ordinary meaning to be given to the terms of the treaty in their context and in the light of its object and purpose", the inevitable conclusion is that discrimination between products of different WTO members is prohibited under GATT, whether it is done in the context of government procurement policies or in any other context.

Taken to its extreme, this reading could mean that there is no legal justification at all for a plurilateral procurement code, since all favourable treatment granted to GPA members must automatically be granted to all other GATT members as well. Such an approach would seriously impair the significance of the national treatment exclusion of GATT and would conflict with the Contracting Parties' express intention to allow preferences to domestic products over imported ones in government procurement. A more modest approach would limit the implications of the interpretation presented above to the more blunt cases described in the previous section, where domestic law requires the procuring agency to prefer one foreign bid over another superior one. One must, in other words, distinguish between discrimination between products from different foreign countries and discrimination between a domestic and an imported product. The latter form of trade discrimination is dealt with under Article III of GATT, which requires national treatment, and there we find an express exclusion of government procurement policies. The former type of discrimination, however, is dealt with under Article I of GATT, and it contains no such exclusion.

GPA Parties could therefore claim to be justified in putting only products from GPA Parties, and not products from other GATT Parties, on an equal footing with their own domestic products when competing with the latter. Non-GPA parties could not challenge the fact that domestic products are preferred over their own since they do not grant reciprocal national treatment to other countries' products. Put differently, they cannot criticise other Parties' reliance on the national treatment exception when they rely on it themselves. However, where no domestic products are involved and the competition is between two foreign products, they should be entitled to equal opportunities.

Further support for this position can be found in a decision by the GATT Contracting Parties at the end of the Tokyo Round with regard to the plurilateral codes, including the Procurement Code, concluded in that round. The decision noted "that existing rights and benefits under the GATT of contracting parties not being parties to these Agreements, including those derived

[105] Vienna Convention on the Law of Treaties, signed 23 May 1969, 1155 UNTS 331; 8 ILM 679.

[106] *Supra*, note 52.

from Article I, are not affected by these Agreements".[107] This clearly suggests that while non-parties to the codes may not be entitled to claim new rights under these Agreements, they should nevertheless not be harmed in relation to their existing position prior to the Code. A situation where they are barred from any procurement opportunities following the conclusion of the Code, or where they are rejected in favour of an inferior bid from a GPA Party, would hardly conform to this decision of the Contracting Parties, nor to their intention.

This outcome would also be in line with the general policy of GATT toward non-multilateral arrangements. For instance, in relation to free trade areas and custom unions that are permitted as an exception to the MFA, Article XXIV of GATT requires that tariffs and other regulations of commerce affecting non-members of the arrangements "shall be no higher or more restrictive" than those existing in the members of the arrangements prior to its formation.[108] It would also keep the important non-discrimination principle of the GATT intact while at the same time not impairing the incentive to join the GPA. Since the more important national treatment privilege in government procurement is reserved only to GPA Parties, governments still have most significant gains to reap from joining the GPA. Only National Treatment can ensure real and predictable procurement opportunities for their suppliers, so the prospects for "free riders" under the GPA would be very meagre.

In view of this conclusion, it is doubtful whether a complete exclusion of non-GPA suppliers from participation in government tenders can be justified under GATT, particularly given prior to the inception of the Tokyo Code and the GPA there was no such exclusion.

(f) Is Trade Discrimination in Government Procurement Required under the GPA?

This leads us to the third question posed above: can the GPA be understood as requiring its signatories to practise trade discrimination, in the sense of their having to grant preference to GPA products, services and suppliers over non-GPA products, services and suppliers? The answer to this question depends on the proper interpretation of the national treatment obligation of the GPA. This obligation is found in Article III:1 of the GPA:

> "With respect to all laws, regulations, procedures and practices regarding government procurement covered by this Agreement, each Party shall provide immediately and unconditionally to the products, services and suppliers of other Parties offering products or services of the Parties, treatment no less favourable than:

[107] Action by the Contracting Parties on the Multilateral Trade Negotiations, GATT, BISD 26th Supp., 201 (1980).

[108] GATT, *supra* note 1, Art. XXIV:5.

(a) that accorded to domestic products, services and suppliers; and
(b) that accorded to products, services and suppliers of any other Party."

A literal reading of this obligation would appear to require that any preference given to national products over products from non-GPA countries must also be extended to imports from GPA members. For example, if for a certain US contract subject to the GPA there are only two bids, a low-price bid from Australia, which is not a Party to the GPA, and a slightly higher bid from the EC (a GPA Party), the EC supplier would be entitled to demand "treatment no less favourable" than that which would have been accorded to US goods, i.e. application of the 6 per cent price preferential. If this reading is correct, the US government agency conducting the procurement would be required under the GPA to purchase the more expensive EC products.[109]

Such an interpretation of the GPA's national treatment obligation must be rejected for several reasons. First of all, it would bring the GPA into direct conflict with the GATT's prohibition on trade discrimination, as explained in the previous section. It would create a head-on collision between the two agreements, since the GPA would command what the GATT prohibits. A GPA Party's fulfillment of its obligations toward one GPA Party would amount to a violation of its obligations toward another GATT Party.

Secondly, such an interpretation of the GPA's national treatment obligation would be in conflict with the Vienna Convention's rule of interpretation, which requires us to interpret a treaty in its "context" and "in the light of its object and purpose".[110] The context of the GPA is one of liberalisation of government procurement policies[111] and its declared objective is that "laws, regulations, procedures and practices regarding government procurement . . . should not discriminate among foreign products or services or among foreign suppliers".[112] The GPA was created in order to eliminate distortions to international trade and not to create new ones. It would be very unreasonable to assume that the GPA requires signatories to duplicate existing domestic distortions to the international level. The national treatment obligation must therefore be construed solely as requiring signatories to eliminate policies which discriminate against foreign suppliers or products (who are GPA members) in relation to domestic suppliers, with the intention of putting them all on an equal footing and ensuring that procurements are conducted only on the basis of commercial consideration. It cannot be understood as forcing governments to prefer GPA bids over non-GPA bids.

Finally, the literal interpretation suggested above is not in line with the traditional understanding of the national treatment concept, as reflected in

[109] It should again be stressed that the current discussion is based on the GPA and the obligations originating from it. The fact that US domestic law may require the procuring entity, in certain cases, to prefer the more expensive EC bid is a different issue that has been discussed above in para. (d).

[110] Art. 31:1 of the Vienna Convention on the Law of Treaties, *supra* note 105.

[111] See the Preamble to the GPA, first sentence.

[112] *Ibid.*, second sentence.

particular in Panel rulings on GATT's Article III. In the Panel Report on *Italian Discrimination against Imported Agricultural Machinery*,[113] it was held that the national treatment obligation of GATT was intended to prevent any adverse modification of "the conditions of competition *between the domestic and imported products* on the internal market".[114] "Toward this end, Article III obliges members of the WTO to provide equality of competitive conditions for imported products in relation to domestic products."[115] Applied to the GPA, this would mean that as long as equal conditions of competition are maintained between GPA imports and domestic goods, the national treatment obligation is met, even if GPA imports are not given advantages *vis-à-vis* other imports which domestic goods would have had.

It has also been held by GATT Panels that the purpose of the national treatment obligation "is to ensure that internal measures not be applied to imported or domestic products so as to afford protection to domestic production".[116] One could therefore persuasively argue that if its purpose is to ensure that no protection is afforded to domestic production, then, *a fortiori*, it should ensure that no such protection is afforded to any imports.

(g) The Case of the Mixed Tender: Domestic v. GPA v. GATT

Armed with the conclusions reached in the previous sections regarding the mutual relationships between the various parties, we can now try to grapple with a more complex problem involving three bids falling into different categories. Such problems are likely to occur in procurements by GPA Parties who apply preference policies in favour of their domestic products in relation to non-GPA products, as most parties appear to do. The type of solution adopted to the problem is likely to affect the extent of the trade diversion that will be caused by the GPA.

To illustrate the problem, assume that in a tender of an Israeli government agency for a contract subject to the GPA, three bids, identical in quality and in all other aspects, are received:

Israeli supplier:	$210,000
US supplier:	$205,000
Australian supplier:	$200,000

Note that the USA is a GPA Party while Australia is not. Israeli government tender regulations require that preference be given to domestic products over

[113] BISD 7th Supp., 60 (1959).
[114] *Ibid.*, para. 12 (emphasis added).
[115] *United States—Taxes on Petroleum and Certain Imported Substances*, BISD 34th Supp., 135, in para. 5.1.9. cited in the Appellate Body decision: *Japan—Taxes on Alcoholic Beverages*, *supra* note 104, at p. 16.
[116] *United States—Section 337 of the Tariff Act of 1930*, BISD 36th Suppl., 345, para. 5.10.

imports up to a price margin of 15 per cent.[117] This requirement does not apply *vis-à-vis* imports originating from GPA Parties where the procurement is covered by the GPA.

In this example the Australian bid is the superior bid, assuming that the quality of all offered products is identical. From an efficiency standpoint, the contract ought to be awarded to the Australian producer, who is the most efficient, and doing so will also save Israeli taxpayers money. Any other award would divert trade from its most efficient source to a less efficient source and impose a deadweight social loss. However, approaching the problem from a rule-based perspective, it would seem that the outcome depends on the order in which we evaluate one bid against the others.

If we first pit the Israeli bid against the Australian bid, the Israeli bid takes precedence as a result of the domestic price preference. If next we compare the Israeli and US bids, the US bid must win since it is lower and no price preference may be applied. Result: the *US bid* wins the contract. If, however, we first pit the US bid against the Australian bid, the Australian bid wins, given my earlier conclusion that the GPA does not require a GPA bid to be preferred over a superior non-GPA bid. We next compare the Australian and Israeli bids and must then give preference to the domestic product over the Australian. Result: the *Israeli bid* wins the contract. Finally, if we first pit the Israeli bid against the US bid the US bid wins, since it is lower. But when pitted against the Australian bid, the US bid loses. Result: the *Australian bid* wins the contract. Three approaches and three different results!

How, then, do we resolve this conundrum? A protectionist approach would claim that the domestic bid should win since in any case the US bid has no right to win the contract. From the standpoint of international law, we have already established that the GATT prohibits preferring of the US bid over the Australian, and that the GPA also does not require such a preference. From the domestic law perspective, the US bid is not the lowest one, so there is no reason to let it win. When left with the domestic and Australian bids the answer is clear: the domestic bid must win under the existing domestic preference policy.

However, I would argue strongly against such an approach. The only reason why the domestic bid has been chosen over the lower US bid is because of a domestic preference policy, even if the causation is indirect. The fact that there is a lower bid from a non-GPA party cannot be used as an excuse to bypass the US bid and to award the contract to an inferior domestic bid. That in itself would constitute a violation of the national treatment obligation. It is a manifestation of protectionism, which is prohibited under the GPA. If my earlier conclusion is correct, according to which the central thrust of the GPA is to liberalise trade in the public sector and to ensure that awards of procurement contracts subject to the Agreement are conducted solely on the basis

[117] The Public Tenders Regulations (Preference for Domestic Products and Obligation of Industrial Cooperation), 5755–1994.

of commercial considerations, then it must mean that in the case at hand domestic preference policies may not be applied in any way to the detriment of the GPA bidder. The contract must therefore be awarded to the lowest bidder, the Australian one.

This is my conclusion in terms of international law. Whether it is actually implemented in national law depends of course on the legal system of each GPA Party.

In Israel, the requirement to grant domestic preference is found in regulations[118] issued under the Public Tenders Law, 5752–1992.[119] However, section 5A(b) of the Law provides that regulations issued pursuant to the Law shall apply only to the extent that they do not conflict with any obligation of the State of Israel under an international treaty. It is therefore clear, and has been established judicially,[120] that when a domestic product competes with a GPA product for a government contract, the domestic preference requirement does not apply and the contract will be awarded on purely commercial criteria. In my opinion, the same rule should apply when there is a non-GPA as well as a GPA bidder participating. The reasoning is as follows. Israeli law, in contrast to US law,[121] does not contain any requirement to exclude non-GPA suppliers from participation in tenders. As previously argued, awarding the contract to the Israeli supplier when a superior GPA bid exists, amounts to a violation of the national treatment obligation of the GPA. To apply the preference regulations would therefore be in conflict with the GPA. As a result, the regulations do not apply and we are required to fall back on the basic rule of the Law that contracts shall be awarded by means of tenders "which gives *every person* an equal opportunity to participate".[122] In other words, the contract must be awarded to the most advantageous bid which, in our example, is the Australian one.

However, this will only be the rule in States which do not bar non-GPA suppliers from participating in government tenders.[123] Our conclusion, then, only reiterates the problematic nature of such exclusions, both from an economic and international law standpoint.[124]

[118] Ibid.

[119] SH 1992, 114. Act that requires all Israeli government agencies and public entities to conduct their procurements by means of public tenders and that sets out the rules governing such tenders.

[120] HP 417/96 (Tel-Aviv District Court) *Heiman Systems GmbH v. The State of Israel (Customs Administration)*, not yet published.

[121] See *supra* note 000, and accompanying text.

[122] S. 2 of the Public Tenders Law, 5752–1992.

[123] Such as the USA, for example. See *supra* note 000, and accompanying text.

[124] See *supra*, para. (f).

IV. CONCLUSION

In this paper, I have tried to show the complex problems in connection with plurilateralism and strict reciprocity, as reflected in the new Government Procurement Agreement, one of the few plurilateral agreements left after the Uruguay Round. What we have here is a clash between the principle of non-discriminatory multilateralism, on the one hand, and the quest for reciprocity, the so-called "fair trade" approach, on the other. In this clash, the quest for reciprocity—in my view an exaggerated, almost obsessive quest—has clearly had an upper hand and has resulted in a myriad of derogations from the Agreement's application. Instead of being a multilateral agreement in the traditional sense, the GPA has to a large extent turned into a set of bilateral agreements, in particular in Category B and C procurements. The Agreement currently harbours various types of trade discrimination, both between Parties and non-Parties to the GPA as well as between GPA-Parties and each other. This has many negative implications, from both a political and economic point of view, and has caused serious problems for the GPA regime. It was in protest against this development that Hong Kong, one of the founding members of the Procurement Code which had participated actively in the negotiations leading up to the new code, eventually refused to sign it. This was because it felt that the GPA had departed too far from the traditional GATT standard of non-discrimination.[125]

I have tried to show in this paper how some of the potential trade diversion likely to be caused by the GPA can be prevented if the GATT and the GPA are properly interpreted and enforced. The blunt cases of trade discrimination between Parties and non-Parties to the GPA ought to be neither required nor permitted under international or national law. In particular, the complete exclusion of non-Party suppliers, such as implemented by the US Government, would appear to be in clear conflict with GATT principles of non-discrimination. On the other hand, the claim that such harsh measures are necessary in order to encourage countries to join the GPA has hardly proven itself during the fifteen years since the GPA's adoption.[126] It has, however, caused a significant amount of trade diversion and increased expenditures of US tax-dollars.

Since a large part of the problems discussed here results from the negotiation approach taken by the Parties to the GPA, one must ask oneself whether there is any superior alternative to this approach. It has been claimed that the insistence on reciprocity was instrumental in helping to expand the GPA

[125] Information derived from talks with WTO officials. Hong Kong joined the GPA again in 1997. See supra note 54.

[126] The exclusion was introduced in the implementation of the Tokyo Code in 1979. Nevertheless, the new GPA has not enjoyed a much higher membership than the Tokyo Code. While two Parties seceded—Singapore and Hong Kong—only Korea and Aruba has joined (except for countries joining as a result of their accession to the European Communities). Israel joined the Tokyo Code in 1983.

beyond a simple agreement at Category A level to a much more far-reaching agreement that extends to lower levels of government and several major utilities sectors.[127] According to this opinion, if MFN treatment had been the basis for the negotiations, the offers would have been scaled down to the level of the lowest common denominator in order to achieve a balance in coverage.[128] It seems to me, however, that this would only have occurred if coverage negotiations had started from the premise of entity-for-entity bargaining. Under such conditions, Parties are naturally inclined to withhold as many entities as possible, hoping to get a "free ride" as a result of other Parties' bilateral bargains.[129]

If, on the other hand, negotiations first centre on defining a common objective, stated in general principled terms, of the coverage expansion to be achieved, and only then move on to translate the objective into lists of entities and services, the negotiators would be much more likely to agree on a broad coverage without compromising the MFN principle.[130] The common objective could be defined, for instance, in terms of value of procurement opportunities (calculated by an agreed methodology) in relation to the size of each Party's economy but possibly also subject to some qualitative criteria. An agreed mechanism for determining whether each Party's subsequent coverage offer meets the common objective should also be established. The Parties could for that purpose hire the services of an independent consultant, as was done toward the end of the bilateral negotiations between the EC and the USA, in order to assess the value of their respective offers under the GPA.[131] It would then be incumbent upon each Party to submit a list of entities and services meeting the agreed requirements as a condition for membership in the new Agreement. Just as the whole WTO package was defined as a "single undertaking" with a uniform number of components, so ought the GPA have been presented with an agreed uniform definition of coverage to be met by anyone wishing to join the GPA. The move to such an approach would also

[127] De Graaf and King, *supra* note 32, 446.

[128] *Ibid.*, n. 49.

[129] It appears indeed from the account of de Graaf and King, *supra* note 32, 442–3, that from the outset the GPA negotiations centered on the entities which each Party wanted the other Party to include, while relentlessly withholding its own entities from possible inclusion. The same applies to the Parties' inability to reach satisfactory results in relation to services: "The reciprocity rule was also applied to service contracts in all categories, because it was impossible to agree on any meaningful list of common services." (*ibid.*, 447). Instead of trying to define a list of common services to be included, the negotiators ought to have defined the principles of the common objective, which must be fulfilled by each Party as a condition for membership, and the mechanism to establish whether the condition has been met. Then it would be up to each Party to make sure that its coverage offer meets these requirements.

[130] The importance of principled negotiations using objective criteria has been well expounded by the Harvard Negotiation Project. See Roger Fisher and William Ury, *Getting to Yes: Negotiating Agreements Without Giving In* (Boston, Mass., Houghton Mifflin, 1981).

[131] See *Study of Public Procurement Opportunities, European Union, Government of the US*, Prepared at the request of the European Union and the USA, 22 Mar. 1994. See also de Graaf and King, *supra* note 32, p. 445, and 448–9.

reflect the transition from product-by-product tariff negotiations, employed in the first five negotiation rounds under GATT, to agreed linear cuts[132] employed in the subsequent Kennedy, Tokyo and Uruguay Rounds.[133] This common objective approach has proven itself to achieve more extensive tariff cuts than the previous method.[134]

To be sure, the notion of reciprocity is not unique to public procurement agreements; it has always featured in GATT agreements. Nevertheless the parties have usually managed to reconcile it with multilateralism. There is no reason to believe that the same cannot be done within the GPA as well.

[132] Under this approach the Parties first negotiate toward an agreed formula of across-the-board tariff cuts. For instance, in the Kennedy Round a 50% reduction of all tariffs on non-primary products was agreed. Only then could Parties request specific exceptions, based on uniform agreed criteria. See Jackson, *supra* note 78, 121.

[133] Michael J. Trebilcock and Robert Howse, *The Regulation of International Trade* (London, Routledge, 1995), 79.

[134] *Ibid.*

PART V

The Challenges of Adapting to Market Economies

16

The Development of Securities Regulation in Emerging African Capital Markets

S. K. DATE-BAH*

I. INTRODUCTION

In the past decade, there has been an increasing trend towards the liberalisation of markets in Africa and the promotion of market-friendly policies. The Bretton Woods institutions and the donor community have encouraged so-called "structural adjustment" in which the promotion of liberalised markets and the development of the private sector, occupy a central position. The development of capital markets in Africa has been part of this trend in the last decade. A decade ago, there were only four African stock exchanges: in Kenya, Nigeria, South Africa and Zimbabwe. Now there are at least nine stock exchanges that trade regularly: Botswana, Côte d'Ivoire, Ghana, Mauritius and Namibia, besides the four already referred to. Three more African exchanges, Sudan, Swaziland and Zambia, are making progress towards regular trading. Malawi enacted a Capital Market Act in 1990. It has subsequently licensed a stockbroker to offer brokerage services for securities in Malawi and also established a Stock Exchange Committee to oversee the emergence of securities trading in Malawi. However, as at the end of 1995, there were still no listed companies in Malawi. Tanzania (in 1994) and Uganda (in 1996) have enacted regulatory legislation for stock exchanges and securities and the authorities there have taken steps towards the establishment of stock exchanges in these two jurisdictions.

These newly-emerging African capital markets have had to devise a regulatory regime for securities and stock exchanges from scratch. In the Commonwealth jurisdictions, some of which will be the focus of this paper, the starting point has usually been the existing companies' legislation. This has usually been insufficient

* LL.B (Univ. of Ghana), LL.M (Yale), Ph.D (London). Special Adviser (Legal), Economic and Legal Advisory Services Division, Commonwealth Secretariat, London. The views expressed in this paper are the personal views of its author and are not necessarily the views of the Commonwealth Secretariat. The author thanks Mr Makbul Rahim, Chief Project Officer (Legal) of the Commonwealth Secretariat, for his constructive comments on this paper.

to provide a framework for orderly securities trading. Accordingly, supplemental legislation has had to be formulated. The Economic and Legal Advisory Services Division of the Commonwealth Secretariat has assisted Ghana, Tanzania and Uganda to enact modern regulatory legislation to buttress the process of capital market development in these jurisdictions. As an illustration of the development of law in response to changing market conditions, the development of the law on securities regulation in these jurisdictions will be discussed here and compared with the systems of regulation in Botswana and Zambia, which were developed without assistance from the Commonwealth Secretariat.

II. GHANA

As far back as 1968, the Government of Ghana initiated steps directed at the establishment of a stock exchange in Ghana. It commissioned an external consultant's report that recommended the establishment of a stock exchange over a period of two years. As a result, the Stock Exchange Act 1971 was enacted. In concert with the Companies Code 1963, it was intended to provide a framework for the establishment of a stock exchange. The civilian government which took this initiative was however overthrown in a *coup d'état* in 1972. The military government that succeeded it showed no interest in pursuing the initiative. The ultimate establishment of a stock exchange in Ghana resulted from a new initiative taken in 1989 by the Secretary for Finance and Economic Planning of the Provisional National Defence Council (another military government), who in February 1989 appointed a National Committee on the Stock Exchange Project.

It was this Committee that invited the Commonwealth Secretariat to assist it in developing listing rules and membership rules for the proposed exchange and to prepare draft regulatory legislation that was more comprehensive than the then existing Stock Exchange Act 1971. The Commonwealth Secretariat proposed for the consideration of the Ghanaian authorities a draft Securities Industry Law based ultimately on the Securities Industry Act 1980 of the Commonwealth of Australia, which had also been adopted by the individual Australian States. This Australian precedent was also that which had been followed in Malaysia and Singapore.

This legislative model, which was borrowed and adapted to the Ghanaian context, involved a scheme of investor protection through a licensing regime. The Australian scheme seems to have been a development of the idea embodied in the Prevention of Fraud (Investment) Act 1939 of the United Kingdom, later repealed and re-enacted by an Act of 1958 and finally repealed by the Financial Services Act 1986. The essence of this idea was the prevention of dealings in securities except by persons licensed to deal in them or expressly made exempt from the requirement of a licence. This was the idea that was pressed into use in the Ghanaian statute as well. No person is to carry on the business of dealing in securities unless he holds a dealer's licence or is an exempted dealer (a term embracing primarily financial institutions already regulated by separate legislation).

In addition to the licensing regime, the legislative scheme proposed for Ghana included the establishment of a freestanding regulatory body, the Securities Regulatory Commission, and the retention of existing provisions on the registration of prospectuses which could be said to represent a kind of halfway house between UK law and US law. The UK law provides for prospectuses relating to unlisted securities to be submitted for registration to the Registrar of Companies,[1] while prospectuses relating to securities to be admitted to dealings on an approved stock exchange are to be submitted for approval by the exchange and then delivered to the Registrar of Companies for registration.[2] The US law relating to registration statements under the Securities Act 1933 makes it unlawful for any issuer, underwriter or dealer to use the mails or any means of interstate commerce to sell securities to any person, unless a registration statement has been filed and is in effect in relation to such securities and he has delivered a specified prospectus. The US Securities and Exchange Commission has the power to examine the statement and to issue a "stop order" to prevent its effectiveness if the SEC decides after a hearing that the statement is materially deficient. In practice, one understands that the SEC in most cases exercises its regulatory authority over registration statements through issuing letters of comment which issuers take into account in preparing amendments to their registration statement. The contrast with UK law and practice is the active and interventionist role of the SEC in relation to ensuring that the registration statement is accurate and not misleading. At the level of the States in the USA, securities administrators carry out a similar interventionist role. UK companies law does not give an activist examining role to the Registrar of Companies in respect of prospectuses relating to unlisted securities (although there are penal and civil sanctions for misleading prospectuses). The Registrar merely inspects the prospectus to see that it is complete and regular on its face. However, the stock exchange will scrutinise a prospectus relating to listed securities before approving it.

In Ghana, in contrast, under section 279 of the Companies Code 1963, provision is made for the active scrutiny of prospectuses in all cases. If the prospectus relates to securities to be dealt in on an approved stock exchange, the task of scrutiny and approval is given to the exchange which, upon approving the prospectus, will issue a certificate that the prospectus has been scrutinised by it and that the exchange's requirements relating to the contents of the prospectus have been satisfied. The Registrar of Companies, upon receipt of such a certificate, is to register the prospectus within forty-eight hours of the delivery of the prospectus to him, unless it is incomplete or irregular on its face or unless, prior to registration, any consent of an expert required under the Code has been withdrawn. Secondly, if the prospectus

[1] See s. 160 of the Financial Services Act 1986.

[2] See s. 159 of the Financial Services Act 1986.

relates to an invitation in respect of securities to be made through an "exempted dealer" (within the meaning of the Companies Code), the exempted dealer is to issue a certificate that he accepts personal responsibility for the contents of the prospectus and that it complies in all respects with the provisions of the Companies Code. An "exempted dealer" under the Code is any person, firm or body corporate carrying on business in Ghana declared by an order of the Minister published in the *Gazette* to be an exempted dealer for the purposes of the Code.

Professor Gower of the United Kingdom, who prepared the draft Bill which eventually became the Code, expressed the view that the Minister should exercise the power to declare exempted dealers sparingly and that he expected only the banks and government corporations to be granted the privilege of being exempted dealers.

The Registrar, upon receipt of an exempted dealers's certificate, is required to register the prospectus within forty-eight hours of its delivery to him, unless it is incomplete or irregular on its face or unless, prior to registration, any consent of an expert required by the Code has been withdrawn.

Finally, in all other invitations to the public in relation to securities which do not involve an approved stock exchange or an exempt dealer, the Registrar is given power to act like a Securities Administrator of a State in the USA and is required to subject the prospectus to careful scrutiny. The Code gives him twenty-one days within which to carry out this scrutiny unless he decides to abridge the period. If, in his opinion, the prospectus does not comply with the provisions of the Companies Code or contains any untrue statement or omits to state any material fact or is otherwise incomplete or misleading, he is obliged to refuse to register the prospectus until it has been amended to his satisfaction.

This was the Ghanaian law that was in place before the formulation of any specific legislation on securities. With the creation of the Securities Regulatory Commission ("SRC") under the Securities Industry Law 1992, which is the regulatory statute eventually enacted by the Ghanaian Government on the advice of the Commonwealth Secretariat, it was considered prudent that the Registrar of Companies be enabled to seek the assistance of the SRC in his task of scrutiny, particularly as many observers believed that the track record of the Registrar (and the institutional capacity of his department) in the scrutiny of prospectuses were not impressive. Accordingly, the Securities Industry Law 1992 provides[3] that, in cases not involving an approved stock exchange or an exempt dealer, the Registrar may, for the purpose of reaching an opinion on whether a prospectus does not comply with the provisions of the Companies Code; contains any untrue statement; omits to state any material fact; or is otherwise incomplete or misleading, refer the prospectus to the SRC for its opinion. This reference procedure thus enables the SRC to play a

[3] See s. 145(1).

role in regulating the disclosure of information in connection with the issue of securities over the counter.

Moreover, the licensing regime administered by the SRC under the Securities Industry Law gives the SRC regulatory control over the secondary market in securities over the counter through the monitoring and enforcement of the obligations placed on securities market intermediaries by the Law and rules made under the Law. The listed securities market is, of course, also under the regulatory authority of the SRC, but with the GSE allowed a large measure of self-regulation.

The Securities Industry Law facilitates the SRC's general regulatory role by imposing obligations on stock exchanges and securities market intermediaries. The monitoring and sanctioning of the observance of these obligations thus becomes one of the central functions of the SRC. Indeed the bulk of the provisions of the Securities Industry Law consists of these obligations.

The full functions of the SRC are spelt out in the Law as follows:

"(a) to advise the Secretary [i.e.Minister] on all matters relating to the securities industry;
(b) to maintain surveillance over activities in securities to ensure orderly, fair and equitable dealings in securities;
(c) to register, license, authorise or regulate, in accordance with this Law or any regulations made under it, stock exchanges, investment advisers, unit trust schemes, mutual funds, securities dealers and their agents and to control and supervise their activities with a view to maintaining proper standards of conduct and acceptable practices in the securities business;
(d) to formulate principles for the guidance of the industry;
(e) to monitor the solvency of licence-holders and take measures to protect the interest of customers where the solvency of any such licence holder is in doubt;
(f) to protect the integrity of the securities market against any abuses arising from the practice of insider trading;
(g) to adopt measures to minimise and supervise any conflict of interests that may arise for dealers;
(h) to review, approve and regulate takeovers, mergers, acquisitions and all forms of business combinations, in accordance with any Law or Code of Practice requiring it to do so;
(i) to create the necessary atmosphere for the orderly growth and development of the capital market;
(j) to perform the function referred to in section 279(1) of the Companies Code 1963;
(k) to undertake such other activities as are necessary or expedient for giving full effect to the provisions of this Law; and
(l) to perform other functions specified under this Law".

It may be useful to consider these functions of the SRC in greater detail, since an examination of the functions of the regulator of the Ghanaian securities market may give a general indication of what governments in emerging African capital markets expect of their regulatory systems for securities trading.

(a) Advice to Minister on the Securities Industry

Where a securities industry is at an early stage in its development, it is useful to have a focal point for strategic thinking on the industry and for promotion of the industry. While in a developed market the securities regulator may concentrate on its regulatory role, in an emerging market the regulator will have to play a promotional role as well as a problem-solving role for the securities industry. It is in this connection that the SRC's formal statutory function of advising the Minister assumes importance. The SRC can generate ideas on the development of the capital market and communicate these ideas to the Minister.

(b) Surveillance over Activities in Securities to Ensure Orderly, Fair and Equitable Dealings in Securities

Under this rubric comes the general regulatory function of the SRC which has to be exercised alongside the promotional role mentioned above. Indeed, regulation is an essential element in the promotion drive. For, as is well known, the securities industry is sustained by confidence: the confidence of investors that their capital when invested in securities will not be exposed to dishonest and unfair practices. Regulation should therefore secure protection from fraud, dishonesty and unfair practices. Regulation should also ensure that market operations in securities measure up to the rules of the market place. Protecting the integrity of the markets is therefore another objective of regulation independent of, but supplementary to, the need to protect from dishonesty and unfair practices (which might be considered the ethical objective of regulation). The ethical objective, of course, has an impact on the integrity of the markets (which might be considered the economic objective) since fraud and dishonesty can subvert the proper interplay of market forces. As William O. Douglas, then Chairman of the New York Stock Exchange, observed in a press statement in 1937:[4]

> "I have always regarded the exchanges as the scales upon which that great national resource, invested capital, is weighed and evaluated. Scales of such importance must be tamper-proof, with no concealed springs—and there must be no laying on of hands. Such an important instrument in our economic welfare must be surrounded by adequate safeguards".

Maintaining market surveillance in order to achieve these ethical and economic objectives of regulation will entail exercising some of the other more specific functions of regulation which are listed separately in the Securities Industry Law as functions for the SRC. These include:

[4] Quoted in L. Loss, *Fundamentals of Securities Regulation* (2nd edn., Boston, Mass., 1988) at 616.

(i) Registration, Licensing, or Authorisation of, Stock Exchanges, Investment Advisers, Unit Trust Schemes, Mutual Funds, Securities Dealers and their Agents and the Control and Supervision of their Activities with a View to Maintaining Proper Standards of Conduct and Acceptable Practices in the Securities Business

As already discussed above, this licensing control is at the heart of the regulatory regime introduced into Ghana. The function of the SRC in relation to such licensing control and the supervision of licensees to ensure their compliance with their obligations is one of the core responsibilities of the SRC.

(ii) Formulation of Principles for the Guidance of the Industry

Formulation of principles embodied in a code of practice or in subsidiary legislation is one of the techniques available to the SRC in exercising its strategic role of guiding the orderly development of the securities market in Ghana.

(iii) Monitoring the Solvency of Licence-holders and Taking Measures to Protect the Interest of Customers where the Solvency of any Licence-holder is in Doubt

This is a specific function which could be said to be subsumed under (c) above, but which has been separated out for emphasis.

(iv) Protection of the Integrity of the Securities Market Against any Abuses Arising from the Practice of Insider Trading

At the start of the development of a securities market, there is a policy choice whether insider trading should be regulated from the beginning or whether it should be introduced at a later stage. The Ghanaian authorities decided to institute right from the beginning a fair and transparent trading framework, and therefore opted for the regulation of insider trading immediately.

(v) Adoption of Measures to Minimise and Supervise any Conflict of Interests that may Arise for Dealers

This again is a specific function which is subsumed under (b) but which presumably has been given individual mention for emphasis.

(vi) The Review, Approval and Regulation of Takeovers, Mergers, Acquisitions and All Forms of Business Combinations, in Accordance with any Law or Code of Practice Requiring it to do so

Under this head, the function intended for the SRC is to exercise regulatory authority to foster investor protection by ensuring that shareholders in target companies in takeover transactions are treated fairly and equally. There is a second level of regulatory need in this area which is not traditionally addressed by the regulator of the securities market. This is the need for regulatory control to ensure that mergers and acquisitions activities do not result in anti-competitive effects or other effects against the public interest. Such regulatory authority over merger control policy is usually vested in a ministry responsible for trade, industry or finance or a freestanding regulatory body to which such authority is delegated.

In Ghana, the action taken on mergers and acquisitions in relation to the securities industry has been the incorporation of rules on takeover offers and on substantial acquisition of shares in the Listing Rules of the Ghana Stock Exchange. It is the supervision of the application of these rules by the Council of the Stock Exchange which would thus be the function of the SRC.

(vii) Creation of the Necessary Atmosphere for the Orderly Growth and Development of the Capital Market

It could be said that all the other functions of the SRC already discussed build up to this broad function. The fulfilment of the earlier functions will contribute to the attainment of this general function.

This overview of the functions ascribed to the SRC in the Ghanaian legislation gives some indication of the aspiration of African governments in relation to the development of their capital markets. These functions are in broad terms not dissimilar to the functions exercised by regulators on other continents.

Three main themes characterise these functions: investor protection; the maintenance of orderly markets; and development of the capital market. The difference between the regulation of a developed market and an emerging market is probably reflected in the difference in emphasis of these themes. In an emerging market, one would expect greater emphasis to be placed on active promotion and development of the market. An analysis of these functions of the regulators must, however, also take account of the role of government generally in capital market development. Beyond the specific promotional and regulatory roles of the statutory apex industry agencies established in several African jurisdictions in recent years, there is the role that governments themselves must play in developing capital markets.

This includes a coherent policy on private-sector development and the government's commitment to the development of a market economy; the provision of macro-economic stability by the government through appropriate fiscal, monetary, trade and exchange-rate policies; and an adequate regulatory framework for the whole financial system within which is contained the securities market. For instance, a dynamic programme on privatisation will often be a necessary complement to efforts to develop a capital market in an economy where the principal means of production are in State hands. Thus the divestiture by the Government of Ghana of part of its majority shareholding in the Ghanaian company of Ashanti Goldfields Ltd. through the Ghana and London Stock Exchanges exponentially boosted the market capitalisation of the Ghana Stock Exchange and attracted international attention to the Ghana Stock Exchange. The privatisation programme of the Government of Ghana has played a significant role in the development of the capital market in Ghana. The total market capitalisation of the GSE at the end of 1995 was about 2,400 billion cedis or about US $2.4 billion. There were nineteen listed companies as at the end of 1995.

Below the apex regulation by the SRC, the Ghanaian legislative scheme permits a large measure of self-regulation by an approved stock exchange. The Ghana Stock Exchange ("GSE") was incorporated as a private company limited by guarantee under the Companies Code in July 1989. This was before the enactment of the new Securities Industry Law. Accordingly, it was under the Stock Exchange Act 1971 that it was given recognition as an authorised stock exchange in October 1990. In November 1991, the Council of the GSE, exercising an enabling power under the Stock Exchange Act, promulgated as subsidiary legislation, with the approval of the Secretary responsible for Finance (i.e. the Finance Minister), Listing Regulations and Membership Regulations, the initial drafts of both of which had been prepared by the Commonwealth Secretariat. The Council also adopted trading and settlement rules that enabled trading to commence. Upon the coming into force of the Securities Industry Law, the GSE's existing rules were saved pursuant to provisions in the Law. In April 1994, the GSE was converted into a public company limited by guarantee.

In fact, the main actor in promoting capital market development in Ghana has been the GSE, rather than the SRC. The Council of the GSE has won itself respect from the public and the Government and the regulation of the market has largely been left to it. Indeed, the SRC, which is a collegiate body, has still not been fully constituted. However, provision was made for this contingency in the Securities Industry Law under which,[5] until the SRC commences operation, the Governor of the Bank of Ghana is authorised to exercise its functions and powers. It is therefore the Governor who has to date exercised the functions of the SRC. He has been supported by staff from the Non-Banking Financial Institutions Department of the Bank of Ghana. Steps are being taken by the Government to enable the SRC to commence operations,

[5] See s. 148.

and it is thought that by the end of 1996 it will have been established. The membership of the Commission is as follows: a Chairman; the Director General and his two deputies; one High Court judge; a representative of the Bank of Ghana; the Registrar-General or his representative; and four other persons, including a lawyer qualified to be appointed a High Court judge, these being persons who by reason of their ability, experience or specialised knowledge of securities and investment matters or of business or professional attainments would, in the opinion of the Government, be capable of making useful contributions to the work of the Commission.

The Ghana case thus illustrates the development of an emergent capital market where the dominant force in the promotion and regulation of the infant market has been the self-regulatory stock market itself. This underlines the fact that systems for regulating securities usually have to rely on co-regulation, with the stock exchange being allowed a fair degree of autonomy and self-regulatory authority. Given the need for a degree both of self-regulation and of regulation by government, the critical issue is how to structure a regime of co-regulation which is balanced and allows efficient market operations without undue government interference, but at the same time enables government intervention to protect the public interest.

An illustration of such regulatory intervention in Ghana occurred when the Governor of the Bank of Ghana, exercising the powers of the SRC, directed the Council of the GSE by public notice in 1995 to terminate the representation of a stockbroking company and a discount house on the Council; to remove the incumbent Council Chairman; and to suspend a named brokerage company from membership of the GSE. The reasons for this directive were that the Council of the GSE had fined, for failing to protect its clients' interest adequately, the stockbroking company the termination of whose representation on the Council the Governor had directed, and the discount house was being investigated by the Bank of Ghana in connection with certain operational irregularities. The Chairman of the Council was also chairman of the discount house under investigation, hence the direction for his removal. Finally, the reason for the suspension of the named brokerage company was that it had failed to deliver securities within the prescribed settlement period. It had also infringed the Governor's directive relating the enforcement of limits on the trading of non-residents in certain securities.

By a notice under the Exchange Control Act, the Governor had made a rule that non-residents could not hold more than 74 per cent of the equity of any listed company. This limit had been breached in transactions brokered by the suspended brokerage company. Trading in the securities of the seven listed companies affected by this breach of the limit of non-resident shareholding was temporarily suspended. The Council of the GSE met the Governor and a procedure agreed on how the size of the non-resident shareholding was to be reduced. It was agreed that Ghanaians were to have the first right to purchase any shares to be sold by non-residents until the holdings of the latter fell below the permitted 74 per cent. This first option of Ghanaians was to be exercisable over three consecutive trading days from the day the shares were first brought to the market. On the fourth trading day, it would be permissible for non-residents to buy the shares. In effect, the breach of limits would then be condoned. Subsequent to this agreement, the suspension of trading in the affected securities was lifted and the Governor issued another public statement, stressing that his earlier directive had been intended to preserve the health as well as the integrity of the market and to send a clear signal that the SRC would not condone any wrong-doing in the market. He expressed his satisfaction with the steps taken by the Council of the GSE to ensure compliance with his directive.[6]

Another regulatory intervention which the Governor has made in his capacity as the interim SRC has been to invite the Commonwealth Secretariat to elaborate detailed draft proposals on a regulatory framework for mutual funds and unit trusts in Ghana. Although Part IV of the Securities Industry Law provides for a skeletal framework for unit trusts and mutual funds in Ghana, its provisions are not detailed enough to provide a working framework for these collective investment schemes. Accordingly, the Governor, in an initiative reflecting both his regulatory and promotional roles in relation to Ghana's emerging capital market, made the request referred to above. Draft subsidiary legislation under the Law has been prepared which is currently being processed for promulgation in due course.

III. TANZANIA

Since 1986, Tanzania has been engaged in a process of structural adjustment to its economy similar to that undertaken by Ghana. Its objectives have been to improve macro-economic management, to tackle underlying structural weaknesses and to encourage more active private-sector participation. As part of this process of reform, the Government initiated in 1991 a financial sector reform programme. The objective of the reform programme was:

> "to create a system that would operate on the basis of market-oriented principles, that was efficient in mobilizing and allocating resources, and effective in fostering long-term economic growth".[7]

It was in this context of financial reform that the Government committed itself to the development of capital markets in Tanzania. Among its stated objectives were: "to address the financing needs of the private sector, and to promote broad-based ownership of the parastatal enterprises that are being

[6] See Ghana Stock Exchange, *Handbook 1995*, 25.

[7] See Inaugural Address by the Honourable Prof. K. A. Malima, Minister for Finance of the Government of Tanzania, at the Workshop on the Regulation of Securities Business in Tanzania convened by the Bank of Tanzania in Arusha in November 1994.

privatized".[8] It was in pursuance of this policy that the Capital Markets and Securities Act 1994 was enacted by Tanzania. The underlying concepts of this legislation are similar to those of the Ghanaian legislation which has already been discussed. The Commonwealth Secretariat served in an advisory role to the Government of Tanzania in relation to this legislation, and since the Secretariat's experience indicated that the legislative scheme embodied in the Ghanaian statute seemed reasonably well adapted to African conditions, it recommended a similar legislative scheme for Tanzania, and this recommendation was accepted. The main difference between the Ghanaian and the Tanzanian statutes is that unit trusts and mutual funds are not dealt with in the Tanzanian principal statute, but rather in regulations formulated under the principal legislation, and the Tanzanian statute contains provisions on an Interim Stock Trading Facility.

The idea of an Interim Stock Trading Facility is to provide a trading mechanism for securities before conditions are right for the establishment of a full-scale stock exchange. Under both the Ghanaian and Tanzanian statutes, the regulator may not approve a stock exchange unless it has at least three members able to carry on "the business of dealing in securities independently of and in competition with each other".[9] The rules of the exchange also have to measure up to particular standards set out in the statutes. These obligations are made inapplicable to the Interim Stock Trading Facility by the Tanzanian statute.[10] The regulator in Tanzania, which is called the Capital Markets and Securities Authority ("CMSA"), is authorised to permit one or more holders of a dealer's licence under the Act to establish and maintain an Interim Stock Trading Facility in which other holders of dealer's licences may participate until an approved stock exchange has been established.

For such a Facility, the Authority may itself make such rules as may be required for the purpose of ensuring orderly and fair trading in securities on the Facility and the protection of investors. As will be seen in our subsequent discussion of Botswana, there can be a stock trading system operated by only one broker, and therefore the provisions on the Interim Stock Trading Facility were intended to give the Tanzanian authorities the flexibility to adopt that kind of an option as a transitional stage in the development of the capital market. Provision is made that when an approved stock exchange is established pursuant to the Capital Markets and Security Act, the management and operation of the Interim Stock Trading Facility shall be assumed by the approved stock exchange in accordance with rules made by the CMSA.

The functions of the CMSA under the Tanzanian statute are identical to those of the SRC under the Ghanaian statute and therefore do not need fur-

[8] See Inaugural Address by the Honourable Prof. K. A. Malima, Minister for Finance of the Government of Tanzania, at the Workshop on the Regulation of Securities Business in Tanzania convened by the Bank of Tanzania in Arusha in November 1994.

[9] See s. 26(1) of the Capital Markets and Securities Act 1994 of Tanzania and s.25(1) of the Securities Industry Law 1992 of Ghana.

[10] See s. 114 of the Act.

ther elaboration here. The CMSA has been established and is actively planning the establishment of a stock exchange. Its membership consists of:

(1) a Chairman appointed by the President on the recommendation of the Minister;
(2) four other members who in the opinion of the Minister have experience and expertise in either legal, financial, business or administrative matters to be appointed by the Minister;
(3) the Principal Secretary to the Treasury or his nominee;
(4) the Governor of the Bank of Tanzania or his nominee;
(5) the Registrar of Companies or his nominee;
(6) the Attorney-General or his nominee; and
(7) the Chief Executive of the Authority.

The CMSA has decided against encouraging the establishment first of an Interim Stock Trading Facility and is, rather, actively promoting the establishment of a stock exchange. This evolution in the Tanzanian market is in contrast to the Ghanaian market, where the Ghana Stock Exchange has emerged as the main forum for action, rather than the SRC. The difference in the relative strength of the private sectors of the two countries may be an explanation for this.

IV. UGANDA

The context for the development of capital markets in Uganda is similar to what has already been discussed in relation to Ghana and Tanzania. Uganda has pursued liberalisation policies for a decade under the guidance of the Bretton Woods institutions and is currently one of the exemplars of successful structural adjustment, having achieved GDP growth rates of 10 per cent and 8+ per cent in the last two years. In the 1996 election manifesto of President Museveni (on the basis of which he was re-elected), he indicated that among the objectives for which he was seeking re-election was the maintenance of:

> "the present economic policy framework, whose centrepiece is liberalisation and macro-economic stabilisation".[11]

This is the context in which the Capital Markets Authority Statute 1996 was enacted. The Statute follows the Ghana/Tanzania precedents. Again, the Economic and Legal Advisory Services Division of the Commonwealth Secretariat has played an advisory role. The Ugandan Statute has provisions similar to the Tanzanian provisions on an Interim Stock Trading Facility. The regulator in Uganda, the Capital Markets Authority ("CMA"), has decided to follow the route of first promoting the establishment of an Interim Stock Trading Facility before the establishment of a full-scale stock exchange. As in

[11] See Y. K. Museveni, *Tackling the Tasks Ahead: Election Manifesto* (Kampala, 1996), 47.

Tanzania also, and in contrast to the Ghana case, the main player in the process of developing a market for securities has been the regulator, rather than private-sector entities. The CMA was inaugurated earlier this year and it is currently finalising the subsidiary legislation under the Statute which will enable the licensing of securities market intermediaries, stock exchanges and an Interim Stock Trading Facility. The CMA consists of a Chairman appointed by the Minister in consultation with relevant bodies; six other members from the private sector appointed by the Minister; the Permanent Secretary of the Ministry responsible for Finance and Economic Planning or his nominee; the Governor of the Bank of Uganda or his nominee; the Registrar of Companies or his nominee; the Solicitor-General or his nominee and the Chief Executive of the Authority.

The Ugandan Statute also deliberately excludes collective investment schemes from its purview for a subsequent separate enactment. The CMA has requested assistance from the Commonwealth Secretariat in developing an appropriate regulatory framework for such collective investment schemes.

V. BOTSWANA

The regulatory framework for securities trading in Botswana involves a model different from the model so far discussed in this paper. While the Ghana/Tanzania/Uganda model contemplates an exchange organised as a company and then approved by the regulator, the Botswana model involves the establishment of the stock exchange by statute. The Botswana Stock Exchange ("BSE") is established by the Botswana Stock Exchange Act 1994 as a corporate body. The Act provides for the affairs of the BSE to be managed and controlled by a committee to be known as the Committee of the BSE. The Committee consists of three members appointed by the Minister; and not fewer than two or more than six other members as the Committee may from time to time determine. These other members are to be elected by members of the Exchange. Not more than two of such members shall be members of any one partnership or company.

The Act also makes provision for the appointment of a public officer, to be known as the Registrar of the Stock Exchange. It is the Registrar's duty to establish a Register of Stockbrokers in which are to be recorded their names, addresses and such other particulars as may be prescribed. Regulatory authority over the securities industry in Botswana is shared between this Registrar, the Committee of the BSE and the Minister.

Every registered stockbroker is statutorily a member of the BSE.[12] To be registered as a stockbroker, a prospective stockbroker has to apply in writing to the Secretary of the BSE who is required to refer the application to the

[12] See s. 31 of the Botswana Stock Exchange Act 1994.

Committee. The Committee is authorised to recommend to the Registrar whether an applicant is suitable for registration. The Registrar is free to accept or reject the Committee's recommendation. But before the Registrar can refuse any application for registration, he must notify the applicant of his intention and give him an opportunity to show cause in writing why his application should not be refused. An applicant for registration as a stockbroker must be proposed and seconded in writing by registered stockbrokers, except that in respect of the first four stockbrokers to apply for registration it is sufficient that their applications are approved by the Minister. After the registration of the first four stockbrokers, therefore, the existing stockbrokers will have a decisive say in who else may become a stockbroker in Botswana.

The Committee is given disciplinary powers over registered stockbrokers. If the Committee is of the view that a stockbroker has contravened the Stock Exchange Act, has been guilty of disgraceful conduct or negligence in his capacity as a registered stockbroker or has come within the ambit of other stated reasons for becoming subject to discipline, the Committee may suspend the stockbroker from practice for such period as it deems appropriate or may reprimand him and notify the Registrar of that fact.[13] If the Committee is of the view that the delinquent stockbroker should have his registration cancelled, it must inform the Registrar of this opinion and the reasons supporting it. It must then suspend the stockbroker immediately, pending action by the Registrar to cancel the registration. The Registrar is not obliged to act upon the Committee's recommendation for the cancellation of the registration of a stockbroker. However, if he does decide to cancel the registration, he may do so only after he has given the stockbroker concerned an opportunity to show cause why his registration should not be cancelled.

Independently of the Registrar, the Minister also has regulatory authority under the Act. The Minister may appoint one or more inspectors to investigate the affairs of the Exchange or of a stockbroker and to report to the Minister on the matters referred to them for investigation. The precise circumstances under which the Minister may invoke his power to appoint inspectors are set out in the Act.[14]

[13] See s. 34 of the Act.

[14] See s.61 of the Act. They are where:

"(a) the Exchange or a stockbroker has failed, within a period of 60 days after receiving notice in writing from the Registrar to render, correct or complete a return required by or under this Act, to render, correct or complete that return; or

(b) the Registrar is in possession of information which, in the opinion of the Minister, makes it desirable to investigate the affairs of the Exchange or of a stockbroker; or

(c) not fewer than two registered stockbrokers apply in writing to the Minister for an investigation to be made into the affairs of the Exchange or of a stockbroker; or

(d) a person submits a written complaint of alleged conduct such as is referred to in s. 70(1)(d) or s. 70(1)(e) on the part of a stockbroker. (These subsections referred to relate to prohibited acts in respect of manipulative or deceptive methods of dealing in listed securities and fictitious transactions or the spreading of false reports in order to influence the prices of listed securities.)"

The Botswana Stock Exchange Act, which was passed by Parliament in August 1994, came into force at the end of October 1995 at the same time as the publication of regulations[15] made under it to give the BSE operational guidance. Currently only one stockbroker has been licensed under the Act. This sole stockbroker administers the BSE under the supervision of the Committee, as well as operating as the sole securities market intermediary in Botswana. As at February 1996, there were twelve listed companies on the BSE with a market capitalisation of US$395 million.

The Botswana regulatory system discussed above is based on the Zimbabwe Stock Exchange Act 1974. It is understood that the Zimbabwe authorities are currently considering a new draft securities and exchange law to replace that Act. Nevertheless, the simplified regulatory system embodied in this model seems to fit the Botswana circumstances well. There is no full-time freestanding regulator. This reduces the overhead costs of regulation. The Registrar of the Stock Exchange appointed by the Government is in fact a serving senior official of the Ministry of Finance. The self-regulatory governing body of the BSE is *de facto* the focal point for promoting the development of the capital market. Since the Minister appoints the Committee, he is able to satisfy himself that its membership is reliable. The Committee is not given a statutory high-profile advisory role on the industry to the Government as is the case with the Ghana/Tanzania/Uganda statute. The general functions of the Committee are expressed as follows:[16]

(a) to manage and control the affairs of the Exchange;
(b) to regulate the transaction of business on the Exchange;
(c) to manage and invest the funds of the Exchange;
(d) to raise or borrow moneys for the purposes of the Exchange in sums not exceeding in aggregate Pula 50,000 in any financial year, unless otherwise authorised at an Exchange meeting;
(e) to suspend the operation of the Exchange, if it appears desirable to the Committee to do so, and after consultation with the Registrar; and
(f) to do all things required to be done by the Committee in terms of this Act, and such other things not being inconsistent with the terms of this Act as, in the opinion of the Committee, are necessary for ensuring;
  (i) fair and efficient dealing in listed securities; and
  (ii) that the competence and conduct of registered stockbrokers are of a standard sufficiently high for the protection of the public.

Through the Registrar of the Stock Exchange, who is an official of the Ministry of Finance, and through the Minister's own regulatory powers under the Act, the Ministry of Finance in Botswana has a more direct regulatory role

[15] The Botswana Stock Exchange Regulations 1995.

[16] See s. 15 of the Stock Exchange Act 1994. Cf. s.16 of the Zimbabwe Stock Exchange Act 1974.

over the securities industry than is the case under the Ghana/Tanzania/Uganda model.

VI. ZAMBIA

Zambia presents yet another model of regulation. 1991 was a landmark year for Zambia. After decades of one-party rule and "socialist" economic policies, Zambia began a reform programme involving the usual elements of market liberalisation and the promotion of the private sector, including the privatisation of public enterprises. It was in this context that the Zambian Government decided to establish a Zambian securities market, a Zambian securities regulatory regime and a Lusaka-based stock exchange. To assist the Government to achieve these objectives, the International Finance Corporation ("IFC") made available to the Government a consulting team which prepared a blueprint for the development of the securities market and enabled the Lusaka Stock Exchange to be opened in February 1994. Other donors, including the UNDP, contributed to the process of capital market development in Zambia.

Before the commencement of the accelerated reform movement in 1991, the Zambian Stock Exchange Act of 1990 had already been enacted to provide the legal framework for a stock exchange. Following the adoption by the Zambian Government of the blueprint for the Zambian Securities Market prepared by the IFC consultants, the Zambian legislature enacted the Securities Act 1993, which established the Zambian Securities and Exchange Commission ("SEC") and repealed the Stock Exchange Act of 1990. The Bill for the Securities Act was prepared by a group consisting of representatives of the Stock Exchange Council (the Council being a body appointed by the Minister under the Stock Exchange Act 1990) and of the Ministry of Legal Affairs and members of the IFC consulting team. Among the precedents they considered were the Stock Exchange Act 1990 of Zambia, the Jamaican Securities Act 1993 and the Hong Kong Securities Ordinance.

The Zambian SEC is a freestanding regulator with extensive regulatory authority, somewhat in the US mould. The functions of the Commission are expressed as follows:[17]

"(a) to take all available steps to ensure that this Act and any rules made under this Act are complied with;

(b) to supervise and monitor the activities of any securities exchange and the settlement of transactions in securities;

(c) to license and monitor the activities of securities exchanges, dealers, investment advisers and their respective representatives and of

[17] See s. 4 of the Securities Act.

persons who, within the meaning of rules made under this Act, are non-bank custodians or service registrars;

(d) to approve the constitutions, charters, articles, by-laws, rules and regulations governing and pertaining to any securities exchange;

(e) to make, issue, monitor and enforce rules for the conduct of participants in the securities industry and for the supervision and investigation of that conduct, including rules relating to licensing and for the revocation and suspension of licences;

(f) to promote and encourage high standards of investor protection and integrity among members of any securities exchange;

(g) to support the operation of a free, orderly, fair, secure and properly informed securities market;

(h) to regulate the manner and scope of securities on any securities exchange, the exchange rules, listing requirements, margin requirements, capital adequacy requirements, disclosure and periodic reporting requirements, trade settlement and clearing requirements;

(i) to take all reasonable steps to safeguard the interest of persons who invest in securities and to suppress illegal, dishonourable and improper practices in relation to dealings in securities, whether on the securities exchange or otherwise;

(j) to take all reasonable steps to promote and maintain the integrity of persons licensed under Part IV and encourage the promulgation by such persons of balanced and informed advice to their clients and to the public generally;

(k) to consider and suggest proposals for the reform of the law relating to the securities industry;

(l) to encourage the development of securities markets in Zambia and the increased use of such markets by investors in Zambia and elsewhere;

(m) to promote and develop self-regulation by securities exchange;

(n) to co-operate, by the sharing of information and otherwise, with other supervisory bodies in Zambia and elsewhere;

(o) to exercise and perform such other powers, authorities, duties and functions as may be conferred or imposed upon it by or under this or any other Act."

The Zambian regime borrows from the US practice of requiring the filing of a registration statement with the SEC in respect of any security of a public company that is to be traded publicly. The Commission has the right to approve the statement. The Commission may only register it after it has scrutinised and approved the statement. It is a criminal offence to trade in securities in respect of which a registration statement has not been registered by the Commission.[18] In subsidiary legislation, the Securities (Registration of

[18] See s. 32.

Securities) Rules 1993, the SEC has elaborated more detailed rules governing the registration of securities. These rules provide that the registration statement includes, in the case of a public offer, a prospectus that complies with the rules set out in the subsidiary legislation. The Zambian SEC's role, at least at the level of the law in the books, appears to be interventionist in relation to both listed and unlisted securities.

The Lusaka Stock Exchange, however, is accorded a measure of self-regulation. It is a private company owned by its members operating under the regulatory jurisdiction of the SEC.

As at the end of 1995, the Exchange's market capitalisation was US$ 442 million, with eight companies, two listed and six unlisted. The Zambian regulatory regime provides for a unified market in which all securities trading is mediated through the stock exchange, whether the security is listed or not. It is an offence for any person to deal in any unlisted registered security otherwise than through a stock exchange.[19] Accordingly, there is no lawful unlisted over-the-counter market in securities in Zambia.

VII. CONCLUSION

The unifying theme of the various regulatory regimes discussed above has been the concern of the relevent governments not to leave the securities market unregulated. The overview presented here has of necessity been sketchy, given the time constraints within which this presentation has had to be made. But it is hoped that it has given a flavour of this evolving area of law in the African jurisdictions as the law develops in tune with the changing economic conditions in the African countries. The law developed so far may need fine-tuning or even radical overhaul in the light of experience. But it is believed wise that these African governments have moved to fill the regulatory gaps in their law. The crucial issue of judgement is the degree of regulation that is appropriate for an emerging market. An interesting counterpoise to the philosophy reflected in this paper is contained in the opinion expressed by a fund management company operating in the emerging African markets as follows:

> "When governments start stock markets they get advice from all the wrong people: the IFC, the World Bank, USAID, the British 'know-how' fund, and planeloads of consultants from Wisconsin and Chicago. All these people know how first world stock markets work, markets which turn over billions of dollars a year and which are home to large equity-hungry savings institutions. Applying the rules of these markets to the new markets of Africa and the Middle East is like creating traffic lights in the middle of the desert. An expensive waste of time until there is some traffic. Too many traffic lights and the traffic will take another route altogether".[20]

[19] See s. 36 of the Act.
[20] See Blakeney Management, *Working Notes*, 2nd Quarter 1996, 7.

This quotation makes a valid point in that any regulatory regime devised for a particular jurisdiction should take account of the realities of that jurisdiction and not indulge in over-regulation. However, it remains true that securities trading must be conducted within a framework of law; it cannot prudently be left unregulated in the world of today with its concern for investor protection.

17

Process of Transition and Commercial Law in Central and Eastern Europe

ATTILA HARMATHY*

I. COMMERCIAL LAW AND THE EMERGING MARKET ECONOMY

Since the end of the 1980s important changes have taken place in the countries of Central and Eastern Europe. The political and economic systems of these countries has been transformed fundamentally. Those who have an interest in social sciences have started studying the process of transformation, making use of an extraordinary opportunity to witness a change of system. Social science research usually cannot rely on experiments in laboratories, but this time it has acquired a kind of laboratory or a special aquarium for watching and for trying to influence the changing picture.

Several years have passed since the beginning of the process of transformation and it seems to me that many people, both in the countries concerned and abroad, are disappointed by the results and the lack of expected results. Experience shows that the process of transforming a system is slow and painful. The road to be followed cannot be seen, steps have been taken with much hesitation, mistakes have been made, and we sometimes have the feeling that the proper way has been lost. The present paper is an illustration of the problems.

Superficially the task seems to be easy. Countries with a system of planned economy should establish a market economy and put into effect the commercial laws needed for the proper functioning of the market economy. However, the task becomes complicated when one tries to implement it. Without attempting to compile a list of the most important questions connected with the task, I would mention some very basic questions that seem to play a central role.

Although we are concerned with questions related to law, the first question is what kind of market economy should be established. It is not enough to say

* Professor of Law, HEötvös University, Budapest, and Vice-President, Hungarian Academy of Sciences.

that socialism should be replaced by capitalism. These phenomena are too abstract. It has been pointed out that there are different levels and types of capitalism and market economies. So we need to study the conditions that existed in the former socialist countries and consequently what level of capitalism can replace socialism. Put differently, the question is whether a 19th or an early 20th century level of capitalism (corresponding with the level of economic development of a given country) should replace socialism and whether levels of development can be ignored when there is a fixed objective to which the system to be transformed should move. To put the question again in a different way, we need to clarify whether the aim of the countries concerned is simply to move from one system to another and nothing else, or whether the goal is fundamental change and, *in addition*, attainment of a different level of development.

Once we have agreed on what should be done the following questions arise: *who* should do it, *what* should be done and *in what way* should it be carried out. Thus, we face a series of challenges starting with the role of the state, continuing with the role of the law and then to the road of legal development.

It is not enough, however, to contemplate realizing a plan without also considering the *context* of the given society. This means we must also understand the effect of the existing social conditions is fixing the objective and on the appropriate method for realizing it. Here again only a possible starting point for an analysis can be attempted.

This paper focuses on legal questions but it also takes into consideration the economic and social factors influencing the legal solutions. John K. Galbraith has emphasized that the greatest political and economic issue of our time is the dangerous disarray in the countries of the former Soviet Union that are negotiating their uncertain and difficult way to a different economic and political system. He has also referred to the great changes which have taken place in the social and economic structure of the advanced industrial countries.[1] It is an important statement from the point of view of our topic. This is because it calls attention to the dilemma whether states of the former Soviet Union as well as the other states of Central and Eastern Europe can rely on their recollection of the market economies and their experience with capitalism of the 19th century or early 20th century, when setting their objectives for their own, or whether they must start again from the beginning.

II. CHANGES SINCE THE 19TH CENTURY

The question then, is whether the essential features of the market economy and capitalism at the end of the 20th century are the same as those of the 19th century. We must also ask ourselves what kind of view to take of the 19th

[1] J. K. Galbraith, "The Good Society Considered: The Economic Dimension", (1994) 21 *Journal of Law and Society* 165.

century market economy as the basis for our expectations. Economic doctrines expressing the principle of *laissez-faire* and, in close connection with it, a view of the role of the state in the economy restricted to that of a night watchman, may appear as the dominant picture without the benefits of a careful analysis of the history and theories of economics. It has been pointed out, however, that there were two different directions in the individualist movement of the 18th and 19th century. Only one of them represented the night watchman view, while the other direction, that the English classical economists conceived the role of the state in a more positive and experimental spirit.[2] On the other hand, it has also been argued that the theory of *laissez-faire*, free trade, universally advantageous effects of the pursuit of profit by competitive private enterprises did not really reflect the true position.[3]

Although modern economic theory does not deny similarities in the development of market economies in different countries, nevertheless it lays a great emphasis on different economic structures, social conditions, political and administrative factors and consequently on the widely different policies of the countries analysed. As a result of the institutional framework, legal institutions differ to a great extent from country to country and even in the same country according to phases of development.[4]

During the 20th century the views of economic theorists have changed about the character of a market economy. At the same time it has become evident that a market economy cannot be considered to be static. In an often cited book, Schumpeter pointed out that *capitalism has never been stationary*; by nature it has been a form or method of economic change. The economic structure has constantly changed and as a result the institutional framework has changed as well, eroding even the fundamental legal institutions of property (ownership) and freedom of contract.[5] Like many other authors, Schumpeter points to the changing position of shareholders to explain the erosion of property rights.

As property is a fundamental institution of the market economy, it is important for our topic that the changing role of ownership has become an essential element of new theories on contemporary society. The new theory relies on the thesis of Berle and Means, published in 1932, according to which the unity of ownership and control has been severed in the modern corporation.[6] Nevertheless, it should be noted that the foundation and general applicability

[2] L. Robbins, *The Theory of Economic Policy*, London, 2nd ed. 1978, 46.

[3] J. Robinson, *Economic Heresies*, London, 1971, ch. VII, VIII.

[4] J. A. Schumpeter, *History of Economic Analysis*, New York, 1954, (Paperback in 1986) 396–401. For similar opinion in a different context, see B. F. Hoselitz, "Economic Policy and Economic Development", in: *The State and Economic Growth*, ed. H. G. J. Aitken, New York, 1959, 330–46.

[5] J. A. Schumpeter, *Capitalism, Socialism and Democracy*, London, 1942, new edition 1982, 82–83, 140–1.

[6] A. A. Berle and G. C. Means, *The Modern Corporation and Private Property*, New York, revised ed. 1968, 304–5.

of the Berle and Means thesis have been questioned by eminent economists and it has been stressed that the main stream of economic theory continues to work in complete disregard of the thesis. The attention their views have received in other fields has been due to "the popularity of the underlying philosophical outlook".[7] Thus the Berle and Means thesis remains relevant for the general topic even if its application remains is doubtful in the corporate sphere.

While the claim that ownership has lost its importance has been questioned, it cannot be denied that revolutionary changes in industrial and agricultural production have taken place in the last 200 years. Services have grown greatly in importance. Developments in transportation and telecommunications have also had profound effects on both the economy and society. It has become common in the literature to speak of de-industrialisation and of late-modern or post-modern economy and society. However, there are warning signs about drawing conclusions prematurely. For example, the summary of a conference in which eminent economists participated stated that de-industrialisation meant "a new label for an old problem".[8] Consequently, caution is needed if we want to develop the law of Central and Eastern European countries on the basis of modern theories. The facts of development need to be carefully analysed.

Remaining at the level of facts, there have been important structural changes in the economy which have also led to serious social changes. Thus the household has ceased to function as a small factory remaining, however, a consumption unit. Since the 1960s a new revolution has again diminished the role of the family as demand has shifted toward individualized consumption.[9] Another important element has been the transformation of enterprises. The modern enterprise, which became dominant in the US economy by World War I and subsequently adopted in other parts of the world usually comprises several effectively coordinated units administered by salaried middle and top managers. The new organisation has resulted in changes in market structure and has led to imperfect competition.[10] At the same time, small industry has not disappeared in developed European countries and it is of particular importance in Asian countries, including Japan, where it corresponds to special features in the development of those economies.[11]

[7] G. J. Stigler and C. Friedland, "The Literature of Economics: The Case of Berle and Means", (1983) 26 *Journal Law and Econ.* 259.

[8] *De-industrialisation*, ed. F. Blackaby, National Institute of Economic and Social Research, London, 1979, 268.

[9] J. de Vries, *The Industrial Revolution and the Industrious Revolution*, (1994) 54 *Journal Econ. History* 254–65.

[10] A. D. Chandler, *The Visible Hand. The Managerial Revolution in American Business*, (Cambridge, Mass.—London, 1977). 3 ff.

[11] B. F. Hoselitz, "Small industry in Underdeveloped Countries", in: *Development Economics and Policy*, ed. I. Livingstone, London, 1981, 203–7.

III. ECONOMIC DEVELOPMENTS IN CENTRAL AND EASTERN EUROPE

The process of transition in Central and Eastern European countries is mostly considered to be an economic problem and social aspects are usually neglected. In my opinion, the social consequences of programmes of transition cannot be ignored. A legal system cannot operate in isolation from the society which is expected to apply its norms. Although the focus of this paper is on commercial law, it is necessary at least to locate the starting point for an understanding of societies with a market economy at the end of the 20th century.

If the study of the process of transition covers social aspects as well, it must be remembered that developed countries have also experienced important changes since the beginning of the 19th century. I have already mentioned that it has become usual to speak of post-modern societies because of the changes that have occurred. Just as in the field of economic changes, it cannot be claimed that the theory has elaborated a greatly accepted concept of social changes. Even Daniel Bell has emphasized in the preface to the German edition of his book on post-modern society that he understands the concept of post-modern society as a social science fiction that may become a reality.[12]

Being aware of the tentative character of the investigation and of the need for caution if we want to draw conclusions on the basis of modern theories, I believe some statements of Dahrendorf can be used as a starting point. He has summarised the social consequences of changes in the economy in a cautious way, given the fact that the separation of ownership and control has been overrated. In his opinion, the situation found in European and North American countries on the road to industrialisation in the 19th century was the result of special historical factors. It cannot be considered a model for every country. The most important change was the dispersal of capital among a plurality of groups. At the same time, labour (and the new middle class) have also been disintegrating. From the point of view of the countries in a period of transition, this insight is of particular importance. It means that social mobility has become one of the crucial elements of the social structure of industrial societies and the rate of mobility corresponds roughly to the degree of industrialization of the countries concerned.[13]

I have tried to present a picture of changes in the market economies and the societies of developed countries of Europe and North America since the beginning of the 19th century. I should now indicate the level of economic development of the countries of Central and Eastern Europe prior to World War II. At the end of the 19th century they were emerging slowly from a feudal system and attempted to increase the pace of industrialization by state intervention and relied heavily on imported capital. Several of them became

[12] D. Bell, *Die Nachindustrielle Gesellschaft*, Frankfurt-New York, 1975, 10.

[13] R. Dahrendorf, *Class and Class Conflict in Industrial Society*, Stanford, 1959, 39–58.

independent states after World War I and these are the states I refer to hereafter (I do not deal here with the history of the states of the former Soviet Union). There were considerable differences among them. The most industrialized country was Czechoslovakia. Poland and Hungary were agricultural states with some significant industry. Industry was less developed in Rumania, Bulgaria and Yugoslavia. The role of the state grew during World War I and in the interwar period. Direct state participation was largest in Poland and probably less in Czechoslovakia and Hungary although even in these states defence industries (e.g. the Skoda Works) were under state ownership. The development of industry was hampered by the Great Depression and later by World War II.[14]

The Central and Eastern European countries suffered much and were exhausted by World War II, so the most important task after 1945 was the reconstruction of their economies. Land reform took place, which meant the distribution of the great landed estates among small-holders or peasants who did not have any land. The development was somewhat quicker in industry. Intensive industrialization started almost immediately after the war. As the economic structure changed, the importance of heavy industry increased quickly.[15]

The transformation of the political and economic system started later at the end of 1940s. Massive nationalisation was carried out. Centralized state direction of the economy grew. In most countries, a one-party political system was created and the institutional structure of the economy changed profoundly. The political and economic system of the socialist countries is well-known and I need not describe it here.[16] I refer only to an element which is not always stressed. This element is the complete transformation of the financial sector creating a one-level specialized state owned banking system and the role of money, credit and banking. In this system finances were subordinated to the fulfilment of planned targets and became a part of state administration.

Economic reforms were introduced in the 1960s. Hungary tried to build up a system harmonizing state planning and a market economy (Yugoslavia had a special development differing in several respects from that of the other Eastern European countries). As a result of the reforms, the system of planning changed considerably compared with the system of the early 1950s. Nevertheless, the basic features of the system remained the same.

Returning to the question put at the beginning of this section, it can be stated on the basis of experience since the end of World War II that no fundamental change has taken place in the sense of these countries having reached the level of developed economies. It has been suggested that the rel-

[14] N. Spulber, "The Role of State in Economic Growth in Eastern Europe since 1860", in: *The State and Economic Growth*, ed. H. G. J. Aitken, New York, 1959, 262–77.

[15] T. I. Berend—Gy. Ránki, *Közép-Kelet-Európa gazdasági fejlõdése a 19–20.században* (*Economic Development of Central and Eastern-Europe in the 19th–20th Centuries*), Budapest, 1976, 594–621.

[16] For comprehensive analysis see J. Kornai, *The Socialist System*, Princeton 1992.

ative backwardness inherited from the past was perpetuated by the system prevailing between 1948 and 1987.[17] In addition to the inherited backwardness there are not only the problems of transition from a planned economy to a market economy but also structural problems in the financial sector were created during the last forty years.[18]

Bearing in mind the present position, the level of development of the countries concerned and the task of setting the goals to be achieved, we face the question whether some stages of development can be omitted or whether all the stages have to be followed and the speed of the process analysed from this perspective.[19] There is no clear answer to the question. However, the history of the former socialist countries shows that attempts to by-pass some steps of the development have serious economic and social consequences. The question implicates the general problems of development and to a comparison with the position of the less developed countries.

It is instructive too from the point of view of our topic to note what Simon Kuznets said about modern economic growth in the lecture delivered on the occasion of receiving the Nobel Prize in economic science. He explained that a country's economic growth depends on the state of its technology, on institutional and ideological adjustments,[20] and here I would call attention to the last two elements. The institutional and ideological conditions of development are not always sufficiently considered in countries during a period of transition.

Studying problems of development and in particular the problems of underdeveloped countries, one can understand the importance of social and human factors. An essential condition of any development is the social environment.[21] There may be legal and political impediments and society as a whole may react in a hostile way to changes. If we accept the importance of social factors, we shall find the conclusion that a legal order cannot focus only on the economy but must pay attention to social aspects as well, taking into consideration what changes a society can absorb and what endangers stability. Concern for social stability means a relatively slow process of transition while maintaining the central position of the state. Rapidly enforced changes (shock treatment) do not diminish the role of the state because order must be maintained by means of state action.[22]

17 D. F. Good, "The Economic Lag of Central and Eastern Europe: Income Estimates for the Hapsburg Successor States, 1870–1910", Journal of Economic History 54 (1994) pt. 4, 888.

18 There is an abundant literature dealing with problems of transition. Here I refer only to a report of the OECD Centre for Cooperation with European Economies in Transition: *Transformation of Planned Economies*, ed. H. Blemmestein—M. Marrese, Paris, 1991, 19–20.

19 Bell has put a similar question in connection with the Russian industrialisation before the political changes, Bell *supra* n. 12, 17–18.

20 S. Kuznets, "Modern Economic Growth: Findings and Reflections", *American Economic Review* 63 (1973) 247.

21 J. A. Schumpeter, *The Theory of Economic Development*, Cambridge, Mass. 1949, 86 7.

22 J. Habakkuk, "The Entrepreneur and Economic Development", in: *Development Economics and Policy: Readings* ed. I. Livingstone, London, 1981, 19–20., H. Chenery and M. Syrquin with the assistance of H. Elkington, *Patterns of Development* 1950–1970, Oxford, 1975, 4–5.

In a socialist system the state has a central role to play. It is natural to assume that if something of considerable importance is to be done it will be carried out by the state. The transition to a democratic system and to a market economy means dispensing with the omnipotence and omnipresence of the state. A central question therefore is *what the role of the state should be* in the process of transition. Different aspects of the role of the state in this process must be considered. Here I refer only to two. The first one concerns the participation of the state in the economy. As a result of the ideology prevailing in socialist countries private economic activity was restricted. In most socialist countries only retail merchants and artisans could pursue what are limited forms of business. State enterprises were the most important economic actors. In countries in course of transition an important part of the changes has been the increase in importance of private economic activity and abolition as far as possible of the state's direct participation in economic life. State enterprises have been and are being privatised. The question is put, nevertheless, where the limits of privatisation are to be drawn, whether there are some factors, such as high risk aversion, poorly developed financial markets, market imperfections, maintenance of a level of employment and distributional issues which rationalise the existence of state enterprise. In this respect the situation in countries in course of transition is similar to that of underdeveloped countries.[23]

The other aspect of the role of the state is more general than the state's direct participation in the economy. It is the manner in which the state guides the economy or, in another formulation, how the state acts. During World War II the state placed a direct and central role in the administration of the economy and in several countries also allocated resources.[24] Socialist states used to find political solutions instead of economic ones. This way proceeding was close, with the fact that labour organizations had no real importance, if they functioned at all.[25]

It is a widely accepted idea in the former socialist states that a market economy and an active role for the state are incompatible. The aim of reducing state activity to that of a night watchman is not unappealing to some politicians, particularly if the state budget is in deficit and expenditures must be cut. Nevertheless, it is worth recalling that the 19th century liberal states were not passive either and their role was not restricted to setting the rules of the game (forming institutional framework) and maintaining law and order. Polanyi, in a much discussed work, has emphatically explained that self-

[23] C. H. Kirkpatrick, "Business Behaviour in the Public Sector", in: C. H. Kirkpatrick—N. Lee—F. I. Nixson, *Industrial Structure and Policy in Less Developed Countries*, London, 1984, 156–9.

[24] M. MacLennan, M. Forsyth and G. Denton, *Economic Planning and Policies in Britain, France and Germany*, New York—Washington, 1968, 38, J.C.R. Dow, *The Management of the British Economy 1945–1960*, Cambridge, 1968, 1, 7–9..

[25] R. Aron, *Dix-huit leçons sur la société industrielle*, Paris, 1962, 138–9, T.Parsons, *Structure and Process in Modern Societies*, Glencoe, Ill., 1960, 100–1, A. Etzioni, The Active Society, London—New York, 1968, 107, 441.

regulation of the economy was utterly beyond the horizons of politicians during the transformation of society. Some central elements of the market economy, such as labour, land and money, could not be left to self-regulation. Instead, a network of measures and policies was integrated into institutions designed to regulate the market relative to these elements.[26]

Whether or not Polanyi's view has been accepted there seems to be agreement in contemporary economic literature that the state was active in all states in the 19th century (including the United States of America) and that the English classical economists were not opposed to state activity as such. Rather, their distrust of government stemmed from the type of government that existed in England at the beginning of the 19th century and which was known as corrupt, inefficient and arbitrary in its actions. In connection with state activity, Tomlinson notes that no one opposed government intervention to create the framework for banking and to regulate the money supply. Also during this period, the idea of the limited liability of joint stock companies which was approved in England as a shareholder protection against the claims of workers under the newly adopted Factory Acts was contested and considered a significant deviation from the principles of *laissez-faire*. (In France the principle of limited liability of shareholders was admitted earlier in the Commercial Code but these companies were created under strict state control and the system changed only in the second half of the 19th century).[27]

There is no need to speak about the present role of the state in developed states. For most of the 20th century, under the pressure of wars and economic depressions, influential political ideas have strengthened the role of the state in all fields of economic and social life. In the last twenty years, the environment has changed and neo-Keynesian doctrines have been replaced by neo-liberal, monetarist ideas hostile to major state involvement. Although a policy aimed at diminishing the role played by the state in the economy and supporting privatisation and deregulation seems currently to prevail,[28] it cannot be denied that the state is not passive and its role cannot be neglected.

IV. COMMERCIAL LAW DEVELOPMENTS

Given the contrasting roles of the state in former socialist and developed countries, it is not surprising that the process of transformation had to be

[26] K. Polanyi, *Origins of our Times: The Great Transformation*, London, 2nd impression 1946, 73–82.

[27] See Robbins, *supra* n. 2, 38, 41, 46, 48, 56, J. Tomlinson, *Government and the Enterprise since 1900*, Oxford, 1994, 4–11. With respect to the US economy, see H.W. Broude, "The Role of the State in the American Economic Development, 1820–1890", in: *The State and Economic Growth*, ed. H.G.J. Airken, New York, 1959, 12–15. in French Company Law, see C. Ducouloux-Favard, "L'histoire des grandes sociétés en Allemagne, en France et en Italie", *Revue Internationale de Droit Comparé* 1992, pt 4, 850–1.

[28] For a more detailed explanation with bibliographical notes, see A. Harmathy, *General Report on: Legal Aspects of Privatisation*, Council of Europe, Strasbourg, 1993, 206–10.

started anew in Central and Eastern European states. It seems to be evident that the state initiative takes the form of legislation. I shall confine the following remarks to the role of the state and in particular the role of legislation in the development of law and, mainly, the development of commercial law. While the importance of legislation is obvious there is no clear answer to several other questions concerning legal developments. I will mention only three questions. The first concerns the role of codification, the second the importance of the role of other non-legislative means of developing the law, and the third question is the kind of model that should be followed.

It seems to me that when we try to find answers to the legislative question, our guide should be the history of commercial law of developed countries and the present conditions of legal development in Central and Eastern European countries. Some features are of particular importance in the light of the history of commercial law. It is my impression, based on the history of other countries (particularly those countries whose commercial codes have been very influential), that the history of commercial law has differed to some extent from the history of other branches of law. It has been pointed out that customs have played an important role in the development of commercial law. Different contractual forms, clauses, practices and usages established first by Italian merchants and later by merchants in other parts of the European Continent, often written down by notaries and then approved and sometimes transformed by the commercial courts, became after several hundred years the basis of legislation. The first statutes incorporating important parts of commercial law were adopted at a time when the state (in Germany, the princes) became stronger and it became a part of state policy to establish some general uniform rules of trade.[29]

Another interesting feature in the development of commercial law was the connection between the development of a special mechanism for dispute resolution between merchants and the development of commercial law as a separate body of law. In Italy and France merchant guilds established a special tribunal to decide disputes between a guild and its members and between the members themselves. Later, a market dispute resolution system started functioning. In the German states a similar solution evolved somewhat later. The development was supported by the medieval attitude according to which rights belonged to a person and depended on his status as a person.[30] The French Revolution declared the equality of citizens, abolished the corporative system and did away with the rule in which the legal position of a person depended on guild membership. As a result of the new approach, the French

[29] L. Goldschmidt, *Handbuch des Handelsrechts*, Stuttgart, 3.Aufl. 1891. I. Bd. I. Lieferung, 33–8; V. Ehrenberg, Einführung and P. Rehme, *Geschichte des Handelsrechts*, both in: *Handbuch des gesamten Handelsrechts*, hrg. V. Ehrenberg,Leipzig, 1913. I. Bd. 6–8. G. Ripert et R. Roblot, *Traité de droit commercial*, 15e éd. M. Germain, Paris 1993. 12–14.

[30] L. Rosenberg, "Handelsgerichtsbarkeit", in: *Handbuch des gesamten Handelsrechts*, hrg. V. Ehrenberg, Leipzig, 1913. I. Bd. 451–7.

Commercial Code could not maintain the principle that commercial law was the law concerning merchants but had to work out an objective principle for determining which topics belonging by nature to commercial law. Another aspect of the equality principle affected lawyers and the court system. Radical revolutionaries hated lawyers as servants of the *ancien régime*. At the same time they attacked the profession because of its corporatist character. The Revolution granted free access to legal positions and reorganised the court system. The new court system comprised specialised commercial courts but uncertainty was felt concerning its competence.[31] This uncertainty surrounded both the commercial law and the search for the defining features of commercial law.

The above description mainly applies to the development of French and German law. A different approach, leading to similar results but by different means, can be found in the law of other countries. The Swiss developments show some similarity with the French developments. The *Bundesrat* adopted the unified Law of Obligation in 1881 and repealed the separate Act for Merchants of 1879, grounding the decision on the democratic attitude of the Swiss people, which was against conferring special rights on persons depending on their professional status. Separate commercial courts were not typical in Switzerland.[32] The development of the Common Law is another example of the importance of usages and court practice in developing the law and the significance of a separate court system for developing a commercial law. In general, the flexibility of the forms of action facilitated adaptation of the legal system to changing conditions throughout the history of the Common Law. Whether there is some dispute about how the law merchant became part of the Common Law and if there was a separate system of principles at all. It is, however, clear that towards the end of the medieval period the local mercantile courts suffered a decline and commercial customs were incorporated in the judgements of the regular courts.[33] So far as the development of American commercial law is concerned, we need not concern ourselves with what the position was before the 19th century. It is undisputed that American courts played a vital role in the 19th century development of American law and this is equally true of the development of commercial law as an integral part of the Common Law as well.[34]

[31] Ripert—Roblot, *supra* n. 29, 16, J. L. Halpérin, *Haro sur les hommes de loi*, Droits, *Revue Française de Théorie Juridique* 1993, 55–65.

[32] E. A. Kramer, "Handelsgeschäfte", in: *Beiträge zum Zivil- und Handelsrecht*, Festschrift für Rolf Ostheim, red. W. Posch, Wien, 1990, 306, Rosenberg, *supra* n. 30, 457.

[33] A. W. B. Simpson, *A History of the Common Law of Contract*, Oxford, 1975, 283–4, J. H. Baker, "The Law Merchant and the Common Law before 1700", *The Cambridge Law Journal* 38 (1979), 295–306, 320–2.

[34] M. J. Horwitz, *The Transformation of American Law*, Cambridge, Mass.—London, 1977, 1–5, 211–12, A. W. B. Simpson, "The Horwitz Thesis and the History of Contracts", *University of Chicago Law Review* 46 (1979) pt. 3, 533–5, 568, 600.

These short remarks seem to me necessary to emphasize the fact that legislation is not a necessary and probably not even the normal way of developing market law. In the former socialist countries history is often forgotten or neglected. This is for several reasons but I will refer only to one. People became accustomed to the philosophy of the former regime and to the fact that is a command economy legislation by government decrees was the usual means of achieving goals. It is therefore understandable that in the new era as well politicians and, even lawyers, looked on legislation as the natural route to bring about changes and to establish rules for the market economy.[35]

Nevertheless, it is obvious that legislation is the only means for working out new rules and probably not the best one for market purposes. Judicial decisions and the practice of businessmen must also play their proper role.

V. ROLE OF CODIFICATION

The question of the role of legislation is closely connected with the role of codification. Some years ago several eminent lawyers reasoned that the era of civil law codification is over. However, the mood seems to have changed and a growing interest in codification can be observed in several countries, not counting the Netherlands and Quebec.[36] The former socialist countries were among the countries which were not only interested but enacted new Civil Codes after 1945 (such as Czechoslovakia) and have enacted new civil or commercial codes since the political changes. Examples are the new Civil Code in the Russian Federation, important amendments to the Civil Code in Poland and the former Czechoslovakia, Hungary, the new Commercial Code covering mainly companies in the former Czechoslovakia, and in Bulgaria.[37] Most likely, the wave of codification has not yet come to an end in these countries.

The series of codes of these countries in transition is not the result of cooperation among them. It is doubtful whether the countries concerned have a

[35] T. W. Waelde and J. L. Gunderson, "Legislative Reform in Transition Economies: Western Transplants—A Short-cut to Social Market Economy Status?" *International and Comparative Law Quarterly* 43 (1994) pt. 2, 348–9, B. Rudden, "Civil Law, Civil Society, and the Russian Constitution", *Law Quarterly Review* 110 (1994) January, 68.

[36] See e.g. on the end of the era of codification R. Sacco, "La codification, forme dépassé de législation?" in: *Rapports Nationaux Italiens au XIe Congrès de Droit Comparé*, Milano, 1982, 65–9. On the possibilities of codification see: H. Kötz, "Taking Civil Codes Less Seriously", *Modern Law Review* 50 (1987) pt. 1, 11–14, A. L. Diamond, "Codification of the Law of Contract", *Modern Law Review* 31 (1968) 372.

[37] See e.g. for a survey of the position before the changes: A. Harmathy, "General Problems of Civil Law Codification in the Law of CMEA Countries", in: *Questions of Civil Law Codification*, ed. A. Harmathy and Á. Németh, Budapest, 1990, 52–66. On some problems involving the recent Codes: F.J.M.Feldbrugge, "The New Civil Code of the Russian Federation", in *Review of Central and East European Law* 21 (1995) pts. 3–4, 237–43, E.A.Sukhanov, "Russia's New Civil Code", *Parker School Journal of East European Law* 1 (1994) pts. 5–6, 619–36, O.Sadikov, "Das neue Zivilgesetzbuch Rußlands", *Zeitschrift für Europäisches Privatrecht* 4 (1996) pt. 2, 259–72, V. Knapp, "Unity or Diversity in Civil Law", *Parker School Journal of Eastern European Law* pt. 1. (1994) 5–6, 637–46.

codification plan or any medium term concept of legislation. The countries which have made an Association Agreement with the European Union have a legislative programme for the approximation of their laws with the EU laws and directives, but the programme does not include provisions for new civil or commercial codes. New codes are considered a necessity by politicians and lawyers and many people assume that new commercial codes will be enacted in the near future. It has not happened so far.

The reasons for expecting a new commercial code is only partly the result of perceiving legislation as a principal means for the development of law. People usually do not think it necessary to give reasons why a commercial code is necessary because it seems self-evident. If one tries to find the reasons, several answers suggest themselves. One of the answers is tradition. Most of Central and Eastern European countries had a commercial code before the socialist era and so the wish to return to a code system is understandable. Another possible reason is the established model for the creation of the capitalist system. People remember that capitalism started with the enactment of commercial codes in the 19th century. Therefore, the return to a market economy should also start with a new commercial code as the constitution of the economic life. A further explanation is the traditional influence of German and French law. Prior to 1945, the Central and Eastern European law was influenced by German (including Austrian) or French law or by both and these systems had, and continue to have, separate commercial codes. The Common Law had no direct contact with legal developments in Central and Eastern European countries and common law concepts and institutions. This above brief survey of the development of the capitalist system and that of commercial law shows that the obvious answers are not necessarily the right ones. Some additional comments are needed, however, about codification.

Codification may serve several purposes.[38] In our case, the purpose is the establishment of a new market based economic system by fixing the rules necessary for its functioning.[39] When adopting this goal it is often overlooked that codification with a similar purpose can be found in the case of the Prussian Code (*Landrecht*). This was the work of an enlightened absolute monarch before the advent of capitalism and it is regarded today as an utopian attempt.[40] The French Civil Code was not intended to establish a new system of rules for the new political and economic regime. It has been characterised as compromise law intended to unify the rules for all of France,

[38] For overview of the possible purposes, see B. Oppetit, "De la codification", *Receuil Dalloz Sirey* 1996, pt. 5, Chr. 33–6.

[39] A more detailed description of my opinion appears in another paper so it will not be repeated here. See A. Harmathy, "Systemwende, Rechtssytemveränderung in den Mittel- und Ost-Europäischen Staaten", in Festschrift für E. J. Mestmäcker, hrsg. U. Immenga and W. Möschel—D. Reuter, Baden-Baden, 1996, 167–75.)

[40] F. Wieacker, *Privatrechtsgeschichte der Neuzeit unter besonderer Berücksichtigung der deutschen Entwicklung*, Göttingen, 2.Aufl. 1967, 323.

mostly on the basis of the existing practice.[41] The question has not been put with respect to the German Civil Code as it was not the result of a revolutionary change and did not usher in a new social and economic system. Laymen usually think of the French Civil Code as the enactment of a new era but this is because they are not aware of its sources and antecedents. In our case, however, the question is not so much the need for a new Civil Code as the need for a new Commercial Code. Why is the search for a commercial code neglected and not put in the forefront when the goal is creation of a new economic system? It is strange that the Civil Code is expected to bring about a new economic system and not the Commercial Code. The reason why this is not the case is probably because there are no revolutionary Commercial Codes establishing a new economic system.

The French Commercial Code has been characterised as a work of mediocre quality containing mostly the rules in 17th century decrees. Its enactment was largely due to the need to prevent bankruptcy speculations.[42] The official commentary on the German Commercial Code of 1895 stressed the importance of learning from the experience under the old Code with respect to the unification of rules, the importance of harmonizing of rules of commercial law with the new Civil Code, and it emphasized the importance of customary law from the point of view of commercial life.[43]

VI. DEVELOPMENT WITHOUT CODIFICATION

When we look for some points of comparison with the development of the Common Law, we see that an important number of statutes were passed by the English Parliament in the second part of the 19th century changing the previous law and interfering with the freedom of contract. Several statutes adopted in the second part of the 19th century concerned company law and the law of negotiable instruments. These Acts did not introduce a new economic system. On the contrary, they were characterised as indifferent to commercial needs or as not breaking new grounds but reproducing existing law.[44] We can find a similar trend in the development of American law where the U.S. Supreme Court played a particularly important role during the creative period of American law in the second part of the 19th century.[45]

[41] J. Carbonnier, *Droit civil, Introduction*, Paris, 21e éd. 1992, 128, 131–3, P. Malaurie and L. Aynès, *Droit civil, Introduction générale*, Paris, 1991, 142–4. J. Gordley, "Myths of the French Civil Code", 42 *American Journal of Comparative Law* 1994, pt. 3, 460–3, 476, 480.

[42] Ripert and Roblot *supra* n. 29, 15–16.

[43] *Quellen zum Handelsgesetzbuch von 1897*, hrg. W. Schubert, O.B. Schmiedel and C. Krampe, II/1.Bd. Frankfurt, 1–4.

[44] R. Cranston, "Commercial Law and Commercial Activity", in: *Commercial and Consumer Law*, ed. R. Cranston and R. Goode, Oxford, 1993, 286–7, P. S. Atiyah, *The Rise and Fall of Freedom of Contract*, Oxford, 1979, 693.

[45] J. R. Commons, *Legal Foundations of Capitalism*, 1924, reprint Madison-London,1968, 7.

These observations seem to support the hypothesis that the development of commercial law does not favour introducing new systems by means of codification. Even discrete separate statutes quite often reproduce solutions grounded in existing practice. The hypothesis is in harmony with a statement of Hayek who points to the fact that a revolution often changes the whole structure of government but that most rules of just conduct of the civil law will remain as before. The different nature of the development of civil and public has not been appreciated by legal theorists because the development of civil law has been almost entirely in the hands of public lawyers "who think of law primarily as public law".[46]

VII. CONCLUSION

The development of commercial law raises as well the question of which model should be followed. There are two parts to the question. The first question is whether a separate commercial law (a Commercial Code) is needed or the principle of the unity of the civil law should be accepted. To put it differently, which country model should be followed? The second part of the question is whether legal transplantation should be applied. There is an abundant literature on both these questions. I shall confine myself to some short remarks on each of these problems.

So far as the need for a separate commercial law is concerned, I agree with the proposition that the civil law could meet the requirements of commercial life and that there are no theoretical objections to this happening.[47] It means that acceptance of the principle of duality or unity depends on the conditions of the given country, and particularly on the question whether the society and its economy are sufficiently influential to shape the civil law rules in a commercial way or whether the great majority of its citizens have a very uncommercial mentality. Traditions may also have some effect but it is of secondary importance. A similar view was expressed by Czachorski who, until his death in 1995, was the head of the Polish codification committee dealing with civil law codification.[48] In other countries the debates on economic law during the socialist period seem to have influenced this question of codification.[49]

As far as legal transplants are concerned, I would refer to the distinction emphasized by Schwarz between law and statute (code). Drawing on several examples from legal history he observes that transplantation and reception

[46] F. A. Hayek, *Law, Legislation and Liberty*, London, 1973. reprint 1979. 134–5.

[47] Goldschmidt, *supra* n. 29, 10, Ehrenberg, *ibid*., 20–1.

[48] W. Czachorski, "De la séparation à l'unification du droit des obligations civiles et commerciales en Pologne Populaire", in: Rotondi Inchieste di Diritto Comparato, Vol. III. Padova, 1973, 33–5, 42.

[49] Knapp, *supra* n. 37, 642–3, V. A. Dozortsev, "One Code or Two?" *The Parker School Journal of East European Law* 2 (1995) pt. 1, 27–57.

occurs most easily at the level of statutes but it will not be law.[50] A foreign legal institution can serve as a model if the conditions necessary for its functioning exist in the host country and if the mentality of the donor law is close enough to that of the host country so that the alien institution can be transplanted and find a fertile ground. The countries in transition have the choice to decide whether or not to borrow from other legal systems. Nevertheless, there are limits on their freedom of choice. If they want to join the European union they must take the rules of the Community as they find them. The countries of Central and Eastern Europe are slowly starting to understand what this means.

Finally, the social consequences of the legal changes must be emphasized again. In the old economic order the state took responsibility for many services and did not permit them to be offered by private organizations. The transition to a market economy means a fundamental change, the role of the state becomes very different from what it used to be. If the state ceases to provide services without promoting the creation of new systems the consequences can be very serious in health care, education and other essential services and the long-range effects of this change can be important for the whole society.[51] The legal regulation of social security and labour relations is not part of commercial law. Nevertheless, no acceptable commercial law regime can be established without proper consideration of its social consequences.

[50] A. B. Schwarz, "Reception und Assimilation ausländischer Rechte" (published first in Receuil Lambert in 1938), reprinted in the collection of his papers: *Rechtsgeschichte und Gegenwart*, Karlsruhe, 1960, 150–8.

[51] A team working at the World Bank has published a book on these important issues: see *Labour Markets and Social Policy in Central and Eastern Europe*, ed. N. Barr, New York, 1994.

18

The Challenges of Adapting Law to Market Economies in Post-communist Central European Countries

JERZY RAJSKI*

I. INTRODUCTION

The process of transition from communist political and economic systems to democratic and market-oriented economies has been carried out in Central Europe through a sequence of political decisions progressively changing the former regime. The communist systems imposed by force on Central Europe have been gradually dismantled by non-revolutionary means, with full observance of the rule of law.

Enormous changes have had to be made simultaneously in both the political and economic systems. This has been without precedent in modern history. The earlier radical reforms undertaken in other countries during recent decades concentrated on either the political or economic systems. For example, the reforms undertaken in Spain in the late 1970s and the Republic of Korea in the 1980s aimed at the democratisation of the political systems. They were carried out in the framework of the existing market economy which created a proper economic environment for political changes. On the other hand, the reforms undertaken more recently in Mexico concentrated on the economic system and were carried out within the framework of the existing political structure.

Radical reforms which focus on either the political or economic system are of course less complex than those aiming to transform both systems simultaneously. In the latter case, not only are the risks in the reforms doubled but the interaction between the two systems further complicates the reform process. The reformers in the post-communist countries were confronted with an enormous task and faced the challenge of breaking out of a vicious circle: the political reforms had to be carried on without the necessary support of a market economy, while the economic reforms lacked a proper political (democratic) framework.

* Professor of Law, Warsaw University, Poland.

The post-communist Central European countries accomplished quite quickly the fundamental political reforms which radically transformed their political systems. A political pluralism and free elections, supported by the right of free association of citizens in political, social and professional organisations, has been established. Individual liberties have been guaranteed and the economic liberties and protection of private property rights have established the legal basis for economic development.

However, the conversion of the socialised, State-owned and directed economy has proceeded more slowly than expected. This means that the historical sequence of events—market economy first and political democracy second—has been reversed, thus further complicating the process of economic reforms. The communist economic systems were a total failure. The living standards of the population declined dramatically. The post-communist economies, now gradually being transformed, could not meet the great social expectations. This led to a rapidly growing rate of unemployment, a phenomenon previously unknown in communist countries. The challenge confronting the reformer countries was to reconstruct the whole economy in an unfavourable economic and social environment.

The political and economic reforms could not be undertaken and carried out without a fundamental transformation of the whole system of law inherited from the communist regimes. It was therefore decided that a proper legal framework for political democracy and a market economy should progressively be established.[1] Fundamental changes have been adopted in new constitutions or have been introduced into those constitutions inherited from former regimes. The principle that the State must be governed by law (*Rechtsstaat*) was introduced as the foundation of the new legal order. The Constitutions guarantee the protection of private property and the freedom of economic activities, which are at the basis of the liberty of the individual.

At the same time, the legal infrastructure for a market economy has been introduced gradually. The massive law-making effort resulted in codification or recodification of certain branches of law and the adoption in each of the post-communist countries of hundreds of statutes which profoundly changed their systems of laws. The enormous law reforms carried out in these countries have been facilitated by the possibility of going back to their pre-communist legal traditions. For a long time, the legal systems of these countries had been developed in the framework of romano-germanic legal tradition.

The "coming back to the roots" tendency, visible during this process of law reform, has been supplemented by a modernisation approach aiming to establish a legal framework adjusted to the requirements of a modern market econ-

[1] J. Rajski, "L'établissement d'un nouvel ordre juridique dans les pays en transition" in *La Banque Européenne pour la Reconstruction et Développement et les mutations en Europe centrale et orientale*, Paris 1994; J. Rajski, "Quelques aspects juridiques du passage de l'économic d'Etat planifiée à l'économie de marché en Polgne", *Revue internationale du droit comparé, RiDP* no. 1991, 119 ff, and V. Zlatescu, "Droit de la transition en Romanie", RiDP no. 4/1995, 975 ff.

omy. This was expressed in several *travaux préparatoires* in a comparative law approach, in which the law and practice of a number of economically developed countries were taken into account. Thus, the modern law of contemporary democratic States has contributed at least indirectly, as a source of inspiration or a model, to the success of law reforms in post-communist countries. It has led in some cases to a "transplantation" or "reception" of normative concepts and structures, and even sets of rules of law. This attitude towards the law-making process has been reinforced by the Association Agreements recently concluded by all the post-communist Central European countries with the European Union (Community) and its members. Under these agreements the central European countries have undertaken to harmonise their laws progressively with European law in large areas involving the (market) economy.

A major part of the process of adapting the law to a market economy in post-communist Central European countries has resulted in the adoption of laws concerning:

(1) privatisation and de-monopolisation of the economy;
(2) transformation of property law and ownership structures;
(3) liberalising economic activities of both domestic and foreign operations;
(4) developing commercial law and commercial law structures;
(5) developing capital markets regulations;
(6) establishing competition regulations;
(7) developing banking and insurance regulations;
(8) liberalising currency exchange rules; and
(9) conversion to an independent judiciary and the establishment of specialised economic (commercial) courts for the settlement of business disputes.

The laws adopted in various Central European post-communist countries, although showing fundamental similarities, often differ (sometimes to a great extent) both as to the legislative form and as to content. This is why in the following comments on some of these issues I take mainly Polish law as an example.

II. PRIVATISATION

Profound and large-scale changes in ownership structures in all post-communist countries have constituted a decisive factor in the process of conversion of State command economies to market economies.[2] The communist

[2] C. Jones, *Privatization in Eastern Europe and The Former Soviet Union*, London 1992; P. Šarčevic (ed.), *Privatization in Central and Eastern Europe*, London 1992; A. Rapaczynski, J.S. Earle, R. Frydman (eds), *The Privatization Process in Central Europe*, Budapest 1993; N. Horn, "The Lawful German Revolution: Privatization and Market Economy in a Re-Unified Germany", 39 *American Journal Comparative Law* 725 (1991).

economy was based extensively upon State ownership. Privatisation of this economy has been a necessary precondition for its marketisation. The scope, rate and nature of the privatisation process have greatly influenced the emerging post-communist economic and social system. Privatisation has lead to a global redistribution of property and power in post-communist States. Privatisation has in all post-communist countries been a complex and difficult political, social and economic issue. It has been a task without precedent in modern history, the implementation of which required the establishment of a proper legal and institutional framework.

Such a framework has been established in Poland through a series of acts passed by the Polish Parliament in 1990. This includes the Privatisation of State-owned Enterprises Act of 13 July 1990 and the Establishment of the Office of the Minister for Transformation of Ownership Act of the same date.[3] Both Acts have been based upon compromise solutions reached after heated parliamentary debates. They provide for a State-controlled privatisation concept, taking into account the legitimate interest of the employees.

The first of the above Acts has been replaced by a new Act on State-owned Enterprises, Their Commercialisation and Privatisation, which was adopted by the Seym (lower chamber of the Parliament) on 28 June 1996. This entered into operation on 1 January 1997, after having been approved by the Senate and signed by the President of the Republic.

The 1990 Privatisation Act provides two main methods for the privatisation of State-owned enterprises (SOEs), which are retained under the 1996 Act. The first method involves two stages. Since the specific legal nature of an SOE excludes any possibility of changing its owner, privatisation must begin with the transformation of an SOE into a corporation in order to give it proper corporate form. The privatisation of the State-owned corporation is then effected by selling its shares to third parties. The second method of privatisation involves the liquidation of an SOE as a separate legal (but not necessarily economic) entity in order to dispose of its assets.

The 1996 Act provides for a general policy of transforming SOEs into corporations (described as a policy of commercialisation of SOEs), which has been hampered by the existing prolonged and cumbersome procedures, as well as the problem of how to deal with the interests of employees. The State-owned shares in privatised corporations are sold in open, competitive procedures to guarantee proper protection of State interests and to facilitate effective public control over their disposition.

The 1996 Act provides for the right of employees to acquire free of charge up to 15 per cent of the total amount of shares belonging to the State (Treasury) in order to secure their support for privatisation of SOEs. Under the 1990 Act they were given the right to purchase up to 20 per cent of the total amount of shares on preferential terms at a 50 per cent discount.

[3] J. Rajski, "Privatization of State-owned Enterprises in Poland", 4 *Hastings Internat. & Comparative Law Rev.* 767 (1994).

The 1996 Act determines in greater detail the procedures for liquidating an SOE for privatisation or other purposes. An SOE may be liquidated for any of the following purposes:

(1) to sell the enterprise's assets, in whole or in part;
(2) to contribute the enterprise's assets to a corporation;
(3) to transfer the enterprise's assets for a specific period of time for use under contract by third parties.

The great majority of the liquidated SOEs have been transferred by lease to employees who have satisfied the requirements laid down in the 1990 Act. The 1996 Act expressly limits this possibility to SOEs which do not have more than 500 employees and the value of whose sale of products or services does not exceed 6 million ECU.

III. MASS PRIVATISATION

A concept of so-called mass privatisation has been widely accepted in post-communist countries as an unconventional method of effective privatisation of State property allowing the achievement a number of important political, social and economic goals.[4] One of its objectives has been to speed up the privatisation process which was hampered by a lack of sufficient capital. The main political and social aim has been to revive declining public support for privatisation. Giving citizens a direct stake in privatised corporations has contributed to the acceleration of radical changes in society through widespread distribution of corporate ownership. This wide distribution of State property has been recognised as corresponding to the principles of social justice: because all citizens have contributed by their heavily unpaid work to the development of State property, therefore they should participate directly in its privatisation.

Different mass privatisation concepts and programmes have been carried on in various post-communist countries. A unique programme has been adopted in Poland.[5] It has been designed not only—I would even say not mainly—to fulfil the above objectives of mass privatisation, but also to assist the SOEs included in the programme in their transition to a market economy. An appropriate legal framework was created by the Act of 30 April 1993 on National Investment Funds and their Privatisation. A programme encompassing over 500 SOEs and representing approximately 10 per cent of Polish industry has

[4] R. Wisner, "A Socialist Shortcut to Capitalism? The Role of Worker Ownership in Eastern Europe's Mass Privatization", 19 *North Carolina Journal of Int'l Law & Commercial Regulation*, Fall 1993; Mass Privatization—an Initial Assessment. Centre for Cooperation with Economies in Transition, OECD Publications, Paris 1995.

[5] J. Rajski, "Polish Law on National Investment Funds and their Privatization", *Revue de droit des affaires internationales/ International Business Law Journal*, no.2/1994, 211 ff.

been linked to the capital markets. Fifteen specially constituted National Investment Funds (NIF) have been established in the form of closed-end funds registered as joint stock corporations to assist in the restructuring of SOEs. The latter were transformed into corporations and were included in the programme by holding their shares. Each corporation initially has the same shareholding structure: 33 per cent of the shares are held by a lead NIF; 27 per cent are held by other NIFs, each holding almost 2 per cent; 25 per cent are retained by the State Treasury; and 15 per cent are distributed free of charge to the employees.

The principal purpose of the NIFs is to increase the value of their assets, in particular through an increase in the value of the shares held in their portfolios. The NIFs are expected to attain this purpose by:

(1) exercising their shareholder rights with a view to improving management of those companies in which the Funds hold a controlling share, including the strengthening of their position in the market and the acquisition of new technologies and credits on their behalf;
(2) the conduct of economic activities consisting of the acquisition and transfer of company shares and exercise of the acquired rights;
(3) the granting of loans, and the contracting of loans and credits, to accomplish the above purposes as well as for other statutory purposes (Article 4 of the NIFs Act).

The shareholding in each NIF is initially represented by share certificates which began to be distributed on 22 November 1995 among all resident adult Polish citizens for a nominal value equivalent to less than US$10. The distribution process was closed on 21 November 1996. On receiving the share certificate, the owner is immediately able to trade it in bearer form. The market price of the shares has risen nearly seven-fold over the nominal price. That the share certificates have been introduced for trading on the stock exchange. They can now be placed on deposit with the National Securities Depository.

The owner may convert the share certificate through a broker into one share in each relevant publicly-quoted NIF. Because the value of the share certificate is not linked solely to the performance of a single corporation or a group of corporations, but represents a broad spread of investments in over 500 corporations, it offers Polish citizens a direct, but diversified, interest in a variety of Polish industries.

Each NIF is managed by a management firm which has been carefully selected from a number of competing consortia comprising leading Polish and foreign consulting firms, investment banks and other investment institutions. The team managing each firm works on the basis of a management and performance contract which provides for financial incentives to increase the long-term value of the fund. A supervisory board, initially appointed by the Minister for Privatisation from among the persons selected through a competition conducted by a special Selection Commission, controls the activity of the managers.

Implementation of the programme has contributed to speeding up privatisation of over 500 SOEs. Interposing NIFs has ensured that shares in privatised corporations are not so dispersed as to make effective corporate governance impossible. Calling in Western managers and Western experience to help run the Funds and stimulating a measure of competitive pressure between them should help improve efficiency and restructuring of the companies included in the programme. Finally, postponing trading in shares of the Funds creates a breathing space in which the NIFs managers could evaluate the companies under their charge and prepare them for the market.

IV. RE-PRIVATISATION AND RESTITUTION TO FORMER OWNERS

Restitution to former owners of property illegally nationalised or expropriated by the communist regime is one of the most politically contentious and difficult issues in Poland. Poland is the last post-communist Central European country not to have solved these problems.[6] A number of arguments against restitution has been advocated by leftist parties and organisations. The main argument has been based on the economic and financial hurdles facing Poland and the devastated economy inherited from the former Communist regime. Populist social reasons are also added, and it is said it would be unjust to compensate only former owners and not all employees who were deprived of honest remuneration and whose work contributed to the growth of State property. This is augmented by the argument that everybody is entitled to compensation for damage caused by the communist State. Finally, some legal arguments have also been raised involving the protection of legally acquired rights and complications in evaluating the legal status of a number of property rights. Because of these arguments, moral obligations (which should be accepted by the law) to restore property rights that have been confiscated by communist regime have not been recognised.

Since 1991 several reprivatisation proposals have been prepared by various Polish governments. Some of them have even been submitted to the Polish Parliament. However, none of them has been adopted. A new proposal providing for a restricted and partial compensation of specified owners of illegally nationalised or expropriated property has recently been introduced in the Seym and is treated as one of the priority items of the new government.

[6] A. Gelpen, "The Laws and Politics of Reprivatization in East-Central Europe: A Comparison", 14 *U.Pa. J. Int'l Bus.L.* (1993) 315 ff.

V. LAW ON OWNERSHIP

Property law has had to be fundamentally changed in all post-communist countries in order to eliminate the socialist concept of ownership and to establish rules of law. Under the communist regimes, the term ownership was assigned a special economic characteristic and a specific legal meaning.[7] The legal de-personification of "the property of the whole people" led to a pervasive system of entitlements, vested in those who were appointed to make the proper decisions. The classification distinguished among various "types" and "forms" of ownership aimed at the establishment of different levels of legal protection. The highest form was exclusively reserved for "socialist State property", i.e. "the property of the whole people"; the lowest level of protection was reserved for private property which was treated as a remnant of the past capitalist epoch.

This differentiation among various types of ownership and different scope and intensity of their legal protection had to be abolished. In addition, the traditional unitary concept of law reflecting the equality of all owners, be they private or public, has been reintroduced by appropriate provisions of the Civil Codes and other statutes. Consequently, all rules providing for a privileged legal status and protection of State ownership have been repealed.

VI. REVIVAL AND DEVELOPMENT OF COMMERCIAL LAW

Commercial law disappeared in communist countries as a branch of law serving the interests of private business and capitalist market economy. It was replaced by either a new branch of law (economic law) or sets of specific rules governing economic relations between State economic organisations as well as other socialist economic organisations (units of socialised economy). The traditional business organisations, partnerships and corporations were also eliminated (with very few exceptions in the area of foreign trade) and replaced by new State-owned enterprises and other socialist economic units. In addition, formal abandonment of commercial law was confirmed by either a total or at least a partial repeal of the commercial legislation inherited from the former, capitalist regime.

Given these circumstances, revival or re-establishment of commercial (business) legislation became indispensable after the fall of the communist economic system.[8] The dormant provisions of the Commercial Code which were not

[7] A. Baev, "Civil Law and the Transformation of State Property in Post-Socialist Economies: Alternatives to Privatization", 12 *UCLA PAC. L. J.* (Fall 1993), 131 ff.

[8] G. Baracks, "Revival of Commercial Law in Hungary", in Ross Cranston and Roy Goode (eds.) *Commercial and Consumer Law*, Oxford 1993, 326 ff.; J. Rajski, "Revival of Commercial Law in Poland", *ibid.*, 340 ff.; S. Luc, Y. Maltsev, "The Development of Corporate Law in the Former Soviet Republics", 45 *International & Comparative Law Quarterly no.* 2 (1996), 365 ff.

formally repealed by the Communist regime have been revived and progressively amended or supplemented. The Czech and Slovak Republics as well as Bulgaria have had to prepare and adopt new Commercial Codes. The law of commercial companies has been modernised in several post-communist countries in the form of separate enactments on business organisations. Other commercial laws, such as those on bankruptcy and reorganisations, have either been revived (see e.g. Polish Bankruptcy Act of 24 October 1934 and the Arrangement Proceedings Act of the same date) or newly enacted, as for example in the Czech and Slovak Republics. Appropriate *travaux préparatoires* have also been undertaken in order to harmonise commercial law with European rules and regulations.

VII. FOREIGN INVESTMENT LAW

Separate rules and regulations on foreign investment inherited from the former regime have been maintained to some extent, although far-reaching measures have been introduced in order to create a proper legal environment for foreign investment.[9] Foreign investors are free to make all kinds of investments by establishing their own enterprises ("green field investments") or investing in existing enterprises, both private and State-owned (including privatised State-owned) enterprises. The requirement for a foreign investor to obtain a government permit to set up a corporation has been abolished. Such permission is needed only in exceptional cases enumerated by law. Foreign investors may use corporate vehicles which essentially resemble continental European corporate forms. The law also enables them to shape their enterprises according to their wishes and specific needs. No less important, the majority of central European post-communist laws enable foreign investors to repatriate all profits after payment of taxes.

Guarantees aiming at the protection of foreign investments have been reinforced at the international level by a number of multilateral and bilateral foreign investment treaties to which the central European post-communist countries are parties.

VIII. LEGAL INFRASTRUCTURE FOR STOCK MARKETS

The capital markets, which functioned well before the Second World War in all central European countries, disappeared after the establishment of Communist economies. Government planning authorities closed securities and commodity exchanges. The abandonment of socialist planned economic systems and the progressive re-establishment of a market economy required the revival of capital markets.

[9] J. B. de Servigny, Investir en Hongrie, Paris 1996; D. Philippe, Les investissements en Roumanie, Revue de droit des affaires internationales/International Business Law Journal, no. 2/1994, 179 ff.

The decisions to reconstruct stock markets were made first in Hungary and Poland. The legal framework for a stock exchange in Hungary was created by Act VI of 1990 and in Poland by the Public Trading in Securities and Trust Funds Act of 22 March 1991. The Polish law was prepared with the assistance of American and French experts. Regulatory and supervisory functions on the Polish securities market are exercised by the Securities Commission. Its functions include the supervision of publicly-traded securities and to issue licences to brokers seeking to trade on the exchange. The Commission also monitors market performance with a view to protecting the interests of investors.

Polish law has been based upon a regulated securities market concept. The de-materialised book-entry form of securities has been adopted. European disclosure standards have been accepted, as well as high initial capital and high net-capital maintenance requirements for brokerage houses in line with European Union Directive 93/6 on capital adequacy. Poland has also introduced a central securities depositary.

Generally speaking, the Polish Act of 1991, as amended, has been harmonised with the legislation of the European Union Member States. The Warsaw Stock Exchange was reopened on 12 April 1991 as a joint stock corporation which was initially owned by the State Treasury. Shares in the Exchange were subsequently sold to the Exchange's member brokers and banks.

IX. COMPETITION RULES

A legal framework for the protection of economic competition (unknown in communist States) has been progressively established in all central European post-communist countries. In Poland, it has been set out in two Acts: the Anti-Monopoly Law of 24 February 1990, and the Unfair Competition Law of 16 April 1993. Both regulations have been harmonised with current European Union regulations. An Anti-monopoly Office has been established to implement anti-monopoly law and to adopt policies affecting the evolution of a free market in Polish economy. The law regarding protection against unfair competition protects Polish and foreign economic operators from activities which are recognised as violating fair competition standards in European Union Member States.

X. REFORM OF THE LAW OF CONTRACTS

The civil law codified in post-communist central European countries has had to be changed substantially in order to eliminate the socialist distortions to the civil law and to adjust it to a market economy. The fundamental principle of the law of contracts, freedom of contract, which was almost totally eliminated from the law governing contracts concluded between different entities of "socialist" economy, has been fully reintroduced. The provisions concerning commercial contracts have regained their dispositive nature. The previously existing restrictions have been eliminated. The catalogue of contracts expressly regulated in the Civil Codes and other statutes has been enriched by including new types of contracts which have been developed in modern market economies.

This catalogue is neither complete nor exhaustive. The parties are, therefore, free to depart from these provisions and to arrange their contractual relations according to their wishes and with very few exceptions. As a result, the parties are at liberty to agree on variations from the Civil Code provisions, to agree on combinations of the types of contracts regulated by the provisions of the Civil Code (and other statutes) and to develop entirely new contractual relations.

Further reforms of the law of contracts are to be expected during coming years. They will aim at modernising this part of the civil law in order better to adjust it to modern market requirements. They will certainly take account of the emerging European Law of Contracts.

XI. REFORM OF JUDICIAL SYSTEMS

The reform of judicial systems aimed at the re-establishing of an independent judiciary includes the following elements. The principle of the independence of judges declared in the Constitutions has been supported by a number of legal guarantees included in the regulations on the organisation of courts and the status of judges. The two-level court structure composed of the courts of first instance (regional or district voivodship) and the courts of second instance called the courts of revision (voivodship or the Supreme Court) has been replaced by a traditional three-tiered judicial system composed of the courts of first instance, courts of appeal and the Supreme Court as a court of cassation.

The extraordinary rights of appeal against final court judgments established by communist countries in the form of an "extraordinary revision" and available to the Minister of Justice, the Prosecutor General and the First President of the Supreme Court have been eliminated. The so-called State Arbitrage, a specific semi-judicial and semi-administrative system of dispute settlement between socialist economic organisations, has been eliminated.

Economic or commercial courts corresponding to the romano-germanic tradition of commercial tribunals have been established as an integral part of the independent judicial system. The economic courts have suffered, however, at least in certain post-communist countries, a case load crisis due to a sharp increase in the number of disputes submitted to them for resolution and the lack of sufficient numbers of qualified judges. The problem has been exacerbated because the available business lawyers, who disappeared in the communist countries for almost a half of century, have largely been absorbed by industry and law firms. The relatively low wages of overloaded judges have not helped to make the position attractive enough for business lawyers, who are in great demand.

XII. REVIVAL AND DEVELOPMENT OF ARBITRATION

Arbitration has become a popular dispute resolution mechanism in business transactions, both international and domestic. In the communist States genuine arbitration was banished from domestic economic life. Quasi-arbitration by the courts attached to the national chambers of foreign trade exerted a monopolistic jurisdiction over disputes between authorised economic organisations belonging to the COMECON member states.

Foreign trade enterprises dealing with non-COMECON partners were strongly recommended to negotiate for the jurisdiction of the Court of Arbitration attached to the national (Polish, Czechoslovak, Bulgarian etc.) Chambers of Foreign Trade. An alternative choice was use of an arbitration clause providing for the jurisdiction of an arbitration court in the country of the respondent party or arbitration in a third "neutral" country.

All Central European post-communist countries have eliminated the restrictions imposed on arbitration in domestic economic relations.[10] The jurisdiction of the Courts of Arbitration at the National Chambers of Commerce has been extended to cover disputes arising out of domestic economic relations. The parties are free to agree on the jurisdiction of other institutional or *ad hoc* arbitral tribunals.[11] In the late 1980s the COMECON compulsory quasi-arbitrations system ceased to operate.

International arbitration has become a generally accepted means of resolving disputes arising out of international commercial relations. The Central European post-communist countries have joined the ranks of countries supporting international arbitration by adopting laws establishing a proper legal framework to that effect harmonised with internationally accepted standards.

[10] E. Horvath, "Arbitration in Central and Eastern Europe", 11 *Journal of International Arbitration* 5 (1994).

[11] E. Horvath, "The New Arbitration Act in Hungary", *Journal of International Arbitration* 3 (1995); T. Szurski, Arbitration in Poland, International Commercial Arbitration in Europe, Special Supplement, the ICC International Court of Arbitration Bulletin, Nov. 1994, 101–8; A. Wiszniewski, Arbitration in Poland: Arbitrating Local Disputes, East-European Business Law, June 1991, s. 3.

XIII. CONCLUSION

Central European post-communist countries have profoundly changed their legal systems in order to create a proper legal framework for the transformation of the economy inherited from the communist regime to a market economy. The institutions and rules on which an efficient functioning of a modern market economy is based have been progressively introduced. This has been done in spite of a number of difficulties due to the absence of a proper legal framework, sometimes also of political will to make the necessary law reforms, and to the lack of legal experts in various areas of the law, which ceased to exist under the communist regimes. The process of law reform has been also been complicated by the fact that it had to be carried on by instalments—a feature that rendered more difficult the task of erecting a new coherent legal system. The present system is still composed of a mixture of old and new regulations which sometimes impairs the coherence of the whole system of law.

The adoption of laws adjusting the existing system to the requirements of a market economy is but the first stage in the process of creating the necessary legal framework. Equally important is the need for a proper law enforcement process and to create a business climate necessary for effective operation of a market economy. This will require more time for preparing and adopting the necessary legal regulations. A favourable climate for both domestic and foreign private economic activities has been progressively created. The private economic sector is developing rapidly in all central European post-communist countries and in generating the major part of the GDP and employing the major part of the labour force. Foreign investment has also been growing steadily, although not as rapidly as was hoped. The fact that all post-communist Central European countries have for hundreds of years shared European values and a common cultural and legal heritage provides a promising setting for the evolution towards an effective market economy.

The Association Agreements establishing an association between the European Community and its members and all the Central European post-communist countries may be expected to speed up the process of law reform. The process of formal reintegration of post-communist Central Europe into a United Europe will influence decisively the progress of Central European post-communist countries towards a modern market economy with a proper legal framework.

19

Integrator Companies in Mexico, Lifesavers of Micro, Small and Medium-sized Industries

ELVIA ARCELIA QUINTANA ADRIANO*

I. INTRODUCTION

Micro, small and medium-sized companies in Mexico currently account for 98 per cent of the national industry.[1] Concepts such as quality, productivity, excellence, technological modernisation and competitiveness are frequently encountered in relation to these enterprises and reveal the problems micro, small and medium-sized companies are facing in Mexico.

These problems are a consequence of the globalisation of trade, which is also affecting Mexico, and the evolving rules governing international trade. In response to these challenges, the Federal Government, through the Secretariat of Commerce and Industrial Development (SECOFI), has established the integrator companies scheme to solve some of the problems faced by micro, small and medium-sized businesses.

II. DEFINITION OF INTEGRATOR COMPANY

An integrator company can be defined as a company incorporated for the purpose of providing specialised services to its members, who may be individuals or corporations, in the various productive sectors of the economy at the micro, small and medium-sized levels, and whom it assists and advises on the modernisation and expansion of their involvement in the national Mexican economy.

The integrator companies were established by the Mexican government within the framework of the *1991–1994 Program for Modernization and*

* Ph.D; Full-Time Resident Researcher, Law Research Institute, National Autonomous University of Mexico, Mexico City; Professor in the Postgraduate Study Division; and Resident Professor of Commercial Law, Faculty of Law, National Autonomous University of Mexico, Mexico City.

[1] Instituto Nacional de Estadística Geografía e Informática (INEGI), "Micro pequeña y mediana Empresa", *Nacional Financiera* No. 7, 28 Feb. 1993, 120, *Universo Económico*, 15.

Development of the Micro, Small and Medium-Sized Industry. The aim of the programme is to try to solve the problems of micro, small and medium sized companies by proposing various types of co-operative organisations with a view to facilitating the establishment, operation and growth of the companies by using pragmatic instruments that respond to changing markets and the special characteristics of the various types of companies. The programme also defines the companies forming part of the programme and establishes supporting regulations to be observed by the Federal administrative agencies.

The Decree authorising the incorporation of integrator companies was published in the *Diario Oficial de la Federación* on 7 May 1993 as a consequence of the views expressed by various industrial organisations and individuals attending the public consultative fora. The objectives of the Decree are to improve national economic structures, to assist micro, small and medium-sized enterprises to adapt to international competition and to foster a stronger development through the better use of material and human resources. The Decree also seeks to improve productivity through inter-industry co-operation, delegating specialised tasks to the integrator companies and establishing integrator companies in specific areas of the economy that have a very large export potential.

The Decree was amended on 30 May 1995 to strengthen the virtues of the old Decree, which was considered an efficient instrument for removing administrative obstacles, supporting improved productivity in the business sector and in seeking horizontal integration. The purpose of the new Decree is to ensure the supply of goods and services of high quality and at competitive prices, to equip the integrator companies with an operational flexibility that will enable them, on behalf of the integrated companies, to obtain the highest return on their productive capacity. In addition, an integrator company is legally authorised to market a percentage of the goods and services produced by the integrator companies to third parties. The amended Decree will not only permit the operational improvement of integrator companies but will also relieve them from regulatory burdens to face the challenges and opportunities of the export market. In addition, by way of further support for the micro, small and medium-sized enterprises, the Program of Industrial Policy, which is co-ordinated by SECOFI, was established and began operating in June 1996.

It appears the growth of these companies has been modest, mainly because of their size. This is the reason the Mexican Government is anxious to accelerate their growth through effective changes in the way they purchase or produce their products, thus consolidating and enhancing their presence in the export markets. An additional objective is to improve the technological competence of the companies and consequently the quality of the goods produced by them. The government will also play its own role in deregulating the economy and simplifying the administrative rules. The programme will also have a positive impact on regional development by creating permanent jobs and will promote investments in the manufacturing sector. Nevertheless, we must bear in mind that effective penetration of international markets requires inter-industry co-operation to ensure that individual companies make use of the best modern technology.

III. GOVERNMENT POLICY TOWARDS INTEGRATOR COMPANIES

The emergence of international markets has brought about large economies of scale, and this in turn has been a key factor in encouraging States to establish free trade zones. If micro, small and medium-sized companies learn this lesson they should be able both to survive and face the domestic market challenges, and to compete with companies in similar lines of business within the NAFTA (North American Free Trade Agreement) framework.

The organising scheme for integrator companies has been inspired by these insights. Mexico has borrowed from European countries their experience and know-how for this type of business organisation. Through the Ministry of Commerce and Industrial Promotion, the Federal Government is responsible for promoting and co-ordinating the development, operation, incorporation, organisation, and registration of integrator companies. It performs these functions in co-operation with State governments, business development banks and industry associations. Among the inducements used by the Government to encourage micro, small and medium-sized businesses to join an integrator company is the assurance that the integrated companies will retain their independence and autonomy. In other words, any company that is affiliated with an integrator company will not lose its decision-making capacity regarding its own business, and the proprietors will still be able to raise their own capital and acquire the resources and technology needed to improve the company's productivity.

Today, the Federal Government is actively promoting the contemporary and obvious market for integrator companies, which is the export market as reflected by the gradual increase in non-oil exports, which reached 88 per cent in 1994.[2] It also represents a true opportunity for economic and technological growth, as well as improvements in quality and competitiveness for the micro, small and medium-sized integrated companies. These developments are due to Mexico's participation in the 1994 Uruguay Round of GATT and the inflow of new foreign investments. This in turn is a challenge for the integrator companies by putting them face to face with highly qualified competitors and forcing them to make the necessary adjustments to compete successfully with them.

[2] SECOFI. Encuentro Nacional de Empresas Integradoras. Octubre 13 de 1994.

IV. REQUIREMENTS FOR INCORPORATION OF INTEGRATOR COMPANIES

Integrator companies must be incorporated pursuant to the Mexican corporations legislation and must have legal capacity of their own, regardless of the type of incorporation they choose. They must have a minimum share capital of MP$50,000. No shareholder can hold more than 30 per cent of total outstanding shares. The integrator companies must submit an economic and financial feasibility study supporting the integration, a draft of the articles of incorporation and an organisational chart for providing specialised support services to existing micro, small and medium-sized companies to be integrated with the integrator company and expected to be potential users of services provided by the integrator company.

The shareholders of an integrator company may be individuals or micro, small or medium-sized corporations performing similar economic activities, either in industry, trade or services. They may be engaged in different economic activities but must have a common business purpose or be entities that wish to integrate to supply another larger-scale company. In addition to these requirements, an integrator company must have a defined geographical scope which may be national, regional, State or municipal, depending on the integrated company's needs.

With respect to income, the integrator companies will be allowed to earn income only from the provision of services or from fees established by the shareholders. An integrator company is not permitted, directly or indirectly, to hold any shares in the integrated corporations.

V. NATIONAL REGISTRY OF INTEGRATOR COMPANIES

SECOFI is responsible for controlling the national registry of integrator companies. There are currently 168 registered companies involving 8,000 micro, small and medium-sized companies with a total capitalisation of MP$220 million, with an average capitalisation of MP$1 million per company.[3] Integrator companies are principally located in the following sectors: agriculture and livestock, trade, food, handicrafts, machine tool production, leather and footwear, processed foods, furniture manufacturing and plastic products. They are to be found in the following states: Chihuahua (thirty-four), Mexico City (sixteen), Queretaro (thirteen), Puebla (ten), Jalisco (ten), Mexico (seven), Veracruz (five), Sinaloa (five), Guanajuato (four), Oaxaca (four) and Tlaxcala (one). These companies represent 75 per cent of all integrator companies already operating in our country.[4]

[3] SecretarÍa de Comercio y Fomento Industrial, Datos proporcionados en el RNEI. México, D.F. Nov. 1995.

[4] *Ibid.*

VI. SERVICES PROVIDED BY INTEGRATOR COMPANIES

As part of their objectives, integrator companies seek to raise the competitiveness of micro, small and medium-sized companies, to encourage specialisation in any of the various stages of the productive process, to consolidate their positions in the internal market and to increase their share of the export market. The functions and services of integrator companies can be classified under the following headings:

(1) *Technological.* The purpose of this service is to simplify access to specialised technical data or state-of-the-art equipment, machinery and scientific and technological laboratories, as well as qualified personnel, to increase productivity and the quality of products produced by integrated companies;
(2) *Promotion and marketing.* The purpose here is to improve and diversify the integrated companies' share of the internal and export markets, as well as to reduce distribution costs, through consolidating offers, jointly performing market research and preparing promotional catalogues in addition to taking part in fairs and exhibitions;
(3) *Design facilities.* The integrator companies will help integrated companies to select their models by reviewing current fashion trends in the market, by improving the companies' competitiveness and to develop and apply innovations with creative elements that will distinguish their products from competitor's products.
(4) *Sub-contracting of industrial products and processes.* The purpose here is to complete the manufacturing chains and support the co-ordination of various plant sizes, and promote specialisation while looking for opportunities to manufacture parts or components, to integrate the finished products of other companies, and to supply various industrial processes.
(5) *Financing.* The integrator company will advise the member companies on their financial needs and assist them in negotiating credits with various types of financial intermediaries.
(6) *Joint activities.* Because the use of intermediaries in industry is expensive in Mexico, companies being integrated try to avoid intermediaries and seek direct access to raw materials, inputs, assets and common technology, favourable price terms, and conditions of quality and timely delivery. The role of the integrator companies in promoting these goals may be summarised as follows: to sell production on behalf of member companies; to assist them by consolidated their market positions; to acquire raw materials, spare parts or machinery and equipment on favourable terms of price, quality and timely delivery, which are a function of larger purchase volumes; to obtain technology, technical assistance; to support renewal and innovation of machinery and equipment; to train the work force and individuals at executive levels; and to implement programmes to improve quality and productivity.

7. *Management of industrial wastes.* Member companies will be advised on how better to manage industrial wastes for recycling purposes, thus contributing to the preservation of the environment and encouraging the development of recycling technology.
8. *Administrative arrangements.* Member companies will be advised and assisted in making arrangements affecting the administrative, informational, accounting, legal, fiscal, credit and other areas appropriate for the company's operation.

Integrator companies seek, through being incorporated, to reduce production costs. They provide their member companies with greater access to sources of finance such as financing for the acquisition of anti-pollution technology, with administrative assistance, sub-contracting, export and access to foreign trade. All these steps provide the integrated companies with higher productivity, better organisation, production and technological development standards, and enable them to share costs and increase their efficiency without competing among themselves. However, integrator companies continue to experience problems implementing these goals.

VII. FINANCING

Nacional Financiera (NAFIN) is part of the development banking programme within the Mexican financial system, and its goal is to preserve productive plant and employment; and to support the financial intermediation system with credits for the micro, small and medium-sized company. The latter goal eases their access to financing through the Program of Financing for Industrial Modernisation (PROMIN), and, currently, the entrepreneurial development programme (PRODEM).

NAFIN has established specific schemes which, together with the commercial banks, credit unions and financial leasing companies (all being financial intermediaries) allow the micro, small and medium-sized companies to have access to credit. Nacional Financiera, pursuant to its regulating law, is restricted in the types of financing it may provide, mainly because all credit applications must be supported by warranties and must be structured on the basis of various plans of credit support granted to Mexican businessmen, which will allow the institution to recover the loan if default occurs. One of the solutions to this problem is the establishment of integrator companies that, among other functions, may grant credits to their integrated companies with institutional support from the financial intermediaries. Additionally, an integrator company that is supported by the development banking sector must develop different credit options. These must be comparable to those generated by the commercial banking sector with feasible and accessible terms that are attractive and have optimal financial schemes for the proper functioning of the integrator companies. In this respect, they need to create a special scheme permitting the development bank and integrator companies to work together but whose main interest will be different from that of financial intermediaries.

Among the financial support schemes designed by Nacional Financiera to operate within the commercial banking area are schemes related to working capital, fixed investments, support for technological modernisation; environmental improvement; restructuring of liabilities; support for importing goods and services from abroad; and the importing of raw materials and other inputs, spare parts, machinery and equipment.

The Decree promoting the incorporation of integrator companies[5] provides that the development banks "will promote the integration scheme" through specific support programmes for the integrator companies and their integrated companies. The support is in the form of credits, warranties and risk capital terms of five to fifteen years with preferential rates of interest to stockholders "so that they can make their contributions to the capital stock of Integrator Companies". The Development Bank can participate in up to 25 per cent of the amount of the project. Also, NAFIN and the National Bank for Foreign Trade are important participants in the proper operation of integrator companies, since they must counsel businessmen regarding the international purchase and sale of merchandise, products and processes.

(a) Fiscal Aspects

When an integrator company begins operating, it may resort to the Simplified System of Corporations established by the Income Tax Law,[6] for a ten-year period. This imposes no ceiling on income so the integrator company is able to build up its capital assets and also resort to a resolution that eases administrative conditions for taxpayers. If integrator companies use this provision they will be able to perform transactions on behalf of their integrated companies, but only if they fulfill the requirements issued by the Ministry of Finance "through general rules".

(b) Management and Administration

There is a National Council of Integrator Companies.[7] It is a legally incorporated body with non-commercial purposes, and is a private organism for business consultation and services for the micro, small and medium-sized businessmen grouped by integrator companies. The National Council represents

[5] *Diario Oficial*, 7 May 1993, as amended in *Diario Oficial*, 30 May 1995, Art. 60

[6] Ley del Impuesto sobre la Renta, Title II, Legal Persons; Decreto of 30 May 1995, Art. 50; Administrative Resolution on the simplified regime for legal persons, SHCP 16/JUN/1995.

[7] Se crea por acuerdo en el Encuentro Nacional de Empresas Integradoras en la Ciudad de México, D.F., 13 Oct. 1994.

the common interests of this productive sector and co-ordinates the efforts of integrator companies with respect to their consolidation, growth and development. The Council serves those areas identified by its members who wish to have a modern organisation that provides a quick and immediate response. Membership is not mandatory and the individual integrator companies preserve their autonomy and independence.

The National Council's objectives are, among others, to promote an inter-business organisation that contributes to group work; promotes export of sector production; provides legal advice; creates an advisory databank for decision making; improves working conditions, productivity and training of integrator companies; functions as a mediator in disputes that arise among companies; designs proper co-operative mechanisms among businessmen to preserve the environment; promotes funding and financing channels; and consolidates the micro, small and medium-sized company presence in the private sector.

The Nacional Financiera and the National Bank for Foreign Trade also have a development scheme which is intended to promote the business culture of the industrial, commercial and services sectors, but which basically focuses on the demand rather than the supply sector of the private market. Additionally, both institutions train the micro, small and medium-sized companies on managerial and administration topics, and on continuous improvement of processes and total quality. The object is to create the most favourable business environment for the companies and to enable them to understand the advantages of integration. There is also an explicit commitment on the part of these institutions to meet their objectives and to provide leadership for their client companies.

Training and advising integrator companies in lines of business and basic areas of training, management and administration must be jointly performed by the National Council of Integrator Companies, the Ministry of Commerce and Industrial Promotion, the Nacional Financiera, the National Bank for Foreign Trade, the Chambers of Commerce related to an industry's specific lines of business and the integrator companies themselves in order to optimise their development.

(c) Sub-contracting and Foreign Trade

Sub-contracting is an indirect means of exporting that offers excellent growth prospects to those who use it. This is because the system increases the final quality of products to be exported. This comes about because each manufacturer does not export a fully finished product, but is part of a process of producing a composite product, which is achieved through several sub-contracting companies, each of which exclusively manufactures a specific part. Thus, margins of error in the production of commodities are greatly reduced since products need only to be assembled and exported. Consequently, the time applied to machinery in all companies taking part in the process is reduced.

The Program to Develop the Micro, Small and Medium-Sized Companies has established mechanisms to promote sub-contracting, but further initiatives are needed. The Mexican Center of the Network of Sub-contracting Exchanges is currently designing new procedures to advise companies who need a special process about other companies using the process. The Center is working jointly with the National Bank of Foreign Trade, the Ministry of Commerce and Industrial Promotion, and the National Chamber of Transformation Industry (CAINTRA). All these institutions are working to create a positive atmosphere and to maximise the joint effort of all the existing sub-contracting exchanges in the country.

Currently, sub-contracting exchanges are operating in the states of Queretaro, Puebla, Yucatan and San Luis Potosi. The sub-contracting exchanges seek to participate in domestic and international exhibitions to promote integrator companies performing specialised functions. The sub-contracting exchanges do not yet have a homogenous database. However, the Mexican Center of Network of Sub-contracting Exchanges is working on it with a view to reaching a higher degree of organisation and to improve the training capabilities in all exchanges. In other words, if all sub-contracting exchanges co-operate with each other, a complete knowledge of all companies and their services will be achieved enabling subcontracting not only inside the corresponding state but also all over the country or even in the international sector.

The strategy expected to be followed by the exchanges through sub-contracting is to make technical processes available. To this end, the exchanges must have the development banking's support and the subcontracting companies must have a good technological capacity and a proper infrastructure that allows them to attract integrator companies or micro, small or medium-sized businesses seeking to contract out work.

All these steps will allow domestic companies to be promoted in international markets. In addition, it will make for easier communications among sub-contracting companies in different countries to satisfy the volume of requested orders. To achieve successful promotion abroad of exporting processes, it is necessary to form technological alliances that will allow the incorporation of integrator companies with the potential of being sub-contracted out as suppliers for export companies. This will eliminate intermediaries and thus provide better profits for the integrator companies.

The federal government should encourage the establishment of sub-contracting exchanges throughout the country, so that integrator companies attempting to associate with them will have greater growth possibilities. This must be achieved with short-term plans, by means of feasible and special credits to create and integrate the sub-contracting exchange, thus providing the domestic market with better access to the world economy and globalisation. In addition, governmental institutions should provide informational support concerning micro, small and medium-sized integrator companies suitable to engage in subcontracting work worldwide, and about financing programmes for labour training.

(d) Final Consideration

Micro, small and medium-sized companies in Mexico are the foundation for large corporations, while the latter are decisive for the growth and well-being of the population and the country. Therefore, any attempt by large corporations to operate in isolation will be a waste of effort and resources. If integrator companies manage to combine the potential of micro, small and medium-sized companies, they will match the large corporations in resources, be more competitive and successfully face the modern challenges of the global economy.

Mexico has a modern economic and administrative structure, an efficient system of development and commercial banking and a proper legal framework. However, the procedures and laws regulating business activity must be further studied and improved truly to support what productive companies at this level need most: timely and cheap financing. This is the only way for their products to become more competitive in the international market. Most importantly, it will also ensure the survival of these companies.

VIII. CONCLUSION

Integrator companies are established pursuant to Mexican commercial law in order to provide specialised services to their members who are also business corporations from different productive sectors, these being classified as micro, small and medium-sized companies. Their objectives are to increase competitiveness, promote specialisation of companies in any of the various stages of the productive process and to consolidate the activities of the integrated companies. This inter-business structure is intended to solve the problems faced in isolation by companies at these levels, such as quality, productivity, excellence and technological modernisation. This will make it possible for them to face the general challenges of economic globalisation and, particularly, that of the Free Trade Agreement with Canada and the USA, competitively penetrating the international markets.

Aware of the advantages of integrating micro, small and medium-sized companies, the Mexican Government supports and promotes the companies. To this end, the Mexican Government makes sure that the companies' constitutions meet the prescribed requirements. When the requirements have been met, the companies are registered in the Ministry of Commerce and Industrial Promotion, the department in charge of controlling the National Registry of Integrator Companies. Integrator companies have legal capacity and are legal persons and may issue shares according to the type of corporate organisation adopted by them. Participation of the integrated companies in the integrator company's share capital is restricted, and they must be users of services provided by the integrator company while preserving their independence and autonomy.

The main industries where integrator companies are located include agriculture and livestock, trade, processed foods, handicrafts, machine tools, leather footwear, agroindustry, wood manufacturing and plastic products.

The Mexican Government's policy is to support such integration. For this purpose, it acts through Nacional Financiera, a development institution, that implements support schemes for micro, small and medium-sized companies through financial intermediaries in the commercial banking sector. One of the very important roles of the integrator companies (among their many functions) is to assist their members to obtain financial assistance on favourable terms. The taxation area is another source of support for integrator companies, since they are entitled to make sure of the simplified taxation system for a ten-year period, therby facilitating the capitalisation and administration of the companies.

To promote co-operation among the groups, the National Council of Integrator Companies, a non-profit organisation, provides consultative and advisory services for micro, small and medium-sized businessmen. The Council is organised on a geographical basis and is integrated by its members. Membership is not mandatory. Integrator companies are also encouraged to join foreign trade associations in order to improve the quality of products intended for export.

PART VII

Consumer Law Developments

20

Canadian Perspectives on the Challenges of Consumer Bankruptcies

JACOB S. ZIEGEL*

I. INTRODUCTION

Over the past 15 years many industrialized countries have encountered the problem of chronic overindebtedness by consumers and have sought solutions for it. In Canada, it has led to a startling growth in the number of consumer bankruptcies. In turn, this has set off alarm bells among creditors and federal bankruptcy officials. The complaint is that going into bankruptcy and obtaining a discharge from one's debts is too easy and threatens the integrity of Canada's credit system.

These concerns are responsible for important provisions in Bill C–5, a bill to amend Canada's Bankruptcy and Insolvency Act (BIA),[1] which is currently before Canada's Parliament[2] and is expected to be enacted over the next year. The cumulative effect of the amendments will be to make straight bankruptcy a much less attractive route for overindebted consumers and to encourage them to make a statutory "proposal" to their creditors involving repayment of at least a part of the debts. The provisions are encountering increasing

* Professor of Law Emeritus, University of Toronto. This paper has also been published, with minor differences, in the *Journal of Consumer Policy*, vol. 20, 199–221 (1997).

[1] Rev. Stat. Can. 1985, c.B–3, as am. (Prior to 1992, the Bankruptcy and Insolvency Act was known as the Bankruptcy Act.) Bill C–5 was originally introduced in the House of Commons of the Canadian Parliament on November 24, 1995, as Bill C–109. Following the prorogation of the Canadian Parliament in December 1995, it was re-introduced in identical form as Bill C–5 and given first reading in the House of Commons on March 4, 1996. Bill C–5 was eventually approved by both Houses of the Canadian Parliament and given Royal Assent on April 25, 1997. See now Stat. Can. 1997, c.12.

[2] Under Canada's constitution, the federal government has exclusive jurisdiction over matters of bankruptcy and insolvency. Constitution Act 1867–1982, s.91(21). However, the BIA is not a complete insolvency code and the BIA itself provides (s.72(1)) that federal and provincial law continues to apply unless inconsistent with the BIA. Apart from this provision, the courts have vacillated over the years over the matters that fall within the exclusive jurisdiction of the federal government and have allowed substantial play for provincial intrusions.

criticisms[3] on the grounds that they ignore the source of the problems, the desperate financial condition of many of the consumer bankrupts, and the credit industry's own role in precipitating the current crisis.

The purpose of this paper is to provide a preliminary exploration of these issues. Much of the relevant data are still missing or uncertain. Nevertheless, enough is known to give us a reasonably reliable picture about Canadian consumer bankrupts and their problems and to enable us to ask pertinent questions about the role of modern bankruptcy law in a credit driven society.

II. GROWTH OF CONSUMER BANKRUPTCIES

The number of consumer bankruptcies in Canada more than tripled between 1985 and 1995, from 19,752 in 1985 to 65,432 in 1995.[4] It is almost certain that the 1996 figure will comfortably exceed 70,000. The number of consumer bankruptcies during this 10 year period was nearly 20 times greater than the increase in Canada's population[5] and was more than 4 times greater than the increase in the real outstanding volume of consumer credit, great though this increase was.[6] On the other hand, real disposable personal income only grew by a very modest 13 per cent.[7]

Very troubling though the bankruptcy statistics are, they must be seen in perspective. As the following table (Table 1) shows, on a percentage basis there have been even higher growth rates in earlier years. In 1969, the number of consumer bankruptcies was only 1,725, but between 1970 and 1979 it escalated by about 600 per cent as compared with an increase of approximately 50 per cent between 1980 and the end of 1989. It is clear, then, that the growth pattern in Canadian bankruptcies is not a uniform one but surges and abates in response to a variety of factors. Since some of the blame for the

[3] See e.g., Canadian Insolvency Practitioners Association, *Submissions to the Industry Committee of the House of Commons on Bill C–5*, June 1996, and J. Ziegel, "Canadian Bankruptcy Reform, Bill C–109 and Troubling Asymmetries" (1996) 27 Can. Bus. L.J. 108. (The present paper borrows heavily from those parts of the latter article dealing with the consumer bankruptcy provisions in Bills C–109 and Bills C–5.) Prof. Iain Ramsay of the Osgoode Hall Law School of York University and the author also gave evidence, on behalf of themselves and three other Canadian academics, on the consumer bankruptcy aspects of Bill C–5 before the Industry Committee of the House of Commons and subsequently before the Senate Committee on Banking, Trade and Commerce.

[4] CANSIM Series Data, D370477, Annual Consumer Bankruptcies, and Industry Canada, Office of the Superintendent of Bankruptçy, *Annual Statistical Summary*, 1995, Table 2.

[5] Between 1985 and 1995, Canada's population grew from 25.9 million to 29.6 million, an increase of about 14%. CANSIM Series Data C241089.

[6] The outstanding balance of consumer credit was $60.443 billion in Dec. 1985 and $119.279 billion in Nov. 1995. CANSIM Series Data B153. Corresponding figures, in constant 1981 dollars, are $47.537 billion in Dec 1985 and $68.370 billion in Nov. 1995. Constant dollar values were computed using the CANSIM Series Data P700000 and D484000: C.P.I. Canada on all items.

[7] The figure was $336.370 billion in Dec. 1985 and $381.225 billion in Nov. 1995. CANSIM Series Data E205160, both figures being expressed in constant 1981 dollars. Corresponding nominal dollar figures are $427.694 billion for Dec. 1985, and $665.119 billion for Nov. 1995.

Table 1. Growth in consumer and business bankruptcies 1966–1996

Year	*Consumer Bankruptcies*	*Business Bankruptcies*
1966	1,903	2,774
1967	1,549	2,474
1968	1,308	2,481
1969	1,725	2,354
1970	2,732	2,927
1971	3,107	3,045
1972	3,647	3,081
1973	6,271	2,934
1974	6,992	2,790
1975	8,335	2,958
1976	10,049	3,136
1977	12,772	3,905
1978	15,938	5,546
1979	17,876	5,694
1980	21,025	6,595
1981	23,036	8,055
1982	30,643	10,765
1983	26,822	10,260
1984	22,022	9,578
1985	19,752	8,663
1986	21,765	8,502
1987	24,384	7,659
1988	25,817	8,031
1989	29,202	8,664
1990	42,782	11,642
1991	62,277	13,496
1992	61,822	14,317
1993	54,459	12,526
1994	53,802	11,810
1995	65,432	13,258

Source: Industry Canada

current escalating number of bankruptcies is being put on the amendments to the BIA adopted by the Canadian Parliament in 1992,[8] it is relevant to note that the number of consumer bankruptcies was substantially higher in the

[8] Stat. Can. 1992, c.27. The particular amendment, which is the target for this criticism, is s.168.1 of the BIA entitling an individual first time bankrupt to obtain an automatic discharge from bankruptcy nine months after the bankruptcy order unless the discharge is opposed.

immediate years before the 1992 amendments became effective and that the number of consumer bankruptcies actually *declined* in the two years (1993 and 1994) after the amendments came into force.

III. SOCIOECONOMIC PROFILE OF CONSUMER BANKRUPTS

A comprehensive government sponsored study of the characteristics of Canadian consumer bankrupts and their financial condition appears in a 1982 study by Brighton and Connidis.[9] There are several more recent, also government sponsored, studies which, while less comprehensive and more particularistic, provide an equally convincing, and depressing, picture of the bankrupts and their problems.

Brighton and Connidis reported that consumer bankrupts did not "fit the stereotype of 'high rollers walking away from their debts' while holding on to substantial assets".[10] The authors also found[11] that consumer bankrupts were primarily drawn from the lowest socioeconomic levels although they emphasized (as later studies have also emphasized) that consumer bankrupts are not a homogeneous group. The median indebtedness was $10,865, but median assets were only $400. The median realized assets amounted to $528, and only about 6 per cent of the sample of consumer bankruptcies yielded $2,000 or more.[12] In only about one third of the cases was any money available for distribution among creditors after meeting the trustee's fees and expenses. The typical amount available for distribution was $100 to $250.

Equally revealing is a *Study of Receipts and Disbursements: Summary Administration* published by the Office of the Superintendent of Bankruptcy (OSB) in October, 1994. In 1993, 73,549 bankruptcies were closed. Of this number, 70,235 were consumer bankruptcies or 95.6 per cent of the total number. 91 per cent of the consumer bankruptcies were summary administration cases;[13] only 9 per cent were regular consumer bankruptcies. The consumer bankruptcy estates aggregated[14] $6.4 billion in liabilities, and $2.5 billion in

[9] J. W. Brighton, J.A. Connidis, *Consumer Bankrupts in Canada*, Consumer and Corporate Affairs Ottawa, 1982.

[10] *Ibid*., 76, para. 7.

[11] *Ibid*., Summary of Findings (unnumbered pages).

[12] The median realized assets are higher than the median declared assets because apparently they include intangible assets, such as postbankruptcy income tax refunds, which are not included in the statement of assets at the time of bankruptcy. See Report, 40, 60. Realized assets would not include household furniture and other personal items and professional equipment and trade tools exempted under s.68(1)(c) of the BIA.

[13] Summary administration cases are those where, in the opinion of the official receiver, the realizable assets of the bankrupt, after the claims of secured creditors are deducted, will not exceed $5,000 or such other amount as is prescribed. BIA, s.49(6). A larger amount has not been prescribed. Summary administration estates receive the benefit of a much simpler procedure. BIA s.155.

[14] For ease of description the following numbers have been rounded off to the first decimal point.

assets, leaving a deficit of $3.9 billion. Only $800 million was actually realized from the assets, i.e., 12.5 per cent of the amount of the liabilities. The liabilities of the summary administration estates amounted to $3.3 billion compared with assets of $1.4 billion. The amount realized from available assets was $166 million, or about 4.25 per cent of the liabilities. In terms of the sources of realized assets, the largest share (53 per cent) came from pre-bankruptcy and post-bankruptcy income tax refunds. The rest were made up as follows:[15]

voluntary payments	– 28 per cent
GST refunds	– 5 per cent
asset sales	– 6 per cent
miscellaneous	– 8 per cent

Of the $166 million realized, $93 million (56 per cent) went to cover the costs of administration and $73 million (44 per cent) was available for the payment of dividends. On this basis, and ignoring the claims of preferred creditors, each unsecured ordinary creditor would have received $2.21 for each $100 owing to it.

Two other studies should also be mentioned. *A Sociodemographic Profile of Consumer Bankrupts in Canada* by David R. Forde and Lance W. Roberts, also prepared for the OSB in 1994,[16] found that income levels among consumer bankrupts was generally low and that about 22 per cent of the bankrupts reported no personal monthly income. 6 per cent reported no family income.[17] 58.6 per cent of the bankrupts were between 20–39 years old. The median monthly personal income was $1,089. The median level of family income was modestly higher at $1,460. The average monthly level of family income for Canadians is estimated to be $4,343 and the median income $3,815.[18] The median level of assets (presumably unrealized assets at the time of compilation of the data) was $2,400 compared with a median level of liabilities of $24,300.[19] The principal types of debt by creditors were financial institutions (83 per cent), credit card companies (79 per cent), and government agencies (67 per cent).[20]

[15] *Study*, 3.

[16] And dated April 24, 1994. The study was prepared for the OSB as part of a study of the bankruptcy counselling process, and was based on a random sample of 10% of consumer bankruptcy filings across Canada between November 30, 1992, and November 30, 1993.

[17] *Ibid.*, Summary, 9.

[18] Statistics Canada, *Family Incomes: Census Families—1993* (Ottawa: Statistics Canada, February 1995) 9, 21.

[19] *Ibid.*, 6.

[20] *Ibid.*, 7. The government debts relate to unpaid income taxes and premiums, and refunds due for overpaid unemployment benefits. One of the many troubling phenomena of the 1990s is the number of employers said to have converted their employees into independent contractors even though they continue to do the same work. The conversion relieves the employer from regulatory and tax burdens and shifts them on to the 'contractor', even though the contractor may be ill equipped to carry them. Waiters, construction workers, and drivers working for courier companies are examples of employees who have been converted to contractor status. (The

IV. CAUSES OF CONSUMER BANKRUPTCY

Data collected by the OSB as part of the three year review indicate the following bankruptcy causes as recorded by trustees. (See Table 2). The data were recorded in 108 cases from a database of approximately 500 files. They suggest that trustees perceive the central reasons for bankruptcy to be excessive consumer debt and unemployment.

Table 2. Cause of bankruptcy as recorded by trustees

Cause	*Number*	*Percentage*
Excessive Borrowing	9	8
Excessive Consumer Credit	27	25
Marital	6	6
Guarantor	3	3
Mismanagement	4	4
Unemployment	35	32
Health/Dependents medical expense	7	6
Other	17	16
Total	108	100

Source: Office of the Superintendent of Bankruptcy: Bankruptcy Database Sample.

Another OSB sponsored study, *Re-Engineering Consumer Bankruptcy and Insolvency Systems: A National Assessment*,[21] also contains valuable information based on replies given by six groups of respondents with strong stakes in the administration of consumer bankruptcies and proposals.[22] When asked to indicate what they perceived to be the major causes of consumer insolvencies, credit counsellors and proposal administrators gave highest ranking to unemployment, with financial mismanagement being well behind in second place.[23] When asked to indicate whether consumers choose the bankruptcy solution because they perceive it to be "an easy route", 51 per cent of the trustee respondents thought it a "small" or "very small" consideration. 19 per cent

author's source for this information are statements made by trustees in bankruptcy at a roundtable meeting on Bill C–5 held at the Faculty of Law, University of Toronto, on August 7, 1996.)

[21] Office of the Superintendent of Bankruptcy, *Insolvency Bulletin*, 2nd–3rd semester 1995, vol.15, nos.2–3, 115 et seq.

[22] The six groups were credit counsellors, proposal administrators, trustees, OSB staff, court officials and creditors. Consumer debtors and consumer bankrupts were not included in the survey.

[23] Pp. 121–2, Question 5. Unemployment was mentioned as a very frequent contributing factor by 46% of the credit counsellors and 50% of the proposal administrators. The corresponding figures for financial mismanagement were 34% and 36%.

thought it was a "neutral" consideration. Only 9 per cent thought it was a very large consideration.[24]

The above causes of bankruptcy deserve much closer analysis than can be provided here, and should be interpreted in conjunction with the following comments.

(a) Importance of Unemployment Factor

Compared with many other industrialized countries, Canada has long suffered from a relatively high unemployment rate. An unemployment ratio of 6 per cent is often considered to be equivalent to full employment in the Canadian context. Between 1985 and 1995, the percentage was persistently closer to 10 per cent. Equally disturbing is the fact that Canada's weak economic performance over the past decade and the downsizing by many enterprises has led to a marked increase in unemployment rates among skilled and professional workers and executives. It has also meant that many two-family incomes have been reduced to one income, and heavily indebted consumers who previously relied on second jobs to augment their regular incomes no longer find it possible to do so.

Nevertheless, as Chart 1, below, indicates, the correlation between the number of consumer bankruptcies and the general unemployment rate in the economy, while statistically significant, is not as strong as might be expected. This suggests that the interplay between bankruptcy and unemployment is complex and that the high rates of unemployment reported among bankrupts may, to a substantial extent, be due to factors other than the general level of activity in the economy. In any event, the connection between the two requires further investigation.

(b) Overindebtedness: the Consumer Credit Phenomenon

All the Canadian studies make it clear that the liability of consumer bankrupts are predominantly composed of consumer credit debts. Chart 2 (*infra*) also shows a strong correlation between the growth in consumer credit and the number of consumer bankruptcies. The volume of consumer credit in Canada has grown 1600 per cent since 1966 (in absolute dollar terms) and doubled between 1985 and 1995.[25] Consumer credit in Canada has been a well established phenomenon since the late 19th century but until after World War II it was a predominantly middle class facility.[26] This selectivity has long been

[24] P. 199, Question 11.

[25] In constant 1981 Canadian dollars the increase between 1985 and 1995 was 44%.

[26] *Report of the Royal Commission on Banking and Finance*, esp. ch. 7, 9, 11 and 18–22 (1964, Queen's Printer, Ottawa.)

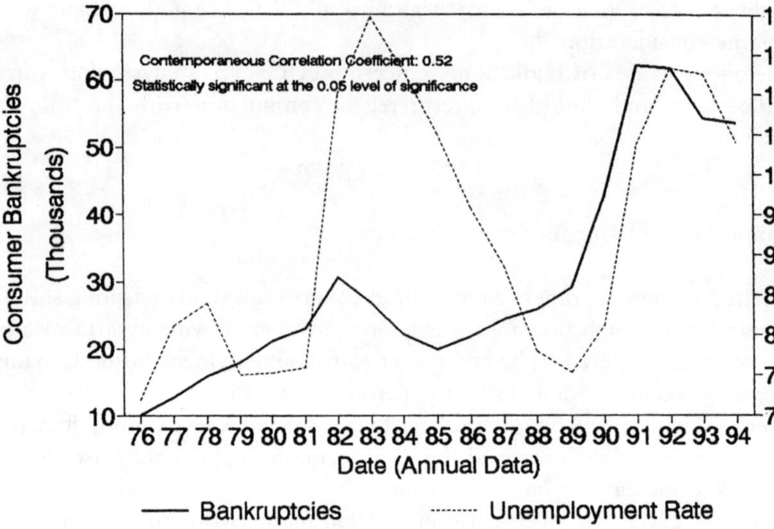

CHART 1 Consumer bankruptcies and unemployment rates in Canada.
Graph prepared by Douglas J. Cumming, a joint LL.B./Ph.D. (Economics) student at the University of Toronto

abandoned and it is notorious how accessible consumer credit is to all classes of Canadian consumers, regardless of their income levels and often, it would seem, with little regard for their capacity to repay the newly incurred debts. Equally important is the development of new forms of credit, particularly multipurpose and single purpose credit cards. Chart 3, though reflecting US figures, shows that credit card debt per household grew from US$310 in 1980 to $3,090 in 1995, and is still growing. It may be safely assumed that the growth figures are comparable for Canada.[27] Canadian trustees tell many anecdotal stories about the number of credit cards held even by unemployed bankrupts and how often a debtor will make a cash withdrawal on one credit card in order to keep another credit account in good standing. It is conventional wisdom that credit cards are regularly used as a proxy for income by income poor Canadians.

(c) Consumer Credit's Popularity

The Canadian bankruptcy scene cannot be properly understood without explaining the basis for consumer credit's enormous popularity with credit

[27] Between 1986 and 1995 the outstanding balances owing on credit cards to the Canadian chartered banks grew (in absolute dollars) from $5,862 million to $17,707 million. See *Bank of Canada Review*, Jan. 1996, Table C7.

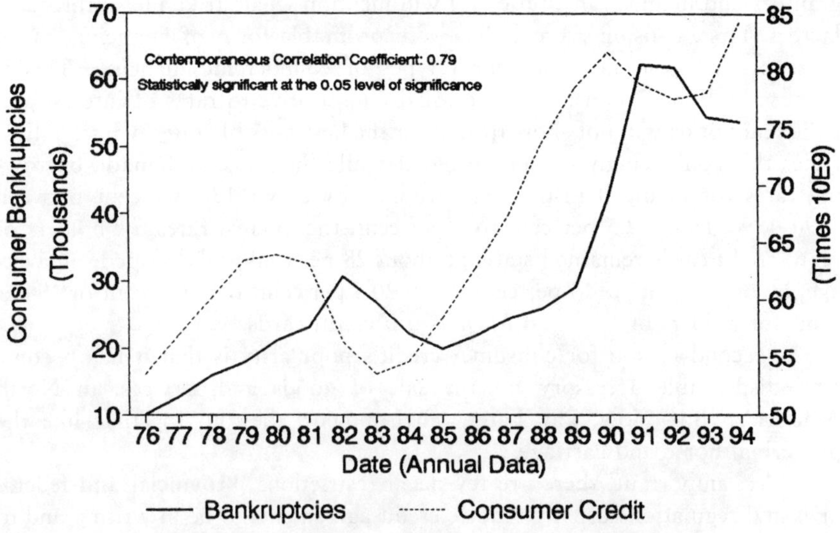

CHART 2 Consumer bankruptcies and consumer credit in Canada.

Graph prepared by Douglas J. Cumming, a joint LL.B./Ph.D. (Economics) student at the University of Toronto

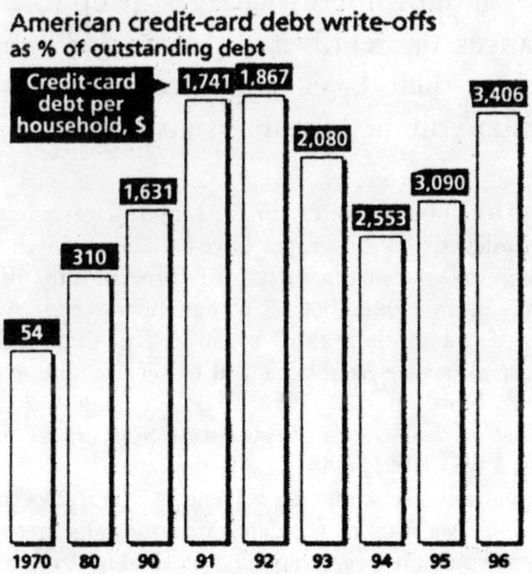

CHART 3 American credit-card debt write-offs as % of outstanding debts

Source: The Economist, July 27, 1996, p. 64

grantors and financial institutions. I will mention what strike me as three key factors. First, consumer credit is a very profitable form of financing, much more profitable in fact than most types of commercial financing. This is because "rationed" consumers are usually insensitive to rates of interest and either cannot or will not shop around for the best possible rates. Chart 4 illustrates this convincingly by showing that while the Bank of Canada borrowing rates for financial institutions dropped by about 150 per cent between 1990–1996, from 12.5 per cent to 5 per cent, the interest rates for holders of retail credit cards remained static at about 28 per cent and dropped, on average, by only about 10–15 per cent (from 20.5 per cent to 18 per cent or 19 per cent) for holders of *Visa* and *MasterCard* credit cards.[28]

The second reason for consumer credit's popularity is that it has become an indispensable accessory for the sale of goods and services; in North America's "Buy Now, Pay Later" environment, they go together like the proverbial horse and carriage.

No less important, there are few legal restrictions. Provincial and federal laws and regulations usually require credit agreements to be in writing and to disclose the terms of the agreement, including the cost of the credit expressed as a nominal annual interest rate.[29] There are also some advertising regulations but these, like the other disclosure requirements, are not policed and rarely enforced.[30] With one exception, there are no ceilings on interest rates[31] and the consumer's principal recourse for extortionate rates is the common law doctrine of unconscionability or, where applicable, the provincial business practices and unconscionable transactions relief Acts.

However, the problem is not so much of black sheep in the credit industry gouging unsuspecting consumers (although it undoubtedly happens) but of the ballooning effect of standard interest charges of up to 28 per cent per annum on outstanding balances on retail credit cards for overextended consumers who cannot meet even their basic expenses. High interest rates, generous profit margins and high volume customers also allow credit grantors to diver-

[28] At the present time (December 1996) credit card interest rates have become a lively topic of controversy because it is alleged that the rates have failed to match the dramatic reduction in general interest rates occurring in Canada in the first nine months of 1996. "Dozens" of members of Parliament announced in November 1996 that they would try to pressure the Canadian banks and large retailers to reduce their rates by 50%, and that, if this moral suasion did not work, they would consider a Private Member's Bill to set a ceiling on credit card interest rates (Toronto) Globe and Mail, November 20, 1996, B7).

[29] See for example Cost of Borrowing Regulations SOR/92 as am. SOR/94–367, adopted under the federal Bank Act, S.C. 1991, c.46.

[30] Cf. J. Ziegel, "Is Canadian Consumer Law Dead?" (1995) 24 Can. Bus. L.J. 417, 419–20.

[31] The federal Small Loans Act used to regulate rates on loans up to $1,500. provided by small loan companies, but these provisions were repealed in 1980 and replaced by s.347 in the federal Criminal Code making it an offence for persons to charge an effective interest rate exceeding 60% of the amount of credit advanced. See further Ziegel, "Repeal of the Small Loans Act and Enactment of a New Usury Law" (1981) 59 Com. Bar Rev. 188. (The prohibition is not restricted to consumer credit and was intended to outlaw loan sharking. There have been very few prosecutions under the section.)

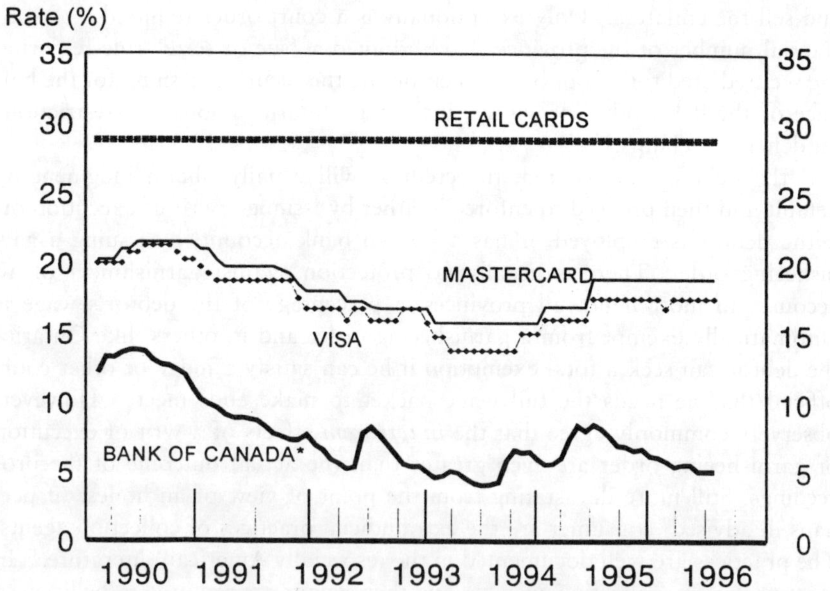

CHART 4 Credit card rates and the Bank of Canada rate.

- One Visa and one MasterCard issuer are used as examples. Rates of other cards vary.
- The spread between the sample Visa rate and the Bank of Canada rate is 12.5 percentage points as of June 30.
- The spread for the lowest Visa and MasterCard rate is 5.9 points while the spread for the highest is 13.9 points.
- The spread between retail card rates and the Bank rate is 23.8 points while the spread for gasoline cards is 19 points.

Source: Office of Consumer Affairs, Industry Canada, Ottawa

* The Bank of Canada rate is the rate at which banks can borrow money from the Central Bank.

sify their risks and not to be too fussy about the consumers to whom they extend credit. Canadian statutory law imposes no sanctions on reckless credit grantors and has no doctrine corresponding to the European doctrine of the responsible lender.[32]

Though the details vary from province to province,[33] Canadian law is generally equally favourable to enforcement of the creditor's rights against a defaulting consumer. If the debt is secured (as it invariably will be for motor vehicle purchase money loans and purchases of other high unit items), many of the provinces impose few if any restrictions on the creditor's right to seize

[32] Arguably, however, irresponsible credit practices are vulnerable to attack under provincial business practices Acts, but I am not aware of a reported case where the attack has been successfully made.

[33] See R. C. C. Cuming, "Consumer Credit Law" in G. H. L. Fridman (ed.), *Studies in Canadian Business Law* (1971), 87 et seq.

and sell the collateral. Only exceptionally is a court order required.[34] A substantial number of the provinces have adopted a "sue or seize" rule requiring the secured creditor to opt between enforcing the security or suing for the balance of the debt; other provinces, including Ontario, impose no restrictions on deficiency claims.[35]

If the debt is not secured, the creditor will usually obtain judgment by default and then proceed to enforce it either by issuing a writ of execution or, if the debtor is employed or has a known bank account, by issuing a garnisheeing order. There is usually no protection against garnishment of an account. In most if not all provinces, a percentage of the debtor's wage is automatically exempt from a garnisheeing order and in others, like Ontario, the debtor can seek a total exemption if he can satisfy a judge or other court official that he needs the full wage packet to make ends meet.[36] However, observers commonly agree that the *in terrorem* effects of a writ of execution or garnisheeing order are even greater than the actual outcome of the proceedings. Still more devastating from the point of view of an honest (if perhaps ill advised) consumer are the extrajudicial practices of collection agents. The practices are well documented in the (especially American) literature.[37] In most provinces, collection agencies and their agents are required to be licensed but this counts for little since the rules are largely unenforced. They will be even less enforced in the current anti-enforcement environment encouraged by government cost cutting and the dismantlement, in one fashion or another, of the consumer protection machinery adopted over the past 25 years.[38]

[34] Some provinces, including Ontario, require a court order where two thirds or more of the credit price has been paid. However, if there is default, overwhelmingly it occurs long before this cut-off point is reached and the two third provision has little practical effect. Stronger restrictions exist, or existed, in Saskatchewan and Alberta. For the details see Cuming, *supra* n.33. All the provinces allow sellers of durable goods to retain title in the goods, even after they have been delivered to the buyer until the credit price has been fully paid. Purchase money financing, especially by banks in relation to motor vehicles, is also a major phenomenon in Canada.

[35] Until Ontario adopted a revised Personal Property Security Act in 1989, some courts disallowed a deficiency claim if the secured party had not complied with the notice requirements under Part V of the Act. The revised Act makes it clear (s.64(3)) that non-compliance only entitles the debtor to claim actual damages or the liquidated damages provided for in s.66(2), whichever is greater. See J. S. Ziegel and D. D. Denomme, *The Ontario Personal Property Security Act: Commentary and Analysis* (Can. Law Book, Toronto, 1993), 475–81.

[36] Wages Act R.S.O. 1990 c.W.1.s.7(5); 80% of wages are automatically exempt from seizure or garnishment unless a court order is made reducing the percentage.

[37] Complaints about abuses led to the adoption of the Federal Debt Collection Practices Act (FDCPA) 15 U.S.C. ss. 1692–1692o (Supp.1 1977); see Geltzer and Woocher, Debt Collection Regulation: Its Development and Regulation for the 1980s (1981) 37 Bus. Lawy. 1401, and Goldston, "Federal Regulation of Debt Collection Practices . . . " (1979) 13 Univ. S.F. Law Rev. 575. Canada does not have federal legislation corresponding to the FDCPA and so far the federal government has been content to leave the regulation of debt collection practices to the provinces.

[38] Cf. Ziegel, *supra* n.30.

V. THE CANADIAN BANKRUPTCY REGIME

(a) Choice of Regime

An insolvent Canadian consumer seeking relief from her indebtedness has a number of alternatives. On the one hand, she may opt for a straight bankruptcy by making an assignment in bankruptcy pursuant to s.49 of the BIA. I consider this below. On the other hand, she may prefer a statutory consolidation of her debts under Part X of the BIA or make a proposal to her creditors under Part III Division 2 of the BIA.[39] The critical difference between a statutory consolidation and a proposal under Division 2 is that the former provides for no remission of any part of the debt whereas Division 2 clearly contemplates it, although it is not mandatory.[40] Still another route open to a consumer is to seek the assistance of a non-profit debt consolidation and credit counselling service, such as the ones that have been active in Ontario for more than 20 years, or of a commercial debt prorating service. I will limit my remarks to the debt adjustment regimes under the BIA.

Neither regime has made a significant impact on the Canadian insolvency scene. Part X has its genesis in 'orderly payment of debts' legislation adopted in Alberta during the Depression and subsequently copied in Manitoba. In a 1960 decision,[41] the Supreme Court of Canada held the legislation ultra vires the provinces as an encroachment on the federal government's exclusive insolvency jurisdiction, and this forced the federal government to enact substitute legislation. It did so in 1965 by adding Part X to the BIA. Part X only applies in those provinces which have elected to adopt it; only 6 provinces have done so.[42] The total number of consolidation orders made in 1995 amounted to 2,078 or somewhat less than 4 per cent of the number of personal bankruptcies declared that year.

Division 2 of Part III was added to the BIA in 1992 so as to give consumer insolvents a more flexible and attractive regime than Part X. The hope has not been realized. The number of consumer proposals filed in 1995, 2,419,[43] was only 341 more than the number of Part X orders. There appear to be several reasons for this disappointing performance. Any debt prorating or adjustment programme requires considerable self-discipline on the consumer's

[39] The consumer may also make a proposal under Part III Division 1 of the BIA and must use Division I if her total indebtedness, excluding a mortgage debt on the consumer's principal residence, exceeds $75,000. BIA s.66.11. Until 1992, only one set of provisions were available for both commercial and consumer proposals. What is now Part III, Division 1, was extensively revised in the 1992 BIA amendments and a new Division 2 was added to cater to the needs of consumers debtors.

[40] See BIA s.66.11, definition of "consumer proposal" and s.2, definition of "proposal".

[41] *Reference Re The Orderly Payment of Debts Act 1959, (Alta).c.61*, [1960] S.C.R. 561.

[42] For the list, see Industry Canada, Office of the Superintendent of Bankruptcy, *Annual Statistical Summary for the 1995 Calendar Year*, 38.

[43] *Ibid.*, Table 4B, 6.

part for several years. This may not be too difficult where the consumer makes a comfortable living and the monthly payments do not cut too deeply into the consumer's life style. The prospects are distinctly gloomy if the consumer's income is close to the poverty level and the cumulative debts represent many years of the consumer's annual income. A second reason is that a Division 2 proposal is not binding on secured creditors, a serious omission in a society which depends as heavily on automobile transportation as Canadians do. Another disadvantage is that default in payment of the committed amounts for 3 months or more results in an *automatic* annulment of the proposal.[44]

These features of a Division 2 proposal should be contrasted with the ease of making an assignment in bankruptcy and of obtaining an early discharge from most of one's debts, particularly if the discharge is not opposed. It seems that the strongest incentives for a consumer to opt for the proposal route are avoidance of the bankruptcy stigma, to the extent it still remains a stigma, and the consumer's right to retain all her assets.

(b) The Bankruptcy Option

It is remarkably easy for an insolvent consumer to go bankrupt under Canadian law provided the debts amount to a minimum of $1,000. All that is required is a written assignment (this is a standard document running to a couple of pages), the nomination of a trustee who has agreed to act (rarely a problem since trustees widely advertise their availability on cable T.V. and in the Yellow Pages of the local telephone directory), and "acceptance" of the assignment by the official receiver.[45] The last step is perhaps the easiest since the official receiver cannot refuse his acceptance if the assignment is in order. A modest filing fee is payable, but it only amounts to $50.

Acceptance of the assignment turns the consumer into a legal bankrupt and automatically vests all the consumer's present and future property in the trustee.[46] There are two exceptions to this rule. First, certain types of assets are exempt from the trustee's grasp. These exemptions are determined not by federal standards but by the exemption rules obtaining in the province of the debtor's residence at the time of bankruptcy.[47] In the second place, post-bankruptcy income does not automatically enure for the estate's benefit but

[44] BIA s.66.31.

[45] BIA s.49. The term "official receiver" is misleading since under the BIA the official receives nothing, except documents, for even the shortest period. The term was borrowed from English bankruptcy law where the official receiver is responsible for the insolvent's property between the date of filing of the assignment and the making of the bankruptcy order.

[46] BIA, s.67(1), s.2 (definition of property), and s.71(2).

[47] BIA s.67(1)(b). As in the US, efforts to substitute a uniform federal exemption standard have so far foundered because of provincial resistance and unwillingness by successive federal governments to impose a single standard. However, unlike the US position, the Canadian bankrupt does not even have the option of choosing between a federal exemption and those in force in the province of the bankrupt's residence.

the trustee must seek a payment order under s.68 of the BIA. Under the existing Act the making of such an order is entirely in the discretion of the judge and will usually be determined by what the judge determines is necessary to enable the bankrupt to maintain a reasonable life style. Except where the debtor is making a large income, trustees dislike making formal applications since they are time consuming and the results may not warrant the effort. They prefer instead to reach an informal agreement with the bankrupt.[48] Given the percentage of bankrupts who are unemployed and the poverty level median incomes of consumer bankrupts in general,[49] in most cases s.68 is more an aspiration than a reality.

(c) Discharge From Bankruptcy and Release from Debts

By all accounts, Canadian debtors' primary reason for choosing personal bankruptcy is to stop creditor harassment and to obtain an early discharge of their debts. In most cases the prospects for obtaining relief from at least the second burden are very good. Until the Bankruptcy Act of 1919, Canadian law provided no mechanism for discharge from bankruptcy or release of one's debts without the creditors' concurrence. The 1919 Act replaced the need for creditors' consent with a broadly based judicial discretion in which creditors have a right to object but not to veto. This approach still governs the existing statutory provisions.

Since the 1992 amendments, every receiving order or assignment operates as an application for discharge nine months after the date of bankruptcy unless the debtor serves a notice of waiver.[50] Before the date of the hearing the trustee is required to prepare a report on the debtor's estate and the debtor's conduct, before and since the bankruptcy, and to serve a copy of it on the creditors and the SOB.[51] Both the creditors and the SOB are then entitled to appear at the hearing and to oppose the discharge. If the case does not fall under s.173 of the Act, the court has a complete discretion to grant or refuse the discharge, to make a suspended order of discharge, or to give a conditional discharge contingent on the debtor making future payments out of his earnings or other income or turning over future property.[52]

Section 173 lists 13 grounds on which a discharge must be refused or suspended or granted conditionally. All the grounds but the first involve mis-

[48] The Superintendent of Bankruptcy has issued a directive for the guidance of trustees with respect to the share of the bankrupt's income they should seek to obtain for distribution among creditors. So far as I have been able to ascertain, since the guidelines are not mandatory, trustees interpret them non-uniformly and very flexibly in practice. See Directive 17R2 as amended to April 2, 1993.

[49] See text accompanying nn. 9–20 *supra*.

[50] BIA ss.168.1, 169.

[51] BIA s.170.

[52] BIA s.172.

conduct by the debtor before or since the bankruptcy. In practice, the first ground is the most important and applies when the debtor's assets are not equal to 50 per cent of the amount of the debtor's liabilities, unless the court is satisfied that the debtor is not to blame for the diminished value of the assets.[53] Section 173(1)(a) very much reflects a Victorian ethos and bears little relevance to the ccircumstances of most contemporary Canadian consumer bankrupts. As a result, the section has lost most of its sting.

Even before the addition of s.168.1 in 1992, the courts routinely found that s.173(1)(a) created no obstacle and freely granted an absolute discharge in the absence of special circumstances (such as concealment or fraudulent conveyance of assets) or unless the debtor was making a tidy income. New section 168.1 recognizes these realities and provides that, in the case of first time bankrupts, the bankrupt is entitled to an automatic discharge at the end of 9 months unless a creditor, the SOB, or the trustee himself objects.[54] However, both under the pre- and post-1992 provisions, eight types of debt remain non-dischargeable.[55] None of these exclusions is likely to affect consumer credit debts unless the debtor obtained the credit by false pretences or fraudulent misrepresentations.[56]

(d) Mandatory Counselling

One conceptually important but controversial requirement added to the discharge provisions in 1992 deserves to be noted. The House of Commons committee holding hearings on what was then Bill C–22 was persuaded that consumers should not be entitled to an automatic discharge under s.168.1 unless they had received mandatory counselling under new s.157.1. The underlying rationale was that since many bankruptcies were said to be caused by consumers' inability to manage their budgets and to use credit wisely, some instructions on these matters would serve a beneficial purpose.

The new provisions are controversial because they do not discriminate between the actual grounds of bankruptcy—between poor budgetary skills, for example, and financial problems precipitated by loss of a job—and because they draw an invidious distinction between consumer bankrupts and non-consumer bankrupts. There is also a striking difference of opinion between bankrupts and trustees about the effectiveness of postbankruptcy counselling. As Table 3 indicates, bankrupts think well of the counselling requirements and believe they do much good; the trustees are much more sceptical.[57]

[53] BIA ss.173(1)(a), 174.

[54] It appears that trustees frequently object if the debtor has not paid the trustee's fees and expenses!

[55] BIA s.178(1).

[56] BIA ss.178(1)(e).

[57] The SOB's directive provides for two mandatory counselling sessions for which the trustee is entitled to be paid $85 per session by the bankrupt if the counselling is not provided on a group

Table 3. Comparison of trustees' and bankrupts' perceptions of counselling outcomes

OUTCOMES ON KNOWLEDGE	5*	4	3	2	1
Counselling effects on knowledge of financial management					
Trustees' perceptions	0%	8%	54%	35%	3%
Bankrupts' perceptions	24%	27%	21%	12%	16%
Counselling effects on understanding of the causes leading to bankruptcy					
Trustees' perceptions	1%	17%	50%	29%	3%
Bankrupts' perceptions	25%	23%	22%	13%	17%
Counselling effects on ability to avoid future bankruptcy					
Trustees' perceptions	1%	11%	52%	30%	6%
Bankrupts' perceptions	48%	20%	12%	8%	12%
Counselling effects on ability to keep financial affairs in good order					
Trustees' perceptions	0%	9%	55%	33%	3%
Bankrupts' perceptions	41%	26%	15%	8%	10%
OUTCOMES ON RESPONSIBILITY					
Counselling effects of understanding of consequences for creditors					
Trustees' perceptions	2%	9%	26%	46%	17%
Bankrupts' perceptions	30%	25%	22%	11%	12%
Counselling effects on willingness to act in a financially responsible manner					
Trustees' perceptions	0%	10%	58%	28%	4%
Bankrupts' perceptions	45%	26%	12%	7%	10%

* Outcomes rated on a 5 point scale including: 5 = Extensive effect 4 = Considerable effect 3 = Moderate effect 2 = Little effect 1 = No effect.
Source: Sociometrix Inc., *A National Assessment of Bankruptcy Counselling Services, Final Report,Office of the Superintendant of Bankruptcy, Ottawa,* June 13, 1994, p. 32.

basis. The first session takes place at the time of the first interview before the bankruptcy decision is made and its purpose is really, as is generally recognized, to assess the consumer's condition and to determine the best course of action. The second session takes place after the bankruptcy order has been made, and before discharge from bankruptcy and may last between 30 minutes and 2 hours. The average appears to be between 30 minutes and 1 hour. See Directive No. 1R2, Dec. 21, 1994.

VI. THE COUNTERREVOLUTION AND THE BILL C–5 PROVISIONS

In preparation for the Bill C–5 amendments, the federal government established an advisory committee (BIAC), which in turn established a series of Working Groups which focused on particular aspects of the BIA. Working Group I was responsible for consumer bankruptcies and consumer proposals. The Group contained a large number of bankruptcy officials and creditors, but only a few trustees and no debtor representative, or sociologists or social workers. The officials and creditor representatives were convinced that the bankruptcy process had become too easy, that there were many bankrupts who should have chosen the proposal route, and that the BIA should be amended to encourage consumers much more energetically to travel in the proposal direction. Their views prevailed and Bill C–5 contains the following provisions to accomplish these goals:

(1) in the light of standards to be determined by the Superintendent of Bankruptcy (SOB), the trustee will be expected to fix an amount of the bankrupt's total income that the consumer will be obliged to pay over to the trustee unless the consumer appeals the decision;[58]

(2) a trustee, in making his report under s.170 of the BIA prior to the expiration of the 9 months' period, may include a recommendation that the discharge be granted conditionally;[59]

(3) in making a recommendation, the trustee is required to consider (i) whether the bankrupt has met the bankrupt's obligations under a s.68 requirement, (ii) the total amount paid by the bankrupt to the estate, having regard to the bankrupt's indebtedness and financial resources, and (iii) the fact that the bankrupt chose the bankruptcy route and not the proposal route to resolve her debt problems.[60] If the bankrupt disagrees with the trustee's recommendation, she may request to have the dispute resolved by mediation; and if this does not resolve the issues, the Bankruptcy Court may be asked to do it;[61] and

(4) apart from the trustee's new powers and obligations, and in addition to the existing grounds of objection, any creditor may object to the bankrupt's discharge on grounds similar to those available to the trustee. Even more significant (and presumably more inhibiting from the bankrupt's point of view) is the fact that the court, in considering an application for discharge, must also take into account the bankrupt's payment record under s.68 and the fact that the bankrupt chose the bankruptcy route instead of making a proposal.[62]

[58] Bill C–5, s.30(2), amending s.68 of the BIA.
[59] *Ibid.*, s.101(1), adding new s.170.1(1).
[60] *Ibid.*, s.170.1(2).
[61] *Ibid.*, s.170.1(4), (7).
[62] *Ibid.*, s.103(1) adding s.173(1)(m) and (n).

(a) Objections to Provisions

The proposed provisions have attracted much opposition from trustees and some academics and raise the following practical and principled questions:

1. *Where Is the Evidence?* The claim that large numbers of debtors, in a position to pay, are avoiding their obligations by opting for bankruptcy is, as we have seen, not supported by the available evidence. The proponents of the amendments have not adduced any contrary evidence. This does not mean that such cases do not exist (undoubtedly they do), but if they exist creditors can discourage them by exercising much more regularly their right to object to a discharge or by requiring the trustee to apply for a s.68 payment order before the discharge.

2. *Too much Bureaucracy and Paper Shuffling.* No convincing case has been made for substituting the trustee's judgment with respect to what the debtor should be asked to pay over voluntarily without a s.68 order, and for substituting the bankruptcy court's judgment where the trustee and the bankrupt cannot reach voluntary agreement.

3. *The bankruptcy process should not be converted into a collection agency for credit grantors.* This is a key issue which so far has received surprisingly little discussion in Canada and appears to have been totally neglected in Working Group I. If credit grantors deem it profitable to extend credit without verifying the credit worthiness of the borrower, it may be argued, they should be willing to accept the consequences. The large number of borrowers and the generous profit margins presumeably enable creditor grantors to absorb the losses. In any event, credit grantors should be able to look after themselves.

An important weakness about this argument is that it penalizes the careful as well as the reckless creditor. Avoiding this result by forcing the bankruptcy court to hold a detailed enquiry into the conduct of each credit grantor would be too costly and time consuming. A more profitable alternative, it may be thought, would be to establish a priority ranking for unsecured creditors comparable to the priorities applying to competing secured claims under Article 9 of the American Uniform Commercial Code and the Canadian provincial personal property security Acts.[63] Such an approach would require unsecured credit grantors to file a notice of their financing intentions with a public registry (again based on the well established precedents for secured claims) on pain of dropping to the bottom of the ladder if they fail to do so.

4. *Canadian bankrupts, like their American cousins, should be entitled to a Fresh Start; consumer proposals should always be optional and voluntary.* This is another key issue which so far has been little debated in Canada. I know

[63] For example, the Ontario Personal Property Security Act, R.S.O. 1990, c.P10 as am., s.30(1), provides that, unless other provisions of the Act apply, secured creditors' claims rank in order of priority according to the date of registration of the financing statement which is required to be filed. The first to file rule does not apply to purchase money security interests (s.33(2)) and these enjoy priority over prior perfected secured claims provided the statutory requirements are met.

of at least one very experienced master and registrar in bankruptcy in Toronto and of an equally experienced and thoughtful insolvency practitioner who subscribe to this philosophy.[64] I doubt however, that many other Canadians would endorse it in this unqualified form. I see several difficulties about it. It fails to explain why the debtor should be expected to surrender his present property but none of his future property. If the reason is undue hardship to the debtor, should the hardship to the creditor (especially an involuntary creditor, a separated or divorced spouse, an offspring claiming maintenance or support payments, or a friend or government agency making a non-profit loan) not also be considered? Is this not the rationale for a category of debts not affected by a discharge order found in all common law bankruptcy systems?

If these distinctions are well founded then there is much to be said for the current Canadian provisions allowing a judge to consider each objection to a discharge on its own merits. Perhaps the judges should be provided with guidelines (the existing BIA contains none). If, as I have suggested as worthy of consideration, consumer credit debts are hived off as not entitling a consensual creditor to object to a discharge or entitling the creditor only to object in specified circumstances, this will greatly simplify the task of adjudication. Even if this approach is not acceptable, it seems to me entirely appropriate for the bankruptcy court to ask to what extent the creditor has voluntarily assumed the risk of non-payment. Canadian creditors seem to accept the fairness of such a test since we are told they rarely bother to object to a discharge in a typical consumer bankruptcy.

VII. CONCLUSION

There will surely be no disagreement about the importance of consumer bankruptcies as a major legal, social, and economic phenomenon. What is surprising is how little attention the problem has so far attracted among Canadian sociologists, social workers, and legal scholars.[65] This has meant that the debate has largely been dominated by creditor oriented interest groups and other parts of the picture have been ignored.

So far as the Canadian legal academy is concerned, until quite recently bankruptcy law was either not taught at all as a separate subject or was taught by downtown practitioners more interested in the practical aspects of the discipline than its conceptual foundations. The scholarly interest is beginning to grow. My hope is that this paper will help to nurture and expand both the scope and depth of that interest.

[64] The practitioner is John D. Honsberger, Q.C., who is also a highly respected bankruptcy scholar. The judicial officer is Master Murray Ferron, Q.C., whose views appear in Ferron, "Rehabilitation" and "fresh start": Concepts that never were. (1996) 16 *National Insolvency Review*, 39.

[65] Among Canadian legal academics, Iain Ramsay of the Osgoode Hall Law School is a notable exception.

21

A European Concept of Consumer Rights: Some Reflections on Rethinking Community Consumer Law

NORBERT REICH*

I. INTRODUCTION

(a) The Concept of "European Economic Constitution"

(i) Rights Theory in the Union Context

This paper is concerned with the development of consumer rights granted to European citizens—individuals as well as groups—within the context of Union or rather, to be more precise, Community law. It uses the notion of "European Economic Constitution" as a metaphor to describe a fundamental process even though there may be some confusion about its content. The paper does not want to suggest that the European Union or Community resembles a State and that its "basic constitutional charter"[1] can be compared to the State constitutions of the Member States. Similarly, it does not want to suggest that the "constitution" should be regarded as something irrevocably laid down in some norms or principles beyond positive Community law that cannot be changed or modified by Member States or by appropriate Community legislative processes.

The paper does not comment on the discussion of whether the Union

* Professor of Civil, Commercial and European Law, University of Bremen. A longer version of this paper was first presented as a special course at the summer seminar of the University Institute, Florence in 1995 and will be published in *Collected Courses of the Academy of European Law* (1997), forthcoming. The present version concentrates on consumer rights in a broad sense only and was presented at the 8th Conference of the International Academy of Commercial and Consumer Law at Bar Ilan University, Israel, in Aug. 1996.

[1] Case 294/82, *Les Verts* v. *Parliament* [1986] ECR 1339 at 1365 No. 23, repeated in *Opinion 1/91* [1991] ECR I–6079 at 6102.

"needs a constitution"[2] or not. Rather it suggests that it already has one, though not in the traditional sense of (political) constitutions of States rather as an (incomplete and dynamic) body of laws which protect the "ordinary" European citizens in their economic role as consumers, in their functions as ecologically responsible subjects and in their individual and collective access to courts of law in case of need of protection. The other areas of citizens' rights, especially in social policy and a Union citizenship, will not be treated here because they go beyond the concept of the European consumer as a "passive market citizen"[3] but are concerned with citizens as active participants in markets for the supply of labour, the provision of professional services or of political discourse which are not the topic of this paper.

The concept of "European Economic Constitution" tries to describe a process of establishing, guaranteeing and implementing individual and collective rights as *subjective rights*[4] (*subjektive Rechte—droits subjectifs*) to EC citizens in the dynamics of European integration. This concept may be useful to describe a process of "constitutionalisation" which will never be finished but which has already left some conceptual signposts that cannot simply be removed without endangering the entire Union structure. This is especially true at a time when a rather traditional critique of the Union insists upon its retreat while competences and powers are at the same time extended, as has been done with regard to consumer policy in Article 129a of the EC Treaty as amended. The concept of subsidiarity[5] has been the vehicle for attempts at a "de-constitutionalisation" of the Union. It should be remembered that the European Court of Justice (ECJ) has so far resisted these tendencies by insisting that the principle of subsidiarity "cannot lead to a situation in which the

[2] Cf. the scepticism voiced by Grimm, "Does Europe Need a Constitution?" [1995] 1 *European Law Journal (ELJ)* 282; and a somewhat broader approach by J. H. H. Weiler, "Does Europe Need a Constitution? Reflections on Demos, Telos and the German Maastricht Decision", *ibid.*, 219.

[3] Cf. N. Reich, "European Consumer Law and its Relationship to Private Law" [1995] 3 *European Review of Private Law (ERPL)* 285.

[4] It is frequently said that the common law does not know the concept of "subjective rights" but uses instead the concept of "cause of action"; cf. Legrand, "European Legal Systems are not Converging" (1996) 45 *International and Comparative Law Quarterly (ICLQ)* 52 at 70; but cf. the detailed conceptual framework towards rights theory much earlier elaborated by Hohfeld in *Fundamental Legal Conceptions* (1919), distinguishing between rights, claims, powers and immunities, discussed in Reich, *Sociological Jurisprudence und Legal Realism im Rechtsdenken Amerikas* (1966), at 34–6.

[5] A. Toth, "The Principle of Subsidiarity in the Maastricht Treaty" (1992) 29 *CMLRev.* 1079; N. Reich, "Competition Between Legal Orders—A New Paradigm for EC Law?" (1992) 29 *CMLRev.* 861 at 889–95; R. Dehousse, "Community Competences—Are There Limits to Growth?"in R. Dehousse (ed.), *Europe after Maastricht* (1993), at 107–25; Bernhard, "The Future of European Economic Law in the Light of the Principle of Subsidiarity" (1996) 33 *CMLRev.* 633; D. Curtin, "The Constitutional Structure of the Union—A Europe of Bits and Pieces" (1993) 30 *CMLRev.* 17; for the German position cf. Bericht der Bundesregierung über die Anwendung des Subsidiaritätsprinzips im Jahre 1995, BT–Drucks. 13/5180 2 July 1996; for a new initiative to amend the Maastricht Treaty by a Protocol on subsidiarity, cf. draft of the German government of 13 June 1996 and the critique of Reich, "Zur Problematik eines Protokolls über die Anwendung des Subsidiaritätsprinzips" [1996] *Verbraucher und Recht (VuR)* 358–62.

freedom of private associations to adopt supporting rules restricts the exercise of rights conferred on individuals by the Treaty".[6] In a different yet comparable context, the ECJ has justified minimum harmonisation of workers' rights with respect to health and safety under Article 118a because this must necessarily be done uniformly throughout the Union and cannot be used as an argument against Community jurisdiction under Article 3b(2) of the EC Treaty as amended.[7]

This paper follows the position adopted in and extends Opinion 1/91 of the European Court of Justice[8] regarding the compatibility of the European Economic Area Treaty and its provisions of judicial control with the EC Treaty. There, the Court insisted on the specificity of Community law, which contains the rights and duties not only of Member States but also of citizens:

> "The essential characteristics of the Community legal order which has thus been established are in particular its primacy over the law of the Member States and the direct effect of a whole series of provisions which are applicable to their nationals and to the Member States themselves."

Whenever the concept of "subjective rights" is used, these words should be kept in mind and should be linked to those provisions of Community law that create a direct effect in favour of individuals in their capacity as citizens. The ECJ has recently repeated its concept of subjective rights in its case law that "the principle of State liability for loss and damage caused to individuals as a result of breaches of Community law for which the state can be held responsible is inherent in the system of the Treaty".[9]

(ii) From "Wirtschaftsverfassung" for Economic Citizens to a Charter of Subjective Rights

The concept of a European Constitution has mostly been used in the context of the discussion of an economic constitution concerned with activities of active market subjects *vis-à-vis* Member States and the Community itself. Economic freedoms as guaranteed by the Treaty were transformed into fundamental rights. Especially influential in this context have been so-called "neo-liberal" (*ordoliberale*) concepts of "Wirtschaftsverfassung".[10] They have found some confirmation in new Article 3a of the Community Treaty as

[6] Case C–415/93, *ASBL* v. *Bosman* [1995] ECR I–4921 at 5065, para. 81.

[7] Case C–84/94, *UK* v. *Council* [1996] ECR I–5755, para. 47

[8] [1991] ECR I–6102 No. 21.

[9] Joined cases C–46/93 and C–48/93, *Brasserie du Pêcheur and Factortame* [1996] ECR I–1029 at 1149 para. 31; Joined cases C–178 etc./94, *Dillenkofer et al.* v. *Federal Republic of Germany* [1996] ECR I–4845, comment by Reich, [1996] *Europäische Zeitschrift für Wirtschaftsrecht (EuZW)* 709; W. van Gerven, "Towards a European Ius Commune?", in Reich/Mernik, *Umweltverfassung und nachhaltige Entwicklung in der Europäischen Union* (1997) at 179.

[10] Joerges, "European Economic Law, the Nation State, and the Maastricht Treaty" in R. Dehousse (ed.), *supra* n. 5, at 37–8; D. Gerber, "Constitutionalizing the Economy: German Neo-Liberalism, Competition Law, and the New Europe" (1994) 42 *American Journal of Comparative Law* 25.

amended by the Maastricht Treaty whereby co-ordination of Member States' economic policies will be "conducted in accordance with the principle of an open market economy with free competition". Several other new provisions repeat the principle of an open market economy, e.g. Article 102a(2) for the economic policy of the Member States, and Article 130 on industrial policy where reference is made to a system of "open and competitive markets".

This open market economy is characterised by the recognition of economic freedoms, especially freedom of entry into markets, freedom from discriminatory treatment and freedom against unreasonable restrictions on trade.[11] Neo-liberal theory combines the case law on free movement and free competition with the principle of an open market economy by subjectivising the European Constitution in an economic sense: market subjects, especially undertakings and professionals, have an irrevocable right of entry and right to competition, not only against Member States but also *vis-à-vis* the Union as a Community. Freedom of professional activity is not just an objective principle generously granted and revoked by law, but a subjective right which can be enforced in courts of law.

To some extent this subjectivisation of the Economic Constitution can be found in the case law of the European Court, which has recognised in many judgments that Community law protects private property and free professional activity. The *ADHBU* judgment of 7 February 1985 insists that:

> "the principles of free movement of goods and freedom of competition, together with freedom of trade as a fundamental right, are general principles of Community law of which the Court ensures observance . . . [T]he principle of freedom of trade is not to be viewed in absolute terms but is subject to certain limits justified by the objectives of general interest pursued by the Community provided that these rights in question are not substantially impaired".[12]

The "*Banana*" judgment of 5 October 1994 repeats that the right to property and the right to pursue a trade or business form part of the general principles of Community law.[13] At the same time the Court insists that these principles are not guaranteed without restrictions and must be seen in relation to their social function. Community law therefore protects only the essence and substance of property rights—a principle well established in the case law on intellectual property.[14] This is of course a somewhat more cautious formula than the one used by neo-liberals.

[11] Mestmäcker, "Zur Wirtschaftsverfassung der EG" in *Festschrift Willgerodt* (1994), 275.

[12] Case 240/83, *Procureur de la République* v. *ADHBU* [1985] ECR 531 at 548 Nos. 9–12.

[13] Case C–280/93, *Federal Republic of Germany* v. *Council of the Union*, [1994] ECR I–4973 at 5065; cf. the critique voiced by U. Everling, "Will Europe Slip on Bananas? The Bananas Judgment of the Court of Justice and National Courts" (1996) 33 *CMLRev*. 401–37; N. Reich, "Judge-made 'Europe à la carte' " (1996) 7 *European Journal of International law (EJIL)* 103–11.

[14] N. Reich, *Europäisches Verbraucherrecht* (3d edn., 1996), No. 109.

(iii) The Evolution of the European (Economic) Constitution towards a "Charter for Citizens"

Even though the scepticism voiced by Weiler[15] and Joerges[16] against the neo-liberal concept of economic constitution is justified, it still may be useful in the context of developing a Euro-specific theory of subjective rights transgressing the boundaries of free movement. The main reason is the recognition by neo-liberals that constitutional principles need to be transformed into *individual rights*. Entry into markets, guarantee of private property and free exercise of profession and trade need to be implemented by individuals. They must therefore enjoy effective judicial protection and access to law. The Community law concept of "direct effect" tries to transfer these objective principles into subjective rights. This transformation is certainly part of the a*cquis communautaire* and hardly needs justification today, despite the manifold criticism voiced by traditional theories on State sovereignty.

In the conceptual framework of this paper, the idea of subjectivisation of principles guaranteed under Community law will be extended further to general citizens' rights in their roles as consumers and their functions as ecological subjects. The main criticism of the idea of *Wirtschaftsverfassung* can be summarised in its one-sided approach to rights theory. Economic rights of active market citizens are certainly the nucleus of any right granted by the European Community. In reality only those citizens who are actively engaged in free movement and competition will profit from these. Therefore, in the course of evolution of Community law these active economic rights have been supplemented by additional rights which will be analysed here as consumer rights, ecological rights and citizens' rights of access to law. One should look at the European constitution like a Russian *matrioshka*, which at its core contains the basic structure but has several layers of coats and dresses around it showing us the actual shape of the figure. This is the very reason why consumer rights (in a broad sense including ecological as well as citizens' rights) remain somewhat at the periphery of the European Constitution. This is fine even though the expanding consumer rights are challenging the traditional concepts of Community law which were mostly concerned with the interests of suppliers in the common market.

(b) The Concept and Legal Basis of Consumer Rights in the European Union

(i) "Human Rights" v. *"Citizens' Rights"*

When discussing rights within the European Union, one must avoid the same misunderstanding as arises when using the term Constitution. Since the

15 "The Transformation of Europe" (1991) 100 *Yale LJ* 2403 at 2477–8.

16 *Supra* n. 10.

European Union is a legal creation, fundamental rights to be protected by it can only be created by law and do not exist before, above or beyond law. The classical human or fundamental rights theory is therefore not applicable to the Union. Rights in this context will not necessarily be "everyone's" rights but may be limited to Union citizens.[17]

Consumer rights are not explicitly recognised by the EC Treaty. Article 129a on consumer policy is concerned with jurisdiction, not with conferring rights, even though, together with Article 3(s) and 100a(3), it insists on a high level of protection to which the Community is contributing. It is difficult to see how an individual consumer or a consumer association could enforce an eventual "right to a high level of protection". Article 130r lists the objectives of environmental policy which are also related to health issues, e.g. quality of drinking water and air. We will discuss later whether a right to safety and environmental quality can be deduced from these norms.

The European Court of Justice, on the other hand, has indirectly recognised the existence of consumer rights in its case law on free movement. The fundamental freedoms of the EC Treaty—free movement of goods, freedom to provide services, right to non-discriminatory treatment on grounds of nationality—support not only the active but also the passive market citizen. Examples will be given later. In this context the ECJ is also referring to the European Human Rights Convention (EHRC) despite the Court's opinion that the EC has no jurisdiction to adhere to this convention.[18] The EHRC may be used for applying and interpreting certain provisions of EC law. The Court has consistently held that certain fundamental rights which are common to all Member States, like the right to property and effective juridical protection, are part of the Community legal order, even though it has hesitated to use them to control the legality of Community law measures themselves—a point of critique correctly observed by Coppel and O'Neill.[19] Fundamental rights are also "binding on the Member States when they implement Community rules".[20] When measuring the legality of Community or Member State measures under the fundamental freedoms, respect must be paid to the EHRC, especially Article 10 on freedom of expression. In Case C–260/89,[21] the Court has insisted that possible restrictions of freedoms under Community law, especially the freedom to provide services, must be interpreted in the light of the Convention. The protection of a pluralistic system of broadcasting is con-

[17] Cf. the critique by J. Weiler, "Thou Shalt not Oppress a Stranger: On the Protection of Human Rights of Non EC-nationals—A Critique" (1992) 3 *EYIL* 65; Peers, "Towards Equality: Actual and Potential Rights of Third-country Nationals in the European Union" (1996) 33 *CMLRev*. 7.

[18] *Opinion 2/94* [1996] ECR I–1759 at 1789, para. 35.

[19] "The European Court—Taking Rights Seriously?" (1992) 29 *CMLRev*. 669 and the (somewhat exaggerated) critique by Weiler/Lockhart, " 'Taking Rights Seriously' Seriously—The European Court and its Fundamental Rights Jurisprudence" (1995) 32 *CMLRev*. 51 at 81.

[20] Case 5/88, *Wachauf* v. *Bundesamt für Ernährung* [1989] ECR 2609 at 2639.

[21] *ERT* v. *Dimotiki* [1991] ECR I–2925 at 2973 No. 43.

nected with the freedom of expression and reception as protected by Article 10 of the EHRC which "is one of the fundamental rights guaranteed by the Community legal order".[22]

(ii) The Union Treaty and Human (Citizens') Rights

An interesting new impetus to fundamental rights has been introduced by Article F(2) of the Maastricht Treaty. It gives a correct although contradictory restatement of the state of fundamental rights in the European Union:

> "The Union shall respect fundamental rights, as guaranteed by the European Convention for the Protection of Human Rights and Fundamental Freedoms signed in Rome on 4 November 1950 and as they result from the constitutional traditions common to the Member States, as general principles of Community law."

Article F(2) restates the already existing *acquis* under the case law of the European Court of Justice even though it cannot substitute a non-existing catalogue of fundamental rights, as Judge Grimm, a member of the German Constitutional Court, has correctly said.[23] Its legal character is ambivalent due to the specificities of judicial control.[24] Article F is part of the Union Treaty and therefore cannot be invoked under Article L in proceedings before the European Court. On the other hand, fundamental rights will be respected as general principles of Community law. According to Article 164, the Court must ensure that "the law" is observed in the interpretation and application of the Treaty. Principles of Community law on fundamental rights can certainly be regarded as "the law" according to Article 164.[25] Therefore, one must conclude that even though the Community is not directly bound by the European Human Rights Convention, it is indirectly under an obligation to respect it as a general principle of Community law. Member State courts are similarly bound and may, under the procedure of Article 177, refer to the Court of Justice preliminary questions on the interpretation of this Treaty to which the general principles of Community law belong, thus indirectly guaranteeing human rights. It might therefore be said that the rather restrictive approach of the Court in the *ERT* judgment should be overruled by a broader recognition of the importance of the EHRC. This is of course restricted to areas which are covered by Community law and does not extend to areas which are not under its jurisdiction, for instance criminal matters. Article F(2) has therefore created a dynamic element in the recognition of fundamental

[22] Cases C–353/89, *Commission* v. *Netherlands* [1991] ECR I–4069 at 4097 No. 30; C–288/89, *Stichting Collectieve Antennevoorziening Gouda* v. *Commissariat voor de Media* [1991] ECR I–4007 at No. 23.

[23] Grimm, "Europäischer Gerichtshof und nationale Arbeitsgerichte aus verfassungsrechtlicher Sicht" [1996] *Recht der Arbeit (RdA)* 66–71.

[24] D. Curtin, *supra* n. 5 at 65; S. O'Leary, "The Relationship Between Community Citizenship and the Protection of Fundamental Rights in Community Law" (1995) 32 *CMLRev.* 519 at 551.

[25] J. Bengoetxea, *The Legal Reasoning of the European Court* (Oxford, Clarendon Press, 1993).

rights, provided they fall in areas which are covered by the Treaty or by secondary Community law.[26] So far as consumer rights come under the ambit of the EHRC, they will indirectly increase the position of the consumer within the Community context.

(iii) The Importance of Secondary Law

Many provisions of primary Community law only contain enabling provisions and try to give Community law a certain direction. This is especially true with regard to consumer and ecological policy which is supposed to be based on a high level of protection. Frequently, therefore, it sets out minimum standards and contains provisions enabling Member States (not individuals) to opt out if this high level of protection is not attained by Community law.

On the other hand, once the Community legislator has acted by adopting directives aiming at a high level of protection, these directives become the starting point for guaranteeing rights. It is therefore a matter of the theory of "direct effect" how far these rights are guaranteed by the directives themselves and how far they can be enforced in the judicial process of Member States. Community rights theory presupposes a close link between primary and secondary Community law, a phenomenon unknown to Member States' constitutional law. The latter usually contain a hierarchy of sources of law whereby fundamental rights enjoy the highest place in the constitution and are placed above legislative and administrative acts. Such a hierarchy does not exist in Community law. Primary and secondary Community law intermingle where the guarantee of subjective rights is concerned. Outside the area of free movement, directives concretise or implement the rather general provisions of Community law.

It might be argued that secondary Community law can always be changed according to the procedures provided for by Community law. This is certainly true, but that does not affect the thrust of the argument. Community directives establishing subjective rights and being capable of direct effect are usually the result of complicated negotiations where many actors participate according to the relevant Community provisions, which makes their adoption, but also their amendment or even abolition, difficult. Horizontal directives in particular are not only hard to adopt but also hard to change. If this observation is correct, they frequently establish and implement fundamental rights in favour of Union citizens. In practice, the discretion of the Community law maker to amend and even revoke them exists only with regard to technical adaptations, not in fundamental aspects.[27]

[26] N. Neuwahl, "Principles of Justice, Human Rights and Constitutional Principles within the EU" in E. Paasivirta/Rissanen (eds.), *Principles of Justice and the Law of the EU* (1995), 76–9.

[27] Cf. Case C–303/94, *Parlament* v. *Council* [1996] ECR I–2943 concerning Dir. 94/43 amending Dir. 91/414/EEC on pesticides.

(iv) Direct Effect

The theory and practice of direct effect is the pivotal point of a European charter for citizens in general and consumer rights in particular. There is hardly any topic which has given rise to so much debate and controversy as the theory of direct effect. However, it can now be said that, after some hesitations and confusion in ECJ practice, the basic principles are well settled and can be said to form part of the *acquis communautaire*.

As far as primary Community law is concerned, there is no doubt that the rules on free movement and competition enjoy direct effect. The Maastricht Treaty has extended direct effect to the free movement of capital, which was previously excluded.[28] It is, however, not yet clear how far reciprocal rights are guaranteed to passive market consumers, e.g. free choice under the freedom to provide goods and services rules (the so called "passive *Waren-bzw. Dienstleistungsfreiheit*"),[29] a right to safety as a corollary to Article 36 allowing restrictions on free movement[30] and protection of consumers against anti-competitive practices.[31]

Secondary Community law will enjoy direct effect under certain limited conditions, and only with the help of either a Member State's legislature or a court. It is well known that direct effect can only take place if the delays for implementation of a directive have expired. It is then up to the national or eventually the Community judge to verify whether the provisions of a directive are sufficiently specific and unconditional to be invoked by private citizens in litigation against Member States. This must be determined on a case-by-case approach. Several directives on consumer protection, as I will show below, have been recognised to have direct effect.

Directives concerned with ecological and citizens' rights are much more difficult to interpret as having direct effect. Direct effect may be given, as will be shown, only to a limited extent for certain but not for all provisions, e.g. in relation to the directive concerning an environmental impact statement. The theory of direct effect must be seen in relation to the area in which it is supposed to create, guarantee or support citizens' rights.

As far as horizontal direct effect in private law relations is concerned, it should be remembered that the Court allows it against public bodies; this includes not only the Member States as such but also the public institution within its territory. Public bodies are also found in the private sector if enterprises are controlled by State regulation, e.g. privatised public utilities.[32]

So far as horizontal relations between private bodies are created and changed by directives, e.g. by consumer law, there has been a long debate on

[28] Case 203/80, *Casati* [1981] ECR 2595.

[29] N. Reich, *supra* n. 14, No. 43.

[30] Cf. the argument put forward by H-W Micklitz, *Internationales Produktsicherheitsrecht* (1995) at 216–40.

[31] N. Reich, "Garantien unter Gemeinschaftsrecht" [1995] *EuZW* 71.

[32] Case C–188/89, *Foster* v. *British Gas* [1990] ECR I–3313 at 3349.

the possibility of direct effect. The Court has always been hesitant and at first rejected a direct effect in its *Marshall* I case.[33] The Court's position was not only opposed by legal scholars[34] but also by three of its Advocate Generals, namely Van Gerven in Marshall II,[35] Jacobs in *le Foyer*[36] and Lenz in the *Dori* case.[37] The *Dori* judgment of 14 July 1994 allowed the Court to settle the conflict through a compromise. On the one hand, the Court rejected direct effect among citizens. On the other hand it repeated what it had said in many earlier judgments:

> "the national court that has to interpret that law must do so, as far as possible, in the light of the wording and the purpose of the directive so as to achieve the result it has in view and thereby comply with Article 189."[38]

The Court thereby shifts the responsibility for enforcing Community law to Member State courts. These courts have to apply both national and Community laws and have to merge them in a spirit of co-operation and loyalty according to Article 5 of the EC Treaty.[39] They should try to go as far as possible in interpreting national law in a Community-like manner in order to avoid conflicts between their national and Community laws.[40] There will of course be limits to the interpretation of national law through Community law, e.g. in criminal law.[41] On the other hand, the mechanism of interpretation can hardly be distinguished any longer from application because it extends not only to new law under the impact of the directive, but also to old law enacted before the directive.[42] It depends therefore on how national judges handle this power. This may be expected to lead to considerable differences in the application of Community law and thereby endanger its uniformity. The power of national judges is also limited to cases which do not lead to a *contra legem* application, as the Court indicated with its reference to interpretations of the national law "*as far as possible* in the light of the wording and purpose of the directive" (italics added).

[33] Case 152/84, *Marshall* v. *South-West Hampshire Health Area Authority (Teaching)* [1986] ECR 723.

[34] N. Reich, "Competition between Legal Orders" (1992) 29 *CMLRev*. 861 at 881–3; S. Prechal, *Directives in European Community Law* (Oxford, Clarendon Press, 1995), 205–305; G. Winter (ed.), *Sources and Categories of EU Law* (1995), 487–506 with references.

[35] Case C–271/91, *Marshall* v. *South-West Hampshire Area Health Authority (Teaching) (No. 2)* [1993] ECR I–4367 at 4387.

[36] Case C–316/93, *Vaneetveld* v. *Foyer* [1994] ECR I–763 at 770.

[37] Case 91/92, *Paola Faccini Dori* v. *Recreb Srl* [1994] ECR I–3325 at 3344; confirmed by Case C–192/94, *El Corte Inglés* v. *Rivero* [1996] ECR I–1281 at 1303.

[38] At 3357 No. 26.

[39] J. Temple-Lang, "Art. 5 as an Element of Community Constitutional law" (1990) 27 *CMLRev*. 645.

[40] Lutter, "Die Auslegung angeglichenen Rechts" [1992] *Juristenzeitung (JZ)* 593.

[41] Case 80/86, *Kolpinghuis* [1987] ECR 3969.

[42] Case C–106/89, *Marleasing* v. *La Comercial Internacional de Alimentación* [1990] ECR I–4135.

(v) State Liability as a New and Universal Remedy?

Another instrument to guarantee effectiveness of Community law stopping short of horizontal direct effect is State liability in case of non-implementation of directives. This principle was first developed in *Francovich*[43] and has been restated several times.[44]

The extent of this State liability has been modified by later decisions of the ECJ, which in some areas of free movement have in effect considerably narrowed down this newly created remedy.[45] Liability now depends on a "sufficiently serious breach" of Community law by the Member State,[46] even though negligence or some other form of fault is not necessary. However, the prerequisite of "sufficiently serious breach" may create a new and obscure defence for Member States who have, allegedly in good faith, misinterpreted primary Community law or the sphere of application of a directive which leaves room for different constructions.[47] This qualification, which will be fulfilled where the State has "manifestly and gravely disregarded the limits on the exercise of its powers",[48] makes subjective rights created by Community law dependent upon Member State discretion in the interpretation of Community law. The Court's argument, namely that wide discretion in the exercise of law-making functions by Member States should not be hindered by the prospect of actions for damages, is a political one and should not be used where directives create clear and unequivocal obligations of Member States in favour of citizens.

The *Dillenkofer* judgment of 8 October 1996[49] is much more explicit in protecting consumer rights conferred upon individuals by Community law directives. The case before the ECJ concerned the right of a traveller to have money refunded and the right to passage home in the event of insolvency of the travel organiser according to Article 7 of Directive 90/314/EEC of 13 June 1990.[50] The Court made clear that State liability is not merely an objective principle guaranteeing the effectiveness of Community law and forcing Member States to implement directives, but also a means to ensure the protection individual rights:

[43] Cases C–6/90 and C–9/90, *Andrea Francovich and Others* v. *Italian Republic* [1991] ECR I–5357.

[44] Case C–334/92, *Teodoro Wagner Miret* v. *FGS* [1993] ECR I–6911; for an overall discussion of the underlying legal principles cf. Caranta, "Judicial Protection Against Member States: A New Ius Commune Takes Shape" (1995) 32 *CMLRev*. 703.

[45] W. van Gerven, "Bridging the Unbridgeable" in Micklitz/Reich, *Public Interest Litigation before European Courts* (Baden Baden, Nomos, 1996), 69.

[46] Cases 46 and 48/93, *Brasserie du Pêcheur and Factortame* [1996] ECR I–1029 with note by Streinz [1996] *EuZW* 201; Case C–5/94 *Hedley Lomas* [1996] ECR I–2553.

[47] Case C–392/93, *The Queen* v. *HM Treasury ex parte British Telecommunications* [1996] ECR I–1631, repeated in Joined cases C–283 etc./94, *Denkavit et al.* [1996] ECR I–5063.

[48] *Ibid*., at para. 42.

[49] Joined cases C–178 etc./94 [1996] ECR I–4845; note by Reich [1996] *EuZW* 709.

[50] [1990] OJ L158/59.

> "the full effectiveness of the third paragraph of Article 189 of the Treaty requires that there should be a right to reparation where the result prescribed by the directive entails the grant of rights to individuals, the content of those rights is identifiable on the basis of the provisions of the directive and a causal link exists between the breach of the State's obligation and the loss and damage suffered by the injured parties" (paragraph 22).

A "sufficiently serious breach" will exist where a Member State fails to take any of the measures necessary to achieve the result prescribed by the directive within the period laid down; in that case the Member State "manifestly and gravely disregards the limits on its discretion" (paragraph 26).

This pronouncement of the Court will considerably strengthen individual rights, even though several problems persist, e.g. in cases where the directive has been only partially implemented, where loss and damage may be difficult to ascertain and where a relevant (direct) causal link may be missing.[51] Everything depends, of course, on whether secondary Community law intends to and has given an individual or a group of individuals enforceable subjective rights. This is a question which will be analysed in the following parts of the paper.

(vi) "Soft Law"

So-called "soft law"—an apparent contradiction but still a useful concept—has had some importance in the development of subjective rights in the Community context, even though some criticise it as an excuse not to legislate norms which may enjoy direct effect.[52] It may also be said to be a contradiction that soft law, e.g. instruments which do not have binding force such as recommendations, declarations of parliaments and so on which have become popular in consumer law, can have any legal importance at all. However, in the *Grimaldi* judgment,[53] the Court recognised that a recommendation issued by Community institutions according to Article 189 paragraph 5 can serve as a guideline for the judge to interpret his/her national law which is supposed to "implement" the recommendation. The same may be said of other recommendations in the area of consumer. Unfortunately, the European Court has no monopoly of interpretation in these cases and cannot prevent completely divergent results.

[51] The ECJ is not very clear on that point: *Francovich* refers to any type of causation; *Brasserie* restricts it to a "direct causal link"; while *Dillenkofer* only mentions a "causal link" ; cf. my annotations in [1996] *EuZW* at 713.

[52] Gibson, "Subsidiarity—Implications for Consumer Policy" (1993) 16 *JCP* 323.

[53] Case C–322/88, *Grimaldi* v. *FNF* [1989] ECR 4407.

II. CONSUMER RIGHTS AS ECONOMIC RIGHTS

(a) Free Movement and Free Choice

The European Community was originally an economic union, and therefore economic rights still constitute the central point of its Constitution. The movement of goods, persons, services and capital and non-distorted competition in the internal market are the basic structures of the Economic Constitution of the EC, as restated in Article 3a of the EC Treaty and amended by the Maastricht Treaty on the European Union.

These rights are directed mostly against Member States and prohibit, overtly or covertly, discriminations as well as unreasonable restrictions on access to markets within the Union. There is ample case law and literature on these subjective rights of active market citizens in the EC and therefore no need to comment on them. The important questions now are whether the free movement rules can be understood as having a common source allowing for a uniform interpretation of their sphere of application, their ambit of protection, and the restrictions on free movement imposed by the Community itself.[54]

This part of the paper is more concerned with economic rights of "passive market citizens", e.g. consumers. The issue will be examined with regard to information, fairness and protection against insolvency.

(b) Choice and Information

(i) Primary Law

A consumer's right of access to information has been recognised by primary Community law as being part of the free movement rules. From the abundant case law, I may single out three trends.

(1) An indirect right to information by the consumer has been recognised by the European Court in its case law concerning justifiable restrictions on trade under the *Cassis* principle. Whenever a Member State has good arguments to justify its restrictive legislation *vis-à-vis* the goods coming from other Member States, it should, under the proportionality principle, prefer information-type regulations to standard setting.[55] The case law of the European Court of Justice, as has been repeatedly pointed out by many scholars,[56]

[54] Cf. the interesting paper by Tesauro AG, "The Internal Market of the EC in the Light of the Recent Case-Law of the Court of Justice", Zentrum für Europ. Wirtschaftsrecht, Bonn (1996).

[55] N. Reich *supra* n. 14 at Nos 34, 55.

[56] S. Weatherill, "The Evolution of European Consumer Law and Policy: From Well Informed Consumer to Confident Consumer?" in Micklitz (ed.), *Rechtseinheit oder Rechtsvielfalt in Europa?* (1996), 423 at 463; Reese, *Grenzüberschreitende Werbung in der EG* (1994).

departs from the model of the informed or the confident consumer who is best protected by information and not by strict standard-setting. Whenever labelling is sufficient to protect the consumer, a prohibition of the marketing of the product may not be necessary. Where two interpretations of national legislation concerning intra-Community trade are possible, the one which provides for more information of the consumer should be preferred. The European consumer should be seen as one whose habits and patterns change due to the influence of the internal market. Paternalistic regulations, in the opinion of the Court, should not be imposed when they restrict trade or discriminate against foreign producers. There are of course exceptions to this rule, e.g. in cases where information is not enough to protect the consumer against aggressive marketing methods as in the case of door-to-door sales.[57]

(2) Spectacular litigation resulted in the *GB-INNO-BM* judgment of 7 March 1990.[58] In this case, the European Court explicitly recognised consumers' right to information by referring to the first EC Consumer Programme of 1975. The litigation arose in a cross-border context where a Luxembourg business organisation sought an injunction against a Belgian supermarket chain which had also distributed its leaflets in Luxembourg. The leaflet made special bargain offers indicating the amount of money to be saved and time limitations. This practice was illegal in Luxembourg but not in Belgium. The European Court restated and extended its "state of origin principle" whereby goods legally marketed in one Member State may also be sold in other Member States unless mandatory provisions of the receiving State prohibited the practice, provided they meet the proportionality test. Since the practice of the Belgian supermarket chain was in no way deceptive and the Luxembourg legislation did not protect the informed consumer but only protected traditional trade patterns, the Court held that the Luxembourg Law violated Article 30. The same principle was restated in the *Yves Rocher*,[59] *Estée Lauder*[60] and *Mars* cases.[61]

(3) Similar but more complex litigation arose in the context of services in the Irish *Grogan* case.[62] A student group had supplied young women with information on abortion clinics in England. In Ireland, abortion and all advertising for it were strictly prohibited while the United Kingdom had liberal advertising rules. The Irish Society for the Protection of Unborn Children asked for an injunction against the Irish student group distributing this material. The Irish court asked the ECJ for advice whether Article 59 applied in this context. The ECJ emphasised that information on abortion clinics in

[57] Case 382/87, *Buet* v. *Ministère Public* [1989] ECR 1235.

[58] Case C–362/88, *GB-INNO-BM* v. *CCL* [1990] ECR I–667 at 687 No. 14.

[59] Case C–126/91, *Schutzverband gegen das Unwesen in der Wirtschaft* v. *Yves Rocher* [1993] ECR I–2361.

[60] Case C–315/92, *Verband Sozialer Wettbewerb* v. *Clinique Laboratoires and Estée Lauder* [1995] ECR I–317.

[61] Case C–470/93, *Verband gegen Unwesen in Handel und Gewerbe* v. *Mars* [1995] ECR I–1923.

[62] Case C–159/90, *SPUC* v. *Grogan* [1991] ECR I–4621.

another country may be regarded as a service and, where it is furnished on a transborder basis, is protected by Article 59. However, since the service was free of charge, Article 59 did not apply.

With this compromise ruling the European Court avoided the possible conflict of Article 59 with Irish constitutional law, as well as avoiding a detailed examination of the relationship between Article 59 of the EC Treaty and Article 10 of the Human Rights Convention,[63] as it had done in the broadcasting cases. For our purpose, it remains instructive that cross-border information, provided it is commercial in character, comes under the protection of Article 59.[64] This protection extends not only to the supplier but also to the receiver of information.[65] This means that the consumer wanting to obtain information is protected by Article 59. The consumer has a Community-guaranteed right to information. This information is not only protected as part of the free movement of goods or services but is guaranteed as an intrinsic right, provided always that it is supplied for remuneration. It is an important task of legal theory to develop further this right of the consumer and user to information, especially in telecommunications, data processing and storage, and eventually to abolish the requirement of remuneration as in the *Grogan* case.[66]

(ii) Information Guaranteed by Secondary Law

The consumer's right to information is indirectly referred to in Article 129a and now provides a basis for specific actions in the field of consumer protection, even though it does not have direct effect.[67] This right is enshrined in many Community directives, e.g. with regard to labelling, price indication, product and service quality, consumer credit, life assurance, etc. The real debate in Community law is concerned not with the principle of information as such but with its extent and with regard to language requirements. The case law of the European Court has recognised:

> "The fact that consumers in a Member State in which the products are marketed are to be informed in the language or languages of that country is therefore an appropriate means of protection. In this regard it should be held that the hypothesis referred to by the national court that another language may be easily comprehensible to the purchaser is only of marginal importance".[68]

[63] Neuwahl, *supra* n. 26, at 74.

[64] J. Jacqué, "Liberté d'information" in Cassese/Clapham/Weiler, *Human Rights in the EC* (1991), iii, 330–43.

[65] Reich, *supra* n. 14, No. 43.

[66] S. O'Leary *supra* n. 24, at 548.

[67] Cf. Lenz AG in Case C–192/94, *El Corte Inglés* v. *Rivero* [1996] ECR I–1281 at 1292, para. 35.

[68] Cf. Case C–51/93, *Meyhui NV* v. *Schott Zwiesel Glaswerke* [1994] ECR I–3879 at 3900 No. 19 with Cases C–369/89, *Piageme I* (1991] ECR I–2971; C–85/94, *Piageme* v. *Peters* [1995] ECR I–2955.

New Community directives, for instance in the area of life assurance by the Annex to Directive 92/96[69] and Article 3 of Directive 94/47/EEC on time-share,[70] provide informational requirements, especially by insisting that consumers must receive information in the language of their State of residence. However, there is no general principle to that effect in Community law.

The insistence of many Community directives that indications, labels and advertising should not be deceptive is an indirect recognition of the importance of information. This is particularly true with regard to the different advertising directives, particularly Directive 84/450.[71] Article 4 contains remedies which may be invoked by consumer associations before courts of law or administrative agencies and which insist on a preventive, effective and speedy control of misleading advertising. It is up to the Member States to determine how to implement these principles but they must do so effectively.

Transparency of contract conditions is another part of the information paradigm written into secondary Community law. Most important is Directive 93/13,[72] which insists on plain and intelligible language for all standard terms in contracts.[73] Article 11 of Directive 93/22 of 10 June 1993[74] obliges Member States to adopt binding rules on the supply of investment services, including "adequate disclosure of relevant material information in its dealings with its clients".

It should be mentioned that the scope of secondary Community law is much wider than that of primary Community law, because it is not limited to cross-border aspects but extends to all transactions taking place within the European Union. The European citizen should be able to obtain information, to be protected from deception and to know about his/her contractual rights and duties in all EC jurisdictions wherever he or she resides or consumes. Usually, the relevant Directives are sufficiently specific and unconditional to allow for a vertically direct effect, as was stated by the Court in *Dori* with regard to the doorstep selling directive 85/577.[75]

On the other hand, information may sometimes be required as a substitute for more stringent regulation for the consumer's protection. This makes it important to develop fairness standards in the EU.

(c) Fairness

There is no Community law principle of fairness, but it is emerging and developing in several areas in an incremental way, as Wilhelmsson[76] has

[69] [1992] OJ L228/1.
[70] [1994] OJ L137/42.
[71] [1984] OJ L250/17.
[72] [1993] OJ L95/29.
[73] T. Wilhelmson, *Social Contract Law and European Integration* (1995), 145; N. Reich, "Kreditbürgschaft und Transparenz" [1995] *Neue Juristische Wochenschrift (NJW)* 1857.
[74] [1993] OJ L141/27.
[75] *Supra* at 3354 Nos. 16/17

shown. This right must be created by secondary law on trade practices by imposing a still rather limited obligation of fairness on the trader *vis-à-vis* the consumer or sales agent.[77] The misleading advertising directive has, however, rejected such an approach; it leaves commercial fairness to a later stage of harmonisation which so far has been attempted only with regard to comparative advertising where a Commission proposal has been transformed into a Common Position.[78] Other directives try to maintain fairness by allowing the consumer a right to rescind or cancel his contractual consent, e.g. in doorstep, timeshare and life insurance contracts. Similar proposals are under discussion with respect to distance selling where Directive 97/7/EC of the Euopean Parliament and Council was adopted on 20 May 1997.[79] Fairness may also relate to the performance of the contract, e.g. in giving the consumer a right to compensation which cannot be excluded, especially in connected lender liability[80] and package holiday contracts.[81]

More important has been horizontal Community legislation on unfair terms in consumer contracts. Directive 93/13 contains an Article 3 paragraph 1, which provides that :

> "a contractual term which has not been individually negotiated shall be regarded as unfair if, contrary to the requirement of good faith, it causes a significant imbalance in the parties' rights and obligations arriving under the contract, to the detriment of the consumer."

This is a very broad provision obliging every trader who uses a pre-formulated contract clause in the EU after 1 January 1995 to respect the requirements of good faith and to ensure a fair balance of the parties' rights and obligations. This obligation exists only in contracts between sellers or suppliers and consumers, as defined by Article 2 of the directive. It is not a general obligation in other contracts, even though this might be useful.[82] Articles 6 and 7 try to enforce this fairness obligation in an international context and by an effective implementation mechanism.

The fairness obligation has not been concretised in a mandatory blacklist, as was proposed by the Commission and the European Parliament. The list in the annex is now, according to Article 3 paragraph 3, only an indicative, non-exhaustive list of terms which may be regarded as unfair. The actual

[76] *Supra* n. 73, 181–3.

[77] Cf. Dir. 86/653/EEC of 10 Dec. 1986 [1986] OJ L382/17.

[78] [1996] OJ C219/14.

[79] [1997] OJ L144/19.

[80] Art. 11(2) of Dir. 87/102/EEC of 22 Dec. 1986 [1987] OJ L42/48; cf. opinion of Lenz AG in Case C–192/94, *El Corte Inglés* v. *Rivero* [1996] ECR I–1281 at 1288 No. 13 insisting on a minimal protection standard conferred by the Dir.; Howells/Weatherill, *Consumer Protection Law* (Aldershot, Dartmouth, 1995) at 267.

[81] Art. 5 of Dir. 90/314/EEC of 23 June 1990 [1990] OJ L158/59.

[82] H. Collins, "Good Faith in European Contract Law" (1994) 14 *OJLS* 229; Tenreiro, "The Community Directive on Unfair Terms and National Legal Systems—The Principle of Good Faith and Remedies for Unfair Terms" (1995) 3 *ERPL* 373.

decision depends upon the Member State. However, as Wilhelmsson[83] has shown, the annex is not completely devoid of legal effect. Member State's courts of law must interpret their law in accordance with Community law, especially the general clause which can be concretised by reference to the annex. There is some argument to give indirect effect to the annex, e.g. when taking account of the case law of the ECJ concerning the importance of recommendations. This rather "soft" approach to the fairness principle in European law makes it difficult to develop it into a genuine consumer right to fairness which could be enforced individually or by consumer associations in litigation against undertakings using unfair terms. But legal evolution may allow the development of general principles from the annex, especially with regard to exemption clauses which are forbidden not only by the annex but also in many other directives, as well as in most Member State's legislations. It may perhaps be possible to formulate some minimum consumer rights based on the annex. One of these minimum rights would be directed against unilateral decision making of the trader *vis-à-vis* the consumer.[84] Another would impose a ban on exemption clauses depriving the consumer of rights accorded to him or her under European contract law. Exclusion clauses may also be unenforceable under private international law rules according to Article 5 or 7(2) of the Rome Convention. Micklitz[85] derives from the somewhat scattered Community provisions on fairness the general principle that the legitimate expectations of the consumer should be protected.

The limits to the fairness concept under Community law have been clearly pointed out by Wilhelmsson[86] and Huls.[87] Fairness is not concerned with the redistributive aspects of consumer contracts.[88] It is therefore not applicable to cases of "social *force majeure*", e.g. cases of consumer over-indebtedness. Fairness is evaluated at the moment of conclusion, not at the time of performance of the contract, and is not concerned with the subject matter of the contract or the adequacy of the price and remuneration, *per* Article 4 of Directive 93/13. Since all contract directives are only minimum directives, it is up to Member States (including private international law) to guarantee social protection to consumers.

(d) Solvency

Choice will be effective only if the consumer can be assured of protection against loss of money in contracts where he or she is obliged to make advance

[83] *Supra* n. 73, at 66–8.

[84] *Ibid.*, at 173–5.

[85] "Principles of Justice in Private Law within the EU" in Paasavirta/Rissannen, *supra* n. 26 at 284–90.

[86] "Control of Unfair Contract Terms and Social Values" (1993) 16 *JCP* 435.

[87] *Overindebtedness of Consumers in the EC* (1994).

[88] Cf. however C. Willet, "Can Disallowance of Unfair Contract Terms be Regarded as a Redistribution of Power in Favour of Consumers?" (1994) 17 *JCP* 471.

payments, as in insurance, banking deposit and package holiday contracts. This is not so much a problem of free movement of goods but of free movement of services and capital. The European Court, in its *German Insurance* judgment,[89] recognised the solvency argument as a justification for the restriction of free access of transborder services to a member country. Therefore, it is up to secondary Community law to allow for consumer (policy-holder, depositor) protection where a supplier of services becomes insolvent. This relatively new phenomenon of a European charter for citizens first found recognition in labour law under Directive 80/987/EEC.[90]

As far as consumer law is concerned, Article 7 of the package holiday directive has a similar protective ambit. The organiser is under an obligation to "provide sufficient evidence of security for the refund of money paid over and for the repatriation of the consumer in case of insolvency". On 8 October 1996,[91] the European Court of Justice decided, on a reference from the Landgericht Bonn, supported by German consumer associations, that this provision has direct effect. As suggested by Advocate General Tesauro in his Opinion of 28 November 1995, it answered the question in the affirmative because the content of the rights guaranteed in Article 7 is "sufficiently identifiable". German law may not impose a minimum threshhold on this right or allow for advance payments of up to 10 per cent with a maximum of 500 DM. The German government was therefore liable to tourists who lost their advance payments or had to pay twice for being repatriated due to the insolvency of the tour operator because the government had not enacted the directive into German law in due time. Since then, German legislation has implemented Article 7, with effect from 1 November 1994, by providing for mandatory insurance of tour operators established in Germany; it would not have done so without the threat of State liability, which therefore becomes an important weapon to enforce consumer rights, not only in the past but also in the future.[92] Nevertheless, the transformation of the directive is still not complete, because the consumer may still be required to make a down payment of up to 10 per cent, up to DM 500, without sufficient evidence of security; this has only recently been changed.[93]

A deposit guarantee scheme has been introduced in the regulation of credit institutions by Directive 94/19 of the European Parliament and the Council of 30 May 1994.[94] The coverage must attain a minimum level of 20,000 ECU after 1 January 2000. Before that time it must have a minimum coverage of 15,000 ECU. The export of "better systems" from one country to another via branches is explicitly forbidden. Article 7 paragraph 6 confers a direct right

[89] Case 205/84, *Commission* v. *Germany* [1986] ECR 3755 at 3808.

[90] [1980] OJ L283/23.

[91] Joined cases C–178, 179,188, 189 and 190/94, *Dillenkofer et al.* v. *Federal Rep of Germany* [1996] ECR I–4845.

[92] Tonner, Der Reisevertrag, 3. A. (1995) at 147–61.

[93] Cf. Reich [1996] *EuZW* 712.

[94] [1994] OJ L135/5.

of action on depositors if the credit institution becomes insolvent which must be insured by Member States; the wording does not make it clear whether this implies direct effect or depends entirely on the discretion of the Member State. This must eventually be decided in litigation. So far, most existing deposit protection schemes as in Germany do not allow for a direct remedy in favour of the depositor.[95]

A similar scheme has been proposed for investment services and has only recently been enacted.[96] As far as insurance services are concerned, the relevant directives do not contain a policyholder protection system, but Member States, like the United Kingdom, are free to continue or to impose such a system. Protection of the policyholder will be implemented through rules of supervision and guarantee funds. With regard to distance selling, provision for guarantee funds has been left a voluntary code of conduct for providers of services, as provided in Recommendation 92/295/EEC.[97]

III. ECOLOGICAL RIGHTS AND THE CONSUMER

(a) Consumer Safety and Ecological Quality as Objectives of the Community

(i) Origins

Ecological rights in a broad sense are concerned with both product safety and environmental quality. They are closely related to each other because modern product regulation takes into account safety, health and ecological aspects of goods moving freely in the internal market.[98] To some extent, environmental quality may be the broader concept because it extends also to resource planning and protection, process regulation and waste management.[99]

Ecological aspects play an increasingly important role in Community/Union policies. They cannot be separated from consumer policy, which requires more than "value for money".[100] Product safety and ecological quality were among the EEC objectives from the beginning. This can be seen in Article 36, which allows Member States to derogate from the rules of free movement on grounds of "the protection of health and life of humans, animals or plants" unless the Community has itself acted.

Law approximation through Article 100 of the EC Treaty was always concerned with aspects of health (especially in foodstuffs) and safety (especially

[95] Reich [1996] *EuZW* 712.

[96] Directive 97/9/E6 of EP and Council of 3.3.1997, OJ 1. 84/22 of 26.3.1997.

[97] [1992] OJ L156/21.

[98] N. Reich, *supra* n. 14 at Nos. 209, 225.

[99] Rehbinder/Stewart, *Environmental Protection Policy* (1985), at 404–20.

[100] Cf. Kye (ed.), *EU Environmental Law and Policy and EC Consumer Law and Policy: Converging or Diverging Trends?* (1995); L. Krämer, "On the Interrelation between Consumer and Environmental Policies in the EC" (1993) 16 *JCP* 455.

in technical products, pharmaceuticals and chemicals). Free movement of goods could not be attained without acceptable safety levels for products in the Community or, if this was not possible, in Member States. The threat of unilateral action by Member States under Article 36 imposed a strong incentive upon the Community legislative process.

To some extent environmental concerns were addressed in Article 36 and were recognised in later case law of the European Court of Justice as being part of Community policy.[101] This broad reading of the Treaty provisions allowed, on the one hand, Community action, and, on the other, subject to the somewhat obscure limits of the proportionality principle,[102] Member State measures impeding free trade and free movement if the Community remained inactive or acted only unsatisfactorily.

The Single Act, with its ambitious objective to attain an internal market by 31 December 1992, gave safety and environmental regulation a new impulse. This can be seen from the new enabling provisions of Articles 100a and 130r–t. There has been some discussion on how to delineate the different competences of the Community under Articles 100a and 130s and the Court has been asked to rule on the question several times.[103] The Court seems to apply the theory of the primary goal of a Community measure.[104] The internal market programme outlined several important directives concerned with establishing consumer rights to safety and environmental quality, which will be analysed later.

(ii) Modifications by the Maastricht Treaty

The Maastricht Treaty on European Union continued the road to expanding Union competences in the area of consumer safety and ecological quality. Article 3(k) includes, among the Community activities, a policy in the sphere of the environment and Article 3(s) a contribution to the strengthening of consumer protection. The internal market competences of the Community were left untouched, with the exception of the introduction of the co-decision procedure of Article 189b, which now provides for joint directives of the European Parliament and the European Council. The environmental provisions were extended and the decision-making procedures were specified.[105] However, the general framework introduced by the Single Act was left untouched, especially the opting out possibilities of Articles 100a(4) and 130t.

[101] Case 240/83, *Procureur de la République* v. *ADBHU* [1985] ECR 531 at 459 No. 13.

[102] Case 302/86, *Commission* v. *Denmark* [1988] ECR 4607 (Danish bottles) and the critique by Hedemann-Robinson (1997) 20 *JCP* 1–43.

[103] Cases C–300/89, *Commission* v. *Council* [1991] ECR 2867 (re Titanium Dioxide); C–155/91, *Commission* v. *Council* [1993] ECR I–939 (re Waste); C–187/93, *Parliament* v. *Council* [1994] ECR I- 2857 (re shipment waste).

[104] Cf. Krämer, *EC Treaty and Environmental Law* (2nd edn., London, Sweet and Maxwell, 1995) at 91 who prefers objective criteria.

[105] *Ibid.*, 71–80.

Finally, Article 129a introduced a specific provision on consumer protection. This commits the Community to contributing to the attainment of a high level of consumer protection through measures of internal market policy under Article 100a and specific action "which support and supplement the policy pursued by the Member States to protect the health, safety and economic interest of consumers and to provide adequate information to consumers". This specific action will contain only minimum standards and will not prevent Member States from maintaining or introducing more stringent protective measures.[106]

(iii) Direct Effect?

Both environmental and consumer policy in the area of ecological quality and product safety are subject to the so-called subsidiarity principle of Article 3b. There has been extensive debate on the importance and impact of this principle to Community policy and law in the abovementioned areas. My concern here is to analyse the rights which may arise out of these provisions and policies to persons in their individual sphere as citizens or consumers and for the defence of collective or diffuse interests by actions of environmental groups or consumer associations. It is relevant to note that neither the Single Act nor the Maastricht Treaty mentions ecological rights as part of a citizens' charter which can be directly enforced by interested parties as individuals or by accredited groups. Krämer[107] correctly writes:

> "The Treaty does not provide for environmental enforcement bodies nor for individual rights with regard to the environment—right of information, right of participation in decision-making, right of access to justice—nor for sanctions."

A similar critical analysis has been offered by Micklitz and Weatherill[108] with regard to future prospects of the European Union in the area of product safety:

> "These [expectations concerning Union citizenship] must now be satisfied by both Community and by Member States. Here, in fact, is a yet further illustration of the momentum inherent in the process of Treaty revision. Conferral of citizenship provokes an expectation of conferral of rights; rights with substance, rights which can be enforced. Yet what do rights really mean in the modern context of a European Community and a European Union?"

Micklitz[109] has tried to develop a "consumer right to safety", including ecological quality, in the context of the EC Treaty. His analysis departs from the

[106] For an account cf. Micklitz/Reich, "Verbraucherschutz im Unionsvertrag von Maastricht" [1992] *EuZW* 593–8; Lenz AG in Case C–192/94, *supra* n. 80, at 1293 No. 32.

[107] L. Krämer, *supra* n. 104, at 146; Krämer, "Public Interest Litigation in Environmental Matters before European Courts" in Micklitz/Reich, *supra* n. 45 at with proposals for an improvement, at p. 297.

[108] *Federalism and Responsibility* (1995), 35.

[109] At n. 30.

concept of "shared responsibilities for safety" of the Community and Member States in the Union structure. These responsibilities are transformed into obligations, which in turn may become rights of citizens. This concept is already present in the case law of the ECJ which, as will be seen, places a high emphasis on safety and ecological quality in free movement matters. The Court insists that directives relating to health, safety and ecological quality must be implemented not by simple administrative guidelines, but by binding, precise, clear and transparent legal rules which can eventually be enforced by citizens themselves.[110] Micklitz[111] therefore writes:

> "Rights direct towards intervention and regulation. Art. 100a provides a high level of protection, Art. 129a 'shall contribute to the attainment of a high level of consumer protection'. It is possible to deduce from these Articles the principle of 'best possible consumer protection' and as its counterpart 'the prohibition of deterioration'."

The opening of markets, in his opinion, is accompanied by a duty to protect citizens against increased risks to their health and safety interests, which are implicitly guaranteed in Articles 36, 100a, 129a and 130r, read together with Article 5.

It is difficult to agree with Micklitz's stimulating concepts, and they can hardly be regarded as a statement of existing Community law principles. A reading of secondary Community law should be preferred which, depending on the circumstances, may grant explicit or implicit ecological and safety rights where appropriate. It is important to look at horizontal directives specifying these rights, including the availability of compensation in cases of violation,[112] and thereby become part of the "European Charter for Citizens" in the broad sense which is presented here. It will be shown that these instruments already contain a minimum level of protection of European citizens with regard to environmental quality and consumer safety. In some respects they even confer, however modestly, directly enforceable rights on the citizens. This process is an open-ended one.

(b) Access to Safety and Environmental Quality

(i) General Product Safety

Most important in this context is Community Directive 92/59[113] on general product safety. It imposes on the producer and, to a lesser extent, the supplier

[110] Cf. Cases C–131/88, C–361/88, C–59/89, *Commission* v. *Germany* [1991] ECR I–825, 2567 (2601 at No. 16), 2607 (2633 No. 28).

[111] "Principles of Justice in Private Law within the EU" in E. Paasivirta/Rissanen (eds.), *supra* n. 26, at 280–1.

[112] W. van Gerven in Reich/Mernik, *supra* n. 9.

[113] [1992] OJ L228/24.

the duty to market only safe products in the Community. In accordance with the general safety requirement, producers are obliged, first, to place only safe products on the market and, secondly, to provide consumers with the relevant information to enable them to assess the risks inherent in a product throughout its normal or reasonably foreseeable lifetime, and, where such risks are not immediately obvious without adequate warning to take precautions against risks. A third obligation is to adopt measures commensurate with the characteristics of the product to enable consumers to be informed of risks which a product may present and to take appropriate action, including, if necessary, the withdrawal of the product from the market. Distributors are required to act with due care to help ensure compliance with the general safety requirement.

The safety obligation must then be implemented by Member States which have to devise appropriate administrative provisions to make producers and distributors comply with their obligations in such a way that products placed on the market are safe. There are very detailed information duties between Member States and the Community. Article 9 provides for a Community procedure for acting against hazardous products circulating in the internal market, which was challenged by Germany but upheld by the ECJ in its judgment of 9 August 1994.[114] The Court justified it in the following words:

> "The free movement of goods can be secured only if product safety requirements do not differ significantly from one Member State to another. A high level of protection can be achieved only if dangerous products are subject to appropriate measures in all the Member States."[115]

The Court also insisted that the Community procedure was proportionate. It first restated that not only Member States but also the Community is bound to the principle of proportionality in relation to product safety and, as one might add, environmental quality matters. The Court justified the powers conferred upon the Commission on the following grounds:

> "The powers conferred on the Commission by Article 9 are appropriate for the purpose of attaining the objectives pursued by the directive, that is to say, ensuring a high level of protection for the health and safety of consumers whilst eliminating barriers to trade and distortions of competition arising as a result of disparities between national measures taken in relation to consumer products."

(ii) The Importance of Liability Rules

The Court's judgment confirms Micklitz's perception of shared responsibilities in product safety law which do not confer rights upon the individual. Can they be imposed by liability rules? With regard to producers and distributors, this is an aspect of product liability law.

[114] Case C–359/92, *Germany* v. *Council* [1994] ECR I–3681.
[115] At 3860 No. 34.

Community liability for not taking appropriate safety measures could arise out of Article 215(2). In the *Francesconi* case,[116] the Court denied consumers an individual right of redress with regard to measures relating to adulterated wine:

> "It must first of all be observed that the Commission has no power to withdraw adulterated wines from the market, that being a matter for the national authorities. The Commission is under no obligation to publish the identity of traders who may be involved in scandals. The information system established to detect fraud and irregularities in the wine sector and avert dangers which might arise from the use of consumable products leaves it to the national authorities to take steps to inform the consumer."[117]

It is a question of interpretation of Article 9 of the Product Safety Directive whether or not it contains an obligation of the Commission to take appropriate measures against hazardous products on the internal market. Since the procedure can be initiated only when certain requirements are fulfilled, the Commission is under no obligation to intervene and hence cannot be held liable under Article 215(2) in cases of inaction. If, however, these requirements are fulfilled one could argue that the Commission may be held liable in case of non-action.

As far as Member State liability is concerned, this must be seen in the light of the *Francovich* and later *Dillenkofer* judgments, which were concerned with situations where a directive has not been transformed into Member State law. It depends on a "sufficiently serious breach" of Community law and must, according to new case law, be balanced against the legislative discretion of Member States. These prerequisites are satisfied in the case of Germany, which has not implemented the Product Safety Directive. The Directive may trigger a direct effect in favour of injured consumers if, by taking measures possible under it, Germany could have prevented consumer harm.[118]

As a result, subjective rights are conferred upon European citizens only in those cases where they may claim damages arising out of unsafe products. Therefore, Directive 85/357 on product liability[119] is important in this context. While the general Safety Directive is concerned with obligations and duties of producers, distributors, governments and the Community, without giving directly enforceable rights to citizens or consumers, the Product Liability Directive confers individual rights on the consumer, which he or she may enforce in case of injury. The basis of this right is the legitimate safety expectations of consumers. They depend on factors similar to those mentioned in the general Safety Directive, for instance the presentation of the product, the use to which the product could reasonably be expected to be put and the time when the product was put into circulation. Under Community

[116] Cases 326/86 and 66/88 [1989] ECR 2087.
[117] At 2113 Nos. 21–2.
[118] N. Reich [1996] *EuZW* 713; Dir. 92/59 was implemented only in Apr. 1997 (!).
[119] [1985] OJ L210/29.

law, this right to safety can be enforced against manufacturers, importers and, eventually, suppliers for products which come under the Directive. The consumer has a right to compensation under Community law, with the exclusion of non-pecuniary damage which may or may not be provided for by Member States.

The Directive, which has been enforced in most Member States, with the exclusion of France, can be said to take direct effect.[120] In those cases where it has not yet or incorrectly been enacted the principles of the *Marleasing* and *Dori* judgments must be applied.

However, the weakness of this directive so far as a consumers' right to safety is concerned is quite obvious. The Directive is aimed only at compensation, not at prevention. There is no compensation for pain and suffering imposed by Community law, which considerably weakens the position of the consumer. There are many exclusions and limitations which put the consumer on an unequal footing with the producer who uses his/her right to free entry without being obliged to pay adequate compensation in case of consumer loss.

(iii) Environmental Quality as Directly Enforceable Right?

Environmental quality is even less regarded as a directly enforceable right under secondary Community law. This is especially true for waste regulation which is limited to adequate management. Citizens do not have a Community-wide right to environmental quality.

One could at least envisage a right to compensation in cases where environmentally hazardous products, waste or production methods are used. The Commission has therefore put forward proposals for liability for hazardous waste and environmental damages.[121] These proposals attempted to transfer the "polluter pays" principle into systems of civil liability, which would give injured persons a right to compensation under certain circumstances. Most interesting in this respect was the amended Commission proposal of 1991 concerning liability for hazardous waste.[122] According to Article 3, the producer of waste shall be liable under civil law for the damage and impairment of the environment caused by waste, irrespective of fault on his part. The producer is under an obligation to include in his annual report the name of his insurers for civil liability purposes; this reporting obligation indirectly amounts to an obligation to conclude mandatory insurance. Article 4 leaves it to Member States to determine the person who may take legal action in the event of damage to or impairment of the environment caused or about to be caused by waste. Member State law will also determine remedies, including the availability of injunctions. The Member States are also competent to decide

[120] N. Reich, *supra* n. 14 No. 198.

[121] Cf. Commission Communication of 14 May 1993, COM(93)47 final.

[122] [1991] OJ C251/3; cf. Seibt, *Zivilrechtlicher Ausgleich für ökologische Schäden* (1994), at 120–31.

whether and to what extent damages for loss of profit or economic loss may be recoverable. Finally, the Directive shall be without prejudice to national provisions relating to non-material damage.

If this Directive had been adopted, it would for the first time establish in the law of the Community and many Member States an individual or group right to enjoin against or compensate for environmental damage caused by hazardous waste. There would be limits to the damages but the Directive makes it clear that certain types are recoverable, that certain persons must be entrusted with bringing actions against Member States and that this action can include injunctions. The Directive would also have allowed parallel enforcement of legislation against hazardous waste and would therefore give new ecological rights to citizens and citizens' groups. Unfortunately, the European legislator has rejected the adoption of this Directive.

(c) **Participation in Environmental and Safety Decision-making**

(i) Information as the Basis for Participation

Participation of citizens and citizens' groups in decision-making relating to environmental and product safety matters is a relatively new issue for Member States. This eventual right to participation will not be found in constitutional documents of Member States, but rather in administrative regulations and procedures which differ considerably.

So far Community law has not been very explicit on this issue. Environmental and safety policy is seen as a joint responsibility of Member States and the Community/Union on the basis of the subsidiarity principle. Citizens do not play an important role in environmental and safety policy and enforcement.[123]

So far as secondary law is concerned, only early indicators aimed at increased participation can be seen. In this area, environmental law is more developed than consumer law, and may therefore serve as a model for increasing consumer participation in safety decisions. It is also important for the theory of Community subjective rights because it is not concerned with individual rights but with *collective rights and group participation* as part of a "post-modernist" theory of rights.[124]

(ii) Access to Information

The provision of information on environment and product safety is part of many vertical Community directives which will not be discussed in any detail

[123] Koppen/Ladeur, "Environmental rights" in Cassese/Clapham/Weiler, III *supra* n. 64, at 38–41.

[124] N. Reich, "Reflexive Law and Reflexive Legal Theory" [1995] *Melanges Argyrios* 773 at 767.

here. Most important for horizontal information provision is Council Directive 90/313/EEC of 7 June 1990 on the freedom of access to information on the environment.[125] The object of the Directive is to ensure freedom of access to and dissemination of information on the environment held by public authorities and to set out the basic terms and conditions on which such information should be made available. Article 3 obliges public authorities, when so requested, to give access to environmental information to all natural or legal persons on their request and without their having to prove an interest. Conversely, the Directive must be interpreted in such a way as to give every person a right to environmental information, subject only to the limits set forth in the Directive and the procedures provided for by national law. This individual right is very broad and unconditional.

There is some debate about the extent of this informational right and its limitations, e.g. to protect trade secrets.[126] It is not certain whether it also relates to product information, for instance the licensing of chemicals or pesticides that may be harmful to the environment and health. Article 2 defines environmental information as:

> "information on the state of water, air, soil, fauna, flora, land and natural sites, and on activities (including those which give rise to nuisances such as noise) and measures adversely affecting, or likely so to affect these, and on activities or measures designed to protect these, including administrative measures and environmental management programmes."

The Directive makes it clear that a broad concept of environmental information is intended to be used. Whenever public authorities, for instance in product licensing procedures, have to assess environmental qualities of products, especially chemicals and pesticides, by toxic tests, this information should be disclosed to any person legitimately asking for it.

The Directive is not concerned with the use of this information, for instance to stop the marketing of a certain product or to improve the environment. This is left to other, if any, regulations of Member States.

The Directive has been extended to grant access to information held by Community institutions.[127]

The instrument of information could certainly be used to a greater extent to create environmental rights in relation to internal market measures. EC law is quite underdeveloped in this respect. It imposes certain informational obligations, for instance producers and public authorities, but hardly ever gives private persons informational rights. The Product Safety Directive enables Member States *inter alia* to disseminate information in case of hazardous products. But there is no right of citizens to ask for disclosure of such information.

[125] [1990] OJ L158/56.
[126] G. Winter (ed.), *Öffentlichkeit von Umweltinformationen* (1990), at 57–67.
[127] [1993] OJ L340/43; [1994] OJ L46/58.

An interesting new direction has been taken by Directive 94/62/EC of the European Parliament and Council of 20 December 1994 on packaging and packaging waste.[128] It provides for information of users of packages two years after its entry into force. They must be informed about recycling and reuse systems, about their contribution to recycling and reusing, about labelling systems and about packaging waste management systems.

Finally, Council Directive 96/61/EC of 24 September 1996 on integrated pollution prevention and control[129] imposes on Member States the obligation:

> "to ensure that applications for permits for new installations or for substantial changes are made available for an appropriate period of time to the public, to enable it to comment on them before the competent authority reaches its decision. That decision, including at least a copy of the permit, and the subsequent updates, must be made available to the public" (Article 12).

(iii) Environmental Impact Statement

With regard to projects which have a substantial environmental impact, citizen participation can only indirectly influence these projects to the extent that the impacts on the environment are made transparent and information on this impact is made public. If environmental impact studies are not undertaken, this should be reason enough to stop the project until the environmental impact is clarified.

Council Directive 85/337/EEC of 27 June 1985, as amended by Directive 97/11/EC of 3 March 1997,[130] is concerned with the assessment of the effects of certain public and private projects on the environment. According to Article 2, Member States are under an obligation to ensure that, before consent is given, projects likely to have significant effects on the environment by virtue, *inter alia*, of their nature, size or location are made subject to an assessment with regard to their effects. The Directive then goes on to describe the projects and the assessment in more detail. Article 6 contains detailed rights of information and consultation of citizens. Member States are therefore obliged to ensure that the public is given the opportunity to express an opinion before the project is initiated or, under the amended Directive, before consent is given. It is up to Member State law to make detailed arrangements for such information and consultation by ascertaining the public concerned.

There has been some debate on how far the Directive takes direct effect after the deadline of 3 July 1988. This problem came before the European Court in its judgment of 9 August 1994.[131] The case concerned German

[128] [1994] OJ L365/10.

[129] [1996] OJ L257/26; for a discussion cf. Krämer, "Der Richtlinienvorschlag über die integrierte Vermeidung und Verminderung der Umweltverschmutzung" in *Rengeling, Integrierter und betrieblicher Umweltschutz* (1996), at 51–78.

[130] [1985] OJ L175/40 and [1997] OJ L73/5.

[131] Case C–396/92, *Bund Naturschutz in Bayern* v. *Freistaat Bayern* [1994] ECR I–3317, confirmed by Case C–431/92, *Commission* v. *Germany* [1995] ECR I- 2189.

legislation implementing the Directive, which had transitional provisions avoiding environmental impact statements for projects where the consent procedure was initiated before the entry into force of the Directive but the consent was delivered after 3 July 1988. The Court did not directly answer the question of direct effect. It simply stated that:

> "the directive in any case precludes the introduction in respect of procedures initiated after that date of rules such as those at issue in the main proceedings by a national law which, in breach of the directive, transposes it belatedly into the domestic legal system."[132]

The Court indirectly recognises the direct effect of the Directive, as had been suggested by the Advocate General. This means that, if the date of the consent arises after 3 July 1988, an environmental impact statement must be prepared. Citizens or citizens' groups can therefore oppose under national law any project covered by the Directive which is not accompanied by an appropriate environmental impact statement. As a result, it can be said that Community Directive 85/337 gives citizens a right to demand an environmental impact statement of projects described there. This is certainly an important step towards increased participation of citizens in environmental matters.

IV. CONSUMER RIGHTS AS CITIZENS' RIGHTS

(a) Non-discrimination

(i) Generalities

Citizens' rights form the core of the nation State and are part of fundamental rights. In this context however, they will not be developed in full, but only with regard to the position of the consumer as a passive market citizen. Most important are the principles of non-discrimination and effective judicial protection. An important integrating factor has been the European Court of Justice. Its case law has developed so-called derivative rights, that is citizens' rights which are derived from a broadly interpreted principle of non-discrimination enshrined in Article 6 of the EC Treaty (formerly Article 7 of the EEC Treaty). The most important criterion has been the requirement of Community law that "within the scope of application of this Treaty . . . any discrimination on grounds of nationality shall be prohibited".

Because the scope of application of the Treaty changes dynamically and provides for the transfer of an increasing amount of jurisdiction to the Community, the prohibition of non-discrimination extends to fields which formerly did not form part of Community jurisdiction. Some examples of consumer protection as citizen protection will be given below.

[132] At 3753 No. 19.

(ii) Derivative Rights

Non-discrimination among nationals is a fundamental principle of Community law. It was first developed with regard to economic rights, especially those of free movement and entry, by the specific provisions of the Treaty on free circulation of goods, persons, services and capital. The rights were extended to a right of equal treatment, regardless of gender, by Article 119 and specific directives. These provisions unfortunately apply only to the supply side of market relations (labour, access to employment, social benefits), not to the consumption area. There is still no EC rule banning discrimination against consumers on grounds of gender, e.g. in financial services.

Article 6 of the EC Treaty, (formerly Article 7 of the EEC Treaty), is the cornerstone of the fundamental Community law principle of non-discrimination. It forbids any discrimination based on nationality. The Court has on several occasions tried to strike down institutional discrimination which is allowed by international law but not by EC law, especially the requirement of mutuality as a precondition for the granting of rights. EC rights do not depend on reciprocity—a radical departure from well-established principles of international law the importance of which cannot be stressed too much.[133]

The most important criterion for the Court has been an extensive reading of the wording "within the scope of application of this Treaty". Since the Treaty gives citizens a right to move freely and to shop for goods and services anywhere in the Community, derivative rights can be deduced from these entitlements. The following examples appear from case law and are important for consumer protection:

(1) A Luxembourg citizen of German origin residing in Belgium, which in certain regions allows German to be used as an official Court language, may insist on the right to use German to defend his case.[134]

(2) A British citizen who visits Paris and rides on the Metro is entitled to victim compensation under French criminal law if he is criminally assaulted. The requirement of reciprocity of victim compensation in the French legislation is not compatible with Article 7 of the EEC Treaty (now Article 6 of the EC Treaty).[135]

(3) The necessity of executing a judgment abroad cannot be regarded as a sufficient justification for an immediate seizure of the defendant's assets, as provided for in Article 917 paragraph 2 of the German Code of Civil Procedure. The Court said that execution of judgments comes within the scope of application of the Treaty, because Article 220 empowers Member States to conclude international agreements on the recognition

[133] Wolf, "Die faktische Grundrechtsbeeinträchtigung als Systematisierungsmethode der Begleitfreiheiten nach dem EGV" [1994] *JZ* 1151.

[134] Case 137/84, *Mutsch* [1985] ECR 2681.

[135] Case 186/87, *Cowan* v. *Trésor public* [1989] ECR 195.

of judgments, which they did in the Brussels Convention of 1968. They thereby wanted to guarantee "free movement" of judgments in civil matters and to form a "single entity", eg. a uniform European legal space. Therefore, the mere fact that the judgment has to be executed abroad cannot be regarded as a valid reason for immediate seizure of assets.[136] This ruling can be expanded into a general principle of non-discrimination in procedural matters involving consumer protection.

(b) Access to Law

(i) Limited Competence of the Union

Access to law is a fundamental right in most Member States. It is guaranteed under Article 6 of the EHRC and, via Article F(2) of the Maastricht Treaty, indirectly in the EU as a fundamental principle of Community law. It means, on the one hand, that in civil disputes a court system should exist where citizens may obtain a speedy, authoritative, independent and binding decision on their dispute. In administrative matters it means that citizens are entitled under certain conditions to oppose acts of governments and municipalities infringing upon their rights. Access to courts should not depend on income and be a privilege of the rich.

Not being a State, the Community, respectively Union, can guarantee legal access only indirectly.[137] Access to law depends on substantive powers. Since Member States are, with certain exceptions, competent to apply Community law and to transform directives into their own law and thereby make them part of their legislation, citizens will usually seek protection by courts of law in the States of which they are nationals or where they reside. Access to law is a right which must be guaranteed by the Member State, not by the Community.

On the other hand, if a national judge directly or indirectly applies Community law, the court will at the same time be a "European court".[138] This is confirmed by the specificity of the reference procedure under Article 177. Whenever questions of validity or interpretation of Community law are in dispute, the Member State's court may, and in certain conditions must, refer the case to the European Court, which will give a binding judgment. The European Court has exclusive competence to annul secondary Community law.[139] Article 177 institutes a dialogue and a co-operative system between

[136] Case C–398/92, *Mund & Fester* v. *Hatrex Internationaal Transport* [1994] ECR I–467 at Nos. 11, 19.

[137] N. Reich, *supra* n. 16 at No. 253.

[138] D. Curtin, *supra* n. 5, at 25.

[139] Case 314/4199, *Foto-Frost* v. *Hauptzollamt Lübeck* [1985] ECR 4199 at 4232 Nos. 15/16; certain exceptions are possible for interim measures: Cases 143/88 and C–92/89, *Zuckerfabrik Süderdithmarschen* v. *Hauptzollamt* [1991] ECR I–415 at 541 No. 19; the national court must pay

national and European judges. The order referring a case to the European Court is a decision by a national court which ordinarily is binding on the European Court. Without such order, the European Court has no jurisdiction unless other procedures are put in place. This relationship of mutual co-operation is a two-sided and not, as the German Constitutional Court seems to think, a one-sided process. Therefore, even the German Constitutional Court has to submit questions concerning the validity or interpretation of Community law to the European Court, in accordance with Article 177(3).[140]

(ii) Access to EC Courts

Direct access to European courts is possible only under the very limited conditions of Article 173 paragraph 4:

> "Any natural or legal person may . . . institute proceedings against the decision addressed to that person or against the decision which, although in the form of a regulation or a decision addressed to another person, is of direct and individual concern to the former."

This jurisdiction over actions by individuals has now been assumed by the Court of First Instance. The requirement of direct and individual concern has been interpreted narrowly by the case law of the European Court, and recently by the Court of First Instance. As a basic requirement, the persons concerned must be individualised by circumstances in which they are differentiated from all other persons who may also be affected by a regulation or decision, not a directive.[141] Usually, a mere competitive disadvantage, a risk of loss or the eventuality of consumer or environmental harm will not be sufficient to grant standing to potentially injured persons or associations.[142] This restrictive reading of Article 173 means that public interest actions are usually not possible before European courts.[143] A group of individuals or association of consumers or environmentalists will, according to the case law, not be individually affected by a Community regulation, directive or decision and will therefore not enjoy access to the Court of First Instance.

due respect to decisions of the ECJ: Case C–465/93, *Atlanta Fruchthandelsgesellschaft* v. *Bundesamt für Ernährung und Forstwirtschaft* [1995] ECR I–3761 at 3794, para. 46.

[140] Cf. BVerfGE 37, 271 at 282, *Solange I*; recent conflicts concern competence regarding the Banana Reg., 404/93, cf. N. Reich, "Judge made 'Europe à la Carte' " (1996) 7 *EJIL* 103; U. Everling, "Will Europe Slip over Bananas" (1996) 33 *CMLRev*. 401.

[141] Cf. Case C–309/89, *Codorniú* v. *Council* [1994] ECR I–1853 at 1886 as disinguished from Case C–10/95P, *Asocarne* v. *Council* [1995] ECR I–4149; Case C–270/95P, *Christina Kik* v. *Council and Commission* [1996] ECR I–1987.

[142] A. Arnull, "Private applicants and the action for annulment under Art. 173 of the EC Treaty" (1995) 32 *CMLRev*. 7 at 35–40; N. Reich, "Public Interest Litigation before European Jurisdiction" in Micklitz/Reich, *supra* n. 45, at 3–20.

[143] Case 246/81, *Lord Bethell* v. *Commission* [1982] ECR 2277 at 2291 No. 16; confirmed by the CFI, Case T–585/93, *Greenpeace* v. *Commission* [1995] ECR II–2205 for more details cf. the papers by Krämer, Bercusson, Christianos and Micklitz in: Micklitz/Reich, *supra* n. 45.

A more flexible reading has been adopted in competition matters where the Commission exercises jurisdiction of its own. Since persons showing a legitimate interest can file an application with the Commission and have a right to be heard and to receive a reply, they may enforce those rights in legal proceedings. The Court of First Instance, in its judgment of 18 May 1994,[144] conferred a right of participation by consumer associations in competition litigation. A similar right has been rejected in anti-dumping matters but can be (and in the meantime has been) introduced by Community law.[145] Under certain circumstances, consumer or environmental associations may participate in proceedings as interveners supporting the position of one of the parties.

Because of the unsatisfactory state of standing rules, former ECJ judge Zuleeg[146] has made the following proposals for a "moderate extension of *locus standi* to associations and institutions in favour of public interests":

> "*Article 173 paragraph 4*:
>
> Any natural or legal person may, under the same conditions, institute proceedings against acts other than those addressed to that person, provided that he or she is directly and individually concerned.
>
> *Article 173 paragraph 6*:
>
> Persons concerned by legislative acts shall institute proceedings in due time as soon as they are affected by such act or it becomes sufficiently enviseagable that they will be so affected.
>
> *Article 173 paragraph 7*:
>
> By legislative act, associations or institutions pursuing a public interest may be entitled to institute proceedings for this purpose . . ."

This proposal supports the cautious criticism made by the European Court of Justice, in its report to the intergovernmental conference of 1996, on "whether Article 173 is sufficient to guarantee for [individuals] effective judicial protection against possible infringements of fundamental rights arising from the legislative activity of the institutions".[147]

(iii) Procedural Rights as Part of Substantive Rights

Community law may, of course, adopt legislation to improve its citizens' access to justice. This is particularly important in cases where Community law

[144] Case T–37/92, *BEUC & NCC* v. *Commission* [1994] ECR II–285; for a discussion cf. S. Weatherill, "Public Interest Litigation in EC Competition Law" in Micklitz/Reich, *supra* n. 46 at 169.

[145] Case C–170/89, *BEUC* v. *Council* [1991] ECR I–5709; for new tendencies cf. Depayre/Wenig, "Public Interest Litigation in Anti-Dumping Law" in Micklitz/Reich, *supra* n. 45 at 209–24.

[146] "Public Interest Litigation before European Courts" in Micklitz/Reich, *supra* n. 45 at 439–50.

[147] (1995) 32 *CMLRev*. 883 at 891.

confers substantive rights on citizens which can only be effectively enforced by Member States.

(1) Consumer protection has been guaranteed through a number of directives, the most important of which are Directives 84/450 on misleading advertising and 93/13 on unfair contract terms. Articles 4 and 7 of the respective Directives contain detailed requirements as to the standing, *inter alia*, of consumer associations in proceedings before courts of law or administrative authorities enabling them to eliminate misleading practices or unfair terms from the market. The Misleading Advertising Directive provides for injunctive relief, which is not the case with regard to unfair terms legislation.[148] On a reference by the English High Court, the European Court will have to decide whether a right of action of consumer associations is required by Directive 93/13 because the British regulation implementing this Directive had only forseen a right of action by the Office of Fair Trading and not by Consumers' Associations.[149]

(2) According to decision 93/371/EEC, the Court of First Instance has recognised the right of citizens to access to Community documents, which right can be enforced before European courts;[150] any restriction of this right requires a reasoned balancing of interests by the Community institutions ("giving reasons requirement" in the sense of Article 190).

Access to law must of course be guaranteed by the courts of the Member States, not so much by courts of the Community. This is a result of the subsidiarity principle enshrined in Article 3b, which limits the jurisdiction of the Community courts to matters of Community law. On the other hand, violation of the principle of effective remedies by non-implementation of directives may give rise to State liability.

(iv) Cross-border Litigation

Consumer access to justice has been the subject of many Community documents and resolutions, the most recent of which were a Commission Green Paper of 16 November 1993 on access of consumers to justice and the settlement of consumer disputes in the Single Market.[151] The Green Paper gives an assessment of the actual situation and makes some rather hesitant proposals

[148] T. Wilhelmsson, "Public Interest Litigation on Unfair Terms" in Micklitz/Reich, *supra* n. 45, at 385.

[149] Case C–26/96; cf. also C. Willet, "From Reindeers to Confident Consumer" in Micklitz/Reich, *supra* n. 45, 403–18; the litigation may be mooted because the new labour government intends to modify the restrictive approach of the UK regs.

[150] Case T–194/94, *John Carvel and Guardian Newspapers* v. *Council* [1995] ECR II–2767 at 2789; cf. the discussion by J. Shaw, "Citizens' Rights and Access to Law" in Micklitz/Reich, *supra* n. 45 at 243–60.

[151] COM(93)576 final.

for improvement. It is particularly concerned with voluntary mechanisms improving transborder settlement of disputes. It wants to use the existing cross-border information centres to handle consumer complaints.

Another area of concern has been difficulties encountered by group actions for injunctions against cross-border misleading advertising or unfair contract terms. A proposal for a Community directive on mutual recognition of public interest actions is now before the Parliament and Council.[152]

So far as cross-border litigation is concerned, this is to some extent already covered by the Brussels Convention, which contains specific provisions on consumer cases.[153] These provisions will not be analysed here in detail since they are not so much concerned with guaranteeing access to justice as much as with the free circulation of judgments, thereby designating jurisdictions and competences. The purpose of these provisions is to allow a consumer the privilege of suing in his or her home forum as defined in Article 13/14, and this right may not be excluded by jurisdiction conventions. It is left to the Member States, however, to determine how and at what costs citizens or citizens' groups will obtain access to justice. The Brussels Convention is silent on this point and takes Member State provisions as they are.

V. CONCLUSION

The analysis presented here shows that there is a legal framework for a European Charter for citizens as consumers in the areas of economic, ecological and legal protection. This framework has to some extent gone beyond free movement of persons and been transformed into genuine citizens' rights. Weiler[154] insists on "a second and third generation protection" following the access-to-justice movement and developing "institutional devices to ensure effective vindication".

On the other hand, the European Charter still has its roots in the economy of free movement which has been restated in Article 8a of the EC Treaty as amended by the Maastricht Treaty on European Union. Citizens' rights are still fragmented and are subject to many limitations, as we have shown in the area of consumer rights, but this is also true for other areas of Union activity, such as social policy. The citizens' charter is, as Curtin[155] said with regard to the European Constitution, a charter of "bits and pieces". Some bits include interesting innovations, especially those introduced by the case law of the European Court; some are the results of compromise, especially in horizontal

[152] COM(95)712 final; [1996] OJ C107/3.

[153] N. Reich, *supra* n. 14, Nos. 266–7; Morin and Koch, "French resp. German Perspective, Cross Border Consumer Complaints" in Micklitz/Reich, *supra* n. 45 at 419–26, 427–38; Micklitz, "Cross-border Consumer Conflicts—A French–German Experience" (1994) 17 *JCP* 411.

[154] "Methods of Protection: Towards a Second and Third generation of protection" in Cassesse/Clapham/Weiler, *supra* n. 64 at 562.

[155] *Supra* n. 5.

directives of the Council and in certain cases through the joint action of the European Parliament and Council.

Since many citizens' rights need implementation by secondary Community law, its legal effects are particularly important for the protection of European citizens. The Court has taken many courageous steps in this direction, especially through the theory of direct effect and the principle of State liability in cases where Community law obligations are not fulfilled by Member States.[156] The recent *Dillenkofer* judgment of 8 October 1996 is an excellent example in this direction where the ECJ insisted that:

> "First, the recitals in the preamble to the Directive [90/314] repeatedly refer to the purpose of protecting consumers. Secondly, the fact that the Directive is intended to assure other objectives cannot preclude its provisions from also having the aim of protecting consumers. Indeed, according to Article 100a(3) of the Treaty, the Commission, in its proposals submitted pursuant to that Article, concerning *inter alia* consumer protection, must take as a base a high level of protection" (paragraph 39).

As a result, there is no doubt that the European Union/Community as it stands has, despite its contradictions and limitations, developed an impressive set of consumer and citizens' rights in a broad sense. Enforcement, however, is still weak. It is left to courts of law. To entrust the establishment and the implementation of the European charter of citizens' rights to courts of law is a very ambitious project. Its future remains to be seen. An emerging discussion of "public interest litigation" may be the outcome.

[156] W. van Gerven, *supra* n. 45 at 66.

22

Saying Nothing with Words

ANTHONY J. DUGGAN*

I. INTRODUCTION

This Panel Discussion is about the future of consumer protection. The future of consumer protection is assured, in the sense that hardly anyone is opposed to the concept. It is easy to make a commitment to consumer protection—politicians do it all the time. However, a commitment to consumer protection does not exhaust the policy choices that need to be made. On the contrary, it marks only the beginning. For example, who does the word "consumer" cover? The consumer interest is not necessarily a homogeneous one. Where there is a clash between different consumer interests, which set of interests is to prevail? Short-term and longer term consumer interests may sometimes conflict. In that event, which is to take precedence? Again, what does "protection" mean? One school of thought holds that consumers are protected best by laws which facilitate their freedom of choice. This suggests that consumers need protection against fraud and other forms of exploitation in the bargaining process, but it also suggests that consumers should bear responsibility for their own mistakes. Another school of thought holds that consumers are not necessarily the best judges of their own interests, and that the law should make choices for them. A corollary of this view is that consumers should be relieved of the consequences of their own mistakes. With all these variables in mind, it does not make much sense to talk about the future of consumer protection at large.

In keeping with the tenor of these introductory remarks, I plan to argue in what follows that a significant threat to the future of effective consumer protection is posed by fuzzy thinking at the policy-making stage. I will take as my text Arthur Leff's withering statement about the unconscionability provision in section 2–302 of the United States *Uniform Commercial Code*:[1]

> "The gist of the tale is simple: it is hard to give up an emotionally satisfying incantation and the way to keep the glow without the trouble of the meaning is continually to increase the abstraction level of the drafting and explaining language

* Henry Bournes Higgins Professor of Law, Monash University, Clayton, Victoria, Australia.

[1] "Unconscionability and the Code—The Emperor's New Clause" (1967) 115 *University of Pennsylvania Law Review* 485 at 558–9.

> . . . but the lesson of its drafting ought nevertheless to be learned: it is easy to say nothing with words. Even if the words make one feel all warm inside, the result of sedulously preventing thought about them is likely to lead to more trouble than the draftsman's cozy glow is worth, as a matter not only of statutory elegance but of effect in the world being regulated. Subsuming problems is not as good as solving them."

My focus will be on three major Australian consumer protection initiatives about which precisely the same observation could be made, namely:

(1) Australia's own unconscionability legislation;
(2) Recently revised truth in lending requirements; and
(3) Commonwealth reforms to product liability law.

The underlying problem in each case is the legislature's failure to resolve key policy choices. The problem is disguised by resort to drafting at a high level of abstraction, and this serves to make rhetorical claims in support of the new laws seem plausible. The truth, however, is that laws drafted according to this model are bound to be indeterminate—hence Leff's characterisation of UCC section 2–302 as the "Emperor's new clause". The courts are left with the task of resolving the indeterminacy problems, but they can only do this by confronting the policy choices that the legislature itself has overlooked. This is not a legitimate judicial function. It is one thing to say that courts should be required to take policy into account when interpreting legislation. It is quite another to have them invent policy as part of the interpretation process.

II. UNCONSCIONABILITY LEGISLATION

Unconscionability legislation has been high on the Australian legislature's agenda for the past decade or so. New South Wales enacted a *Contracts Review Act* in 1980, and a modified version of this legislation has been adopted by other States and Territories as part of the uniform consumer credit laws. Section 51AB of the *Trade Practices Act* 1974 (Cth) prohibits unconscionable conduct by corporations in trade or commerce, and complementary provisions have been enacted in the uniform State fair trading legislation. For ease of reference, the following discussion will focus on the *Contracts Review Act* 1980 (NSW).

The *Contracts Review Act* (along with the other measures just mentioned) was substantially influenced by UCC, section 2–302. References to section 2–302 lie at the heart of reform proposals which led to the enactment of the provisions,[2] and the proposals themselves are justified in terms which echo the

[2] Committee of the Adelaide Law School, *Report to the Standing Committee of State and Commonwealth Attorneys-General on the Law Relating to Consumer Credit and Money Lending* (South Australian Government Printer, Adelaide, 1969), 58; Peden, *Report to the Minister for*

Official Comment to section 2–302. For example, the *Peden Report*, which was the basis of the *Contracts Review Act* 1980 (NSW) states as follows:[3]

> "While often paying lip-service to the sanctity of contract doctrine, the courts have felt the need to respond to changing needs and expectations in the community and have developed a number of devices to subvert the doctrine of sanctity of contract in order to do justice in individual cases. These devices include the extension of the existing principles of duress, undue influence and illegality, and principles of construction such as the implication of additional terms, the doctrines of fundamental breach, reading down of exclusion clauses, the collateral warranty device, and the doctrine of frustration and equitable estoppel.
>
> The main criticisms of the devices referred to in the last paragraph are not that they failed to achieve justice in the individual cases to which they were applied, but that
>
> (a) they do not make a frontal attack on the root cause of the problem, and by using technical devices the courts invite the contract draftsman to try again;
> (b) they tend to present a multitude of individual decisions which fail to accumulate experience or authority in marking out the minimal requirements of fairness;
> (c) since they often turn upon construction of terms which are necessarily misconstrued to avoid injustice, difficulties are created for the construction of similar terms in subsequent wholly legitimate contracts."

The *Contracts Review Act* 1980 (NSW) provides for the re-opening of a contract if it is found by a court to be unjust.[4] "Unjust" is defined to include "harsh, unconscionable or oppressive".[5] In deciding whether a contract is unjust, the court is directed to have regard to the public interest and all the circumstances of the case,[6] as well as to a list of other factors, including:[7]

(1) whether or not there was any material bargaining inequality between the parties;
(2) whether or not the provisions of the contract were the subject of negotiation;
(3) whether or not it was reasonably practicable for the partys seeking relief to negotiate for alteration or removal of any of the provisions of the contract;
(4) whether or not any of the provisions of the contract imposed conditions which were unreasonable;
(5) whether or not a party to the contract was unable to protect their interests because of age or physical or mental incapacity;

Consumer Affairs and Co-operative Societies and the Attorney-General for New South Wales on Harsh and Unconscionable Contracts (Sydney, 1976), 13 and App. B (the "*Peden Report*").

[3] *Peden Report*, 5–6.

[4] *Contracts Review Act* 1980 (NSW), s. 7(1).

[5] S. 4(1).

[6] S. 9(1).

[7] S. 9(2).

(6) the relative economic circumstances, educational background and literacy of the parties;
(7) the form and intelligibility of the contract;
(8) whether independent advice was obtained by the party seeking relief;
(9) the extent to which the contract was explained to, and understood by, the party seeking relief;
(10) whether there was any undue influence, unfair pressure or unfair tactics exerted on the party seeking relief;
(11) the conduct of the parties in relation to similar dealings; and
(12) the commercial setting of the contract.

The Act binds the Crown, but the Crown may not be granted relief under the Act.[8] Also barred from seeking relief are public and local authorities, corporations and a person who enters into a contract in the course of, or for the purpose of, a trade, business or profession (other than a farming undertaking).[9] In its application to buyers, the Act is therefore effectively limited to consumer dealings.[10] However, subject to the limitations just mentioned, a supplier can claim relief under the Act. In granting relief, the court may:

(1) refuse to enforce all or any part of the provisions of the contract;
(2) declare the contract void in whole or part; or
(3) vary the contract.[11]

The Act may be relied on either by way of application to the court, or as a defence to an action brought against the party claiming relief.[12]

The *Contracts Review Act* is contentious. Its architect, Professor John Peden, claimed that it was drafted with a view to making the law "sharp in focus, conceptually sound and explicit in its policy underpinnings", preserving judicial rigour in the application of the legislation and avoiding "ad hocery" in decision-making.[13]

These claims are open to challenge. I have previously argued that the legislation is:[14]

(1) not "sharp in focus", because it does not distinguish between procedural unconscionability (where the contract is unjust because of deficiencies in the bargaining process) and substantive unconscionability (where the contract is unjust because the outcome is otherwise one-sided or unfair). The list of factors which the courts are directed to

[8] S. 5.
[9] S. 6(2).
[10] *Baltic Shipping Co* v. *Dillon ("The Mikhail Lermentov")* (1991) 22 NSWLR 1 at 20 *per* Kirby
[11] *Contracts Review Act* 1980 (NSW), s. 7(1).
[12] *Commercial Banking Co of Sydney Ltd* v. *Pollard* (1983) 1 NSWLR 74.
[13] Peden, *The Law of Unjust Contracts* (Butterworths, Sydney, 1982), 95.
[14] "Some Reflections on Consumer Protection and the Law Reform Process" (1991) 17 *Monash University Law Review* 252 at 274–6.

consider when deciding whether to grant relief is a jumble of process-oriented and outcome-oriented considerations and no attempt is made to give them any relative weighting;

(2) not "conceptually sound", because in so far as proof might be required of procedural unconscionability, no guidance is given as to how far this proof might legitimately be derived by inference from one-sided outcomes (the more readily such inferences are drawn, the less the distinction between procedural and substantive unconscionability will matter); and

(3) not "explicit in its policy underpinnings", because it is quite unclear whether the legislation is motivated primarily (or at all) by economic efficiency considerations, loss distribution considerations or paternalistic concerns (depending on how it is interpreted, it could be made to relate to any of these goals).

In short, the legislation is indeterminate. This must be counted as a fundamental defect, given that the objective was to make the law more, rather than less, certain. The indeterminacy is a function of the legislature's failure to address key policy choices.

Three examples will serve to demonstrate the problem. Assume that A mortgages the family home to B as security for repayment of a loan made by B to C. C defaults in repayment, and B takes steps to enforce the security against A. Faced with eviction, A brings proceedings under the *Contracts Review Act* 1980 (NSW) to have the contract set aside.[15] Neither B nor C was guilty of any wrongdoing towards A in the period leading up to the signing of the mortgage agreement. A might nevertheless argue that the contract is unjust within the meaning of the statute because it was not in her best interests, and that had she received independent advice at the time she would never have agreed to go ahead with the transaction. If the court is moved by compassion for A's plight, it may well be prepared to accept this argument. It might reason that the consequences to B if the mortgage is set aside will be less severe than the consequences to A if it is not, and that B is in a better position to spread the loss. This is essentially a loss distribution case in favour of intervention. Alternatively, the court might conclude that in the absence of any proof of wrongdoing on B's part, the contract is not unjust. To set aside a contract simply on the basis of the complaining party's assertion that she did not understand it would substantially undermine the security of transactions, and in this sense would be contrary to the public interest. Third party mortgages and guarantees would become less valuable to lenders as forms of security, and some classes of borrower might find it harder to obtain credit. This is essentially an economic efficiency case against intervention. Which of

[15] Apart from the statute, A might be entitled to relief if she could prove unconscientious dealing on B's part (e.g. *Commercial Bank of Australia Ltd* v. *Amadio* (1983) 151 CLR 447) or undue influence by C with notice on B's part (e.g. *Barclays Bank plc* v. *O'Brien* [1994] 1 AC 180).

these competing views is correct—should the court be guided by loss distribution or economic efficiency considerations? For present purposes, the answer does not matter. What does matter is that the statute itself provides no guidance one way or the other. The statute is indeterminate.

Assume now that A agrees to buy property from B for $45,000. The market value of the property is $30,000. A has Alzheimer's disease, but the condition is in its early stages and there is nothing in A's behaviour during negotiations which might lead B to suppose that there is anything amiss. A later brings proceedings against B under the *Contracts Review Act* 1980 (NSW) to have the contract set aside. The issue in this case is whether proof that B knew of A's disability is required to support a finding that the contract was unjust. The question turns on whether the underlying concern of the statute is with relief of A's misfortune (a loss distribution concern) or prevention of B's wrongdoing (an economic efficiency concern).[16] Which approach should the courts take? Again, the statute provides no guidance one way or the other. Not surprisingly, the courts have divided on the question.[17]

Finally, assume that A holds a garage sale. Among the items for sale she includes a painting which she prices at $20. B, an art dealer, attends the sale and immediately recognises A's painting as a long lost masterpiece. B buys the painting from A for $20, without disclosing what he knows. The true value of the painting is $250,000. Could A have the contract set aside under the *Contracts Review Act* 1980 (NSW)? One approach might be to say that the contract is unjust within the meaning of the statute because, given B's superior information, there was a material inequality of bargaining power between the parties at the time of transacting or, alternatively perhaps, because B used unfair tactics in failing to disclose the information. This approach is consistent with a view that information should be shared between contracting parties (a distributive concern). An alternative approach might be to say that there is nothing wrong with a party trading on the basis

[16] From an economic perspective, intervention without proof of B's knowledge would be unwise. A disadvantaged person can take various precautions to avoid misfortune in dealings. The most obvious course is to seek advice before entering into substantial transactions, or to entrust all business matters to a third party (such as a lawyer or an accountant). Of course, A may be so seriously disadvantaged as not to appreciate the need for taking precautions at all. However, if that is the case, A's incapacity is almost certain to be obvious to B. If the courts intervened regardless of whether B actually knew of A's disability—or, at least, wilfully disregarded it—parties in A's position would in future be less inclined to take whatever steps might be within their capacity to protect their own interests. Correspondingly, parties in B's position would be faced with the prospect of investing resources to discover whether the other party might be the subject of a disadvantage likely to result in the transaction being set aside. The alternatives would be to incur this expenditure, or to take the risk of judicial intervention. Either way, transactions would become more costly.

[17] *Baltic Shipping Co* v. *Dillon ("The Mikhail Lermentov")* (1991) 22 NSWLR 1 at 20 *per* Kirby P. and *Collier* v. *Morlend Finance Corp (Vic) Pty Ltd* (1989) ASC 55–716 at 58,433 *per* Meagher JA (proof of knowledge not required); *Custom Credit Corporation Ltd* v. *Lupi* (1991) ASC 56-024 (a decision of the Full Court of the Supreme Court of Victoria under the *Credit Act* 1984 (Vic), Part IX) (proof of knowledge required).

of superior information. On the contrary, if B were required to disclose, he would end up having to share the gains from his discovery with A. A disclosure requirement, routinely imposed, would act as a disincentive to search and discovery. This approach is consistent with economic efficiency considerations.[18] How should the court choose—in favour of a sharing rule, or in favour of exclusivity?[19] Once again, the statute is no help. It is indeterminate.

A justice of the Australian High Court recently made the following observations about the *Contracts Review Act* 1980 (NSW):[20]

> "Civil litigation has . . . increased because courts are increasingly directed by legislatures to re-arrange people's legal rights by reference to vague standards which sound attractive but which are so indefinite that they are extremely difficult to apply to everyday disputes . . .
>
> The difficulties in applying such vague criteria [as those contained in the *Contracts Review Act*] mean that parties to contracts have difficulty in knowing what their rights are. Litigation is forced upon them. When courts have to apply vague standards, consistency of decision-making—which is one of the primary benefits of the rule of law—is difficult to achieve. Moreover, the decision of a court applying such vague criteria often seems arbitrary. Dissatisfaction with the decision-maker in particular cases is often the result. In time, confidence in the judicial system is undermined."

This statement is a clear echo of Leff's eloquent attack on the indeterminacy of UCC, section 2–302: "it is easy to say nothing with words".

III. TRUTH IN LENDING

A uniform *Consumer Credit Code* has been enacted in all Australian States and Territories, and came into effect on 1 November 1996. The *Consumer Credit Code* will replace credit laws enacted just over a decade ago.

The objectives of the *Consumer Credit Code* are as follows:[21]

> "To provide laws which apply equally to all forms of consumer lending and to all credit providers, and which are uniform in all jurisdictions in Australia.
>
> The legislation is based on the principle of truth-in-lending which will allow borrowers to make informed choices when purchasing credit.
>
> [It] applies rules which regulate the credit provider's conduct throughout the life of a loan, but without restricting product flexibility and consumer choice. The policy of the legislation is to rely generally on competitive forces to provide price

[18] A. J. Duggan, Bryan and Hanks, *Contractual Non-Disclosure: An Applied Study in Modern Contract Theory* (Longman Professional, Melbourne, 1994), chap. 5.

[19] The common law favours an exclusivity rule: *ibid.*, chap. 2.

[20] The Hon Justice Michael McHugh, "The Growth of Legislation and Litigation" (1995) 69 *Australian Law Journal* 37 at 43.

[21] *Explanatory Note to Consumer Credit (Queensland) Bill* (1994).

restraint but to provide significant redress mechanisms for borrowers in the event that credit providers fail to comply with the legislation.

[The legislation] is designed to apply to a deregulated credit market and provide standards for the provision of credit which will not be overtaken by changes in the financial marketplace."

"Product flexibility" refers to pricing. One objective in enacting the new laws was to introduce a scheme of regulation which did not interfere with the freedom of credit providers to charge how they liked. Accordingly, the legislation leaves credit providers free to impose interest charges only, or to impose interest charges in combination with other charges such as establishment fees, administration fees or credit card joining and annual subscription fees. The legislation also permits variable rates and staggered rates for fixed sum and continuing credit contracts alike.

According to the Second Reading speech made when the new legislation was introduced into the Queensland Parliament:[22]

"One of the key elements of the Consumer Credit Code is to ensure that there is truth in lending. This means that a consumer can make an informed choice between credit providers as to the nature of the credit being offered, *as well as comparative costs between credit providers*" (emphasis added).

In order to compare costs between credit providers offering different repayment terms, consumers need to know the competing annual percentage rates.[23] Furthermore, unless they are mathematically adept or have access to expert financial advice, they need to know that each credit provider's quoted annual percentage rate accurately reflects the total charge for credit. Credit cost comparisons based on annual percentage rates alone will be misleading if there are additional charges that are not accounted for in the annual percentage rate.

With these considerations in mind, earlier Australian consumer credit laws required disclosure in credit contract documents of the credit provider's annual percentage rate, and at the same time prohibited non-interest charges such as establishment fees, and the like. Credit providers argued that the pro-

[22] Queensland Parliamentary Debates, Legislative Assembly, 4 Aug. 1994, Mr Tom Burns, Minister for Consumer Affairs.

[23] The need for statutory intervention is another question. There is empirical evidence to suggest that, even in the absence of legislation, consumers are at least sensitive to the relative cost of credit from different categories of credit provider (banks, finance companies, retailers, and so on), and would use this information as a surrogate for interest rates when shopping for credit: see the studies referred to in A. J. Duggan, "Consumer Credit Rate Disclosure in the United Kingdom and Australia: A Functional and Comparative Appraisal" (1986) 35 *International and Comparative Law Quarterly* 87. This suggests that consumer credit markets may function quite well even in the absence of rate information, with strong competition occurring *between* classes of credit-granting institutions (see Committee of Inquiry into the Australian Financial System, *Final Report* (1982), chap. 32), though not necessarily *within* classes (see United Kingdom, *Report of the Committee on Consumer Credit* Cmnd. 4596 (1971), para. 3.3.3).

The discussion in the text proceeds on the assumption that statutory intervention may assist consumer choice, but it should not be read as necessarily endorsing this position.

hibition of non-interest charges caused cross-subsidisation problems, and for this reason was both inequitable and inefficient. For example, it was argued that the prohibition of establishment fees made it impossible for the credit provider to recoup from the borrower the start-up costs of the loan in the event of early termination. One option for the credit provider in the face of this prohibition might be to disallow early terminations. However, the legislation gives borrowers a non-excludable right to terminate a contract at any time and it limits the credit provider to recovery of interest charges that have accrued to that point. The remaining option is for credit providers to increase interest charges across the board in order to preserve their profit margins. However, the consequence of this is to give the individual borrower who terminates early a windfall at the expense of the credit provider's other customers: the start-up costs of the loan are borne not by the individual borrower but are spread among the credit provider's customers at large.

Similarly, it was argued that the prohibition of joining and annual subscription fees for credit cards gave one class of card-user a windfall at the expense of another. Many credit card issuers give the consumer a choice between paying the amount in full on the due date, or paying less than the full amount on the due date; credit charges are imposed if the second option is taken, but if the first option is taken, consumers get a "free ride". Consumers who take the first option are in effect using the card facility as a charge card, whereas consumers who take the second option are using it as a credit card. The prohibition of card fees resulted in credit providers covering the cost of providing "free" credit to the charge card users by increasing the credit charge payable to the credit card users. In other words, credit card users subsidised charge card users. The reference in the *Consumer Credit Code* statement of objectives to the preservation of "product flexibility" represents a commitment to the eradication of these kinds of cross-subsidisation problem.

The statement of objectives implies an unfettered commitment to both truth in lending and pricing flexibility. However, in trying to achieve the two objectives simultaneously, the legislation succeeds only in compromising them both. In the name of truth in lending, the *Consumer Credit Code* requires disclosure in contract documents of an annual percentage rate. However, the annual percentage rate to be disclosed is no more than the contract rate expressed annually. The legislation does not prohibit other charges, and there is no requirement for non-interest charges to be accounted for in the disclosed annual percentage rate. A requirement for disclosure of annual percentage rates which are unrepresentative of credit providers' total charges is not only unhelpful in terms of enabling consumers to "make an informed choice . . . as to the comparative costs between credit providers", it is positively misleading.[24] Borrowers will be misled to the extent that they rely on the annual

[24] Begg, "No Truth in Lending: The Cost of Credit Under the Code" (1996) 70 *Law Institute Journal* 32. The legislation provides for disclosure of a "comparison rate" which takes account

percentage rate for comparison purposes—as the legislation presupposes that they will—without taking other items of credit cost into account.

The legislation makes some attempt to address this difficulty *via* the re-opening (unconscionability) provisions. These read, in relevant part, as follows:[25]

> "(1) The Court may, if satisfied on the application of a debtor or guarantor that—
>
> . . .
>
> (b) an establishment fee or charge; or
>
> (c) a fee or charge payable on early termination of a credit contract; or
>
> (d) a fee or charge for a prepayment of an amount under a credit contract; is unconscionable, annul or reduce the . . . fee or charge and may make ancillary or consequential orders.
>
> . . .
>
> (3) In determining whether an establishment fee or charge is unconscionable, the Court is to have regard to whether the amount of the fee or charge is equal to the credit provider's reasonable costs of determining an application for credit and the initial administrative costs of providing the credit or is equal to the credit provider's average reasonable costs of those things in respect of that class of contract.
>
> (4) For the purposes of this section, a fee or charge payable on early termination of the contract or a prepayment of an amount under the credit contract is unconscionable if and only if it appears to the Court that it exceeds a reasonable estimate of the credit provider's loss arising from the early termination or prepayment, including the credit provider's average reasonable administrative costs in respect of such a termination or prepayment."

The re-opening provisions in effect impose a ceiling on establishment and termination fees. They go some way towards restoring the credibility of the legislature's expressed commitment to truth in lending objectives. However, at the same time and inevitably, they compromise the pricing flexibility objective. The compromise is only partial, because the re-opening provisions are limited to certain kinds of fee. Credit providers' freedom to impose other fees remains unrestricted. To this extent, the legislation continues to fall short on the truth in lending front.

not only of the contract rate but also other charges: *Consumer Credit Code*, s. 14(3). However, the calculations for the comparison rate are complex and for this reason governments were persuaded to make its disclosure optional rather than mandatory. They might just as well not have bothered at all. Hold-out problems are likely to make the option unattractive for credit providers. Disclosure of the comparison rate will make credit provider A's product seem more expensive relative to those of credit providers B, C and D if B, C and D choose to disclose only the contract rate (assuming A, B, C and D all impose additional charges). Therefore A will have no incentive to disclose the comparison rate unless B, C and D do so as well. However, B, C and D will each be subject to the same disincentive.

[25] *Consumer Credit Code*, s. 72. The credit provider's loss within the meaning of s. 72(4) does not include the interest charges that would have been earned if the contract had run its full term. This is made clear by s. 75. S. 75 confers a statutory right of early termination on the borrower, and it limits the credit provider's entitlement to recover interest charges to interest charges payable up to the date of termination.

In summary, the *Consumer Credit Code* approach to truth in lending is incoherent. According to the statement of objectives, the aim is to achieve truth in lending objectives and also to maintain product flexibility. These are incompatible goals. In trying to achieve them simultaneously, the legislatures have produced a set of provisions which are counter-productive on both fronts. The provisions do not adequately serve the truth in lending objective, but by the same token they make substantial inroads into credit providers' freedom to charge as they like. On both fronts, it would probably have been better if the new legislation had never been enacted. This is what happens when important policy choices are allowed to go by default.

Schedule 2 to the *Consumer Credit Code* contains miscellaneous provisions relating to interpretation. Clause 7 of Schedule 2 reads as follows:

> "(1) In the interpretation of a provision of this Code, the interpretation that will best achieve the purpose or object of this Code is to be preferred to any other interpretation.
>
> (2) Subclause (1) applies whether or not the purpose is expressly stated in this Code."

This rule is hardly helpful in the context of the truth in lending provisions. In the case of ambiguity, which interpretation should a court prefer: the one that favours truth in lending or the one that favours product flexibility?

IV. PRODUCT LIABILITY

Until the enactment of recent reforms discussed below, product liability in Australia was governed by Division 2A of Part V of the *Trade Practices Act* 1974 (Cth), along with corresponding statutory initiatives in some States,[26] and a combination of contract and tort law. Under the *Trade Practices Act* 1974 (Cth), Part V, Division 2A, a manufacturer is made strictly liable to consumers for loss caused by product defects. Liability does not extend to third parties such as bystanders or non-owners who happen to be using the goods, and the legislation is limited to consumer goods. The basic scheme is to make manufacturers liable to consumers on the same footing that the immediate supplier is liable. Accordingly, a manufacturer may be required to pay damages if, for example, the product is not of merchantable quality or fit for its purpose, or if it does not correspond with a description that has been applied to it.

The economic efficiency case for imposing strict liability on manufacturers rests on two grounds, the "pricing effects argument" and the "deterrence argument". The pricing effects argument assumes that consumers systematically

[26] *Manufacturers' Warranty Act* 1974 (SA); *Law Reform (Manufacturers' Warranties) Act* 1977 (ACT).

under-estimate the risk of product-related accidents.[27] Given this, they fail to discount the product price sufficiently, so that more of the product ends up being purchased than would be warranted by its true cost (including the expected accident cost). The imposition of strict liability on manufacturers will cause them to raise their prices, so that the explicit price of the product does include a component for accident costs. The result should be a drop in demand to the optimal level, and a consequent reduction in the number of accidents.[28] The deterrence argument runs as follows. The imposition of liability on a manufacturer should confront it with the incentive to take steps that will avoid the accident and, consequently, the need for it to pay damages (for example, design improvement, provision of warnings, or the adoption of testing procedures). It will be worthwhile for the manufacturer to take precautions so long as the cost of doing so is less than the reduction achieved in the expected accident cost. In the absence of liability, and still assuming consumers' tendency to under-estimate product risks, these precautions might not be taken, with the consequence that avoidable accidents will continue to occur. Accordingly, manufacturers should at least be liable in negligence (for failure to take cost-justified accident precautions). However, plaintiffs may have difficulty in proving negligence and therefore, in the interests of effective deterrence, a strict liability regime may be warranted. The corollary of the deterrence argument in favour of manufacturers' liability is that in so far as there are cost-justified accident precautions that can more easily be taken by the plaintiff (for example, careful handling of the product), the manufacturer should not be liable. Otherwise, the plaintiff may have an insufficient incentive to take the precaution.

The loss-shifting case for strict liability is based on the assumption that insurance is more readily available to the manufacturer than it is to the consumer.[29] Imposition of liability on a manufacturer will induce it to take out

[27] This assumption is made in nearly all the law and economics literature relating to product liability. It is, however, an empirical observation, and it has not gone unchallenged. See, e.g., A. Schwartz, "Proposals for Product Liability Reform: A Theoretical Synthesis" (1988) 97 *Yale Law Journal* 353, 374–84.

[28] S. Shavell, "Strict Liability Versus Negligence" (1980) 9 *Journal of Legal Studies* 1. Contrast M. Trebilcock, "The Social Insurance-Deterrence Dilemma of Modern North American Tort Law: A Canadian Perspective on the Liability Insurance Crisis" (1987) 24 *San Diego Law Review* 929, 987–8, where the contrary view is put. The argument is that activity levels could be reduced just as readily by internalising the cost of the activity to the consumer, as by internalising it to the manufacturer. There is no *a priori* reason for preferring the latter alternative.

[29] In theory, the consumer could take out first-party accident insurance, covering all accident risks however arising. Whether this is a less effective method of risk spreading than product liability insurance taken out by the manufacturer is an empirical question. Observation suggests that first-party accident insurance is rarely sought by consumers and is difficult to obtain. Trebilcock argues that the reason for this has to do with the fact that current liability rules tend to place the risk of product-related accidents on the manufacturer. If the risk was on the consumer, demand for first-party insurance would be higher. On this basis, the loss distribution argument in favour of strict manufacturers' liability is circular: "The Role of Insurance Considerations in the Choice of Efficient Civil Liability Rules" (1988) 4 *Journal of Law, Economics and Organisation* 243 at 258.

insurance, so that if an accident occurs, the loss will be shifted from the victim and spread over a substantial segment of the community. Liability not covered by insurance will be reflected in higher prices, and this also achieves loss-shifting objectives.

In a joint report published in 1989, the Australian Law Reform Commission and the Victorian Law Reform Commission recommended that Australian laws should be changed to give effect to both economic efficiency and loss distribution considerations.[30] The Commissions proceeded on the assumption that both objectives could be achieved simultaneously. The Report says:[31]

> "Accidents are inevitable. Some loss will be caused by products.
>
> That loss may affect Australia and its economy adversely. The adverse effects will be reduced to the extent that
>
> loss is prevented in ways that do not increase the cost of production of goods beyond the optimal level and
>
> cost of spreading the risk of loss is reduced.
>
> Both effects are comprehended by the policy objectives identified in chapter 2. The overall effect of the recommended changes will be to reduce both the incidence of loss caused by goods and the cost of recovering compensation—including both the actual cost of compensation and the necessary transaction costs. While either reduction would benefit the economy, *when the two occur together their effects are greatly magnified*" (emphasis added).

A draft Bill was appended to the Commissions' report, but the Bill was never adopted. Instead, the government claimed to give effect to the Commissions' recommendations by enacting legislation modelled on the *European Community Product Liability Directive*.[32] The new law commenced operation on 9 July 1992. It operates in conjunction with, not in substitution for, the pre-existing laws outlined above.

Does the new legislation simultaneously achieve both economic efficiency and loss distribution objectives, as the Commissions were concerned that it should? The answer is that it does not and, furthermore, that it could not do so because economic efficiency and loss distribution objectives are incompatible. For example, as mentioned above, economic considerations support the inclusion in product liability laws of a contributory negligence defence. However, loss distribution considerations point in the other direction, because a contributory negligence defence makes it harder for plaintiffs to recover. The new legislation incorporates a contributory negligence defence. By contrast, under pre-existing laws the rights of a plaintiff in a product liability case were not subject to contributory negligence, except where the action was brought in negligence. In this respect, the new legislation scores well on economic efficiency grounds, but badly on loss distribution grounds.[33]

[30] *Product Liability* (ALRC Report No 51 and VLRC Report No 27, 1989).

[31] Para. 10.07.

[32] *Trade Practices Act* 1974 (Cth), Part VA.

[33] However, the economic efficiency benefits are substantially undercut because the pre-existing legislation in the *Trade Practices Act* 1974 (Cth), Part V, Div 2A has not been repealed. This

The new legislation, again in contrast to the earlier laws, incorporates a state of the art defence, as follows:[34]

> "In a liability action, it is a defence if it is established that . . . the state of scientific or technical knowledge at the time when [the goods] were supplied by their actual manufacturer was not such as to enable that defect to be discovered."

The economic efficiency case for the inclusion of this provision is problematical. On the one hand, without the defence, the risk of liability may drive manufacturers out of certain industries. On the other hand, because the defence rewards ignorance, one consequence may be to discourage research and development within an industry. In short, a state of the art defence may generate efficiency gains in the product market, but at the expense of efficiency losses in the market for information. From a loss distribution perspective, there is no case for a state of the art defence.

The actual wording of the state of the art defence is ambiguous. The reference to the discoverability of the defect could be read down by taking cost considerations into account, or it could be read without regard to costs. The consequence if it is read the second way will be to give the defence a very narrow application—any defect is discoverable at some cost. How should a court interpret the defence, taking account—as it is supposed to—of the policy underlying the legislation? The policy is indeterminate, for the reasons that have already been stated. Giving the defence a broad application could be justified on economic efficiency grounds, but not on loss distribution grounds. On the other hand, giving it a narrow application could be justified on countervailing economic efficiency grounds and could also be justified on loss distribution grounds. A court would be equally entitled to go either way. In this respect, the legislature appears to have abdicated its policy-making function in favour of the courts.[35]

means that most plaintiffs can avoid the potential application of the contributory negligence defence by suing under the old provisions instead of the new.

[34] *Trade Practices Act* 1974 (Cth), s. 75AK(1)(c).

[35] The point is well illustrated by the peanut butter scare which was current in Australia at the time of writing. A salmonella infection led to the removal of most peanut butter brands from supermarket shelves. There was some suggestion that the problem might be traceable to the peanuts that were used in production. The director of the Peanut Company of Australia, asked whether the company routinely tested peanuts for contamination, replied: "Only very isolated analysis. Historically, the risk of salmonella in peanuts is extremely low. I think there's probably one or two recorded cases in the literature" (*The Age*, 27 June 1996). If the company was sued under *Trade Practices Act* 1974 (Cth), Part VA, could it rely on the state of the art defence? The answer is uncertain. According to the first reading of the defence outlined in the text, the defence would fail because the "state of scientific or technical knowledge" at the time when the peanuts were supplied was clearly such as to enable the defect to be discovered—there were viable testing procedures for salmonella. According to the second reading, however, the defence would succeed because although it is possible to test for salmonella in peanuts, routine testing was thought not to be cost-justified given the then current state of scientific or technical knowledge about the size of the risk.

The policy muddle is compounded by the failure to repeal the earlier laws. If the courts were to give the defence a broad application, plaintiffs in most cases could avoid it by suing under the product liability provisions in *Trade Practices Act* 1974 (Cth), Part V, Div 2A. These provisions do not include a state of the art defence.

Liability under the new legislation is based on proof of a defect. "Defect" is defined in relevant part as follows:[36]

"(1) For the purposes of this Part, goods have a defect if their safety is not such as persons generally are entitled to expect.

(2) In determining the extent of the safety of goods, regard is to be given to all relevant circumstances including:

(a) the manner in which, and the purposes for which, they have been marketed; and

(b) their packaging; and

(c) the use of any mark in relation to them; and

(d) any instructions for, or warnings with respect to, doing, or refraining from doing, anything with or in relation to them; and

(e) what might reasonably be expected to be done with or in relation to them; and

(f) the time when they were supplied by their manufacturer."

This provision is indeterminate, particularly in its application to design defects. What is "safety"? What is it that persons generally "are entitled to expect"? Who does the class of "persons generally" comprise—for example does it mean the public at large, or is it limited to purchasers of the product in question? Does it include experts? These questions are at large. Depending on how the courts answer them, the new legislation could be given a wide application, or a narrow one. A wide application could be justified on loss distribution grounds. However, on economic efficiency grounds, a wide application would be questionable. The wider the application the provision is given, the greater the cost of production to the manufacturer and the stronger the inhibiting effect the legislation is likely to have on manufacturing activity. Higher costs will be passed on to consumers in the form of price increases, and this is the payment exacted for the increased consumer protection the legislation provides. In this respect, the legislation is analogous to a scheme of compulsory insurance against product-related accidents. The higher the price increase, the more likely that consumers would prefer not to pay it and hence the greater the efficiency loss. In any event, two points are clear. First, in the absence of judicial interpretation, neither the economic efficiency nor the loss distribution effects of the "defect" provision can be predicted with any confidence. Secondly, no matter how the courts end up interpreting the provision, there will be gains on one front and losses on the other.

The foregoing discussion bears out Michael Trebilcock's observation that "a single legal instrument seems unlikely to perform simultaneously prospective standard-setting functions and retrospective assignments of liability in an optimal way":[37]

[36] *Trade Practices Act* 1974 (Cth), s. 75AC.

[37] "The Social-Insurance Deterrence Dilemma of Modern North American Tort Law: A Canadian Perspective on the Liability Insurance Crisis" (1987) 24 *San Diego Law Review* 529, 989–90.

"It is futile to attempt to reform the system with social insurance [loss distribution] objectives as the operative criteria. The closer we come to realising these objectives, . . . the further we will have moved from attainment of optimal deterrence [economic efficiency] objectives . . . there is a necessary *inverse* relationship between the two sets of objectives".

This insight appears to have escaped the Australian legislators, and the result is a muddle. As in the case of the truth in lending laws, an important policy choice has been allowed to go by default. Is the new legislation meant to be primarily aimed at better loss distribution, or is its primary objective increased economic efficiency (reducing the incidence of product-related injuries)? The Law Reform Commissions say both, but this is impossible. Which objective, then, is to be given priority? The legislation itself provides no answers. It is indeterminate.

V. CONCLUSION

This paper has canvassed three major consumer law reform initiatives. The New South Wales *Contracts Review Act* 1980 was enacted with a view to making the law "sharp in focus, conceptually sound and explicit in its policy underpinnings", but it achieves precisely the opposite on all fronts. The new truth-in-lending laws were enacted with two incompatible objectives in mind, truth in lending and "product flexibility", with the consequence that neither is achieved. The product liability reform proposals were made without regard to the inevitability of trade-offs between economic efficiency and loss distribution concerns, and the result is legislation that—contrary to the promise held out by its promoters—lacks a clear policy direction. In all three cases, it has been left to the courts to fill in the policy gaps as best they can.

These assessments all point to major shortcomings in the policy-making process. It might be tempting to explain the problem away by characterising it as a political one—everyone knows that compromise is inevitable in politics and that statutes are often imperfect on that account. The trouble is that, at least in the case of the *Contracts Review Act* 1980 (NSW) and the product liability reforms, the proposals were deficient even before they got into the political arena. In the case of the truth-in-lending laws, it is true that politics played a substantial part in the unsatisfactory outcome. However, the politicians have not conceded that the objectives of the legislation have been compromised. On the contrary, they continue to assert that it delivers sound consumer protection for their constituents.[38] If principled law reform counts for anything, such claims should not go unchallenged.

I hope I may be forgiven for having chosen all Australian examples. However, it is not the examples that matter so much as the underlying mes-

[38] See text at n. 22, above.

sage. There is a lesson in the Australian experience for other countries to heed. The lesson is not that unconscionability legislation, truth-in-lending requirements or product liability laws are necessarily bad. Rather, it is that, when enacting these—or other—measures, it is important to be clear about the underlying policy objectives and associated trade-offs. Otherwise, the commitment to consumer protection they are supposed to reflect will be just words.

23

Comparative Publicity in the Honduran Commercial Code and Consumer Protection Law

DR. LAUREANO F. GUTIÉRREZ FALLA*

I. INTRODUCTION

According to Díaz Ruiz,[1] comparative advertising can be defined as an act by which a message is sent to the public comparing the advertiser's goods or services to those of a competitor and claiming that the advertiser's goods or services are better than the competititor's. Comparative advertising is regulated in Honduras by two different laws with two different protected interests and two different subjects: the Commercial Code of 1950, Articles 422 ff., particularly Article 425(II)(e), and the Consumer Protection Law (Decree 41–89 of 7 April 1989; hereafter "CPL") Articles 11 ff., and Article 17 ff. of Executive Order No. 264–49 of 25 June 1989 (hereafter "Regulation"), more particularly Article 17(e) and (f).[2]

In the Commercial Code, which was adopted in 1950, comparative advertising is prohibited, a prohibition based on the classical juridical concept of unfair competition.[3] The much newer CPL follows the more modern doctrine

* Member of the Honduras Bar.

[1] Emilio Díaz Ruiz, "Competencia Desleal a través de la Publicidad Comparativa", *R.D.M.* No. 215, January–March 1995, 59, 134.

[2] However, it is true that Art. 92(e)(iii) of the Industrial Property Law (Decree 142–93 of 7 Sept. 1993) prohibits the use in commerce, without the consent of the owner, of a distinctive sign identical or similar to a registered trade mark in circumstances that could induce in the public error or confusion, or could cause the owner of the trade mark unjust economic or commercial damage by reason of the dilution of the distinctive force or commercial value of the trade mark or an unjust use of the reputation or distinctive force of the trade mark. Since the rule is expressly limited to the use of distinctive signs in comparative advertising as regulated by Honduran legislation, it would in effect be ruled by the CPL and Commercial Code. However, although Art. 425(II)(a) of the Honduran Commercial Code forbids the improper use of commercial names, symbols, samples, trade marks, patents or other elements of an enterprise or its establishments, it does not forbid the "proper use" as allowed, for example, by the comparative publicity regulations under the Commercial Code.

[3] The classical concept is clearly analysed by Anxo Tato Plaza in "Publicidad Comaparativa y Movimiento de Defensa de los Consumidores en Derecho Comparado", *R.D.M.* No. 206, October–December 1992, 863 ff. Tato explains that under classical French law comparative

and accepts comparative advertising as legitimate if it is not false or denigrating.[4]

The fundamental reason for this difference resides in the character of the protected interests. The Code protects the entrepreneur and the CPL protects the consumer. From the point of view of the entrepreneur, comparative advertising by a competitor can affect his clientèle. This is the reason it is considered unfair competition. From the consumer's point of view, comparative advertising has an important function, that of offering additional information to the consumer. This will permit a more informed choice of the product or services while imposing at the same time some restraint on monopolies for, as Díaz Ruiz has explained,[5] comparative advertising permits less well-known trade marked products to enter the market and, in that way, to weaken monopolistic competition.[6]

The same system of double regulation also exists in Spain. This is because while the *Ley General de Publicidad* (Ley 34/1988 of 11 November) states that comparative advertising is unlawful if it is not based on the essential characteristics, related by affinity and objectively provable, of the products or services being advertised or when goods or services are compared with other non-similar or unknown products or services with products or services with a limited penetration in the market, the *Ley de Competencia Desleal* (Ley 3/191 of 10 January) establishes that the public comparison of the competitor's activities, services or establishment with those of another competitor or third party will be unfair when it refers to products that are not analogous, relevant or comparable.

(a) Unfair Competition

Unfair competition is regulated in Honduras by Articles 425 ff. of the Commercial Code, which form part of Title III, "On the Limits to Commercial Activity and Unfair Competition", of Book II, "On the

publicity was a case of denigration (at 864 ff.) and, therefore, unlawful. However, since Law 60–92 was enacted in order to reinforce the protection of consumers, comparative publicity is lawful if it meets the conditions set out in Art. 10. The products or services being compared must be of the same nature and interchangeable. In addition, the publicity cannot infringe on a competitor's distinctive signs, and it must be lawful, true and objective and not confuse the consumer.

[4] According to Baylos Corroza (Hermenegildo, *Tratado de Derecho Industrial* (Madrid, Editorial Civitas, 1978), 314), the notion of unfair competition, without losing the common principle of morality which appears in other manifestations, is nevertheless a relative notion, that is relative to the time, place and social *mores* under consideration.

[5] *Supra* n. 1, 135.

[6] An example is the judgment of the Tribunal of Brussels in *Pepsi-Cola* v. *Coca-Cola*, 7 June 1983, in which the court authorised comparative advertising because Coca-Cola held more than 80% of the market. Therefore, if Pepsi-Cola were not permitted to advertise its new products by mentioning Coca-Cola's products or by comparing them with Pepsi-Cola, Coca-Cola's monopoly would not be broken, a result that would be contrary to the interests of the market place. See Emilio Díaz Ruiz, *supra* n. 1, 135.

Professional Obligations of Merchants". Following the classical Italian doctrine, Article 425 defines unfair competition as:

> "*Article 425.*—The execution by a merchant of acts, such as the following, intended to wrongfully attract clientele . . .".

The Article goes on to enumerate, non-exhaustively, a series of factual situations illustrating cases of unfair competition. These include cases under Subtitle II ("Directly Damaging another Merchant without infringing Contractual Duties") involving "the direct and public comparison of the quality and prices of the merchant's merchandise or services with those of another merchant identified by name or in a manner that makes his identity conspicuous". All the examples of unfair competition in the Honduran Commercial Code are based on the wrongful (*indebida*) attraction of clientèle of a merchant, even though Article 425 does not define the term "wrongful".

The concept is essential, because the governing philosophy now holding sway in Honduras is that of free enterprise, which entails that competition is of the essence of commerce. Therefore, as part of the right to compete, it is also lawful to look for new customers, even though it involves attracting them from a competitor. Modern doctrine is unanimous in the view that a merchant does not have title or proprietary rights in his customers[7] (as was originally suggested by Vivante[8]) but must rely on his own efforts to retain his customer base as well as to attract new customers.[9]

Nevertheless, limits exist on the scope of permissible competition, one of them being that it must not be wrongful competition. This restriction is included in the word "unduly" in Article 425, an Article that must be read in conjunction with Article 422 of the Honduran Commercial Code. This states:

> "*Article 422.*—Merchants must exercise their professional activity in accordance with the law and commercial usage and custom without injuring the customer or the national economy and without violating public morality. The violation of this obligation for competitive purposes enables the injured party to demand cessation of the illegal conduct and the payment of damages if damages are suffered."

It should be kept in mind that Article 422 refers to the general limits on commercial activities by merchants and is not restricted to unfair competition, which is a subset of wrongful trading conduct. In other words, the right to compete has two different limitations. The first limitation, which is acceptable

[7] See, e.g., Tulio Ascarelli, *Iniciación al Estudio del Derecho Mercantil* (Barcelona, Bosch Editorial, 1964), 293.

[8] César Vivante, "La Proprieta Commerciale delle Clientela", *Riv. Dir. Com.* 1930, T.XXVIII, 1 ff.

[9] According to Francisco Ferrara, *Teoría Jurídica de la Hacienda Mercantil* (trans. José María Navas, Editorial Revista de Derecho Privado, 1950), 330: "the commercial enterprise is not protected against any attack; in principle, competition is legitimate because it is politically, morally and economically useful . . . all merchants have the right to reinforce and strengthen their own organisation and extend the scope of their busines, even when in doing so they damage other enterprises or endanger their existence, but it must be done honestly."

in a system of free enterprise, is not to distort the free circulation of goods and services in the market place even though it may appear to be in the consumer's interest. However, according to Goldner, it serves a different purpose. As he writes:[10] ". . . the real reason for the enactment of a great deal of law dealing with mergers, monopolies and restrictive trade practices would appear to be the prevention of concentration of business power, which has political implications, rather than protecting consumers. Competition law has great relevance to consumers, and parts of it are just as much parts of consumer law. This does not mean that consumer law is part of—or an outgrowth of—competition law".

The second limitation is that of not unduly attracting the clientèle of other merchants, as shown by two different factual situations.[11]

The first situation, which many authors describe as part of the *droit de la concurrence* (competition law) is not specifically regulated in Honduran law.[12] This is true even though Article 339 of the Honduran Constitution prohibits monopolies, oligopolies, hoarding and similar tactics in industrial and commercial activity. Likewise, Article 42(d) of the Regulations under the CPL authorises the Executive to prevent or combat hoarding or any other manipulation that tends unduly to alter the price or to restrict or limit the sale and circulation of goods or services and ". . . (d) to take any other measures that are necessary to control and avoid restrictive practices in the offering and free circulation of the goods or services". Nevertheless, competition law is regulated by Article 422 of the Commercial Code, because any infraction of the rules of the market place would undoubtedly injure the national economy in its various ramifications.

Unfair competition, on the other hand, protects the *aviamiento* (goodwill)[13] of an enterprise, and is defined as a subjective right of an entrepreneur *vis-à-vis* all competing enterpreneurs, entitling complainants to an injunction, inde-

[10] John Goldring, "Consumer Law and Legal Theory: Reflections of a Common Lawyer", in Donald B. King (ed.), *Essays on Comparative Commercial and Consumer Law* (Colorado, Fred B. Rothman & Co., 1992), 316, 328 ff.

[11] According to Cl. Champau, "Les sources du droit de la concurrence au regard du droit commercial et des autres branches du droit commercial en France", in *Etude a l'honneur d R. Houin*, 60 ff. quoted in *Rev. Int. du Droit Economique*, T.10 1986, 25 ff.: " the action against unfair competition is of a disciplinary nature, and competition law, whose sources are foreign to commercial law, is placed outside private law, as far from being the expression of the will of merchants as is the private right to fair competition, it not only assures a free competition of the enterprises, but also forces them to compete effectively."

[12] Such legislation exists in many industrialised countries. Examples are the *Ley Federal de Competencia Económica*, Ley 110/1963 of 20 July, of *Represiones Prácticas Reflectivas de la Competencia in Spain*, the U.S. Sherman Antitrust Act of 2 July 1899 (which for many was the first legislation to that effect), and the Canadian Competition Act of 1985. I understand the Honduran authorities are in the process of elaborating a law to the same effect.

[13] According to Mario Rotondi (*Diritto Industriale* (lst edn., Padua, Cedam, 1965), 480), the object protected by this Act is, in reality, the value of the "goodwill" of the enterprise, i.e. the organisation of the enterprise objectively understood, the personality of the subject that holds title to the enterprise, in that one and the other concur in the formation, maintenance and increase of the goodwill of a concrete individual enterprise.

pendent of any damage suffered resulting from negligence or fraud (elements that would be necessary to claim damages).[14] Competition is considered unfair when the result of the infraction is immoral under the concept of the "moral value of the infractor's conduct".[15] Therefore, a double requirement must be met: that of the inmorality (unfairness) of the means used and the capability of the acts to sway the clientèle of a third party.[16]

Article 425 of the Commercial Code describes four different situations as constituting unfair competition:

"1. Deception of the public in general or of particular persons.
II. Directly damaging another merchant without violating contractual obligations (such as the unlawful use of intellectual property rights, comparative advertising, denigration of competitors and obstructing access of the competitor's clientèle to their places of business).
III. Directly damaging another competitor by violating contractual obligations, not only with respect to contracts to which the infractor is a party but also those where the infractor is not a party.
IV. Any similar act intended to sway directly or indirectly the clientèle of another competitor."

An analysis of the above examples confirms that the use of deception or denigration or discrediting or creating confusion as to the products of a competitor is an essential element of unfair competiton. Honduran legislation follows closely Article 2598 of the Italian Civil Code of 1942 which considered acts of unfair competition as:

"1. . . . Using a name or distinctive signs capable of producing confusion with the name or distinctive signs used by others, or slavishly imitating the competitor's products, or executing by any other means acts capable of creating confusion with the products and the activity of the competitor;

2. Divulging information and opinions on the competitor's products and activities which are capable of discrediting the competitor, or appropriating to oneself the merits of the competitor's products or enterprise;

3. Using, directly or indirectly, any other means not in accordance with the principles of professional ethics and capable of damaging another enterprise."

[14] Tulio Ascarelli, *Teoría de la Concurrencia y los Bienes Inmateriales* (Spanish trans. A.Ventura and R. Suárez Yánez, Barcelona, Bosch, 1970), 160.

[15] The concept can be traced to the Eighth Congress of the Hague of 6 November 1925, which considered unfair competition as all acts contrary to honest usage in industrial or commercial matters. The concept has substantially evolved in legislations such as Germany's (see Paz-Ares.-Cándido.-El "Ilícito Concurrencial: de la dogmática monopolística a la política antitrust", *R.D.M.* No. 159, January–March 1981, 7, 13 ff.). In the area of protected interests, the concept has evolved from the protection of competing entrepreneurs to the protection of the economic public order. With respect to the relevant yardstick, it has evolved from a standard of unfairness based on extrajudicial moral codes and conventions of the entrepreneurs, to the understanding that the standard is substantially of a political and economic nature. Finally, with respect to the the nature of the institution itself, the parallel transformation of the rule, classically understood as a law of conflicts, has evolved into a rule of organisation and control.

[16] Ascarelli, *supra* n. 14, 203.

Based on the above rules Rotondi[17] correctly affirmed that, for Italian law and, we believe, for the Honduran Commercial Code, unfair competition is not a simple application of the principles of extracontractual liability,[18] and does not require indemnifiable damage or an intent to defraud; nor is guilt or negligence required for an act to be deemed unfair competition, the only requirement being that the activity performed by one competitor be potentially damaging to another.

(b) Comparative Publicity in the Commercial Code

Article 425 II (e) of the Honduras Commercial Code states:

> "*Article 425*.—The execution by a merchant of acts such as the following which are intended unduly to attract clientèle will be considered as unfair competition . . . II.—Directly damaging another merchant without violating contractual duties, such as: . . . (e) Direct and public comparison of the quality and the prices of the merchant's products or services with those of another merchant identified by name or in a manner that renders his identity notorious."

Article 425 sets out the following conditions that must be met in order to constitue unfair comparative advertising.

(i) *The existence of a direct and public comparison*. This requirement is fulfilled when the advertising specifically compares the prices or qualities of the advertiser's goods or services with those of another merchant, and when the means used to execute such an act are public knowledge, i.e. utilising any existing means of communication, whether oral, written, images or of any other type.[19] This is an essential requirement for all acts of unfair competition: that it be executed for the purpose of diverting the clientèle of another competitor, which means that the comparison must have been made known to consumers in general and not only to a specific client.

(ii) *The comparison must relate to the quality or price of the advertiser's merchandise or services with those of a competitor*. Therefore, it is necessary that the advertising compare the quality or price of the advertiser's merchandise or services to the quality or price of the merchandise or services of third par-

[17] Diritto, *op. cit*., 482.

[18] It should be remembered that this was its origin in France as a result of the rulings of the French Supreme Court.

[19] According to Art. 2.1 of EC Directive 450/84 relating to deceptive advertising, advertising consists of: ". . . all forms of communication executed in the area of commercial, industrial, artesanal or liberal professional activity for the purpose of promoting the supply of goods or the rendering of services". Jose Antonio García Cruz González, "Derecho Comunitario y Derecho del Consumo", *R.D.M.* No. 192 April–June 1989, 327, interprets the above definition as encompassing all forms of communication occurring in the course of commercial activity. For the application of this concept under Honduran legislation, see Laureano F. Gutiérrez Falla, "La Publicidad Ilícita y la Competencia Desleal a la Luz del Derecho Comunitario Europeo", *R.D.C.O.* No. 139/141, January–June 1991, 145,149 ff.

ties, which could, but not necessarily would, constitute a case of denigration. (iii) *The comparison refers to the goods or services of one or more other competitors identified by name or in such a manner that their identity is notorious.*[20] This requirement needs no further explanation: for comparative advertising to be considered unfair competition, it is necessary that the merchants whose goods or services are being compared with those of the advertisers be identified directly or unmistakably; in other words, as the English Advertising Standards Authority Code of Advertising Practices states: "designating them in such a manner in which there is no probability that the consumers could incur in an error".[21]

Therefore, unfair competition will not occur when goods or sevices are compared to those of a competitor who is not identified or who is difficult to identify. For example, a mere exaltation of the attributes of the advertiser's goods or services would not constitute unfair competition. This is the reason advertising Café El Indio as "the best coffee" is not considered unfair competition.

As Ascarelli[22] has observed,"Italian case law has not considered as unfair the generic affirmations of the excellence of the advertiser's products, although comparative references, because they are unfair, are forbidden". Ascarelli cites ample case law under that same comparison doctrine, which German case law[23] has labelled as "savage critical comparisons U.S. style".[24]

(iv) Under Honduran legislation, publicly and directly to compare the quality and price of the advertiser's goods with those of an identifiable merchant constitutes unfair competition, even though no falsehood, deception or denigration exists. The Honduran rule was clearly established when the Milan

[20] According to C. J. Zavala Rodríguez, *Publicidad Comercial*, (Depalma, 1947), 416–19, comparative advertising will be acceptable in principle when it sets forth the merits of a particular product in relation to all other goods in general but not when it designates them individually by their trade marks or characteristics.

[21] A comparison, e.g., with well known trade marks without identifying their owners, as would be true in referring to the trade marks of Coca-Cola, Ford or Toyota. It is also relevant to remember that in cases such as *Rolex C. Grent* (CNFed. Civil and Commercial, chamber 2, *Rolex S.* v. *Oriente, S.A. and others*, 20 Dec. 1971, La Ley Año LIX No. 202, 20 Oct. 1995), the Argentine Tribunal held that the mere fact of comparing the trade mark of a watch with that of another already known, without the consent of its owner, constitutes a case of unlawful advertising. This criterion is also followed in England based on section 41 (b) of the Trade Mark Act 1938 in cases such as *Bisnag Ltd* v. *Amblis Chemist Ltd* 1940). This is not necessarily the case in Honduras; see *supra*, n. 1.

[22] *Supra* n. 14, 216. I believe the Italian jurisprudence quoted by Ascarelli would also be applicable in Honduras.

[23] Quoted by Anxo Tato Plaza, *supra* n. 3, 889.

[24] According to Otto Kleppner, *Publicidad* (9th edn., Mexico, Prentice-Hall Hispanoamericana, 1988), 624, quoted in B. O'Farrell-Miguel "La Publicidad Comparativa en el Derecho Argentino", La Ley, Año LIX No.202, Oct. 20, 1995, 3: "The impulse for comparative advertising arose in the United States in 1972 when the Federal Trade Commission urged ABC and NBC to permit commercials where other competitors were named. Until that date, only CBS had permitted such messages while NBC and ABC only permitted that the comparison be with 'Brand X'. Since then comparative publicity has become a popular technique although extremely controversial."

Court of Appeals held on 12 March 1926[25] that when reference is made to a better quality or a reduced price in relation to a firm that is identified by name, such act constitutes an insidious or inmoral act, as it is inspired by the desire to obtain benefits for the name and reputation of the advertising firm.[26]

(v) Finally, comparative advertising falling under the aforesaid requirements constitutes unfair competition from an objective point of view, as there is no requirement as to the presence of guilt or negligence[27] or proof of any damage. It is sufficient that the act may potentially divert clientèle, as can be deduced from the word "intended" in Article 425 of the Commercial Code. Nevertheless, the existence of some damage is a requirement for claiming indemnity.

In conclusion, it appears that Honduran commercial legislation agrees with Bourgoignie's opinion,[28] in that foreign experience has shown the extreme difficulty experienced by the legislator in defining the permissible limits for comparative advertising. It creates great juridical insecurity, is a source of substantial conflict, is costly for enterprises and is hurtful to the image of trade marks in general. It is doubtful whether comparative advertising yields any positive results since the technique is used primarily by large enterprises who own trade marks already known to the public.

(c) **Unlawful Advertising**

Unlawful advertising is regulated by Article 11 of the CPL. This states:

> "*Article 11.* Any kind of advertising or propaganda which by inexactitude or concealment may induce to error, deception or confusion with respect to the characteristics, properties, nature, origin, quality, quantity or price of all kinds of products and services, is forbidden."

The concept is broadened by Article 17 of the Regulations, which provides:

[25] Quoted by Ferrara, *supra* n. 9, 365.

[26] I believe Honduran courts would also follow Rotondi's thesis (*supra* n. 13, 509 ff.) that comparative advertising is internationally recognised as lawful when objective references are used to illustrate the quality and merits of the advertiser's product and are made in an honest and objective manner against the corresponding quality of other products. An example is publicity stating the result of a sporting event to confirm that the advertiser's product is the best because it has won an international competition.

[27] Rotondi (*supra* n. 13, 476) says: psychological investigation as to the subjective motive of the person committing the act of unfair advertising is rejected. Only the purely objective elements, which are the acts that should be repressed as acts of unfair competition are taken into account. Ferrara holds a contrary opinion. In *Teoría Jurídica*, *supra* n. 9, 334, he states: "innocent unfair competition is, in our understanding, a *contradictio in terminis* because unfair competition is distinguished from unlawful competition precisely by the occurrence, in the first instance, of malice or a guilt that is lacking in the second; therefore, there can be no unfair competition without guilt."

[28] Thierry Bourgoignie, *Elements pour une Theorie du Droit de la Consommation* (Story Scientia 1988), 69, n. 17.

"*Article 17*. For the effects of the law and this Regulation, unlawful advertising will be considered, and therefore forbidden, as that which in a direct or indirect manner implies falsehood, inexactitude, omissions, ambiguity, exaggeration or any other circumstances that could induce the consumer to deception, error or confusion, such as the following practices and actions . . . ."

Article 17 is followed by a non-exhaustive series of fact situations that should be considered as examples of unlawful advertising.

As stated above, the juridical purpose behind the rules of unlawful advertising is to protect the interests of the consumer and, therefore, the public good, as is clearly stated in Article 1 of the CPL:

"*Article 1*. The purpose of the present law is to establish the legal system necessary to obtain and maintain adequate protection of the consumer and of the nation,in order to guarantee just and equitable treatment in the procurement and use of products and services."

The rules governing unfair competition and unlawful advertising complement each other to a high degree,[29] and in the majority of cases in which a situation of unlawful advertising exists under the CPL there would, at the same time, be unfair competition under the Commercial Code. Nevertheless, there are exceptions to this rule, as in the case of comparative publicity which is regulated differently in the Code and the CPL.

In general, the rules governing unlawful advertising in the CPL closely follow the rules contained in Article 2.2 of EC Directive 450/84 which concerns the harmonisation of legislation of Member States in matters of deceptive advertising. It defines deceptive advertising as:

"all advertising which in any manner, including its presentation to whom it is directed or affects, and which, due to its deceptive nature can affect their economic behaviour or which, for those reasons, damages or is capable of damaging its competitor."

An analysis of Directive 450/84 indicates that it contains three different requisites for constituting unlawful advertising:

(1) the advertising be deceptive per se;
(2) the advertising can lead to deception, that is to say, it can be potentially deceptive;
(3) the advertising contains untrue affirmations.

Nevertheless, as García Cruz González has noted:[30] "in accordance with community law, not only would absolutely or partially false advertising be deceptive advertising, but also advertising which, although exact on an abstract basis, is deceptive because it induces consumers to error".

[29] See Laureano F. Gutiérrez Falla, *supra* n. 19, 148.
[30] "Derecho Comunitario y Derecho del Consumo", R.D.L. No. 192, April–June 1989, 335.

Under the CPL rules, unlawful advertising occurs when it satisfies the the following conditions:

(1) it must be inaccurate or conceal the truth (Article 11 of the CPL) in a direct or indirect manner (Article 17 of the Regulation). Therefore, it encompasses not only advertising that contains explicit inaccuracies but also advertising which, by intentional or unintentional omission, misleads the consumer.
(2) such inaccuracies or concealment, because they contain falsehoods, obscurities, ambiguities, exaggerations or other distortions of a similar nature, could induce deception, error or confusion (Article 11 of the CPL, 17 of the Regulation). This requires a cause and effect relationship between the misrepresentation or concealment and the potential for deception, error or confusion by the consumer. It includes not only false or deceptive advertising as such but also advertising that could potentially produce a false impression, error or confusion in the consumer.

Therefore, under the CPL, unlawful advertising has the following characteristics:

(1) it encompasses not only the element of falsehood but also of confusion, a concept more frequently found in cases of unfair competition than in those involving consumer protection.[31]
(2) no limitation exists in Honduran legislation on the means utilised for communicating the advertising if it produces misrepresentations or concealment in a direct or indirect manner.
(3) damage is not an essential requirement of unlawful advertising, although proof of damages is required to claim indemnity.[32]
(4) unlawful advertising is of an objective character and, therefore, the good or bad faith of the advertiser is not a factor.

II. COMPARATIVE ADVERTISING IN THE CPL

The Regulations governing comparative advertising in subparagraphs (d) and (f) of Article 17 read as follows:

[31] The term is used specifically in Art. 2598(1) of the Italian Civil Code, quoted in the text, deception being typified by Ascarelli (*supra* n. 14, 203) as those acts that violate competitor's differing interests.

[32] For an opposing view, see the Argentine thesis expressed in the judgment in *Rolex* v. *Orante*, 1971 (quoted by Miguel B. O'Farrel, "La Publicidad Comparativa en el Derecho Argentino", La Ley, Año LIX No. 202, 20 October 1995, 1): "In this theme [of comparative advertising] it must be accepted that the mere fact of making an unlawful comparison entails the presumption that it will cause damage by attracting customers, therefore Article 165 of the Argentine Code of Civil Procedure should be utilised . . .". In other words, if the unlawful conduct is proven, it is presumed that the damage exists and that the only remaining question is that of to the amount of the indemnity.

"*Article 17*. For the effects of the law and this Regulation, unlawful advertising will be considered, and therefore forbidden, as that which in a direct or indirect manner implies falsehood, inexactitude, omissions, ambiguity, exaggeration or any other circumstance that could induce the consumer to deception, error or confusion, such as the following practices and actions: . . .

. . .

(b) The making of false statements with respect to the disadvantages or risks of any product or service of a competitor.

. . .

(f) The bringing into disrepute or detracting from, in any manner, the characteristics, qualities or conditions of other products and services. . . ."

It can be seen from this that Honduran consumer legislation has adopted the modern system of permitting comparative advertising because of the advantages it offers a consumer in making a better selection of the products or services he or she requires.[33] Therefore, as a general rule, Honduran consumer protection legislation considers comparative publicity to be lawful, with the following two exceptions:

(1) false statements about the disadvantages or risks associated with a competitor's product or services,[34] It is not an essential requirement, as is the case with unfair competition, that the competitor be explicitly mentioned or identified by name. The mere fact that mention is made in the advertisement of the competitor's goods or services is sufficient.

(2) a comparison that denigrates or impairs in some manner the characteristics, qualities or conditions of another's products or services. This second exception to the general rule allowing comparative publicity involves bringing a competitor's goods or services into disrepute. It refers to statements affecting the merits or the characteristics, qualities or conditions of other products or services in the market place, even where the information contained in the statement is true. As may be noted, the exception encompasses not only unlawful publicity but also unfair competition, because disrepute is an essential characteristic of unfair competition.

[33] This concept is set out in regulations such as the Brazilian *Code of Advertising Self-Regulation*, s. 7. Art. 32 states that comparative advertising is acceptable if its main purpose is not only to illustrate but to defend the consumer (a concept that is also followed by the Colombian Code of Advertising Self-Regulation). Art. 33 affirms that one of the minimum requirements to be met by comparative advertising is that its main purpose is protection of the consumer.

[34] The CPL rule is similar to that contained in Art. 6(c) of the Spanish *Ley General de Publicidad* (Ley 34/1988 of 11 November) on unfair competition. It makes it unlawful to engage in comparative publicity when the comparison "(c) . . . is not based on essentially analogous and objectively provable characteristics of the products or services, or when the comparison is made with other goods or services that are not similar to, known in or only with limited distribution in the market place."

III. THE HONDURAN LEGAL POSITION

Given the fact that there is an apparent conflict between the rules of the CPL and the Commercial Code on comparative advertising, what should be the solution under Honduran law? As the CPL is a law of public order which was enacted after the Commercial Code, the general rule is that the later law overrides the previous one in all cases of discrepancy between the two. Therefore, comparative advertising should be considered to be governed by the CPL and not by the Commercial Code.[35]

Nonetheless, a more detailed analysis of the issue could lead to different conclusions. First, both unfair competition under the Commercial Code and unlawful advertising under the CPL regulate two different institutions with different interests to protect and different procedures. For example, under Article 299(3) of the Honduran Penal Code,[36] unfair competition is considered a felony. This is not the case with unlawful advertising. Therefore, in as much as both laws are unique, one law cannot repeal the other. The rules of comparative advertising under the Commercial Code will apply to the case of merchants while the rules of unlawful advertising under the CPL will apply to cases involving consumers. This can give rise to the anomalous possibility of an entrepreneur invoking the application of the CPL rules based on the manner in which Article 2(b) of the CPL regulation is drafted and under which all entrepreneurs are simultaneously consumers,[37] whereas the consumer could not invoke the rules of unfair competition of the Commercial Code because he would not be considered a merchant from the point of view of that legislation.

From a practical standpoint, the following conclusions may be reached. Though it is true that the CPL sets out rules prohibiting false statements with regards to the disadvantages or risks of a competitor's products or services or the bringing into disrepute of the characteristics, qualities or conditions of a competitor's products or services, the CPL rules are, in effect, included in the concept of unfair competition under the Commercial Code. Article 425(II)(b) of the Code considers the making of claims capable of discrediting the products or services of another's enterprise as a case of unfair competition.

[35] Art. 43 of the Civil Code affirms: "The repeal of the law can be express or tacit. It is express where the new law expressly states that it repeals the previous one. It is tacit when the new law contains rules that cannot be reconciled with those of the previous law".

[36] "*Article 299.*—A person will be punished with imprisonment from six months to two years and a fine of Lps.500.00 to Lps.2,000.00: if he . . . (3) engages in acts of unfair competition according to the rules set forth in the Commercial Code . . .".

[37] "*Article 2.*—For the purposes of this Regulation the following terms have the meaning indicated: . . . (b) CONSUMER: Any individual or juridical person who acquires, utilises or enjoys products or services, whatever their nature, public or private, individual or collective, or the person who produces, facilitates or supplies them". As will be noted, Honduras applies the broad concept and not the restrictive concept of consumer. See Laurenao F. Gutiérrez Falla, "El Derecho Mercantil y el Derecho del Consumidor, El Consumidor y la Clientela", in course of publication in the *Anuario de Derecho Commercial*, Montevideo, Uruguay).

Paragraph IV of the same Article specifies that any similar acts intended directly or indirectly to divert the clientèle of another merchant constitute unfair competition. This does not occur under the comparative advertising rules of the Commercial Code, which differ from the CPL rules in that the latter generally permit comparative advertising. Therefore, since comparative advertising would constitute unfair competition, it is effectively prohibited in Honduras even though it is permitted under the CPL. Any merchant negatively affected by the comparison of his products can invoke the rules against unfair competition in the Commercial and Penal Codes.

Nevertheless, because the unfair competition rules in the Code only apply to merchants, nothing forbids a non-merchant (such as a government agency or department, or a non-profit organisation) from comparing the price and quality of the different products or services offered in the market place by means of publications issued for the purpose of informing consumers, as occurs in other countries.

IV. DE LEGE FERENDA

As stated above, the governing rule in Honduras, as found in the Commercial Code, prohibits comparative publicity, by applying doctrine and principles now considered outdated because they do not take into account the importance of the consumer in commercial law. I have previously written elsewhere[38] that the commercial law "has ceased to be the law of a class, the merchant, and is now being converted into the governing law of commercial traffic with all its components: the entrepreneur, producer, intermediary, financier, investor and consumer, all of whose rights must be protected". I believe that Honduran legislation should be modified to accept the modern trend that is applied in many of the more advanced nations. In those countries, with certain limitations, comparative publicity is accepted as a legitimate mode of advertising, mainly for the benefit of consumers and, consequently, the national economy. I would suggest that this new modification follow the general outline of the EC Directive of 21 April 1995, which was proposed in order to modify Directive 84–450 on deceptive advertising.[39] In my opinion, the rationale behind the proposed Directive should inspire any future Honduran legislation. Comparative advertising should be authorised because it helps to demonstrate the merits of diverse products or services; it stimulates competition in the supply of products and services for the benefit of the consumer; and it provides a means of guaranteeing the basic right of a consumer

[38] Laureano F. Gutiérrez Falla, "The Commercial Code of the Future and the Future of Commercial Law", paper presented at the biennial conference of the International Academy of Commercial and Consumer Law held in Stockholm, 18–23 August 1992.

[39] In making this recommendation I follow the views of Emilio Díaz Ruiz, *supra* n. 1, 110 ff.

to be able to access correct information in order to make an informed selection of the goods or services he wishes to acquire in the market place.[40]

I also believe that the proposed Directive's definition of comparative advertising should be adopted in Honduras. Advertising is comparative if it explicitly or implicitly mentions a competitor or similar goods or services offered by a competitor. The limits to comparative advertising contained in Article 3 of the proposed Directive should also be adopted. Article 3 provides that comparative advertising is authorised if it objectively compares essential characteristics that are permanent and verifiable, if it is equitably selective and representative of the goods or services that compete against one another, and if it is not deceptive and does not create confusion in the market place. It must not also cause the discrediting or denigration of the trade marks, commercial names, goods or services, or activities of the competitor and it must not take advantage of the goodwill attaching to a competitor's trade mark or commercial name. Finally, it must not be directed to the person or the personal situation of a competitor.

Provided the above outline is followed, I believe the new Honduran legislation would comply with the basic requirements of comparative advertising. These requirements are that the advertising must not be denigrating or lead to confusion or error, that it be true and objective, and that it not be directly or indirectly unfair by having abusive effects on the competitor.

[40] As Thierry Bourgoignie has stated (*supra* n. 28, 66): "Information appears as a prime condition for the rationalization and liberty of choice of the consumer; it contributes directly to the good performance of the market." Nevertheless, he denies the advantages of comparative publicity for the consumer's welfare.

Index